OXFORD HISTORICAL MONOGRAPHS

PAPAL JUDGES DELEGATE IN THE PROVINCE OF CANTERBURY
1198—1254

*A Study in
Ecclesiastical Jurisdiction
and Administration*

BY

JANE E. SAYERS

OXFORD UNIVERSITY PRESS

Oxford University Press, Great Clarendon Street, Oxford OX2 6DP

Oxford New York
Athens Auckland Bangkok Bogota Bombay
Buenos Aires Calcutta Cape Town Dar es Salaam
Delhi Florence Hong Kong Istanbul Karachi
Kuala Lumpur Madras Madrid Melbourne
Mexico City Nairobi Paris Singapore
Taipei Tokyo Toronto
and associated companies in
Berlin Ibadan

Oxford is a trade mark of Oxford University Press

Published in the United States by
Oxford University Press Inc., New York

First published by Oxford University Press 1971
Special edition for Sandpiper Books Ltd., 1997

British Library Cataloguing in Publication Data
Data available

Library of Congress Cataloging in Publication Data

ISBN 0-19-821836-2

1 3 5 7 9 10 8 6 4 2

Printed in Great Britain by
Bookcraft Ltd
Midsomer Norton, Somerset

FOR

H.G.S. AND J.S.

ACKNOWLEDGEMENTS

THIS book began its life as a thesis. In the course of collecting material for it, I have become indebted to the librarians, keepers of the manuscripts, muniments, and records, and archivists, of the following institutions and collections: the British Museum; the Public Record Office; the Bodleian Library, Oxford; the Cambridge University Library; the Dean and Chapter libraries at Canterbury, Exeter, Norwich, Peterborough, St. Paul's, Wells, Westminster, and Windsor; the Duke of Devonshire's Collections at Chatsworth; the Duke of Rutland's muniments at Belvoir; the Carlisle County Record Office; the Colchester Town Hall; the East Riding County Record Office; the Essex County Record Office; the Eton College Library; the Lincoln Archives Office; the Lambeth Palace Library; the college libraries of Magdalen, New College, and St. John's at Oxford; the diocesan registry at Salisbury; and the Vatican Archives at Rome. To all these I offer my thanks, and also to Professor Kathleen Major and Mrs. Marjorie Chibnall for the loan of various transcripts and photostats.

My particular gratitude in preparing this work first as a thesis is due to Professor Major, who expertly supervised it and kept it firmly based on the sources, and then as a book to Professor R. W. Southern, an editor of the present series, who rationalized its plan and gently moulded it into a much better book than it would otherwise have been. Professors Southern, Major, and C. R. Cheney, have generously given time to read the revised version throughout and to offer much helpful advice and criticism, and Dr. Diana E. Greenway has saved me from many errors and inconsistencies. I wish to thank them all here. I also wish to acknowledge the use of three unpublished theses by Eleanor Rathbone, James Foster, and R. A. McKinley, of which full details are given in the bibliography.

For material assistance towards the completion of the research, I am grateful to the Council of Bedford College, London, who appointed me to a Tutorial Research Assistantship for two years, and to the Leverhulme Trustees for a grant enabling me to effect the transition between thesis and book. Finally, among many friends, colleagues, and teachers who have encouraged and helped me, I would like specifically to record Dr. Pierre Chaplais, Mrs. Marjorie Chibnall, Mrs. Audrey Cornwall, Professor Peter Herde, Dr. B. V. E. Jones, Canon E. W. Kemp, Professor Stephan Kuttner, the Reverend Dr. F. D. Logan, Dr. Eleanor Rathbone, Dr. Brian Scott, and Professor Walter Ullmann.

J. E. S.

London, 1967

CONTENTS

CONTENTS

ABBREVIATIONS

(I) GENERAL

al.	alien
App.	Appendix
Aug.	Augustinian
Ben.	Benedictine
Cart.	Cartulary
Ch.	Charter
Cist.	Cistercian
Clun.	Cluniac
doc.	document
Gilb.	Gilbertine
H.M.C.	Historical Manuscripts Commission
M.G.H.	Monumenta Germaniae Historica
n.d.	not dated
N.S.	new series
Prem.	Premonstratensian
(re)pd.	(re)printed
trans.	translated

(II) PRINTED BOOKS, ETC.

A.N.C. — S. Kuttner and E. Rathbone, 'Anglo-Norman Canonists of the Twelfth Century', *Traditio*, vii.

Ann. Mon. — *Annales Monastici*, ed. H. R. Luard.

Arnulphus — 'Summa Minorum', *Quellen zur Geschichte*, i, pt. ii, ed. L. Wahrmund.

Bresslau — H. Bresslau, *Handbuch der Urkundenlehre*, 2nd. edn.

C. — 'Code', *Corpus Iuris Civilis*, ii, ed. P. Krueger.

C.F. — 'A Judge Delegate Formulary from Canterbury', ed. Jane E. Sayers, *Bulletin of the Institute of Historical Research*, xxxv.

Chertsey Cart. — *Chertsey Abbey Cartularies* (all references are to pt. i).

C.P.L. — *Calendar of Entries in the Papal Registers*, ed. W. H. Bliss and others.

C.R.R. — *Curia Regis Rolls*.

C.S. — *Councils and Synods*, ii, ed. F. M. Powicke and C. R. Cheney.

D. — 'Digest', *Corpus Iuris Civilis*, i, ed. T. Mommsen and P. Krueger.

D.D.C.	*Dictionnaire de Droit Canonique.*
Drogheda	'Summa Aurea', *Quellen zur Geschichte*, ii, pt. ii, ed. L. Wahrmund.
Dunstable Cart.	*A Digest of the Charters preserved in the Cartulary of the Priory of Dunstable*, comp. G. H. Fowler.
E.H.R.	*English Historical Review.*
Emden, *Oxf. Reg.*	A. B. Emden, *A Biographical Register of the University of Oxford.*
Eubel	C. Eubel, *Hierarchia Catholica Medii Aevi* (all references are to vol. i).
Fournier	P. Fournier, *Les Officialités au Moyen Âge.*
Glos. Cart.	*Historia et Cartularium monasterii Sancti Petri Gloucestriae*, ed. W. H. Hart.
Godstow Reg.	*The English Register of Godstow Nunnery near Oxford*, ed. A. Clark.
J.S.L.	*The Letters of John of Salisbury*, i (1153–61), ed. W. J. Millor and H. E. Butler, revsd. C. N. L. Brooke.
Letters of Inn. III	*The Letters of Pope Innocent III (1198–1216) concerning England and Wales*, cal. C. R. and Mary G. Cheney.
Lewes Cart. N.P.	*The Norfolk Portion of the Chartulary of the Priory of St. Pancras of Lewes*, cal. J. H. Bullock.
Lewes Cart. S.P.	*The Chartulary of the Priory of St. Pancras of Lewes*, cal. L. F. Salzman.
Malmesbury Reg.	*The Register of Malmesbury Abbey*, ed. J. S. Brewer and C. T. Martin.
N.L.C.	*Newington Longeville Charters*, ed. H. E. Salter.
Oseney Cart.	*The Cartulary of Oseney Abbey*, ed. H. E. Salter.
P.L.	*Patrologiae Cursus Completus—Series Latina*, ed. J.-P. Migne.
P.U.E.	*Papsturkunden in England*, ed. W. Holtzmann.
Reg. Antiq. Linc.	*The Registrum Antiquissimum of the Cathedral Church of Lincoln*, ed. C. W. Foster and K. Major.
Reg. Greg. IX	*Les Registres de Grégoire IX*, ed. L. Auvray.
Reg. Hon. III	*Regesta Honorii Papae III*, cal. P. Pressutti.
Reg. Inn. IV	*Les Registres d'Innocent IV*, ed. E. Berger.
R.S.	Rolls Series.
Russell	J. C. Russell, *A Dictionary of Thirteenth Century Writers.*
St. Frideswide's Cart.	*The Cartulary of the Monastery of St. Frideswide at Oxford*, ed. S. R. Wigram.
Stickler	A.-M. Stickler, 'Ordines Judiciarii', *D.D.C.* vi.

Tancred	'Tancredi Bononiensis Ordo Iudiciarius', *Pillii, Tancredi Gratiae Libri de Iudiciorum Ordine*, ed. F. Bergmann.
V.C.H.	*Victoria County Histories.*
W.P.	G. B. Flahiff, 'The Writ of Prohibition to Court Christian in the Thirteenth Century', *Mediaeval Studies*, vi and vii.
X.	'Decretales', *Corpus Iuris Canonici*, ii, ed. E. Friedberg.
6.	'Liber Sextus Decretalium D. Bonifacii Papae VIII', *Corpus Iuris Canonici*, ii, ed. E. Friedberg.

(III) UNPRINTED SOURCES

A	Lambeth Palace Library MS. 105
Abingdon Cart.	Bodleian MS. Lyell 15
Alvingham Cart.	Bodleian MS. Laud Misc. 642
B	Baltimore, Walters Art Gallery MS. W 15
Bardney Cart.	B.M. Cotton MS. Vesp. E xx
Bayham Cart.	B.M. Cotton MS. Otho A ii
Beaulieu Cart.	B.M. MS. Loans 29/330
Belvoir	Archives belonging to the Duke of Rutland at Belvoir Castle
Biddlesden Cart.	B.M. Harley MS. 4714
Binham Cart.	B.M. Cotton MS. Claudius D xiii
Blythburgh Cart.	B.M. Add. MS. 40725
B.M.	MSS. and charters in the British Museum, London
Bodleian	MSS. and charters in the Bodleian Library, Oxford
Boxgrove Cart.	B.M. Cotton MS. Claudius A vi
Bradenstoke Cart.	B.M. Stowe MS. 925
Bromholm Cart.	C.U.L. MS. Mm 2. 20
Burton Cart.	B.M. MS. Loans 30
Byland Cart.	B.M. Egerton MS. 2823
C	Cambridge, Gonville and Caius College MS. 150 (44)
Canons Ashby Cart.	B.M. Egerton MS. 3033
Canterbury	Dean and Chapter Archives at Canterbury
Carisbrooke Cart.	B.M. Egerton MS. 3667
Castle Acre Cart.	B.M. Harley MS. 2110
Chatteris Cart.	B.M. Cotton MS. Julius A i

Christchurch (Twynham) Cart.	B.M. Cotton MS. Tiberius D vi (all references are to vol. i)
Combe Cart.	B.M. Cotton MS. Vitellius A i
Crowland Cart.	Spalding Gentlemen's Society. Transcripts and rotographs in the Lincoln Archives Office
Croxton Transcript	B.M. Stowe MS. 928
C.U.L.	MSS. in the Cambridge University Library
Daventry Cart.	B.M. Cotton MS. Claudius D xii
Dover Cart.	Lambeth Palace Library MS. 241
Dunmow, Little, Cart.	B.M. Harley MS. 662
Dunstable Cart.	B.M. Harley MS. 1885 (cal. *Dunstable Cart.*, see Abbreviations (ii), Printed Books, etc.)
Easby Cart.	B.M. Egerton MS. 2827
Eton	Archives at Eton College, Bucks.
Exeter	Dean and Chapter Archives at Exeter
Exeter Cart.	Exeter, MS. 3672 (paginated)
Eye Cart.	Essex Record Office, Chelmsford, D/D By Q 19
Godsfield Transcript	B.M. Harley MS. 6603
Kenilworth Cart.	B.M. Harley MS. 3650
Kirkham Cart.	Bodleian MS. Fairfax 7
Kirkstead Cart.	B.M. Cotton MS. Vesp. E xviii
L	B.M. Royal MS. 10 B iv
Lambeth	MSS. and charters in Lambeth Palace Library, London
Langdon Cart.	P.R.O. E 164/29
Lanthony Cart. A 1, etc.	P.R.O. C 115/A 1—
Leeds Cart.	Kent Record Office, Maidstone, U/120 Q/13
Lewes Cart.	B.M. Cotton MS. Vesp. F xv (cal. *Lewes Cart.*, see Abbreviations (ii), Printed Books, etc.)
Lichfield Cart.	Bodleian MS. Ashmole 1527
Northampton, St. Andrew's Cart. (A)	B.M. Cotton MS. Vesp. E xvii
(B)	B.M. Royal MS. 11 B ix
St. James's Cart.	B.M. Cotton MS. Tiberius E v
Norwich	Dean and Chapter Archives at Norwich
Nun Cotham Cart.	Bodleian MS. Top. Lincs. d 1
O	Bodleian MS. Laud Lat. 17

Oxford, Magdalen, New College, St John's	MSS. and charters in the college libraries
Pershore Cart.	P.R.O. E 315/61
Peterborough	Dean and Chapter Archives at Peterborough
Pipewell Cart. (A)	B.M. Cotton MS. Caligula A xii
(B)	B.M. Add. MS. 37022
(C)	B.M. Stowe MS. 937
P.R.O.	MSS. and charters in the Public Record Office, London
Ramsey Cart.	B.M. Cotton MS. Vesp. E ii
Reading Cart.	B.M. Cotton MS. Vesp. E xxv
St. Albans Cart. (A)	MS. belonging to the Duke of Devonshire at Chatsworth
(B)	B.M. Cotton MS. Otho D iii
Almoner's Cart.	B.M. Lansdowne MS. 375
St. Augustine's Cart.	B.M. Cotton MS. Julius D ii
Red Book	B.M. Cotton MS. Claudius D x
White Book	P.R.O. E 164/27
St. Neots Cart.	B.M. Cotton MS. Faustina A iv
St. Paul's	Dean and Chapter Archives at St. Paul's Cathedral, London
St. Radegund's (Bradsole) Cart.	Bodleian MS. Rawlinson B 336
Shaftesbury Cart.	B.M. Harley MS. 61
Sibton Cart.	B.M. Arundel MS. 221
Spalding Cart.	B.M. Add. MS. 35296
Stixwould Cart.	B.M. Add. MS. 46701
Thorney Cart.	C.U.L. Add. MS. 3020
Tintern Cart.	B.M. Arundel MS. 19
Torre Cart.	P.R.O. E 164/19
Walden Cart.	B.M. Harley MS. 3697
Walsingham Cart.	Bodleian MS. Top. Norfolk b 1
Waltham Cart.	B.M. Cotton MS. Tiberius C ix
Warter Cart.	Bodleian MS. Fairfax 9
Welbeck Cart.	B.M. Harley MS. 3640
Wells	Dean and Chapter Archives at Wells
West Dereham Cart.	B.M. Add. MS. 46353
Westminster	Dean and Chapter Archives at Westminster

Whalley Cart.	B.M. Add. MS. 10374
Wherwell Cart.	B.M. Egerton MS. 2104A
Windsor	Dean and Chapter Archives at St. George's Chapel, Windsor
Wymondham Cart.	B.M. Cotton MS. Titus C viii

INTRODUCTION

O N E of the first steps taken by Parliament at the Reformation, in extinguishing papal jurisdiction and power in England, was the Act in Restraint of Appeals to Rome. This act was not novel. It had its predecessors in the Second Statute of Praemunire of 1393, which threatened those appealing to Rome with the confiscation of their goods and imprisonment, and in clause 8 of the Constitutions of Clarendon, where Henry II tried to stop appeals to Rome. But it is a testimony of the position which the appeal system was held to occupy and to have occupied in maintaining papal government in pre-Reformation England.

Nearly 350 years after the Act in Restraint of Appeals, F. W. Maitland contended that medieval England was in no way exempt from the jurisdiction of the papacy, as Bishop Stubbs had argued, and that the canon law was equally binding in English courts Christian as in other ecclesiastical courts of Europe. Maitland's view is now generally accepted, but the details of papal judicial administration and the effectiveness of the system in England have not been fully investigated, although it is only on the basis of such details that any judgement can be formed. This work sets out to examine the influence of the medieval canon law, as reflected in the operation of the papal system of judicial delegation in the province of Canterbury, between the accession of Innocent III to the papacy in 1198 and the death of Innocent IV in 1254, when it has commonly been asserted that this influence was at its height. It has not been my purpose to examine in great detail the relatively few sensational cases which have long attracted the attention of historians, but rather to construct a general picture of the day-to-day administration of the courts.

The sources for such a study are abundant. There are the central records, consisting of the papal registers, which form an almost complete series, and the official law compilations including the *Decretales* of Gregory IX. There are also extensive local records of the courts, both original documents

and copies in cartularies, and private records such as formularies and legal commentaries, which have not hitherto been
used for this purpose. My original intention was to include
both English ecclesiastical provinces in this study, but the
quantity of the surviving evidence (much of it merely com-
plementary and repetitive) made this impracticable, and the
following investigation has been limited to the southern
province.

The history of the bishops' courts in England still waits
to be written. The lack of any comprehensive work on this
subject has imposed a definite limitation on my study. It has
not been my place to attempt a detailed analysis of the bishop's
court and its place in society at the time, but where the
bishop's court seems to be inextricably connected with, or
its influence directly dependent on, the papal delegated
courts, certain observations have been made. Maitland suggested that the rise of the papal delegated courts in the
twelfth century heralded a subsequent decline in the amount
of business going before the ordinaries,[1] and Z. N. Brooke
accepted and repeated this argument.[2] Professor Cheney,
however, finds it 'hard to believe in a decline of the bishop's
court, even though appeals to Rome often removed cases
from his hearing'.[3] As yet one can do little more than believe, if one approaches the subject from the starting-point
of the bishop's court. In 1929 F. M. Stenton showed where
some of the sources for such a history lay, and pointed out
that 'the ecclesiastical judges of whom we read in charters
coming from the reign of Stephen or the earliest years of
Henry II are usually the bishops of the sees within which
the churches, lands, or dues at issue lay'. He wrote of 'the
obscurity which overhangs the whole organization of the
English church in the twelfth century', and commented
that the 'records of routine administration fill a place which
no other source of information can supply'.[4]

Since 1929 some of the documents for a study of the
bishops' courts, particularly in the twelfth century, have

[1] F. W. Maitland, *Roman Canon Law in the Church of England* (1898), p. 107.
[2] Z. N. Brooke, *The English Church and the Papacy* (Cambridge, 1931), p. 214.
[3] C. R. Cheney, *From Becket to Langton* (Manchester, 1956), p. 144.
[4] F. M. Stenton, '*Acta Episcoporum*', *Cambridge Historical Journal*, iii, no. 1 (1929),
1–14, and esp. pp. 3, 9, and 13–14.

been printed.[1] More sources have survived than has hitherto been thought, but even so it is doubtful whether they are as rich as for the papal delegated courts. An analysis of Gilbert Foliot's *acta* reveals evidence of about forty judge-delegate cases, and some thirty-four references to the courts of the ordinaries, between the 1140s and the 1180s. For the thirteenth century, the bishops' registers might well be expected to yield much information on diocesan courts, but they are sadly disappointing. Apart from Lincoln, there are no surviving bishops' registers for the period before 1254, with the exception of that of Archbishop Walter de Gray of York. In Gray's register five or perhaps six settlements were made by judges delegate as opposed to thirteen by the archbishop, although most of the latter were not judicial settlements before a court. Furthermore, if examined for episcopal court material, the two Lincoln registers of Hugh of Wells and Robert Grosseteste, disclose very little. That of Hugh of Wells is mainly concerned with institutions and the ordination of vicarages, and reveals seven cases which came before judges delegate (possibly nine) and a handful of references to appeals, as opposed to four suits which the bishop or archdeacon heard. Grosseteste's register contains references to six suits in which judges delegate were concerned, and it is of note that of these one went to the ordination of the bishop, one to the official, and one from the bishop of Lincoln, after appeal, to judges delegate, and then finally to the ordination of the official of Lincoln. There are no references to suits that went straight to Grosseteste as ordinary and were terminated by him. The number of suits recorded in these registers is therefore small, but there is considerable evidence of recourse to Rome.

Maitland pointed out that an examination of the second printed volume of the cartulary of St. Frideswide's showed seventeen ecclesiastical lawsuits brought between 1150 and 1240, all of which were begun before papal commissioners.[2]

[1] Notably *The Letters and Charters of Gilbert Foliot*, ed. A. Morey and C. N. L. Brooke (Cambridge, 1967); *The Acta of the Bishops of Chichester 1075–1207*, ed. H. Mayr-Harting (Canterbury and York Ser. lvi, 1964); and A. Saltman, *Theobald, Archbishop of Canterbury* (1956).
[2] Covering both volumes, I make the total number of cases that were delegated to judges delegate between *c.* 1150 and 1247 to be thirty, as against one case which

Salter, too, in his edition of the Oseney cartulary, noted fifty-five such cases almost equally divided between the period before 1198 and the period after, but he did not count the number of suits which came before the ordinary.[1] From his discovery Maitland argued a decline in episcopal jurisdiction. For the first half of the thirteenth century, a study of many cartularies from southern religious houses has shown that, at this period at least, the monasteries favoured the delegated courts of Rome and took their judicial business there rather than before the ordinary. Indeed by 1198 the monasteries were looking upon the papal delegated courts as their special tribunals, and they continued to do so until the mid-thirteenth century, after which Maitland detected that the bishops' courts appeared to be used more freely. But cartularies, as the products of religious houses, faithfully reflect the interests of these corporations in the acquisition of privileges and territories, and carefully record documents which grant and confirm their rights, frequently after judicial dispute. They are not, therefore, good evidence for where parties other than the monasteries took their suits.

Some light is thrown on the more difficult problem of where secular clerks and laymen initiated cases by the survival of documents that show at least some of them to have come before papal courts. But this may be far from a complete picture of the situation. The chance survival of a group of documents connected with Archbishop Hubert Walter's archiepiscopate shows something of provincial and diocesan business, and some of the *sede vacante* material of 1242–3 refers to diocesan courts.[2] Cases coming before Archbishop Hubert's provincial court, most of which were dealt with by delegation, include a case of certain clerks against the bishop of Llandaff, and a case between two clerks.[3] Another case,

came before the bishop of Lincoln in 1162 × 1167 (no. 1012). An agreement of c. 1129 took place before the vice-archdeacon in a synod (no. 651).

[1] Twenty-eight of the fifty-five cases belong to the period 1198 to 1254, when, according to my reckoning, only five cases came before the ordinary's jurisdiction.

[2] I hope to deal with the growth of the archiepiscopal courts more fully elsewhere. On the discovery of these documents in 1879 and 1893–4, see M. M. Morgan, 'Early Canterbury Jurisdiction', *E.H.R.* lx (1945), 394; H.M.C., *Var. Coll.* i. 205–81, which she cites; and the notes on the flyleaves of the *Sede Vacante* volumes.

[3] Canterbury, Ch(rist) Ch(urch) Letters, ii, nos. 245 and 250. Professor Cheney has suggested that some of the appeals from the lower diocesan courts to the

where an appeal was made to Rome and for the tuition of the
see of Canterbury in Hubert Walter's time, had started
before the archdeacon of Middlesex. It was between John de
Nettleswelle the chaplain, and Alice and Richard the black-
smith.[1] Similarly, a case brought by Peter fitz Payn, clerk,
against Alan de Herteland over the church of Shebbear
(Devon), which went on appeal to Rome, appears to have
begun in the court of the bishop of Exeter's official.[2] Another
case, of 1242, where an appeal was made to Rome and for the
tuition of the see of Canterbury, had commenced before the
archdeacon of Salisbury, from whom John Bacun, clerk, appealed.[3] From the vacancy of 1242–3 also, we possess some
material which shows marriage suits, between apparently
ordinary lay people, being brought to the official of the bishop
of Hereford and the dean of Essex[4] before appeals were made
to the provincial court.[5] Thus this 'cache' of documents fills
a definite gap in our knowledge and shows the continuous
functioning of the diocesan courts, although doubtless some
cases which were formerly settled there were now going on
appeal to Rome.

A study of Archbishop Stephen Langton's surviving *acta*
gives an over-all picture of the different courts in the first
half of the thirteenth century.[6] He acted as judge delegate
in four suits, and three of these were major ones. Probably in
1214–15 he settled a case between the bishop and chapter of
Lincoln and the master, prior, and canons of Sempringham,
over churches and benefices that the canons wished to appropriate. Between March and April 1222 he dealt with the
complaint of the bishop of London against the abbey of
Westminster over the status of the abbey and its liberty, and

---

archbishop were made during vacancies, for example from Lincoln after the death
of St. Hugh in 1200, when the see remained vacant for two and a half years (*Hubert
Walter* (1967), pp. 64 and 73 n. 2). Gilbert Foliot's letters contain ten references to
the archbishop's court, some of them to cases on appeal (e.g. no. 246).

[1] Canterbury, *S(ede) V(acante)*, bk. i, p. 50.   [2] Ecclesiastical Suits, no. 341.

[3] Canterbury, *S.V.*, bk. ii, p. 200; the proceedings recorded in M 364, no. 12
may also have been initiated by a case in the archdeacon's court, in this case that of
the archdeacon of Taunton.

[4] MS. *sic*, and see p. 318 for the dean of Middlesex.

[5] Canterbury, M 364, nos. 11 and 17.

[6] See *Acta Stephani Langton*, ed. K. Major (Canterbury and York Ser. l, 1950),
pp. xxxvii–xxxix and the references cited there.

in January 1224 in company with Bishop Richard Poore, he
heard the suit of the convent of St. Frideswide against Fulk
of Rycote, knight, about violence done to certain of the
canons—a matter of some importance. The fourth suit was
over a matter of small importance, a portion in the church of
Bexley, but the plaintiffs were a powerful religious corporation, the prior and convent of Holy Trinity, London. There
is also evidence of four cases which came before the archbishop's court, two of them on appeal. Another case came
before his arbitration, and in four more he made awards or
ordinations, two of them as diocesan, but in as many as three
of these he was acting as a party, and they were not, therefore,
court settlements.

Two points are suggested by this survey. First, if the
nature of episcopal jurisdiction is considered, it can be
roughly divided into instance jurisdiction, where the cases
were brought by the parties, and *ex officio* jurisdiction, covering cases of correction initiated by or on behalf of the bishop.
The *ex officio* jurisdiction naturally enough remained with the
bishop and his subordinates, and was not affected by the other
growing jurisdictions. Indeed, with the administrative ad-
vances of the twelfth century, this type of jurisdiction presumably expanded. With instance jurisdiction, it seems that,
as the twelfth century progressed, more provision was made
for judicial decision, at least if we are to judge by the appearance of the bishop's legal official in the 1150s to 1160s and
the growth of a caucus of legal men, the *magistri*, round
the bishop. But the real development was that by the end of
the century the accusing party had more choice as to where
he might take his case. We shall probably not be far wrong
if we assume that a majority of important persons, both lay
and ecclesiastic, and the most important cases, went to Rome,[1]
while those of lesser note, which were brought by ordinary

---

[1] It seems indisputable that two important cases of the mid-twelfth century, the
Battle case over the exemption of the abbey from the diocesan and the Sackville/
Anstey case about marriage and inheritance, would have gone straight to Rome
fifty years later. As it was, the Battle case came before the king's court and was
settled there, and the Sackville marriage case started in the court of the archdeacon of
London and then went to the diocesan synod before finally being decided by Pope
Innocent II, while the marriage section of the Anstey case started in the archbishop
of Canterbury's court before transfer to Rome.

individuals, stayed in England and were dealt with by the diocesan, or perhaps the archbishop. It is not necessary, therefore, to imagine a decline in the bishop's or archbishop's jurisdiction so much as a possible alteration in the kind of persons and cases which came before them. The papal courts provided an attractive alternative for many litigants, particularly the ecclesiastical corporations, but not for all people, and not in all types of case and circumstances. Moreover, at a time when all jurisdictions were expanding, it does not necessarily follow that there was a marked diminution in the number of suits coming before the ordinary and the archbishop.

The other point is that in questioning the nature of the surviving evidence for the bishops' courts, which appears so fragmentary for the thirteenth century, it is well to bear in mind that it is probably far from representative of the actual jurisdiction. There is a greater likelihood of destruction if these records did concern smaller matters, as has been suggested, and persons of lesser importance, who had not the same facilities for preservation and registration, just as the lack of lay records illustrates an almost certain distortion. In view of the legal and administrative developments which were made in the bishops' courts in the twelfth century, especially the frequent use of the bishop as a judge delegate and of his diocesan machinery for the administrative purposes of the delegated courts, it is, indeed, hard to accept a decline of the bishop's court, as Professor Cheney has said. But it is possible to argue in favour of adaptation and change in the thirteenth century.

I

THE ORIGINS AND DEVELOPMENT OF PAPAL DELEGATED JURISDICTION

1. *Appeals to Rome*

'Praefuit [Petrus—Papa] in appellatione quia ipse solus cephas, id est, caput dictus est.'[1]

No period was more influential in determining the subsequent course of the history of the papacy as an institution of government than the pontificate of Gregory VII. The constant reiteration of the theme that the Roman Church had the primacy, and that for western society to function successfully this had to be realized by both ecclesiastics and secular rulers alike, may be regarded as the foundation of the appeal system as it was known in the twelfth century. The events of this pontificate led to a re-forming of society, and new life was soon breathed into the old canonical texts which outlined the primacy of the Church of Rome and accentuated the importance of the Petrine commission.[2]

Subsequent to the activities of Gregory VII and the new attitudes towards society which were born at that time, the legal revival of the late eleventh century was no less important. According to Gregory VII, the Roman Church alone knew the *norma iustitiae* which only the pope could declare.[3]

[1] Huguccio, *Summa ad Dist.*, Pembroke College, Cambridge, MS. 72, f. 129ᵛ, cited by B. Tierney, *Foundations of the Conciliar Theory* (Cambridge, 1955), p. 29. Huguccio was one of the masters of Innocent III, see J. de Ghellinck, *Le Mouvement théologique du douzième siècle*, 2nd edn. (Museum Lessianum, Section Historique, x, 1948), p. 463.

[2] *Decretum* (*Corpus Iuris Canonici*, i, ed. E. Friedberg, Leipzig, 1879) C. 9 qu. 3 c. 16: 'Prima sedes a nemine iudicatur', see G. Phillips, *Kirchenrecht*, i (Regensburg, 1846), pp. 258–77; and *Decretum*, dist. xxi cc. ii, iii, and iv: 'Romana ecclesia a Christo primatum accepit', 'Primatum Romanae ecclesiae non aliqua synodus sed Christus instituit', and 'Inferiores a superioribus iudicandi sunt'. See also Matt. 16:17–19.

[3] W. Ullmann, *The Growth of Papal Government in the Middle Ages* (1955), p. 275 and nn. 1–2. Professor Ullmann considers that the *norma iustitiae* theory is

The provision of a law book which calendared previous papal decisions, therefore, was of prime importance in the development of the pope's jurisdictional powers and the provision of a Church legal system. The connection between the compilation of the *Decretum* and the rediscovery of more complete Roman law texts has long been realized, even if direct influence of the *Corpus Iuris Civilis* on Gratian's compilation is disputed.[1]

The appeal system was Roman in origin, dating from the time of the Republic and receiving further definition under the Empire.[2] With the lack of any evidence to the contrary, it seems probable that the idea of a system of appeals had been adopted by the papacy from the Roman law, and was given further impetus by the newly discovered texts. As early as 343, the Council of Sardica had made Rome the court of appeal for ecclesiastical disputes between bishops,[3] and in 378 the edict *Ordinarium Sententias iudicum* of the Emperor Gratian established the Roman see as a court of first instance for all metropolitans, and made it a final court of appeal, with provisions for overriding metropolitical jurisdiction, for all other bishops.[4] This was now gradually extended in the course of the twelfth century to cover other appellants.

the seed out of which grew the later ideas that the pope was judge ordinary of all, as expressed, for example, by Huguccio. According to Innocent II the Roman Church was the 'sedes justitiae' and to Innocent III the 'fundamentum legis totius Christianitatis'.   [1] See below, p. 42.

[2] M. Fournier, *Essai sur l'histoire du droit d'appel* (Paris, 1881), p. 17, and G. Le Bras, 'Le Droit romain au service de la domination pontificale', *Rev. hist. de droit français et étranger*, 4e série xxvii (1949), 391. Cf. Acts 25:11-12: 'Caesarem appello. Tunc Festus cum concilio locutus, respondit: Caesarem appellasti? ad Caesarem ibis.' St. Paul's appeal unto Caesar illustrates the form of Roman civil appeal from a provincial court to the central government. See also *Registrum Simonis de Gandavo*, ed. C. T. Flower and M. C. Dawes (Canterbury and York Ser. xl, 1934), p. 334: 'Delatio iudicis infidelis appellacioni beati Pauli ad Cesarem interposite deferentis arguit nos fideles, quos obediencie et reverencie debitum plus astringit, si appellacionibus legitimis ad summum Pontificem, qui maior est Cesare, interiectis minime deferamus', cited by R. Brentano, *York Metropolitan Jurisdiction and Papal Judges Delegate (1279-1296)* (University of California Publications in History, lviii, 1959), p. 148.

[3] C. J. Hefele, *Histoire des conciles d'après les documents originaux*, i, pt. ii (Paris, 1907), 762-6 and 769-77; and see H. Hess, *The Canons of the Council of Sardica* (Oxford, 1958), chapter vi.

[4] *Collectio Avellana*, ed. O. Guenther (Corpus Scriptorum Ecclesiasticorum Latinorum, xxxv, 1895), 13, p. 54, and see Le Bras, 'Droit romain', p. 381.

Appellate and first-instance jurisdiction, as developed between the 1120s and the 1180s, is the most striking aspect of the growing power of the twelfth-century papacy, which was felt in many different walks of life, and which long ago attracted the attention and fed the imagination of Church and legal historians alike. But although the implications of a functioning appeal system are great, and appellate jurisdiction was one of the strongest aspects of medieval papal government, it is in no way to detract from this movement to point out that the machinery of the appeal system developed from an inchoate state to a more ordered one. The development took almost a century, extending from the right to deal with the cases of bishops and to hear *causae majores*, to the duty to receive appeals and first-instance cases of lesser importance from lesser ecclesiastics and laymen.

England is fortunate in having more material to illustrate the development of papal delegated jurisdiction before 1198 than probably any other country. The *acta* of judges delegate in summarizing the process *in toto* provide much information, and cartulary sources reveal a fair amount of evidence of this kind. For the pontificate of Adrian IV (1154–9), the potentialities for investigation are shown in the letters of John of Salisbury, a unique and most revealing source.[1] Finally, the English legal sources from the pontificate of Alexander III (1159–81) onwards, of which the importance has only recently been realized, are without parallel in any other European country.

The position of England, however, in the general scheme of the papal judicial system was by no means exceptional. The canon law itself was not a clearly defined set of rules and injunctions, but a jurisprudence built on precedent, in this respect resembling the later English common or case law. By its nature canon law had to be deemed universal in its application. This has been overlooked by those scholars who have seen an English Church separate from the general trends. They have also ignored the fact that the appellate system was in its infancy all over Europe before the end of the papacy of Alexander III.[2] The fallacy of thinking that delegated

---

[1] Professor Brooke makes this point in vol. i on p. xxxii.

[2] Professor G. Barraclough in a review of Professor Stephan Kuttner's *Repertorium der Kanonistik (1140–1234) (Studi e Testi* lxxi, 1937) in *E.H.R.* liii (1938),

jurisdiction was fully developed by 1172 has led to the 'false edifice' of the Compromise of Avranches[1] and the opinion that the disproportionately large number of English decretals, which are incorporated in the Gregorian compilation of 1234, point to England's backward position in the understanding and implementation of the canon law.[2] The appellate system in England developed certain peculiarities, but at no point was it exempt or severed from the general application of the Church's law.

The activities of Henry of Blois, bishop of Winchester (1129–71), have been investigated closely by Dr. Voss.[3] For our purposes, interest centres on him because the introduction of the appeal system to England has been connected with him by the chronicler Henry of Huntingdon, who says that appeals were not commonly known in England until Henry, bishop of Winchester, introduced the system as legate.[4] This is true as to period, but Henry of Huntingdon undoubtedly exaggerated the part played by Henry of Blois between 1139 and 1143, and if Henry had intended to prevent appeals, it is very doubtful whether he could have succeeded. During Theobald's tenure of the see of Canterbury from 1139 to 1161, appeals to the pope became a normal part of the procedure in English Church suits, but this

494 n. 3, writes: 'It is in this background alone, and as part of this development of church institutions—not as a result of a temporary crisis in English history—that the situation in England towards the end of Henry II's reign is to be interpreted. The turning point is in the history of the "ecclesia Romana" rather than in that of the "ecclesia Anglicana"; for it is in the law and procedure of the Roman church that the essential change is to be found, and the problem which arises in England arises at the same time in the rest of Europe.'

[1] See S. E. Thorne, 'Le Droit canonique en Angleterre', *Rev. hist. de droit français et étranger*, 4ᵉ série xiii (1934), 499–513; Z. N. Brooke, *The English Church and the Papacy*, p. 212; and A. Morey, *Bartholomew of Exeter* (Cambridge, 1937), p. 45. The 'false edifice' has been undermined by M. Cheney, 'The Compromise of Avranches and the Spread of Canon Law in England', *E.H.R.* lvi (1941), 177–97.

[2] Z. N. Brooke, *The English Church and the Papacy*, pp. 212–14, and 'The Effect of Becket's Murder on Papal Authority in England', *Cambridge Hist. Journal*, ii (1928), 213–28.

[3] L. Voss, 'Heinrich von Blois, Bischof von Winchester, (1129–1171)' (*Historische Studien*, ccx, 1932). Documents are printed in the appendices; see especially in this connection appendices VII, VIIIa, IXh, i, l.

[4] Henry of Huntingdon, *Historia Anglorum*, ed. T. Arnold (R.S. lxxiv, 1879), p. 282; and see also Gervase of Canterbury, *Opera Historica*, ii, ed. W. Stubbs (R.S. lxxiii, 1880), 384; both cited by M. Cheney, 'Compromise of Avranches', p. 178.

may have been due to the special circumstances of political disturbance in Stephen's reign rather than to Theobald's policy. Theobald watered the seeds of the growing canon law and acted conscientiously as a papal representative, but an 'atmosphere of informality and improvisation' surrounds his work as a delegate.[1] The John of Salisbury correspondence (between 1153 and 1161) shows evidence of some fifty appeals to Rome in which Theobald was concerned, the majority of which belong to the pontificate of Adrian IV (1154–9). Professor Brooke thinks that this number is in proportion about half of the actual appeals which took place from England at that time.[2]

2. First-Instance Cases

Maitland was the first to draw attention to the number of first-instance cases that were taken directly to Rome without a prior hearing in a lower court.[3] It is probable that they increased in number, and Canon Kemp thinks that it was Alexander III who 'more than any other single person, . . . established the papal curia as not only a court of appeal for all Christendom, but also a court of first instance'. He continues that in the second half of the twelfth century first-instance cases became increasingly common, and vied with appeals from the various local tribunals in the amount of business which was created.[4] Certainly, for the first half of the thirteenth century, it would be no exaggeration to say that the majority of cases which reached Rome were of first instance. Indeed, the papacy's own contribution to the Roman idea of appeal lay in this development of the supposition that Rome was in fact the one court of Christendom, and not merely a tribunal of last resort.

This was bolstered by earlier texts, which were collected and glossed to mean that the Roman Church was judicially and administratively the head. Of particular importance, was the Gelasian passage to be found in Gratian:

---

[1] This phrase is C. N. L. Brooke's in *J.S.L.*, p. xxxiv.
[2] *J.S.L.*, p. xxxii n. 1.
[3] Maitland, *Roman Canon Law*, p. 104.
[4] *Papal Decretals relating to the Diocese of Lincoln in the Twelfth Century*, ed. W. Holtzmann and E. W. Kemp (Lincoln Rec. Soc. xlvii, 1954), p. xviii.

Cuncta per mundum novit ecclesia, quod sacrosancta Romana ecclesia
fas de omnibus habet iudicandi, neque cuiquam de eius liceat iudicare
iudicio. Siquidem ad illam de qualibet mundi parte appellandum est:
ab illa autem nemo est appellare permissus,[1]

which appeared to state categorically that the Roman Church
was the fount of justice. In a sense this was the position
which litigants required of it. They wanted an authoritative
lead and a firm judgement. For this reason the statements of
popes and clerics, which augmented Gratian's text—that all
people, especially the oppressed, might appeal to the Roman
Church—were particularly welcome.[2] St. Bernard elaborated this with 'Appeals are made to you [the pope] from all
over the world as a proof of your unique primacy',[3] and in a
letter, which was probably addressed to Adrian IV, Archbishop Theobald stated:

The limbs derive their vigour from the head, and the holy Roman
church is by God's grace the salvation of all other churches; and so it
is essential for all men to have recourse to you when they are in the
grip of some necessity from which they cannot free themselves by
their own efforts.[4]

In 1155 Pope Adrian IV wrote to Archbishop Basil of
Thessalonica, emphasizing papal claims and declaring that
previous councils had ordained the reference of every ecclesiastical dispute to the judgement of Rome. This idea
had always seemed ludicrous to the Eastern Church, particularly during the period of the degradation of the papacy in
the ninth and tenth centuries.[5] Even now it did not attract
the East, but for the Western Church it was a different
matter.

---

[1] *Decretum*, C. 9 qu. 3 c. 17, cited by Maitland, *Roman Canon Law*, p. 104.

[2] *Decretum*, C. 2 qu. 6 c. 8: 'Ad Romanam ecclesiam ab omnibus, maxime tamen
ab oppressis appellandum est.'

[3] Bernard: 'Appelatur de toto mundo ad te. Id quidem in testimonium singularis
primatis tui.' *De Consideratione*, *P.L.* 182, col. 761. And see Stephen of Tournai,
ep. 143 to Clement III in *P.L.* 211, col. 429, and *P.U.E.* i, no. 58 (28 Feb. 1164).

[4] *J.S.L.*, no. 57 (c. 1154–9 prob. late). A full expression of this idea is found with
Innocent III, see *P.L.* 214, no. cccl, col. 324: 'ut ad eam [apostolica sedes] tanquam
generalem omnium matrem et singulare fidelium Christi refugium appelletur per
quod et minorum tollatur oppressio et superiorum praesumptio refrenetur.'

[5] S. Runciman, *The Eastern Schism* (Oxford, 1955), p. 119, citing *Sacrorum
Conciliorum Nova et Amplissima Collectio*, xxi, ed. J. D. Mansi (Florence and Venice,
1776), p. 795.

The opening up of the papal court to first-instance jurisdiction was made possible by constant legal definition on the
part of the pope, in which no one was more diligent than
Alexander III, by the decretal collections of the 1180s,
which incorporated many commissions to judges delegate,[1]
and by the new type of papal mandate, for gradually more
and more cases were being delegated for hearing in the
provinces from whence they came. The early mandate, as
issued under Innocent II (1130–43), had been devised
specifically for each case.[2] With Lucius II (1144–5), it is
possible to discern something approaching a 'common
form',[3] although minor changes occur under Eugenius III
(1145–53), when, for instance, the clause *per presentia scripta*
became *per apostolica scripta*, and the number of judges to
whom the mandate was addressed had not yet settled down
to three.[4] By the time of Alexander III's pontificate it became
possible to write to a set of delegates: ' . . . you shall enquire
into the facts and truth of the matter simply and straight-
forwardly according to the procedure of the canons and the
institutes of the holy fathers',[5] and the activities of this
pontificate are clearly crystallized in the Alexandrian mandate.[6] The mandate was now addressed to three judges, 'for
a threefold cord is not quickly broken', the *appellatione remota*
clause is the norm, and the *sane si non omnes*, allowing two
judges to hear the suit if one excused himself, and the *fine
canonico* or *fine legitimo* phrase become common.[7] The significance in general is not only in the number of the new
Alexandrian sources but also in the number of first-instance
cases, two factors which were inextricably connected. In the

[1] See below, pp. 35–8.
[2] See M. Cheney, 'Compromise of Avranches', p. 179, citing *P.U.E.* ii, no. 32.
[3] Ibid., p. 179, citing *P.U.E.* i, no. 29, but this should not be exaggerated.
[4] *P.U.E.* iii, nos. 47 and 90, and *Papsturkunden in Frankreich*, i (Normandy), ed.
J. Ramackers (Abhandlungen der Gesellschaft der Wissenschaften zu Göttingen,
Philologisch-Historische Klasse, 3. Folge, nr. 21, 1937), no. 37.
[5] *Papal Decretals relating to Lincoln*, no. xiii.
[6] e.g. *P.U.E.* i, nos. 156, 159, 169, and 173, in which certain stereotyped phrases
appear. Alexander used the mandate to judges delegate to inquire about the charges
of certain lay brothers against the order of Sempringham, see *Le Livre de Saint
Gilbert de Sempringham*, ed. R. Foreville (Paris, 1943), App. II.
[7] *Papal Decretals relating to Lincoln*, no. vi; and, e.g., *P.U.E.* i, no. 84, and *Papsturkunden in Frankreich*, iv (Touraine) (Göttingen, Philologisch-Historische Klasse,
3. Folge, nr. 35, 1956), no. 173.

same way the rapid spread of the canon law in England ran parallel with the extension of papal delegated jurisdiction, and was a reciprocal development.

Although these extensions were welcomed by the litigants, they were not welcomed by the secular rulers, who had their own jurisdictions to build up and maintain.[1] There is evidence of increasing royal interference with appeals, but it was the first-instance cases that contained the greater threat to royal power. Paschal II had rebuked Henry I for interfering with appeals to Rome, and Stephen had attempted to try clerks several times, as Theobald was forced to admit to the pope, 'according to the custom of our nation'.[2] From the beginning of his reign Henry II tried to create a separatist English Church which would be cut off from continental developments.[3] The Constitutions of Clarendon were the expression of this desire. He intended to keep a close watch over relations with the papacy,[4] and as firm as possible a grip over the English Church. Royal interference also spread in a more surreptitious way: 'He [Geoffrey] appealed Gregory to the judgement of the Apostolic See. There he will say things which he dared not say in England, because Gregory is a servant of the king.'[5] The Compromise of Avranches took place on 21 May 1172. Nearly four months later, on 2 September 1172, Alexander III wrote to Henry ordering him not to interfere with appeals to Rome nor to allow interference with them.[6] It would be wrong to suppose that the king took no further interest in ecclesiastical suits. Avranches allowed the English Church to continue in contact with Rome, but royal intervention and interference did not cease altogether.

[1] See Barraclough in *E.H.R.* liii (1938), 494 n. 3, who draws attention to the royal protests in France and Germany also against the new developments.

[2] *P.L.* 163, no. cdxxv, col. 379, and Saltman, *Theobald*, p. 124.

[3] On Henry II's obstructing appeals to Rome see Saltman, *Theobald*, chapter iv and pp. 128–31, and H. Mayr-Harting, 'Hilary, Bishop of Chichester (1147–69) and Henry II', *E.H.R.* lxxviii (1963), 211.

[4] e.g. *J.S.L.*, nos. 108 and 112.

[5] Ibid., no. 81. Cf. no. 102, for local interference, in this instance by Earl Reginald of Cornwall.

[6] *P.U.E.* iii, no. 189.

3. Developments at Rome

(i) Delegation

As early as the pontificate of Paschal II (1099–1118) delegation was used for the settlement of cases that were brought to
Rome.[1] However, it appears to have been rather more an
expedient for ascertaining local knowledge than a means of
shouldering some of the work off the papacy. For this reason
too it was used by Innocent II in the course of the suit
between Bernard, bishop of St. Davids, and Urban, bishop
of Llandaff; but by the time of this pontificate appeals were
increasing in number, and it must soon have become obvious
that delegation could lessen the burden.[2] It appears that
delegation expanded with increasing momentum, and that
this impression is not entirely due to the better legal sources
for the pontificate of Alexander III. Eugenius III possibly
extended delegation. To him were addressed St. Bernard's
remarks on the desirability of delegating more frequently,
cutting down on the number of cases heard by the pope, and
introducing firm measures to deal with frivolous appeals.[3]
But it was the increase in first-instance cases under Alexander
that really got the system under way.[4]

The part played by the bishops in the extension of the
papal judge-delegate system has not gone unrecognized. By
about 1130 the bishops were called upon to fulfil this new
function.[5] In the early days in England the bishops Henry
of Winchester (1129–71), Theobald of Canterbury (1139–
61), and Hilary of Chichester (1147–69), heard some cases.[6]

---

[1] Phillips, *Kirchenrecht*, vi (1864), 756, citing three instances. Phillips thinks that
delegation is to be found with the earliest appeals.

[2] M. Cheney, 'Compromise of Avranches', p. 180; *Liber Landavensis*, repro-
duced by J. Rhys and J. G. Evans (Oxford, 1893), pp. 62 and 66–7 (cited M.
Cheney, 'Compromise of Avranches,' p. 178); and, e.g., *Papsturkunden in Frankreich*, i (Normandy), no. 10, and *P.U.E.* ii, no. 32 (dated 1131 and 1143 respectively). Mrs. Cheney has argued that delegation was employed because of the
advantages of local inquiry rather than because of the pressure of business.

[3] See *De Consideratione*, bk. i chapters iii, vi, x, and xi, in *P.L.* 182.

[4] Barraclough in *E.H.R.* liii (1938), 494 n. 3, dates the beginnings of appellate
jurisdiction as about the pontificate of Eugenius III.

[5] See, e.g., *Papsturkunden in Frankreich*, i, ed. J. Ramackers, no. 10 (a case of
1131).

[6] See Voss, *Heinrich von Blois*, App. ix *h*; Saltman, *Theobald*, Chs. nos. 16, 101,
207, and 212; and *Acta of the Bishops of Chichester*, ed. H. Mayr-Harting, nos. 21,

During the 1160s and 1170s mandates grew noticeably more frequent. Gilbert Foliot of Hereford (1148–63) and later of London (1163–87), Bartholomew of Exeter (1161–84), and Roger of Worcester (1164–79) received sixty or seventy delegations each.[1] As judges in their own diocesan courts, the bishops were presumably familiar with the elements of procedure, and they could be expected to be reasonably knowledgeable about the latest legal pronouncements. New methods became necessary owing to the increase in the number of suits going to Rome and the limited number of bishops in the hierarchy, who were in any case becoming increasingly concerned with other business. As early as the pontificate of Innocent II subdelegation had been made possible.[2] This was usually made to juniors and lesser men. Also delegation was gradually extended to other clerks, particularly regulars. In 1162 the anti-pope Victor IV delegated a suit to an abbot and an archdeacon.[3] Delegation to abbots and lesser dignitaries became common once the bishops had set up the system, so that by the 1180s the bishops were no longer the only ecclesiastics to act as judges delegate.[4]

The earliest instance of a specific body exercising the papal function of delegation is presumably that of the Cistercian General Chapter for hearing causes within the order.[5] The system of delegating cases seems to have followed the papal policy. The parallels in organization are remarkable; for instance, subdelegation occurs, and the phraseology of the mandates and the methods of conducting

36–7, and 43–4. Mayr-Harting in *E.H.R.* lxxviii (1963), 211 and n. 5, says that he has noted fifteen occurrences of Hilary as judge delegate.

[1] M. Cheney, 'Compromise of Avranches', pp. 180–1; A. Morey and C. N. L. Brooke, *Gilbert Foliot and his Letters* (Cambridge, 1965), p. 243, note about forty letters and *acta* of Gilbert dealing with delegated cases, and twenty surviving papal decretals which were addressed to him. See also Morey and Brooke's edition of *The Letters and Charters of Gilbert Foliot*, and Morey, *Bartholomew of Exeter*, chapter iv.

[2] *Decretum*, C. 2 qu. 5 c. 17.

[3] *Papsturkunden in den Niederlanden*, ed. J. Ramackers (Göttingen, Philologisch-Historische Klasse, 3. Folge nr. 8 and 9, Berlin, 1933–4), no. 98, cited by C. N. L. Brooke in *J.S.L.*, p. xxxv n. 1 as the earliest instance in the *Papsturkunden* volumes of delegation to lesser clerics.   [4] See below, pp. 118ff.

[5] For a full discussion of this question, see my article 'The Judicial Activities of the General Chapters', pts. i and ii, in *Journal of Ecclesiastical History*, xv (1964), 18–32, and 168–85.

the hearing of cases and enforcing sentences are similar.[1] It is reasonable to suppose that delegation arose on account of the Cistercians' privileged position and the administrative advantages which it offered with the rapid increase in the number of houses. It was probably well established by 1190, when the General Chapter dealt with eight cases in this way. There are grounds for asserting that the Cistercians were not immediately entirely independent of the papal orbit of justice. Clause 71 of the 1190 *Statuta* stated that the suit between the abbot of Cercamp (dioc. Amiens) and the provost of Douai (dioc. Arras) had been committed to the abbots of Longpont (dioc. Soissons) and Clairmarais (dioc. Thérouanne), and that if an appeal had been made to the pope, it should be withdrawn,[2] and clause 9 of the 1197 *Statuta* threatened excommunication to those Cistercians who tried to take their lawsuits outside the order.[3]

(ii) *The Chancery and the Court of 'Audientia Litterarum Contradictarum'*

Increasing delegation brought considerable pressure to bear on the Chancery. The attraction of the court of Rome to the litigant brought petitioners there in ever-growing numbers, for confirmations of their rights, for concessions, and for mandates to judges delegate to hear their cases in the provinces. This is nowhere more noticeable in the twelfth century than during the pontificate of Alexander III, when hundreds of petitions reached Rome each year. The flood did not abate until the mid-thirteenth century, but by that time development had taken place in the old central offices and new methods had been devised to deal with the increased business.

The papal Chancery or writing office has been credited with a degree of sophistication that was unknown to secular governments until the thirteenth century.[4] Detailed studies have recently shown, however, that Chancery observances and organization were less inflexible and rigid than has

---

[1] See, e.g., *Statuta Capitulorum Generalium Ordinis Cisterciensis*, i, ed. J.-M. Canivez (Bibliothèque de la revue d'histoire ecclésiastique, ix, 1933), 1191, no. 29, 1196, no. 28, and 1192, no. 38.

[2] *Statuta*, 1190, no. 71.   [3] Ibid. 1197, no. 9.

[4] In general on the papal Chancery, see Bresslau.

hitherto been supposed.[1] This is not to say that there were
not distinct types of documents and distinct methods of
applying for them, but that adjustments could be made in
type and method of issue, at least on an exceptional occasion.[2]

The differentiation in style and format between letters of
grace, grants, and privileges, and letters of justice, mandates
of varying kinds, and mainly judicial commissions,[3] suggests
possible different methods of issue, at least in so far as it was
necessary to discriminate between them before a document
could be drawn up. We do not know whether there was a
central clearing-house within the Chancery for sorting and
allocating all types of petitions when they were presented.
But we do know that some documents received the attention
of the pope, whereas others did not,[4] and that a distinction
was made between supplications for grants and petitions for
mandates. A differentiation was also made between important legal petitions, which would possibly demand careful
treatment at Rome and which concerned an important person
or an important principle, and matters of smaller moment
which might safely be delegated and which presented little
problem.[5] The distinction was always fine in so far as at any
time what appeared to be a small matter might in the course
of the hearing develop an importance which could not be
foreseen at the delegation.[6] And conversely, but less frequently, major cases might become minor or at least require
partial delegation for settlement. Such were the cases that
came before curial officials but were at some point delegated
to local judges for ascertaining answers to specific questions.[7]

The role played by the *audientia litterarum contradictarum*
in the issue of the mandate, consequent upon a petition and

---

[1] See, e.g., P. Herde, *Beiträge zum Päpstlichen Kanzlei und Urkundenwesen im
13. Jahrhundert* (Münchener Historische Studien, i, 1961), p. ix.

[2] The difficulty of classifying papal documents into the accepted categories is
perhaps best illustrated by the form of the conservatory mandate. This document
was a hybrid with some features of a letter of grace and some of a letter of justice.

[3] See R. L. Poole, *Lectures on the History of the Papal Chancery* (Cambridge,
1915), pp. 115–19.

[4] Ibid., pp. 118–19.

[5] See *P.L.* 214, *Gesta*, section xli, cols. lxxx–lxxxi, where Innocent III differ-
entiates between the two.   [6] See below, p. 17.

[7] See below, p. 18.

impetration, will be dealt with below.[1] Its importance to be noted here is as a department of the Chancery, necessitated by the growing amount of delegation and acting as a control point in the delegation of suits. It is possible that it existed prior to the time of Innocent III, but it is more likely that it originated during that pontificate. Under Innocent III there was much definition in the papal Chancery. In 1203, for example, he thought fit to write about the exactitude of clauses in mandates.[2] The function of the court of *audientia litterarum contradictarum* was to filter the causes and safeguard the defendant in delegation if he sent his proctor to Rome. Its significance for the thirteenth century is embedded in its establishment as a new office, albeit part of the Chancery, with its own officer who acted under the vice-chancellor.[3] In the Wells case their proctors sought if possible a hearing at Rome, and failing this, delegation to certain named judges who were listed in order of preference. This presupposes the notion that the client instructed his proctor as to which sort of hearing he wanted. The proctor presumably then acted accordingly. His method or choice of action is not clear to us, but behind the formal approaches we may suspect a network that could be broken into by personal contacts, which might momentarily alter the common system of which too we know almost nothing.

The resultant document from a petition for delegation, the mandate, was made clearly distinguishable from the papal grant or privilege, not only because it was important to have set forms to avoid forgery and alteration, but also because speedy execution was needed. The terse nature of the mandate and the arrival at common forms meant that it could be speedily drawn up. Set phrases were used, small cuts of parchment utilized, and the scribe in many instances only varied from the common form in writing the names of the parties and of the judges. Of course, if variations were ordered, the process was slowed up, but otherwise the issue was swift and easy. The general run of mandates passed

---

[1] See below, pp. 55–8.

[2] *P.L.* 215, no. cxc, col. 209 (c. 15. *X.* I. 3); and see below, pp. 65–70.

[3] See below, pp. 20 ff; and Herde, *Beiträge*, pp. 164–73. *Reg. Inn. IV*, no. 7295 is an instance of the *auditor litterarum contradictarum* being designated to act for the vice-chancellor, presumably during his absence.

without being contradicted by the defendant's proctor, and were dispatched to the provinces as soon as they were sealed and paid for.[1]

(iii) *The Court of Auditors*

The growth of the court of Auditors, or *Rota*,[2] is comparable with the establishment of the court of *audientia litterarum contradictarum* as a product of the governmental needs of the thirteenth century. The origins of the court of Auditors are equally obscure, but its purpose was clearly to hear cases of importance at Rome for the pope.[3]

Major suits were reserved for the pope to hear himself, and in these cases he might take counsel of the cardinals. The pope heard them in synod or *in Curia*, or in the consistory. In front of Leo IX (1049–54), in a synod in the church of the Saviour, John, bishop of Porto, brought his complaint against Crescentius, bishop of Silva Candida, about the church of St. John the Baptist and St. Adalbert on the island of Licaonia in the Tiber;[4] and in May 1126 Honorius II decided *in Curia* a suit between the church of St. Maria Nova and the monastery of St. Saba.[5] By the time of Innocent II (1130–43) strain on this personal system is becoming evident. The hearing of the case between Peter, abbot of SS. Andrew and Gregory, and Odo de Polo was begun in front of Innocent II in the Lateran Council, but because the pope was busy with other affairs it was deferred until after the Council had met.[6] During this Council also, the numerous charges were heard of Azo, abbot of the monastery of St. Paul, against a host of defendants.[7] Governmental business increased considerably during this pontificate and the cardi-

---

[1] See below, pp. 54–8.

[2] *Rota* is a later name for the court, and is supposed to have come from the round table at which the auditors sat, see Phillips, *Kirchenrecht*, vi (1864), 449.

[3] In general see N. Iung, 'Auditeur', *D.D.C.* i, cols. 1399–1403; E. Cerchiari, *Capellani Papae et Apostolicae Sedis Auditores Causarum Sacri Palatii Apostolici seu Sacra Romana Rota*, 3 vols. (Rome, 1919–21), esp. vol. i, chapter i; Phillips, *Kirchenrecht*, vi. 449–72; and P. Hinschius, *Das Kirchenrecht der Katholiken und Protestanten in Deutschland*, i (Berlin, 1869), 392–6.

[4] *Regesta Pontificum Romanorum—Italia Pontificia*, ii, ed. P. F. Kehr (Berlin, 1907), 20, no. 12 (9–15 Apr. 1049).

[5] *Italia Pontificia*, i (1906), 67, no. 7, and cf. 122, no. 2 (1153–4).

[6] Ibid. 106, no. 8 (4 Apr. 1139–43).

[7] Ibid. 169, no. 20; and ii, 28, no. 5, and 34, no. 1.

nals were now claiming a greater share in the government of the Church, so that cases were heard more frequently in consistory than in the old synod.[1]

As the pope heard cases with the counsel of his most trusted advisers, the practice soon arose of delegating certain cases to the officers of his household, the subdeacons and chaplains, and the cardinals. These men fulfilled the duties of the archdeacons and officials in other dioceses, with the difference that their powers were not permanent. The practice was an old one. Between 1099 and 1118 Paschal II ordered his chancellor John of Gaeta to hear a cause between the church of the Twelve Apostles and the church of St. Mark,[2] and in the presence of Gerard, vicar of Lucius III, and of Hyacinth and Peter de Bono, cardinals, the quarrel between the Terracinenses and the Frangipani was related.[3] The pope's vicar seems to have acted as a counterpart of the bishop's official, deciding causes when the pope was absent or busy.[4] Delegation to cardinals became increasingly common in the twelfth century.[5] They are found frequently dealing with cases on appeal for the pope, and in about 1154–9 certain cardinals decided a suit between the pope himself and a bishop.[6] The method was well established by the time of Celestine III, but as yet there was nothing approaching a corporate and permanent institution.

The impermanent nature of the auditor's status during Innocent III's pontificate is illustrated by his various appointments; for instance, that of P(eter Suarez de Deza), archbishop of Compostella, and Odo, bishop of Terdona (Italy) when both men were visiting Rome during 1198. The pope, however, took the necessary precaution of stating that if the bishop should have left the city by this time, M. (a papal subdeacon and chaplain) should be substituted in his place.[7] Between 1206 and 1209 a cause was commited to T., papal subdeacon and chaplain, as auditor, but because T. was absent,

---

[1] See C. R. Cheney, *From Becket to Langton* (Manchester, 1956), p. 52.

[2] *Italia Pontificia*, i. 72, nos. 2 and 3. For John of Gaeta, see Poole, *Papal Chancery*, pp. 74–5.

[3] *Italia Pontificia*, i. 194, no. 17 (1184–5), and see 80, no. 6 (1147).

[4] Ibid. 51, no. 6 (1148).   [5] e.g. ibid. 142, no. 36 (1158).   [6] Ibid. ii. 38, no. 3.

[7] *P.L.* 214, no. cclxxxiii, col. 237 (c. 13. *X*. II. 27 and *Regesta Pontificum Romanorum*, i, ed. A. Potthast (Berlin, 1874), no. 292).

it had to be recommitted to the bishop of Albano.¹ At the end
of the St. Davids case between Gerald of Wales, archdeacon
of Brecon, and the archbishop of Canterbury, the question
of costs was referred to Hugolinus, cardinal deacon of St.
Eustace (later cardinal bishop of Ostia, and Pope Gregory
IX).² In 1206 Guala, cardinal deacon of St. Mary in Porticu
and later legate in England, dealt with one of the issues in
the protracted case between the bishop of Worcester and the
abbot of Evesham about churches in the Vale of Evesham.³
These were sporadic appointments, and as yet no continuity
in the office of auditor had been attained.⁴

It is soon possible to detect the use of the same men under
at least two popes, for instance Peter de Collemedio under
Honorius III and Gregory IX, and John de Sancto
Germano under Gregory IX and Innocent IV.⁵ There is no
evidence in the *Decretales* of Gregory IX of 1234 that the
auditors were yet an established tribunal, but some time
during the middle years of that pontificate that is what they
came to be. With the pontificate of Innocent IV, the auditors
assumed or were granted the description *generalis*, either
auditor generalis causarum palatii or *auditor generalis causarum
curie*.⁶ This permanent body received its power to hear cases
directly from the pope.⁷

The auditor was appointed to hear a particular suit, much
as the judge delegates in early cases. His powers were to
make inquiries only, unless he was given a special mandate to
pass a definitive sentence.⁸ An auditor was thus defined in the

---

¹ *Reg. Hon. III*, no. 119 (c. 10. X. II. 22 and *Reg. Pont. Rom.* i, ed. Potthast,
no. 3872).

² Giraldus Cambrensis, *Opera*, iii, ed. J. S. Brewer (R.S. xxi, 1863), 274.

³ *Chronicon Abbatiae de Evesham*, ed. W. D. Macray (R.S. xxix, 1863), p. 191.

⁴ With Innocent III the phrase '*concessimus auditores*' or '*dedimus auditores*',
e.g. *Reg. Greg. IX*, nos. 2134 and 2621, was used.

⁵ Cerchiari, *Capellani Papae et Apostolicae Sedis Auditores*, ii (1920), 8–10.

⁶ Under Innocent IV there were four auditors *generales causarum palatii*, Bonus
Johannes, J. Spata, Simon, and John Astensis, and three auditors *generales curie*,
Guillelmus Bardini, Martinus, and Vernacius; F. E. Schneider, *Die Römische Rota*
(Paderborn, 1914), p. 7. See also *Reg. Inn. IV*, nos. 2363, 2456, 2598–9, 3141, and
3921; and nos. 6960 and 7530.

⁷ See Appendix A (i), Auditors appointed by Gregory IX and Innocent IV to
hear English lawsuits.

⁸ *P.L.* 214, no. cccxiv, col. 274 (Inn. III); and Cerchiari, *Capellani Papae et
Apostolicae Sedis Auditores*, iii (1919), 7.

Decretales: 'he to whom the middle of a case is committed is called a *cognitor* or an *executor* or better still an auditor.'[1] The canonist William Durand, who was an auditor under Clement IV (1265–8),[2] says:

In curia autem Romana auditores dicuntur, qui aliorum vice causas examinant; sed sine illorum mandato potestatem diffiniendi non habent: unde et generales auditores palatii domini Papae vice et loco ipsius domini, causas examinant et audiunt, et postea eidem domino referunt; ut secundum eius imperium, et beneplacitum sententias eius auctoritate promulgent, et causas decidant . . .[3]

The glossator Baldus de Ubaldis summed this up as 'general auditors of the sacred palace have ordinary jurisdictional powers in hearing cases but not in deciding'.[4]

The auditors were used increasingly to hear suits that had already opened before judges delegate, but had not been settled, and which thus acquired the status of major causes. Such were the Rochester, Cliffe-at-Hoo (Kent), and Buckingham cases. The Rochester case between the prior and convent of Rochester and the archbishop of Canterbury, over the election of the bishop of Rochester, began before the abbot of Walden, the prior of Merton, and the archdeacon of Northampton, who were ordered to bring the case to an end within four months or to remit it to Rome. The case is next discovered before Stephen, cardinal of St. Mary in Trastevere, but with the appeal of the convent of Rochester it was delegated again, with the same instructions, this time to the abbot of St. Albans, the prior of Merton, and the archdeacon of St. Albans. The case was still not settled by delegation, and it was not brought to an end until Giles, cardinal deacon of SS. Cosmas and Damian, heard it.[5] The Cliffe-at-Hoo case followed an almost identical course. Four commissions of judges were involved in it before delegation to the abbot of St. Albans, the prior of Dunstable, and the archdeacon of Northampton, with orders to decide the cause with the consent of the parties or to return it to the pope. After a hearing

---

[1] c. 17. *X*. I. 29.
[2] Cerchiari, *Capellani Papae et Apostolicae Sedis Auditores*, ii. 13–15.
[3] Durand, *Speculum Juris* (Frankfurt, 1668), p. 92, lib. 1, pt. 1, '*De Auditore*'.
[4] Durand, *Speculum Juris*, p. 92.
[5] *Reg. Greg. IX*, no. 2731, and App. A (i), nos. 4 and 28.

in front of Sinibald, cardinal priest of St. Laurence in Lucina, it came finally for settlement before Giles, cardinal deacon of SS. Cosmas and Damian.[1]

A similar array of judges delegate and auditors appeared in the case between John de Vercellis, canon of Lincoln, and the archdeacon of Buckingham. This time the case appears to have begun before an auditor (the plaintiff was a papal subdeacon), who was not able to settle it and appears to have needed more detailed evidence. The archbishop, dean, and chancellor of York were accordingly ordered to examine the witnesses and muniments which both parties could produce, and to settle the cause or remit it to Rome. The auditor, Giles, cardinal deacon of SS. Cosmas and Damian, was away from Rome when the case was returned there, so this time it was commited to Thomas, cardinal of St. Sabina, who gave sentence in favour of John de Vercellis. On 20 April 1239 the legate in England, Cardinal Otto, was ordered to execute the sentence and to induct John into Buckingham church.[2] A year later the archdeacon went to Rome and obtained that R(ichard de Annibaldis), cardinal of St. Angelo, should hear his cause, and while the suit was in progress he ordered his men to occupy the church. When this became known, the pope immediately ordered the archbishop-elect of Canterbury (Boniface of Savoy) to have the archdeacon's men ejected from the church and John restored, citing the archdeacon to appear before him. This time the suit was committed to Octavian, cardinal deacon of St. Mary in Via Lata who, having heard the case in his house near the cathedral at Lyons, decided that the church of Buckingham belonged to the prebend of Sutton, which was held by the archdeacon, and that the church of St. Margaret Pottergate, Lincoln, belonged to John de Vercellis as prebendary of Walton. The sentence was confirmed by the pope.[3]

The step was short from the auditor's having ordinary powers of hearing a case to gaining ordinary powers of settling. In practice the auditors seem usually to have been granted the necessary power to pass sentence, at least from the time of their establishment as a court. By 1326 a

[1] App. A (i), nos. 3 and 27.   [2] Ibid., nos. 2 and 30.
[3] Ibid., nos. 19 and 25.

fully established and permanent court can be seen working smoothly. A petitioner wishing to take his case before an auditor would go to the vice-chancellor, who, if he thought the suit important enough, designated an auditor.[1] By 1331 the auditors had attained an ordinary power of passing sentence, a power which sprang from the continuing high pressure in the number of cases which found their way to Rome, just as the development of auditors making inquiries for the pope had done.[2]

(iv) *The New Officers*

The establishment of new offices meant an increase in the number of men who were directly concerned in the judicial administration of the Church, both at the centre and in the provinces. The pope turned firstly to the officers of his household to fill the chief positions within the *Curia*. The main qualification for advancement was the possession of a legal training and legal experience. It is a commonplace that the thirteenth century was the age of lawyer popes, but it has perhaps been overlooked how far these qualifications permeated the whole hierarchy of the *Curia Romana*. As Adam, abbot of Perseigne and confessor to Richard I, remarked, the road to advancement in the Church was by way of legal studies.[3] This was to become more marked in the thirteenth century. An aptitude for legal studies, together with some training from one of the famous law schools of the thirteenth century, could bring a promising career within the *Curia*. Distinct methods of progress and a definite ladder of advancement from office to office were becoming apparent.

Connection with an Italian or Roman noble family, or with a member of the *Curia Romana*, was a further important and useful qualification. The family of Savelli produced the popes Honorius III and Honorius IV, the family of Fieschi included the popes Innocent IV and Adrian V, while the counts of Segni supplied the popes Innocent III, Gregory IX, and Alexander IV. Each of the Segni popes owed his

---

[1] G. Mollat, 'Contribution à l'histoire de l'administration judiciaire de l'Église romaine au XIVe siècle', *Rev. d'histoire ecclésiastique*, xxxii (1936), 877–928, and esp. 878–90.

[2] Ibid. 891, and D. Bouix, *Tractatus de Curia Romana* (Paris, 1859), pp. 279–94.

[3] Cheney, *Becket to Langton*, p. 16.

appointment as cardinal to a kinsman. Innocent III was promoted by Clement III, and Gregory IX, who was formerly
Hugolinus cardinal deacon of St. Eustace and cardinal
bishop of Ostia, was promoted by Innocent III.¹ John de
Camezano, *auditor litterarum contradictarum*, William Fieschi,
an auditor and cardinal deacon of St. Eustace, and Ottobon
Fieschi, later legate to England and Pope Adrian V, all
curial officers, were the relatives, probably nephews, of
Innocent IV.² Richard de Annibaldis, an auditor and cardinal
deacon of St. Angelo, was a nephew of Rainald of Segni,
cardinal bishop of Ostia and later Pope Alexander IV. He
had as his chaplain John of Somercotes who was a relative
of Cardinal Robert of Somercotes, one of the few Englishmen
at the *Curia* and *auditor litterarum contradictarum*, auditor and
finally cardinal.³ Promising nephews and sons of influential
nobles, particularly of the great Roman clerical dynasties,
might be rapidly promoted, but the positions which were
granted to them were far from sinecures.

One of the key positions for a young man was the office of
auditor litterarum contradictarum. The first office holder who is
known is Master Otto, papal chaplain and subdeacon, who
was *auditor litterarum contradictarum* between 1216 and
1217.⁴ On 13 August 1225, as an auditor, he was ordered
to inquire into an English plea with Stephen Langton,
archbishop of Canterbury.⁵ He may be the same Master
Odo, Octo, or Otto who appears as a subdeacon, chaplain,
and papal auditor under Innocent III and Gregory IX.⁶

¹ For Cardinal Hugolinus, and particularly for his connections with Christ
Church, Canterbury, for whom he acted as advocate, see especially *Epistolae Cantua-
rienses*, ed. W. Stubbs (R.S. xxxviii, 1865), pp. 471, 476, and 506.

² The observations in this paragraph are compiled from A. Mercati, 'The New
List of Popes', *Mediaeval Studies*, ix (1947), 78; Eubel, pp. 3–7; and A. Ciaconius,
Vitae et Res Gestae Pontificum Romanorum et S.R.E. Cardinalium, ii (Rome, 1677),
cols. 1–207.

³ Richard de Annibaldis heard two English cases, see App. A (i), nos. 25–6. For
John of Somercotes, see Lanthony Cart., A I, VI, no. xli; *Close Rolls (1242–7)*, p. 146.

⁴ *Quinque Compilationes Antiquae*, ed. E. Friedberg (Leipzig, 1882), p. 153. For
a list of *auditores litterarum contradictarum* see Bresslau, p. 284 n. 1. Master Otto
was added by G. Barraclough, '*Audientia Litterarum Contradictarum*', *D.D.C.* i,
col. 1390. To these may be added Master Robert of Somercotes, auditor between
1 Mar. and 20 May 1238.   ⁵ *Reg. Hon. III*, no. 5601 (*C.P.L.* i. 103).

⁶ Cerchiari, *Capellani Papae et Apostolicae Sedis Auditores*, ii. 7 and 9. See also
Regesta Chartarum Italiae—Regestum Volaterranum, ed. F. Schneider (Rome, 1907),
p. 154, no. 440.

Unfortunately no more is known of him, and he may well represent the type of papal officer acting in a temporary, rather than in a permanent, capacity. His successor was Master Sinibald Fieschi, a Genoese, who was born at the end of the twelfth century. He was therefore a man of approximately thirty when he was appointed *auditor litterarum contradictarum*, for he occupied the position at least by 14 November 1226.[1] Before entering the service of the *Curia*, he had lectured at Bologna and he had been a canon at Parma.[2] His tenure was short. By 8 June 1227 he is found as vice-chancellor.[3] In the September of that year he was created cardinal priest of St. Laurence in Lucina at the first promotion of Gregory IX.[4] As cardinal he figured frequently as an auditor, and he took part in the hearing of the case between the rector of Cliffe-at-Hoo and the officials of the archdeacon of Canterbury about archidiaconal rights in the church of Cliffe.[5] In 1235 he became bishop of Albenga, and on 28 June 1243 he reached the highest office, being consecrated pope under the name of Innocent IV.[6] As pope he sanctioned the foundation of a law school within the Lateran Palace, wrote a commentary on the *Decretales* of Gregory IX, and promulgated three important collections of decretals.[7]

The career of Master Vernacius was less brilliant, but he reached the archiepiscopate via the offices of *auditor litterarum contradictarum* and papal auditor. In 1229 he held the office of the *contradictarum*.[8] He is also mentioned as a papal chaplain.[9] From February 1231 to October 1247 he was a canon of Treviso, resident at Paris, and possibly attached to the university law school in some capacity; during this time he acted frequently as a judge delegate.[10] In about 1252 he

---

[1] Bresslau, p. 284 n. 1.

[2] Tierney, *Conciliar Theory*, p. 259, and Ciaconius, *Vitae et Res Gestae*, ii, col. 99.

[3] *Reg. Greg. IX*, no. 100.   [4] Eubel, p. 6.

[5] Ciaconius, *Vitae et Res Gestae*, ii, col. 81; and, e.g., *Reg. Greg. IX*, nos. 1019, 1034, 1364, 1671, 1900, and 2215. See App. A (i), no. 27.

[6] Tierney, *Conciliar Theory*, p. 259; P. B. Gams, *Series Episcoporum Ecclesiae Catholicae* (Regensburg, 1873), p. 810; and Eubel, p. 7.

[7] Tierney, *Conciliar Theory*, p. 259.   [8] Bresslau, p. 284 n. 1.

[9] Binham Cart., f. 141ʳ, document dated 1251, but presumably he had held this minor office for some while.

[10] *Reg. Greg. IX*, no. 549, and *Reg. Inn. IV*, nos. 3154 and 3272.

became archbishop elect of Reggio in Calabria.[1] He was by
now presumably at the papal court again, for from before 19
June 1251 to 22 May 1254 he was a general auditor of the
Curia and heard a Norfolk case.[2] He died in possession of
the church of Loddon in Norfolk.[3] His successor at the
audientia litterarum contradictarum, Master Robert of Somercotes, who reached the status of cardinal after holding the
offices of *auditor litterarum contradictarum* and papal auditor,
was the only Englishman to hold the former post. He had
been at the schools of Paris and Bologna. A former friend,
Stephen of Lexington, abbot of Savigny, wrote to him as
auditor litterarum contradictarum, commending his proctor
G. in the cause which he was bringing to Rome.[4] He was
appointed a cardinal in 1239, and it is said by Matthew
Paris that he would have been elected pope if he had not died
in 1241 in the course of the conclave which finally elected
Celestine IV. His rise can probably be accounted for by his
legal training.[5]

The claims of lawyers on these offices are nowhere better
exemplified than by two successors at the *audientia litterarum
contradictarum*, Geoffrey de Trani and William de Cathadego.
Geoffrey de Trani had taught civil law at Naples and canon
law at Bologna before entering the service of the Roman
Curia.[6] He came from the same family as Celestine IV, but
the exact relationship between them is not clear. He was a
chaplain under Honorius III, and by 11 July 1240 he was
a papal subdeacon and *auditor litterarum contradictarum*. He
probably remained at the *audientia litterarum contradictarum*
until his death.[7] Besides his most famous work the *Summa in
Titulos Decretalium*, he produced *Questiones* and glosses on

---

[1] *Reg. Inn. IV*, no. 5646.

[2] See App. A (i), no. 32, and *Reg. Inn. IV*, no. 7626. In 1224 he had witnessed
a Norfolk charter, Norwich, Reg. III, f. 239ʳ⁻ᵛ.

[3] *Reg. Inn. IV*, no. 8222. He was allowed to keep the church as archbishop. Gams,
Series Episcoporum, p. 916, gives 1252 as the date of his confirmation, but it would
seem to have been between 22 May (*Reg. Inn. IV*, no. 7626) and 12 Nov. 1254
ibid., no. 8220).

[4] See 'Registrum Epistolarum Stephani de Lexinton', pars ii, ed. P. B. Griesser,
Analecta Sacri Ordinis Cisterciensis, viii (1952), 315–16, no. 101.

[5] See my article, 'Canterbury Proctors at the Court of *Audientia Litterarum
Contradictarum*', *Traditio*, xxii (1966), 325 n. 87, for a more detailed account of his
career.

[6] Tierney, *Conciliar Theory*, p. 258.   [7] Bresslau, p. 284 n. 1.

the Gregorian compilation, the *Decretales*.[1] His legal aptitude was recognized by Innocent IV. He was created cardinal deacon of St. Adrian at the first promotion in September 1244, but he died in March of the following year before the important achievements of that pontificate had taken place.[2] He had been granted by the pope two parts of the fruits from the church of Gainford (Durham).[3] William de Cathadego had been master of the schools at Parma, a celebrated Italian law centre, before he was appointed a papal chaplain and *auditor litterarum contradictarum*. He occupied this position in 1246 and presumably remained there until appointment as vice-chancellor, an office which he held from 31 December 1251 to 5 May 1256.[4] A document, which was composed in his name as *auditor litterarum contradictarum* and dated 18 March 1249 at Lyons, is copied into the Easby cartulary.[5] He was himself engaged in a suit about the priory of Villa Petrosa, which he won.[6] He seems to have been followed at the *audientia litterarum contradictarum* from 1252 to 1256 by Master John de Camezano, papal chaplain and relative of Pope Innocent IV, who was the last of Innocent IV's *auditores litterarum contradictarum*.[7] He was involved in a lawsuit with St. Augustine's, Canterbury, about the church of Lenham, which was heard by John de Sancto Germano, subdeacon and chaplain of the pope, acting as auditor.[8]

The office of papal auditor was at first a temporary appointment, often held by lesser curial officials, but by Innocent IV's pontificate it had come to be an important permanent position, usually occupied by cardinals. Master Peter de Collemedio's career witnessed this transition. He was a papal chaplain under Honorius III and Gregory IX,

---

[1] Tierney, *Conciliar Theory*, p. 258.

[2] Eubel, p. 7.   [3] See below, p. 274 n. 3.

[4] Bresslau, pp. 251 and 284 n. 1, and *Reg. Inn. IV*, nos. 5572, 6443, and 8184.

[5] Easby Cart., ff. 319ᵛ–20ʳ.

[6] *Reg. Inn. IV*, nos. 1734 and 1795.   [7] Bresslau, p. 284 n. 1.

[8] App. A (i), no. 9. His nephew was rector of Brize Norton (Oxon.), and engaged in a suit with Thame before the dean of Arches, acting as judge delegate. His proctor, on seeing Thame's privileges, renounced the claim; *Thame Cartulary*, ed. H. E. Salter (Oxfordshire Rec. Soc. xxv–xxvi, 1947–8), no. 234. Another canonist to hold the office was Guy de Baysio, archdeacon of Bologna, and *auditor litterarum contradictarum* from 1304 to 1312; he wrote a gloss on the *Sext*, an apparatus of glosses on the *Decretum*, and a work called the *Rosarium* (Bresslau, p. 284 n. 1, and Tierney, *Conciliar Theory*, p. 258).

and was used as an auditor.[1] In 1217 Honorius III sent him as legate to Frederick II. Gregory IX dispatched him on legation to the count of Toulouse, and in June 1229 he held a council at Toulouse.[2] He was a master of decrees, and archbishop of Rouen from 1237 to 1244.[3] As a recognition of his service to the *Curia*, Innocent IV created him cardinal bishop of Albano in September 1244. He died in this office on 25 May 1253.[4] He had continued to hear causes as an auditor, and in 1252 he settled the dispute between the archbishop of Canterbury, and the dean and chapter of St. Paul's and the priors and convents of St. Bartholomew and of Holy Trinity, London, over the archbishop's right to visit them.[5] His previous connection with Pandulf's household and his tenure of a prebend of St. Paul's in the 1220s must have given him a knowledge of English affairs, and may well explain his appointment on this occasion.[6]

The ear of a friendly cardinal or curial official might be decisive not only in the treatment of the case, as to whether it was major or not, but also as to which auditor was appointed to hear it. In the course of the Bath and Wells election case of 1242–3, overtures were made to several cardinals —to John of Colonna, cardinal priest of St. Prassede and a member of the old Roman family of Colonna, to Richard de Annibaldis, and to the former legate in England, Cardinal Otto.[7] The number of English cases heard by John of Toledo, cardinal priest of St. Laurence in Lucina and auditor under Innocent IV, seems attributable to his English origin, and suggests something of the forces at work in the conduct

---

[1] Cerchiari, *Capellani Papae et Apostolicae Sedis Auditores*, ii. 8–9; *Reg. Hon. III*, no. 656; and *Reg. Greg. IX*, nos. 445 and 477.

[2] Gams, *Series Episcoporum*, p. xxii; *Reg. Greg. IX*, no. 477; and *Sacrorum Conciliorum . . . Collectio*, xxiii, ed. Mansi, cols. 99–100.

[3] Eubel, p. 7, and Gams, *Series Episcoporum*, p. 614.

[4] Eubel, p. 7, and Gams, *Series Episcoporum*, p. xxii.

[5] See App. A (i), no. 22.

[6] *Patent Rolls of the Reign of Henry III 1216–25* (1901), p. 205; St. Bartholomew's Hospital Muniments, Box St. Andrew Holborn, no. 19, cal. N. Moore, *History of St. Bartholomew's Hospital*, i (1918), 354; and Le Neve, *Fasti 1066–1300*, i (St. Paul's, London) (1968), revsd. and ed. D. E. Greenway, p. 54.

[7] See Wells, Lib. Albus I, ff. 75ʳ, 79ᵛ, and 98ᵛ. Cardinal Richard received £50 as a gift from the chapter, and f. 86ᵛ mentions that a yearly pension of 100 marks was being paid to Octavian cardinal deacon of St. Mary in Via Lata by the dean and chapter in 1268.

of major suits.[1] He was probably at the medical school of Toledo, becoming a monk of Clairvaux, abbot of l'Épau in the diocese of Le Mans,[2] vicar of Rome, and on 24 May 1244 a cardinal.[3] He played a notable part in the canonization process of the English archbishop, Edmund of Abingdon.[4] Matthew de Alperino, who figured in two of the English cases which Cardinal John heard, was himself a papal auditor.[5] Two more of the suits heard by John of Toledo concerned English benefices; and he was involved in the settlement of the case between Daventry and La Charité, and in the Paxton suit.[6] The case between Godfrey de Toffetes, clerk of the bishop of Winchester, and Anthony, canon of Piacenza, about Alresford church (Hants), was passed to him by John Orsini, cardinal of St. Nicholas in Carcere and later Pope Nicholas III, who also heard English cases.[7]

4. Contact with the Provinces

(i) Legates

None of the papal officers wielded as much power as the legates. They acted as the main connection between the *Curia* and the provinces of the Church. Since Gregory VII's pontificate the possibilities of their function had been realized, and legations were regarded as forming one of the principal instruments of papal authority in the Church.[8] Under Alexander III new impetus was given to the legatine system, and he declared:

As we have been elevated to the Apostolic See by the will of God to watch over the whole Church, we ought to enlarge the field of our

---

[1] See App. A (i), nos. 10–15.

[2] Dom L. H. Cottineau, *Répertoire topo-bibliographique des abbayes et prieurés*, 2 vols. (Mâcon, 1935–7), col. 1054.

[3] J.-B. Mahn, *L'Ordre cistercien et son gouvernement* (Bibliothèque des Écoles françaises d'Athènes et de Rome, clxi, 1945), pp. 166–7. In 1262 he was promoted to the cardinal bishopric of Porto. He died on 13 July 1275.

[4] C. H. Lawrence, *St. Edmund of Abingdon* (Oxford, 1960), pp. 15, 17–18, and 46.

[5] App. A (i), nos. 11 and 14; and Cerchiari, *Capellani Papae et Apostolicae Sedis Auditores*, ii. 10.

[6] App. A (i), nos. 13 and 15, and see below, p. 176.

[7] Ibid., nos. 16–18.

[8] See, e.g., *Das Register Gregors VII*, ed. E. Caspar (Berlin, 1920), i, 17.

vigilance by approving of visitation of those whom we cannot visit personally by men in whom we have complete confidence.[1]

He also made it possible for the legates to exercise direct judicial powers.[2]

The visitation of the provinces by the pope's representatives secured contact between the policy at Rome and the local developments. The legates intervened directly in details of ecclesiastical administration, reform, and correction, and they supervised the smooth working of the machinery of justice.[3] They dealt with any abuse which might come to the notice of a bishop on tour of his diocese, introduced methods of improvement, and held councils.

Legates empowered with judicial and corrective authority were usually legates *a latere*, although clear distinctions between them and *legati nati*, apostolic vicars, and *legati missi* or nuncios with a special mission, are not apparent until the first half of the thirteenth century.[4] The appointment of legates chosen from the local hierarchy in England in the twelfth century is accounted for by the difficulty of access for legates *a latere*.[5] The legates *a latere* were papal plenipotentiaries, usually cardinals, whose mandates could only be resisted by an appeal to the pope. They enjoyed full authority and confidence by sharing in the pope's *plena potestas*.[6] They could enforce jurisdiction over metropolitans, bishops, and exempt houses, and could command obedience from them. In the course of time they came to hear causes

---

[1] *P.L.* 200, no. cxxxi, col. 197: 'In apostolicae sedis specula, disponente Domino, constituti ad universum corpus Ecclesiae ita debemus aciem nostrae considerationis extendere, ut de his, quos nos ipsi non possumus corporaliter visitare, per alios, de quibus plenam fiduciam habeamus, curam et sollicitudinem gerere comprobemus', quoted by M. Pacaut, 'Les Légats d'Alexandre III (1159–81)', *Rev. d'histoire ecclésiastique*, l (1955), 821–2. Cf. *Decretum*, dist. xciv c. 1: 'Valde necessarium perspeximus, ut . . . ubi nos presentes esse non possumus, nostra per eum, cui precepimus, representetur auctoritas', quoted by K. Ruess, *Die Rechtliche Stellung der Päpstlichen Legaten* (Paderborn, 1912), p. 1.

[2] c. 1. *X.* I. 30.   [3] See, e.g., *P.L.* 215, no. ccix, cols. 523–4.

[4] Pacaut, 'Les Légats d'Alexandre III', p. 838. Archbishop Hubert Walter was appointed legate in 1195 with judicial powers in both provinces, and in June of that year he heard certain ecclesiastical lawsuits at York (Cheney, *Hubert Walter*, p. 120).   [5] Pacaut, 'Les Légats d'Alexandre III', p. 824.

[6] See Phillips, *Kirchenrecht*, vi. 684 ff., and esp. 711–46; and *P.L.* 214, no. cxxiii, col. 677 (Inn. III): 'In diversas provincias legatos a nostro latere destinamus, quibus tanto amplius credatur a subditis, quanto specialius eis apostolicae sedis auctoritas delegatur.'

which would otherwise have been taken to the pope.[1] John of Salerno, cardinal priest of St. Stephen on the Caelian Hill, as legate for Scotland in 1201, heard a suit about boundaries between Melrose and Kelso. According to the Chronicle of Melrose, he stayed two months, accepted presents, and made promises to both parties, but came to no decision. He did, however, ask the king to deal with the case.[2] While he was in England, the abbot and convent of St. Augustine's plaint about the church of Faversham was made before him, and he reported on this matter to the pope.[3]

John of Ferentino, cardinal deacon of St. Mary in Via Lata, arrived in England at the end of May 1206 and stayed until October of the same year. Unfortunately little is known of his judicial activities except for the following few instances. He heard a tithe case between the abbot and convent of Beaulieu and William de Bodeham, parson of Inglesham (Wilts.), which was settled by arbitration under penalty of ten marks; he commissioned the abbots of Lilleshall and Haughmond to proceed with the Evesham inquiry; and an appeal was made to his court by the nuns of Harrold priory, who had been engaged in a fluctuating suit against Baldwin the clerk who was son of Baldwin of Guines, an influential magnate. Only the tenacity of the nuns and their refusal to be outwitted and outdone had brought them this far. The legate heard the case in person, but as difficulties arose and he was about to leave England, he thought it best to refer the matter to the pope.[4] From these few scraps of evidence, it seems that appeal to the legatine court was firmly established by this time.

As appeals to their courts became numerous, the legates began to delegate causes to judges in the localities.[5] The

---

[1] Phillips, *Kirchenrecht*, vi. 730.

[2] H. Tillmann, *Die Päpstlichen Legaten in England bis zur Beendigung der Legation Gualas* (1218) (Bonn, 1926), p. 90, and Thomas Mackay, Lord Cooper, *Select Scottish Cases of the Thirteenth Century* (Edinburgh and London, 1944), p. 3, no. 2.

[3] St. Augustine's White Book, f. 106ʳ.

[4] See C. R. Cheney, 'Cardinal John of Ferentino, papal legate in England in 1206', *E.H.R.* lxxvi (1961), 654–60, where the legate's known *acta* are listed; and also the same author's 'The Papal Legate and the English Monasteries in 1206', *E.H.R.* xlvi (1931), 446, and 'Harrold Priory: a Twelfth Century Dispute', *Beds. Hist. Rec. Soc.* xxxii (1952), no. 13.

[5] See c. 11. *X*. I. 31 (*Pastoralis*), and c. 7. 6. I. 14 (*Si delegatus*).

delegation of causes by the legates was a common European occurrence, similar to the calling of legatine councils. In yet another respect it is possible to show that England was in touch with the latest canonical developments. Her reception of them, however, may have been retarded by political circumstances. At least as early as 1172–3, legates to the Empire were delegating cases for both inquiry and settlement. An instance is the delegation by Conrad, cardinal bishop of Sabina, of a cause between the canons of Vicenza and the prior and monks of St. Silvester, necessitated by the legate's preoccupation with other affairs.[1] Records of many other instances survive, a witness to the increasing amount of judicial business which came with the pontificate of Alexander III.[2] The first known delegations by a legate *a latere* in England occur during the visit of Nicholas, cardinal bishop of Tusculum, between September 1213 and December 1214, and thus may be associated with the relaxation of the Interdict and the submission of John.[3] In one suit the legate had delegated a case to the priors of Coxford, Binham, and Walsingham, which the defendants alleged concerned lay fee, and a writ of prohibition was therefore obtained.[4] In another, the judges were W(illiam) de Muschamp, archdeacon of Derby, and William and John, canons and chaplains of All Saints, Derby. The parties were Simon, sacristan of Darley, and Hubert fitz Ralf, and the case concerned a debt

---

[1] See W. Ohnsorge, 'Päpstliche und gegenpäpstliche Legaten in Deutschland und Skandinavien 1159–1181', *Historische Studien*, clxxxviii (1929), 51 and 112, citing *Regesta Pontificum Romanorum—Italia Pontificia*, vii, pt. i. 140, no. 3 (cf. no. 2).

[2] e.g. *Regesta Pontificum Romanorum—Germania Pontificia*, ii, pt. i, ed. A. Brackmann (Berlin, 1923), 186, no. 8 (1181); and I. Friedlaender, 'Die Päpstlichen Legaten in Deutschland und Italien am Ende des XII. Jahrhunderts (1181–1198)', *Historische Studien*, clxxvii (1928), 144 and 147–8. For Spain and Portugal, Saebekow has worked on legations to the end of the twelfth century, G. Saebekow, *Die Päpstlichen Legationen nach Spanien und Portugal bis zum Ausgang des XII Jahrhunderts* (Berlin, 1931), but no judicial material of legatine delegation has come to light. The various monographs for France are very incomplete; but a legate who was instituted in several of the provinces by Innocent III was granted powers 'to correct and decree . . . to hear and to decide, and also to commit cases', *P.L.* 214, no. cxxii, col. 676.

[3] Tillmann, *Päpstlichen Legaten*, pp. 98 and 105, and see A. Mercati, 'La Prima Relazione del Cardinale Nicolò de Romanis sulla sua Legazione in Inghilterra', *Essays in History presented to R. L. Poole*, ed. H. W. C. Davis (Oxford, 1927), pp. 274–89.

[4] *C.R.R.* vii. 143–4.

of four shillings.[1] Nicholas, cardinal bishop of Tusculum, landed in England on 27 September 1213 and set about restoring the papal administration and control. Considerable interruption had been caused in the administration of the papal judicial system by the Interdict. Restoration of the system was needed, and speedy action was required for the number of suits that awaited attention.[2] Suits were consequently laid before this legate, probably in increasing numbers,[3] and in one instance, in September 1214, where a writ of prohibition had been served on the judges, the priors of Stoke by Clare (Suff.) and Earls Colne (Essex), the legate exhorted them to proceed.[4]

Cardinal Nicholas's legation was followed by that of Cardinal Guala Bichieri, a trusted papal adviser. In 1205 he had been created cardinal deacon of St. Mary in Porticu, and in 1211 he was promoted to the cardinal presbyterate of St. Martin, a title which he held until his death.[5] In 1208 he had been sent on legation to France.[6] From 20 May 1216 to about 11 December 1218 he was legate in England. He must have left the country very soon after this date, as he reached Vercelli, of which he was archbishop elect, by the end of January.[7] At least four reports of delegation by this legate survive. In all the cases the plaintiffs were religious corporations of some importance, the delegations were made to local judges, and the suits seem to have been conclusively settled. A suit between the prior and convent of Newnham (Aug. Beds.) and Geoffrey Rufus, about a yearly rent of

---

[1] *Cartulary of Darley Abbey*, ii, ed. R. R. Darlington (Kendal, 1945), 537–8 (L12). For a third delegation by this legate, see Peterborough, MS. I, f.III^r.

[2] See below, pp. 268–70. The legate was also diligent in filling vacant sees and appointing to lesser dignities, F. M. Powicke, *King Henry III and the Lord Edward* (Oxford, repd. 1966), p. 262.

[3] Montacute Cartulary, *Two Cartularies of the Augustinian Priory of Bruton and the Cluniac Priory of Montacute*, ed. members of the Council (Somerset Rec. Soc. viii, 1894), no. 143; and *Letters of Inn. III*, nos. 1015 and 1024.

[4] *C.R.R.* vii. 275.   [5] Eubel, p. 4.

[6] H. Zimmermann, *Die Päpstliche Legation in der ersten Hälfte des 13. Jahrhunderts* (Paderborn, 1913), p. 41. He was granted *plena potestas*, *P.L.* 215, no. lxxxv, col. 1402; cf. the institution of a legate in Hungary, ibid., no. cxxxvii, cols. 1231–2.

[7] Guisseppe Frova (pseud. Philadelfo Libico), *Gualae Bichierii . . . vita et gesta* (Milan, 1767), p. 109, cited by H. G. Richardson, 'Letters of the Legate Guala', *E.H.R.* xlviii (1933), 251; and Eubel, p. 4. Gams, *Series Episcoporum*, p. 825, does not mention him as archbishop of Vercelli.

threepence from land in Tilwick and Salpho (Beds.), was delegated to Walter, prior of Warden (Cist. Beds.), and Master Alexander, prior of Caldwell (Aug. Beds.).[1] A quarrel about tithes, between the abbot and convent of Bruern (Cist. Oxon.) and the rector of Guiting (Glos.), was delegated to Master Robert de Clipstone and W., dean of Rissington (Glos.).[2] Local judges, William, prior of Thetford (Aug. Norf.), and Adam, prior of Ixworth (Aug. Suff.), heard a case on behalf of Guala between the abbot and convent of Thorney (Ben. Cambs.) and Roger Curpeil, knight of Hempnall (Norf.), about an annual rent of ten shillings from the mill of Tasburgh (Norf.) in probably 1217–18.[3] Likewise, two Oxford masters, Robert de Bingham and William Scot, were commissioned by a mandate of the legate, dated at Oxford, to hear a case between the leper hospital of St. Bartholomew outside the city and Fulk Basset about an annual payment of ten shillings, which Fulk's ancestors had granted to the hospital.[4] In August 1216 Guala was ordered to inquire into an election at Hereford;[5] and he was also delegated to hear a case between Alexander, abbot elect of St. Augustine's, Canterbury, and Master Richard, messenger of the archbishop, and to remit it, fully documented, to Rome.[6] In 1217 Guala acted as judge delegate in another important election case,[7] and in about 1218 he issued a mandate to the abbots of Bindon and Cerne to examine a case concerning an election at the nunnery of St. Edward at Shaftesbury.[8] After he had left England, he continued to hear cases and concern himself with judicial affairs.[9]

Cardinal Hugolinus, nephew of Innocent III and later Pope Gregory IX, kept a register of his legation in Italy

---

[1] *Cartulary of Newnham Priory*, ed. J. Godber (Beds. Hist. Rec. Soc. xliii, 1963), no. 443. Tilwick is in Ravensden, and Salpho in Renhold.
[2] P.R.O. E 326/3943 (App. B (i), no. 1).
[3] Thorney Cart. ii, f. 324ᵛ.
[4] *Oriel College Records*, ed. C. L. Shadwell and H. E. Salter (Oxford Hist. Soc. lxxxv, 1926), no. 431. For these two men see below, pp. 49, 105, 115, and 174.
[5] *Reg. Hon. III*, no. 28 (*C.P.L.* i. 40).
[6] St. Augustine's White Book, ff. 118ᵛ–19ᵛ.
[7] *Reg. Hon. III*, no. 846 (*C.P.L.* i. 49).
[8] Ibid., nos. 757, and 1810 (*C.P.L.* i. 49 and 61), and see below, p. 174.
[9] See, e.g., *Reg. Hon. III*, nos. 2159 and 3640.

from 1219 to 1222, which has survived.[1] The material for
his legation is thus probably as complete as can be found.
He heard cases himself, parties compromised before him,
and he delegated.[2] His activities are comparable with those
of Pandulf, who was legate in England from 1218 to 1221.[3]
Pandulf had begun his curial career as chamberlain of the
pope. In 1211 he had come as a nuncio to England,[4] and
in 1218 he was elected bishop of Norwich, although he was
not consecrated until 29 May 1222. His work was similar to
that of Hugolinus as legate in Italy: he acted as a judge
delegate himself (settling the difficult Oakley case),[5] delegated cases, and referred some suits to the pope.[6] As a judge
delegate of Honorius III he settled a case between the bishop
of Carlisle and Stephen (a clerk of Durham diocese) about
the church of Warkworth, and, in a letter dated from Vaudey
on 18 February (1220 or 1221), ordered the priors of Hex-
ham and Tynemouth to enforce his sentence.[7] Reports of his
delegations survive, and they illustrate clearly the position
held by the legates in the administration of the papal judicial
system in normal times.[8] As during the visit of Guala, delegation was made to local judges, for instance to the abbot and
prior of Sherborne in a case between the prior and convent of
Bruton (Aug. Som.) and the abbess and convent of St.
Edward, Shaftesbury (Ben. Dors.).[9] Very often delegation

1 *Registri dei Cardinali Ugolino d'Ostia e Ottaviano degli Ubaldini*, ed. G. Levi
(Fonti per la Storia d'Italia, Istituto Storico Italiano, 1890), no. 8.

2 Ibid., nos. 41, 50, 79, and 96.

3 Pandulf's letter of appointment, dated 1 Sept. 1218, is in *Reg. Hon. III*, no.
1609 (*C.P.L.* i. 58). No. 1621 states that he is to replace Guala, who wants to return
(12 Sept. 1218). See also *Reg. Hon. III*, nos. 2181, 2287 (*C.P.L.* i. 68 and 70), and
Royal and Other Historical Letters illustrative of the Reign of Henry III, i, ed.
W. W. Shirley (R.S. xxvii, 1862), for many of Pandulf's letters.

4 Tillmann, *Päpstlichen Legaten*, pp. 94–5.

5 *Reg. Hon. III*, nos. 1680, 2073, 2146 (*C.P.L.* i. 60, 67, and 68); *St. Frideswide's
Cart.* ii, nos. 820 and 822–7; and W. Prynne, *An exact Chronological Vindication
. . . of our . . . Kings Supream Ecclesiastical Jurisdiction*, ii (1665), 381.

6 e.g. *Reg. Hon. III*, no. 4047 (*C.P.L.* i. 88).

7 Carlisle County Record Office, Mounsey-Heysham Collection, no. 4.

8 Cooper, *Select Scottish Cases*, no. 15, gives an example of a case delegated in
1221 by James the papal legate in Scotland.

9 Shaftesbury Cart., f. 106ʳ (App. B (i), no. 2). The legate's mandate, which is
included in this report, is also in the Bruton Cartulary (belonging to the earl of
Ilchester) calendared in *Two Cartularies of the Augustinian Priory of Bruton and the
Cluniac Priory of Montacute*, ed. members of the Council (Som. Rec. Soc. viii, 1894),
no. 252.

was to lesser clerics, such as John of Farthingstone (Northants.), rural dean, and Master Thomas, rector of Badby
(Northants.), who heard a suit between Daventry and
Thomas, rector of Lubbenham (Leics.), about the payment
of six and a half marks for tithes and four marks debt.[1] The
trivial nature of many of the suits brought before the legates
is exemplified by a case that was delegated to the abbot of
Alnwick in 1221, about one shilling payment as tithe from a
mill.[2] When Pandulf ordered the precentor and treasurer of
Salisbury to proceed with the hearing of a suit after a writ of
prohibition had been received, on the grounds that it was
not about advowson, he was exercising his legatine powers.[3]
The standing of his court is illustrated by a mandate to the
abbot and prior of Westminster, ordering them to hear a
cause between King John's former nurse Maud de Herlaue[4]
and her son Thomas, and the archdeacon of London, who
had excommunicated Maud after an appeal had been legitimately made to the legate's court. The archdeacon, meanwhile, was ordered by the legate to relax his sentence of
excommunication within eight days of the receipt of his
letter.[5]

The legate Otto Candidus, cardinal deacon of St. Nicholas
in Carcere Tulliano, was sent to England in 1237 'ad refor-
mandum statum ecclesiae et regni'.[6] From 1229 to 1231 he
had been legate in North Germany and Denmark.[7] The
prestige that was accorded to him and his powers was such
that he was given the nickname of 'second pope'.[8] He set

---

[1] Daventry Cart., f. 150ᵛ (App. B (i), no. 3).

[2] E. Bateson, History of Northumberland, i (1893), 295–6, from Nostell Cart.,
f. 121.

[3] Bracton's Note Book, iii, ed. F. W. Maitland (1887), no. 1388. See also no. 74
(1219).

[4] i.e. the nurse to King John's children, see M. Cheney in E.H.R. lxxxii (1967),
760.   [5] P.R.O. SC1, vol. 62, no. 3 (App. B (i), no. 4).

[6] See D. M. Williamson, 'Some Aspects of the Legation of Cardinal Otto in
England, 1237–1241', E.H.R. lxiv (1949), 145–73; Zimmermann, Päpstliche Legation, p. 111; and Reg. Greg. IX, nos. 3509–13.

[7] E. Winkelmann, 'Die Legation des Kardinaldiakons Otto von S. Nicolaus in
Deutschland, 1229–1231', Mitteilungen des Instituts für Oesterreichische Geschichtsforschung, xi (1890). He is recorded as being angry because few princes and ecclesiastics came to one of the provincial councils which he held (p. 31), and on p. 38 as
confirming a settlement; but no evidence remains of his delegation of causes.

[8] Chronica Majora, iii, ed. H. R. Luard (R.S. lvii, 1876), 56, and Flores
Historiarum, ii, ed. H. R. Luard (R.S. xcv, 1890), 462 ff., cited by O. Marti,

sail from England on 5 January 1241, and later, in 1244, was consecrated bishop of Porto and Silva Candida, one of the six cardinal bishops. He died at Lyons in 1251.[1] The machinery of papal authority can be seen operating normally during this legation. People came to put cases before him as they had become accustomed to do before the legate.[2] His court was a court of first instance like that of his predecessors. He heard cases as a judge delegate as they had done,[3] and on his own authority he delegated in the course of his perambulations or while at his residence in London.[4] Frequently delegation was to one judge—such as the dean of Arches, the prior of Battle, the archdeacon of Surrey, the official of the archdeacon of Bedford, and the official of the archdeacon of Canterbury[5]—sometimes to two, such as the priors of Milton and Cerne, and the prior of Dunstable (Richard de Mores) and the master of the schools there.[6] It is possible that the judge or judges were suggested by the plaintiff from within the immediate locality of the parties, rather than selected by the legate. There is no indication of subdelegation. The two instances pointed out by Miss Williamson are not subdelegations but direct delegations by the legate.[7] The subject-matter of the suits differed in no way from those which were taken to Rome—pensions, institutions, tithes,

'Popular Protest and Revolt against Papal Finance in England from 1226 to 1258', *Princeton Theological Review*, xxv, no. 4 (1927), 621.

[1] *Chronica Majora*, iv (1877), 84; Eubel, p. 6; and Gams, *Series Episcoporum*, p. ix.

[2] *Ann. Mon.* i. 107; *Reg. Greg. IX*, no. 4738; and see, e.g., Merton College, Oxford, Ch. 562 (cited in M. Hope Dodds, *History of Northumberland*, xii (1926), 408–9).

[3] *Reg. Greg. IX*, nos. 3614, 3758, and 4372.

[4] e.g. *Oseney Cart.* iv, no. 424; Dunstable Cart., f. 55ᵛ, cal. *Dunstable Cart.*, no. 549; Lewes Cart., f. 112ʳ, cal. *Lewes Cart. S.P.* ii. 27–8; and *N.L.C.*, no. 54. Examples of the legate Ottobon delegating cases are to be found in the Binham Cart., f. 186ʳ, and Chatteris Cart., f. 133ʳ.

[5] *N.L.C.*, no. 54; Lewes Cart., f. 112ʳ, cal. *Lewes Cart. S.P.* ii. 27–8; Magdalen College, Oxford, Selborne Ch. 252, pd. *Calendar of Charters and Documents relating to Selborne and its Priory*, i, ed. W. D. Macray (Hants Rec. Soc., 1891), 24–5; Dunstable Cart., f. 55ᵛ, cal. *Dunstable Cart.*, no. 549; and Canterbury, Cartae Antiquae, M 364, no. 9 (App. B (i), no. 5).

[6] *Charters and Documents . . . of Salisbury*, ed. W. R. Jones and W. D. Macray (R.S. xcvii, 1891), nos. ccxxiv and ccxxxi (hereafter cited as *Sarum Chs.*), and *Oseney Cart.* iv, no. 424. For Richard de Mores see below, pp. 114–18.

[7] *Sarum Chs.* ccxxiv and ccxxxi, and *Dunstable Cart.*, no. 549, cited by Williamson, 'Legation of Cardinal Otto', pp. 152–3.

church rights[1]—and the attraction of the legate's court as a court of first instance seems to have been that on occasion it might save the time and expense of a visit to Rome, especially if the proctor or messenger had only just left to transact business there. But the legatine court was by no means a substitute for the papal court.

Appeals were sometimes made to the pope from the courts that were erected by the legate. Both remaining instances point to error on a specific point of canon law. One delegate of Otto, the archdeacon of Surrey, was accused of citing the parties, the prior and convent of Selborne and Master G. de Haya of Winchester diocese, on feast days at the time of mass.[2] The other appeal was placed by S. de Sinethe, citizen of Canterbury, from the court of Master R., official of the archdeacon of Canterbury, who had been delegated by Otto to hear the case. He said that he had been summoned against his will, and protesting, to appear in court to answer Gregory, palmer, on the feast of St. Margaret virgin and martyr, whose festival he alleged was celebrated in the town of Canterbury and almost everywhere else in the land.[3] On occasion Otto referred a case to the pope, for instance the case about presentation to the archdeaconry of Norfolk, where one of the parties had been presented by the king. After a long hearing Otto decided to remit the cause to the pope, who decided against the royal candidate.[4] There remains evidence of Otto revising his judgement in the St. Kaveran case on receiving new instructions from the pope.[5]

(ii) *Law Collections*

Another basic link between Rome and the provinces was provided by the law compilations. The pope acted as lawgiver. In the 1140s mandates often demanded of the delegates an investigation of fact only,[6] or, if a decision was to be made,

---

[1] e.g. *Dunstable Cart.*, no. 549; *Reg. or Rolls of Walter Gray, Lord Archbishop of York*, ed. J. Raine (Surtees Soc. lvi, 1872), p. 86; *N.L.C.*, no. 54; and *Sarum Chs.* ccxxiv and ccxxxi.

[2] Magdalen College, Oxford, Selborne Ch. 252, pd. Macray, *Calendar*, i. 24–5. See 'De Feriis', c. 5. *X.* II. 9.

[3] Canterbury, Cartae Antiquae, M 364, no. 9 (App. B (i), no. 5).

[4] *Reg. Greg. IX*, no. 4738.

[5] Beaulieu Cart., ff. 129ᵛ–31ʳ.

[6] e.g. *P.U.E.* iii, no. 47 (Eug. III, 8 June 1145).

the pope clearly defined how the judge delegate should proceed and what ruling should apply in the event of certain facts being proved.[1] If the judges were in any doubt how to act, reference might be made to Rome. Before the appearance of the *Decretum* or *Concordia Discordantium Canonum*, which issued from the Bolognese law schools in 1139–40, there was no law book to which the inquirer might easily turn. With the issue of the *Decretum*, some system was imposed on the previous tangled mass of earlier papal decrees, some of which were conflicting. Certain norms of behaviour were defined and some of the pope's law made generally known. It is a commonplace that this law book was enthusiastically received and that its influence was widespread. It seems to have reached England early. Some manuscripts of the *Decretum* that are known to have been in English libraries have glosses attributable to the period during the first thirty years after its appearance.[2] Professor Holtzmann has suggested that the infiltration of the *Decretum* into England may have been connected with John of Salisbury.[3] Yet as Professor Brooke has pointed out:

The evidence of these [John of Salisbury's] letters suggests that it [the *Decretum*] was in normal use in Theobald's curia in the late 1150's, and the reception of it in this country may well have been due to the Archbishop's court; but there seems no sufficient reason to attach the event to John rather than to another of the circle—for instance to John of Canterbury.[4]

The exact date of the appearance of Gratian's canonical text in England may remain obscure, but it seems reasonable to accept that in the 1150s to 1160s the work was being referred to by the judges of the church courts and was being used for teaching purposes.

As lawsuits increased, necessitating further definition, the *Decretum* became outdated to some extent for practical

---

[1] *P.U.E.* ii, no. 32 (Inn. II, Mar. 1143).

[2] Kuttner, *Repertorium*, pp. 3–9, cited by M. Cheney, 'Compromise of Avranches', p. 184.

[3] W. Holtzmann in *Zeitschrift der Savigny-Stiftung für Rechtsgeschichte*, Kan. Abt., xxxix (1953), 466–7.

[4] *J.S.L.*, p. xx n. 1. See nos. 99 (p. 153 n. 1), 100 (p. 157 n. 5), and 131 (p. 231 n. 10).

purposes, and among the canonists a shift in interest took place from commenting on the *Decretum* to collecting decretals, or further statements of the popes on specific legal points. Some sections of the *Decretum* were fully conclusive, at least at first, but such headings as marriage and ordination were sparse and had hardly been formulated. Thus private and unofficial collections of *extravagantes decretales*, the more recent decisions of the popes, began to appear as books of convenient reference about 1170, and with increasing momentum between 1175 and 1190.[1] These are numerous for England, as has been shown by Professor Kuttner.[2] Holtzmann divided the works into three groups: the English group, the Bridlington group, and the Worcester group; and Dr. Charles Duggan has analysed them.[3] Without the survival of these private collections, our knowledge of the early appeal system would be much less. Out of more than 1,050 decretals which have been found to date, only 540 became part of Gregory IX's official collection of the *Decretales* of 1234,[4] and these were taken mainly from amongst the decretals in the *Quinque Compilationes*. Some of these *extravagantes* decretals, such as one concerning Bridlington, to be found in the *Collectio Sangermanensis* and other collections, became incorporated in one of the Five Compilations composed between *c.* 1191 and 1226, in this case in the *Compilatio Secunda* of John of Wales, but were not included in the *Decretales*.[5] They did, however, form part of the medieval canon law, and were thus used for reference and precedent until superseded by Gregory IX's official compilation. Thus about one half would have been entirely lost, had it not been

[1] C. N. L. Brooke, 'Canons of English Church Councils in the Early Decretal Collections', *Traditio*, xiii (1957), suggests on p. 476 that the stimulus to collecting was due to the 1175 Council of Westminster.

[2] Kuttner, *Repertorium*, pp. 272 ff. See also S. Kuttner, 'Notes on a Projected Corpus of Twelfth-Century Decretal Letters', *Traditio*, vi (1948), 345–51. Kuttner's original list of 1937 was supplemented by W. Holtzmann, 'Über eine Ausgabe der päpstlichen Dekretalen des 12. Jahrhunderts', *Nachrichten der Akademie der Wissenschaften in Göttingen*, Philol.-Hist. Klasse (1945), pp. 21–4.

[3] C. Duggan, *Twelfth-Century Decretal Collections and their Importance in English History* (1963), esp. chapter iv.

[4] These figures are from Holtzmann, 'Über eine Ausgabe der päpstlichen Dekretalen', p. 19 n. 1.

[5] See W. Ullmann, 'A Forgotten Dispute at Bridlington Priory and its Canonistic Setting', *Yorks. Archaeol. Journal*, xxxvii (1948–51), 456–73.

for the small collections which form an unusually valuable corpus of the growing canon law.

The large proportion of decretals addressed to English prelates was noted first by Maitland.[1] This was a momentous discovery. Z. N. Brooke, following up Maitland's assertion, estimated that 219 out of 424 decretals of Alexander III dealt with England.[2] He attributed this high percentage for England to English ignorance of the law of the Church, resulting from Henry II's activities prior to the Compromise of Avranches. These conclusions have had to be modified. The large number of legal letters for England, which found their way into the *Decretales*, has been shown to be due to the energetic activity of the English canonists and the predominant position occupied by their private collections.[3] As Professor Barraclough has argued convincingly, if England was backward in the canon law and her judges were needing undue instructions, the answers to their questions would not have been included in an informative collection of the law of the Church, which was compiled for use and not for record purposes.[4] The English zeal in collecting explains the large number of English decretals in the *Liber Extra* or *Decretales*, although in fact probably as many papal decretals of this period were addressed, for instance, to Spanish recipients.[5] It is not surprising that the masters working in the 1160s and 1170s, in the canon law schools at Worcester, Canterbury, and Exeter, should have collected the decretals, that had been sent to the vicinity, for their compilations. Their purpose was a practical one. Collections grew up around the early judges delegate, the bishops, and sometimes they were appended to copies of the *Decretum*.[6] No collections

---

[1] Maitland, *Roman Canon Law*, pp. 123–4.

[2] Brooke, 'The Effect of Becket's Murder', pp. 219–20. Holtzmann, by spreading his net wider, made a total of 359, 'Über eine Ausgabe der päpstlichen Dekretalen', p. 34.

[3] See Duggan, *Decretal Collections*, esp. pp. 21–2, 43, 66, 118–24, 132–5, and 141 ff. Duggan's argument that this high percentage reflects the origin of the early decretalists is not entirely accepted by Morey and Brooke, who think that 'England may have played a particularly conspicuous part in the story of appeals and decretals . . .', *Gilbert Foliot*, p. 235.

[4] Barraclough, review of Kuttner's *Repertorium* in *E.H.R.* liii (1938), 494 n. 3.

[5] Duggan, *Decretal Collections*, pp. 121 n. 2, and 127 n. 2.

[6] Kuttner, *Repertorium*, pp. 273–6, cited by M. Cheney, 'Compromise of Avranches', p. 181.

have been found prior to the English ones; these went to the
Continent, where they stimulated the making of compilations
and, at Bologna, served as models.[1] This influence of England accounts for the remarkable number of English masters
at Bologna in the late twelfth and early thirteenth centuries,
by which time Italy and France, with more advanced methods
of collecting, were taking over England's lead.[2]

The first official collection of Church law, the so-called
Compilatio Tertia of Peter Collivaccinus of Benevento, was
commissioned by Innocent III, whose pontificate saw several
collections of decretals, official and otherwise.[3] Innocent
commended the *Compilatio Tertia* to the masters and scholars
at Bologna in 1210, saying that they might use it 'as much in
judgements as in the schools'.[4] It was enthusiastically received, and England has about a seventh as many of the
number of manuscripts of this work as survive in France.[5]
The collection, however, included only Innocentian decretals up to the twelfth year of that pontificate. Following
Innocent's example, Honorius III ordered an official compilation of his decretals to be made. He addressed the collection (the *Compilatio Quinta*) to Master Tancred, archdeacon
of Bologna, in a bull of 2 May 1226;[6] outlining the need
for definition, and borrowing the phrase of his predecessor,
he commended the decretals to be used as authoritative 'as
much in judgements as in the schools'.

As an official collection, the *Decretales* of Raymond of
Peñaforte was of a much more ambitious nature. It was
ordered by Gregory IX and promulgated on 5 September
1234 in the bull *Rex pacificus*, which was addressed to all
doctors and scholars residing at Bologna and at Paris, 'ut hac

---

[1] Duggan, *Decretal Collections*, pp. 132 ff.

[2] For Alan, Gilbert, and John, the English masters who made compilations at
Bologna in the opening years of the thirteenth century, see Ullmann, 'A Forgotten
Dispute', pp. 461–4, and Duggan, pp. 124–5.

[3] For two earlier private collections from Innocent III's pontificate, see C. R.
Cheney, 'Decretals of Innocent III in Paris, B.N. MS. Lat. 3922A', *Traditio*, xi
(1955), 149–62, and S. Kuttner, 'Bernardus Compostellanus Antiquus. A Study in
the Glossators of the Canon Law', ibid. i (1943), 277–340.

[4] *Quinque Compilationes Antiquae*, p. 105; *Reg. Pont. Rom.* i, ed. Potthast, no.
4157.

[5] Kuttner, *Repertorium*, pp. 361–5.

[6] *Quinque Compilationes Antiquae*, p. 151; *Reg. Pont. Rom.* i, ed. Potthast, no.
7684.

tantum compilatione utantur universi in iudiciis et in scholis'.
It was a compendium of all important Church law prior to
1234. Gregory IX further forbade the making of any other
compilation without special authority from the Apostolic
See; and it remained the official redaction until the compilation of the *Sext* was completed in 1298 at the direction of
Boniface VIII.[1] At Paris translations of the *Decretales* soon
began to appear. At least nine manuscripts of these translations remain. According to E. Fournier they were made
between 1238 and 1245 under the direction of the Paris law
faculty; and Castilian versions survive in three codices of
the thirteenth or the beginning of the fourteenth century.[2]

Professor Vetulani has traced the receipt of books of
canon law in Poland. By the end of the twelfth century the
Decretum was known in Poland, and the cathedral library at
Cracow has a copy of the *Compilatio Prima* of Bernard of
Pavia. The first manuscript of the *Decretales* may have been
brought by the legate. It was mainly through the legates
that reform of the Polish Church under Innocent III had
come about, and that contact with Rome was maintained.
The legates had brought canonical collections to Poland
before 1234, and they continued transmitting the latest texts
after 1234.[3] It is therefore likely that the *Decretales* as well
was introduced into Poland by them.

No bull '*Rex pacificus*' was addressed to the English law
schools. The Oxford law school at this time was of only
lesser importance. There seems no doubt that the transmission
of this law book to England took place very soon after its

---

[1] *Reg. Greg. IX*, nos. 2083–4; *Reg. Pont. Rom.* i, ed. Potthast, no. 9693; *Chartularium Universitatis Parisiensis*, i (1200–86), ed. H. Denifle and E. Chatelain
(Paris, 1889), no. 104.

[2] E. Fournier, 'L'Accueil fait par la France du XIIIᵉ siècle aux décrétales
pontificales: leur traduction en langue vulgaire', *Acta Congressus Iuridici Internationalis*, iii (Rome, 1936), 247–67, and R. Riaza and M. Torres Lopez, 'Versiones
Castellanas de las Decretales de Gregorio IX', ibid., 291–6.

[3] A. Vetulani, 'La Pénétration du droit des décrétales dans l'Église polonaise
au XIIIᵉ siècle', *Acta Congressus*, iii. 385–405. On canon law manuscripts in
Sweden, see T. Schmid in *Traditio*, vii (1949–51), 444–9, who records a variety of
texts, including all the major ones, and who surmises that they were in early use in
Sweden although they were not written there (p. 446); and for Belgium, see R. C.
van Caenegem, 'Notes on Canon Law Books in Medieval Belgian Book-Lists',
Studia Gratiana, xii (Collectanea Stephan Kuttner, ii, ed. J. Forchielli and A.-M.
Stickler, Bologna, 1967), 269–70.

promulgation, and no credence can be given to the statement that it was introduced by the legate Otto at the Council of London in 1237.[1] There were English scholars at Paris and Bologna, and contacts with Rome and the Continent were many. The chronicler John de Oxenedes mentioned the compilation of the *Decretales* in 1234:

At this time Pope Gregory IX, seeing the tedious prolixity of the decretals, had them extracted and collected in a compendium, and ordered it to be sent everywhere and used as the approved and official text. Brother Raymond of the order of Preachers compiled this useful collection.[2]

The manuscript evidence shows a considerable number of thirteenth-century texts of the *Decretales* in English monastic libraries.[3] The Reading manuscript of the *Decretales*, now in the Bodleian Library, commences by quoting the papal bull which was addressed to the university of Paris.[4] Unfortunately it is not always known when these texts came into the possession of the different libraries, and thirteenth-century library catalogues are rare and perhaps not always fully inclusive, nor have any translations come to light, but the widespread use of the *Decretales* in the Church courts suggests a plentiful and early distribution of copies.

The *Curia Romana* set the standards by which men were supposed to live. It also recognized and provided for their needs. In Rome new government offices and departments were established, and new officers appointed, in response to the demands of an ever increasing number of litigants and lawsuits. For similar reasons legates were dispatched and official law books compiled, maintaining contacts between the *Curia* and the provincial courts. The papacy insisted on its claims as the pivot of Church government, but it was also fulfilling the role which was required of it. The main development in judicial organization was probably that of

---

[1] Refuted by Williamson, 'Legation of Cardinal Otto', p. 164 n. 1.
[2] *Chronica Johannis de Oxenedes*, ed. H. Ellis (R.S. xiii, 1859), p. 164. Cf. Matthew Paris, *Historia Anglorum*, ii, ed. F. Madden (R.S. xliv, 1866), 381, and *Chron. Maj.* iii. 328, who puts it among the events of 1235.
[3] See N. R. Ker, *Medieval Libraries of Great Britain. A List of Surviving Books*, 2nd ed. (Royal Hist. Soc. Guides and Handbooks, iii, 1964).
[4] MS. Bodley 639.

delegation of lawsuits to local judges, which originated in the twelfth century, but the changes that came about in the thirteenth century were no less important. They were as much in answer to the external demand for centralization and strong government as they were the result and expression of a conscious policy, formulated by popes, canonists, and administrators, to enhance the prestige and power of the Roman see.

II

THE PROCEDURE OF THE COURTS
OF THE JUDGES DELEGATE

1. Procedural Books

THE procedure of the Church courts, and consequently of the delegated tribunals, derived from the form of extraordinary procedure by *libellus conventionis* of the late Roman Empire, which divided the suit into three parts, *jus*, *litis contestatio*, and *judicium*.[1] The Roman law had not entirely died out in the lay and Church courts of Rome and North Italy, especially in the commercial centres, and at the end of the eleventh century an increasing interest in it brought to light better and fuller texts of Justinian's compilation, the *Corpus Iuris Civilis*. But that the practical application of its procedure was crude and far from uniform is attested by the eagerness with which the lawyers set to work on the new texts.

The process of digesting, expounding, and explaining the founts of the old Roman law began with Irnerius and the school of glossators at Bologna. The Novels[2] and Digest were newly discovered; the Code and the Institutes were more fully used than ever before. These books were to form the basis of the procedure of the ecclesiastical courts. Recent research has shown, however, that the Roman law sources were not used in the first redaction of the *Decretum* (or compilation of the canons) in 1139–40. But before the book began to circulate they were fed into the text by Gratian's followers, who were attracted increasingly towards the civil law procedure for standardizing and improving the machinery

---

[1] For a general sketch of canonical procedure see C. Lefebvre, 'Procédure', *D.D.C.* vii (1959), cols. 285–96, and for a detailed consideration of procedure by libel, P. Collinet, *La Procédure par libelle* (Paris, 1932).

[2] Until the sixteenth century the Novels were known from two sources, the *Epitome Iuliani* and the *Authenticum*, see *Lib. Pauperum of Vacarius*, ed. F. de Zulueta (Selden Soc. xliv, 1927), p. lii.

of the canon law.¹ To these sources, civilian as well as
canonist, ecclesiastical judges turned when hearing cases.²
The *Decretum* was introduced into England soon after its
compilation, and manuscripts of the twelfth century survive
in some quantities.³ Little is known, however, about the
transmission of the civil law books. The Roman lawyer Vacarius, who came to England probably in the mid 1140s, and
who was teaching in England, presumably at Oxford, before
the study of civil law was prohibited by King Stephen, made
known the Code and the Digest through his *Liber Pauperum*⁴ (and incidentally acted several times as a papal judge
delegate);⁵ but no complete English twelfth-century manuscripts of the *Corpus Iuris* appear to have survived.⁶ Robert
de Chesney, however, is known to have had a copy of the
Digest which he requested Gilbert Foliot to have corrected
and glossed for him;⁷ Abbot Benedict of Peterborough
(1177–94) left a set of the *Corpus Iuris Civilis* to his monastery; and a copy of the Institutes is recorded at Canterbury
in the 1170s.⁸ These cannot have been isolated instances,
and the paucity of the references to civil law texts almost
certainly does not indicate their absence from England.

Procedural difficulties, as distinct from legal, are strongly
evident in the period immediately following the completion of
Gratian's *Decretum*. There is little about canonical procedure

¹ See J. Rambaud-Buhot in *Histoire du droit et des institutions de l'Église en
Occident*, vii, ed. G. Le Bras (Paris, 1965), 51–8, and 119–29.
² See, for example, Morey and Brooke, *Gilbert Foliot*, p. 59: '[His 'Foliot's] letters
show that he applied the authorities of Roman law to problems of procedure in
canon law courts without hesitation.'
³ See Kuttner, *Repertorium*. For a summary of the available legal literature, both
canonist and civilian, and its transmission to England, see now R. C. van Caenegem,
Royal Writs in England from the Conquest to Glanville (Selden Soc. lxxvii, 1959),
pp. 360–73, esp. 365 ff.
⁴ Ed. de Zulueta, pp. xiii–xxiii.
⁵ See *A.N.C.*, p. 287 n. 18: to this list of Vacarius's occurrences as a judge
delegate may be added *Early Yorkshire Charters*, ix, ed. C. T. Clay (Yorks. Archaeol.
Soc. Rec. Ser., Extra Ser. vii, 1952), no. 159.
⁶ See Morey and Brooke, *Gilbert Foliot*, p. 67; they cite W. Senior, 'Roman Law
Manuscripts in England', *Law Quarterly Review*, xlvii (1931), 337–44. Senior,
however, is more concerned with thirteenth- and fourteenth-century manuscripts;
N. R. Ker's *Medieval Libraries* shows no surviving twelfth-century manuscripts of
the *Corpus Iuris Civilis* and few civilian works altogether.
⁷ Morey and Brooke, *Gilbert Foliot*, p. 66.
⁸ Senior, 'Roman Law Manuscripts in England', p. 337.

in the *Decretum*,[1] compared with the plentiful chapters in
the *Quinque Compilationes* and the sections 'De Rescriptis',
'De Appellationibus', 'De Officio et Potestate Judicis', 'De
Excepcionibus', and 'De Dolo et Contumacia' of the *Decretales*. Allusions to procedural troubles in the Church courts,
both ordinary and delegated, of the 1150s occur in John of
Salisbury's letters, which show that the outline of the *ordo
judiciarius* was not yet developed, uniform, or fully under-
stood.[2] For instance, an appeal was made from the court of
Walter, bishop of Coventry, to Theobald, archbishop of
Canterbury, when the bishop who was acting as judge delegate was responsible only to the pope and was sitting in the
superior court, as one of the parties realized.[3] If an answer
could not be found when a difficulty arose, and if technical
details were not provided in the rescript, reference was made
to the pope, who as supreme judge over all the courts defined procedure.[4] Between 1140 and 1191 the development
of decretal legislation took place. Decretal collections, the
earliest of which date from about 1175, reflect procedural
inquiries as well as legal, and procedural sections are found
in the *Collectiones Cantabrigiensis* (the first part), *Cottoniana*
(ff. 225ᵛ et seq.), and *Peterhusensis* (ff. 27ᵛ et seq.). The two
latter are 'Worcester' collections of *c.* 1191 and 1194 at the
earliest.[5] These collections were made by the judges or their
clerks for their own personal use, and were frequently appended to copies of the *Decretum* and filed and bound up
with other legal material.[6] Some of the decretals from
these collections found their way via the Five Compilations

---

[1] *Decretum*, C. II qu. 1–6 and 8; C. III qu. 6–7, 9, and 11; and C. IV qu. 1–6.

[2] *J.S.L.*, nos. 53, 57, 70–1, 74, and 83—an exception is pleaded against the judge
in the latter.

[3] See the letter of Theobald reporting this to the pope, *J.S.L.*, no. 54, of
c. 1154–9.

[4] e.g. *Papal Decretals relating to Lincoln*, nos. iv, vi, xii, xiv–xv, xviii, and xxi.

[5] See Duggan, *Decretal Collections*, pp. 47–8 and 104–7. The '*Wigorniensis
Altera*' is described by Duggan as an illustration of an English primitive collection
devised on a basis of personal and local interest. It is very small, containing ten
decretals sent by Alexander III to judges delegate (Duggan, p. 46).

[6] Important collections come from Worcester, Exeter, and Canterbury, and
were presumably made for important judges delegate, Roger of Worcester, Bartholomew of Exeter, and Richard of Canterbury (ibid., pp. 94, 118, and 149).
M. Cheney, 'Compromise of Avranches', p. 181, citing Kuttner, *Repertorium*,
pp. 273–6.

to Gregory IX's compilation of the canons, and so became general law.

To search through the textbooks of the Roman and canon law for a ruling on a particular procedural point was no easy task. Procedural information is scattered all through the *Corpus Iuris Civilis*, and therefore could not readily be consulted. For this reason procedural treatises were devised to help judges and litigants. Such works are comparable in their private origin to the collections of decretals. Among the first is the *Ordo Iudiciorum* of Bulgarus, which was dedicated to Aimericus, chancellor of the Roman Church, who held office from 1123–41; it is described by Kantorowicz as 'the oldest evidence of a scientific give-and-take connection between the glossators of the Civil law and the Curia'.[1] Gratian's *Decretum* and the legal renaissance of the twelfth century sparked off the composition of a host of such manuals of procedure.[2] Amongst the earliest are the anonymous commentary on Causa II question 1 of the *Decretum*, which begins with the words 'In principio de ordine iudiciario agitur', and which is much disputed as to date but was probably composed between 1160 and 1175,[3] and an anonymous treatise from France, *Incerti Auctoris Ordo Iudiciarius, pars summae legum, et tractatus de prescriptione*.[4] There are also the Anglo-Norman *Ulpianus de Edendo* or *Incerti Auctoris Ordo Iudiciorum of c.* 1140,[5] and two English treatises—the *Ordo Iudiciarius* of 1182–5,[6] probably by an English canonist attached to the court of the archbishop of Dublin, and the *Practica legum et decretorum* of *c.* 1183–9, which was written by William of Longchamp, bishop of Ely, before his

---

[1] H. Kantorowicz and W. W. Buckland, *Studies in the Glossators of the Roman Law* (Cambridge, 1938), pp. 70–1. Acting as a judge delegate of the pope, Bulgarus delivered a judgement in his own lecture room on 8 July 1151 (p. 68), an instance of the close connection between the legal writers and the practitioners, and between the civilians and the canonists.

[2] See *Studies in the Glossators*, p. 72, where Kantorowicz lists them with their editors (his n. 8), and Stickler, cols. 1132–43, esp. 1135–8.

[3] Ed. F. Kunstmann in *Kritische Ueberschau der deutschen Gesetzgebung und Rechtswissenschaft*, ii, ed. L. Arndts, J. C. Bluntschli, and J. Potzl (Munich, 1855), 17–29. Stickler dates this 1171.   [4] Ed. C. Gross (Innsbruck, 1870).

[5] Ed. G. Haenel (Leipzig, 1838). Dated by Stickler.

[6] Ed. J. F. von Schulte, 'Der *Ordo iudiciarius* des Codex Bambergensis P. I. 11.', *Sitzungsberichte der Kaiserlichen Akademie der Wissenschaften*, lxx (Vienna, 1872), 285–326.

chancellorship.[1] Two further treatises, from Christ Church, Canterbury, were discovered by Professor Kuttner and Miss Rathbone,[2] and an *Ordo Iudiciarius* of *c.* 1202–9 is in Baltimore, Walters Art Gallery MS. W 15.[3] Too much importance should not be attached to these treatises. Kantorowicz has said that in the twelfth century they were far ahead of practice.[4] What their circulation was, and whether they were regarded as authoritative by the judges, cannot be known. Much distortion has resulted from using them to explain the practices of a different period; they can only be expected to illuminate contemporary events. Professor Thorne, for instance, in asserting that the mechanism of appeals remained long unknown in England, used William of Drogheda's treatise, of 1239, to discuss all suits after 1172.[5] A more recent writer depended on Tancred, who completed his *Ordo Iudiciarius* in *c.* 1216, to introduce the background to a small collection of Alexandrian decretals.[6] But it may be noted that the *Summa de Ordine Iudiciario* of Ricardus Anglicus (de Mores) of *c.* 1196 and the *Summa Aurea* of William of Drogheda of 1239,[7] as well as the other more numerous works from the Continent which appeared owing to the impetus from the compilation of the *Decretales* in 1234, are not without forerunners. These, although not statutory works, deserve to be studied carefully with the suits of the time.

From the early thirteenth century there survive letter or precedent books giving the forms to be used by the judges and parties of the delegated courts when drawing up documents. Formularies of this kind are another consequence of

[1] See *A.N.C.*, p. 290. Longchamp's work is edited by E. Caillemer in 'Le Droit civil dans les provinces anglo-normandes au XIIᵉ siècle', *Mémoires de l'Académie Nationale des Sciences, Arts . . . de Caen* (1883), pp. 204–26.

[2] B.M. Royal MS. 10 B iv, f. 59ʳ⁻ᵛ, and ff. 33–41, cited in *A.N.C.*, p. 291 n. 7.

[3] *A.N.C.*, p. 291, and see below, pp. 47 ff., on a formulary in this MS.

[4] *Studies in the Glossators*, p. 72.

[5] S. E. Thorne, 'Le Droit canonique en Angleterre', *Rev. hist. de droit français et étranger*, 4ᵉ série xiii (1934), 508.

[6] *Papal Decretals relating to Lincoln*, pp. xx ff.

[7] On Richard see Stickler, col. 1137, and *A.N.C.*, pp. 291 and 338–9. On Drogheda see Stickler, col. 1136; F. de Zulueta, 'William of Drogheda', *Mélanges de droit romain dédiés à Georges Cornil*, ii (Paris, 1926), 641–57; and H. G. Richardson, 'Azo, Drogheda and Bracton', *E.H.R.* lix (1944), 22–47.

the revival of Roman law and procedure in the eleventh and twelfth centuries.[1] Although, as we have seen, procedural treatises survive from the twelfth century, no English examples of judge-delegate formularies appear, at least at first sight, to precede the pontificate of Innocent III, but it seems reasonable to suppose that there must have been such letter books, particularly from the judicially formative pontificate of Alexander III. In any case the distinction between a formulary and a procedural treatise is fine. The procedural writer, William of Drogheda, for example, sometimes gives a form in his treatise, and, as will be shown below, the basic letters in some of these formularies may be earlier than the dates of the pope who is mentioned.

A group of seven English formularies have been described by Professors Cheney[2] and Kuttner.[3] The English origin of London, B.M. Royal MS. 15 B IV, ff. 65ᵛ–6ʳ (L), Cambridge, Gonville and Caius MS. 150 (44), f. 119ʳ (C), Baltimore, Walters Art Gallery MS. W 15, ff. 79ᵛ–81ᵛ (B), and Vatican, MS. lat. 2343 (V) can be traced from the inclusion of a letter concerning 'the custom of the English Church'.[4] Montecassino MS. 136, pp. 223–4 and 231 (M), known only from the catalogue,[5] corresponds so closely with V (both have Italian appendices) and C in the forms, all of which are identical in subject and number (sixteen), as to suggest that it is also one of the group.[6] Lambeth MS. 105, f. 271ᵛ (A) has some relationship with Baltimore (B),[7] and in any case uses English names; while Bodleian MS. Laud

---

[1] H. G. Richardson, 'The Oxford Law School under John', *Law Quarterly Review*, lvii (1941), 324.

[2] C. R. Cheney, *English Bishops' Chanceries 1100–1250* (Manchester, 1950), pp. 124–30, discusses B, A, L, and O.

[3] S. Kuttner, '*Analecta Iuridica Vaticana* (Vat. lat. 2343)', *Studi e Testi*, ccxix (1962), 443–5, adds C, M, and V.

[4] Ibid., p. 444 and n. 6. F. Donald Logan has produced an edition based on C, L, and V, with three of the forms from B; see 'An Early Thirteenth-Century Papal Judge-Delegate Formulary of English Origin', *Studia Gratiana*, xiv (Collectanea Stephan Kuttner, iv, Bologna, 1967), 73–87.

[5] See *Bibliotheca Casinensis*, iii (Monte Cassino, 1877), 228–9. As Professor Kuttner notes, all the rubrics, incipits, and explicits are given.

[6] L has one less form, that concerning revocatory letters, and is therefore only fifteen in number, see Kuttner, *Analecta Iuridica*, p. 445 n. 2.

[7] The forms concerning the matrimonial 'petitio' and letters dimissory for a clerk moving from one diocese to another, which are found in both, are distinctly comparable.

lat. 17, ff. 223^v–4^v (O) makes mention of English places and English ecclesiastics. To these may be added a formulary of English origin in B.M. Cotton MS. Julius D II, ff. 150^r–4^r which uses the names of Canterbury clerics.[1]

The origin of B has been the subject of some dispute. Mr. Richardson has suggested that it is connected with the Oxford law school.[2] Professor Cheney, on the other hand, is convinced that there is 'absolutely no evidence for the repeated statements that the Baltimore MS. was written at Oxford' and that to assert that the forms were assembled there outsteps the evidence.[3] He has seen, however, a common core in B, L, A, and O (C, V, and M were unknown to him), and has associated it with the diocese of Lincoln and the bishop's chancery. But B is the most sophisticated formulary of the group, which contains also part of an *ordo judiciarius* and some secular forms.[4] In view of this and its use in the main of Oxford names—there are also some Northampton ones,[5] and these are crucial to Mr. Richardson's argument that it is a product of the early Oxford law school —an origin in the nascent university still seems the more tenable theory. The relationship between L and C is close, presenting the conclusion that both have been copied from a common source. Both are carelessly written. When collated, the more sensible readings of one correct the obvious corruptions of the other, indicating a common source, although perhaps not an immediate one. Because of the English letter, Kuttner has associated B with these two, and Cheney has seen definite connections between B and A. Two

---

[1] C.F.

[2] Richardson, 'Oxford Law School', pp. 319–38. This argument was accepted by Kuttner and Rathbone in *A.N.C.*, p. 291.

[3] Cheney, *Bishops' Chanceries*, pp. 125 n. 1 and 126–7.

[4] Eleven of the ecclesiastical forms, mainly concerning Oxford, were included in *Formularies which bear on the History of Oxford c. 1204–1420*, ii, ed. H. E. Salter, W. A. Pantin, and H. G. Richardson (Oxf. Hist. Soc. N.S. v, 1942) (cited as *Oxford Formularies*).

[5] The church of Crick (Northants.) is mentioned twice. An investigation of its patronage has not helped towards establishing the origin of the formulary. It passed from Roger de Camvill to the Estley or Astley family t. Henry II (J. Bridges, *History and Antiquities of Northamptonshire*, i, ed. P. Whalley, Oxford, 1791, pp. 557–62), in whose hands it remained at least until 1271 (*Rotuli Ricardi Gravesend Episcopi Lincolniensis*, ed. F. N. Davis, Linc. Rec. Soc. xx, 1925, p. 117).

later formularies in B.M. Add. MS. 8167,[1] mentioning the names of popes Gregory (IX) and Honorius (III), exhibit strains of B, A, L, and C, in format, and one mentions the church of St. Mary at Oxford.[2] A common origin for L, C, V, M, B, and A may therefore be suspected.

O, however, is not related in any obvious way to this group.[3] It is more closely comparable with the Canterbury formulary, which does not perpetuate the common core and which uses local names. To connect O with the diocese of Lincoln seems tenuous, although a connection with Oxford might be argued from the inclusion of some Oxford names.[4] But much more powerful arguments can be put forward for the compilation of the forms at Cirencester. The places which are mentioned are all within thirty miles of Cirencester: Winchcombe, Cerney (North or South), 'Leche' (Northleach, Eastleach, or Lechlade), and 'Culne' (Coln St. Dennis, St. Aldwyn, or Rogers) in Gloucestershire, Malmesbury and Bradenstoke (Wilts.), Blockley and Kempsey (Worcs.), and Oxford. Of the personnel who appear, R., abbot of Cirencester, is mentioned four times; R., abbot of Winchcombe, the prior of Bradenstoke, and Master R(obert) de Clipstone each occur three times; and R., dean of Cirencester, R., dean of Blockley, the prior of Cirencester, R., dean of 'Leche', and R., abbot of Malmesbury, twice. Master Alexander of St. Albans (Alexander Neckham), who entered the abbey at Cirencester between 1197 and 1201 and became abbot in 1213,[5] R., archdeacon of St. Albans, Master R(obert) de Bingham, Master J. de Pratis, J., archdeacon, and A. (? Adam), vice-archdeacon, of Oxford, J., dean of Langford (Oxon.), and G. de Bradewelle are all mentioned once. As meeting-places Cirencester occurs three times, and Winchester, Gloucester, and Salisbury each once.

---

[1] ff. 95ᵛ–7ʳ and 114ʳ–19ʳ.   [2] f. 114ʳ.

[3] Kuttner, *Analecta Iuridica*, p. 444, appears to see it as one of the group, as does Professor Cheney, but apart from the fact that it is a manual of the same type I can see no direct relationship between its letters and those of others in the group.

[4] Masters R(obert) de Clipstone, Alexander of St. Albans, R(obert) de Bingham, and J. archdeacon of Oxford, who is presumably Master John of Tynemouth, all have links with Oxford. See Chapter III, pp. 105, 121, 126, 131; Emden, *Oxf. Reg.* and *A.N.C.*, pp. 317, 325.

[5] See Emden, *Oxf. Reg.* ii. 1342–3, and J. C. Dickinson, *The Origins of the Austin Canons and their Introduction into England* (1950), p. 188.

Furthermore, the formulary is built round two main cases, which give every appearance of being real. The first is a suit about tithes between the abbot of Séez (dioc. Séez, Orne, France), and J., clerk of Kempsey (Worcs.), who is also cited as Master J. de Kempsey, as Master J., rector of Cerney (Glos.) and as J., rector of 'Ebintone' (? Edington, Wilts.). The judges were R., abbot of Winchcombe (Ben. Glos.), and R. and R., deans of Cirencester and Blockley. The last two alternate with R., dean of 'Leche', and Master R(obert) de Clipstone. R. abbot of Winchcombe, is mentioned once as Ralph, and is presumably Ralph II, abbot from 1182 × 84 to (?) 1194.[1] The suit was heard in the parish church at Cirencester.[2] The second case recites a mandate of Pope Innocent III, which was dated at the Lateran on 20 February 1201[3] and appointed as judges the abbot of Cirencester, the prior of Bradenstoke, and the abbot of Malmesbury, who alternates with Master Alexander of St. Albans. The parties were Robert Pictor of Abingdon and J. knight, son of Robert de Rameseia (who is mentioned on one occasion as O. de Rameseia), and the case was about 100 shillings sterling and a pound of cumin which Robert Pictor was supposed to receive in return for some land. The cause must have been heard between 1201 and 1208, by which time Robert of Melun had ceased to be abbot of Malmesbury:[4] the vice-archdeacon of Oxford and J., dean of Langford, were asked to execute the sentence.[5] There seems little doubt that these are real cases, the details of which have been taken from actual documents. Since the first suit was heard in the parish church at Cirencester, it is possible that documents concerning it were deposited at the abbey there; and the inclusion of the abbot in the second commission could account for the presence also of those documents in Cirencester. Eight out of the thirteen forms in O concern these two suits. The prior of Cirencester occurs in two of the other five documents and the convent of Cirencester figures as a party in a third.

[1] V.C.H. Glos. ii. 72. [2] O, f. 223ᵛ, cols. i–ii.

[3] O, f. 224ʳ, cols. i–ii. The mandate comes from the third year of Innocent, for which the register is incomplete, and there is no trace of it.

[4] V.C.H. Wilts. iii. 230. Walter Loring is mentioned as abbot elect in 1208. The final *actum* mentions the abbot of Malmesbury as R.

[5] O, f. 224ʳ, col. i–224ᵛ, col. i.

The other two seem to be strays, the fourth mentioning St. Albans and the archdeacon of St. Albans, and the fifth Master R(obert) de Clipstone again. A plausible explanation of the origin of the formulary is that it was compiled in the Augustinian abbey at Cirencester, between 1182 and 1221,[1] by scribes working from original documents who added anything of use which came their way. During the thirteenth century the formulary was re-copied into the psalter in which it is now found, by which time some of the names had become corrupt.[2]

Another problem in the interpretation of these formulary books is the date of the composition of the forms. The connection between the date of the composition of B, A, L, and O, and the pontificate of Innocent III, was argued by Professor Cheney.[3] B, A, L, O, and C all give that pope's name. Cheney suggested that the hand of A 'cannot hardly be later than the first decade of the thirteenth century' and that H. bishop of Lincoln is Hugh of Avalon (1186–1200).[4] The date of B has been narrowed by Richardson to 1202–9, since the fourth year of King John (1202) is mentioned, and by an ingenious argument concerning the schools of Northampton the *terminus ante quem* is given as 1209. It also includes mention of popes Alexander (III) and Celestine (III). In fact B, like O, gives the impression of having been built up over the years, and some of the basic forms of the group appear to be earlier than Innocent III. Substitution of a contemporary name for an obsolete one is not unknown in letter forms,[5] and the primitive fount might date from as far back as the pontificate of Alexander III. There is the evidence of the additional letter of Pope Alexander III in L and of the use of his name in B,[6] but even if in origin the form of the group is earlier than has hitherto been thought,

---

[1] See above, p. 50 n. 1. The last letter or form (f. 224ᵛ, col. i) mentions J. archdeacon of Oxford, who must be Master John of Tynemouth archdeacon until 1221.

[2] Ker, *Medieval Libraries*, p. 52, attributes the psalter to Cirencester but on the grounds of the Cirencester names in the formulary.

[3] Cheney, *Bishops' Chanceries*, p. 124.

[4] Ibid., pp. 124, 127.

[5] H. G. Richardson, 'An Oxford Teacher of the Fifteenth Century', *Bulletin of the John Rylands Library*, xxiii (1939), 449, speaks of re-fashionings of a letter-writing tract indicated by the name of the pope, etc.

[6] L, f. 69ᵛ, and B, ff. 79ᵛ, col. i, 80ᵛ, col. ii.

the substitution of a later name shows that the form was still applicable when it was copied. If the major form is earlier than Innocent III's pontificate, the question of the date of the transcription arises. Impetus might have been provided by canon 38 of the Fourth Lateran Council (1215), which required judges to have clerks to draw up documents and make copies of the *acta* for each stage of the suit.[1] It may be that the stereotyped productions of L, C, V, and M, which mention only Innocent's name, date from the last year of the pontificate (1215–16) and were made in answer to a demand following the decree. But, on the other hand, such forms must have been needed and provided earlier, just as they were needed and provided afterwards. B.M. Add. MS. 8167 shows that the particular form of the group was copied until the 1240s at least;[2] and the Canterbury formulary, a more advanced type of manual, with an introduction and extended rubrics, and not one of the group, was composed after 1216 and probably soon after 1227,[3] as the forms were still required.

Questions as to the place and date of origin of the form which is common to B, A, C, L, V, and M will remain unanswered until a careful analysis of the manuscripts is made. When that has been done it may well be concluded that the form originated, as Richardson argued, at Oxford, perhaps in the law schools.[4] It is difficult to see otherwise why the writer should have used predominantly Oxford names and places, although his forms do not appear to be based on actual documents.[5] A reconstruction of the

---

[1] c. 11. *X.* II. 19, and see Drogheda, xiv, pp. 19–20, on how to compose *acta*.

[2] f. 96ʳ.

[3] *C.F.*, pp. 200–1.

[4] Richardson, 'Oxford Law School', pp. 319–38. See also "The Schools of North-ampton in the Twelfth Century', *E.H.R.* lvi (1941), 595–605.

[5] The judges mentioned are the prior of St. Frideswide's (3 times, once called D.), the abbot and prior of Oseney (both twice, and once called respectively A. and W.), the abbot of Thame (twice), the subprior of St. Frideswide's, the prior of Thame (called H.), the abbot of Bury St. Edmunds (W.), the abbot of Pipewell, the dean of Oxford, and possibly the prior of Bury and the prior of Pipewell (P. and W.), and several men who may have been attached to the Oxford schools, Master W. de Westal', W. de Branf', and W. of Lincoln diocese (all once). Cf. Cheney, *Bishops' Chanceries*, pp. 125–7, who also comments that the litigants were summoned to Oxford seven times, to the church of St. Peter in the East (5 times) and the church of St. Mary the Virgin (twice), and on the parties; but he connects them all with

transmission of the forms could be as follows. The original production, compiled by someone working in Oxford, served as an exemplar for B, although not directly, for B is very corrupt and must be at some distance from the parent manuscript. There is no hint of the manuscript's provenance. From B and other formularies, A with its extraordinary mixture of names—T., archdeacon of Wiltshire (not identified), H., bishop of Lincoln, the official of the archbishop of Canterbury, C. de Cantuar', a party, and the church of Wig' —may have been composed. The first part of the book containing A has been attributed to Bury St. Edmunds; the book also includes a collection of decretals of Innocent III,[1] but the relationship between A and these two sections is not clear, and therefore whether A belonged to Bury is not ascertainable. After A had been compiled, the basic form of B was then stripped of all proper names except that of the reigning pope, Innocent III, perhaps after his decretal on the making of court *acta*, and circulated in C, L, V, and M, for example. The only suggested medieval ownership for C is Gloucester, but this may not be tenable.[2] L is part of a grammar which belonged to Worcester cathedral, and the manuscript contains besides a collection of decretals.[3] V and M have Italian appendices and were presumably made for an Italian market. The two later formularies in B.M. Add. MS. 8167, which resemble these so closely, form part of a book which belonged to William Haseley, a monk of Westminster, who gave it to the abbey in *c.* 1250. Richardson describes this manuscript as 'an ordinary commercial production', and he notes a collection very similar to Haseley's

the diocese of Lincoln as the underlying link. The name of R. de Log occurs as a party. The Log family had land in the parish of St. Mary the Virgin, Oxford. A John Log is mentioned in *c.* 1210–20, and in 1238 Peter son of John Log gave lands and tenements to the canons of St. Frideswide's (*St. Frideswide's Cart.* i, nos. 431, 433, and 436). There are also four mentions of H. bishop of London (? Lincoln), a mention of the year in which H. bishop of Lincoln died; and London, St. Paul's, the dean of York, and the cathedral of St. Peter at York are also noted.

[1] M. R. James and C. Jenkins, *A Descriptive Catalogue of the Manuscripts in the Library of Lambeth Palace* (Cambridge, 1930), pp. 176–9, and Kuttner, *Repertorium*, pp. 305, 311 n. 1, and see also 335.

[2] See M. R. James, *A Descriptive Catalogue of the Manuscripts in the Library of Gonville and Caius College*, i (Cambridge, 1907), 36.

[3] See Duggan, *Decretal Collections*, pp. 81–4, who seems to favour an association with Exeter for the decretal collection (p. 84 n. 3).

book which was written at Thorney 'a generation or so later' by John Britton, precentor of the house.[1]

The material is too sparse to bear the weight of an elaborate structure of argument, but the tracing of the common core in B, A, L, C, V, and M to one and not several founts would mean little more than that by stripping a particular fount of its names and places it was made a popular and useful form, and that these six manuscripts represent a chance survival. As a contrast to these general or 'commercial' productions, the evidence of the Canterbury formulary and of O suggests that at least some formularies were made primarily for domestic use, being the private collections of the clerks of bishops or abbots. The Canterbury formulary is distinctly traceable to the chancery of Christ Church from whence it was copied by a St. Augustine's scribe.[2] Similarly O has the appearance of originating at Cirencester in the Augustinian house there. Many problems about these formularies have not been solved, but it is sufficient to recognize for the present purpose that such collections must have been common in England between 1198 and 1254, and that these few remaining treatises are examples of the sort of manuals which would have been devised and used by most judges delegate and their clerks.

2. *The Preliminaries of the Suit*

(i) *The Impetration or Application for the Mandate*

Nothing is really known of how the machinery for the issue of papal rescripts worked before the pontificate of Innocent III, and even then the sources are surprisingly meagre.[3] But for a petitioner to open a suit before papal judges delegate it was necessary to procure a mandate from the pope. The petition which was presented was probably a written one. At any rate by the thirteenth century William of Drogheda instructs the applicant to put his case in writing,[4] and forms

---

[1] Richardson, 'Oxford Teacher', pp. 447–50. The Thorney book is now Cambridge, C.C.C. MS. 297.   [2] *C.F.*, pp. 199–200.

[3] For the sources in general, see Barraclough's bibliography to his article *'Audientia Litterarum Contradictarum'*, cols. 1398–9; Herde, *Beiträge*, pp. 164–73, who deals mainly with Innocent IV and later when the sources become more numerous; and below.   [4] Drogheda, i, pp. 7–8.

of petition were made available to plaintiffs and their proctors.[1] The impetration, or application for the mandate, took place in the *Curia Romana*, at least this is the phrase used by the 1230s.[2] The term seems to be used loosely much as one might speak of taking a case to 'the Vatican' today.

There seems to be no evidence to support the supposition of Professor Barraclough that the *audientia litterarum contradictarum*, a court for the regulation of the proctors, existed in embryo, even if not as a separate office, before the time of Innocent III.[3] It may be, as he suggests, that its origins are connected with the development of the system of judicial delegation under Eugenius III and Alexander III; but this cannot be proved, and it was perfectly possible for the Chancery to issue a mandate without the *audientia litterarum contradictarum* playing a part in the process. The system of the *contradictio* is first mentioned in 1199,[4] and the *audientia publica* and the *audientia litterarum contradictarum* are not heard of until this period. Dr. Herde has assumed, indeed, that it was Innocent III who in his Chancery reforms created the institution of the *audientia publica*, and he implies that Innocent instituted the *audientia litterarum contradictarum* also, and with it the regular possibility of stopping the issue of a papal document or of changing its contents.[5] This was

---

[1] e.g. *Oxford Formularies*, p. 275 no. 5. A small book of forms of petition 'secundum cursum Romane curie' was written by the cardinal Guala Bichieri in 1226, ed. R. von Heckel in 'Das päpstliche und Sicilische Registerwesen', *Archiv für Urkundenforschung*, i (1908), 502–10. See also G. Barraclough, 'Formulare für Suppliken aus der ersten Hälfte des 13. Jahrhunderts', *Archiv für Katholisches Kirchenrecht*, cxv (1935), 435–56.

[2] See my article 'Canterbury Proctors', p. 313, and docs. nos. i–iv and vi.

[3] Barraclough, '*Audientia Litterarum Contradictarum*', cols. 1387, 1389. J. Teige, *Beiträge zur Geschichte der Audientia Litterarum Contradictarum*, i (Prague, 1897), esp. 14, argued without any real basis that there was a separate department of the Curia dealing with the expedition of writs as early as 'perhaps in the first half of the twelfth century'.

[4] *Quellen und Forschungen aus italienischen Archiven und Bibliotheken* (Köenigl. Preussisches Historisches Institut in Rom, x, 1907), 378, no. iii.

[5] Herde, *Beiträge*, pp. 164–8. Dr Herde has prepared a study of the *audientia litterarum contradictarum*, and an analysis of the whole group of formularies, to be published by the Bibliothek des Deutschen Historischen Instituts in Rome. The earliest, the Durrieu manuscript, dating from the middle years of the thirteenth century, which R. von Heckel had proposed to edit, is a most crucial source and has long awaited an editor (Barraclough, '*Audientia Litterarum Contradictarum*', col. 1394). On this MS. see also G. Tessier, 'Note sur un manuel à l'usage d'un officier de la Cour pontificale (XIIIe siècle)', *Études d'histoire du droit canonique dédiées à*

the *contradictio*. In the case of judicial business, the Chancery decided whether the suit should be delegated, and if so, what kind of mandate should be sent. The chosen form, detailing judges, etc., which followed the plaintiff's petition very closely, was then drawn up and at some later time read aloud in the *audientia publica*, a public sitting of the Chancery where general pronouncements were declared and comments made.[1] At this point an objection to the contents of the letter might be raised by the defendant's proctor. If no objection was made, the mandate was returned to the writing office for checking, sent for engrossing, and then sealed with the *bulla*. If, on the other hand, a protest was registered, the dispute was handed over to the *auditor litterarum contradictarum* for inquiry into the objection.

The operation of this procedure is described for the first time by Thomas of Marlborough, proctor of Evesham abbey, in 1205–6. He speaks of the reading in the *audientia publica*, where he made an objection, and of being called *ad audientiam contradictarum* on the next day, which might mean either going *for* the hearing of the contradiction in the Chancery or the *audientia publica*, or of going *to* the *audientia litterarum contradictarum*, a separate chamber.[2] The *Chronicon Montis Sereni* speaks of two letters being read in the *audientia* in 1223: one of these the proctor allowed to pass without comment, the other he contradicted. The next day the *magister contradictarum* caused the contradicted letter to be destroyed.[3] The existence of the process of the *contradictio* presupposes the system of reading the documents aloud, but it seems unlikely that the contradiction procedure operated

G. Le Bras, i (Paris, 1965), 357–71, esp. 369, and Herde, 'Der Zeugenzwang in den Päpstlichen Delegationsreskripten des Mittelalters', *Traditio*, xviii (1962), 265 ff. On the Trier MS., Stadtbibliothek Cod. 859/1097, which contains a formulary of the *audientia litterarum contradictarum*, see H. M. Schaller, 'Eine Kuriale Briefsammlung des 13. Jahrhunderts . . .', *Deutsches Archiv für Erforschung des Mittelalters*, xviii (1962), esp. 174.   [1] Herde, *Beiträge*, pp. 166, 168.

[2] *Chron. Abb. Evesham*, p. 199, and also p. 145 referring again to the contradiction process. On the whole case, see M. Spaethen, 'Giraldus Cambrensis und Thomas von Evesham über die von ihnen an der Kurie geführten Prozesse', *Neues Archiv der Gesellschaft für ältere deutsche Geschichtskunde*, xxxi (1906), 629–49.

[3] '*Chronicon Montis Sereni*', M.G.H., *Scriptorum*, xxiii (1874), 200. This is the first known mention of an officer, and the first to be noted by name is Master Otto who appears under Honorius III, see *Quinque Compilationes Antiquae*, p. 153, cited by Barraclough, '*Audientia Litterarum Contradictarum*', col. 1390.

in every case. It is as mistaken to think that proctors objected in all instances as it is to accept the old idea that all documents that were not seen by the pope went through the *audientia publica* and vice versa.[1] This is no longer acceptable. One method of issue did not necessarily preclude the other. According to Herde, the *audientia publica* acted to some extent as a public relations office where documents which the pope had seen could also be read if he thought it desirable.[2] Although there was a ruling for routine matters to follow a defined course and to be divided into either *litterae legendae* or *litterae dandae*, for important matters special rulings could be made.[3] This seems to point to the view that the pope may have played some part in the delegation of important cases. At least it should not be assumed that, because he was not necessary to delegation, he was never concerned with it or that he did not know of what was going on.

It may be that during Innocent III's pontificate the *audientia litterarum contradictarum* represents a stage in the process of the issue of a certain document, rather than a distinct office or court.[4] The *auditor litterarum contradictarum* worked in close conjunction with the vice-chancellor and on his behalf. He was present at the reading, and he heard the objection. In the investigation of its validity he merely took over some of the vice-chancellor's work, and it may have been some time before he got a separate chamber or office.[5]

Whether this procedure antedates 1198 or not, no documents from the *audientia litterarum contradictarum* appear to have survived from before the pontificate of Gregory IX.[6] The first known survival is a letter of Master Richard of Langdon, proctor of Richard le Grand, archbishop of Canterbury, recording his agreement not to bring the convent of Christ Church, Canterbury, before a Church court nor to

---

[1] Bresslau, pp. 282 ff.   [2] Herde, *Beiträge*, p. 168.
[3] Ibid., pp. 171–2.   [4] Ibid., pp. 165–6.
[5] There is an interesting instance in *Reg. Inn. IV* (no. 7295), of the *auditor litterarum contradictarum* being designated to act for the vice-chancellor, presumably in his absence. It illustrates the close relationship which was maintained between the two offices.
[6] On the documents and the procedure in general, see 'Canterbury Proctors'.

prejudice them in any way on account of a mandate which he had procured from Gregory IX, dated 10 September 1230.[1] The document resulted from the protest that Master Philip de Mortimer, proctor of Christ Church, had made in the *audientia publica*, and was a private or unofficial deed. The second is an official document, issued in the name of the *auditor litterarum contradictarum*, Master Robert of Somercotes, some time after 20 May 1238, and called a *cautio*.[2] It noted that the mandate that the archdeacon of Canterbury had obtained would not be valid against the prior and chapter of Christ Church. In other words, at the reading of the mandate in the *audientia publica* the proctor acting on behalf of Christ Church had objected to the issue of letters which might adversely affect his clients. The auditor had then after investigation accepted his protest.

It cannot be argued convincingly that an objection was made in every case.[3] Mandates, as we shall see, could be made out against a large number of people, and not all applicants would have been wealthy enough to employ standing proctors at Rome to look after their interests. No doubt in important cases they endeavoured to do so, but there must have been many documents which passed through the *audientia publica* without comment. The *contradictio* system also allowed for objections against the personnel of the judges and the place of hearing. Again this must have been extraordinary procedure. No documents recording decisions about these matters by the *auditor litterarum contradictarum* survive from before 22 April 1277,[4] but it seems likely that this variety of objection too came into being with the system of contradiction, and was thus in operation from the early years of Innocent III's pontificate.

---

[1] Canterbury, Cartae Antiquae, C 47, pd. 'Canterbury Proctors', App. doc. vi.
[2] Canterbury, Cartae Antiquae, A 206, pd. 'Canterbury Proctors', App. doc. vii.
[3] See 'Canterbury Proctors', pp. 321–3 and 324, and Herde, *Beiträge*, p. 167 and n. 334. Brentano, however, inclines to this view, *York Metropolitan Jurisdiction*, p. 157.
[4] Canterbury, Cartae Antiquae, C 284 and C 285, pd. 'Canterbury Proctors', App. docs. i, ii. See also forms of about the same date in *Die Formularsammlung des Marinus von Eboli*, ed. F. Schillmann (Bibliothek des Preussischen Historischen Instituts in Rom, xvi, 1929).

(ii) *The Place of the Hearing*

The question of the choice of the judges must be dealt with later,[1] but the question of where the delegated court was to sit concerns us now. No decision as to the place of meeting is ever recorded in the mandate, and it is probable that the place was only mentioned at Rome when the bench of judges was challenged. This lack of a specific instruction suggests that unless there was some additional document, as the *littere conventionales*, to make known the place on which the parties had agreed, the judges made their own decision.[2] In all cases, probably, the commissions sat in a church.[3] Also the location was supposed to be a safe one.[4] The place is by no means always specified in the *acta*, but an analysis of the places where the courts are known to have met between 1198 and 1254 suggests the following observations.

Generally speaking, the place of meeting was dictated by the composition of the group of judges. Cambridgeshire judges met at Barnwell or Cambridge; Suffolk judges at Bury St. Edmunds; Kentish judges at Canterbury; Sussex judges at Chichester; Bedfordshire judges at Dunstable; Herefordshire judges at Hereford; Lincolnshire judges at Lincoln; Norfolk judges at Norwich; Peterborough judges at Peterborough; and Stamford judges at Stamford.[5] There is also an indication that cases were heard in major towns, county towns, cathedral cities, towns situated on main routes, and towns where there were important religious houses, such as Oxford, Canterbury, Lincoln, London, Northampton, Cambridge, Dunstable, and St. Albans.[6] Boniface VIII was to

---

[1] See Chapter III, pp. 109–18.

[2] 'Canterbury Proctors', pp. 318–21. Cf. Cooper, *Select Scottish Cases*, p. xxviii, who asserts that 'the judges delegate suited their own convenience as to the venue' without seeking to accommodate parties and witnesses, and see his nos. 17, 18, 22, 34, 40, and 44.

[3] In Anglo-Saxon churches special places were provided for the sitting of Church courts, *The Ecclesiastical Courts*, Report of the Commission set up . . . in 1951 (1954), p. 2.

[4] Bishop Mauger of Worcester, for instance, was granted the right to appeal if summoned to answer lawsuits in Wales, where he said it was dangerous for Englishmen to go (*Letters of Inn. III*, no. 406).

[5] See App. A (ii), A List of some of the Meeting-Places of the Courts.

[6] See ibid., nos. 87–97 (Oxford, 11 examples), 15–23 (Canterbury, 9 examples), 60–7 (Lincoln, 8), 69–75 (London, 7), 78–83 (Northampton, 6), 9–14 (Cambridge, 6), 34–9 (Dunstable, 6), and 102–6 (St. Albans, 5).

declare in 'Statutum quod' that commissions of delegates were to sit in cities where there were generous supplies of experts available,[1] and Innocent IV foreshadowed this ruling in the second canon of the First Council of Lyons, 1245,[2] saying that the judges, who were to be dignitaries, should only summon the parties to cities and large places.

Sometimes the judges heard cases away from their home towns. A commission of Gloucester judges heard a case between two Buckinghamshire houses at Oxford;[3] and a commission of Cambridge judges made a settlement in Wallingford priory church in Berkshire, in a suit between Wallingford priory and Henry of Earley (Berks.) and his chaplain.[4] In these instances, when the judges made considerable journeys, it was probably for reasons of convenience. If, however, a plaintiff sought and obtained a commission to three judges at distance from one another, he ran the risk of objections from both the judges and the defendant. In a case between G(eoffrey de Burgh) archdeacon of Norwich and Master Robert of York about the bishopric of Ely, one of the members of the first commission was the archbishop of York, who was said to be too far from Ely to hear the cause without expense, and of the second commission, the abbot of Coverham (Yorks. N.R.), who was four days' journey from his colleagues, the abbot of Waltham (Essex) and the archdeacon of Huntingdon.[5]

Defendants were not supposed to be brought before judicial tribunals more than two days' journey from their own diocese,[6] but this seems often to have been ignored. William, son of Conan of Holbeach (Lincs.), was brought before a commission of Kentish judges by the prior and convent of Christ Church, Canterbury, and a settlement was made at Canterbury. The suit concerned an annual rent of four shillings from seven acres of land in Holbeach.[7] Beaulieu brought the prior and convent of St. Michael's Mount (Cornw.), in a suit about the tithes of St. Kaveran church,

---

1 c. 11. 6. I. 3.
2 *Sacrorum Conciliorum Collectio*, xxiii, ed. Mansi, p. 619.
3 App. A (ii), no. 94.   4 Ibid., no. 112.
5 *Reg. Hon. III*, nos. 846, 1422 (*C.P.L.* i. 49, 55).
6 c. 28. *X*. I. 3, and see, e.g., Peterborough, MS. 5, f. 135^{r-v}.
7 App. A (ii), no. 19.

before the prior of Christchurch (or Twynham, Hants), and a settlement was made in the church there.[1] Sentence in a suit between Dunstable and Robert, rector of Bradbourne in the Peak (N. Derbys.), was given by St. Albans judges on 18 December 1214 in the abbey at St. Albans, and when Robert failed to pay the expenses, to which he had been condemned, he was brought south again in 1223, and this time heard sentence before the abbot and prior of Warden and the prior of Beadlow in Flitwick church (Beds.), which belonged to Dunstable priory.[2] In another Beaulieu case it was specifically stated in the mandate to the legate Otto, dated 15 October 1238, that Beaulieu, the defendants, might be brought beyond two days' journey but not beyond four or five.[3] The abbot of Lavendon was held to have acted 'maliciose' by the abbot of Prémontré when he impetrated letters from the general chapter to the abbots of Newhouse and Croxton who were six days' journey from his adversary, the abbot of St. Radegund's;[4] and papal examples show the defendants coming from as far away as 100 miles, which must have meant three to four days' travelling according to season and weather.

The plaintiff's choice of commission undoubtedly affected the decision about the place of hearing. In a suit between Lanthony and St. Julian's hospital, St. Albans, when the judges were obtained by Lanthony, they were Gloucester clerics, and the hospital of St. Julian at St. Albans had to come to Gloucester where sentence was given in the church of St. Mary by the abbey gate; and when the judges were obtained by St. Albans, they were Dunstable men, meeting at Dunstable.[5] The dean of Lincoln brought the prior and convent of Tutbury before Southwell judges, who met at

[1] App. A (ii), no. 28.
[2] App. A (ii), nos. 46, 102, and see *V.C.H. Beds.* i. 371.
[3] Beaulieu Cart., f. 130ᵛ. Cf. *Letters of Inn. III*, no. 125, where the Kentish defendants complained of being summoned more than four days' journey out of the diocese of Canterbury and into that of Lincoln, probably to Oxford. The impetrant was a canon of Dover; the judges were from Oxfordshire, namely the abbot of Thame, the prior of St. Frideswide's, and Master W. de Bram[feld ?], for whom see above, p. 52 n. 5.
[4] St. Radegund's (Bradsole) Cart., f. 42, pd. H. M. Colvin, *White Canons in England* (Oxford, 1951), pp. 339–40, and see p. 87.
[5] App. A (ii), nos. 37, 51.

Southwell; while the prior and convent brought the dean before Stafford judges, sitting at Stafford.[1] The prior of Newstead (Notts.) was summoned to answer the abbot of Chertsey (Surr.) by Oxford judges, who made a settlement in St. Mary's church, Oxford, a journey of about 100 miles from Newstead.[2] The abbot and convent of Westminster convened Andrew, vicar of Pershore (Worcs.), before the prior of St. Albans and the dean of Hertford, who gave a decision in the abbey of St. Albans (Herts.). Andrew was represented by a proctor.[3] Another case in which a decision was given at St. Albans, by the archdeacon, was between the convent of Holy Cross, Waltham (Essex), and the convent of Chepstow in Monmouthshire, who were contumacious, perhaps not surprisingly considering the length of the journey.[4] From Worcester to Bury St. Edmunds is again about 100 miles in distance, but it was at Bury that the case between the prior and convent of Eye and the archdeacon of Worcester concerning the church of Badingham (Suff.) was heard by the abbot and prior of Bury St. Edmunds and the prior of Great Bricett (also Suff.).[5]

Although there are instances of the plaintiff coming some distance—as the prior and convent of Lewes (Suss.) who appeared against W., rector of Weston Colville (Cambs.), at Carlton cum Willingham (one of the Lewes properties in Cambs.) before the prior of Merton (Surr.) and his co-judges, who are unspecified;[6] they also appeared against Nicholas parson of Sculthorpe (Norf.) before Huntingdon judges in the church of St. Mary at Huntingdon[7]—they are isolated and can possibly be explained by other factors, such as the likelihood of making a settlement. An analysis of the cases in which some of the religious houses were involved both as defendant and as plaintiff shows that, when they were acting as plaintiff, the suit was usually heard near home, when as defendant, they sometimes had a journey to make. In all the suits where the prior and convent of Christ Church, Canterbury, were acting as plaintiffs, and where the place of settlement is known, it was Canterbury.[8] In an instance

---

[1] *Reg. Antiq. Linc.* iii, no. 759.   [2] App. A (ii), no. 95.
[3] Ibid., no. 104.   [4] Ibid., no. 105.   [5] Ibid., no. 7.
[6] Ibid., no. 24.   [7] Ibid., no. 56.   [8] Ibid., nos. 15, 17–19, 21.

where they were defendants, they went to Boxley parish church in Kent, where the abbot and prior of Boxley and Master Th(omas) of Maidstone heard a case between them and Master Richard, rector of Cliffe-at-Hoo (Kent).[1] The prior and convent of Eye appeared as plaintiffs at Barnwell (Cambs.), Fornham All Saints (Suff.), Ipswich (Suff.), Norwich on two occasions, Bury on two occasions, and Westleton (Suff.),[2] and as defendants at Fressingfield (Suff.) and Lincoln.[3] The prior and convent of Lanthony by Gloucester as plaintiffs went to St. Mary's church Gloucester twice, and to Hereford cathedral and St. Mary's church Oxford,[4] and as defendants they went to Dunstable, Hereford, and St. Paul's, London.[5] St. Frideswide's occur only once as defendants, at Dunstable.[6] As plaintiffs they heard judgements at Flamstead (Herts.), in the churches of All Saints and St. Peter's by the castle at Northampton, in St. Mary's church, Oxford, in St. Andrew's chapel in St. Albans abbey, and at Westminster.[7] Acting by proctor the nuns of St. Michael's, Stamford (Northants.), were brought by the abbot and convent of Owston (Leics.) before the priors of Leicester, Belvoir (Lincs.), and Breedon (Leics.) in Breedon church, which belonged to Breedon priory;[8] but when they brought William Erl of North Luffenham (Rutland) before the deans of Stamford, Rutland, and Carlby (Lincs.), it was in the church of St. Mary at the bridge in Stamford.[9]

In a petition to Pope Innocent IV in 1248 to allow them not to be cited more than two days' journey from their monastery to answer lawsuits, the abbot and convent of Bardney alleged that they had either to expend much energy and money or lose the suit.[10] The archdeacon of the East Riding in seeking a similar indult stated that he had attended causes for eight days at a time. He was given an assurance that he should not be summoned to attend courts outside the diocese of York or more than two days' journey from his domicile.[11]

---

[1] App. A (ii), no. 4.   [2] Ibid., nos. 1, 6–7, 47, 58, 84–5, 116.
[3] Ibid., nos. 49, 63.   [4] Ibid., nos. 50–1, 54, 90.
[5] Ibid., nos. 37, 55, 74.   [6] Ibid., no. 35.
[7] Ibid., nos. 44, 78, 80–1, 91, 103, 118.   [8] *V.C.H. Leics.* ii. 8.
[9] App. A (ii), nos. 5, 110.
[10] Bardney Cart., f. 28 r-v, and *Reg. Inn. IV*, no. 3774.
[11] *Reg. Hon. III*, no. 6205 (*C.P.L.* i. 115).

These examples suggest that not only was the decree of the Fourth Lateran Council concerning impetration and summonses sometimes disregarded, but also that the advantage was with the plaintiff, who by his choice of judges usually indirectly determined the place where the court would sit. This seems to be supported by the above evidence; and the decree 'Statutum quod' of Boniface VIII showed an exact analysis of the state of affairs fifty years earlier by enacting that when the plaintiff and defendant were of the same city and diocese, the cause was not to be committed outside it, and that when the plaintiff and defendant were of different dioceses, the plaintiff should impetrate to delegates within the diocese of the defendant, or in another diocese not his own and not beyond one day distant.[1] The exact advantage gained by the plaintiff is impossible to assess, particularly in minor suits. It was the right of the defendant to object if he felt himself prejudiced. He could also petition for an indult if he was rich enough.

Indults were granted to the convents of Merton in 1231,[2] Oseney in 1232,[3] St. Augustine, Canterbury, in 1236 and 1253,[4] Spalding in 1238,[5] Sempringham, Nostell, and St. Mary, York, in 1245,[6] and St. Frideswide, Oxford, and Abingdon in 1250.[7] An indult granted to Cartmel priory (Lancs.) by Gregory IX conceded that they should not be summoned to courts of judges delegate more than two days' sail from their port, because of the danger from storms, the grave expenses, and the pressure to enter into unsuitable agreements.[8] Similar indults were also granted to seculars —the bishop and officials of Norwich in 1240,[9] the bishop elect of Winchester in 1253,[10] and the bishop of Llandaff in 1254, whose indult was to remain valid for three years.[11] The travelling distance beyond which these petitioners were not to be bound to go varied from one day, granted to Aymer de Valence bishop elect of Winchester by Innocent IV,[12]

---

[1] c. 11. 6. I. 3.   [2] Reg. Greg. IX, no. 728.   [3] Ibid., no. 985.
[4] Ibid., no. 3277; St. Augustine's Red Book, ff. 26ᵛ–27ʳ.
[5] Spalding Cart., f. 417ʳ.   [6] Reg. Inn. IV, nos. 1008, 1300, 1660.
[7] St. Frideswide's Cart. i, no. 55; Abingdon Cart., f. 24ʳ.
[8] Reg. Greg. IX, no. 1554.   [9] Ibid., no. 5269.
[10] Reg. Inn. IV, no. 6475.   [11] Ibid., no. 7967.
[12] Ibid., no. 6475.

to three days granted by Innocent III to St. Augustine's, Canterbury;[1] but the most usual period was two days, and some of the indults specified that they related to suits about goods and property only.[2]

(iii) *The Mandate*

The mandate, or rescript, which was drawn up in the Chancery, sealed with the leaden *bulla* on hemp cords, and issued in the pope's name, started the action, and was the authority by which the judges acted.[3] As such they quoted it when commanding officers to make a citation or execute a sentence on their behalf. When the abbot of Westminster, the prior of Merton, and Master William de Sancte Marie Ecclesia, judges delegate of Gregory IX, instructed the dean of Canterbury to cite the abbot and convent of St. Augustine, Canterbury, to appear at Southwark, they recited the papal mandate that they had received granting them this power.[4] Similarly, when judges delegate had passed sentence in a case between Master Baldwin, canon of Troyes, France, and Master W(illiam), archdeacon of Worcester and the convent of Lanthony, Gloucestershire, in 1235, they ordered the dean of Gloucester to carry it out, and sent him both a copy of their sentence and the papal mandate on whose authority they had proceeded.[5] Professor Le Bras has described the mandate and the appeal system as two of the most powerful means of papal centralization, both of which were provided by the Roman law.[6] Certainly to some extent papal power was disseminated by the mandate, which is comparable with the English royal writ.[7] Although its influence may have been

---

[1] St. Augustine's Cart., f. 66ʳ⁻ᵛ.

[2] *Reg. Greg. IX*, no. 985; Abingdon Cart., f. 24ʳ; *Reg. Greg. IX*, no. 3277; *Reg. Inn. IV*, no. 1660; *St. Frideswide's Cart.* i, no. 55; and *Reg. Greg. IX*, no. 728.

[3] Numerous original mandates survive: e.g. *The Priory of St. Radegund Cambridge*, ed. A. Gray (Cambridge Antiquarian Soc. xxxi, 1898), Ch. 6, p. 77; Lambeth Palace Library, Papal Documents, no. 30; and Windsor, Papal Bulls, no. 1.

[4] St. Augustine's Cart., f. 79ʳ.

[5] Lanthony Cart. A1, XVI, no. xvi. Another example of sending the papal mandate to the executive officer is in the Lewes Cart., f. 260ʳ, cal. *Lewes Cart. N.P.*, no. 135; but the original is not P.R.O. E 40/14071 as Bullock says.

[6] Le Bras, 'Droit romain', p. 391.

[7] William J. La Due wrote a thesis on this subject. An excerpt was published as *Papal Rescripts of Justice and English Royal Procedural Writs, 1150–1250. A Comparative Study* (Pontificia Universitas Lateranensis Institutum Utriusque Juris,

exaggerated, it was usually treated with respect by the judges, and scrutinized. When, for instance, a mandate arrived from which the *bulla* had been detached, the judges delegate, the abbots of Kirkstead, Bardney, and Barlings, declined to acknowledge it without a new order from Rome; and on another occasion the judges refused to act because the mandate lacked the 'o' in 'spoliarunt'.[1]

Broadly speaking, thirteenth-century mandates can be divided into two classes, the first inclusive, covering minor cases and cases of first instance, and the second particular, comprising major cases and cases of appeal. From the evidence of the Oseney cartulary the late Dr. H. E. Salter supposed that groups of cases were set aside for sending to Rome.[2] A wide mandate was then sought which could be used against a number of people on a variety of charges. This at least was the practice in minor cases. Salter's supposition is confirmed by the evidence. The prior and convent of St. Neots brought Robert, parson of Barnwell, Bartholomew, rector of Barton Bendish, and T., rector of Brampton, before judges delegate off one mandate.[3] By a mandate of 27 April 1233, the abbot and convent of Bec succeeded in bringing William Estormy and Elias, chaplain, the priory of St. Frideswide, Oxford, the abbey of Tewkesbury, and the nunnery of Godstow before Dunstable judges in suits about a chapel at Shalbourne (Berks. now Wilts.), tithes at Hidden and Eddington in Hungerford (Berks.), tithes at Lesser Ogbourne (Wilts.), and tithes in Wycombe (Bucks.).[4] The mandate also includes the name of the abbey of Abingdon among the defendants.[5] Thorney got one mandate against the rectors of Pertenhall (Beds.) and Tydd St. Giles (Cambs.) in 1224;[6] and similarly Christ Church, Canterbury, against the parson of Eythorne (Kent) and the brothers of

Theses ad Lauream, no. 155, Rome, 1960). Unfortunately the sections dealing with the English royal Chancery (chapters ii, iv) were omitted from the excerpt; but La Due draws attention in his conclusions to the expansion in the issue of papal mandates under Eugenius III (1145–53), and of royal writs under Henry II (1154–89).

[1] *Reg. Hon. III*, no. 2547 (*C.P.L.* i. 73); and *Letters of Inn. III*, no. 1052.
[2] *Oseney Cart.* vi, p. 339.
[3] See App. A (ii), nos. 12–14.
[4] Ibid., nos. 34–6, and Eton College, Bledlow Ch. C 5.
[5] Eton College, Bledlow Ch. C 5.
[6] Thorney Cart. ii, ff. 257ᵛ and 322ᵛ.

Notre Dame des Dunes in Sheppey;[1] Dover against certain chaplains in Dover;[2] Bardney against the Stixwould nuns and the archdeacon of Cleveland (Yorks. N.R.);[3] and St. Frideswide's against the rectors of Souldern and Beckley (Oxon.).[4]

Besides the parties who were specified by name in the mandate, an unlimited number could be summoned by the clause 'et quidam alii'.[5] The clause 'quidam alii' was not, however, to be taken to refer to more important persons than those actually named.[6] A mandate of Gregory IX, issued from Perugia on 9 November 1229, and made out against the archdeacon of Essex, the rector of the church of East Lavant (Sussex), 'et quidam alii clerici et layci Londoniensis et Cicestrensis diocesum',[7] was used also to bring to justice Robert de Dene, rector of St. Peter's, Lewes, and of the chapel of Smythwick; J., chaplain of the same; Richard, rector, and Gilbert, vicar, of Patcham; Walter, rector of Barcombe; and probably P., rector of Tarring (all Sussex).[8] Philip, rector of East Hendred (Berks.), got a mandate against the convents of Bec, Abingdon, Reading, and Caen, and against William de Ferrieres, earl of Derby, and others ('quidam alii') of the Salisbury, Worcester, and Coventry dioceses.[9] The abbot and convent of St. James, Northampton, summoned through one mandate of Honorius III, dated 4 February 1222, William, son of Richard Cav', Philip, John, and Reginald, clerk, and other parishioners of Hartwell (Northants.), 'auctoritate generalis clausule in

---

[1] App. A (ii), nos. 17–18. The Cistercian abbey of Dunes in Flanders was granted the church of Eastchurch in Sheppey by Richard I, *Calendar of Documents preserved in France*, i (918–1206), ed. J. H. Round (1899), p. 497, and see E. Hasted, *History and Topographical Survey of . . . Kent*, ii (Canterbury, 1782), 665. Presumably they had a cell at Eastchurch.

[2] App. A (ii), nos. 41–2.   [3] Ibid., nos. 60–1.   [4] Ibid., nos. 80–1.

[5] See, e.g., Bradenstoke Cart., f. 119ᵛ; *Reg. Antiq. Linc.* iii, no. 647; Lanthony Cart. A 1, III, no. lv, and A 2, ff. 221ᵛ and 223ʳ (two examples).

[6] c. 15. *X.* I. 3 (Inn. III).

[7] P.R.O. E 40/14190 (cf. E 40/14189), cal. *Lewes Cart. S.P.* ii. 101.

[8] P.R.O. E 40/14157–9, cal. *Lewes Cart. S.P.* ii. 24–5, 34–5; P.R.O. E 40/14156, cal. *S.P.* ii. 26; Lewes Cart., ff. 116ᵛ–17ʳ, cal. ii. 39; P.R.O. E 40/14139, cal. ii. 56; and Lewes Cart., f. 103ʳ, cal. ii. 9–10.

[9] Windsor Ch. xv. 41. 71 and Abingdon Cart., f. 53ʳ. Cf. P.R.O. E 135/21/33, which recites a mandate obtained by the rector of Odell (Beds.) against the prior and convent of Canons Ashby, the rector of Newington, Saer de Odell knight, 'et quidam alii Norwycens' Eliens' et Lincoln' civitatum et diocesum'.

literis domini pape contente scilicet quidam alii'.[1] In the
Council of Lyons Innocent IV legislated that through the
clause 'quidam alii' only three or four people were to be
convened, and their names were to be expressed in the first
citation.[2] When summoned by general letters 'in communi
forma', which made no mention of the Cistercian order to
which he belonged, the abbot of Beaulieu refused to obey
the summons of the judges delegate, the abbot of Hyde, the
prior of Breamore, and the dean of Winchester. An appeal
was accordingly made to the pope by the plaintiffs, the prior
and convent of Selborne.[3] The other defendants in this case,
the abbot of Tiron and the prior of Andwell, also declared
that they could not be summoned by the general clause
'quidam alii'.[4]

If all the defendants were not mentioned specifically by
name in the mandate, it was difficult for the proctors at
Rome to know when to make a contradiction on behalf
of clients who might well be prejudiced. For this reason
indults were sought granting exemption from summons unless mention of the order, rank, or church was made in the
mandate. The Premonstratensians were allowed by Gregory
IX, for example, to treat as invalid impetrated letters containing the clause 'quidam alii' that did not make a note of
their order.[5] The archbishop of Canterbury was allowed not
to answer a judicial summons unless his title was referred to
in the papal letters.[6] The treasurer of York declared that
neither his office nor the parson J. was mentioned in letters
that the convent of Eye had procured, addressed to the
abbot of Langley and his colleagues. After the judges had

[1] Northampton, St. James's Cart., f.109ʳ⁻ᵛ.
[2] c. 2. 6. I. 3, and also *Die Päpstlichen Kanzleiordnungen von 1200–1500*, ed.
M. Tangl (Innsbruck, 1894), p. 56 n. 2.
[3] Magdalen College, Oxford, Selborne Ch. 373 (Macray, *Calendar* i. 24); and
see c. 6. *X*. I. 3 (Alex. III).
[4] Magdalen College, Oxford, Selborne Ch. 373. Cf. O, f. 223ᵛ, col. i, a formulary
example: the prior of Séez appeals to the pope because he was not mentioned in the
mandate which J. rector of 'Ebintone', (? Edington, Wilts.) had obtained about
tithes belonging to the convent of Séez; and c. 21. *X*. I. 3.
[5] *Chartulary of Cockersand Abbey*, i, pt. i, ed. W. Farrer (Chetham Soc. xxxviii,
1898), p. 39.
[6] *Reg. Greg. IX*, no. 2989. Cf. the archbishop of York who was not bound to
answer papal letters addressed to parsons and canons of York, *Reg. Hon. III*, no. 6231
(*C.P.L.* i. 116).

refused to admit this exception, he appealed to the pope, who ordered the dean, the master of the schools, and Master Robert de Gravele, canon of Lincoln, to hear the cause if it was as alleged or to return the case to the abbot of Langley and his commission.[1] When a mandate was sent to the abbot and prior of Warden and the prior of Dunstable in 1215, a special note was made in it that the abbot and convent of Westminster were to answer the charge.[2] Westminster held that they could not be summoned without special letters, and they had presumably received an indult to this effect. A similar indult was granted by Honorius III in 1220 to the prior and convent of Christ Church, Canterbury, conceding that they should not be held to pay attention to letters which did not mention the church of Canterbury.[3]

The charge of the mandate was also elastic enough to enable the plaintiff to summon such groups on a collection of charges, for instance 'super possessionibus, decimis, debitis et rebus aliis',[4] 'super possessionibus, legatis et rebus aliis',[5] and 'super subjectione, obediencia, professione, visitatione, procuratione et rerum ejusdem ecclesie dispositione'.[6] By the use of provisos, furthermore, recent decisions of the pope and *Curia* on points of law and new modes of procedure could be brought to the attention of the judges and the parties without drawing up specific forms for each case. The ruling of the Fourth Lateran Council (canon 32), that vicars' portions should be sufficient, was often called to the attention of the judges by a proviso included in the mandate in causes which concerned benefices, pensions, or apportionment of tithes.[7] Most of the mandates containing this proviso date from the pontificate of Honorius III, but a mandate of the legate Ottobon of 1266 also included it.[8] Other provisos about issuing sentences of excommunication or of interdict

---

[1] Eye Cart., f. 39ᵛ.
[2] Westminster Domesday, f. 228ʳ⁻ᵛ (f. 452ʳ⁻ᵛ ibid.).
[3] Canterbury, Reg. A, f. 33ʳ.   [4] *Montacute Cart.*, no. 171.
[5] Bodleian MS. Dodsworth 76, f. 1.
[6] St. Paul's, Press A, Box 23, Ch. 864.
[7] Hefele, *Conciles*, v, pt. ii. 1359–60; and, for examples, Binham Cart., f. 185ʳ; P.R.O. E 40/14953; P.R.O. E 40/14253, cal. *Lewes Cart. N.P.*, no. 73 (although Bullock has this as E 40/14298); Dover Cart., f. 226ᵛ; P.R.O. E 40/14955; Leeds Cart., f. 10ʳ; *Chertsey Cart.*, no. 92; P.R.O. E 40/14071; and Lanthony Cart. A I, VIII, no. lxxviii.   [8] Binham Cart., f. 187ᵛ.

were sometimes added to the mandate without basic alteration to the stereotyped form.[1]

Specific mandates were issued more rarely, for dealing with cases of importance which might influence the law of the Church, for appeal cases where individual instructions were needed, and when influential persons were involved.[2] Innocent IV wrote on 18 April 1246 to the abbot of Bourne, the prior of St. John, Northampton, and the archdeacon of Buckingham, instructing them how to deal with a case that had been sent to him on appeal by the prior and convent of Spalding.[3] A mandate of Innocent III to the priors of Marton and Malton and H., dean of Ryedale (Yorks. N.R.), mentioned specifically that the church of Branxton (Northumb.), which belonged to Kirkham priory's church of Kirknewton in Glendale, had been seized by certain malefactors in the skirmishes in those parts. The judges were ordered to restore the church to the canons, if this appeared just when they had established the truth.[4] Often specific mandates commanded the judges to decide the cause within a certain time, 'mandamus quatinus, partibus convocatis, audiatis causam et eam infra v. mensium spatium post receptionem presentium studeatis judicio vel concordia terminare', or to remit it with full details to Rome.[5]

3. 'Jus' or the Commencement of the Suit

(i) Citation and Contumacy

On returning from Rome, the plaintiff or his proctor informed the judges of his impetration or appeal, presented his mandate to them, and asked them to summon the defendants. A form is provided in the Lambeth formulary:

A. B. C. judicibus D. clericus salutem. De sanctitatis vestre confidens equitate ad vos litteras summi pontificis inpetravi, ut de causa que

---

[1] Abingdon Cart., ff. 53ʳ–4ʳ, and Windsor Ch. xv. 41. 71: 'proviso ne in terram ipsius comitis [of Derby] excommunicationis vel interdicti sentenciam proferatis nisi super hoc a nobis mandatum receperitis speciale'.

[2] e.g. Westminster Domesday, ff. 228ʳ, 276ʳ, and 448ʳ.

[3] Spalding Cart., f. 418ᵛ. Cf. Magdalen College, Oxford, Selborne Ch. 373 (see above, p. 68).

[4] Kirkham Cart., f. 89ᵛ, and see P.R.O. DL 25/563.

[5] B.M. Harley Ch. 84 F 45, and see Bodleian MS. Chs. Bucks. a 3, Ch. 45.

vertitur inter me et C. super ecclesia illa diligenter congnoscatis (*sic*) et fine debito terminetis. Quapropter sanctitati vestre supplico ut nobis certum diem prefigatis et prefatum C. ut prefixa a vobis die coram presencia vestra juripariturus et sufficienter instructus in ecclesia illa appareat, auctoritate apostolica cogetis vel citetis.[1]

As the abbot of Humberston and the priors of Thornton and Grimsby reported: 'Hujus igitur auctoritate mandati ad instanciam predictorum abbatis et conventus de Neuhus [Newsham, Lincs.] citavimus pluries et legittime . . .'[2] When the plaintiff had presented the mandate to the delegates, he obtained from them a sealed *memorandum* acknowledging their receipt of it. Drogheda makes a note of it: 'Forma memorandi. Memorandum quod R. et J. iudices a domino papa delegati receperunt mandatum domini papae sub hac forma: Gregorius etc.'[3] This step seems to have been a precaution which the plaintiff would take if he were business-like.[4] The archdeacon of Northampton and the dean of Haseley (Oxon.) reported that they had received a mandate of Honorius III, dated 6 July 1222, in which Geoffrey, rector of Steeple Aston (Oxon.), challenged Bradenstoke priory and others to answer him about tithes and other matters.[5]

The procedure followed the formal course of the *ordo judiciarius*. Alongside this plenary procedure, which is outlined below, a second method of judicial procedure was gradually developed, termed summary,[6] to deal with affairs demanding immediate action, such as cases about the validity of an election, the possession of a benefice, or a marriage case. The summary procedure dispensed with the formal charge (the libel) and the formal declaration of disagreement (the *litis contestatio*), and it allowed, for example, no objections against the conduct of the action (dilatory exceptions).[7] But it was not an alternative mode of procedure until

---

[1] A, f. 271ᵛ, col. i, and cf. B.M. Add. MS. 8167, f. 116ᵛ.
[2] B.M. Harley Ch. 44 E 20.   [3] Drogheda, vii, p. 11.
[4] See Maitland, *Roman Canon Law*, p. 112.
[5] Bradenstoke Cart., f. 147ʳ.
[6] On the revival of the concept of summary procedure and its gradual extension, see C. Lefebvre, 'Les Origines romaines de la procédure sommaire au XIIᵉ et XIIIᵉ s.', *Ephemerides Iuris Canonici*, xii (1956), 149–97.
[7] Fournier, pp. 231–2.

Clement V's decretals,[1] although it had an effect on certain elements of the suit at an earlier date.

The judges now summoned the defendant. The first citation was expected to contain details about the suit and to include the papal mandate which outlined the charge or *editio*.[2] As Tancred writes:

Attamen delegati iudices in prima citatione consueverunt tenorem commissionis sibi factae in literis citationis totum de verbo ad verbum inserere et reo, qui ad iudicium vocatur, transmittere, ut sciat, qui sunt, qui eum ad iudicium vocant, et cuius auctoritate. Et in literis citationis contineri debet, quod die tali, loco tali, tali actori, coram ipsis iudicibus responsurus accedat.[3]

The second and third citations, however, omitted both the mandate and the *editio*,[4] and sometimes the defendant may have been issued with a separate copy of the charge.[5] Almost certainly the plaintiff was summoned verbally at the time that he presented the mandate to the judges. At any rate no written examples summoning the plaintiff to court have survived.

A citation was either simple or peremptory. It was usual for simple citations to be made three times,[6] the third summons being peremptory. Tancred says that the parties ought to be summoned by three edicts, or by one peremptory order which substitutes for them all: 'debent vocari tribus edictis vel uno pro omnibus peremtorio'.[7] The judges in the Alvingham case ordered the dean of Walcot to cite the defendant by one peremptory edict: 'Mandamus quatinus uno pro tribus edicto peremptorie scitetis Petrum dictum personam

---

[1] c. 2 *Clem.* ('*Clementis Papae V Constitutiones*' in *Corpus Juris Canonici*, ii, ed. E. Friedberg, Leipzig, 1881) V. 11, and c. 2 *Clem.* II. 1.

[2] *C.F.*, no. (1); C, f. 119ʳ, col. i; L, f. 65ᵛ, col. i; and B, ff. 79ᵛ, col. i; 80ᵛ, col. ii; and 81ᵛ, col ii (the first and last of these examples are printed in *Oxford Formularies* ii, nos. 4 and 11).

[3] Tancred, p. 133; cf., e.g., B.M. Wolley Ch. v. 27.

[4] See *C.F.*, nos. (3), (4), (5), and A, f. 271ᵛ, col. i.

[5] Damasus Hungarus, '*Summa de Ordine Iudiciario*', *Quellen zur Geschichte des Römisch-Kanonischen Processes im Mittelalter*, iv, pt. iv, ed. L. Wahrmund (Innsbruck, 1926), lxxxvii, p. 61. For Damasus Hungarus see Stickler, col. 1137, who dates his work as between 1210 and 1216. On making the *editio*, see *C.* ii. 1; *D.* ii 13; and *Lib. Pauperum*, ii, tit. 1.

[6] This is presumably what 'post legitimas citationes ei factas' means (B.M. Stowe Ch. 58).   [7] Tancred, p. 132.

duarum partium ecclesie de Staynton'.'[1] When the first or second citation was peremptory, it was usually because speed was necessary; for instance in marriage suits when delay might spiritually endanger the parties, and in suits where the thing which was sought in the libel was perishable.[2] In some cases two peremptory citations might be made before punishment was threatened, as, for example, when an important person was summoned.[3] The most frequent practice in England, however, seems to have been to issue simple edicts and then a peremptory one.[4] In most cases when simple citations were issued, the defendants had to be summoned all three times before they came to court. The phrases 'sepe ac sepius et tandem peremptorie fecimus evocari', 'pluries et tandem peremptorie . . . citato', 'sepe et sepius fecimus evocari', are a common occurrence in final *acta*.[5]

Citations were made at definite intervals—'per legittima dierum spacia'.[6] According to the Roman law, ten days were allowed between each simple citation and thirty days for a peremptory one. In 1254 the defendants in a case were summoned 'trinis edictis per intervalla triginta dierum'.[7] A *memorandum* of a citation is dated 4 March 1252, and the party was summoned to appear on 16 March.[8] Presuming that the citation would reach its destination the following day, this would be a period of ten days before the court day. In all citations the charged party was ordered to

---

[1] Alvingham Cart., f. 5ʳ. On this suit see App. B (ii), pp. 315–16.

[2] See *C.F.*, no. (3); A, f. 271ᵛ, col. i—a peremptory citation apparently on the second edict; B, ff. 79ᵛ, col. i; 81ᵛ, col. ii; and B.M. Harley Ch. 84 F 44. Drogheda has examples of the second citation being peremptory and the third being a second peremptory citation (xvi and xvii, pp. 21–2).

[3] See *C.F.*, no. (6). C, f. 119ʳ, col. i, and L, f. 65ᵛ, cols. i and ii, give examples of three peremptory citations.

[4] A, f. 271ᵛ, col. i: 'Hujus igitur auctoritate mandati C. clericum primo ac secundo citavimus et tercio illi diem prefiximus peremptorium'; B.M. Add. MS. 8167, f. 116ʳ⁻ᵛ; B.M. Egerton Ch. 382: 'semel secundo et tercio edicto peremptorio citavimus'; Canterbury, Cartae Antiquae, L 135: 'Et quia jam tercio vocati estis pro eadem causa a nobis predictum diem vobis constituimus peremptorium'; and *C.F.*, no. (5).

[5] P.R.O. E 326/2268; E 40/14953–4; Thorney Cart. ii, ff. 257ᵛ, 383ʳ; and Bodleian MS. Dodsworth 76, f. 1.   [6] Binham Cart., f. 185ʳ.

[7] Magdalen College, Oxford, Steyning Chs. 12, and 16, cal. L. F. Salzman, *Chartulary of the Priory of S. Peter at Sele* (Cambridge, 1923), no. 25.

[8] B.M. Harley Ch. 84 F 35.

desist or come to answer.[1] The defendant in the Canterbury formulary was ordered to make satisfaction within eight or fifteen days or to appear.[2] The fact that the citation had been made would be proved in front of the judges by witnesses or certified by the delegate.[3]

A peremptory summons contained the warning that the suit would be heard whether the defendant appeared before the court or not; and one formulary example orders the defendant to appear ready to put forward any dilatory exceptions so that the suit would not be delayed.[4] Furthermore, if the defendant failed to appear before the court after the legitimate citations, or refused to reply to the accusation, he was declared contumacious, and as such could be punished. He did not automatically lose the suit.

Suspension or inhibition from celebrating the sacraments was the usual penalty for a clerk, although excommunication could also be imposed.[5] In 1195, for example, the archbishop of York was suspended for contumacy.[6] The papal decretal 'Ex Concilio Africano' did not, however, approve of the deprivation of benefices.[7] In a document which was addressed to the judges, the dean of Cirencester reported that he had declared William, rector of Hampton Gay (Oxon.), suspended because of contumacy and that he had cited him again to appear before the court.[8] It was usual in declaring the punishment of suspension to cite the party again peremptorily, as the dean of Ewell reported that he had done in 1235 × 40;[9] for the longer the contumacy continued, the greater would be the penalty to be exacted.[10]

---

[1] *C.F.*, no. (1).   [2] Ibid., nos. (1), (2), and (4).

[3] Ibid., nos. (1), (2); and c. 4. *X*. II. 15 (Greg. IX).

[4] B.M. Add. MS. 8167, f. 114ᵛ.   [5] *C.F.*, no. (7).

[6] *Chronica Magistri Rogeri de Houedene*, iii, ed. W. Stubbs (R.S. li, 1870), 305, 309, and 315. Cf. Canterbury, Christ Church Letters, ii, no. 12, where the judges, the prior of Abingdon and the prior and subprior of St. Frideswide's, declined to suspend the bishop of Exeter for contumacy because it might endanger many souls.

[7] c. 1. *X*. II. 1. 'De iudiciis—Contumax in non comparendo vel non respondendo excommunicari potest; beneficio autem privari non debet.'

[8] Bodleian MS. Chs. Oxon. a 5, Ch. 364. This document is unfortunately torn. It dates probably from *c.* 1260.

[9] *Oseney Cart.* ii, no. 1112.

[10] *C.F.*, no. (7); and, e.g., 'Charters and Muniments belonging to the Marquis of Anglesey', cal. I. H. Jeayes, *Collections for a History of Staffordshire*, ed. Staffs. Rec. Soc. (1937), no. 58 (hereafter cited as 'Burton Chs.'), where the rest of the

Excommunication was used mainly against contumacious laymen. The ordinance of William the Conqueror, probably of 1072, stipulated excommunication as the punishment for not answering a triple citation before the Church courts.[1] Excommunication, and possibly an order to pay costs, may have composed the 'tota poena' which was inflicted on Ivo Wint' (? of Winchester), a layman, for contumacy in a suit against the abbot and convent of Beaulieu about a tenement.[2] The person who remained for more than forty days under sentence of excommunication was liable to be arrested and imprisoned by a writ of 'de excommunicato capiendo' directed to the sheriff, but it is difficult to form any opinion of the actual effect of excommunication at this time.[3]

Following the Roman law practice, in lawsuits of real action over property, interim judgement could be passed against a contumacious party after a summary investigation.[4] Such decisions provided the plaintiff with possession of the thing sought for a year's duration, subject to the case being reopened within this time. If the suit was reopened, the defendant had to pay the costs which he had previously incurred; if the case was dropped, the plaintiff, after the lapse of a year and without further investigation, was declared to be the right and true possessor.[5] The obvious contumacy of Ingeram, a rector of Rousham (Oxon.), in a suit against Oseney resulted in a judgement of the tithes in dispute *causa rei servande* to the abbot and convent.[6] When the bishop and chapter of Le Mans (Sarthe, France) did not

defendants, who had been contumacious, are peremptorily cited to appear to put forth dilatory exceptions on the second court day.

[1] *Die Gesetze der Angelsachsen*, i, ed. F. Liebermann (Halle, 1903), 485.
[2] Beaulieu Cart., f. 136ʳ.
[3] R. Phillimore, *The Ecclesiastical Law of the Church of England*, ii, 2nd edn. (1895), 964. Cf. Curialis, '*Ordo*', *Quellen zur Geschichte*, i, pt. iii, ed. L. Wahrmund (Innsbruck, 1905), i, p. 29. On the whole subject, see F. D. Logan, *Excommunication and the Secular Arm in Mediaeval England* (Pontifical Institute of Mediaeval Studies, Studies and Texts, 15, Toronto, 1968).
[4] R. W. Lee, *Elements of Roman Law*, 3rd edn. (1952), p. 442; P. J. Schierse, 'Legislation on Sequestration in Roman Law and in the Decretals of Gregory IX', *The Jurist*, xxiii (1963), 291–313, esp. 306; X. II. 15: 'De eo qui mittitur in possessionem causa rei servande', and esp. c. 3. X. II. 6 (Inn. III): 'Si lite non contestata reus est contumax, si fieri potest, mittitur actor in possessionem causa custodiae; alias reus excommunicabitur.' For forms, see A, f. 271ᵛ, col. i; B, f. 79ᵛ, cols. i–ii; L, f. 65ᵛ, col. ii; C, f. 119ʳ, cols. i–ii; and C.F., no. (8).
[5] Tancred, p. 137.   [6] *Oseney Cart.* iv, nos. 156 A and B (cf. C and D).

come to the hearing of a suit, nor commission a proctor to act on their behalf, the judges, Stephen, prior of St. Swithun's, and Guy, prior of Southwick, declared in favour of the dean of Salisbury's possession of the lesser tithes of Deverill (Wilts.), *causa rei servande*. Three weeks before the statutory year, the proctor of the bishop and chapter of Le Mans, Wimund of Deverill, appeared and promised to stand in judgement. But against his oath he was again contumaciously absent on the day appointed for the parties to appear, and a final sentence was given in favour of the dean.[1] Some time before 1214, the archdeacon of Exeter and his fellow judges delegate were said by R(ichard de Hegham), archdeacon of Essex, one of the parties, to have proceeded illegally in giving R. Peverel a portion of the church of Ermington (Devon), *causa rei servande*, because their jurisdiction had at that time been revoked.[2] When the rector of Withersfield (Suff.) was contumacious, he was at first fined, and then suffered a judgement *causa rei servande* against him. If he would not pay the one mark fine for the expenses of the opposing party or resisted the *missio in possessionem*, he was to be suspended.[3] These interim judgements were frequent in England, and they must have contributed to a respect for the efficiency of the canon law. For Scotland Lord Cooper records two unusual instances concerning judgements *causa rei servande*. In one instance the defendant appeared before the judges, but refused to reply, and was therefore guilty of verbal contumacy. Interim possession was awarded to the plaintiff, which became *vera possessio*.[4] In the other the judges delegate, being advised that an order of *missio in possessionem* would be attended by risk of bloodshed, placed the defendant's lands under interdict instead.[5]

After Hugh de Bilney, a clerk, had waited in vain for three months at Rome for his adversary Thomas to appear

---

[1] *Vetus registrum Sarisberiense . . . Register of S. Osmund*, i, ed. W. H. Rich Jones (R.S. lxxviii, 1883), pp. 354–6, and for another instance of this practice in operation see Belvoir, Large Cart., f. 77ʳ and Small Cart., p. 29, where the priory of Belvoir was granted an interim *missio* and was then finally adjudged the tithes in question.   [2] *Montacute Cart.*, no. 143.

[3] Windsor Ch. xi G 37 (3). On this suit see App. B (ii), p. 315.

[4] Cooper, *Select Scottish Cases*, p. 36.   [5] Ibid., pp. 9–10.

and answer about the church of Kimberley (Norf.), a mandate was sent to the abbot of Dereham ordering him to condemn Thomas in costs as contumacious unless he could show lawful impediment for his failure to appear.[1] In such an instance the case may well have gone by default; for contumacy could have an effect on the disposition of the cause itself, although the judgement usually depended on other supports as well. A sentence was passed on John, chaplain of the church of Sedlescombe (Suss.), by W., abbot of Combwell, and F., prior of Leeds; John had absented himself throughout the case and had not sent a proctor to make reply. It was decided that he ought not to take tithes from the monks of Robertsbridge, and perpetual silence was imposed on him about them. In this case the judges took counsel of wise and discreet men, and they also examined Robertsbridge's privileges about the tithes.[2] When the prior and convent of Chepstow contumaciously did not appear to hear sentence (nor probably previously), the archdeacon of St. Albans, a subdelegate of the prior, did not hesitate to promulgate sentence against them and in favour of the abbot and convent of Holy Cross, Waltham, in the conventual church of St. Albans on 25 July 1251. The judge acted, he said, after hearing the intention and proofs of Waltham and having taken the advice of men who were learned in the law.[3] These are cases where the defendant was contumacious. If the *actor*, on the other hand, having ignored the first round of citations, still refused to come when cited a year later, sentence would automatically be declared against him.[4]

Forms of letters, which were used for absolving the contumacious from the penalties that they had incurred, are provided in the Canterbury formulary.[5] In these examples the rural dean was ordered to absolve the penitent, when he

---

[1] *Reg. Greg. IX*, no. 4803, where the mandate is addressed to the archdeacon of Dereham; but since there was no such archdeacon, this would seem to be a mistake for the abbot of Dereham, or, possibly but less likely, for the archdeacon of Norfolk.

[2] B.M. Egerton Ch. 382.

[3] B.M. Egerton Ch. 409 (App. B (ii), no. 7). Cf. *Oseney Cart.* iv, no. 415c, where Thomas de Boues, rector of Harwell (Berks.), was contumacious, and sentence was given against him on 7 Aug. 1217.

[4] Magdalen College, Oxford, Steyning Ch. 16, cal. *Sele Cart.*, no. 25.

[5] *C.F.*, no. (9), and cf. Curialis, '*Ordo*', xx, p. 10.

had offered security to attend the court. A form for restoring possession is also given.[1]

(ii) *The Libel, Exceptions, and Altercations*

Once in court, the defendant heard the libel or *editio*.[2] In some instances the papal letters were used as an *editio*, as in a suit between the convents of Bullington (Lincs.) and Garendon (Leics.) in 1251.[3] The libel was expected to contain the following information:

> Conventi nomen et nomen convenientis
> Iudicis et nomen scribes causamque petendi
> Et quascumque petas res, omnes scribere debes,[4]

and had to be in writing.[5] Libels are frequently quoted in full.[6] This, for instance, was the libel that the proctor of the abbot and convent of St. Valéry delivered to the rector of Hinton Waldrist (Berks.) in 1239–40:

> Ego procurator . . . propono quod ipse ecclesiam sancti Walerici decimis provenientiis de dominico quondam Walteri, Widonis et Reginaldi patronorum sancti Walerici contra justiciam spoliavit, unde peto dictas decimas prefatis abbati et monachis restitueri et prefatum rectorem ad restitutionem perceptorum, que decem marcas sterlingorum estimo, condempnari. Hoc dico salvo jure addendi et cetera.[7]

The written *intentio* of the plaintiff, James, rector of Charwelton (Northants.), against the abbot and convent of Biddlesden (Cist. Bucks.) is quoted in a document of 1253:

> . . . recitata partis attricis intentione sub forma subscripta concepta, 'Coram vobis domine precentor de Bernewell [Barnwell, Aug. Cambs.] judex a domino papa delegate, petit Petrus Fannel procurator domini Jacobi rectoris ecclesie de Charewolton quatinus compellatis dominos

---

[1] *C.F.*, no. (10).

[2] Windsor Ch. xi G 14.

[3] P.R.O. E 135/6/13 (App. B (ii), no. 2), and cf. Alvingham Cart., f. 5ʳ (App. B (ii), no. 1) and above, p. 72.

[4] Arnulphus, xii, p. 16. Cf. *Henrici de Segusio Cardinalis Hostiensis Summa Aurea* (Lyons, 1597), lib. ii, p. 91ᵛ.

[5] c. 1. *X*. II. 3. For forms see Arnulphus, pp. 15–20.

[6] e.g. Pershore Cart., ff. 111ᵛ, 113ʳ; West Dereham Cart., f. 60ᵛ; P.R.O. E 42/384; B.M. Stowe Ch. 58; and Thorney Cart. ii, f. 257ᵛ.

[7] New College, Oxford, Takeley Ch. 229. St. Valéry was a Benedictine abbey in the diocese of Amiens (Cottineau, ii, col. 2912).

abbatem et conventum de Bitlesdene et sentencialiter condempnetis eosdem ad solvend' decimas minutas provenientes de manerio . . .'[1]

He sought other things also in several articles.

The final phrase 'salvo sibi jure mutandi vel minuendi vel addendi' follows a set form that allowed the plaintiff to change the libel, to add to it, or to withdraw part of it, up to the moment of contesting the suit.[2] It concluded the series of articles of which the libel consisted. When William of Englefield (Berks.), knight, had delivered his libel, he declared that he would prove either or both of his accusations.[3] If a declaration of what was sought was omitted from the libel, the defendant could appeal;[4] and Innocent III also declared that precision should be aimed at, especially in real actions: 'Quum agitur reali, non sufficit rem generaliter peti, sed debet ita specificari, ut evitetur obscuritas et aequivocatio.'[5] It was usual to include an article seeking expenses, those already incurred and those yet to be incurred, and damages.[6] Roger, rector of Oddington (Oxon.), in his *editio*, sought three marks yearly as expenses,[7] but it was not wise to exaggerate the claim or to be too specific on this point early in the suit.[8]

The defendant did not have to give an answer immediately. He might ask for *inducie deliberatorie*, a term of twenty days, to decide whether he was answering the case or not, and, if he was replying, to decide on his defence.[9] The defendant Peter applied for this period of delay and was granted it by the judges, in his suit with the convent of Alvingham.[10] An entry in the St. Neots cartulary, 'Elapsis postea legitimis induciis deliberandi super eodem libello propositis', shows another instance where the requested delay was granted.[11] The writer of the Canterbury formulary says, however, that

[1] B.M. Harley Ch. 84 F 45. Cf. the *intentio* recited in Norwich Ch. 680, where the prior and convent sought two parts of all the tithes from the demesne of Hubert de Ria the first in Swanton (Norf.).

[2] See *C.F.*, no. (1); Windsor Chs. xi G 15, and xi G 37 (4) (App. B(ii), no. 6); and Warter Cart., f. 46ᵛ.

[3] B.M. Add. Ch. 20372 (App. B(iv), no. 7).

[4] c. 49. *X*. II. 28 (Inn. III).   [5] c. 2. *X*. II. 3, and cf. c. 3.

[6] Dover Cart., ff. 50ᵛ, 51ʳ; cf. Bodleian MS. Chs. Oxon. a 8, Ch. 29b.

[7] *Thame Cart.*, no. 37.   [8] c. 1. *X*. II. 11 (Greg. IX).

[9] B.M. Royal MS. 10 B iv, f. 59ʳ (see above, p. 46 n. 2).

[10] Alvingham Cart., f. 5ʳ (App. B(ii), no. 1).   [11] St. Neots Cart., f. 130ᵛ.

this term could be denied to the defendant if a full account of the charge had been included in the citatory letters.[1] This reflected the decision of Celestine III in 1193: 'Induciae deliberatoriae denegantur reo, si per litcras citatorias plene potuit instrui, et deliberare super eo, de quo quaeritur.'[2] When the proctor of Bec added to his first charge the allegation that the rector of Withersfield had despoiled the convent over six years, the rector sought another period of *inducie deliberatorie*, but the judge ruled against the application.[3] If it was a minor change, a further delay could be refused, but if it was an important addition to the libel, the defendant was usually allowed a new period in which to decide whether to withdraw from or press on with the suit in its altered form.[4]

As soon as the defendant appeared in court he could put forward dilatory or peremptory exceptions.[5] A dilatory exception was directed not against the right on which the action was founded, but against the conduct of the action; while a peremptory exception could relieve the defendant from the duty of contesting the suit, and might be instrumental in deciding it. The loser in a dilatory or peremptory exception was ordinarily punished by being condemned to pay the consequent costs.[6]

Even if the greater number of dilatory exceptions were frivolous and disallowed, instances remain of bona fide objections, which to some extent seem to justify this procedure. Out of numerous dilatory exceptions that were put forward by the rector of Withersfield, the judge accepted three as worthy of discussion and quashed the rest.[7] The three accepted were that the acts in question were invalid, seeing that they contained conflicting evidence, that the papal letters were not valid, because at the time of impetration the cause was not imminent, and that furthermore the rector

[1] *C.F.*, no. (1).   [2] c. 2. *X*. II. 8.

[3] Windsor Ch. xi G 37(4) (App. B (ii), no. 6).

[4] c. 3. *X*. II. 8 (1220).

[5] See W. W. Buckland, *Textbook of Roman Law from Augustus to Justinian*, 3rd edn., revsd. P. Stein (Cambridge, 1963), p. 656; and Collinet, *Procédure par libelle*, pp. 304–15.

[6] cc. 5, 6. *X*. II. 14 (Inn. III). In the same way the loser of the principal cause or main issue was usually bound to pay the expenses, c. 17. *X*. I. 34 (Greg. IX).

[7] Windsor Ch. xi G 37(10).

had been summoned before several different judges over this negotiation. The triple exception of the abbot and convent of Bec, which was put forward by their proctors Peter of Swyncombe and John of Bledlow against the prior and convent of Dover in 1245, alleged that the letters of Dover's proctor could not be counted as valid, because they lacked the necessary clause *judicatum solvi*, because they did not express the name of the proctor, and because they were not sealed by the prior. This was accepted by the judges. Consequently the judges deemed that the prior and convent of Dover were unrepresented, and thus guilty of contumacy until then, and as such they ordered them to pay two marks sterling expenses within twenty days, otherwise they would be censured further. A mandate was sent by the judges to the dean of Dover ordering him to compel the prior and convent to pay or to suspend them, and to summon them to appear on 22 September to answer Bec in the continuation of the suit. The document reporting this is dated 26 July 1245 in the church of Pinner (Middx.).[1]

A decretal of Innocent III stated that all dilatory exceptions were to be put forward on or before a day to be arranged by the judges, and that none was to be admitted afterwards.[2] As soon as the libel had been read, this day was fixed. A document dated on the day after Palm Sunday in Norwich cathedral contains much information about dilatory exceptions. On this day Philip de Fleg, rector of Waxham (Norf.), appeared personally and proposed certain dilatory exceptions, seeking a day for proposing them all, whereupon he was granted the day after 'Quasimodo' Sunday.[3] The year in which this took place is not known, but the lapse of time would have been a fortnight. Compared with this, an *actum* dated at Lichfield in the cathedral church on the Wednesday

---

[1] Windsor Ch. xi G 27 (App. B(ii), no. 3).

[2] c. 4. *X*. II. 25. See also Tancred, p. 142; and, e.g., B.M. Harley Ch. 75 B 2: 'Facta est eis sufficiens editio de terris et rebus aliis super quibus eis injuriari dicebantur, et postea prefixus est eis dies ad omnes exceptiones dilatorias que sibi conpeterent proponendas'; Harley Ch. 84 F 43: 'Cum datus esset dies ad proponendum omnes exceptiones dilatorias . . . '; Harley Ch. 84 F 36; Windsor Ch. xi G 16; and 'Burton Chs.' 58.

[3] Bodleian MS. Chs. Norfolk a 6, Ch. 624. This was not the first day on which the suit was heard. The document refers to the names of the other defendants as being included 'in actis primi diei litis'.

before the feast of St. Leonard (4 November) 1248 stipulated that, with the consent of the parties, the Thursday after the feast of St. Nicholas (10 December) (thus about a month later) had been agreed upon for proposing all dilatory exceptions and proceeding as the law should dictate; meanwhile peace was to be preserved between the parties.[1] In the Alvingham suit, a delay of about two and a half months was granted. The parties appeared before the judges on 17 July 1245 in the chapel of St. Michael at Malton, and were told that 7 October was the final day for proposing all dilatory exceptions.[2] On the day appointed for proposing all dilatory exceptions, Marcellus, rector of Dalham (Suff.), the defendant in a case with the abbot and convent of Bec, was absent. The judge therefore declared that it would no longer be possible for him to propose them, and he ordered him to be cited again to contest the suit.[3]

When the exceptions had been put forward and admitted, they were argued over and discussed, presumably on the same day, until some decision was reached, but sometimes a separate day was appointed. The judges, the master of the schools at Malton, and the subprior of Kirkham and the dean of Buckrose, who were subdelegates, wishing to think more fully about the exceptions which had been proposed by Peter, parson of Stainton, appointed 5 November for discussing them. On 12 November 1245, again in the chapel at Malton, the judges after taking counsel refused to admit the exceptions, and declared that on 4 December the suit should be contested in front of the principal judges, the master of the schools at Malton and the priors of Bridlington and Kirkham, in the church of Winthorpe (Notts.).[4]

An exception against the claim of Richard, rector of Odell (Beds.), who asserted that half of the tithes near Woodend and of Allegho belonged to him, was proved by the defendants, the prior and convent of Canons Ashby. They produced an instrument of a former decision before judges delegate, in which it was shown that the tithes had been adjudged to them. Such a peremptory exception over the

---

[1] Bodleian MS. Chs. Oxon a 1, Ch. 11.   [2] Alvingham Cart., f. 5ᵛ.
[3] Windsor Ch. xi G 16 (App. B (ii), no. 4).
[4] Alvingham Cart., f. 5ᵛ (App. B (ii), no. 5).

thing in judgement, *res judicata*,[1] if sufficiently supported by evidence, could decide the case, as in this instance, when the judges, after satisfying themselves on the authenticity of the document, absolved the prior and convent from the petition of the *actor*.[2] Similarly after Walter, successor of Th', rector of Easton (Suffolk), had impetrated letters to the prior of St. Frideswide's and other judges, the abbot and convent of St. John, Colchester, placed an exception (*res judicata*), saying that the letters included no mention of a former sentence in their favour. This plea was not admitted by the judges, and so an appeal was made, Colchester obtaining letters to the prior of Holy Trinity, Ipswich, and others.[3] The final exception of four, put forward by Peter, parson of St. Andrew's, Stainton, against the convent of Alvingham, namely that having been properly presented to the church and instituted in it he was entitled to the fruits thereof, was held to be peremptory by Alvingham. And seeing that this statement was a direct contradiction of their assertion that they held the church, the prior and convent of Alvingham claimed that the suit was contested. It was not, however, accepted, at least at a later date, that through a peremptory exception the suit was automatically contested.[4]

Frequently altercations are recorded: 'post multas altercationes', 'diutius esset altercatum', 'per multum tempus inter ipsos esset in judicio altercatum super premissis', and altercations usually meant delays.[5] After many altercations the rector of Odell confessed that he had no right to the tithes of Stockinge, Woodend, and of the land which Walter the forester held.[6] Altercations could be over any point, and so might come before or after the contestation of the suit. Sometimes they concerned dilatory exceptions, as was recorded in the Christchurch (Twynham) cartulary.[7] The proctors of Bec and Tewkesbury engaged in long altercations over exceptions in 1233–4 in Dunstable priory

---

[1] *D.* xliv. 2; and *Lib. Pauperum*, viii, tit. 32.   [2] P.R.O. E 135/21/33.

[3] P.R.O. E 42/384. See also O, f. 224ʳ, cols. i–ii, where a peremptory exception was dimissed by the judges and sentence declared in favour of the plaintiff.

[4] c. 2. 6. II. 3 (Bon. VIII).

[5] e.g. Bradenstoke Cart., f. 105ʳ; P.R.O. E 40/14198; and *St. Frideswide's Cart.* ii, no. 980.

[6] Canons Ashby Cart., f. 110ᵛ.   [7] Christchurch Cart., f. 92ʳ.

church.[1] Prolonged altercations concerned the payment of arrears in a suit about tithes between Daventry priory and Thomas, rector of Lubbenham (Leics.).[2] Thomas agreed that he ought to pay six and a half marks yearly for tithes as had been decided before judges delegate of Innocent III,[3] but he insisted that he had only ceased payment because of war. The prior and convent of Daventry also sought four marks debt for non-payment. It was finally agreed that Thomas should pay the six and a half marks yearly in future and that the charge about arrears should be dropped.[4]

4. 'Litis Contestatio'

The contestation of the suit had now been reached. The name and concept of the *litis contestatio* were adopted from the sources of late Roman law.[5] The main purpose of citing the parties was to see if the suit was contested. The *litis contestatio* was an important stage in the procedure. It consisted of the narration or accusation by the plaintiff, and the definite, contradictory, and opposing reply to this, which was made by the defendant in court,[6] such as this example:

. . . facta est litis contestatio in hunc modum: videlicet quod predictus T. actor petiit capellam, decimas et obventiones omnes de Gatesbir' tanquam pertinentes ad ecclesiam suam de Westmeln' jure parrochiali, quas priorem et canonicos sancte Trinitatis London' injuste detinere dicebat occupatas, mere intendens petitorium. Procurator vero dictorum prioris et canonicorum sancte Trinitatis litem contestando respondit quod memorata capella, decime et obventiones de Gatesbir' jure parrochiali spectabant ad ecclesiam suam de Brakyng', eo quod villa de Gatesbir' tota sita esset infra limites parrochie sue de Braking', et etiam eadem ecclesia in possessione erat tam capelle quam decimarum

---

[1] Canterbury, Cartae Antiquae, L 381.
[2] Daventry Cart., f. 150ᵛ.
[3] Ibid., f. 151ʳ.
[4] In 1245 the same case came before the official of Lincoln, and there was a new settlement (f. 152ʳ). In 1289 Daventry conceded these tithes from the fee of Hugh Poherius to the then rector for a sum of money.
[5] C. iii. 9; Collinet, *Procédure par libelle*, chapter vi, section ii; Buckland, *Textbook of Roman Law*, pp. 632, 667, 695; and *D.D.C.* iv, cols. 475 ff.
[6] Tancred, pp. 196–201, and cf. P.R.O. E 40/14953: '. . . Intentione prioris et monachorum contra eundem W. et responsione ejusdem W. ad intentionem eorumdem prioris et conventus . . .'

et obventionum predictarum et ita ad ecclesiam de Westmeln' minime pertinebant.[1]

The formal contradiction signified legally the commencement of the process, and that there was bona fide contention between the parties. Without this there could be no case:

Non per positiones et responsiones, sed per petitionem in iure propositam et responsionem secutam fit litis contestatio, qua omissa nullus est processus.[2]

An agreement to come to a composition or to submit to an ordination would remove the necessity of contesting the suit;[3] and if there was no contested case, there could be no proof or sentence. As the *Decretales* stated, 'lite non contestata non procedatur ad testium receptionem vel ad sententiam diffinitivam'.[4] In a formulary example, when ordering delegates to hear witnesses if they are too infirm to come to court, the judges send a copy of the *litis contestatio* with their seals appended to it to prove that the suit had been contested.[5]

The oath of calumny, which was taken over from the Roman law, was sworn after the suit had been contested.[6] It was probably omitted unless specifically requested on the motion of one of the parties. Notices of it are rare. It was intended to prevent chicanery and vexatious litigation. The plaintiff promised that he had not brought the case in bad faith, and that he would not produce false instruments, corrupt the judges, or ask for unnecessary delays; the defendant, for his part, swore to conduct his defence in an equally honest manner.[7] In 1237 Otto, the legate in England, enacted that the oath should be taken, because after it the truth was more easily shown and cases were more quickly terminated.[8] On 16 April 1238 Gregory IX wrote to the prior

[1] P.R.O. E 212/28, and cf. Canterbury, Cartae Antiquae, L 351.
[2] c. l. *X*. II. 5 (Greg. IX). For this see, e.g., B.M. Harley Ch. 84 F 45; Warter Cart., f. 46ᵛ; and *Malmesbury Reg.* i. 388: 'Dictorum vero abbatis et conventus procurator *litem contestando* reddit quod . . .'
[3] e.g. Abingdon Cart., f. 90ᵛ; *Glos. Cart.* i, no. ccxxxvi.
[4] c. l. *X*. II. 6.   [5] *C.F.*, no. (22).
[6] See *C.* ii. 58(59); *Lib. Pauperum*, ii, tit. 40; 'De Iuramento Calumniae', title 7. *X*. II; Tancred, pp. 201–7; Fournier, p. 175; and St. Neots Cart., f. 130ᵛ: '. . . facta litis contestatione juramento etiam de calumpnia subsecuto . . .'
[7] Fournier, p. 175.   [8] *C.S.* ii, pt. i. 256, no. [24].

and convent of Christ Church, Canterbury, allowing them to force their adversaries to take this oath and the oath *de veritate dicenda*, provided that they were willing to take them themselves.[1] Either the parties or their proctors, if it was specified in the proctorial constitution, might take the oath.[2] The prior and convent of Alvingham granted this power to their proctors in 1245: 'concedentes eisdem plenam potestatem jurandi in animam nostram de calumpnia'.[3] The oath *de veritate dicenda*, of speaking the truth, and not the oath of calumny, was taken in the thirteenth century in spiritual causes.[4] It enforced the oath-taker to say only what he knew to be true.

The Proof

If the defendant denied the charge and contested the suit, the plaintiff was given a probatory term in which to prove his case.[5] Similarly if the defendant put forward exceptions and they were accepted by the judges, it was his duty to prove them within the term which was assigned to him. Interrogatories, or positions, were devised to help towards the proof. The plaintiff, on a day appointed by the judge after the oath of calumny or *de veritate dicenda* had been taken, set forth a series of separate allegations which he had extracted from the libel. He then demanded from his adversary on oath the answer of 'Yes' or 'No' to each one of these. The answers were the *responsiones*. The aim of positions was to fix neatly the points on which the parties disagreed, and to expose exactly what was to be proved.[6] The judges' duty at this stage was to separate and elucidate the opposing statements. The onus of proof was on the *actor*.[7] Negative proof was not accepted, and the aim of the *actor* was to get his adversary to make an admission, or several admissions, that irrefutably proved his case.

---

[1] Lambeth Palace Library, Papal Documents, no. 33.
[2] cc. 3, 4. *X.* II. 7 (Eug. III), c. 3. 6. II. 4, and, e.g., *Reg. Antiq. Linc.* ii, no. 386.
[3] Alvingham Cart., f. 5ʳ.
[4] Fournier, p. 176; c. 2. *X* II. 7; and *C.S.* ii, pt. i. 256, no. [24].
[5] *Ecclesiastical Courts*, p. 15.
[6] Fournier, pp. 178–80. See also Collinet, *Procédure par libelle*, pp. 354–5.
[7] Fournier, pp. 176, 178. The canon law took over the Roman maxims: 'Actore non probante reus absolvitur', and 'Onus probandi incumbit ei qui dicit'.

To commence the proof, each party collected evidence for its case. Evidence was of two kinds: oral, that is the attestations of the parties and of the witnesses, and written, consisting of the information provided by authentic charters. In most cases both varieties of evidence were used to build up the whole proof, and the judges reported:

... propositis, auditis et intellectis attestationibus, instrumentis necnon et rationibus utriusque partis, cum, tam per depositiones testium quam per rationes necnon per inspectiones instrumentorum coram nobis in jure exibitorum, nobis constaret evidenter . . .[1]

Evidence was sent to the *Curia* for suits that were to be decided there. In 1251 a mandate was dispatched from Pope Innocent IV to the bishop of Ely, ordering him to have careful transcripts made and forwarded to the *Curia* of the evidence of the dean and chapter of Hereford in their dispute with Bishop Peter of Aigueblanche.[2]

The oral attestation of witnesses was placed as first rank evidence.[3] When the nuns of Godstow asserted that the croft whose tithes were claimed by Robert, parson of Wytham (Berks.), was not within the boundaries of his parish, and that in any case they had exemption by papal privilege because the croft was newly brought into cultivation, they went on to bring forward witnesses and to prove it, so that the sentence followed in their favour.[4] Because of the necessity of giving witnesses due warning to appear, the judges appointed a distinct and separate court day for their production. Letters were sent to them, ordering them to come and cautioning them to give true testimony.[5] A letter in the Lambeth formulary threatens a witness with punishment for contumacy if he should be absent.[6]

On arrival before the court, the witnesses were sworn in. Admission, as it was called, was followed by examination.

---

[1] P.R.O. E 40/14953.

[2] *Charters and Records of Hereford Cathedral*, ed. W. W. Capes (Hereford, 1908), p. 89.

[3] See *D.* xxii. 5; *C.* iv. 20; and *Lib. Pauperum*, iv, tit. 17. In some cases a jury might be used, see, e.g., New College, Oxford, Writtle Ch. 401.

[4] *Godstow Reg.* i, no. [31]. Cf. Exeter Cart., p. 54, where the proof of several witnesses on oath produced a sentence, and, e.g., Canterbury, Cartae Antiquae, L 351: 'cum nobis postmodum per testes idoneos de jure constaret Cant' ecclesie . . .'

[5] See Wells, Lib. Albus, i, f. 97ᵛ; and *C.F.*, no. (20).   [6] A, f. 271ᵛ, col. iii.

The witnesses were asked specific questions, sometimes framed so as to produce definite answers of 'yes' or 'no'. Witnesses of both sides might be interviewed, those of the plaintiff coming first. They were heard separately and in private,[1] either by the judge or by a commissioner deputed to act for him, who on occasion might take attestations on the spot in order to save the expense of bringing witnesses to court.[2] Meanwhile the clerk was busy noting their replies.[3] In a form in the Cirencester formulary showing how witnesses' attestations were to be recorded, Ralph the chaplain stated on oath that he was present in the church of Cerney when Robert de Rameseia promised to pay 100s. to Robert Pictor at certain times, and that he had watched Robert swear on the altar to keep to this arrangement. Asked about the day and the time, he said that he did not remember except that it was a good while before Easter. Samson the chaplain, on oath, agreed with this testimony, but he could not recall whether it happened before or after Easter.[4]

A singular feature of early attestations is the large number of witnesses who were called upon to give evidence. In a case heard at Rome between the archdeacon of Canterbury and the monks of St. Augustine's, the archdeacon's witnesses were more numerous than the monks', but the delegates were ordered to give judgement for the monks if the quality of their witnesses was better.[5] To remedy a state of affairs which was wasting the time of the courts, Innocent III legislated that not more than forty witnesses might be pro-

---

[1] Gratia of Arezzo, 'Summa de Iudiciario Ordine' in Pillii, Tancredi, Gratiae Libri de Iudiciorum Ordine, ed. F. Bergmann (Göttingen, 1842), p. 371; R. Burn, Ecclesiastical Law, iii, revsd. R. Phillimore, 9th edn. (1842), 310; and P.R.O. E 135/4/17. The hearing in private was contrary to the Roman law procedure of Justinian.

[2] c. 8. X. II. 20 (Eug. III), and c. 52 (Hon. III). See also St. Frideswide's Cart. ii, no. 820, where the abbot of Pipewell and the prior of St. Andrew's, Northampton, examined witnesses on behalf of Pandulf; and B.M. Add. MS. 8167, f. 119ʳ, a formulary example.

[3] Warter Cart., f. 46ᵛ: 'Unde judices testes quos utraque pars duxerat producendos admiserunt, et eosdem diligenter examinaverunt, et eorum dicta in scriptis redigerunt . . .'; and Ecclesiastical Courts, p. 15.

[4] O, f. 224ʳ, col. i. An example of the testimonies of ten men survives from a suit between Lewes priory and the parson of Burnham Thorpe, Norfolk: P.R.O. E 40/14099, cal. Lewes Cart. N.P., no. 72; and of some attestations before arbiters in Belvoir, Small Cart., pp. 36–7.

[5] Letters of Inn. III, no. 659.

duced in any one case.[1] In about 1244 the chapter of Wells appealed to the pope, saying that the subdelegates of the priors of Chacombe and Wroxton, R., prior of the hospital of St. John at Northampton, and Master Thomas de Skireford, summoned an excessive number of witnesses. They appear to have called on all the canons and vicars of Wells, who it was pleaded were 'numerous and in diverse parts'.[2]

The attestations, or depositions, of the witnesses were published and then disputed by the parties: ' . . . attestationibus publicatis, habita quo sufficienti disputatione in testes et eorum dicta . . .'[3] A separate day was usually chosen for discussing the attestations,[4] and when in 1255 a day was fixed for this purpose by the dean of Chichester, the defendant was cited by the dean of Storrington (Suss.) to appear in court so that the suit could proceed.[5] The published reports of witnesses' attestations were sometimes preserved in case of further dispute:

Et de consensu partium examinandi sunt testes quos utraque pars duxerit producendos per viros fidedignos a partibus eligendos, quorum dicta in scriptis fideliter redacta deponentur in ede sacra apud Stokes sub sigillis examinatorum, ita quod si post decessum dicti rectoris super hoc contingat questionem oriri per hoc possit veritas declarari.[6]

Each party was reponsible for paying the expenses of its own witnesses.[7] When a settlement was made in 1208 between the monks of Bardney and the nuns of Stixwould, it was agreed between the parties that if there should be a further controversy, the expenses of witnesses should be shared.[8]

The most desirable proof was the *confessio in jure*, which

[1] c. 37. X. II. 22. Cf. *Reg. Antiq. Linc.* iii, no. 759, where the judges speak of examining a 'multitude' of witnesses of both sides, as is the custom.

[2] Wells, Lib. Albus, i, f. 97ᵛ.

[3] Canterbury, *Sede Vacante*, bk. iii, no. 447, p. 156; P.R.O. E 40/14221: '. . . et ad publicationem attestationum perventum fuisset, illis publicatis predicta causa amicabili compositione conquievit . . .'; and Exeter Ch. 815: '. . . et habita sufficienti dispiccione super attestationibus . . .'

[4] Norwich Ch. 1686 (App. B (ii), no. 8), and see O, f. 224ʳ, col. ii, where the day for discussing the depositions was the same as the sentence day.

[5] Magdalen College, Oxford, Findon Ch. 49.

[6] P.R.O. E 40/14036.

[7] *C.F.*, no. (21); and Burn, *Ecclesiastical Law*, iii. 309.

[8] Bardney Cart., ff. 240ʳ–1ʳ.

the plaintiff endeavoured to extract from his adversary.[1] It had to be conceded voluntarily or it would be held invalid, and it had to be made before the judge in the adversary's presence.[2] Confessions were frequently given. On the day that was selected for the production of witnesses by the prior of Monkton Farleigh and the prior and dean of Malmesbury in 1227, the defendant, Osbert, vicar of Tew (Oxon.), confessed that he had no right to the tithes in question.[3] In a suit which was brought against them by the abbot and convent of Bec in 1225, Laurence and William, rectors of the church of Wimborne All Hallows (Dorset), made a confession, 'tam ex inspectione instrumentorum quam vicinie fama'.[4]

The *confessio in jure* could be made at any point in the procedure, a fact illustrative of its accepted importance. In 1237 in Chichester cathedral, Milo, vicar of West Greenwich, made a confession before contestation of the suit had taken place, admitting that the things which were sought by the abbot and convent of Bayham in their edition belonged to them:

Cum igitur coram nobis in dicta causa isset usque ad litem precise contestandam legitime processum, demum dictus vicarius dictorum abbatis et conventus in judicio plene confitebatur intentionem, dicens res petitas prout in editione continentur ad dictos abbatem et conventum de jure pertinere. Qua confessione coram nobis in judicio legittime facta, omnia in dicta editione contenta dictis abbati et conventui sentencialiter adjudicavimus, in omnibus ordine juris observato . . .[5]

Very often, as in a St. Neots case, a confession was linked with other proofs, and the judgement was made on a broad basis,[6] although a sentence could follow immediately on a confession without any other supporting evidence. When

---

[1] See *C*. vii. 59: *D*. xlii. 2; *Lib. Pauperum*, vii, tit. 55; and Burn, *Ecclesiastical Law*, iii. 324.

[2] c. 3. *X*. II. 18 (Greg. IX), and see, e.g., St. John's College, Oxford, Ch. xix. 2: '. . . partibus coram nobis [the judges] in judicio constitutis, prenominate capelle rector Philippus spontanea et mera voluntate sua recognovit . . .', and Bodleian MS. Dodsworth 76, f. 1.

[3] Bradenstoke Cart., f. 147ᵛ.   [4] Windsor Ch. xi G 12.

[5] Bayham Cart., f. 60ᵛ, and see Pipewell Cart. (A), f. 31ᵛ, for a charter of confession of Reginald, rector of Desborough (Northants.), in a case against Pipewell.

[6] St. Neots Cart., f. 111ᵛ (2 examples). See also Canterbury, Cartae Antiquae, C 1270, and *St. Frideswide's Cart*. ii, no. 732.

Richard, chaplain of 'Crucheston' (? Cruxton in Maiden Newton, Dorset), confessed that he had paid and ought to pay eight shillings yearly to the church of Bruton (Som.) for the chapel of Cruxton, sentence was declared against him at once.[1]

Literal proof in the form of instruments could be produced at any moment before the *conclusio in causa*, when the judges declared that no more evidence might be put forward.[2] Such documentary proof was frequently employed and was obviously important.[3] The abbot and convent of Cormeilles (Ben. dioc. Lisieux, France), whose documents had been burnt in a fire, pleaded with Gregory IX for a mandate to certain ecclesiastics ordering them to examine witnesses and take depositions about the convent's possessions, in order that they might have new documentary evidence compiled, because, as they said, they feared a lawsuit. The request was granted, and the abbots of Strata Florida and Valle Crucis and the prior of Valle Crucis were ordered to set about this task.[4] Many suits were conveniently brought to an end by the production and inspection of instruments.[5] In the Alvingham suit charters were produced of the patron of the church of Stainton, of the bishop of Lincoln, of the chapter of Lincoln, and of the archbishop of Canterbury.[6] Faced with this kind of proof, the party could only recognize the right of its adversary after inspecting the authenticity of the documents. Alexander, parson of Kerdiston (Norf.), on inspecting the original deeds and noting the other proofs of Lewes, declared publicly that he would not claim any right again to the said tithes from the demesne of William of Kerdiston on behalf of his church.[7] Roger de Lurdingdedale, rector of Lenham (Kent), was forced to resign the prebend of Guston when he saw the letters which he had made on receiving the farm and also the letters of a

---

1 *Bruton Cart.*, no. 282.

2 c. 9. *X*. II. 22 (Inn. III); *C*. iv. 21; *D*. xxii. 4; and *Lib. Pauperum*, iv, tit. 18.

3 See, e.g., L, f. 66ʳ, col. 1; C, f. 119ʳ, col. ii; Norwich Ch. 1686 (App. B(ii), no. 8); *N.L.C.*, no. 9; and Eye Cart., f. 41ʳ⁻ᵛ.   4 *Reg. Greg. IX*, no. 1155.

5 e.g. Leeds Cart., f. 10ᵛ; Northampton, St. Andrew's Cart. (A), ff. 56ʳ⁻7ʳ; Pipewell Cart. (A), ff. 29ᵛ⁻31ᵛ; and Dover Cart., f. 226ᵛ: 'Et ad probationem juris sui protulerunt scriptum autenticum H. bone memorie quondam Cant' archiepiscopi . . .'   6 Alvingham Cart., f. 5ᵛ.

7 Lewes Cart., f. 255ᵛ, cal. *Lewes Cart. N.P.*, no. 122.

former abbot of St. Augustine's, Canterbury.[1] In 1229 the plaintiff, Master Richard of Wallingford, rector of Cliffe-at-Hoo, after he had inspected the privileges of the convent of Canterbury, renounced his petition about the tithes of two mills, one water mill, sheep folds, and certain lands.[2] In suits which had been before judges delegate and were reopened, the instrument of a former papal settlement sufficed for sentence to be declared immediately. In 1254 the abbot and convent of Westminster exhibited a fifty-five-year-old decision, which had been made by judges delegate appointed by Celestine III, about a pension of five marks owed to them yearly for the church of Bloxham (Oxon.) by the abbess and convent of Godstow.[3] Master Eustace de Normanvilla, rector of Kenardington (Kent), when he had been brought into court by the prior and convent of Dover, showed the document of a former composition. An arrangement was made on this basis, arbiters being appointed to arrange who should possess the tithes not mentioned in the composition.[4]

5. 'Judicium'

When all the evidence had been put before the court, it was time for the judges to appoint a day on which they would give sentence, and to summon the parties to appear before them then.[5] A final or definitive sentence, which decided the cause itself, entailed a condemnation or an absolution.[6] Whereas in one case the parson of Eythorne (Kent) was condemned to pay five shillings yearly,[7] in another the judges pronounced that the abbot and convent of Bardney were absolved from the charge of Richard, clerk of Bassingham (Lincs.) and parson of Burton by Lincoln.[8] Likewise, either the plaintiff was declared to have succeeded in his proof or to have failed in it, 'pronunciamus R. actorem intentionem

---

[1] St. Augustine's Red Book, f. 274ʳ.

[2] Canterbury, Cartae Antiquae, C 280.

[3] Westminster Domesday, f. 379ᵛ, and see f. 378ᵛ also. Cf. P.R.O. E 135/21/33 (see above, pp. 82–3).   [4] Dover Cart., f. 229ᵛ.

[5] See the *Ordo Judiciarius* in B, f. 81ᵛ, col. i, for comments on the citation to the sentence.

[6] *C.* vii. 45; *Lib. Pauperum*, vii, tit. 41; and Fournier, p. 208.

[7] Canterbury, Cartae Antiquae, L 351.   [8] Bardney Cart., f. 203ʳ⁻ᵛ.

suam sufficienter probasse',[1] or 'pronunciamus R. actorem in probatione intentionis sue defecisse'.[2] The prior and convent of Norwich were declared to have proved their intention by the deposition of witnesses on oath and the production of charters, whereas Robert Buttamund, rector of Thornham (Norf.), was said to have failed in his proof and was condemned to pay the wheat, barley, beans, and peas in question, and six marks to cover arrears and expenses.[3] If the charge of the *actor* was proved, silence was imposed on the defendant about the case and vice versa.[4]

The sentence had to be written,[5] and the papal mandate was to be quoted in full.[6] The form of the sentence, which the judges delivered sitting,[7] began with an invocation.[8] Sentence could not be pronounced on a feast day, nor when the sun had gone down.[9] Egerton Charter 409 in the British Museum provides a fine example of a clerk's draft up to and including the sentence.[10] There are a number of deletions of words which had been written twice, of omission marks, and of rephrasing attempts. The document is unsealed. It is obvious that most final *acta*, owing to their importance, must have been prepared in rough and then checked and scrutinized. Several introductory paragraphs intimate the necessity of the sentence being in writing. As one document commences:

Universis sancte matris ecclesie filiis ad quos presens scriptum pervenerit . . . prior Christi ecclesie de Thwinham Winton' diocesis salutem in domino. Rerum gestarum series idcirco litteris commendatur ne lapsu temporis humana prolabente memoria ex jam sopite litis materia litem suscitandi posteris occasio prepareretur, ne quod provisum est ad concordiam tendat ad noxam et ne innocencie malicia vel ignorancia prejudicium pariat et jacturam sane cum causa que vertebatur . . .,

and although this is the usual kind of 'harangue' it does suggest a basic realization of the threats to which the

---

[1] *C.F.*, no. (23); P.R.O. E 40/14953; and B.M. Cotton MS. Nero C iii, f. 199.
[2] *C.F.*, no. (24); and P.R.O. E 212/28.
[3] Norwich Ch. 1686 (App. B (ii), no. 8).
[4] B.M. Egerton Ch. 382; Bayham Cart., f. 60ᵛ; *Godstow Reg.* i, no. [31]; and A, f. 271ᵛ, col. iii.   [5] *C.F.*, no. (24). See also Arnulphus, i, p. 46.
[6] *C.F.*, no. (23).   [7] Tancred, p. 270.
[8] e.g. Magdalen College, Oxford, Steyning Ch. 16; Alvingham Cart., f. 5ᵛ; and B.M. Harley Ch. 84 F 45.   [9] Tancred, p. 271.   [10] App. B (ii), no. 7.

sentence might be subjected if no authentic record was made.[1] But by no means all suits were terminated by sentences. Many ended with compositions,[2] and some were discontinued.

At any point the suit might be discontinued, if the *actor* voluntarily renounced his petition or the *reus* withdrew his defence. Hugh, the abbot, and the convent of Oseney withdrew their suit against the canons of St. Frideswide's, and promised not to renew the controversy.[3] In most cases such withdrawals followed a confession or realization that the opposite party was in the right, as when Hugh de Lunde, rector of Brocklesby (Lincs.), withdrew from his suit against the Cistercian nuns of Nun Cotham in 1238/9.[4] In 1288 Stephen de Tawelle, rector of Westmill (Herts.), renounced his suit on seeing a document of a previous settlement made by judges delegate;[5] and in the same way in about 1221 Master William of Purleigh, rector of Purleigh (Essex), inspected instruments of the nuns of Wix, recognized their right, and renounced his action.[6] These were renunciations by the *actor* as was that of Master Simon of London, rector of Launton, in 1214,[7] that of the prior and convent of Shelford (Aug. Notts.),[8] and that of the prioress and nuns of Stamford, which was made by their proctor, A., chaplain, in about 1217.[9]

If the defendant renounced the continuation of his defence, he might be rewarded or placated by the judges or by the *actor*, and vice versa. For instance, when the proctor of Newton Longville ceded all right on behalf of the convent, the tithes were declared to be Notley's, but Notley were

---

[1] Beaulieu Cart., f. 132^{r-v}. See also St. Neots Cart., f. 130^v; B.M. Cotton MS. Nero C iii f. 199; and *C.F.*, no. (26).

[2] Formularies give examples: A, f. 271^v, col. iii; L, f. 66^r, col. i; C, f. 119^r, col. ii; and B.M. Add. MS. 8167, ff. 96^v–7^r. See also the very careful composition which Richard, prior of Dunstable, arranged between the abbot and convent of Bec and the rector of Withersfield in 1241, after a prolonged and complicated case lasting some six years, Windsor Ch. xi G 22, and Chapter V for some further comments on compositions.

[3] *St. Frideswide's Cart.* ii, no. 703 (dated by Wigram *c.* 1200).

[4] Nun Cotham Cart., f. 38^v.   [5] P.R.O. E 42/232.

[6] P.R.O. E 40/14044(2).   [7] Westminister Ch. 15684.

[8] Castle Acre Cart., f. 47^r (no date).

[9] Canons Ashby Cart., f. 50^r. Cf. Torre Cart., f. 60^v, where M., the prioress, and the convent of Kington St. Michael (Ben. Wilts.) renounced their suit against the abbot and convent of Torre.

ordered to pay twelve and a half marks yearly to Newton.[1] Similarly, when William, clerk of Lewes, renounced his quarrel against Robert of Little Canfield (Essex) about the church of Canfield, Robert gave William three marks.[2] In a suit between the abbot and convent of St. Augustine, Canterbury, and Henry, archdeacon of Canterbury, about the churches of Milton and Faversham (Kent), the archdeacon remitted all actions against St. Augustine's about the church of Milton, and resigned the papal letters that he had impetrated about it. The abbot and convent, for their part, remitted to the archdeacon the fruits of Faversham, and those in store-houses.[3] Such arrangements were common,[4] and seem to be part of the prevalent desire to make compositions that would last rather than let the cause drag on to a sentence, and perhaps an appeal and the reopening of the suit.

Sometimes suits were reciprocally withdrawn. In 1236 Abbot Luke and the convent of Abingdon, and Andrew, vicar of Marcham (Berks.), renounced all quarrels and suits which were between them before ordinary and delegated judges.[5] In the church of Ware the prior and convent of Lewes and Master E(dmund), rector of Ovingdean, renounced suits reciprocally, and the rector remitted another suit which he was conducting against the monks before judges delegate at Salisbury.[6] In a similar arrangement, the abbot and convent of Thorney abandoned their suit about the church of Twywell (Northants.) against H. de Leckeburn, rector of Whittlesey (Cambs.), while he renounced his plea against Thorney about the lesser tithes of the demesne of Twywell, which he was pressing before the archdeacon of Northampton.[7] Furthermore a mutual agreement might be made between the parties to place the cause before arbiters, or to come to an out-of-court arrangement.

---

[1] *N.L.C.*, no. 62.

[2] Lewes Cart., f. 307ᵛ, cal. *Lewes Cart. S.P.*, ii. 119 (the date is not given—t.N., R., and R., abbots of Buildwas, Haughmond, and Lilleshall, therefore probably c. 1220–40, see R. W. Eyton, *Antiquities of Shropshire*, vi. 333, vii. 300, and viii. 225).   [3] St. Augustine's Red Book, f. 257ʳ.

[4] e.g. Exeter Cart., p. 14; and B.M. Harley Ch. 44 I 25.

[5] Abingdon Cart., ff. 69ᵛ–70ʳ.   [6] P.R.O. E 40/14227.

[7] Thorney Cart. ii, f. 384ʳ. See also *Reg. Antiq. Linc.* iii, no. 759.

Appeal

The discontinuation of the suit might also be caused by an appeal to Rome. The system of appeal was taken over from the Roman law; but whereas in Roman law appeal could only be made after the sentence was given, canon law recognized that appeal could be made at any moment during the course of the suit, although an appeal against a final judgement had to be made within ten days of the sentence.[1] The effect of the appeal to Rome was immediate. As soon as it had been lodged, it was illegal for the judges to proceed further in the suit's conduct, pending instruction. Letters known as *apostoli* were sent by the judges to Rome, in which the grounds of the appeal were stated, as well as the matter of the suit and the point at which the appeal had been made —whether at the beginning of the suit, after contestation, or after the sentence.[2] The judges also usually fixed a date before which the appeal was to be followed up.[3] An appeal which was made by William de Walda, rector of Lamport and Faxton (Northants.), from the sentence of the judges delegate, Elias, prior of Westminster, and Master William of Purleigh, was later renounced by him and he swore not to molest the prior and convent of Lewes again in any way, and consented to submit to compulsion by the official of the archbishop of Canterbury if necessary.[4]

When making an appeal to Rome, the appellant might also appeal to the archbishop of his province, whose right it was, acting as vice-gerent of the pope, to maintain the *status quo* of the plaintiff pending litigation, and to protect his person and property. This right seems to have been granted to provincials remote from Rome; and Canterbury and York had it.[5] As early as 1146, when Bernard, abbot of Cerne, appealed to Eugenius III, Gilbert Foliot, abbot of Gloucester, asked Archbishop Theobald for the protection of

---

[1] *X*. II. 28; and see also A. Amanieu, 'Appel', *D.D.C.* i, cols. 764–807.

[2] *D*. xlix. 6; *Lib. Pauperum*, vii, tit. 62; A, f. 271ᵛ, col. i; and B, f. 79ᵛ, col. i, f. 80ᵛ, col. ii.

[3] Windsor Ch. xi G 37 (4) (App. B (ii), no. 6).

[4] P.R.O. E 40/7896.

[5] For details of the operation of the system, see now P. J. Wood, 'Tuitorial Appeal to the Archbishops of Canterbury and York in the Thirteenth Century' (Edinburgh M. Litt. thesis, 1970).

Bernard's church during his absence.[1] By the time of the archiepiscopate of Hubert Walter (1193–1205) the practice of seeking the tuition of the see of Canterbury while lodging an appeal to Rome was well established. Documents of this period refer to: '. . . ad apostolicam sedem et ad vestram cujus interest appellationes rite factas tueri appellavit . . .',[2] and '. . . post appellationem ad dominum papam pro tuitione juris sui quod in eadem habet ecclesia rite interpositam, et etiam ad nos ne status appellationis ipsius in aliquo turbaretur . . .'[3]

The archbishop on receiving the appeal or *provocatio* was bound to establish whether tuition should be granted. If it was granted, arrangements had to be made for its retention and observance, and an *inhibitio* was sent to prohibit the judges from proceeding any further. In the early years of the tuitorial appeal system it is unlikely that there were any courts to deal with this type of business.[4] Archbishop Hubert Walter invoked the help of local ecclesiastics, issuing mandates to delegates instructing them to establish whether the appeal had taken place legally and to revoke anything which had been done after it.[5] The procedure was still the same under Archbishop Edmund. On 4 April 1236 he ordered the priors of Monks Kirby and Combe to inquire into the appeal that had been made by Hugh, rector of Kenilworth. The priors were told to establish whether the appeal was legal, and if they saw fit, to revoke anything which had taken place after it, and to fix a time within which the appeal was to be prosecuted.[6] Most of the material concerning tuitorial appeals dates from the vacancy in the see of Canterbury between 1240 and 1245, when the prior and convent of Christ

---

[1] *Letters and Charters of Gilbert Foliot*, ed. Morey and Brooke, no. 56.

[2] Canterbury, Christ Church Letters, ii, no. 245.

[3] Canterbury, S(ede) V(acante), bk. i, p. 133 (a). See also Christ Church Letters, ii, nos. 232 and 242, for further appeals 'ad tuitionem' during Hubert Walter's archiepiscopate.

[4] M. M. Morgan, 'Early Canterbury Jurisdiction', *E.H.R.* lx (1945), 394.

[5] Canterbury, S.V., bk. i, p. 133(a), and see Cheney, 'Harrold Priory', no. 9.

[6] B.M. Add. Ch. 21289. Cf. Churchill, *Canterbury Administration*, i. 463, and B. L. Woodcock, *Medieval Ecclesiastical Courts in the Diocese of Canterbury* (Oxford, 1952), p. 65, who state that protection once granted lasted for a year and a day.

Church asserted their right to this jurisdiction.[1] Normal practice in the method of dealing with appeals therefore cannot necessarily be inferred from this period, but their methods seem to be a continuation of earlier practice; and it is noteworthy that the prior and convent dealt at least with some of the business by delegation.[2] An official, however, sometimes made an appearance on their behalf.[3]

The terminology of the appeal indicates the changes which were to take place. The most regular form, which is recorded among the *sede vacante* material of 1240–5, was 'ad ecclesiam Cant' pro tuitione' or 'ad tuitionem sedis Cantuar' '.[4] This gave way to 'ad sedem apostolicam et pro tuitione curie Cantuariensis',[5] and it has been suggested that it is to the archiepiscopate of Boniface of Savoy, who was elected in 1243 and consecrated in 1245, that we must look for the beginnings of an organized court.[6]

The competence of provincial tuition does not seem to have been limited to certain types of cases. Cases among the *sede vacante* material concern tithes, churches, election, the establishment of vicarages, and marriage.[7] Archbishop Pecham, however, declared against tuitorial appeal in matrimonial cases.[8] It is likely that tuitorial appeal was made most frequently in suits about property and possession. The majority of suits going to Rome concerned possessions and property, and this may reflect that predominance. It is impossible to estimate the number of appeals to Rome in which the tuition of Canterbury was also sought, but it would seem valid to conclude that the system must have stopped some frivolous appeals by withholding the grant of protection after examination had been made. This would have been a

[1] It is found mainly in M 364, a magnificent roll of suits, and *S.V.*, bks. ii and iii. The prior and convent of Christ Church asserted their right especially against the bishop of London, who claimed this jurisdiction, see *S.V.*, bk. ii, p. 199.

[2] Morgan, 'Early Canterbury Jurisdiction', p. 394, and *S.V.*, bk. ii, pp. 200(*b*), 202(*a*) and (*b*).

[3] M 364, nos. 12 and 16, and *S.V.*, bk. ii, p. 200(*a*).

[4] e.g. *S.V.*, bk. iii, p. 161(*b*), and Cartae Antiquae, M 364, no. 2.

[5] See Churchill, *Canterbury Administration*, i. 428.

[6] Morgan, 'Early Canterbury Jurisdiction', p. 398.

[7] *S.V.*, bk. ii, pp. 196(*b*), 200(*b*), and M 364, nos. 10 and 11.

[8] Churchill, *Canterbury Administration*, i. 462.

valuable contribution to the efficient working of the machnery of the courts.

Although the Romano-canonical procedure was open to abuse, it had the makings of a system of average efficiency, thoroughness, and fairness. It might be said that the procedural techniques showed too great a concern to be fair by catering for appeal at any point in the suit, which the procedure of the Roman law had not allowed. The central machinery, necessary for the initial stages of the suit, worked in favour of the plaintiff, on the assumption that the defendant could object, at least at a later date. Because the defendant was not safeguarded in the early stages at Rome, he had to be allowed the right of appeal before judgement.[1] Basically this was a weakness, but it was a machinery which in many cases seems to have worked and, what is more, to have worked without serious delays.[2] Legal delays, which were an integral part of the procedure by libel, were an essential device to protect all concerned, plaintiffs, defendants, and judges. In the English southern province, the judges delegate and their entourages demanded increasing procedural definition from the popes, collected instructions and forms, and seem to have made every effort to develop uniformity. If the procedure erred on the side of rigidity, at least it led to uniformity and to a system which was easily administered even by men not specifically trained in the law. A study of the court documents has shown the way in which the procedure before the courts usually corresponded closely to the papal enactments, the procedural treatises, and the formularies.

---

[1] For a contemporary comment on the abuse of this practice, and other malpractices, see the poem 'Bulla fulminante' of Philip the chancellor of Paris and a satirical poet, F. J. E. Raby, *History of Christian Latin Poetry*, 2nd edn. (Oxford, 1953), p. 397. Philip was born at the end of the twelfth century and died in 1236 or 1237 (p. 395).

[2] See below, pp. 216–17, and App. A (iv).

III

THE PERSONNEL OF THE COURTS: THE JUDGES AND OTHER OFFICERS

1. *The Powers of the Judges*

'... iudices delegati saepe constituuntur ab ordinariis.'[1]
'Et nota, quod dominus papa iudex est ordinarius singulorum.'[2]

ROMAN law had differentiated between delegated and ordinary jurisdiction, that is between the powers which proceeded from a special commission and the powers which were bound to a function. This distinction was accepted and retained by the canon law.[3] By 1198 the system of delegating judicial power and setting up *ad hoc* tribunals far from Rome was well established. Although the influence and importance of these proprietary papal delegated courts has been acknowledged, the judge-delegate scheme has never been systematically investigated. The basis was provided by Alexander III who defined the position of the temporary judge in canon law. Of the forty-three chapters in title 29, 'De officio et potestate iudicis delegati', of book i of the *Corpus*, eighteen were declared by him. The next great legislator was Innocent III. He provided fifteen chapters of title 29, and together Alexander III and Innocent III are thus responsible for thirty-three chapters.[4]

One of the greatest problems of canon law was the problem of equity. The legislator, the pope, since he cannot have in view every single case, forms the law according to what he

---

[1] Tancred, p. 95.   [2] Ibid., p. 91.

[3] Le Bras, 'Droit romain', p. 390. See also G. Crisci, '*Evolutio historica delegationis a jure*', *Apollinaris*, ix (1936), 270–99; Phillips, *Kirchenrecht*, vi. 756; and R. Naz, 'Juge délégué', *D.D.C.* vi, cols. 216–18.

[4] Noted by M. Pacaut, *Alexandre III* (Paris, 1956), p. 265, who also notes the relative numbers of their decretals concerning appeals which found their way into the *Corpus*. If this observation is applied to the title 'De Rescriptis' (*X.* I. 3), which also has forty-three chapters, six are found to come from Alexander III, fifteen from Innocent III, and twelve from Gregory IX.

considers the common advantage. It is the judge's duty to apply the general law in specific cases. Canon 20 of the 1917 *Codex* has a historical tradition behind it.[1] The judge has the obligation to render justice in the name of the pope: 'Iudicis est, ut diximus, aequitatem librare audita causa utrimque',[2] and to render it according to the law: 'juris ordine in omnibus observato', as the judges declared in a final *actum* of 1251.[3] It is necessary to consider the powers that were given to the judge, and the checks on his abusing his position, as well as the means devised to help him.

The powers of the judges delegate over the subsidiaries of the case were always immense. They had automatically a plenary jurisdiction over all things and people influencing the case, and preventing the accomplishment of their task.[4] This jurisdiction extended, for example, over those who threatened witnesses, and was thus superior to that of the ordinary and of the metropolitan.[5] By a simple commission, and without the mandate stating it, the judges delegate could cite, punish the contumacious, surrender the cause to arbiters, excommunicate, suspend, pass a sentence of interdict, order the execution of a sentence, reserve powers of compulsion for themselves, and command their superiors to do any of these things.[6] The immense power of these *ad hoc* courts in operation was one of the main attractions for the parties, even though they might come before the same persons acting as judges in the ordinary courts and even the king's courts.

[1] See C. Lefebvre, *Les Pouvoirs du juge en droit canonique* (Paris, 1938), p. 17, and *Codex Iuris Canonici*, ed. P. Gasparri (Vatican, 1948), p. 5. See also I. G. Serédi, 'De Relatione inter Decretales Gregorii Papae IX et Codicem Iuris Canonici', *Acta Congressus Iuridici Internatio ,alis*, iv (1937), 11.

[2] 'Rhetorica Ecclesiastica', *Quellen zur Geschichte*, i, pt. iv, ed. L. Wahrmund (Innsbruck, 1906), p. 6. This treatise was composed before 1179 (Stickler, col. 1136).

[3] B.M. Harley Ch. 53 A 23, and see Lefebvre, *Pouvoirs du juge*, p. 69.

[4] Bencivenna of Siena, 'Invocato Christi Nomine', *Quellen zur Geschichte*, v, pt. i, ed. L. Wahrmund (Heidelberg, 1931), p. 60: 'Hodie autem iure canonum, cum dominus papa causam alicui delegat vel committit, delegatus recipit plenam potestatem super his omnibus, que ad causam illam noscuntur spectare'; formerly attributed to Pillius but more recently to Bencivenna of Siena (see Stickler, col. 1136) and pd. as *'Summa de Ordine Iudiciorum'* in *Pillii, Tancredi, Gratiae Libri . . .*, ed. F. Bergmann, on p. 41.

[5] cc. 1, 11. *X*. I. 29.

[6] cc. 4, 5. *X*. I. 29, and see Durand, *Speculum Juris*, p. 10, lib. 1, pt. 1, *'De Iudice Delegato'*. These powers could, however, be limited by the mandate.

The powers of the judges over the case itself were not usually as impressive. The judge delegate represented the pope, but he was only his spokesman in a limited field. He had no legislative powers, and his jurisdiction was essentially not full, only delegated. His powers of legal interpretation, although existing, were essentially limited. The system was elastic enough to provide for variation in the instructions which were sent to the judges. Because of the widespread use of personnel with varying qualifications the mandate had to be flexible. The inclusion of lower-ranking clergy in the papal judicial administration influenced the powers they were granted and the kind of mandate they received. Just as the papacy used commissions for different activities, so the commission could be altered to suit individual cases. In practice many cases could be dealt with by one of the stock mandates, especially when smaller cases reached the *Curia*. When cases of importance were at stake or there was some doubt about the commission, mandates embodied a general statement of the law of the Church applying to the case and the powers granted to the judges to deal with it. In the early twelfth century this was the practice in almost every case.[1] The mandate for many judges signified their only contact with Rome. It was therefore imperative that it should be explicit, and it was equally stressed that the powers which were granted in it should not be exceeded. The judges had to keep diligently within the powers conceded to them, and sometimes a time limit was imposed for the hearing of the case.[2]

The use of *relatio* or reference back to Rome was not on the whole encouraged, although formularies give examples.[3] In the twelfth century recourse to Rome was frequent. Henry of Winchester reported to Theobald: 'Domnum papam Innocentium [II] et curiam Romanam super hoc consului, et tale super hoc rescriptum accepi.'[4] Soon afterwards Theobald wrote to the pope himself: 'In addition we beg of you to give us a ruling on the punishment to be

---

[1] Morey, *Bartholomew of Exeter*, p. 51.

[2] Durand, *Speculum Juris*, pp. 7 f., lib. 1, pt. 1, '*De Iudice Delegato*'; and Tancred, p. 98: 'Et hoc ideo, quia fines mandati diligenter custodiendi sunt'. For example *Reg. Greg. IX*, nos. 3261, 5142, and *Reg. Inn. IV*, no. 5024.

[3] A, f. 271ᵛ, cols. i–ii; B, f. 80ᵛ, col. i; C, f. 119ʳ, col. ii; and L, f. 66ʳ, cols. i–ii.

[4] Voss, *Heinrich von Blois*, App. VIIa.

inflicted on those who forge your letters; it is difficult for us to wait for your advice on individual cases of this kind every time they arise';[1] and as the prior of Newburgh wrote to Urban III on 17 September 1186: 'ad vestre sanctitatis notitiam ista refero, ut, quod dignationi vestre placuerit, inde statuatur'.[2] No law book could contain all the solutions, so that recourse to Rome for directions how to act, universally common in the twelfth century, continued in the thirteenth century, but with less frequency as the law became more formulated. The famous letter of Innocent III in reply to the bishop of Ely was split into thirteen sections in the Gregorian *Liber Extra*.[3] Often the mandate instructed the judge in an important case to settle it if he could or to remit it to Rome.[4] J(ohn), archdeacon of St. Albans, remitted a suit to the pope in 1251/2.[5] The outcome is unknown. When the abbot of St. Albans and the priors of Dunstable and St. Albans returned a difficult case to Rome, the pope delegated it a second time to Pandulf, bishop elect of Norwich.[6]

Sometimes minor cases presented legal questions during the hearing, which could not be foreseen when the rescript was issued. If a question of the interpretation of the law was involved, the advice of assessors could be sought and this was in fact encouraged. The assessors assisted the judges by giving them an opinion on the case, which was not, however, binding. As often as possible they were chosen with the consent of the parties,[7] but the judges could insist on counsel being taken, and occasionally the mandate or rescript exacted this.[8] The phrase 'juris peritorum freti consilio' or one of

---

[1] *J.S.L.*, no. 57; see also no. 54. Theobald sometimes dealt with cases in provincial and national councils, see, e.g., *J.S.L.*, nos. 14, 16, 70, 92, 124–5, and for other instances of consultation, nos. 5, 16, 56, 72, 74, 80, 84, and 113. These references are given by C. N. L. Brooke, *J.S.L.*, p. xxxv n. 4 and p. xxxvi n. 2.

[2] *P.U.E.* iii, no. 380.

[3] *P.L.* 215, col. 478, no. clxix: c. 8. *X*. II. 22; c. 1. *X*. I. 16; c. 4. *X*. II. 25; c. 14. *X*. II. 1; c. 28. *X*. I. 29; c. 14. *X*. I. 3; c. 11. *X*. I. 31; c. 28. *X*. III. 30; c. 19. *X*. V. 33; c. 29. *X*. III. 38; c. 7. *X*. III. 24; c. 9. *X*. III. 10; and c. 53. *X*. II. 28.

[4] e.g. *Reg. Hon. III*, nos. 846, 2366 (*C.P.L.* i. 49, 70), and *Reg. Greg. IX*, nos. 2948, 5023, and 5142.

[5] 'Ancient Documents relating to Tithes in the Peak', ed. J. C. Cox, *Journal of the Derbs. Archaeol. and Nat. Hist. Soc.* v (1883), no. II.

[6] *Reg. Hon. III*, no. 1680 (*C.P.L.* i. 60).

[7] Fournier, p. 25; Durand, *Speculum Juris*, pp. 93 f., lib. 1, pt. 1, '*De Assessore*'; and Tancred, pp. 108–9.　　　　[8] Lefebvre, *Pouvoirs du juge*, p. 79.

its variants, commonly found in judge-delegate *acta*, denotes the use of assessors.[1] Unfortunately they are not often specified by name. Often the assessors coerced and persuaded parties into compositions. In 1197 Hubert, archbishop of Canterbury, and Hugh, abbot of Abingdon, are described as 'labouring and helping to this composition'.[2] In 1237 the legate Otto in his Constitutions insisted that judges should take counsel in difficult cases.[3]

At any point the mandate might be revoked and a hearing arranged in Rome or different judges substituted. In the event of the latter, revocatory letters were sent to the judges by the new delegates. Examples of this sort of letter are given in the formularies.[4] During the case between the abbot and convent of Bec and the rector of Withersfield, the prior of Dunstable declined to accept the revocatory letters addressed to him by the prior of Langley and his colleagues, and asserted that Bec were prepared to prove that the new letters had been obtained by the rector under false pretences.[5] In the event of a dispute as to who had the jurisdiction, arbiters were called upon to decide.[6] The Montacute cartulary records the archdeacon of Exeter and his co-judges proceeding when their jurisdiction had been revoked and committed to Gilbert, bishop of Rochester, and others, or so it was alleged by R(ichard de Hegham), archdeacon of Essex, the defendant.[7]

Arbiters, Ordainers, and Conservators

The cause might also be removed from the judges by both the parties. Out-of-court arrangements took place,[8] and the parties might transmit their quarrel to arbiters without con-

---

[1] See, e.g., P.R.O. E 212/28; B.M. Cotton MS. Nero C iii, f. 199; and Harley Ch. 84 F 45.

[2] Westminster Domesday, f. 378ᵛ and *Godstow Reg.* i, no. [308].

[3] *C.S.* ii, pt. i. 259, no. [29].

[4] A, f. 271ᵛ, col. 1; B, f. 79ᵛ, col. 1; C, f. 119ʳ, col. ii; and *C.F.*, no. (16).

[5] Windsor Ch. xi G 37(9) (App. B (iii), no. 1).   [6] *C.F.*, no. (17).

[7] *Montacute Cart.*, no. 143. Brentano, *York Metropolitan Jurisdiction*, p. 282, records that the judges did not recognize revocations in the case with which he deals.

[8] See, e.g., *Cartulaire de l'abbaye de S. Victor de Marseille*, ii, ed. B. E. C. Guérard (Paris, 1857), 468, no. 1009, a case of 1163 which the legate was commissioned to hear, but the parties had already transacted; he therefore confirmed their arrangement.

sulting Rome if mutually agreed on this course of action.[1]
This could be a means of saving the expenses of a case. The
process is vividly described in the Register of St. Osmund.[2]
A suit had arisen between the chapter of Salisbury and
Master Ralph de Stokes about 100s. a year that Master Ralph
sought for the church of Kings Somborne (Hants); it had
been delegated by Pope Innocent III to the chancellor and
subdean of Wells. The parties decided to have arbiters.
The chapter chose Master A. de Tylen (? Adam of Tilney),
or Master Robert de Bingham (a canon of Salisbury by 1222),
or Master Thomas de Disce (? Diss), canon of Salisbury,[3]
or any other suitable person. Master Ralph de Stokes, for
his part, elected to have the prior of Dunstable (Richard de
Mores), or Master William of Bardney (archdeacon of Wells
by July 1215), or Master Richard de Tyreton, or Master
Robert de Kington.[4] Together they chose the bishop of
Chichester (Richard Poore) or if he was unable to serve, the
bishop of Rochester (Benedict of Sawston), and failing him,
the bishop of Bath (Jocelin of Wells).[5] It is interesting to
note that all these bishops acted as itinerant justices.[6] The
arbiters were to settle the dispute amicably if possible; if not,
they were to pass definitive sentence, and what the majority
of them decreed was to be observed under penalty of a payment of thirty marks to be made by the recalcitrant party to

[1] Tancred, p. 103.

[2] *Reg. S. Osmund*, i. 256-7 (and see the original register in the diocesan registry
at Salisbury, f. 34ʳ⁻ᵛ).

[3] For Adam of Tilney, see K. Major, 'The *Familia* of Archbishop Stephen
Langton', *E.H.R.* xlviii (1933), 529-30; for Master Robert de Bingham, see Emden,
Oxf. Reg. i. 189 (he became bishop of Salisbury in 1229). He acted as a delegate of
the legate Guala in *c.* 1218, in company with Master William Scot, see *Oriel
College Records*, pp. 344-5, cited by Emden, and above, pp. 30, 49 and n. 4. Master
Thomas de Disce occurs as Thomas de 'Bilee' in *Reg. S. Osmund*, i. 256.

[4] For Richard de Mores, see below pp. 114-18, and App. A (iii), no. 45; for
Master William of Bardney, see *Acta Stephani Langton*, ed. K. Major (Canterbury
and York Ser. l, 1950), p. xlviii n. 1, and H.M.C., *Cal. of the MSS. of ... Wells*, i
(1907), 67; and for Masters Richard de Tyreton (?Tyrington) and Robert de
Kington, see possibly Emden, *Oxf. Reg.* iii. 1925, and Additions in *Bodleian Library Record*, vi (1957-61), 684, and *Oxf. Reg.* ii. 1053. Master R. de Tiringtona
acted again as an arbiter during Innocent III's pontificate in company with Master
Stephen de Melsa, Master (R.) of York, Master R(obert) de Clipstone, and Valen-
tine de Worthe (*Letters of Inn. III*, no. 279, and Belvoir, Stanford Ch. 175).

[5] See below, pp. 125-6 and 130; Russell, pp. 118-19; and M. Gibbs and J. Lang,
Bishops and Reform 1215-72 (Oxford, 1934), pp. 186-7.

[6] Gibbs and Lang, *Bishops and Reform*, p. 167.

the other. In a case in 1247, between the prior and convent
of Sele and Hugh, chaplain of the chapel of St. Leonard of
the forest, the fourth arbiter William, vicar of Angmering
(Suss.), would not give his definite consent to the decision
of his colleagues, the dean, chancellor, and treasurer of
Chichester, but the sentence seems to have held.[1]

The system of choosing arbiters reflected the system of
selecting judges when an objection was made in the *audientia
publica*. In a form of arbitration similar to the Somborne one,
the convent of Hatfield Regis (Ben. alien, Essex) chose
Masters Warner de Tunston, John de Lyndesheye (? Lind-
sey, Lincs.),[2] and Adam of Lincoln; while the rector of
Burgate (Suff.) opted for Master Henry de Nuttel',[3] Hugh
le Waleys, and Ralph de Sutbur'. The common choice was
the archdeacon of Colchester (Robert de Insula), Master
John de Pagrave, and the dean of St. Edmunds.[4] Other
instances of arbitration show the following choices. In a
case between Thorney (Ben. Cambs.) and Richard Mare-
scallus, Thorney chose Ralph de Colingham and Alexander de
Stanford;[5] Richard chose William de Hanewrh' and Con-
stantine of Lynn; while both parties agreed upon Master
Robert de Gravele, canon of Lincoln.[6] In a case brought by
West Dereham (Prem. Norf.) before the deans of Holt
(Norf.) and Norwich, arbiters were chosen; A., the abbot of
Dereham, selecting the prior of Pentney (Aug. Norf.); the
defendant H., rector of Hillington (Norf.), choosing Master
W. de Becko;[7] and both parties consenting to the abbot of
Langley (Prem. Norf.), probably Hugh.[8] In a suit between
Daventry (Clun. Northants.) and Pipewell (Cist. Northants.),
which was brought by Daventry to the abbots of Vaudey
(Cist. Lincs.) and Crowland (Ben. Lincs.) and the prior of

---

[1] *Sele Cart.*, no. 35.

[2] See Emden, *Camb. Reg.*, p. 370, who says he became a canon and official of
Lincoln in 1263.

[3] See ibid., p. 430, who has a Master Henry de Nuttele as a brother of
Sturbridge hospital, Cambridge, in 1279.

[4] B.M. Add. Ch. 28408.

[5] Possibly the Master Alexander de Stanford mentioned in Emden, *Camb. Reg.*,
p. 550.   [6] Thorney Cart. ii, f. 257ᵛ.

[7] A 'W. de Bec' had been steward to Archbishop Langton in 1214, see *Acta
Stephani Langton*, ed. Major, p. xlviii n. 1.

[8] West Dereham Cart., f. 111ᵛ.

Peterborough (Ben. Northants.), two arbiters were chosen who appear to have acted in concert with the judges delegate, perhaps to advise them. They were Master T., official of the archdeacon of Northampton, chosen by Daventry, and Master H. de Stanford, chosen by Pipewell.[1] When Gilbert Glanvill, bishop of Rochester, compromised on arbiters in a case against the monks of Rochester, he composed a document declaring that any letters to judges delegate, which were impetrated before or after the arbitration was entered upon, should be regarded as null and void. By this act he demonstrated that the power of the judges delegate had been superseded.[2]

No distinction appears to be made between arbiters and ordainers. They are mentioned jointly by Matthew Paris: 'tanquam arbitros et pacis ordinatores, consenserunt . . .',[3] and while title 43 of Book I of the *Corpus* concerns arbiters, no mention is made of ordainers.[4] This would suggest that it is merely an alternative name. Many of these settlements were made before diocesans: Robert Grosseteste, bishop of Lincoln, Hugh of Northwold, bishop of Ely, Eustace de Fauconberg, bishop of London, and Robert de Bingham, bishop of Salisbury, are all represented.[5] Archdeacons, officials, and canons, such as John Houton, archdeacon of Northampton (who had been archdeacon of Bedford), Master Roger of Weasenham, archdeacon of Oxford, Master Robert of Cadney, official of the bishop of Lincoln, Master W. de Button, official of the bishop of Bath, and Elias of Dereham, canon of Salisbury, also accepted cases.[6] It is difficult to understand why a party should go to the trouble and expense of acquiring a mandate from

[1] Daventry Cart., f. 156ᵛ, and Pipewell Cart. (C), f. 147ʳ. Possibly Hugh de Stanford, see Emden, *Oxf. Reg.* iii. 1759, and *Camb. Reg.*, p. 550.

[2] Canterbury, *S.V.*, bk. iii, p. 157(a).

[3] *Chron. Maj.* iii. 75. Cf. *Cartulaire de l'abbaye de Saint-Père de Chartres*, i, ed. B. E. C. Guérard (Paris, 1840), 676 no. 86, a composition before arbiters or ordainers.

[4] cc. 1–14. X. I. 43.

[5] *Cartulary of Bushmead Priory*, ed. G. H. Fowler and J. Godber (Beds. Hist. Rec. Soc. xxii, 1945), no. 14; Ramsey Cart., f. 41ᵛ; St. Paul's, Press A, Box 23, Ch. 864; Walden Cart., f. 44ᵛ; and B.M. Add. Ch. 19620.

[6] Northampton, St. Andrew's Cart. (A), f. 94ʳ; B.M. Add. Ch. 10639; Wells Ch. 31; and Magdalen College, Oxford, Selborne Ch. 326 (Macray, *Calendar*, i. 20).

Rome, only to allow the suit to revert to what was in fact very near to the ordinary jurisdiction; but possibly the dual tie of ordinary and papal authority was regarded as more binding than a straight settlement of one kind or the other. The original judges delegate often report arbitrations and confirm them.[1]

Athough the conservators had general commissions, their powers were limited. They were instituted to give protection to certain corporations who might be harmed. Whole orders, such as the Cistercians and Premonstratensians for instance, were granted conservators for the protection of their privileges and property.[2] Innocent III conceded conservators to the Teutonic knights in Livonia and also to the order of Sempringham in England; and the Franciscans and Dominicans received them from Innocent IV in 1245.[3] Individual religious houses might also be granted conservators. The great Benedictine house of St. Albans had a conservator, the abbot of Waltham, as early as 1232, when the parties appeared before him and abandoned certain actions; and Westminster had conservators, the priors of Tandridge (Aug. Surrey) and Blackmore (Aug. Essex), in 1251.[4] Hugh Bluet, prior of Lenton (Clun. Notts.), conservator of the privileges and indulgences of the Cistercian order in the province of Canterbury, exercised coercive powers against the prior and convent of Luffield (Ben. Northants.) and Ralph, vicar of Thornborough, who were molesting the Cistercians of Biddlesden (Bucks.) over property in 1251–2; the documents which survive from this case show clearly the conservators' position.[5] Innocent IV stated in the Council of Lyons in 1245 that a conservator protected from injuries, but did not exercise judicial powers of investigation. This was repeated and upheld by Boniface VIII in a bull of 8 April 1295.[6] Permanent powers of judicial inquiry and the

---

[1] e.g. Dover Cart., ff. 229ᵛ–30ᵛ.

[2] See, e.g., S. Pegge, *An Historical Account of Beauchief Abbey* (1801), p. 46.

[3] *P.L.* 216, col. 918, no. cxxii; and *Letters of Inn. III*, no. 619.

[4] *St. Frideswide's Cart.* i, no. 51. See below, pp. 265–6, for Westminster, and for a similar grant to Kirkham (Aug. Yorks. E.R.) made by Innocent III, *Letters of Inn. III*, no. 1119, and for Peterborough (1245), Peterborough, MS. 1, f. 99ʳ.

[5] B.M. Harley Chs. 84 F 35 and 36, and Bodleian MS. Chs. Bucks. a 4, Ch. 91.

[6] c. 1. 6. I. 14; and Hefele, *Conciles*, v, pt. ii. 1644, can. 4.

right to appoint subconservators were not conceded until the Council of Vienne (1311–12), after which date the appointment of conservators became a common phenomenon.[1] The development of the use of conservators had been slow, and the potentialities of such a system were not exploited until after the end of our period.

2. *Appointment and Choice of the Judges*

Whether in the twelfth century the judges were deputed by the pope or chosen by the parties is not known. The earliest suggestion that the applicant had anything to do with the appointment of the judges comes from Alexander III's pontificate, when a party is found suggesting a judge.[2] This was regarded as abnormal by Dom Morey in his consideration of Bartholomew of Exeter as a judge delegate.[3] But it is common to find forms of petition to the *Curia* making mention of the judges who were required after 1198. William of Drogheda's example shows the plaintiff, W., vicar of 'Asseleia' (? Ashley), seeking the appointment of the dean, precentor, and archdeacon of Hereford in a case against W. Pokevelt, rector, and 'quidam alii', both clerks and laymen, of Lincoln, London, and Hereford dioceses.[4] Similarly, the Oxford formulary has an A. de Crec, knight, bringing a case against B., clerk, over the advowson of the church of Crick (Northants.), and seeking as judges the abbot and prior of Oseney and the subprior of St. Frideswide's.[5] When the dean and chapter of Wells took certain cases to Rome in the thirteenth century they nominated the judges. In one case against the abbot and convent of Glastonbury (Ben. Som.) and 'quidam alii' of Bath, Salisbury, and Exeter dioceses, 'super decimis, possessionibus et rebus aliis', they sought the bishop, dean, and archdeacon of Lincoln. In another, against the abbot and convent of 'Alegnye' (? Athelney, Ben. Som.) and 'quidam alii' of Bath, Salisbury, and

---

[1] *Päpstlichen Kanzleiordnungen*, ed. Tangl, pp. 321–4.
[2] *Quinque Compilationes Antiquae* (Comp. i lib. ii tit. xi c. 2), p. 15.
[3] Morey, *Bartholomew of Exeter*, p. 48.   [4] Drogheda, ii, p. 8.
[5] *Oxford Formularies*, ii. 275, no. 5, and for another example no. 1, where the plaintiff seeks the abbot of St. Edmunds and the prior, presumably of St. Edmunds. There are further examples in the formulary (B) which have not been printed.

Worcester dioceses, they sought the dean, chancellor, and treasurer of Salisbury. In 1242 when they took their case against Bath over the election of the bishop to Rome, they hoped that the case would be heard by the pope in person. If this was not possible they requested judges notwith-standing the constitution 'de duabus dietis', and they sug-gested the bishops of Worcester and Norwich and the archdeacon of Sudbury, or the bishop and dean of Lincoln and the archdeacon of Lincoln (or the archdeacon of Hunt-ingdon), or the bishop, dean, and precentor[1] of Salisbury.[2] These examples suggest that it was the normal practice by this time for the plaintiff to name the judges he wanted.[3]

Unless an objection was made by the defendant's proctor, the *Curia* appears to have appointed as the plaintiff sug-gested. In a form of petition for judges in the French *ordo judiciarius*, which goes under the name of Curialis, G., clerk, who brought a suit against the abbot of St. Just-en-Chaussée of Beauvais diocese,[4] J., knight, and 'quidam alii' of the dioceses of Beauvais, Paris, and Orleans, suggested the dean, precentor, and master of the schools of Orleans.[5] The next form is the papal mandate resulting from this impetration made out in the name of Gregory IX and addressed to the three clerics whose names had been proposed by the plain-tiff.[6] At least from the pontificate of Innocent III it was pos-sible to object to the applicant's proposals for a commission, but such objections would seem to have been limited to those who were wealthy enough to employ a standing proctor at Rome. It is unlikely that objections were frequently made.[7] On 13 April 1237 the priors of St. Oswald's (Aug.) and St. Bartholomew's (Aug. hosp.), Gloucester, were procured as judges by the prior and convent of Lanthony (Aug. Glos.). Their subdelegates, the subprior of St. Oswald's and the dean of Gloucester, gave sentence in favour of the plaintiffs,

---

[1] On one occasion cited as the chancellor, Wells, Lib. Albus, i, f. 96ʳ, noted in H.M.C., *Report on the MSS. of Wells Cathedral* (1885), p. 1.

[2] Wells, Lib. Albus, i, ff. 2, 95ʳ, and 96ʳ (H.M.C., *Rep. on the MSS. of Wells*, pp. 1, 59).

[3] This, too, was the normal practice before the provincial court of Canterbury; see Morgan, 'Early Canterbury Jurisdiction', p. 396, and the references cited there.

[4] Cottineau, ii, col. 2754.

[5] Curialis, 'Ordo', lxviii, p. 22.   [6] Ibid. lxix, p. 22.

[7] See above, Chapter II, p. 58.

whereupon the defendants, the hospital of St. Julian near St. Albans, appealed to Rome and got a mandate to the prior of Dunstable (Aug. Beds.) and the archdeacon of Bedford, who were appointed judges on 13 October 1238.[1] In this case no objections appear to have been made to either of the proposed commissions at Rome.

Instances of the appointment of judges at the suggestion of a party abound in the papal registers. Hugh d'Aubigny got letters addressed to the abbot of Bury St. Edmunds (Ben. Suff.) and then to the prior of Dunstable (Aug. Beds.) and his colleagues; while his adversary the archbishop of Canterbury obtained a mandate to the abbots of Cirencester (Aug. Glos.), Evesham (Ben. Worcs.), and Hyde (Ben. Hants).[2] Similarly, in a suit between the abbot and convent of Kirkstead (Cist. Lincs.) and the rector of Benniworth (Lincs.), mandates were obtained by the rector to the prior of Oseney (Aug. Oxon.) and his fellow judges, the prior of St. Mary Magdalene's, Lincoln (Ben.) and his fellow judges, and the bishop of Lincoln and his colleagues; while Kirkstead got letters to the abbot of Welbeck (Prem. Notts.) and his fellows, and the prior of Waltham (Aug. Essex) and his colleagues.[3] Further references to commissions obtained by one party and then by the other occur in cartularies and charters. In a suit between the abbot and convent of St. John Colchester (Ben. Essex) and the rector of Easton (Suffolk), letters were got by the convent to the abbot of Sibton (Cist. Suff.) and others, and the prior of Holy Trinity, Ipswich (Aug. Suff.) and his fellows; and by the rector to the prior of St. Frideswide's, Oxford (Aug.) and his colleagues, and the prior of Wroxton (Aug. Oxon.). The final judges were the priors of Thoby and Tiptree (both Aug. Essex), who were chosen by Colchester.[4] A papal settlement recorded in the Crowland cartulary speaks of diverse judges delegate and of letters impetrated by both

<hr />

[1] Lanthony Cart., A 1, X, nos. lxxiiii and cviii.

[2] *Reg. Greg. IX*, no. 5182. The original mandate which was procured by the archbishop survives (Lambeth Palace Library, Papal Documents, no. 32).

[3] *Reg. Hon. III*, no. 6257 (*C.P.L.* i. 116). For another register example of mandates obtained by first one party and then the other, see the case between the nuns of Campsey Ash and the canons of Butley, *Reg. Greg. IX*, no. 302.

[4] P.R.O. E 42/384.

parties.[1] In these cases it appears that the defendant played no part in objecting to the commission at the time when the delegation was made, but preferred to get a whole new commission after the case had begun, if he found the judges unacceptable. This was an alternative to making an objection or contradiction in the *audientia publica*.

It was possible for the curial officials to refuse or to alter a commission, but in practice they do not appear to have examined the suggested names with any scrutiny. The *Curia* acted on the assumption that it was for the defendant himself to object if he felt injured. Accordingly, it provided him with the machinery to make his objection or to apply for a new mandate. It was illegal, however, to apply for a new rescript if no mention was made in the petition of the existence of a prior mandate.[2] Furthermore, if the second mandate was obtained by one party when the first had been got by common consent, the first was held to remain valid.[3] When a second mandate was received, the new judges ordered the previous judges to discontinue their hearing of the case.[4]

In allowing the petitioner to nominate his judges, the *Curia* had devised a system that to modern eyes may appear to favour the plaintiff unduly.[5] It accepted his application and his statement of the case prima facie. In so doing, the underlying assumption seems to have been that not only were the defendant's legal rights of protection catered for in the machinery outlined above, but that the plaintiff was already at some disadvantage which had to be allowed for. Cases could not be taken to Rome without considerable trouble and expense. For this reason it was probably assumed that most impetrations expressed a genuine grievance and were not frivolous. In all likelihood the defendant, at the time of the appeal or impetration, was in possession of the thing sought, if it was property or tithes. The possessor's advantage was very great, and so was that of the person who steadfastly refused to pay tithes or a rent. The plaintiff's

---

[1] Crowland Cart., f. 189, and cf. Exeter Cart., p. 79, and New College, Oxford, Writtle Ch. 401.

[2] c. 3. X. I. 3. For examples of mandates obtained surreptitiously, see *Letters of Inn. III*, nos. 5, 55, and 734.   [3] c. 3. X. I. 3.

[4] See above, p. 104, and App. B (iii), no. 1.

[5] Maitland, *Roman Canon Law*, p. 114, saw this as an 'enormous advantage'.

advantage would only be unfair if he managed to obtain, and keep, a biased commission. On the whole he probably came away with a mandate to three local ecclesiastics who might be sympathetic to his cause, but who were not necessarily hostile to the defendant.

What influenced the plaintiff in his choice of judges? The idea that the judges should be local men was basic to the judge-delegate system, and the advantages of local inquiry and knowledge account for the growth of the system of delegation.[1] Considerable expense could be spared by the use of local men, and this was advantageous to the plaintiff. When exemptions from hearing cases were granted by the popes, the exempt clerics were sometimes ordered to make this factor known in their locality, so that parties would not propose them as judges. The abbot of Thornton (Aug. Lincs.) was given an exemption in 1221 from hearing cases and was instructed to make this known in his area.[2] Within the particular area the plaintiff's choice would have been determined by local connections, prejudices, and rivalries— factors which must have been influential but at which we can only guess. It seems, however, that the factor of proximity was not always respected, and that mandates were sometimes acquired to distant judges. For instance, the convent of Thame (Cist. Oxon.) brought the rector of Oddington (Oxon.) before the abbot of St. Mary's (Ben.) and the precentor and treasurer of York.[3] Similarly, the rector of Great Paxton (Hunts.) got a mandate against the warden and ministers of the altar of St. Hugh in Lincoln cathedral, addressed to the abbot and prior of Hyde (Ben. Hants) and the official of the bishop of Winchester.[4] Nor was it unknown for the judges to be a considerable distance from one another as well as from the parties. A mandate of 1217 was directed to the abbots of Waltham (Essex), Coverham (Yorks. N.R.)

---

[1] See *P.U.E.* iii, no. 47 (Eug. III, 8 June 1145): 'Quia igitur in alterius partis absentia super re incerta certam non potuimus dare sententiam, causam ipsam vestre discretioni discutiendam committimus . . .', and similarly no. 90 (Eug. III, 1150–3); and c. 28. *X.* I. 3—Fourth Lateran Council. The factor of proximity also played an important part in Cistercian delegation, see J. E. Sayers, 'English Cistercian Cases and their Delegation in the First Half of the Thirteenth Century', *Analecta Sacri Ordinis Cisterciensis*, xx (1964), 85–102.

[2] *Reg. Hon. III*, no. 3550 (*C.P.L.* i. 83), and see below, p. 146, for further examples.

[3] *Thame Cart.*, no. 37.   [4] *Reg. Antiq. Linc.* ii, no. 385, and iii, no. 830.

and the archdeacon of Huntingdon (diocese of Lincoln), in a suit between G(eoffrey de Burgh), archdeacon of Norwich, and Master Robert of York about election to the bishopric of Ely.[1] Some of these examples might be explained by the personal reputation that certain judges undoubtedly gained, but not all can be accounted for in this way. Many of the secular judges may have held in the locality other benefices of which we have no record. Such uncertain elements as these defy complete analysis.

Richard de Mores, canon of Merton and prior of Dunstable, who has been convincingly identified with the procedural writer Ricardus Anglicus,[2] heard causes in nearly every year of his long reign as prior.[3] His importance as a judge delegate was intimated by Professor Russell and by Professor Kuttner and Miss Rathbone.[4] A new investigation has uncovered forty-eight suits in which he was concerned as an officer of the delegated courts. He was primarily a canonist, who had been at the leading schools of Europe (Paris, Bologna, and Oxford), but after attending the Fourth Lateran Council he remained in Paris from 1215 to 1216 to study theology.[5] Several points of interest come to light if we examine the suits which he heard. His colleagues were usually neighbours. He served with the precentor (on six occasions), subprior, and sacrist of his own house,[6] and frequently with the archdeacon, abbot, and prior of St. Albans (Ben. Herts.), the abbot and prior of Warden (Cist.

---

[1] *Reg. Hon. III*, no. 1422 (*C.P.L.* i. p. 55).

[2] Russell, pp. 111–13, and more particularly by Kuttner and Rathbone in *A.N.C.*, pp. 329–39. Also identified with the Dunstable annalist (*Ann. Mon.* iii pp. x–xi).

[3] 1202–42. See App. A (iii), Richard, prior of Dunstable, as judge delegate.

[4] Russell, pp. 111–13, and *A.N.C.*, p. 338.

[5] *A.N.C.*, p. 338; and *Ann. Mon.* iii. 44. A mandate of Honorius III (*Reg. Hon. III*, no. 1683), dated 16 Nov. 1218, was addressed to a Richardus Anglicus doctor of Paris and others there, but it seems unlikely that this was Richard de Mores, who on 17 or 21 Nov. 1218 settled a case in company with the abbot of Warden and the dean of Berkhamsted, see App. A (iii), no. 8. This is perhaps the Ricardus Anglicus who is mentioned as a regent master in Theology at Paris in 1218, see *Chartularium Universitatis Parisiensis*, i, ed. Denifle and Chatelain, 85, cited by Kuttner and Rathbone in *A.N.C.*, p. 338 n. 77. The suggestion of Charles E. Lewis in *Traditio*, xxii (1966), 469–71, that Richard de Mores had been in the *familia* of Archbishop Hubert Walter rests solely on his attesting one charter. The lack of any further evidence to support this makes it no more than a possibility.

[6] App. A (iii), nos. 29, 33–36, and 38 (precentor); 31 (subprior); and 36 (sacrist).

Beds.), the prior of Caldwell (Aug. Beds.), and the prior of
Wymondley (Aug. Herts.).[1] His other fellow judges were
mainly from the vicinity, the priors of Redbourn (Ben.
Herts.) and Newnham (Aug. Beds.); the abbot and prior of
Missenden (Aug. Bucks.); the abbot and prior of Woburn
(Cist. Beds.); the deans of Berkhamsted and Flamstead
(Herts.), Luton (Beds.), and Newport Pagnell (Bucks.); and
the archdeacons of Bedford and Northampton.[2] He sat also
with the chancellor of Oxford,[3] and in a different case with
Master William Scot, doctor of canon law, living at Oxford.[4]
On one occasion he served with the bishop of Rochester
(Henry de Sandford), on another with the archdeacon of Worcester, and on two occasions with the archdeacon of Dorset,
otherwise his co-judges were reasonably near to Dunstable.[5]
Professor Cheney has suggested that in one of the instances
where A., archdeacon of Dorset, occurs, it is probably a slip
for A(lexander of Elstow), archdeacon of Bedford, since the
mandate implies that both the judges were from Lincoln
diocese,[6] but two occurrences of this officer in independent
sources render this unlikely, especially as there was an A.,
archdeacon of Dorset, in c. 1209 and c. 1210 (the date of the
mandate being 19 December 1208).[7] The association of
Dorset with Lincoln diocese could well be explained by a
curial confusion with Dorchester in Oxfordshire, for the
Latin forms of Dorset and Dorchester were remarkably
similar. W. Basset, dean of 'Wengh'', on the other hand, is
probably not the dean of Wingham in Kent, as Cheney
identifies him.[8] Wingham College in Kent was not founded

---

[1] App. A (iii), nos 8, 10, 12–13, 17, and 37 (abbot of St. Albans); 5, 10, 18–19,
23–6, 28, and 32 (prior); 17, 19, 23–6, 28–9 (archdeacon); 6–7, 9, 11, and 14 (abbot
and prior of Warden, prior in nos. 7 and 9 only); nos 33–5 (prior of Caldwell); and
nos. 41–2 (prior of Wymondley).

[2] Ibid., nos. 4, 5, 8, 11, 16, 18, 20–2, 30, 37, and 43.   [3] Ibid., no. 32.

[4] Ibid., no. 14. See also no. 8, a cause subdelegated to him and two other Oxford
masters by Richard de Mores and his colleagues, and for further suits heard by him
see Emden, Oxf. Reg. iii. 1657, who has identified him with the Master William
Scot, archdeacon of Worcester in 1218, who was elected bishop of Durham in 1226
but whose election was quashed by Gregory IX.

[5] App. A (iii), nos. 2, 3, 16, and 27.   [6] Ibid., no. 2 (Letters of Inn. III, no. 788).

[7] Ibid., nos. 2 and 3, and Sarum Chs. 92 and 94 (pp. 73, 76); presumably
identifiable with Adam (de Ilchester) who occurs definitely on 7 January 1214 in
this office Statutes . . . of (Salisbury, ed. C. Wordsworth (1915), p. 52).

[8] App. A (iii), no. 1; cf. Cheney in Letters of Inn. III, no. 751.

until 1287. It could, of course, be the parson of Wingham in the deanery of Bridge (Kent), but it is much more likely that we have to look nearer to Dunstable. Mursley is the next deanery and includes Wing, where there was a Benedictine cell dependent on the abbot and convent of St. Nicholas, Angers,[1] who were the plaintiffs in this case. In general an analysis of Richard's colleagues shows him serving with Benedictines, Cistercians, Augustinians, and seculars, the factor of proximity being more important than religious order or diocesan boundary.

It may be asked how plaintiffs got to know of suitable judges. Richard was included in a commission with the archbishop of Canterbury (Stephen Langton), the bishop of Winchester (Peter des Roches), and the bishop of Salisbury (Richard Poore), probably as the result of his reputation as a canonist;[2] and in his own area he must have been well known as a lawyer and as an ecclesiastic of importance. He held his own court at Dunstable,[3] and he was a proctor of some repute.[4] He also travelled throughout the surrounding counties on ecclesiastical business. Probably at the end of 1210 he was as far afield as Staffordshire, possibly at the instance of the Augustinian canons of Darley who had brought a suit before Staffordshire judges to whom he may have given legal counsel.[5] In 1213 or 1214 he was engaged in the inquest into church losses in the bishopric of Lincoln consequent upon the Interdict, and he assisted the preachers of the crusade in Huntingdonshire, Bedfordshire, and Hertfordshire.[6] In 1228 he acted as visitor for the Augustinian order in the dioceses of Lichfield and Lincoln.[7] Eight out of the forty-eight suits in which he was

---

[1] D. Knowles and R. N. Hadcock, *Medieval Religious Houses* (1953), p. 92.

[2] App. A (iii), no. 15.

[3] Russell, p. 113.

[4] Kuttner and Rathbone, *A.N.C.*, p. 338 n. 76, citing *Rotuli Hugonis de Welles*, i, ed. W. P. W. Phillimore (Canterbury and York Ser. i, 1909), 109. Richard appeared on behalf of the convent of Dunstable before judges delegate appointed by Honorius III on one occasion, Dunstable Cart., f. 67ᵛ, cal. *Dunstable Cart.*, no. 767.

[5] App. A (iii), no. 44.

[6] *Ann. Mon.* iii. 39–40, cited by Russell, p. 112. As Professor Cheney has pointed out to me, the date given by the Dunstable Annals (1212) must be wrong in this instance.

[7] *Ann. Mon.* iii. 112, cited by Russell, p. 113. He was also appointed a visitor for the order in the province of York in 1223, *Ann. Mon.* iii. 80.

involved concerned the Augustinian house of St. Frideswide at Oxford, in the diocese of Lincoln, to whom he must have been well known.[1] In seven of these cases St. Frideswide's was probably the plaintiff; in the eighth the mandate was obtained by the abbot and convent of Bec.[2] Richard appeared in six suits where Bec was the plaintiff, of which four were dependent on the same mandate, and in one of which he acted as a subdelegate of Archbishop Edmund.[3] Some of the Bec lands were concentrated in the counties around Bedfordshire, within relatively easy reach of Dunstable. He also heard nine cases where the great Benedictine abbey of St. Peter at Westminster had an interest.[4] Westminster was the plaintiff in six of these.[5] Master Thomas Foliot, rector of Ashwell (Herts.), who procured a mandate against Westminster, was a brother of Hugh Foliot, archdeacon of Shropshire, and is perhaps to be identified with Master Thomas Foliot, a canon of Lichfield in 1209.[6] The name of Roger de Moris the clerk, who impetrated a mandate to Richard, the prior of St. Albans and the dean of Luton, is arresting, but whether or not he was a relative of Richard, prior of Dunstable, cannot be stated.[7] Wymondham, a cell of St. Albans, with whose dignitaries Richard occurs so frequently as judge, got mandates to him, probably in 1208 and in 1239.[8] Also in 1208 the almoner of St. Albans procured an inclusive mandate against Alexander, clerk of Norwich diocese, and other persons of Ely and London dioceses, about tithes belonging to the almonry.[9] Master Richard de Tingehurst, who acted with him as a subdelegate of the archdeacon of Bedford in 1238, had been brought before him in 1225/6 by the abbot and convent of Oseney, another Oxford Augustinian house, over tithes in Clapham (Beds.).[10]

The bulk of the cases concerned tithes in Oxfordshire, Hertfordshire, Buckinghamshire, Bedfordshire, and

---

[1] App. A (iii), 8, 10, 19, 23–6, and 33.   [2] Ibid., no. 33.

[3] Ibid., nos. 17, 33–6, and 48.   [4] Ibid., nos. 5, 7, 12–13, 15, 21, 27–8, and 43.

[5] Ibid., nos. 12–13, 21, 27–8, and 43 (where the defendants, Pershore, had also impetrated letters—to the abbot of Dore).

[6] Ibid., no. 7; Westminster Ch. 15684; and P.R.O. E 135/2/28.

[7] App. A (iii), no. 18.   [8] Ibid., nos. 2 and 41–2.

[9] Ibid., no. 4.   [10] Ibid., nos. 16 and 38.

Cambridgeshire,[1] but Richard also heard cases in Worcestershire, Lincolnshire, Norfolk, Kent, Middlesex, Dorset, Surrey, Huntingdonshire, Berkshire, and Wiltshire.[2] It seems possible to detect two circles of influence, the first made up of the counties surrounding Dunstable and Bedfordshire, and the second composed of an outer group of counties with five outliers—Worcester, Wiltshire, Dorset, Lincolnshire, and Norfolk. Two cases were election contests—one at Bury St. Edmunds, the other at Shaftesbury—and several, including these, were of first rank importance demanding a lawyer of skill.[3] The case brought by the prior and convent of Wymondham against the rural dean of Waxham (Master Peter de Ware) in 1239 over who had the right to exercise spiritual jurisdiction in the manor of Happisburgh (Norf.) was a complicated one which was expertly brought to an end.[4] At about the same time the dispute between the archbishop of Canterbury and the bishop of London about the archbishop's right to visit monasteries in the diocese of London, was referred back to the pope with full details for him to make a decision.[5] As has been suggested above, Richard was desirous, it seems, of making compositions rather than passing judgement, which was perhaps another recommendation to petitioners. At least twenty-two of the cases which he heard were ended with compositions, settlements, or arbitrations,[6] and we have several glimpses of Richard sitting in his delegated court citing the latest decretals and coaxing the parties to agreement.[7]

3. The Personnel

With the increase in the number of cases that were taken to Rome by the turn of the century, the applicants mentioned the names of judges from lower grades in the ecclesiastical hierarchy; this was to have important effects. If the personnel are investigated, the inclusion can be appreciated, within the

[1] App. A (iii), nos. 5, 8, 19, 23–6, and 31; 7, 13, and 20; 10, 29, and 36; 16 and 38; and 4.
[2] Ibid., nos. 21; 22; 2 and 42; 9; 12 and 43; 17; 11 and 28; 32; and 33–5 (the last case concerns tithes in Berks. now Wilts.)
[3] Ibid., nos. 6 and 14.   [4] Ibid., no. 41.   [5] Ibid., no. 40.
[6] Ibid., nos 2, 5, 7, 9, 11, 16–17, 19–21, 24, 26–8, 32–6, 42, 43, and 45.
[7] Ibid., no. 48; and see Chapter II, p. 94 n. 2.

orbit of papal judicial administration, of a large number of clerks—both regulars and seculars. They ranged in a downward scale from the bishops and abbots to priors of small alien houses, and rural deans. The extent of the judge-delegate system is far wider than has been imagined, and the amount of legal knowledge which was expected from the average ecclesiastic becomes apparent. Lawyers were by now in great demand, and the main method of advancement was through a legal education. Professor Kuttner and Miss Rathbone have shown the marked enthusiasm for the study of canon and civil law in England in the late twelfth century.[1] The way in which legal knowledge permeated the ecclesiastical ranks in the thirteenth century can be vividly illustrated by examining some of the persons who acted as judges delegate. To some extent the judge-delegate system produced the kind of judge it needed, as with Abbot Samson of Bury, who became a very popular judge[2] and about whom we have the following details:

Seven months had not passed since his election, when lo and behold! letters of the Lord Pope were brought to him, appointing[3] him judge delegate for the hearing of causes, a task of which he had neither knowledge nor experience, though he was learned in the liberal arts and in the Holy Scriptures, being a literate man, brought up in the schools and once a schoolmaster, well known and approved in his country. He forthwith called to him two clerks skilled in the law and associated them with himself, making use of their counsel in ecclesiastical business, and studying the decrees and decretal letters, whenever he had time, so that within a short time by reading of books and practice in causes he came to be regarded as a wise judge, proceeding in court according to the form of the law.[4]

Like Samson, many undoubtedly gained some knowledge of canon law by practice, but others already possessed some skill in the law; and Professor Cheney has suggested that whereas persons holding high ecclesiastical office were

---

[1] *A.N.C.*, esp. p. 280.

[2] See, for example, the references given in *Letters of Inn. III*.

[3] The Latin text says '. . . et ecce offerebantur ei litere domini pape constituentes eum iudicem de causis cognoscendis . . .', which H. E. Butler in *Chronicle of Jocelin of Brakelond* (1949), p. 33, translates as 'when lo and behold! letters of the Lord Pope were brought to him, offering to appoint him judge delegate for the hearing of causes . . .'   [4] Ibid., pp. 33–4.

frequently chosen for their general standing, since they could call in legal advice if necessary, lesser persons, such as canons of cathedrals and schoolmasters, were selected mainly for their legal competence.[1]

Throughout the following analysis of the personnel, the tendency for the judges to come from the towns and legal centres, such as Northampton, Oxford, Lincoln, and Salisbury, will be noticed. Nearly every order of regulars was drawn upon to furnish judges delegate: Augustinians, Benedictines, Cistercians, Cluniacs, Gilbertines, Premonstratensians, and members of the order of Fontevrault. By the middle of the thirteenth century mandates were addressed to friars, both Dominicans and Franciscans.[2] According to the evidence collected, the regulars during this period received slightly more mandates than the seculars.

(i) The Regulars

The main burden of the delegated judicial work seems to have been borne by the Augustinians. Some 420 mandates were sent to them in the southern province between 1198 and 1254, involving abbots, priors, subpriors, precentors, and canons of ninety-four houses. Mr. Dickinson has estimated that by 1215 there were about 173 independent houses of regular canons established in England. Their houses, although frequently very small, were to be found in most parts of England, being particularly numerous in Norfolk, Suffolk, and Essex.[3] The Augustinians were also a learned order, especially it seems in the law. A large number of the canon law collections noted by Fournier and Le Bras owed their origin to regular canons.[4] Several of the English houses were noted as intellectual centres, such as Dunstable, Merton, Cirencester, and St. Frideswide's, Oxford, and their personnel were often used as judges.[5]

[1] C. R. Cheney, 'England and the Roman Curia under Innocent III', *Journal of Ecclesiastical History*, xviii (1967), 180–1.

[2] e.g. the prior of the Friars Preacher of London and the warden of the Friars Minor at Leicester, 'Peak Docs.', no. vii, and the warden of the Friars Minor at Chichester, B.M. Harley Ch. 83 C 32.

[3] Dickinson, *Austin Canons*, p. 153.

[4] Ibid., p. 186.

[5] Ibid., pp. 186–92; and see R. W. Hunt, 'English Learning in the late Twelfth Century', *Trans. of the Royal Hist. Soc.* 4th ser. xix (1936), 19–35, esp. 34.

Richard de Mores had been a canon of Merton before he became prior of Dunstable and a noted judge delegate. Another canon of Merton, Guy, became prior of Southwick, and as such acted as a judge delegate in 1199 and between 1197 and 1216, in commissions with the priors of St. Swithin's and Hyde, Winchester (both Ben. Hants), with S(effrid II), bishop, and L(ewis), the precentor of Chichester, and with the dean and archdeacon of Chichester.[1] He wrote several minor theological works which have survived, and was a friend of John of Salisbury.[2] Master Alexander of St. Albans (Alexander Neckham), canon of Cirencester, whose learning has been described by Dr. Hunt, received a mandate to act as a judge delegate with Robert, abbot of Malmesbury (Ben. Wilts.), and Walter, prior of Lanthony (Aug. Glos.), in 1203.[3] Celestine III had directed a mandate to him and the abbots of Combe (Cist. Warw.) and Stanley (Cist. Wilts.) on 23 January 1195.[4] At about the same time, 1197 to 1205, Alexander, prior of Canons Ashby, who wrote a tract on the art of preaching, heard delegated cases in the Northamptonshire area with Robert, abbot of Eynsham (Ben. Oxon.); Geoffrey, abbot of Bruern (Cist. Oxon.); the abbot, Walkelin, and the prior of St. James's, Northampton (Aug.); Walter, prior of St. Andrew's, Northampton (Clun.); Master Henry de Gylevylle, canon of Lincoln; and Master A. de Wilne.[5] Laurence de Stanesfield, prior of Barnwell (Cambs.), an important convent for the study of canon and civil law, was joint president of the provincial chapter that was held at St. Frideswide's in 1234, and a frequent judge delegate.[6] Giles

---

[1] *Reg. S. Osmund*, i. 354–6; *Letters of Inn. III*, nos. 87 and 1143; and Magdalen College, Oxford, Old and New Shoreham Ch. 4, cal. *Sele Cart.*, no. 17.

[2] Dickinson, *Austin Canons*, p. 187, and E. Rathbone, 'The Influence of Bishops and of Members of Cathedral Bodies in the Intellectual Life of England, 1066–1216', ii (London Ph.D. thesis, 1936), 426 n. 57 and 478.

[3] Hunt, 'English Learning', p. 25, and P.R.O. E 327/45.

[4] Lanthony Cart., A 2, f. 221ʳ. He is addressed here as plain Master Alexander of St. Albans. He occurs in formulary O as a judge delegate, see above, p. 49.

[5] Hunt, 'English Learning', p. 20, and Russell, pp. 12–13; *Oseney Cart.* iv, no. 178 and *St. Frideswide's Cart.* ii, no. 703; P.R.O. E 40/13847(2); Westminster Ch. 2479; and *Letters of Inn. III*, nos. 545 and 563.

[6] *Chapters of the Augustinian Canons*, ed. H. E. Salter (Canterbury and York Ser. xxix, 1922), no. 4. For his occurrences as judge delegate, see Walden Cart.,

of Bourne, prior of Merton (Surr.) from 1222 and an active judge delegate, resigned his office in 1231 in order to become a Cistercian monk at Beaulieu.[1] Another Augustinian, who was on occasion a judge delegate, was Martin, abbot of Missenden (Bucks.), deposed from office in 1236.[2] It is difficult to do more than identify the other Augustinians; and only glimpses of their activities can be obtained. About one third of the mandates were directed to the larger and less remote priories, such as Waltham, Merton, St. Frideswide's, Holy Trinity, Aldgate, and Lanthony. It is noticeable that in the priories of Merton, Holy Trinity, Aldgate, and Barnwell, the precentor was also used as a judge delegate in company with the prior in two of the instances.[3] The remarkably few references to Oseney officials serving as judges delegate, especially after Innocent III's pontificate, seem to be accounted for by their exemptions.[4]

Probably the first regulars to serve as judges delegate were the Benedictines. They were the foremost religious order of Christendom and were particularly well established in the towns. The abbots of the great Benedictine houses ranked equally with the bishops. During the years from 1198 to 1254 some 300 mandates were directed to sixty-eight houses and cells in the south, and twenty alien Benedictine priories received mandates,[5] so that the Benedictines form the second largest group to act as judges delegate. The

ff. 43ᵛ, 44ᵛ, and 48ᵛ; *Reg. Hon. III*, no. 6070 (*C.P.L.* i. 113); *N.L.C.*, nos. 85, 86; Bodleian MS. Chs. Berks. a i, Ch. 17; Leeds Cart., f. 8ᵛ; and Belvoir, Large Cart., f. 87ᵛ.

[1] *V.C.H. Surrey*, ii. 102, and *Ann. Mon.* iii. 128. For causes heard by him, see Lewes Cart., f. 242ᵛ, cal. *Lewes Cart. N.P.*, no. 76; f. 311ʳ⁻ᵛ, cal. *Lewes Cart. S.P.* ii. 128-9; P.R.O. E 40/14070, cal. *Lewes Cart. N.P.*, no. 140; P.R.O. E 40/14197; *Sele Cart.*, no. 40; and P.R.O. E 135/4/17, cal. *Lewes Cart. N.P.*, no. 70.

[2] Westminster Domesday, f. 576ʳ; St. Albans Cart. (B), f. 187ʳ; and *V.C.H. Bucks.* i. 375.

[3] Windsor, Papal Bulls, no. 1; Magdalen College, Oxford, Southwick Chs. 4 (cal. *Sele Cart.*, no. 34) 20 and 23; and *Reg. Greg. IX*, no. 627.

[4] I have evidence of only four mandates addressed to Oseney after 1216: *Reg. Hon. III*, no. 6257 (*C.P.L.* i. 116); *Reg. Antiq. Linc.* iii, no. 647; Eye Cart., ff. 41ᵛ⁻2ᵛ; and *Chertsey Cart.*, no. 92. For exemptions see below, pp. 143-7.

[5] The priors of Boxgrove, Arundel, Newport Pagnell, and Minster Lovell, for instance, received mandates: Lewes Cart., f. 311ᵛ, cal. *Lewes Cart. S.P.* ii. 129; Bayham Cart. f. 60ᵛ; Magdalen College, Oxford, Buddington Chs. 7, and 8 (cal. *Sele Cart.*, no. 30); *Sele Cart.*, no. 35; Northampton, St. Andrew's Cart. (A), f. 241ᵛ; Bodleian MS. Chs. Oxon. a 1, Ch. 13b; *N.L.C.*, no. 9; *Cartulary of . . . Eynsham*, i, ed. H. E. Salter (Oxf. Hist. Soc. xlix, 1907), no. 231; and Carisbrooke Cart., f. 72ʳ.

abbots, priors, and obedientiaries of the exempt convents played an important part: St. Albans, Bury, St. Augustine's, Canterbury, Westminster, and Evesham. Eynsham, Hyde (Winchester), Abingdon, Peterborough, Reading, and Rochester rank high. Individuals who seem to have been important as judges delegate came from these houses; for instance Hugh II, abbot of Bury, Walter de Astone, abbot of Hyde, Robert of Battle, abbot of St. Augustine's, William of Trumpington, abbot of St. Albans, Osbert, prior of Abingdon, Raymond, prior of St. Albans, and N., prior of Eynsham. Of the monastic officials who were appointed, the sacrist of Bury acted as a judge with the priors of Ixworth and Thetford between 1218 and 1222, the precentor of St. Albans with the prior and archdeacon of St. Albans in 1252–3, and the precentor of Rochester with the prior and dean in 1238.[1]

Priors of ten Cluniac houses received mandates: Bermondsey, Castle Acre, Daventry, Lewes, Mendham, Monks Horton, Monkton Farleigh, Much Wenlock, St. Andrew's, Northampton, and Wangford. This is about one quarter of the number of Cluniac houses in England.[2] The prior of St. Andrew's, Northampton, perhaps owing to the convenient location of the house, was frequently sought.[3] The order of Fontevrault provided double houses for monks and nuns living under the rule of St. Benedict, and there were four of these in England. The prior of one of them, Amesbury (Wilts.), acted as a judge delegate on at least two occasions.[4] Grovebury (Beds.), which was also dependent on Fontevrault, was for monks only; its prior heard several cases with the prior of Caldwell (Aug. Beds.).[5]

The Cistercians were soon involved in hearing cases, as more were sent to Rome and delegation increased. Their extra-monastic activities have long been recognized. They

---

[1] Castle Acre Cart., f. 128ᵛ, and on the sacrist's judicial powers by virtue of his office, see M. D. Lobel, *Borough of Bury St. Edmunds* (Oxford, 1935), pp. 31–47. *Reg. Antiq. Linc.* ii, no. 386, and P.R.O. E 40/14036.

[2] See Knowles and Hadcock, *Medieval Religious Houses*, pp. 95–101.

[3] See Crowland Cart., f. 94; P.R.O. E 40/13847(2); St. John's College, Oxford, Ch. xix. 2; Lanthony Cart. A1, VIII, no. lxxxii; and Daventry Cart., f. 141ᵛ.

[4] *Reg. Hon. III*, no. 1810 (*C.P.L.* i. 61), and *Oseney Cart.* ii, no. 1042, and see vi, no. 38.

[5] *Oseney Cart.* iv, nos. 151A, and 403–4, and see vi, no. 48.

were employed by Innocent III to counteract heresy and preach a crusade.[1] In spite of some resistance, and certain checks on the study of canon law within the order, Cistercians often served as judges delegate.[2] Their experience in dealing with their own lawsuits may have made them popular choices.[3] Of the Cistercians of the southern province in England, abbots and priors of thirty houses heard cases, receiving about 130 mandates between them. The abbots and priors of Thame, Warden, and Bruern were frequent judges. Simon, abbot of Thame (Oxon.) between 1205 and 1224, heard several cases in company with local ecclesiastics, and sometimes with his prior.[4] The abbot of Warden (Beds.) was frequently a co-judge of the prior of Dunstable, and the abbot of Bruern (Oxon.) of Simon, abbot of Thame, and N., prior of Eynsham (Ben. Oxon.).[5] The more isolated houses seem to have escaped service. The Premonstratensians copied the Cistercian judicial system,[6] and they too contributed judges delegate. Mandates were addressed to thirteen houses, the abbot and prior of West Dereham (Norf.) and the abbot of Barlings (Lincs.) receiving the most.[7] Barlings was a large convent with its number of canons most likely exceeding thirty by the end of the thirteenth century.[8] West Dereham, which had been founded by Hubert Walter, had much prestige.[9]

---

[1] See J.-M. Canivez, 'Étonnantes Concessions pontificales faites à Cîteaux', *Miscellanea historica in honorem Alberti de Meyer*, i (Louvain, 1946), 505, and *P.L.* 215, col. 358, no. lxxvi, and col. 1024, no. clxxxv, for the activities of Peter and Raoul of Castelnau against the heretics in the south of France.

[2] See P. Colomban Bock, 'Les Cisterciens et l'étude du droit', *Analecta Sacri Ordinis Cisterciensis*, vii (1951), 3–31, who places in perspective the prohibitions against the study of law in the order. See also Canivez, 'Cîteaux', *D.D.C.* iii, col. 777, and A. van Hove, *Prolegomena* (Malines–Rome, 1945), pp. 455, 470.

[3] See Sayers, 'Judicial Activities' II, and 'English Cistercian Cases'.

[4] *St. Frideswide's Cart.* ii, no. 1018; *Oseney Cart.* iv, nos. 156A and 415A, and see vi, no. 30; iv, nos. 401C and 402, 415B and C, v, nos. 571, 854, and 879D, and see vi, no. 31; Canons Ashby Cart., f. 50ʳ; P.R.O. E 212/28; and *Glos. Cart.* i. 25.

[5] Westminster Domesday, f. 228ʳ⁻ᵛ; *Registrum Roffense*, ed. J. Thorpe (1769), p. 655; *Chertsey Cart.*, no. 91; and *Reg. Hon. III*, no. 757 (*C.P.L.* i. 49). B.M. Add. Ch. 20469; *Oseney Cart.* v, no. 879D, and iv, nos. 156A and 415A.

[6] Sayers, 'Judicial Activities' I, pp. 23–4, and II; Colvin, *White Canons*, pp. 196–7.

[7] Eton College, Sporle Ch. 1; *Reg. Hon. III*, no. 6257 (*C.P.L.* i. 116); *Reg. Greg. IX*, no. 4803; Binham Cart., ff. 146ᵛ⁻7ʳ; Bardney Cart., f. 203ʳ⁻ᵛ; *Reg. Antiq. Linc.* iii, no. 730; *Reg. Hon. III*, no. 2547 (*C.P.L.* i. 73); and Bardney Cart., f. 95ᵛ.

[8] Colvin, *White Canons*, p. 75.

[9] Ibid., p. 129.

The use of several Gilbertines and priors of hospitals as judges delegate illustrates the way in which commissions combined various regulars. The prior of the Gilbertine house of St. Katherine at Lincoln acted once with the sub-prior, twice with the subdean of Lincoln, and three times with the prior of St. Mary Magdalene, Lincoln (Ben.),[1] and A., prior of St. Margaret's, Marlborough (Gilb.) made several appearances.[2] The central position of the hospitals at Lincoln and Northampton would account for the inclusion of their priors in commissions.[3]

(ii) The Seculars

A clear picture emerges of the reliance of the papal delegated judicial system on the officers of the permanent diocesan administration. It casts a new light on the interaction between the delegated and the permanent Church courts and on the consequent relations between the officials. The bishops had been the stalwarts of papal judicial delegation in the twelfth century. In the thirteenth, major causes were still often sent to them, but they no longer monopolized the delegated cases, for many of the suits which now reached Rome were of minor importance. Benedict of Sawston, bishop of Rochester, who was also a royal justice,[4] Eustace, bishop of Ely, Richard Poore, bishop of Salisbury, and Stephen Langton and Edmund of Abingdon, archbishops of Canterbury, played an important part in the great suits of the time.[5] As we shall see, many of them would have gained experience in more junior capacities, and parties possibly went

[1] B.M. Add. Ch. 20512; Reg. Antiq. Linc. iii, no. 730; St. Frideswide's Cart. ii, no. 731; and Westminster Ch. 2596.

[2] B.M. Campbell. Ch. xxii 11; and Eton College, Cottisford Ch. 37. The prior of St. Margaret's, Marlborough, also served as a judge between 1232 and 1239, Sarum Chs. ccxxi.

[3] Combe Cart., f. 76ᵛ; Reg. Antiq. Linc. ii, no. 513; and Wherwell Cart., f. 99ʳ. Newnham Cart., no. 156; St. Frideswide's Cart. ii, nos. 732, 978, and 980; Abingdon Cart., f. 90ᵛ; Spalding Cart., f. 418ᵛ; and Oseney Cart. v, no. 802A.

[4] Gibbs and Lang, Bishops and Reform, p. 167, citing Patent Rolls of the Reign of Henry III 1216–25, p. 208. For three minor cases heard by Benedict as bishop, see Chertsey Cart., no. 93; N.L.C., no. 135; and Early Charters of the Cathedral Church of St. Paul, London, ed. M. Gibbs (Camden Soc. 3rd Ser. lviii, 1939), pp. 110–13.

[5] See, e.g., App. A (iii), no. 15, Reg. Hon. III, no. 5792 (C.P.L. i. 108), Reg. Greg. IX, no. 5395, and Reg. Inn. IV, no. 239. For Eustace, bishop of Ely, as a judge delegate, see Letters of Inn. III.

on asking for them after they had received promotion. The average bishop could still reckon to count service as a judge delegate among his duties, and two bishops at least sought exemption.[1] Evidence survives of some ninety mandates to the archbishop of Canterbury, the bishops of Bath, Chichester, Ely, Exeter, Hereford, Lincoln, London, Norwich, Rochester, St. Asaph, Salisbury, Winchester, and Worcester. It was not long before the bishop's legal deputy in the diocese, the official, was involved in hearing cases. The official of the bishop of Worcester sat on a commission with the prior of Lanthony (Aug. Glos.) and the archdeacon of Gloucester in 1223–4.[2] This was Master Robert de Clipstone, proctor of Bishop Mauger of Worcester at Rome in the Evesham suit of 1205.[3] He also appears as a judge delegate in formulary O in the suit of 1182×1194, and as a delegate of the legate in 1215, where he seems to be described as a clerk of John of Tynemouth, archdeacon of Oxford from 1215 to 1221.[4] As delegate of the legate Guala, he was appointed with the dean of Rissington (Glos.) to hear a suit between the abbot and convent of Bruern (Cist. Oxon.) and the rector of Guiting (Glos.) on 23 January (?) 1217.[5] He was official of the bishop of Worcester by 1211.[6] Most of the officials who acted as delegates were masters, such as Master Alan, official of Winchester, and Master Thomas, official of Canterbury, but little more is known of them.[7]

The archdeacon presented himself as a suitable judge delegate. His chief function was to act as the bishop's officer

---

[1] See below, p. 145. [2] Glos. Cart. ii, no. dccxiii.

[3] Chron. Abb. Evesham, pp. 150–1; and see Ann. Mon. iv. 395.

[4] See above, pp. 49–51, and A.N.C., p. 325. A Master Robert de Clipstone is found as a witness to a St. Frideswide's charter of 1200 (Oseney Cart. ii, no. 788), and he occurs twice more as a witness in the Oseney cartulary between 1197 and 1201 (iv, nos. 39B and D) and in 1204 (Pershore Cart., f. 106ᵛ). He also acted as an arbiter probably during 1201 (Letters of Inn. III, no. 279). [5] P.R.O. E 326/3943.

[6] Rathbone, 'Influence of Bishops', i. 317, citing Kenilworth Cart., f. 47ᵛ.

[7] Great Chartulary of Glastonbury, i, ed. A. Watkin (Som. Rec. Soc. lix, 1947), no. (XXII), pp. (viii)–(ix); and Lewes Cart., f. 228ᵛ, cal. Lewes Cart. N.P., no. 231. There are references to the officials of Winchester and Canterbury in 1225–6 (Chartulary of Winchester Cathedral, cal. A. W. Goodman (Winchester, 1927), no. 397, and Lanthony Cart. A2, f. 4ʳ), and in 1220–7 (Cart. of . . . St. Gregory Canterbury, ed. A. M. Woodcock (Camden Soc. 3rd Ser. lxxxviii, 1956), no. 192), but the names are not given.

outside the cathedral precincts and within a defined territorial area. In the cathedral church he had no jurisdiction and
few duties. The centre of his activities was the archdeaconry,
a subdivision of the diocese, where he ranked second only to
the bishop.[1] He held his own court, and his clerks were
mostly lawyers. Often he had his own official, and he too
was sometimes appointed judge delegate. Master P(eter)
Peyure, official of the archdeacon of Bedford, settled a cause
alone in November 1239, as delegate of the legate Otto.[2]
The officials of the archdeacons of Buckingham and Colchester, and Master R., official of the archdeacon of Leicester, and W., official of the archdeacon of Surrey, are also
found acting.[3] The archdeacon who took his title from the
cathedral church was the *archidiaconus major* of the diocese,
but his precedence was merely titular over the other archdeacons. His rights and duties remained limited to the
recognized area of his archdeaconry.[4] Evidence survives of
121 mandates sent to archdeacons of every diocese ordering
them to act as judges delegate. One who seems to have been
of some repute was Master Henry Tessun, archdeacon of
Bath, who acted alone in 1245–6.[5] He had been a canon of
Salisbury as early as *c.* 1222, when he is found acting in a
judge-delegate cause as an arbiter.[6] Master John of Ferentino, who as archdeacon of Norwich from 1228 to 1247
acted as a judge delegate, had been especially active in
carrying out provision mandates for the pope, but he was
one of those who escaped the attack on the foreign clergy of

---

[1] A. Hamilton Thompson, *The English Clergy and their Organization in the Later
Middle Ages* (Oxford, 1947), pp. 248, and 251, and 'Diocesan Organization in the
Middle Ages: Archdeacons and Rural Deans', *Proceedings of the British Academy*,
xxix (1943), 7 and 13.

[2] Dunstable Cart., f. 55ᵛ, cal. *Dunstable Cart.*, no. 549.

[3] B.M. Harley Ch. 43 A 44; Windsor, Arundel White Bk., p. 215; Castle Acre
Cart., f. 47ʳ; and P.R.O. E 135/4/17, cal. *Lewes Cart. N.P.*, no. 70.

[4] Hamilton Thompson, *English Clergy*, p. 58, and 'Diocesan Organization',
p. 9.

[5] Bodleian MS. Chs. Oxon. a 8, Ch. 29b.

[6] *Malmesbury Reg.* ii. 18, and see K. Major, 'The *Familia* of Robert Grosseteste'
in *Robert Grosseteste Scholar and Bishop*, ed. D. A. Callus (Oxford, 1955), p. 239;
he held the prebend of Bedminster in 1243, and retained it as archdeacon of Bath.
He is found as a witness to a charter of judges delegate from Lincoln diocese, the
prior of Luffield and the archdeacon and dean of Buckingham, in 1232, P.R.O.
DL 25/15.

December 1231.[1] The archdeacons of St. Albans, London (St. Paul's), Rochester, Buckingham, Colchester, and Northampton acted frequently.

Each archdeaconry was subdivided into a number of rural deaneries, or deaneries of Christianity.[2] The deanery was a small territorial area which included a group of country or town parishes. Its administrative officer, the rural dean, had no judicial powers unless they were delegated to him by the bishop, but he had an unrivalled knowledge of the locality, arising from his powers of supervising and reporting.[3] He was the immediate officer of the spiritual court or court Christian, responsible to the bishop and appointed by him. Hamilton Thompson has said that it is seldom that we come into contact with the rural dean in the day-to-day execution of his work.[4] Much of the rural dean's work, however, was concerned with the delegated courts, and here he may clearly be seen as judge delegate, subdelegate, and executive officer. In this period at least 118 mandates were dispatched to sixty-six rural deans.[5] The difficulty of identifying persons again prevails. For the most part they remain obscure rectors, but three were

---

[1] St. Augustine's Red Book, f. 274ʳ. See H. Mackenzie, 'The Anti-Foreign Movement in England, 1231–1232', *Haskins Anniversary Essays* (New York, 1950), p. 194 n. 50. Mentioned as papal subdeacon (*C.P.L.* i. 120), and as papal chamberlain (*C.P.L.* i. 157).

[2] Hamilton Thompson, *English Clergy*, pp. 63–4, and 67–8. The title is used indiscriminately, for instance the deans of Wilbraham, Cambridge, and Chesterton are all mentioned in the mandate as deans of Christianity (P.R.O. E 40/13828[c], and E 40/14302).

[3] Hamilton Thompson, *English Clergy*, p. 67, and see also P. Andrieu-Guitrancourt, *Essai sur l'évolution du décanat rural en Angleterre* (Paris, 1935).

[4] Hamilton Thompson, 'Diocesan Organization', p. 36.

[5] The deans of Abingdon, Andover, Bedford, Berkhamsted, Bosmere, Bristol, Brooke, Buckingham, Bury St. Edmunds, Cambridge, Canterbury, Carlby, Chester, Chesterton, Colchester, Covenham, Dartford, 'Depwade', Donnington, Dumbleton, Dunstable, Dunwich, Dymock, Ely, Ewell, Gloucester, Hampton, Haseley, Hertford, Holland, Holt, Hoxne, Huntingdon, Iffley, Ipswich, Islip, Langford, Leicester, Luton, Lynn, Malmesbury, Marlborough, Ness, Newbury, Newport Pagnell, Northampton, Norwich, Oxford, Patney, Preston, Reading, Repps, Rochester, Rutland, Sapey, Southwark, Stamford, Stanton, Walsingham, Warwick, Whitchurch, Wilbraham, Wilton, Winchester, Wisbech, and Witham. Until well into the thirteenth century the title of the deanery depended on the place of the residence of the dean or was taken from the benefice which he held (Hamilton Thompson, 'Diocesan Organization', p. 28), so that is is sometimes difficult to locate the actual area of jurisdiction and to separate the personnel correctly.

certainly masters, Master G., dean of Ipswich in 1225–6, Master S. de Risinge, dean of Hoxne in 1221, and Master W., dean of Canterbury in 1233–4;[1] and many of them may have had some legal knowledge. For instance, one country parson, Master Peter of Paxton, who was appointed a judge delegate in company with the prior of Huntingdon (Aug.) and a Master Aristotle in about 1198,[2] possessed a complete set of civil and canon law treatises.[3] Master A. de Wilne, who acted with Leicestershire and other Midland judges, appears to have been a rector.[4] Two other rectors, R., of St. Antoninus, London, and E., rector of Boxley (Kent), who were employed as judges, were masters, and may have had some legal knowledge; but of Robert, rector of Haddenham (Cambs.), the rector of Aynho (Northants.), C. (?), rector of All Saints, Worcester, and Roger, chaplain of St. Thomas's, Oxford, who served as judges delegate during this period, nothing is known.[5]

The officers of the bishop's cathedral church, as well as those directly responsible to him in the diocese, were also sought as judges delegate. As the immediate head, under the bishop, of the secular cathedral chapter, the dean had administrative and judicial experience. He was also visitor of the cathedral clergy. Like any other dignitary or prebendary, the dean had his own court for the proof of wills and other ecclesiastical causes on the estates belonging to his dignity.[6] If a man with legal knowledge and experience was required as judge the dean was an obvious choice. Some seventy-two mandates were sent to deans of cathedrals: the deans of Lincoln, London, and Salisbury, and the subdeans of Lincoln and Wells, received a large proportion.

The precentor, the dignitary in charge of the ceremonial

---

[1] Eye Cart., ff. 34ᵛ, 36ʳ; and P.R.O. E 40/13828 (f).

[2] Bardney Cart., f. 203ʳ⁻ᵛ.

[3] A.N.C., p. 281, citing Reg. Antiq. Linc. iii, p. 164 (no. 821).

[4] Facsimiles of Early Cheshire Charters, ed. G. Barraclough (Lancs. and Cheshire Rec. Soc. 1957), p. 28; and Letters of Inn. III, nos. 545, 563, and 665.

[5] N.L.C., nos. 45, 46; P.R.O. SC 7/19/14; West Dereham Cart., ff. 239ᵛ, 294ʳ⁻ᵛ; Magdalen College, Oxford, Brackley Ch. 62, cal. W. D. Macray, 'Collection of Brackley Deeds at Magdalen College, Oxford', Bucks. Advertiser (1910); Letters of Inn. III, no. 1187; and Oseney Cart. v, nc. 879D.

[6] K. Edwards, English Secular Cathedrals in the Middle Ages, 2nd edn. (Manchester, 1967), pp. 137, 147.

and the conduct of the services, did not escape acting as a judge delegate. In all the English secular cathedrals with the exception of St. Paul's, Exeter, before 1225, and possibly York in the twelfth and early thirteenth centuries, he was recognized as second dignitary after the dean.[1] Often he was a lawyer or had legal training. Benedict of Sawston, precentor of London, lectured in law at Paris (where he was living in 1214),[2] and later became bishop of Rochester. As Master Benedict, canon of St. Paul's, he had heard cases with the archdeacon of London and S(tephen) Ridell, clerk, in 1201, and with the archdeacon of Colchester and Richard of Stortford, master of the schools of St. Paul's, before or during the early part of 1203.[3] As precentor he heard a delegated case in 1205 and another in 1206/7.[4] Master Robert of Cadney, precentor of Lincoln, who settled a suit in 1251, had been official of Lincoln and one of Grosseteste's *familia*.[5] Thirty-one mandates were sent to the precentors of Chichester, Hereford, Lichfield, Lincoln, London, Salisbury, and Wells. The precentor of Salisbury received the greatest number of mandates.

Of the other dignitaries of the cathedral church, the chancellor was the most obvious choice as a judge delegate. He was the successor of the twelfth-century 'magister scholarum' of the secular cathedrals, lecturing in theology and canon law. The centres of legal teaching of the late twelfth century had been the cathedral schools, the most famous of which were Lincoln, Exeter, and York; and London and Hereford also had some reputation.[6] The cathedral school at Salisbury had a late flowering in the thirteenth century and surpassed all the others in legal studies,[7] and the chancellor of Salisbury

---

[1] Edwards, *English Secular Cathedrals*, pp. 159–60, and see also *Statutes of Lincoln Cathedral*, i, ed. H. Bradshaw and C. Wordsworth (Cambridge, 1892), 105, and 136–8.   [2] *A.N.C.*, p. 289.

[3] *Letters of Inn. III*, no. 348; and *C.R.R.* ii. 267, 298.

[4] B.M. Wolley Ch. v 27; and *Chron. Abb. Evesham*, pp. 191, 193, and 222.

[5] B.M. Harley Ch. 53 A 23, and Major, '*Familia* of Robert Grosseteste', pp. 218 and 223.

[6] Edwards, *English Secular Cathedrals*, pp. 176–203. At Hereford in the fourteenth century, however, it was the penitentiary who was expected to teach canon law (ibid. pp. 197–8). It is not surprising to find the penitentiary of Canterbury, Master John, as a judge delegate in 1218, and an unnamed holder of the office in 1220–7 (P.R.O. E 40/14198; and *St. Gregory's Cart.*, no. 192).

[7] Edwards, *English Secular Cathedrals*, pp. 191–2.

received at least thirteen mandates.¹ Lincoln too produced a notable succession of chancellors, William de Montibus, Roger de Insula, and Master Nicholas de Wadyngham.² The treasurer, who was fourth dignitary in many of the secular cathedrals, also acted as a judge delegate. Twenty mandates were sent to the treasurers of Chichester, Exeter, Hereford, Lichfield, Lincoln, London, Salisbury, and Wells. The continuing importance of the legal schools in the secular cathedrals is reflected in the group of canons who acted as judges delegate. Nearly all of them were masters. Masters John, P., W. Durand, and W. de Kainesham represented Chichester.³ Lincoln provided Masters Henry de Gylevylle, John of Tynemouth, Robert de Gravele, R. de Holm, Thomas de Fiskertona, and Walter Blund.⁴ London provided Masters William of Purleigh and William de Sancte Marie Ecclesia, and from Salisbury came a notable array, including Master Robert de Bingham.⁵ Master John of Tynemouth, canon of Lincoln, and Master Henry of Bishopstone, canon of Salisbury, had connections with the Oxford law school. Master John had taught Thomas of Marlborough in Oxford and later became archdeacon there.⁶ Master Henry had lectured in canon law at Oxford, and was

---

¹ P.R.O. E 210/3736; *Reg. Hon. III*, no. 1810 (*C.P.L.* i. 161); *Oseney Cart.* ii, no. 1042, and see vi, no. 38; *Sarum Chs.* cxlv; *Thame Cart.*, no. 37; Pershore Cart., ff. 109ᵛ-10ʳ; *Cart. of Buckland Priory*, ed. F. W. Weaver (Som. Rec. Soc. xxv, 1909), no. 13; Bradenstoke Cart., ff. 119ᵛ-20ʳ; *N.L.C.*, no. 27; *Selborne Chs.* 252, 326 (Macray, *Calendar*, i. 20, 24–5); *Oseney Cart.* iv, nos. 153, 250, and see vi, no. 47; and Magdalen College, Oxford, Greensted and Stanford Ch. 1.

² Bardney Cart., ff. 92ʳ and 240ʳ; Wherwell Cart., f. 99ʳ; *Letters of Inn. III*, no. 989A; Daventry Cart., f. 151ʳ; and B.M. Harley Ch. 53 A 23. For William de Montibus, see also Hunt, 'English Learning', p. 21. Roger de Insula became dean of York in 1220 (*York Minster Fasti*, i, ed. C. T. Clay (Yorks. Archaeol. Soc. Rec. Ser. cxxiii, 1957), 3).

³ Dover Cart., f. 175ᵛ; P.R.O. E 327/44; Eye Cart., ff. 44ᵛ-5ʳ; and Lewes Cart., f. 311ʳ-ᵛ, cal. *S.P.* ii. 128–30.

⁴ Crowland Cart., f. 94; Northampton, St. Andrew's Cart. (A), f. 241ᵛ; *Winchester Cart.*, no. 484; Eye Cart., f. 39ᵛ; Bardney Cart., ff. 92ʳ, 240ʳ; and the cartulary of Thurgarton priory, owned by the chapter of Southwell, no. 1066, cited in *Reg. Antiq. Linc.* viii, p. 113 n.

⁵ *Malmesbury Reg.* ii. 60–4; P.R.O. E 40/14953; *Reg. Greg. IX*, no. 360; and St. Augustine's Cart., f. 79ʳ, and *Oseney Cart.* v, no. 851B.

⁶ *A.N.C.*, pp. 317 and 325. John was a canon of Lincoln from (?)1206 to 1215, and archdeacon of Oxford from 1215 to 1221. He had acted as a judge delegate when in Archbishop Hubert Walter's household (Canterbury, MS. Scrapbk. A, p. 86, no. 160).

to rule the school at New Salisbury.¹ Two canons of Salisbury, who heard a judge-delegate case in 1250, Master (?)Ralph of York and Peter de Cimba, may well have been products of the school there and pupils of Master Henry.² But by the early thirteenth century most of the canons had been trained at the universities, and the chancellors of the universities were obvious choices as judges delegate. The chancellor of Oxford was a popular judge delegate, acting frequently with the dean of Oxford and the prior of St. Frideswide's,³ and an early reference to the chancellor of Oxford by name (Master G.) is found in a papal commission acting on a mandate of 4 February 1222.⁴ He may be identifiable with Master Geoffrey de Lucy, chancellor, who heard a case in company with T., parson of St. Clement's, Oxford, and rural dean, presumably between 27 June 1214 and the middle of August 1216.⁵ Similarly the chancellor of Cambridge is mentioned, but only twice, and both times with the prior of Barnwell (Aug. Camb.).⁶

Masters of schools were sometimes called upon to make up commissions with other local ecclesiastics. Thus the master of the schools at Lincoln acted with the dean and a

¹ Edwards, *English Secular Cathedrals*, p. 191, and *Malmesbury Reg.* ii. 18. On the Oxford law school see Richardson, 'Oxford Law School', pp. 319 ff.

² *Reg. Inn. IV*, no. 5024.

³ See, e.g., *Reg. Antiq. Linc.* iii, no. 1019; Lanthony Cart. A I, III, no. liv; St. Neots Cart., f. 111ʳ⁻ᵛ; *Oseney Cart.* iv, no. 137A; B.M. Add. Ch. 21888; and P.R.O. SC7 15 (27).

⁴ Northampton, St. James' Cart., f. 109ʳ. A predecessor, Master Alard, rector of the schools, is found excusing himself from serving as a judge delegate in a case settled in 1210 (Abingdon Cart., f. 144ᵛ). J. Grim, master of the schools, was ordered to serve as a judge delegate with the priors of St. Frideswide's and Oseney in 1201 (*Letters of Inn. III*, no. 279).

⁵ Gloucester, D. and C. Library, Reg. B, pp. 21–2; pd. M. G. Cheney, 'Master Geoffrey de Lucy, an early chancellor of the university of Oxford', *E.H.R.* lxxxii (1967), 762–3, who dates the documents. It is unlikely that Master G. can refer to Grosseteste, who would surely occur as Master R., and for the date of whose chancellorship the evidence is very shaky; but there seems no reason to suppose that this Master G. could not be Geoffrey de Lucy, whose earliest known occurrence at St. Paul's is in 1223. The argument that there was a vacancy before 1222 rests on the translation of the phrase 'cancellario non existente', which occurs at the stage of the contestation of a suit which had been delegated to the chancellor of Oxford and others on 23 (*sic*, not 22) March 1221 (*Oseney Cart.* v, no. 851A), but this might mean merely that the chancellor did not put in an appearance from this point onwards. All in all, the evidence suggests that Master G. is Master Geoffrey de Lucy who remained chancellor until early 1223.

⁶ *N.L.C.*, nos. 85–6; and Bodleian MS. Chs. Berks. a 1, Ch. 17.

canon, Master Robert de Gravele, in 1224, and in 1238 a settlement was made by the master in company with the sub-dean and precentor of Lincoln.[1] The master of the schools at Marlborough appeared on the same bench as the prior of St. Margaret's (Gilb.) and the dean of Christianity at Marl-borough, and the master of the schools at Shaftesbury with the local dean.[2]

4. Attitude to Service and Efficiency

Considering the widespread use of many varieties of per-sonnel, it is remarkable that few complaints are to be found about the efficiency of the judges. Reports of ignorance of the law on the part of the judges occur but rarely. A new judge, the bishop of Salisbury (Richard Poore), was appoint-ed in 1220 to replace the dean of Winchester, who was said to be ignorant of the law,[3] and the priors of Binham (Ben. Norf.) and Bordesley (Cist. Worcs.) are found alleging this of themselves in order to gain exemption.[4] These are the only known instances. Unfairness was more seriously re-garded by the papacy than ignorance. A judge delegate could be refused if he did not fulfil the statutory require-ments of the canon law or if he was suspected of unfairness. Legal handbooks provide paragraphs 'De recusatione iudi-cis'.[5] For instance, a judge delegate who was the employer of the impetrant, a relative of one of the parties, or a member of the same household, could be refused.[6] The rector of St. Aldate's, Gloucester, obtained a mandate to Bishop Mauger of Worcester and others, but soon after this he joined the bishop's household. New judges were appointed in 1206 to hear the case unless it was established that Mauger's com-mission was accepted after the rector's appointment to his household.[7] The dean of Patney (Wilts.) was refused by the

---

[1] Eye Cart, f. 39ᵛ; and Westminster Domesday, f. 470ʳ.

[2] *Sarum Chs.* ccxxi; and Reading Cart., f. 114ʳ. The master of the schools at Malton is also found serving, Alvingham Cart., f. 5ʳ.

[3] *Reg. Hon. III*, no. 2366 (*C.P.L.* i. 70).   [4] See below, p. 147.

[5] Bencivenna of Siena, '*Invocato Christi Nomine*', p. 40. Tancred, p. 146; Drogheda, cdli, p. 396; and Damasus Hungarus, '*Summa de Ordine Iudiciario*', xxviii, p. 22.   [6] cc. 17, 25. X. I. 29 and c. 36. X. II. 28.

[7] *Letters of Inn. III*, no. 678. For another example of a judge being replaced because he was the impetrant's employer, see Morey, *Bartholomew of Exeter*, p. 69.

villagers of Combwich (Som.) as a judge in about 1201; unfortunately the reason is not recorded.[1] On grounds of suspecting the judges—the abbots of Malmesbury, Abingdon, and Evesham, who were all Black Monks—of unfairness, Mauger bishop of Worcester appealed to Rome and got a commission to the bishop of Ely, the prior of Coventry, and the archdeacon of Northampton in 1203.[2] Usually arbiters were appointed who considered the complaint about the judges on the spot.[3] Unfairness of action was severely regarded. When the prior of Bolton (Aug. Yorks. W.R.) and his fellow judges were charged with exceeding the mandate and acting unfairly, the papal legate Otto was ordered to suspend them and cite them before the pope if he found that the allegation was justified. These judges were said to have been corrupted by bribes.[4] To proceed when the mandate had been revoked was similarly a grave action.[5]

The duty of serving as a judge delegate was onerous. In theory no ecclesiastic was exempt from it, and from the foregoing evidence the persons used are so diverse as to suggest that almost everyone who held office in the Church must have served from time to time as a judge delegate. A pope such as Innocent III might make it appear a spiritual duty. Occasionally he terminated the mandate with:

Tu denique fili abbas super te ipso et credito tibi grege taliter vigilare procures extirpando vicia et plantando virtutes, ut, in novissimo districti examinis die coram tremendo iudice qui reddet unicuique secundum opera sua, dignam possis reddere rationem.[6]

---

[1] Lanthony Cart. A1, VIII, no. lxxxiii.

[2] *Chron. Abb. Evesham*, p. 123, cited by D. Knowles, *Monastic Order in England* (Cambridge, 1950), p. 336.

[3] Damasus Hungarus, '*Summa de Ordine Iudiciario*', pp. 22–3, and c. 41. *X*. II. 28.

[4] *Reg. Greg. IX*, no. 3764. Cf. the comments of Bulgarus, '*Excerpta Legum Edita a Bulgarino Causidico*', *Quellen zur Geschichte*, iv, pt. i, ed. L. Wahrmund (Innsbruck, 1925), p. 10: 'Judex, si depravatus pretio vel gratia perperam iudicavit, vindictam non modo extimationis, verum etiam litis dispendium sustinebit. Si per inscientiam et inprudentiam male iudicavit, condempnabitur, quantum videbitur aequum religioni iudicis iudicantis de ea re.'

[5] *Montacute Cart.*, no. 143. See above, p. 104.

[6] Westminster Domesday, f. 276[r] (abb. of Woburn: 30 Nov. 1212); f. 228[r] (abb. of Warden: 16 Mar. 1215); Northampton, St. Andrews' Cart. (A), f. 120[r] (abb. of Walden: 11 Jan.—); Lanthony Cart. A1, VIII, no. lxxviii (abbs. of Dore and Flaxley: 23 Jan. 1213); *Oseney Cart.* iv, no. 156A (abbs. of Thame and Bruern: 11 Dec. 1214). Cf. *Lotharii Cardinalis (Innocentii III) De Miseria Humane Condi-*

On a mundane level this service interfered with the judge's normal duties and meant considerable loss of time. Sometimes it necessitated travelling. Furthermore, the receipt of a mandate frequently involved the judge in several different lawsuits. On the other hand, the advantages which these legal duties brought to the individual judge cannot be measured. Innocent III had decreed that judges ought to hear suits without charge, although it was acknowledged as customary to exact a tenth on the suit;[1] it is unlikely that the judges allowed themselves to lose financially. As for the incidence of bribes it is impossible to form any opinion, although French legatine and provincial councils forbade judges to take money and presents, which suggests that gifts were not unusual.[2] Promising clerics may have been brought to the notice of the bishop or superior through judge-delegate service, but it is more likely that it was precisely those men who already enjoyed some reputation who were called upon to serve. At any rate from the evidence available it cannot be held that the judges were actively resisting the hearing of lawsuits, but they had been provided, and to some extent had provided themselves, with methods of exemption.

(i) Subdelegation

From the point of view of both judges and *Curia*, provision had to be made for those who were unable to serve. The inclusion of the *quod si non omnes* clause, commonly found in the mandate by 1198, was devised to avoid delay and to save reference back to Rome if the fulfilment of the commission was impeded. It meant that the judges could proceed without one of their number or, if the delegation was to two judges, that one could act without the other.[3]

---

tionis, ed. M. Maccarone (Lucani–Rome, 1955), p. 95: 'Ipse est iudex iustus, fortis et longaminis, qui "nec prece, nec precio", nec amore, nec odio declinat a semita rectitudinis, sed via regia semper incedens, nullum malum preterit impunitum, nullum bonum irremuneratum relinquit. Hunc nemo potest corrumpere, iuxta quod inquit psalmista: "Tu reddes singulis secundum opera eorum".'

[1] c. 10. *X*. III. 1, and see Aegidius de Fuscarariis, '*Ordo Iudiciarius*', *Quellen zur Geschichte*, iii, pt. i, ed. L. Wahrmund (Innsbruck, 1916), lxvi, p. 121, 'De salario iudicum', where he quotes the same ruling. His work was completed between 1263 and 1266 (Stickler, col. 1138).

[2] Hefele, *Conciles*, v, pt. ii. 1501, can. 43, and 1533, can. 35.

[3] *Decretum*, C. 2 qu. 5 c. 17.

Thus although the abbot of Peterborough, who was appointed a judge in 1209, had died before the mandate was received, and Andrew canon of Ferentino was away from England in 1253, the other members of these commissions legitimately proceeded.[1] This had not been allowed in a case of 1156:

... he [the bishop of London] also explained that without the bishop of Worcester to whom the investigation of the cause had been delegated jointly with himself—although he had not appeared on the appointed day—he neither could nor ought to judge between them.[2]

The *quod si non omnes* clause also enabled a judge to excuse himself from service if, although present, he had for some grave reason to decline to serve.[3] Technically, the judge by excusing himself from service automatically conferred his powers on the other members of the same commission.

A natural development from this was that a judge was allowed to appoint a substitute, to excuse himself and confer his powers on another. There may have been a distinction, which is no longer discernible, between subdelegation if the powers had been granted *simpliciter*, that is in common, and subdelegation if the powers were *in solidum*, or jointly held: namely that, if granted *simpliciter*, subdelegation would be to a member of the same commission, but if made *in solidum* subdelegation could be to any other ecclesiastic. Subdelegation enabled a commission to proceed, without further reference to Rome, if more than one delegate had to avoid service.[4] It may have arisen that the incapability of the majority of a commission to serve necessitated subdelegation. As Professor Brooke has pointed out, acting without a colleague was a prior development to subdelegation.[5] It remained a distinct process in its own right in the thirteenth century, although it does not seem to have been frequently

---

[1] Thorney Cart. ii, f. 322^r; and B.M. Harley Ch. 84 F 45. See also c. 14. *X.* I. 29: in the event of the delegate dying before the mandate reached him, if it was made out to the office and did not mention him by name, his successor to the office might hear the case.   [2] *J.S.L.*, no. 14.

[3] c. 3. *X.* I. 29. Cooper, *Select Scottish Cases*, pp. xxx–xxxi, regards the excuse often made by the judges that they were too busy to serve as without the strict rule stated in this decretal.

[4] c. 3. *X.* I. 29: 'Delegatus Papae impeditus subdelegare potest causam, quae sine ipso commode terminari potest.'   [5] *J.S.L.*, p. xxxiv.

used. A list of judges for this period, who neither served nor appointed subdelegates, is short, comprising some thirty-five names only.

Subdelegation was well established by the time of Innocent III, but appears to have been little used during his pontificate. Throughout the whole period from 1198 to 1254 it was an infrequent practice. A list of the subdelegates who were used in the southern province totals eighty in all. The records suggest, however, that subdelegation may have increased in the two later pontificates, that is between 1227 and 1254. A distinct numerical rise is traceable. Of those subdelegations that can be precisely dated, sixty-eight come from after 1227, as opposed to eight from before this date.[1]

The choice of subdelegates seems to have depended on geographical proximity. Nearby ecclesiastics and those from the same house were appointed. The precentor of Barnwell, for instance, subdelegated to the dean of Cambridge; the prior of Caldwell committed his powers to the sacrist; and the prior of Evesham to the dean of Evesham.[2] Priors often conferred their duties on subpriors, cathedral dignitaries on canons and clerks, and the bishop and archdeacon on their officials.[3] Usually the subdelegates were from a lower stratum in the ecclesiastical hierarchy than the delegates. The general tendency was to delegate lower, in order to be sure to find someone to act. The choice may be said to have been guided more by convenience than by any direct policy. There is no evidence that the parties chose the subdelegates, as Dr. Brentano has suggested for the late thirteenth century; on the contrary, subdelegation letters suggest that the judges chose them, possibly with the consent of the parties.[4]

A prominent class among the subdelegates is formed by the deans, masters, and secular canons. More seculars than regulars were used as subdelegates. The rural deans seem to

---

[1] Four commissions cannot be precisely dated.

[2] B.M. Harley Ch. 84 F 45; *Godstow Reg.* i, no. [94]; and Pipewell Cart. (A), ff. 29ᵛ–31ᵛ.

[3] e.g. *Cartularium Monasterii Sancti Johannis Baptiste de Colecestria*, i, ed. S. A. Moore (Roxburghe Club, 1897), 100; Bodleian MS. Dodsworth 76, f. 44; and *Reg. Greg. IX*, no. 567.

[4] Brentano, *York Metropolitan Jurisdiction*, p. 278. For examples see below, pp. 140–1.

have been frequently chosen, and there is mention of the deans of Abingdon, Buckrose, Cambridge, Cirencester, Middlesex, and Southwark, for example.[1] In many instances ecclesiastics served in both capacities as judge delegate and as subdelegate during their lifetime. There are some who seem to have made frequent appearances as subdelegates. Master Roger de Cantilupe, clerk, served between 1221 and 1224, again in 1226, and again in about 1231.[2] In 1225 he appears as a witness to a document, in 1227–8 he acted as an arbiter, and in 1233–5 as a judge delegate.[3] By 1231 he was being used by the king on business at Rome, and by February 1240 he had been rewarded with a canonry of St. Paul's and the prebend of Cantlers.[4] Master William de Novo Castro figured as a subdelegate in cases as widely separated as one of March 1215 and another of 1250.[5] These men seem to have been gathered in important legal centres, attached to some ecclesiastic's household or to the schools. Master Roger de Cantilupe was active at Oxford, of which university he was probably a master. It is noteworthy that when the chancellor of Oxford subdelegated on three occasions, the commissions included Oxford masters and clerks: Master Elias de Daneis, Master Ralph of Sempringham,[6] and in company with the archdeacon and dean of Oxford, Master (J.) de Poppleton, R. de Thetford, and S. de Dyham.[7] He also subdelegated to Nicholas, deacon, and Bartholomew of Chieveley, a monk of Abingdon.[8] Master William de Novo Castro acted at Lincoln, where the canons and other

---

[1] *Reg. Greg. IX*, no. 5182; Alvingham Cart., f. 5ʳ; B.M. Harley Ch. 84 F 45; *Glos. Cart.* i, no. ccxxxvi; Windsor Ch. xi G 27; and Westminster Domesday, f. 379ᵛ.

[2] *St. Frideswide's Cart.* i, no. 46; ii, no. 721; *Oseney Cart.* iv, no. 45; and *Reg. Greg. IX*, no. 567.

[3] *Oseney Cart.* v, no. 851C; iv, no. 68; *St. Frideswide's Cart.* ii, no. 721; and Lanthony Cart. A1, XVI, no. xvi. He was a canon of St. Davids by 1233–5.

[4] *Patent Rolls of the Reign of Henry III 1225–32* (1903), pp. 423–4, cited with other references by Emden, *Oxf. Reg.* i. 347.

[5] Bodleian MS. Dodsworth 76, f. 44, and P.R.O. E 135/6/13.

[6] He became chancellor of Oxford himself by *c.* 1249 and dean of Lichfield in 1253, see Emden, *Oxf. Reg.* iii. 1669.

[7] *Malmesbury Reg.* ii. 30, 59; B.M. Cotton MS. Nero C iii, f. 199; and Harley Ch. 84 F 43.

[8] *Oseney Cart.* iv, no. 137A. Cf. Pershore Cart., f. 106v—subdelegation to monks, but it was not usual and these subdelegates were helped at the settlement.

officials were often subdelegates.[1] Master Alexander Blund, canon of Lichfield, is another of the genre; he served as a subdelegate in 1248 and *c.* 1250.[2] Other subdelegates with substantial legal training were the officials of the archdeacons of London and Worcester and of the bishops of Winchester and Worcester.[3]

The use of vicars and chaplains was not infrequent, but for the most part they appear to be from town churches, particularly from Oxford and around. The vicars of Cumnor and Haseley, Reginald, chaplain of St. Aldate's, Oxford, and the chaplains of St. Peter's in the East and St. John the Baptist's, Oxford, are all found acting.[4] The chaplain of St. Mary's, Cambridge, served with the subprior and precentor of Barnwell as a subdelegate of the prior and dean of Huntingdon; and Thomas of St. Botolph's, London, priest, was a subdelegate of the dean of London in 1233–4.[5] Not all these minor clerics, however, who served as subdelegates were from town churches. Walter, vicar of Croxton (Leics.), heard a case with the dean of Framland in 1241, and in 1245 the rector of Edvin Loach or Ralph (Heref.) and the vicar of Martley (Worcs.) gave sentence in a subdelegation *ad totam causam.*[6] In probably 1252 an objection was made by the abbot and convent of Dore (Cist. Heref.) against the vicar of Talgarth (Breconshire), who had been constituted a subdelegate, probably *in parte,* by the prior of Carmarthen (Aug.). Dore argued that the vicar was not able to act as a judge because he was not in possession of any dignity.[7] This reflected the decision of Innocent IV in the First Council of Lyons of 1245, where it was stated that only dignitaries, canons, and the like should be asked to act as judges and

---

[1] See, e.g., Bardney Cart., ff. 105ᵛ, 213ʳ; Lichfield, Magnum Registrum Album, f. 187; and *Cartularium Abbathiae de Rievalle*, ed. J. C. Atkinson (Surtees Soc. lxxxiii, 1889), no. ccclxvi.

[2] Bodleian MS. Chs. Oxon. a 1, Ch. 11, and B.M. Harley Ch. 84 F 44.

[3] *Reg. Greg. IX*, no. 567; *Reg. Antiq. Linc.* ii, no. 355; and *N.L.C.*, no. 9.

[4] *Oseney Cart.* ii, no. 1112; *St. Frideswide's Cart.* ii, no. 1053; *Oseney Cart.* iv, no. 45; and 'Burton Chs.' 58.

[5] B.M. Stowe Ch. 163, and P.R.O. E 40/13828(f).

[6] Belvoir, Large Cart., f. 54ʳ, and P.R.O. E 40/12969.

[7] P.R.O. E 135/24/4 (App. B (iii), no. 2). See c. 27. *X.* I. 29, and Damasus Hungarus, '*Summa de Ordine Iudiciario*', xxviii, p. 22: if a subdelegate is refused, the cause of refusal ought to be proved in front of the delegate of the pope.

subdelegates.[1] The procedural writer, Aegidius de Fuscarariis, says under the head 'Quando delegatus et quibus personis et sub qua forma debet committere vices suas':

Et debet subdelegare personis in dignitate constitutis vel institutis in ecclesiis cathedralibus et aliis collegiatis honorabilibus.[2]

There is every reason to suppose that delegation had penetrated lower in the hierarchy than the *Curia* intended, and that subdelegation had taken this a stage further. This ruling may have had some effect. The examples appointing chaplains and vicars date mainly from 1245 or before, but rural deans, rectors, and chaplains continue to occur as subdelegates after this date.[3]

Like the powers of the delegate, those of the subdelegate depended exclusively on his mandate, which could be limited or complete. The subdelegate was therefore either an officer appointed by the delegate and responsible to him or an equal with equivalent powers. When the prior of Bridlington subdelegated to the dean of Buckrose and Walter of Malton, clerk, in the Alvingham case, it was a partial subdelegation, and he wrote to his colleagues as follows:

Viris venerabilibus et discretis priori de Kirham [Kirkham] et magistro scolarum Maltone prior de Brideligton' salutem. Quoniam cognitioni cause vobis et nobis auctoritate apostolica commisse que vertitur inter tales et tales interesse non possumus, vices nostras decano Bukeros et Waltero de Malton clerico usque ad sentenciam diffinitivam committimus, ratum et gratum habituri quicquid utrique vel eorum alteri quem adesse contigerit una vobiscum subdelegatis vestris justicia mediante fecerit.[4]

But when the precentor of Barnwell subdelegated to the dean of Cambridge in 1253, he committed complete powers to him:

Precentor de Bernewell judex a domino papa delegatus discreto viro decano Cantebrug' salutem in domino. In causa que vertitur inter Jacobum rectorem ecclesie de Charewolton' ex una parte et religiosos

---

[1] *Sacrorum Conciliorum Collectio*, c. 2. ed. Mansi, xxiii, col. 619. Reiterated by Boniface VIII in his 'Statutum quod', c. 11. 6. I. 3.
[2] Aegidius de Fuscarariis, '*Ordo Iudiciarius*', v, p. 12. Cf. Ottobon in the Council of London (1268), *C.S.* ii, pt. ii. 772, no. [24].
[3] e.g. Westminster Domesday, f. 379ᵛ; Northampton, St. Andrew's Cart. (A), f. 208ʳ; and *Glos. Cart.* i, no. ccxxxvi.   [4] Alvingham Cart., f. 5ʳ.

viros abbatem et conventum de Bitlesdene ex altera, que nobis a domino papa commissa est, vobis vices nostras committimus insolidum, ratum et gratum habituri quicquid super dicta causa totaliter duxeritis faciendum. Idem partibus significamus.[1]

The stages of a suit were long and complex. The intricacy of the procedure, which defeated some commissions, made partial delegation useful. Subdelegates could also be used to make full inquiries, and collect all the data on the suit. For instance, the subprior and precentor of Barnwell and the chaplain of St. Mary's, Cambridge, were ordered by the prior and dean of Huntingdon to investigate a case, to send all the details they had elicited, and to summon the parties to appear on a certain day in St. Mary's church at Huntingdon to hear sentence.[2] Most partial subdelegations were for hearing the suit up to the sentence, *usque ad sentenciam diffinitivam.*[3] The main responsibility therefore rested with the delegates, and if an appeal was made, it went first to them.[4] A partial delegation to Thomas of St. Botolph's, London, priest, and his colleagues resulted in an appeal to the delegates, because one of the subdelegates wrongly proceeded alone with the assent of the others. The appeal continued on its way to the pope after the delegates had denied its validity.[5] The delegate was never free of the responsibility of a partial subdelegation. The subdelegates might bring about a composition, but for this to be made legal, confirmation by the delegates was needed. In a quarrel between the prior and convent of St. Martin, Dover, and the rector of Snargate (Kent), the judges delegate—the abbot and prior of Battle—committed the hearing to the abbots of Langdon and St. Radegund's. During the course of the hearing the parties desired to come to an amicable composition, and having done so, the rector of Snargate subjected himself to

---

[1] B.M. Harley Ch. 84 F 45. Arnulphus, lii, p. 55, gives some forms, as do most of the procedural writers, showing the various grades of subdelegation.

[2] B.M. Stowe Ch. 163.

[3] Bodleian MS. Chs. Norf. a 6, Ch. 624. See also, e.g., Bodleian MS. Chs. Oxon. a 1, Ch. 31, and MS. Chs. Bucks. a 3, Ch. 45; and B.M. Harley Ch. 84 F 43.

[4] P.R.O. E 135/24/4 (App. B (iii), no. 2).

[5] P.R.O. E 40/13828(f), and cf. the appeal of W., vicar of Elmdon, which went from subdelegates, the dean of Welton (Lincs.) and John, vicar of Brigstock (Northants.), to the principal judges, the abbot of Bourne and the prior of Newburgh, and thence to the pope in 1242 (Canterbury, *S.V.*, bk. ii, p. 202).

the jurisdiction of the principal judges for coercion, as the power still remained with them. The commissaries drew up a document, which the judges delegate confirmed, appending their seals.[1] Mandates which limited in time, rather than in extent of power, gave the subdelegate more freedom. The sacrist of Faversham was appointed by the prior to act for him until Christmas 1246 with full powers, and as commissary he passed two sentences, one of them on or soon after 31 October.[2]

Total subdelegation put the subdelegate on equal terms with the other members of the commission. It was a method of substitution. The judge merely transferred his mandate, handing over the powers which had been granted to him *in totum* or *ad totam causam* or *totaliter*.[3] The subdelegate was then directly responsible to the pope. When the abbot of Wigmore subdelegated to a certain canon in this way, not reserving sentence for himself and his colleagues, Gerald of Wales, the plaintiff, appealed to Rome.[4] As with proctorial commissions, subdelegations could be made to two people and could include the clause *sub alternatione*, whether the case was delegated totally or in part.[5] It eased, in some part, the exacting demands of the delegates on the subdelegates, and lessened the judges' responsibility.

A subdelegate could not refuse to serve, nor does he himself appear to have been able to subdelegate.[6] Furnished, however, with a reasonable excuse, or an indult exempting him from hearing cases, he might request exemption, as the prior of Repton did some time after 1234.[7] Subdelegation by one judge to several officials foreshadows the irresponsible practice, noted by Dr. Brentano in the late thirteenth cen-

[1] Dover Cart., ff. 228ᵛ–9ʳ.

[2] Ibid., ff. 50ᵛ–1ʳ.

[3] *Glos. Cart.* i, no. ccxxxvi; cf. Northampton, St. Andrew's Cart. (A), f. 208ʳ. B.M. Egerton Ch. 409; P.R.O. E 40/12969; *Reg. Roff.*, p. 457; *St. Frideswide's Cart.* ii, no. 721, and Belvoir, Large Cart., ff. 54ʳ and 88ʳ–ᵛ.

[4] Gerald of Wales, *Opera*, iii, ed. J. S. Brewer (R.S. xxi, 1863), 212–13.

[5] 'Peak Docs.', no. ii, pp. 135–6; Exeter Ch. 640; Windsor Ch. xi G 27; B.M. Harley Ch. 84 F 43; Bodleian MS. Chs. Oxon. a 5, Ch. 364; and a 1, Ch. 13b.

[6] c. 28. *X.* I. 29: 'Delegatus Papae, nisi malitione se exoneret, subdelegatum compellit ad suscipiendam subdelegationem' (Inn. III). Curialis, '*Ordo*', ii, p. 3.

[7] Burton Cart., ff. 62ᵛ–3ᵛ (xliiᵛ–xliiiᵛ), cal. G. Wrottesley, 'Abstract of the Contents of the Burton Chartulary', *Collections for a History of Staffordshire*, ed. William Salt Archaeol. Soc. v, pt. i (1884), 56.

tury, of conferring powers on as many as six or even nine men.[1] Undoubtedly the reason for this was to ensure the procuration of a subdelegate.[2] In 1246 Master Robert of Leicester, archdeacon of Ely, subdelegated to John,[3] prior of Canons Ashby, and Master Thomas de Syreford, rector; and the other member of the same commission, the precentor of Norwich, conferred his powers on John, chancellor, and the subprior of St. Frideswide's, Oxford, and the prior of the hospital of St. John at Northampton.[4] In the same way the abbot of Eynsham subdelegated to the parochial chaplain, the master of the schools, and the custodian of the hospital at Cirencester. His colleague, the prior of St. Frideswide's, committed his duties to the sacrist and succentor of Cirencester; while the third member of the commission, the dean of Oxford, subdelegated to the dean of Cirencester and Richard Pestevin. The settlement of 1242 was headed by the names of the sacrist, dean, and master of the schools at Cirencester.[5] Both these instances illustrate another unfortunate aspect of subdelegation, which was becoming more frequent: all the original judges of these commissions had declined to serve.

(ii) *Indults*

Subdelegation could only free the judge from a mandate which had been received. A more lasting step was to forestall the dispatch of judicial mandates. The judge might seek an indult exempting him from the duty of hearing lawsuits. Professor Cheney has noted a reference to an indult of this kind as early as 1141.[6] Complaints from the abbot of Fountains and the abbot of Oseney persuaded Lucius III and Urban III to grant them exemption if they

---

[1] *York Metropolitan Jurisdiction*, pp. 278, 280, and 'An Endorsed Subdelegation: 1284', *Traditio*, xiii (1957), 452–6.

[2] Bodleian MS. Chs. Bucks. a 3, Ch. 45.   [3] Mentioned also as 'G'.

[4] Northampton, St. Andrew's Cart. (A), ff. 208r–9r. The third member of the commission, the official of Norwich, excused himself from hearing the case.

[5] *Glos. Cart.* i, no. ccxxxvi.

[6] Cheney, *Becket to Langton*, p. 69, citing 'Der Bericht des Abtes Hariulf von Oudenburg über seine Prozessverhandlungen an der Römischen Kurie im Jahre 1141', ed. E. Müller, *Neues Archiv*, xlviii (1930), 112: 'Cancellarius ait: Non tibi dabitur dominus Carnotensis, quia . . . nec Laudunensis, quoniam optinuit, ut nulla sibi causa preter propria imponatur . . .'

were unwilling to serve.[1] Likewise on 25 October 1195 Celestine III exempted the prior of Snape (Ben. Suff.).[2] These few isolated and rare instances would suggest an expected reaction to a novel and irksome system on the part of a minority of officials, rather than any concerted effort to obtain exemption.

No indults of this kind, addressed to individual English ecclesiastics, remain from the pontificate of Innocent III. It is possible that he did not grant any. A concerted advance on this topic in 1211 by the Cistercian order, who were making use of their corporate organization, seems to have been ignored.[3] If single attempts were made by abbots and priors, they were probably rejected and dismissed. Just as the earlier indults follow the active pontificate of Alexander III, so the main body of indults for English judges comes after Innocent III. The development is almost peculiar to the pontificate of Honorius III, and twenty-three instances date from that period. The documents follow distinct formal patterns.[4] The Cistercians also received some satisfaction on the same score from Honorius III in 1219.[5] Yet taken over all the incidence of these grants is fractional.

Of the thirty-one indults that were conceded between the pontificates of Innocent III and Innocent IV, thirteen were addressed to Augustinians: the abbot of St. Augustine's, Bristol; the prior of Butley; the abbot of Cirencester (exempted by Honorius III and Innocent IV); the priors of Holy Trinity, Aldgate, and St. Bartholomew's, London; the

---

[1] *P.U.E.* iii, no. 368; *Oseney Cart.* iii, no. 12, and *P.U.E.* iii, no. 389.

[2] P.R.O. SC7 9 (4); sealed with a *bulla* on silk cords.

[3] Canivez, 'Étonnantes Concessions . . . à Cîteaux', pp. 505–9, cited by Cheney, *Becket to Langton*, p. 69; and *Statuta Ordinis Cisterciensis*, i, ed. Canivez, 385, no. 34: 'De eo quod Dominus Papa facit commissiones causarum abbatibus, prioribus et cellerariis Ordinis unde domus nostrae gravantur et Ordo, committitur Domino Cistercii, ut supplicet Domino Papae quatenus saltem de prioribus et subprioribus et cellerariis nobis, dignetur parcere, si placet.'

[4] The similarities in the wording of some of the indults, for example those granted to the prior of Holy Trinity, Aldgate, and the abbot of Bayham, may possibly suggest the use of the same proctor or the same formulary, *Foedera, Conventiones, Litterae etc.* i, ed. T. Rymer (Rec. Comm., 1816), 184–5 (P.R.O. SC7 18 [27] and [1]). Cf. also Waltham Cart., f. 73ʳ (App. B (iii), no. 4) with Canterbury, Reg. A, f. 20ʳ.

[5] Canivez, 'Étonnantes Concessions . . . à Cîteaux', pp. 507–8. Similarly the Franciscans received a general exemption from Gregory IX on 22 Apr. 1241 (*Reg. Greg. IX*, no. 5995).

abbot of Missenden; the prior, subprior, precentor, and sacrist of Oseney; the prior of Repton; the abbot and prior of St. Osyth's; the abbots of Thornton and Waltham; and the prior of West Acre.[1] Ten went to Benedictines: the abbots of Abingdon and Bardney; the priors of Belvoir and Binham; the abbot and prior of Bury St. Edmunds (separately); the prior, subprior, and precentor of Christ Church, Canterbury; the abbot and prior of St. Augustine's, Canterbury; the abbot, prior, archdeacon, and precentor of St. Albans; and the abbot and prior of Westminster.[2] Two were granted to Cistercians, the priors of Bordesley and Thame; one to a Premonstratensian, the abbot of Bayham; one to a Gilbertine, the prior of North Ormsby; and one to the prior of the hospital at Brackley.[3] Finally, three indults were given to seculars; to Alexander Stavensby, bishop of Coventry and Lichfield, to Robert Grosseteste, bishop of Lincoln, and to the treasurer of Salisbury, Master Edmund of Abingdon, afterwards archbishop of Canterbury.[4] These numbers correspond with the general conclusions that have been drawn about the proportionate use of the different regulars and seculars as judges delegate. A further assessment of the recipients seems to show that indults were limited to clerics of importance, and for the most part to regulars: abbots of houses such as Bury St. Edmunds, St. Augustine's Canterbury, Cirencester, and Westminster; priors of convents such as Christ

---

[1] Bradenstoke Cart., f. 105ʳ; *Reg. Hon. III*, no. 3205 (*C.P.L.* i. 79); *Cart. of Cirencester Abbey* i, ed. C. D. Ross (Oxford, 1964), nos. 163 and 169; *Foedera*, i. 184 (P.R.O. SC7 18 [27]); Thorney Cart. ii, f. 384ʳ; Westminster Domesday, f. 576ʳ; *Oseney Cart.* iii, no. 34, and *Reg. Antiq. Linc.* iii, no. 647; Burton Cart., ff. 62ᵛ–3ᵛ (xliiᵛ–xliiiᵛ) (cal. Wrottesley, *Coll: Hist. Staffs.* v, pt. i. 56); *Reg. Hon. III*, no. 3550 (*C.P.L.* i. 83); ibid., no. 3350 (*C.P.L.* i. 81); Waltham Cart., f. 73ʳ; and *Reg. Hon. III*, no. 6257 (*C.P.L.* i. 116).

[2] Abingdon Cart., f. 18ᵛ; Bardney Cart. f. 23ᵛ; Belvoir, Large Cart., f. 12ʳ; Binham Cart., f. 36ᵛ; *Pinchbeck Reg.* i, ed. F. Hervey (privately printed, 1925), 42; *Reg. Hon. III*, no. 3101 (*C.P.L.* i. 79); Canterbury, Reg. A, f. 20ʳ; St. Augustine's Red Book, f. 25ᵛ; St. Albans Cart. (A), f. 47ʳ⁻ᵛ; and Westminster Domesday, f. 14.

[3] *Reg. Hon. III*, no. 4378 (*C.P.L.* i. 92); Bradenstoke Cart., f. 146ᵛ; *Foedera*, i. 185, and P.R.O. SC7 18 [1]; *Reg. Inn. IV*, no. 884; and Magdalen College, Oxford, Brackley Ch. 106, cal. Macray, *Bucks. Advertiser* (1910). The abbot of Easby (Prem. Yorks. N.R.) gained exemption in 1224–5, Easby Cart., f. 317ʳ; the indults for the northern houses have not been included in the assessments.

[4] Lichfield Cart., f. 15ᵛ; *Reg. Inn. IV*, no. 2832; and *Cirencester Cart.* ii, no. 489, p. 432. Grosseteste, as Master Robert Grosseteste, had been a judge delegate on at least one occasion during Innocent III's pontificate (*Letters of Inn. III*, no. 1156B).

Church, Canterbury, Holy Trinity, Aldgate, and St. Bartholomew's, London. Likewise, they were granted to the bishop of Coventry and Lichfield and the bishop of Lincoln, persons who were most likely to have kept permanent proctors at the *Curia*. Edmund of Abingdon's indult, as treasurer of Salisbury, seems to confirm both the importance of the legal school there and the frequent use of the officers of that cathedral as judges delegate.[1]

A fee was certainly charged for an indult, and a further fee for registration. By no means all indults of this kind were registered. A mandate of 25 February 1227 ordered the prior of West Acre, whose exemption was not registered, to hear a case notwithstanding.[2] It is possible that some sort of list of exempt judges was kept at the *Curia*, but it is more likely that the plaintiff informed the chancery clerks of the proposed judge's exemption if he knew him to have an indult but particularly wanted him as judge. Often mandates were dispatched that made no mention of these exemptions, and their existence had to be claimed and proved by the judges. In 1223 the prior of St. Bartholomew's, London, declared that he was exempt, and in 1233 the abbot of Missenden made a similar claim.[3] The prior of Thame also claimed his exemption during Honorius III's pontificate.[4] Evidence remains of instructions to certain exempt judges— for instance the abbots of St. Augustine's, Canterbury, Waltham (Aug. Essex), and Thornton (Aug. Lincs.)—to make their indults known throughout their vicinity, so that petitioners would not ask for them as judges in the *Curia*: 'Ne autem aliqui per ignoranciam ad vos commissionis litteras impetrantes exinde dampnum incurrant, volumus ut per partes vicinas hanc indulgenciam publicetis.'[5]

In granting these indults the *Curia* clearly maintained the right to compel judges to serve, safeguarding itself by the phrase 'nisi commissionis ad te obtinende littere plenam

---

[1] See above, pp. 129–32.   [2] *Reg. Hon. III*, no. 6257.
[3] Thorney Cart. ii, f. 384ʳ; and Westminster Domesday, f. 576ʳ.
[4] Bradenstoke Cart., f. 146ᵛ. Cf. *Regesta Chartarum Italiae—Regestum Volaterranum*, ed. Schneider, p. 141, no. 398: 'alter [judex] indulgentiam asserit se habere . . .'
[5] St. Augustine's Red Book, f. 25ᵛ (App. B (iii), no. 3). See also Waltham Cart., f. 73ʳ (App. B (iii), no. 4).

fecerint de hac indulgencia mentionem', whereas the indulgences from before 1198 merely stated that the judges need not act if they were unwilling. Indults probably lasted only for the pontificate in which they were granted, although the name of the abbot of Oseney who had gained an exemption from Pope Urban III is not included in an Oseney indult of Gregory IX, which was addressed to the prior, subprior, precentor, and sacrist of Oseney.[1] This might suggest that the abbot of Oseney's indult still held good; but for the abbot of Cirencester two indults survive, one granted by Honorius III and the other by Innocent IV.[2] On the whole it is more likely that such grants expired with the grantor.

The main argument put forward by those who petitioned for exemption from hearing causes was that delegation upset the normal conduct of monastic life. The expense and work of hearing suits was also mentioned. Some applicants for indults stressed their lack of knowledge of the law. The prior of the Cistercian house of Bordesley claimed that he was not skilled in the law and that he was now aged.[3] The prior of Binham, the abbot of Bayham, and the prior of Holy Trinity, Aldgate, sought exemption on the same grounds. As the indults recited, 'cum asseris juris peritiam non habeas'.[4]

5. The Officers who were employed by the Judges

The officers of the permanent diocesan administration were at the disposal of the judges delegate for performing subsidiary duties. The delegate of the pope, sharing in the papal *plenitudo potestatis*, had a temporary jurisdiction for the suit in question over the ordinary of any diocese and over ecclesiastics who were normally his superiors.[5] He could order anyone to cite a party and to carry out his sentence, and he could penalize anyone who disobeyed him.[6] Such was the power of the judge delegate that, in theory at least, he could

---

[1] *P.U.E.* iii, no. 389, and *Oseney Cart.* iii, nos. 12 and 34. Cf. *Reg. Antiq. Linc.* iii, no. 647, where the prior claims exemption some time between 1238 and 1242.
[2] *Cirencester Cart.* i, nos. 163 and 169.
[3] *Reg. Hon. III*, no. 4378. Cf. *Cirencester Cart.* i, no. 163.
[4] Binham Cart., f. 36ᵛ; P.R.O. SC7 18 [1]; and 18 [27].
[5] c. 11. *X.* I. 29 (Alex. III).
[6] c. 28. *X.* I. 29 (Inn. III) (cf. c. 11. *X.* I. 31), and c. 7. *X.* I. 29 (Alex. III).

call on an archbishop or a bishop to carry out his sentence; but in practice those ecclesiastics whose offices had been created to lessen the work of the bishop in the diocese seem to have been called upon most frequently to act in a delegated as well as in an ordinary capacity. It has been noted that at first it was almost exclusively the bishops who were commissioned as judges delegate. But the evidence for the period before 1198 is not sufficient to reveal definitively how the bishops summoned and made inquiries, and how they implemented their sentences. Probably they used diocesan officers, who were rapidly becoming concerned in the work of the ordinary courts and who seem later to be accustomed to the duties that they were called upon to perform for the delegated courts.

Through the bishops a close connection was established between the judge-delegate system and the diocesan organization.[1] When ecclesiastics other than bishops were appointed judges delegate in the early years, they referred their sentences to the diocesans for execution and for the maintenance of their observance. In probably 1183 × 1184 judges delegate (the abbot of Evesham and the prior of Reading) ordered the bishop of Lincoln to see that their sentence was observed.[2] In the Harrold case, at the beginning of Innocent III's pontificate, as Professor Cheney records, 'The delegates, in transmitting their record of the case to the diocesan late in 1198 or early in 1199, called upon him in the usual fashion to execute their sentence.'[3] Similarly in about 1214 the abbot of St. Augustine's, the prior of St. James's, and the dean of Bristol ordered the bishop of Exeter to execute their sentence about the church of Colyton (Devon).[4] Usually the bishop transmitted such orders to his subordinates. When Mauger, bishop of Worcester, was asked by the judges delegate to see that the canons of Kenil-

[1] Relations, however, between ordinaries and judges delegate were not always good, and Professor Cheney cites an example of an ordinary resisting the sentence of a judge delegate in his diocese, Cheney, 'England and the Roman Curia', p. 183.

[2] *Oseney Cart.* iv, no. 400A. The bishop is Walter de Coutances, consecrated on 3 July 1183. and the abbot of Evesham, Adam (1161–91).

[3] Cheney, 'Harrold Priory', p. 6 and no. 4.

[4] Exeter Ch. 815.

worth were inducted into corporal possession of the church of Brailes (Warw.), he delegated this task to his officials—Ralph of Evesham, prior of Worcester, and Master Robert de Clipstone.[1]

By the thirteenth century commands were usually sent directly to the diocesan officers asking them to deal with administrative details. In 1219, for example, the abbots of Battle, Robertsbridge, and Hastings, judges delegate, wrote to R(anulf) de Harpley, official of the bishop of Norwich, ordering him to carry out their sentence and punish any resistance.[2] This machinery, already established for the ordinary ecclesiastical courts, was borrowed by the delegated courts. However, the choice by the judges delegate of officials of varied standing—including regulars—for attending to subsidiaries of the case illustrates the lack of a rigid organization within the diocese, although it is noticeable that in choosing clergy to perform subsidiary duties connected with their courts, the judges delegate favoured the rural deans. The rural dean was in most cases a beneficed clerk, and he had a definite connection with a distinct locality.[3] In area his territory was small. To command the rural dean to cite a party, to investigate about tithes or expenses, to execute a sentence of suspension or excommunication, to carry out an induction or to seize possession, did not, therefore, involve him in too onerous a task. Furthermore, because the rural deaneries were small enough for the deans to know the inhabitants well, it would soon be brought to their notice when sentences were not kept. The rural dean was becoming recognized as the familiar officer of the delegated court. He sat as judge delegate, and probably even more frequently as subdelegate, and on occasion he was chosen as an arbiter.[4] His appointment by the judges delegate as an administrative officer of the temporary court suggests that he already held an important, though ill-

---

[1] Kenilworth Cart., f. 47ᵛ.

[2] Lewes Cart., f. 260ʳ, cal. *Lewes Cart. N.P.*, no. 135.

[3] F. Barlow, *Durham Jurisdictional Peculiars* (Oxford, 1950), p. 102.

[4] Master R., dean of Lympne (Kent), and B. dean of Dover were chosen as arbiters in 1228 (Dover Cart. f. 229ᵛ), Master W(alter) dean of Malling in *c.* 1218 (P.R.O. E 40/14198 and E 40/14221), and the deans of Cambridge, Wilbraham, and Chesterton (Cambs.) in or before 1233 (P.R.O. E 40/13828[c]).

defined, position in the administration of the diocese by the early thirteenth century.

The evidence for the activities of the diocesan officers on behalf of the delegated courts is slight, consisting of only a fractional proportion of the number of suits for which documentary information remains. It is unusual for subsidiary documents, such as the orders of the judges and the reports of the officers, to survive, and administrative details were seldom mentioned in the final *acta*. In spite of these deficiencies, however, it is possible to offer a tentative reconstruction of the use of diocesan officers and others by the delegated courts.

(i) *Duties of Citing, Censuring, and Inquiring*

The judges delegate could cite the defendants directly; and they probably did so if the defendants lived nearby. But they might hold their courts at some distance from the dwelling place of the defendants, and in many cases numerous defendants from widespread areas were charged, so that the citation was frequently delegated to someone else.[1] When Alard, the dean, and Benedict of Sawston, the precentor of St. Paul's, London, cited R., a knight of Coventry diocese, by a direct command to appear before them on 14 January (presumably 1206) at St. Paul's to reply to the charges of the abbot and convent of St. Evroult, it is most probable that they gave the letter of citation to someone else to convey to the party.[2] Citation could be a dangerous business. When the judges' messengers, including a clerk, presented the citation to Master William de Cerneia some time before 1237, they were set upon and wounded.[3] A decree of the legate Otto, which was issued in the Council of London in 1237, reveals that hitherto citation had been frequently performed by the plaintiff or his representative.

[1] Cf. Gratia of Arezzo, '*Summa de Iudiciario Ordine*', p. 331, on citation by the ordinaries. Gratia was writing after 1234, Stickler, col. 1138. Cf. also Aegidius de Fuscarariis, '*Ordo Iudiciarius*', viii, p. 15.

[2] B.M. Wolley Ch. v. 27, and cf. *N.L.C.*, no. 45, where R(ichard of Ely), archdeacon of Colchester, and Master R., rector of the church of St. Antoninus, summoned the prior and monks of Newton Longville to come on the Monday after 6 May 1200 or 1201 to St. Paul's, London, to answer R., rector of Loughton (Bucks.).

[3] *Reg. Greg. IX*, no. 3419.

The legate enacted that, in future, officers of the court, and not the representatives of an interested party, should call the defendant to appear, and the rural dean was specified for this duty.[1] From the evidence of actual citations the rural dean appears as the usual choice. The officers who were ordered to carry out citations are mentioned only in eleven cases for the whole period between 1198 and 1254, but the rural dean was involved in ten of these suits as the officer who cited the party.[2]

The rural dean of the locality or an ecclesiastic resident in the area was chosen for this purpose. The dean of Brackley (Northants.) cited the nearby abbot and convent of Biddlesden (Bucks.) in 1250.[3] The dean of Canterbury cited the abbot and convent of St Augustine, Canterbury.[4] The dean of Walcot (Lincs.) summoned Peter, parson of the church of Stainton-le-Vale (Lincs.); the dean of Moulton (Northants.) went in pursuit of Thomas de Eastleigh, a clerk; and the subprior of Canons Ashby (Northants.) and the rector of Cottisford (Oxon.) were told to cite respectively the prior and convent of Luffield (Northants.) and Ralph, who was vicar of Thornborough (Bucks.) and dean of Buckingham.[5] Canons Ashby is about eight miles from Luffield, and Cottisford about nine from Thornborough. It seems probable that the rural dean or officer who had been selected to make the citation summoned the party personally. There is no evidence to the contrary, although Mr. Foster thinks that very often rural deans did not implement mandates themselves.[6] An example of a subcitation, or delegation

---

[1] *C.S.* ii, pt. i. 256, no. [26]. See also Drogheda, xi, p. 17: 'Potest fieri citatio parti per nuntios, huic tamen obviat legati constitutio', and xvi, p. 21, and *C.F.*, nos. (2) and (4), where a dean, a prior, and a chaplain are mentioned for this duty.

[2] B.M. Harley Ch. 84 F 44; Harley Ch. 84 F 35; P.R.O. E 135/24/4; St. Augustine's Cart., f. 79^r; Bodleian MS. Chs. Oxon. a 5, Ch. 364; '*Burton Chs.*' 58; Windsor Ch. xi G 27; *Oseney Cart.* ii, no. 1112; Northampton, St. Andrew's Cart. (A), f. 209^r; and Alvingham Cart., f. 5^r. Of the eleven citations (two of them were issued in the course of the same suit), two date from the 1230s, three from the 1240s, and four from the 1250s. The final two are of uncertain date; neither of of them is positively earlier than the 1230 decade.

[3] B.M. Harley Ch. 84 F 44.   [4] St. Augustine's Cart., f. 79^r.

[5] Alvingham Cart., f. 5^r; Northampton, St. Andrew's Cart. (A), f. 209^r; and Bodleian MS. Chs. Bucks. a 4, Ch. 91.

[6] J. Foster, 'The Activities of Rural Deans in England in the Twelfth and Thirteenth Centuries' (Manchester M.A. thesis, 1955), pp. 75–6.

at second-hand, is given by Curialis. He writes of an official who had been ordered by the judges delegate to cite a party, and shows him subdelegating this duty to certain priests, ordering them to return the letters appended with their seals when they had done this.[1]

It was the duty of the officer to inform the judges when he had executed the citation, either in a written document or by some other recognized sign.[2] The earliest certificate of citation that has survived seems to be one of the dean of Ewell, who was ordered to cite Thomas de St. John, priest, at his brother's house.[3] Its date is before 20 January 1236, and thus precedes the order of the legate Otto in the Council of London, which declared that officials of the courts were to inform the judges of the completion of their activities.[4] The legate Ottobon later echoed Otto's statute and added that no punishment would be inflicted on a person who ignored a mandate of citation that had been delivered to him, unless the diocesan official who was responsible for its delivery certified that he had presented it.[5] The judges often ordered the officer to report in letters patent.[6] The dean of Walcot reported to the judges, the priors of Bridlington and Kirkham and the master of the schools at Malton, that he had cited the defendant. The judges had cautioned him to certify *per literas vestras patentes*; he did so, and put his seal on the document.[7] Similarly, in the citation forms included in the Canterbury formulary the judges instructed the prior of St. Gregory's or the dean or the chaplain of St. Paul's, Canterbury, to report in letters patent.[8] When the judges had ordered an officer to summon a party they caused a memorandum of their order to be made. A memorandum of the prior of Lenton, conservator of the privileges and indults of the Cistercians in the province of Canterbury, states that on 4 March 1252 a mandate had been directed to the dean

---

[1] Curialis, '*Ordo*', lxxii, p. 23.

[2] Fournier, p. 59. Woodcock, *Medieval Ecclesiastical Courts*, p. 50, says that in the thirteenth and fourteenth centuries, before the ordinary courts, the 'certificate' consisted of the signature of the apparitor written on the dorse of the original mandate. This was returned to the registrar.

[3] *Oseney Cart.* ii, no. 1112.   [4] *C.S.* ii, pt. i. 256, no. [26].

[5] Ibid. ii, pt. ii. 772, no. [25].

[6] e.g. Bodleian MS. Chs. Bucks. a 4, Ch. 91. Cf. Drogheda, xii, p. 18.

[7] Alvingham Cart., f. 5ʳ.   [8] *C.F.*, nos. (2) and (4).

of Brackley bidding him to cite the defendants to appear on 16 March. The document was dated on the day of the dispatch of the command.[1] A memorandum, which recorded that the judge had ordered the dean of Brecon to cite the abbot and convent of Dore, appears among the notes about this suit and is followed by a copy of the dean's certificate.[2]

If the defendant failed to come to court after he had been cited, an officer might be ordered to censure him for his contumacy and to cite him again. The writer of the Canterbury formulary gives examples of the enforcement of punishment by the delegated courts. In the first example the judges themselves imposed the penalty; in the second they delegated this undertaking to the dean of Canterbury. The dean was instructed to suspend or excommunicate H., chaplain, until he should offer a sufficient pledge that he would appear. The dean was further directed to report on his actions in letters patent.[3] Various local clerks acted as sequestrators in judgements *causa rei servande*, and again the sequestrator or inductor was often the rural dean. In the Canterbury formulary the dean is told to induct the plaintiff into possession of a church or of land forming part of the endowment or of tithes; and since such a sentence is useless if it is not maintained, he is to safeguard and enforce the induction, threatening ecclesiastical censure on those who attempt to contravene it.[4] In the Harrold case, the abbot of Lavendon, at the command of the judges delegate, gave the nuns custody of the church of Stevington (Beds.) *causa rei servande*.[5] Furthermore, the archdeacon of Bedford, Master Alexander of Elstow, was instructed by the judges to see that the nuns retained undisturbed the possession that had been adjudged to them.[6] In the Lambeth formulary the judges ordered the delegate to induct C., clerk, into a church *causa rei servande*, and to maintain his occupation of it until they should send further instructions.[7] Similarly the judges appointed officers to execute other intermediary sentences. The dean of Dover was ordered to compel the prior and convent of Dover to pay two marks sterling as expenses to the abbot and convent

[1] B.M. Harley Ch. 84 F 35.   [2] P.R.O. E 135/24/4 (App. B (iii), no. 2).
[3] *C.F.*, no. (7).   [4] *C.F.*, no. (8).   [5] Cheney, 'Harrold Priory', no. 16.
[6] Ibid., no. 17.   [7] A, f. 271ᵛ, col. 1.

of Bec. This order followed an intermediary sentence over an exception. If the prior and convent of Dover refused or neglected to pay the sum, which the dean was to receive on behalf of the abbot and convent of Bec before 15 August 1245, the dean was to suspend them and publicly declare them excommunicated in each of the churches of Dover until they should make full satisfaction. He was also instructed to summon them to appear on 22 September for the resumption of the hearing of the suit.[1]

After the dean, or other officer of the court, had issued such sentences, he might be ordered at a later date to absolve the penitent from the censures that he had incurred. The officer announced the absolution in the same place as he had declared the offender excommunicate, and he reported about the absolution in letters to his superiors.[2] Bishop Robert Grosseteste, acting on the authority of the abbot of Pershore a delegate of the pope, directed the archdeacon of Lincoln to absolve a clerk who had been excommunicated by the legate Otto.[3] In the case of an absolution from a judgement *causa rei servande*, the officer was ordered to restore possession until sentence had been given.[4]

One of the greatest advantages of the papal system of delegating judicial cases was that evidence from the locality could be easily collected and used. Inquisitions were delegated to rural deans who acted as investigators for the ordinaries.[5] The deans of Burnham and Walsingham (Norf.) were ordered by the prior, archdeacon, and dean of Huntingdon, the judges delegate, to inquire about the tithes that had been withdrawn from the lordship of Sculthorpe in the deanery of Burnham, and to send the result of their inquiry under seal. In St. Mary's church, Huntingdon, sentence was given in favour of the prior and convent of Lewes and against Master Nicholas, rector of Sculthorpe. The sentence declared that the tithes of the lands in question had been taken away from the lordship of Sculthorpe after they had been conferred on the monks.[6] In another suit R., dean of

---

[1] Windsor Ch. xi G 27 (App. B (ii), no. 3).   [2] *C.F.*, no. (9).
[3] *Epistolae Roberti Grosseteste*, ed. H. R. Luard (R.S. xxv, 1861), p. 245.
[4] *C.F.*, no. (10).
[5] See, e.g., St. Neots Cart., f. 110ᵛ.
[6] Lewes Cart., f. 253ʳ, cal. *N.P.*, no. 113; and f. 260ᵛ, cal. *N.P.*, no. 138.

Langford (Beds.), and the rural chapter made an inquisition about the vicarage of Henlow, which was in the deanery of Langford, at Warden (Beds.) on 25 October 1200.[1] Subsequently the same dean was ordered by the abbot of Winchcombe and the prior of Gloucester to put the plaintiffs, the canons of Lanthony, into possession of two portions of the altar dues of the church of Henlow and the third part of the third part of the garb tithes from the demesne of the canons.[2]

(ii) Executing Sentences

The judges delegate depended on the officers of the ordinary diocesan administration for the execution of sentences. The canon law specified that it was the duty of the ordinary to assist the judges delegate in this way.[3] A judge could only order the execution of his sentence when he had been authorized to do so, but in practice almost every mandate included the necessary clause which gave him this power. By the mid-thirteenth century the rural dean was the usual official for this duty.[4] For the southern province eighteen instances remain of the rural dean serving, as opposed to six orders from which he was excluded. There are examples of nine rural deans acting before and during the 1220s, four in the 1230s, one in the 1240s, two in the 1250s, and one at an unknown date between 1227 and 1241. The rural dean did not, however, monopolize the duty. Sometimes he acted in the company of the archdeacon.[5] On one occasion a rural dean, the dean of Hoxne (Suff.), was commissioned to execute a sentence at Stradbroke (Suff.) with a regular, the abbot of Leiston (Suff.).[6] In 1219 the dean of Darley (Derbys.) was appointed an executor with William de Cornhull, bishop of Coventry, and his officials and the archdeacon

---

[1] Lanthony Cart. A 9, f. 165ʳ, pd. Cheney, Becket to Langton, pp. 192–3.

[2] Lanthony Cart. A 1, X, no. cxi.

[3] c. 7. X. I. 29 (Alex. III), and c. 10. X. II. 1 (Cel. III).

[4] The rural dean was also often commanded to exact payment of the expenses of the suit under penalty of excommunication if the loser refused to pay, see, e.g., Westminster Domesday, f. 379ᵛ, where the dean of Oxford in 1254 was ordered to see that the abbess and convent of Godstow paid 40s. expenses to Westminster by the feast of St. Peter ad vincula (1 Aug.).

[5] St. Frideswide's Cart. ii, nos. 732 and 978.

[6] Eye Cart., ff. 40ʳ–1ʳ.

of Derby.[1] Sometimes the rural dean was omitted altogether from the number of those who were ordered to execute sentences, as in the following two instances: Henry de Sandford, archdeacon of Canterbury, was ordered by judges delegate to execute a sentence some time after October 1225; and the subdean of Wells was directed by the prior of Ivychurch and the chancellor and succentor of Salisbury to give the prior and convent of Bradenstoke possession of the tithes of a mill.[2]

In all instances it was an officer of the locality who carried out the sentence. The dean of Burnham was to see that a sentence about twenty shillings rent yearly from the church of Burnham Thorpe was carried out.[3] The dean of Heyford and the archdeacon of Oxford were ordered to attend to a sentence about the tithes of one hide of land at Souldern (Oxon.).[4] The dean of Islip (Oxon.) was entrusted with the execution of a sentence about the tithes at Fritwell (Oxon.); and the dean of Aston Rowant (Oxon.) was to induct Oseney into possession of tithes within the parish of Watlington.[5] In 1220 R., dean of Waddesdon (Bucks.), was instructed to induct the Augustinian canons of St. Frideswide's, Oxford, into possession of the church of Oakley (Bucks.). (Oakley is about nine miles from Waddesdon.)[6] When the abbot of Winchcombe and the prior of Gloucester passed sentence about the church of Henlow (Beds.) and its tithes, probably in 1202 × 1203, they ordered the dean of Langford (Beds.) to put the canons of Lanthony into possession as was usual.[7] But they also ordered two monks from the abbeys of Gloucester (Ben.) and Woburn (Cist. Beds.) to assist in the execution of the sentence. Each monk came from the locality of each of the parties—Lanthony and St. Julian's hospital at St. Albans.[8] In another Henlow case the judges, the subprior of St. Oswald's and the dean of Gloucester, ordered the official of the archdeacon of Bedford and John, vicar of Langford, and Geoffrey, vicar of Chicksands (both Beds.),

---

[1] *Reg. Antiq. Linc.* iii, no. 731.
[2] Leeds Cart., f. 10ᵛ (App. B (iii), no. 5); and Bradenstoke Cart., f. 119ᵛ.
[3] P.R.O. SC1, vol. 11, no. 70, cal. *Lewes Cart. N.P.*, no. 69.
[4] *St. Frideswide's Cart.* ii, no. 978.
[5] Ibid., no. 976; and *Oseney Cart.* iv, nos. 404 (and 403).
[6] *St. Frideswide's Cart.* ii, nos. 820–1.
[7] Lanthony Cart. A 1, X, no. cxi.   [8] Ibid., no. cx.

all or two of them, to carry out a sentence of 1238 in favour of Lanthony.[1]

In executing sentences the officers were granted powers to deal with anyone who impeded them. The dean of Marlow (Bucks.), when ordered by the prior of St. Frideswide's and the dean of Iffley to carry out a sentence by putting the nuns of Godstow into possession of the tithes of all the mills of Wycombe (Bucks.), was bidden to curse solemnly anyone who should attempt to prevent him.[2] Sentence of excommunication was the usual penalty for resistance.[3] In 1251 the dean of Shefford (Beds.) was ordered by the archdeacon of St. Albans, the judge delegate, to carry out a sentence in favour of the abbot and convent of Holy Cross, Waltham, about tithes in the parish of Arlesey (Beds.). He was urged to pass sentence of excommunication and interdict against anyone who resisted him and to report to the judges on his actions.[4] The delegates remained responsible to the judges until they sent back a document recording the completion of their duties. In a document dated 29 August 1235 the dean of Gloucester reported that he had received the mandate of the judges delegate, and that he had executed their sentence by instituting Master Baldwin in the church of Painswick (Glos.).[5] When Henry de Sandford, archdeacon of Canterbury, had committed to his official Master Roger the duty of execution, which was demanded of him by the priors of Rochester and Lesnes and the archdeacon of Rochester, he made a notification of its completion, the official having carried out the duty.[6]

The ordinary of the diocese was expected to compel the observance of sentences without receiving a specific mandate

---

[1] Lanthony Cart. A 9, f. 164ʳ (and in A 1). Cf. Welbeck Cart., f. 80ʳ, where the chaplains of Elton and Scarrington (both Notts.) were ordered by the prior of Mattersey (Gilb. Notts) and the dean of Laneham, subdelegates of the dean of Lichfield and the archdeacon of Derby, to induct the abbot and convent of Welbeck (Prem. Notts.) into possession of the tithes of two mills in the parish of Whatton (Notts.).

[2] *Godstow Reg.* i, no. [92].

[3] See, e.g., Lanthony Cart. A 1, X, no. cx.

[4] B.M. Egerton Ch. 409. Sometimes the mandate included a proviso that such sentences of excommunication and interdict should not be promulgated, presumably either during the course of the suit or after it (see above, pp. 69–70).

[5] Lanthony Cart. A 1, XVI, no. xv, and see no. xiv.

[6] Leeds Cart., f. 10ᵛ (App. B (iii), no. 5).

to this end from the judges delegate. Sometimes, however, he was specifically charged with this duty as well. In 1227 the prior of Barnwell, the chancellor, and the dean of Cambridge committed delegated powers to compel the observance of a composition, about tithes of the lordship of Bottisham (Cambs.), that had been made between the priors and convents of Anglesey (Cambs.) and Newton Longville (Bucks.), to 'the ordinary of the place', the bishop of Ely.[1] Similarly, the chancellor and the dean of Oxford and the dean of Iffley, the judges delegate, provided that if William, rector of Croxton (Cambs.), ceased to pay two and a half marks yearly to the prior and convent of St. Neots (Hunts.) in return for the tithes in the parish of Croxton, he should be compelled to do so by the diocesan. The diocesan, Hugh, bishop of Ely, made an *inspeximus* and confirmation of the judge-delegate settlement on 30 May 1231.[2]

The names of diocesan officers sometimes occur among the witnesses to judge-delegate settlements; and rural deans might seal the final *acta* together with the judges. As early as 1191 × 1196, a rural dean, Master Ralph of Evesham, is found witnessing a papally delegated settlement.[3] The name of Gilbert, dean of Beltisloe in the archdeaconry of Lincoln, appeared in the witness list to a judge-delegate charter in a case about Bytham (Lincs.) soon after 1225.[4] Simon, dean of Hoxne (Suff.), and William, dean of Redenhall (Norf.), were witnesses to an arrangement between the prior and convent of Butley and G. of Fressingfield (both Suff.), and so were G(eoffrey), archdeacon of Suffolk, and Warin his chaplain.[5] The deans of Colchester and Witham in the archdeaconry of Colchester added their seals to the report of the settlement, which had been made before the priors of Thoby and Tiptree (both Essex), in a suit between the abbot and convent of St. John, Colchester, and Walter, rector of Easton (Suffolk). The settlement was made in 1240, and

---

[1] *N.L.C.*, no. 86. Cf. Whalley Cart., f. 153ʳ⁻ᵛ, where the prior of St. Frideswide's, the subdelegate of the dean of St Mary's, Warwick, issued a firm warning in 1241 to the archdeacon of Chester not to upset his sentence.

[2] St. Neots Cart., ff. 110ᵛ–11ᵛ.

[3] W. de Gray Birch, *Descriptive Catalogue of the Penrice and Margam Abbey Manuscripts*, 1st ser. (1893), no. 46.

[4] *Reg. Antiq. Linc.* iii, no. 1019.   [5] B.M. Harley Ch. 44 I 25.

the deans are described by the judges delegate as *nobiscum assidentium*.[1] Similarly rural deans sometimes witness the charters of parties recording settlements. The dean of Lewes acted as a witness to a letter of a party recording the restoration of certain tithes in a suit which had been settled before judges delegate in 1230.[2] Hugh, dean of Wirral (Ches.), was among the witnesses to a charter of 1198 × 1216 of Thomas Patrick, in which he recorded the renunciation of his claim that the church of Tarporley was a chapel of Bunbury church (both Ches.).[3] When in about 1252 Master Thomas Crispin, rector of Bytham (Lincs.), made a notification that he had returned to Walter son of Roger de Colevill the two acres of meadow which had been conceded to him, in return for two shillings yearly, H., dean of Beltisloe, added his name to those of the witnesses.[4]

The witnessing or sealing of these charters by the deans in whose localities the parties resided illustrates the close dependence of the delegated courts on the local ecclesiastical administration. The officers of the ordinary administration were present when the final *acta* of the temporary courts were drawn up; they were there also when the parties made charters. Whether they were present on such occasions at the command of the judges or at the request of the parties, and whether this presence was usual, are questions which cannot be answered. But as it is known that on occasion they were ordered by the judges delegate to execute and maintain the observance of sentences, it does not seem unreasonable to suppose that when their names appear among those of the witnesses, these attestations may denote an order to fulfil a definite commission. Even if they were not ordered to carry out sentences and safeguard arrangements, their presence suggests that they would announce the sentence in the ruridecanal chapter, and that if it was not kept, they would inform the diocesan.[5]

---

[1] P.R.O. E 42/384.
[2] P.R.O. E 40/14157, cal. *Lewes Cart. S.P.* ii. 24–5.
[3] *Early Cheshire Charters*, ed. G. Barraclough (Lancs. and Cheshire Rec. Soc., 1957), no. 13. See also *Middlewich Cart.* ii, ed. J. Varley and J. Tait (Chetham Soc. cviii, 1944), 297–8.
[4] *Reg. Antiq. Linc.* iii, no. 1021.   [5] Cf. Foster, 'Rural Deans', p. 121.

The judges delegate were instructed by the pope to ensure that their decisions were carried out. To this end they had great powers over their temporary officers. When Roger of Weasenham, archdeacon of Oxford, a judge delegate, ordered the dean of Arden (Warw.) to carry out a sentence, he threatened him under pain of suspension from his benefice.[1] If the rural dean did not wish to execute a mandate, he could seek to be relieved of the duty. In the Canterbury formulary the dean says that he has received the judges' mandate telling him to cite, excommunicate, suspend, or announce a sentence of excommunication terminated, but since he is frightened, and also threatened with ill treatment by the person he is to cite, he says that he has not yet fulfilled their command. He beseeches the judges to release him from this duty and to entrust it to someone who is powerful enough to execute their mandate, whom this person would not be able to resist, so that the authority of the Church should not be weakened by his arrogance.[2] If a good reason was provided, such a plaint presumably produced the desired release from the task; but if the rural dean failed to request exemption or failed to do what had been ordered or return a certificate, he might be summoned to present himself before the judges and be punished by them.[3] The form of such a summons is included in the Canterbury formulary.[4] A similar summons for disobedience over the fulfilment of a mandate is included by Curialis in his commentary.[5] There it is followed by a threatened penalty—suspension from office—for non-appearance before the court and a subsequent absolution, which enjoined penitence for the contumacy and disobedience.[6] When the dean of Gloucester was ordered to execute a sentence, he was instructed also to summon again by peremptory edict the dean of Easton Neston (Northants.) to appear by proctor on (?)11 September 1235 at St. Paul's, London. The dean of Easton Neston was to be required both to satisfy Master Baldwin, who had won the suit, about expenses caused by his disobedience, and to reply to the judges delegate about his

---

[1] Bodleian MS. Chs. Bucks. a 3, Chs. 43, 44.   [2] *C.F.*, no. (29).
[3] Drogheda, xi, p. 17.   [4] *C.F.*, no. (28).
[5] Curialis, '*Ordo*', cxlvii, p. 42.   [6] Ibid., cxlviii–cxlix, p. 43.

contempt. The dean of Gloucester was also instructed to excommunicate the dean of Easton Neston for his disobedience and contempt.[1] It appears that the dean of Easton Neston had been ordered to execute the sentence of the judges delegate but had failed to do so. That such duties could be tiresome for the officers is illustrated by the following instance. In 1230 the prior of Christ Church, Canterbury, sought, and was granted, a papal exemption from executing sentences of judges delegate outside the diocese of Canterbury. He alleged that he had been ordered by French judges delegate to carry out sentences, some concerning the debts of merchants, in 'remote parts of England', with much trouble and expense.[2]

Although the judicial powers of the judges delegate, arbiters, and conservators were necessarily circumscribed, administratively their powers over the conduct and subsidiaries of the case were almost unlimited. In choosing judges, the plaintiff had the initial advantage, but the defendant might secure different men either by objecting in the *audientia publica* or by applying for a new mandate. Most of the judges were local men, and commissions might include both regulars and seculars from the district in question, often from the nearest towns and legal centres. Among the regulars the Augustinians were active, apparently both because their houses were numerous and because their priors were often legally trained. Among the seculars, diocesan and cathedral officers, particularly legal officers like the officials, chancellors, canons, and members of the bishops' *familiae*, were popular choices. The demands made upon the judges by the papal delegated system were heavy. A general assessment of their acts and attitudes suggests a smoothness of operation, and complaints and troubles appear to be the exception; but after 1227 subdelegation increased, and during Honorius III's pontificate indults exempting ecclesiastics from judicial service were sought by and granted to important religious and secular clergy. Lower clergy were chosen more frequently as delegates and subdelegates during the 1230s

[1] Lanthony Cart. A 1, XVI, no. xiiii (App. B (iii), no. 6).
[2] Canterbury, Reg. A, ff. 19ᵛ–20ʳ.

and 1240s, and to counter this a papal decree of 1245 ordered that judges and subdelegates must be dignitaries and men of substance. In carrying out subsidiary duties connected with their courts, such as citing parties and executing sentences, the judges delegate used the bishop's administrative officers, and in particular the rural deans of the localities, who were already important in the administration of the diocese and who now became an accepted part of the judge-delegate court.

IV

THE BUSINESS OF THE COURTS
AND THE LITIGANTS

1. *The Competence of the Courts*

De divisione jurisdictionum sacerdotii et regni.

Sunt enim causae spirituales, in quibus judex secularis non habet cognitionem nec executionem, cum non habeat coertionem. In hiis enim causis pertinet cognitio ad judices ecclesiasticos, qui regunt et defendunt sacerdotium. Sunt autem causae seculares quarum cognitio pertinet ad reges et principes, qui defendunt regnum, et de quibus judices ecclesiastici se intromittere non debent, cum eorum jura sive jurisdictiones limitatae sunt et separatae, nisi ita sit quod gladius juvare debeat gladium, est enim magna differentia inter sacerdotium et regnum.[1]

In these words Bracton tried to rationalize the clash that had taken place between the two jurisdictions of Crown and papacy in the twelfth century. Historians since Le Bras in 1922 have sought to minimize the idea of a necessary rivalry between Church and State, clergy and laity, persisting from this first encounter; and Flahiff, in extending the investigation, has shown that in practice where the jurisdiction was disputed, either court was used by the litigant.[2] Looked at from any point of view, it is impossible to deny that there was some clash between Church and lay courts in England during Henry II's reign as to the relative competence of tribunals, but it is possible to over-emphasize the importance

---

[1] *Henrici de Bracton de Legibus et Consuetudinibus Angliae*, ii, ed. T. Twiss (R.S. lxx, 1879), 170, and cf. vi (1883), 248–51, and 296.

[2] G. Le Bras, 'Le Privilège de clergie en France dans les derniers siècles du Moyen Âge', *Journal des savants*, N.S. xx (1922), esp. 164; G. B. Flahiff, 'The Use of Prohibitions by Clerics against the Ecclesiastical Courts in England', *Mediaeval Studies*, iii (1941), 101–16, who cites Le Bras on p. 101; and Powicke, *Henry III*, pp. 776–7. J. W. Gray, 'The *Ius Praesentandi* in England from the Constitutions of Clarendon to Bracton', *E.H.R.* lxvii (1952), 481–509, sees, however, 'a corporate church policy' (p. 507), and suggests that the argument can be taken too far.

of principles in the quarrel.[1] That it was to some degree a sincere attempt to reach a compromise over disputed points of jurisdiction and competence has perhaps been overlooked. At any rate it was in a diluted form that the dispute between the two jurisdictions reached the thirteenth century, although theoretical legal writers tended to dress it up in terms of a deep-rooted and incompatible rivalry.

The expansion of the king's court in England was made at the expense of smaller local and private courts.[2] A stronger jurisdiction was devouring the work of the localities by attracting cases and litigants to itself. Through the device of writs, which became increasingly varied, the Crown extended its jurisdiction.[3] Parallel developments took place with the papacy, which spread its influence through the expedient of the papal mandate, and through the system of delegated courts competent to deal with a growing variety of business. In broad terms the areas of jurisdiction in dispute between Church and State did not increase or change. It was rather the amalgamation of courts that brought matters to a head and pitted the royal courts in England against the growing ecclesiastical jurisdiction, particularly that of Rome.

It is certainly true that both powers endeavoured to maintain their positions by high-flown arguments as to their relative position in society, but underneath this surface they strove, perhaps more purposefully, to perfect the efficiency of their administrations. Within this environment the litigant brought his case. Where did he take it? He took it to the most suitable court, that is to the one which seemed to him most competent to deal with his case, where he could get the most appropriate writ or mandate, and whose enforcement was most likely to operate. By and large by the thirteenth century the most suitable tribunal was obvious

---

[1] On the outcome of the dispute in terms of jurisdictional powers, see the Constitutions of Clarendon, *Select Charters*, ed. W. Stubbs, 9th edn., revsd. H. W. C. Davis (Oxford, 1913), pp. 164–7, esp. cc. 1, 9, 14, and 15.

[2] *W.P.*, pt. i. 261.

[3] Ibid. 264. See also T. F. T. Plucknett, *Early English Legal Literature* (Cambridge, 1958), pp. 30–1, and 36, and *Treatise on the Laws and Customs of the realm of England commonly called Glanvill*, ed. G. D. G. Hall (1965), and on the authorship and date, pp. xxx–xxxiii.

for most cases, and it was only in a few small areas that there was any real doubt, and here self-interest undoubtedly prevailed. But it is well to remember that in most instances higher ecclesiastics would favour their own tribunals, and more important laymen the king's courts. There were, however, exceptions for personal reasons. With lesser persons, both laymen and clergy, there were other considerations, and the question was by no means so clear or so important. Similarly, in cases where the impetrant chose a delegated papal court rather than the local diocesan one, many considerations of practicality would influence the choice. An important religious house would obviously rather come before a papal tribunal than the local diocesan one, and an important layman would naturally prefer to take a marriage suit to Rome rather than before his bishop.

The writ of prohibition has been seen as an important weapon in the hands of the lay courts.[1] It was rather an instrument by which a dividing line could be maintained between the two jurisdictions.[2] It was indeed important that by this device the Crown claimed the right to decide where the jurisdiction was in question, but the initiative in procuring a writ of prohibition rested with the party and not with the king.[3] If both parties agreed to come before a Church court in a matter of advowson, for example, little could be done about it unless there was direct intervention.[4] It is also worthy of comment that, according to Flahiff's calculations, in no less than one-third of the prohibition cases of the thirteenth century, the king's court recognized the ecclesiastical character

---

[1] Flahiff makes this point in 'Use of Prohibitions', p. 101, and cites as an example of this interpretation, H. D. Hazeltine, 'The Early History of English Equity', *Essays in Legal History*, ed. P. Vinogradoff (Oxford, 1913), p. 277. The similar institutions of 'inhibitio' and 'l'appel comme d'abus' in France are of later date, see R. Génestal, *Les Origines de l'appel comme d'abus* (Bibliothèque de l'École des hautes études — sciences religieuses, lxiii, 1951), esp. the foreword by J. Dauvillier, and pp. 9 and 27.   [2] *W.P.*, pt. i. 261.

[3] Ibid. 282; and N. Adams, 'The Writ of Prohibition to Court Christian', *Minnesota Law Review*, xx, no. 3 (1936), 277.

[4] As, for example, in the Oakley (Bucks.) case, between the prior and canons of St. Frideswide's and W. son of Richard, clerk of Lincoln diocese, where the king, who asserted that he was patron of the church and the judge in this cause affecting its advowson, forbade the judges to proceed, see *Royal Letters*, i. 533; *Reg. Hon. III*, no. 1680 (*C.P.L.* i. 160); *St. Frideswide's Cart.* ii, nos. 820 and 822-7; Prynne, *An Exact Chronological Vindication*, ii. 381; and *Bracton's Note Book*, iii, no. 1545.

of the original plea and sent it back.[1] It seems, therefore, that this dissection of interests was considerably more dispassionate and less influenced by high theory than has been supposed, and that the evolution of the two jurisdictions was a calmer and less dramatic process than Bracton and others would have us believe. Such theorists, however, show that neither power was prepared to lose whole realms of influence or to allow definite encroachments, but in the long run it was the court that showed itself the most suitable and experienced in a particular sphere of competence that gained the jurisdiction.

The jurisdiction of the canon law was claimed to extend over certain persons and certain cases.[2] The Church claimed litigants *ratione personae* and *ratione materiae*. The *privilegium fori*, that is the right of the clerk to have his case tried only before a Church court, was well defined and largely accepted by the thirteenth century.[3] Secular judges were not to concern themselves with the affairs of clerks, and Innocent III sharply reproved the archbishop of Pisa for maintaining that, at least in temporal matters, a clerk could renounce his right of exemption and appear before a secular court.[4] Benefit of clergy, a part of the *privilegium fori*, was the exemption of members of the clergy from the jurisdiction of the temporal courts in certain criminal cases which would normally have come before the lay courts.[5] At about the same time as the spread of the *Decretum*, criminal cases in

---

[1] Flahiff, 'Use of Prohibitions', p. 107, and *W.P.*, pt. ii. 233; and see Adams, 'Writ of Prohibition', pp. 284–5. Similarly, in 1215 Innocent III issued a mandate ordering secular pleas to be left to the lay courts (*Letters of Inn. III*, no. 1020).

[2] Fournier, p. 64.

[3] See the introduction to R. Génestal, *Le Privilegium Fori en France*, i (Bibliothéque de l'École des hautes études—sciences religieuses, xxxv, 1921), pp. i–xix; c. 1. X. II. 2: 'De foro competenti. Clericus coram suo episcopo conveniri debet'; and Fournier, p. 66. Note, however, the limits and qualifications which were imposed by the king's court in England (see below, pp. 178, 183–4, and 210). Henry II also excluded offences against the forest law in both England and Normandy. According to the Council of Lillebonne (1080) the violation of forest laws by clerks was beyond the sphere of the bishop's jurisdiction (W. S. Holdsworth, *History of English Law*, iii (1923), 297, and C. H. Haskins, *Norman Institutions* (Cambridge, Mass., 1918), pp. 30 and 32).

[4] c. 12. X. II. 2.

[5] L. C. Gabel, *Benefit of Clergy in England in the Later Middle Ages* (Smith College Studies in History, xiv, nos. 1–4, 1928–9), p. 7. For examples of proof of clergy, see P.R.O. SC1, vol. 3, nos. 164 and 192; and *Bracton's Note Book*, ii, no. 490.

which clerks were involved were coming under the jurisdiction of the Church, although not without question. In a
case about poisoning in 1156, it was stated:

Osbert [archdeacon of York] however most steadfastly denied the
charge and replied that by privilege of his dignity and order he was not
subject to lay jurisdiction, but only to that of the Church, and that he
was ready, come what might, to abide by its judgement. . . . Meanwhile King Stephen was succeeded by our most serene lord, King
Henry, from whose hands we just and only just succeeded in recalling
the case to the judgement of the Church, with much difficulty and by
strong pressure, to the indignation of the king and all his nobles.[1]

Henry II's attack on the question in England was prefaced
by similar activities in Normandy.[2] Part of Henry's complaint was that the punishments which were imposed by
courts Christian in England were too lenient. The murder
of Becket, however, prevented Henry from making good
his claim, and he was forced to recognize the right of
the Church alone to try criminous clerks. Apart from a
reference in the *Causa Magistri Gaufredi*, a poem of 1210
dealing with the clerk Geoffrey of Vinsauf,[3] little is known
about appeals to Rome in criminal cases.

By the thirteenth century the Church courts' civil competence was established over certain actions *ratione materiae*.
It included cases over Church rights and jurisdiction, such
as cases about ecclesiastical correction and jurisdiction, visitation, elections, and conventual jurisdiction, which were at
no time claimed by the lay power as being within secular
competence. It also embraced, or attempted to embrace, cases
relating to Church property and income—land and rents,
advowson and benefices, pensions and portions, and chapels,
although certain limitations were gradually imposed on
cases affecting property and advowson. Finally the Church
claimed spiritual cases, cases concerning marriage and

---

[1] *J.S.L.*, no. 16.

[2] Constitutions of Clarendon, c. 3, *Select Charters*, ed. Stubbs, pp. 164–5, and
Haskins, *Norman Institutions*, pp. 32 and 171.

[3] Translated by Richardson, 'Schools of Northampton', p. 598, and printed in
full in Latin by E. Faral, 'Le manuscrit 511 du "Hunterian Museum" de Glasgow',
Studi Medievali, N.S. ix (1936), 57. M. Faral has written that this is an appeal to
the archbishop of Canterbury, which Mr. Richardson questions. It seems indisputable that it is an appeal to Rome.

legitimacy, and wills, and although rights to judge questions relating to bastardy, chattels, and debts were closely guarded by the lay courts, yet the Church had some successes here.

2. Church Rights and Jurisdiction

(i) Ecclesiastical Correction, Jurisdiction, and Visitation

The exercise of the right of ecclesiastical correction was not questioned by the lay courts. In a long and intricate case between Edmund, archbishop of Canterbury, and Hugh d'Aubigny, earl of Arundel, resort was made to Rome. The quarrel, it seems, was first brought by Hugh d'Aubigny before the abbot of Bury St. Edmunds and a colleague. Then on the exception of the archbishop, it was delegated between 2 and 4 February 1238 to the abbots of Evesham, Cirencester, and Hyde, who subdelegated to the dean of Abingdon and others. It is not known why Hugh appealed again to Rome, nor why the archbishop's proctor acted similarly some time afterwards. On the proctor's appeal, papal letters were addressed on 15 February 1240 to the abbot of St. Augustine's, Canterbury, and the archdeacons of Wiltshire and Berkshire. The case concerned the sentences of excommunication and interdict which the archbishop had issued against the castle and town of Arundel. Hugh asserted that the archbishop by excommunicating him had illegally by-passed the diocesan. The archbishop replied that the earl had infringed his hunting rights in the forest of Arundel.[1] The plaint of the abbot and convent of Marmoutier at Tours against the bishop of Lincoln alleged that he had excommunicated the monks of the priory of Tickford (or Newport Pagnell), a cell of theirs. The case was placed in the hands of an auditor, William, cardinal deacon of St. Eustace, who decided in favour of the bishop on 2 June 1249 at Lyons.[2] Likewise the bishop of Worcester's

---

[1] The entry in *Reg. Greg. IX*, no. 5182, reviews the history of the case down to 1240. Lambeth Palace Library, Papal Documents, no. 32, is the papal bull addressed to the abbots of Evesham, Cirencester, and Hyde.

[2] *Reg. Inn. IV*, no. 4601, and see *V.C.H. Bucks.* i. 361–2. A similar case had been brought by the abbot elect of Glastonbury against Bishop Savaric of Bath about the sentences of interdict and excommunication which he had imposed on the monks (*Letters of Inn. III*, no. 159).

excommunication of William de Beauchamp, sheriff of Worcester, and several of his household, was challenged by the excommunicates, but was confirmed by the auditor John, cardinal deacon of St. Nicholas in Carcere, on 4 January 1251 and by the pope on 11 January.[1]

Suits about archiepiscopal and episcopal rights of jurisdiction and visitation were referred to Rome and often committed to delegates. On 1 June 1252 Innocent IV sent a mandate to the abbots of St. Albans, Bury St. Edmunds, and Waltham, in answer to a complaint made to him by the bishops of Bath and Wells, Chichester, Coventry and Lichfield, Ely, Exeter, Lincoln, London, Norwich, Rochester, St. Asaph, St. Davids, Salisbury, Worcester, and the bishop elect of Winchester, that the metropolitan was hindering the jurisdiction of his suffragans, particularly in the matter of appeals.[2] A suit between the archbishop of Canterbury and the archdeacon of Rochester concerned the archbishop's right to institute parsons in churches in Rochester diocese, to hear matrimonial causes, and to exercise jurisdiction over the manors of the bishop of Rochester *sede vacante*. It was delegated on 22 May 1238 to the legate Otto.[3] The question about the archbishop of Canterbury's right to visit the churches of St. Paul, London, St. Bartholomew, Smithfield, and Holy Trinity, Aldgate, and to receive procurations as metropolitan, came first before the priors of Christ Church, Canterbury, and St. Radegund's, then the bishop of Albano, and finally the pope. It was settled in 1252, when the defendants were condemned to admit the archbishop to visit their churches as metropolitan and to pay procurations.[4]

Bishops' rights of jurisdiction were frequently asserted before delegated courts against claims of exemption. The claims of Eustace, bishop of London, and the dean and chapter of St. Paul's over the abbot and convent of Westminster were contested before judges delegate. The suit was submitted to the ordination of Stephen, archbishop of Canterbury, Bishops Peter of Winchester and Richard of Salisbury,

---

[1] *Reg. Inn. IV*, no. 5194.
[2] *Wells Cathedral Miscellany*, ed. A. Watkin (Som. Rec. Soc. lvi, 1941), p. 97, *C.P.L.* i. 278.
[3] *Reg. Greg. IX*, no. 4372.
[4] *Reg. Inn. IV*, nos. 5670–2. See also *Early Charters of St. Paul's*, no. 229.

and Priors Thomas of Merton and Richard of Dunstable, and was settled in favour of Westminster in 1222.[1] In the church of St. Paul, London, on 4 November 1228, M(artin of Pattishall), dean of London, R(eginald), archdeacon of Middlesex, and Master R(obert) de Arches,[2] a subdelegate of the bishop of Rochester, decided a quarrel between Thomas Blundeville, bishop of Norwich, and the priors of Binham and Wymondham. The dispute had broken out over the obedience and reverence due to the bishop from the priors for their parish churches, and over visitation, procurations, and the appointment of vicars. It was decided that the priors were to be presented to the bishop and were to profess canonical obedience to him, and that the vicars were to be instituted on the presentation of the priors. The bishop's visitation fees and the taxation of the vicarages were also settled.[3]

The decision of the bishop, dean, and precentor of Hereford, in a case between the bishop of Llandaff and the abbot and convent of Gloucester about the inspection of the church of Newport (Mon.), followed a similar pattern of composition. The bishop was to visit the church and to receive procurations: he was also to admit suitable clerks presented by the abbot and convent.[4] In c. 1234 Alexander Stavensby, bishop of Coventry, challenged the prior and convent of Coventry about visitation;[5] and in 1246 Roger of Weasenham, bishop of the same see, prosecuted the abbot and convent of Burton and the abbots, priors, rectors, and vicars of other monasteries and churches about procurations from his visitation, which they declined to pay.[6] The complicated arrangements and stipulations of the award of the judges in 1219 in a suit between Bishop Hugh II of Lincoln and William, abbot, and the convent of St. Albans, about the ordination of a vicarage in the church of Luton, and about

---

[1] Westminster Ch. 12753, pd. *Acta Stephani Langton,* ed. Major, no. 54.

[2] He occurs as official of the bishop of London on 26 Jan. 1223/4 (B.M. Harley MS. 6956, f. 136ʳ, a transcript from St. Paul's Pyx F), and as a witness to a composition made before M. Reginald, official of the bishop of London, in Oct. 1221/2 (Westminster Ch. 2185).   [3] Binham Cart., f. 46ᵛ.

[4] *Glos. Cart.* ii, nos. dxix–dxx. Cf. the abbot and convent of Malmesbury against the bishop and chapter of Salisbury about procurations, etc. (*Malmesbury Reg.* i. 378 and 370–2).

[5] *Reg. Greg. IX,* no. 2197.   [6] Lichfield Cart., f. 14ᵛ.

the subjection of the cells of Belvoir, Hertford, and Beadlow, show how it was necessary to formulate detailed decisions if further disputes were to be successfully avoided.[1] The well-known dispute between Robert Grosseteste and the dean and chapter of his cathedral church of Lincoln about the bishop's jurisdiction, which the dean and chapter refused to acknowledge, his right of visitation, and the churches belonging to the dignitaries, was finally settled by Innocent IV on 25 August 1245. This was five years after its commencement, when every judicial trick and hindrance had been exploited by both parties.[2]

The exercise of archidiaconal jurisdiction was sometimes challenged by monastic houses and by the rectors of churches within the archdeaconry. Thomas, archdeacon of Lincoln, brought the abbot and convent of Bardney before papal delegates in a dispute about his jurisdiction in the parish of Bardney. He claimed the right to visit the parish church and to receive an annual payment from the church of All Saints, Barton. The suit was settled at Freston (Suff.) on 23 April 1246.[3] Similarly Adam of Bury St. Edmunds, archdeacon of Oxford, asserted his rights of jurisdiction against St. Frideswide's in the churches of Headington, Marston, and Elsfield (Oxon.), and in the parish of St. Frideswide in Oxford, and this came before the abbot of Bardney and the priors of St. Katherine and of St. Mary Magdalene, Lincoln, in 1231.[4] When Master Walter (de Salerne), archdeacon of Norfolk and chaplain of Pope Innocent IV, initiated a suit against the prior and convent of Wymondham, he managed to get it heard by a papal auditor. It concerned his right to visit and exercise archidiaconal

---

[1] St. Albans Cart. (B), f. 110ʳ, and *Reg. Antiq. Linc.* iii, no. 653. Cf. the case between the abbot and convent of Evesham and the bishop of Worcester about the churches in the Vale (*Reg. Inn. IV*, no. 4378).

[2] The documents in this suit are *Reg. Greg. IX*, nos. 5023, 5142; *Reg. Inn. IV*, nos. 239, 349, 1457; *Reg. Antiq. Linc.* ii, nos. 355–6; and P.R.O. KB 26/123 m. 7, and 131 m. 6. Cf. the Hereford case, *Hereford Charters*, pp. 92–5.

[3] Bardney Cart., f. 30ᵛ, and cf. Burton Cart., ff. 62ᵛ-3ᵛ (cal. Wrottesley, *Coll. Hist. Staffs.* v, pt. i. 56), the case of William de Luceby, archdeacon of Derby, against the abbot of Burton, about the privileges and liberties of the convent before judges delegate of Gregory IX.

[4] *St. Frideswide's Cart.* ii, no. 731. See also Exeter Ch. 812 for another suit of the same kind about archidiaconal jurisdiction in the church of Colyton (Devon) between the archdeacon of Exeter and Master Michael de Buketon.

jurisdiction in the churches of Wymondham and Happis-burgh (Norf.). The sentence in Walter's favour was delivered by John, cardinal of St. Nicholas in Carcere, on 10 June 1249 at Lyons.[1] A case about archidiaconal jurisdiction between Master R., rector of the church of Cliffe-at-Hoo (a parish in the archbishop's peculiar of Shoreham within the diocese of Rochester), and the officials of the archdeacon of Canterbury, opened in 1231.[2] The rector alleged that the officials had exceeded the archidiaconal rights in his church. The suit was delegated to at least five commissions of judges before it was recalled to the *Curia*. A papal mandate of 19 December 1236 ordered the bishop and treasurer of Chichester to compel the archdeacon and his officials to appear at the papal court, in person or by agent, within four months, taking with them all the documents concerning the case.[3]

Sometimes the officials and officers of the bishop threatened the archdeacon's jurisdiction. Walter, archdeacon of Surrey, complained to the pope that Master Geoffrey de Foring (*sic*)[4] and other officers of William de Raleigh, lately bishop of Winchester, exercised an undue jurisdiction in his archdeaconry and oppressed his subjects, presumably by financial exactions and extortions. The judges, the treasurer of Salisbury and Master Ralph of York and Peter de Cimba, canons of Salisbury, were ordered by Innocent IV on 26 November 1250 to bring the case to an end within six months, or else to summon the parties to Rome.[5] It was at no time disputed that this field of jurisdiction belonged to the Church courts, and particularly to those of Rome.

(ii) *Elections*

The popes increased their jurisdiction over election cases in the thirteenth century, and there was considerable growth and standardization in the electoral law under Innocent III.[6]

---

[1] *Reg. Inn. IV*, nos. 4645–6.   [2] *Reg. Greg. IX*, no. 2375.

[3] Ibid., no. 3406. This is probably the same Master R. (Richard of Wallingford), rector of the church of Cliffe-at-Hoo, who brought the prior and convent of Christ Church, Canterbury, before judges delegate about the tithes of two mills, one water mill, and other tithes in 1228–9 (Canterbury, Cartae Antiquae, C 280).

[4] Master Geoffrey de Fering was official of Winchester from December 1239 (Eye Cart., f. 29^{r-v}).

[5] *Reg. Inn. IV*, no. 5024.   [6] cc. 16–44. X. I. 6.

The papal rights of postulation, translation, and confirmation were elaborated during this pontificate, and the right to decide between rival candidates was freely exercised.[1] After 1215 there was little new development in the law, but ignorance about the actual application of the law, and questions about the rights of electoral bodies and the form of election, led to continual reference to the papal court.[2] Twenty-five disputed elections were referred to the papacy in the period between November 1214 and 1273.[3]

The enactments of Alexander IV and Gregory X, which ruled that disputed elections were reserved, or major, cases, confirmed at a comparatively late date an accepted custom.[4] Although contested elections were major cases, they were frequently delegated for settlement because of the need to obtain exact evidence. The Rochester election case of 1235–8 was delegated to two commissions of judges delegate and heard by two auditors before it was concluded.[5] A papal mandate of Gregory IX, issued on 16 June 1237, ordered the legate Otto to examine witnesses and hear the suit about the election of the prior of Norwich as bishop, or to remit it to Rome with all the information he had gleaned.[6] An order of Honorius III was dispatched from Rome on 9 June 1217 exhorting the judges to proceed actively in the lawsuit of G(?Geoffrey de Burgh), archdeacon of Norwich, against Master Robert of York, about election to the see of Ely, or to remit it to Rome, lest the suit should become interminable.[7] The royal power did not contest at any time the papacy's right to legislate about elections and to decide in disputed cases. Within these bounds, however, all means were tried to secure the election of suitable candidates.[8]

[1] See G. Barraclough, 'The Making of a Bishop in the Middle Ages', *Catholic Historical Review*, xix (1933), 278–9 and 293, and c. 1. X. I. 7 (Inn. III).

[2] Gibbs and Lang, *Bishops and Reform*, pp. 56–7.

[3] Ibid., p. 70. See also A. H. Sweet, 'Control of English Episcopal Elections in the Thirteenth Century', *Cath. Hist. Rev.* vi (1927), 579. He says that of 141 effective elections to English bishoprics between 1216 and 1307, it appears that about 17 per cent were decided by the pope.

[4] Barraclough, 'Making of a Bishop', p. 294, citing c. 10. 6. I. 6; Powicke *Henry III*, p. 260; and c. 1. X. I. 7.

[5] *Reg. Greg. IX*, nos. 2731, 3261, and 4197.

[6] Ibid., no. 3758.

[7] *Reg. Hon. III*, no. 1422.

[8] Powicke, *Henry III*, p. 266.

Exactly the same principles of conduct were applied to conventual elections.[1] Adam, sacrist of Coventry, appealed to the pope against the bishop, who had refused to confirm him as abbot of Shrewsbury. Adam then renounced his claim, and Innocent IV, after annulling the bishop's appointment of William, monk of Coventry, promoted Henry, monk of Evesham, to the abbacy.[2] This was a case of postulation. In a disputed election in 1217 at St. Edward's, Shaftesbury, an appeal was made to Rome by A., sacrist of the house, who had been elected abbess. As it was said that one part of the nuns had elected J., the legate Guala refused to confirm A.'s election, until further inquiries were made; and he appointed the abbots of Bindon and Cerne for this purpose. Before them A. was said to have renounced her election and appeal. Judges delegate, the abbot of Warden, the prior of Dunstable, and Master William Scot, doctor of canon law living at Oxford, now examined A.'s case; and she claimed that she had been coerced into renouncing her election and appeal. Shortly after this, on 18 January 1218, a papal mandate was obtained by J., who complained that she was tired of the labours and expenses of the suit. It was addressed to the bishop and chancellor of Salisbury and the prior of Amesbury, who were instructed to impose silence on A. if they found that the facts were as J. alleged, or else to remit the case to the abbot of Warden and his commission.[3] The outcome of the case is unknown, but the stages thus far illustrate that the methods used to deal with disputed elections to abbacies or priorates were similar to those employed in episcopal election disputes.

(iii) *Conventual Jurisdiction*

Another plentiful group of cases, which went almost exclusively to Rome and were delegated, concern conventual jurisdiction and the relationship and rights of certain monastic houses. Such suits were often between convents of different dioceses and between houses which were separated

---

[1] See U. Berlière, 'Les Elections abbatiales au Moyen Âge', *Academie Royale de Belgique*, fasc. 3 (Brussels, 1927), esp. pp. 53–5.

[2] *Reg. Inn. IV*, no. 5188.

[3] Rome, Vatican Archives, Reg. Vat. 9, f. 150ᵛ, and 10, ff. 48ᵛ–9ʳ (*Reg. Hon. III*, nos. 757, 1810, and *C.P.L.* i. 49, 61).

by the Channel. Rome was therefore the obvious tribunal. Sometime after 4 April 1209, R(ichard de Dalham), dean, N (?Matthew),[1] precentor, and Master Thomas Foliot, canon of Lichfield, heard a quarrel about the subjection of the convent of Langley (Ben. priory, Leics.) to the house of Farewell (Ben. abbey, Staffs.), and the appointment of a prioress at Langley. It was decided that the prioress of Langley was to be elected by the prioress (*sic*) of Farewell and the convent of Langley, that the prioress of Langley was to retain Alice of Ely in her house for five years, and that Farewell should renounce all other rights over Langley.[2] The quarrel reopened, and in 1248 another settlement was made by which Langley agreed to pay four marks to Farewell.[3]

A similar case between the prior and convent of Castle Acre and the convent of Bromholm in Norfolk, an alien priory dependent on Cluny, concerned the subjection of Bromholm to Castle Acre and the election of the prior of Bromholm. The judges delegate, the abbots of Swineshead, Vaudey, and Bourne, formulated a composition by the terms of which the prior of Castle Acre was to nominate three monks of his house, one of whom was to be chosen prior of Bromholm by the convent of Bromholm. All was not finally settled, however, for the convent of Bromholm soon petitioned the pope that on the death of the present prior they should elect, notwithstanding this arrangement. The pope, therefore, on 20 January 1226 ordered the bishop and prior of St. Andrew's, Rochester, and the prior of St. Mary's, Strood, to hear the case.[4] In 1229 another settlement was made by judges delegate, the abbot of Owston and the deans of Stamford and Rutland, acting on a mandate of Gregory IX. They decreed that the prior of Castle Acre was in future to nominate six monks, three of Acre and three of Bromholm, out of whom the convent of Bromholm should elect a prior.[5]

---

[1] N. is possibly a slip for M., since a Matthew was appointed precentor in *c.* 1177, occurs in *c.* 1208 and in 1219, and was still in office in 1229/30; see *Magnum Registrum Album*, ed. H. E. Savage (Collections for a History of Staffs., ed. William Salt Archaeol. Soc. 1926), nos. 42, 180, 189, 191, 358, and 658.

[2] P.R.O. E 135/2/28 (App. B (iv), no. 1).   [3] *V.C.H. Leics.* ii. 3.

[4] Bromholm Cart., ff. 11ʳ–12ʳ; and *Reg. Hon. III*, no. 5792 (*C.P.L.* i. 108).

[5] *V.C.H. Norf.* ii. 359–60.

Another Cluniac case concerned the obedience of the priory of Daventry to the mother house of La Charité. Such an important case, in which the abbot and convent of Cluny acted as plaintiffs, was brought before two auditors at the command of Innocent IV: first John Astensis, chaplain of the pope, and then John of Toledo, cardinal priest of St. Laurence in Lucina. It appears that the prior of La Charité had nominated the prior of Daventry until 1231, 'when it [Daventry] slipped out of the Order'.[1] Daventry was treated as non-exempt by the bishops of Lincoln, but La Charité continued to assert its claims.[2] The document which records the suit before the auditors is an *inspeximus* by Robert Grosseteste, bishop of Lincoln, of the report of Cardinal John, dated 29 May 1250 at Ile-Barbe near Lyons.[3]

The general movement towards freedom for monastic dependencies is reflected in suits of this nature, between alien houses, which came before judges delegate. The abbot and convent of St. Melaine at Rennes in Britanny challenged the bishop of London (probably Roger Niger) and the patron, the earl of Oxford, about the right of instituting a prior at Hatfield Regis or Broad Oak (Ben. al. Essex). The monks had said that the abbot had the right of appointment, whereupon the bishop had excommunicated them. The abbot had requested that the sentence should be relaxed, but the bishop had refused. He therefore appealed to the pope. The bishop and the earl instituted William, monk of St. John's Colchester, as prior, who so persecuted the monks that they had to return to St. Melaine, and a second appeal was made to the pope. On 17 April 1236, Gregory IX ordered the dean, precentor, and treasurer of Salisbury to hear the cause or remit it to the *Curia*,[4] but it was not finally settled until 11 November 1254, when Fulk, bishop of London, made an award declaring the priory to be independent.[5] In a similar case of this nature, the abbot and convent of St. Nicholas at

---

[1] R. Graham, *English Ecclesiastical Studies* (London, 1929), p. 99; and see *C.P.L.* i. 126, this is Daventry not Coventry.

[2] Knowles and Hadcock, *Religious Houses*, p. 96, and *V.C.H. Northants.* ii. 11.

[3] Bodleian Northants. Ch. 181, cal. N. Denholm-Young, *Cart. of the Mediaeval Archives of Christ Church* (Oxf. Hist. Soc. xcii, 1931), p. 50.

[4] *Reg. Greg. IX*, no. 3090.

[5] *V.C.H. Essex*, ii. 108, and Knowles and Hadcock, *Religious Houses*, p. 67.

Angers conducted a long suit against the prior and convent of Spalding about their subjection to Angers.[1] The suit began well before 1235, and was not settled until 2 January 1242 in the palace of the pope.[2] This composition differed little from the 'Compositio Prima' of 1232.[3] There were only slight changes in the amount paid to the abbot, in the restriction of visitation rights to every three years, and in the stipulation that the profession of novices was to be held at Spalding in future. The election of the prior of Spalding was to be made by the convent, and the prior was to have full administration of temporals and spirituals.[4]

A case between the prior of Nostell and Gervase, prior of Breedon,[5] about the control of Breedon (Aug. Leics.) by its mother house Nostell (Aug. Yorks. W.R.), came first before the bishop of Lincoln as ordinary, and then before papal judges delegate. Eventually both parties agreed to renounce all appeals and to accept the bishop's official's ordination. It was decided that the prior and convent of Nostell should retain their control over Breedon and that Prior Gervase should resign with a pension of twenty marks to be paid by Breedon.[6] Similarly a suit between the prior and convent of St. Botolph's, Colchester,[7] and the prior and convent of Holy Trinity, Aldgate, over subjection, obedience, profession, visitation, procurations, and disposition of things in the latter church, which came before the abbot of Langley and the prior and the dean of Norwich, was finally submitted to the ordination of Eustace, bishop of London.[8]

[1] Knowles and Hadcock, *Religious Houses*, p. 77. Spalding was dependent upon St. Nicholas at Angers until 1397.

[2] *Reg. Greg. IX*, nos. 2416, 4240–1; *Reg. Inn. IV*, no. 1203; and Spalding Cart., ff. 11ᵛ and 14ᵛ.

[3] *V.C.H. Lincs.* ii. 118–24. The 'Prima' is in Spalding Cart., f. 11ᵛ, and in W. Dugdale, *Monasticon Anglicanum*, iii, ed. Caley, Ellis, and Bandinel (1846), 220 num. xv.   [4] Spalding Cart., f. 14ᵛ.

[5] The priory was founded for a prior and five canons of Nostell (Knowles and Hadcock, *Religious Houses*, p. 129).

[6] *Rotuli Roberti Grosseteste*, ed. F. N. Davis (Linc. Rec. Soc. xi, 1914), pp. 440–2, and see p. 424; and *Close Rolls* (*1237–42*), p. 449, cited by R. A. McKinley, 'The Cartulary of Breedon' (Manchester M.A. thesis, 1950), p. xix. See also *V.C.H. Leics.* ii. 8.

[7] This was the first house of the Augustinian order in England (see Knowles and Hadcock, *Religious Houses*, p. 134).

[8] St. Paul's, Press A, Box 23, Ch. 864 (App. B (iv), no. 2). See also *V.C.H. Essex*, ii. 148.

Another category of suit concerned the relationship between convents and hospitals, and here again there was no challenge to the Church's jurisdiction. A cause between the prior and canons of St. Bartholomew's, London, and the master and brothers of the hospital, which concerned the election of a master, his obedience to the prior, and the receiving of brothers, was delegated to Benedict of Sawston, bishop of Rochester, and his colleagues. The parties, however, submitted to the ordination of Eustace de Fauconberg, bishop of London, which was given on 1 July 1223 in the church of St. Paul, London.¹ A suit of the master and brothers of the hospital of St. John at Huntingdon against the abbot and convent of Thorney, about the hospital's right to say masses for, and hear the confessions of, the ill and poor inmates of the hospital, was committed by Innocent IV on 18 July 1245 to the bishop of Lincoln, who subdelegated to the archdeacon of Huntingdon. The hospital was situated in All Saints parish where Thorney and the prior and convent of Huntingdon were the joint patrons. It was decided, with the consent of Robert, bishop of Lincoln, that the abbot and convent of Thorney should concede what the hospital sought, saving the rights of the mother church, the prior and convent, and the rector. For this concession the hospital was to pay Thorney three shillings yearly.²

3. Church Property and Income

The subject-matter of many cases was closely connected with property and income. Lay fee constituted non-sacred, immovable goods, and was therefore in England a plea which belonged to the Crown. This was conceded in principle by Alexander III.³ Clause 9 of the Constitutions of Clarendon declared:

Si calumnia emerserit inter clericum et laicum, vel inter laicum et clericum, de ullo tenemento quod clericus attrahere velit ad elemosinam, laicus vero ad laicum feudum, recognitione duodecim legalium

---

¹ *Early Charters of St. Paul's*, no. 146.   ² Thorney Cart. i, f. 42ʳ.
³ c. 7. *X.* IV. 17. On the king's claims to decide competence and Alexander III's position, see F. W. Maitland, 'Frankalmoign in the Twelfth and Thirteenth Centuries' in *Collected Papers*, ii, ed. H. A. L. Fisher (Cambridge, 1911), 205–22, esp. 215.

hominum, per capitalis Justitiae regis considerationem terminabitur, utrum tenementum sit pertinens ad elemosinam sive ad feudum laicum, coram ipso Justitia regis. Et si recognitum fuerit ad elemosinam pertinere, placitum erit in curia ecclesiastica, si vero ad laicum feudum, nisi ambo de eodem episcopo vel barone advocaverint, erit placitum in curia regia . . .[1]

In a notification addressed to the abbot and prior of Hyde and the prior of Sherborne, judges delegate, William de Vernon, earl of Devon, and the barons and knights of the Isle of Wight informed the judges that it was recognized on the order of the king, by the oath of twelve free and lawful men of the island, that the land in Freshwater about which there was a dispute between the abbot and convent of Lyre and Thomas Griffin, parson of Freshwater, belonged to the abbey and not to the church of Freshwater. They declared that they were prepared to prove their testimony.[2] In this instance, where the case was between a religious house and a clerk, one party, presumably Lyre, had brought the case before a Church court. The clerk, Thomas Griffin, in an attempt to have it established that the land belonged to his glebe, meanwhile applied for the assize *utrum*.[3] But in 1202 the assize declared the land in question to be lay fee belonging to the abbot and convent.[4] The judges delegate were notified to this effect.

(i) *Land and Rents*

From the group of cases concerning land, which came before the papal courts, it is difficult to tell how many dealt with land held in lay fee and not with free alms. That the Church courts sometimes dealt with disputes which were really about lay fee is confirmed by a letter in the Special Correspondence volumes in the Public Record Office, in which it is stated that the citizens of Scarborough (Yorks.) complained to the king that Master Walter of Wisbech, archdeacon of

---

[1] *Select Charters*, ed. Stubbs, pp. 165–6. The writ of prohibition *de laico feodo* covered not only manors, lands, pastures, woods, marshes, but also houses, grain standing in the field, the right of pasturage, and the services and customary dues on certain land (*W.P.*, pt. i. 273).   [2] Carisbrooke Cart., f. 72ʳ.

[3] On this point see D. M. Stenton, *English Justice between the Norman Conquest and the Great Charter 1066–1215* (Jayne Lectures for 1963, London, 1965), pp. 46–7.   [4] *Curia Regis Rolls*, ii. 110.

the East Riding, and his dean greatly injured them by bringing pleas concerning lay fee to the court Christian;[1] but the frequency with which such suits were brought before Church courts cannot be ascertained. Between 1220 and 1230, however, the majority of pleas in writs of prohibition claimed to be about lay fee.[2]

Suits concerning property and land that was in dispute between religious houses and clerks, or between different religious houses, came before judges delegate. The abbot of Westminster brought John de Templo, parson of the Holy Innocents, before judges delegate about eight messuages which the abbot said belonged to the parish of St. Margaret's.[3] The abbot of Warden, the prior of Chicksands, and A dean of Edworth (Beds.) were appointed by the pope to deal with a quarrel about a virgate of land between the canons of Lanthony and Robert, clerk of Henlow (Beds.).[4] Innocent III instructed Robert, abbot of Walden (Essex), William, prior of Barnwell, and Robert, rector of Haddenham (Cambs.), to hear a suit about the land of Hervey Walter in the town of Ickleton (Cambs.) disputed between Hericus,[5] abbot, and the canons of West Dereham and Eufemia, prioress, and the convent of Ickleton (Ben. Cambs.). Arbiters (Eustace, bishop of Ely, and Master Elias of Dereham) settled the suit: each convent was to have some of the land, and the canons of West Dereham were to pay the nuns one pound of cumin each year.[6] A suit between the dean (Alexander) and the chapter of Wells and Ernisius, a canon of Wells, about land at Biddisham (Som.) that Ernisius possessed in the name of his prebend was settled by John,

---

[1] P.R.O. SC1, vol. 6, no. 73. On the other hand, the abbess and convent of Holy Trinity, Caen, complained to the pope that the earl of Oxford brought them before a lay court over certain English manors, which they alleged they had always held in pure alms (*Letters of Inn. III*, no. 661).

[2] *W.P.*, pt. i. 310. On p. 274 Flahiff says that the comparatively small number of prohibition pleas arising out of a lay fee in the mid and late thirteenth century shows the success achieved by the king's courts. It must be remembered that these calculations are based not on the number of writs taken out during these years, but on the number of cases that were not dropped by the plaintiff and judges on receipt of the writ.

[3] Westminster Domesday, ff. 346ᵛ–7ʳ, t. Hen. III.

[4] Lanthony Cart. A 1, X, no. cv. Date probably *c.* 1173 × 1178. MS. 'Adeano', but ? read 'A. decano'.

[5] Mentioned also as Henry.   [6] West Dereham Cart., f. 293ᵛ.

abbot of Ford, Humphrey, prior of Ford, and Baldwin, prior of Axmouth.[1]

In cases about land, laymen were frequently the defendants. The prioress and convent of St. Michael, Stamford, sued William Erl of North Luffenham (Rutland) about land;[2] the abbot and convent of Bardney charged Philip de Kyme about land in Bawburgh (Norf.);[3] and the abbot and convent of Beaulieu brought Ivo Wint' (? of Winchester) before the prior of Christchurch and his co-judges about a tenement.[4] On 25 July 1239 a private arrangement about land was made between the abbot and convent of Pipewell and Robert Basset of Rushton (Northants.), after suits had been brought *in foro ecclesiastico* and *in foro seculari*.[5] The abbot and convent of Beaulieu, when they made a chirograph with William de St. Clare about a footpath near the bridge of Soberton (Hants) and about free right of way for horse vehicles and pedestrians, remitted all actions that they had brought against him *in curia Christianitatis* by letters of the pope.[6] In 1241 a composition about certain pastures was made between, on the one hand, the abbot and convent of Combe, and, on the other, Nicholas, knight of Withybrook (Warw.), and the free tenants of the same place, in front of the priors of Newnham and Caldwell.[7]

Rather more infrequently, it seems, laymen brought ecclesiastics before delegated courts in questions about land. William de Mowbray got letters from Innocent III, addressed to Simon the dean and Hamo the treasurer of York, in a dispute with the abbot and monks of Byland about the forest of Middlesmoor in Nidderdale. The suit was settled on 4 August 1204 at York.[8] W., called *pincerna*, and his sons, got papal letters, addressed to the dean, chancellor, and subdean of Wells, against the abbots of Margam and Neath 'super terris et rebus aliis'.[9] Walter, son of Geoffrey, and others said in front of William, prior of St. Frideswide's, and the archdeacon and chancellor of Oxford that their

---

[1] Exeter Ch. 26 and Wells Ch. 26.
[2] P.R.O. E 326/2268 (App. B (v), no. 3).   [3] Bardney Cart., f. 95ᵛ.
[4] Beaulieu Cart., f. 136ʳ.   [5] Pipewell Cart. (B), f. 25ʳ.
[6] Beaulieu Cart., f. 47ʳ⁻ᵛ.   [7] Combe Cart., f. 77ʳ.
[8] Byland Cart., f. 77ʳ⁻ᵛ, and see below, p. 218.
[9] B.M. Harley Ch. 75 B 2 (App. B (iv), no. 3).

ancestors had given certain meadow-lands to Daventry in return for tithes of hay and of the courtyard, which belonged to the church of West Haddon. Daventry, they alleged, had taken both.[1]

Disputes about manors were also brought before the delegated tribunals. A suit of 1175 between Albin, abbot of Darley, and Hubert, son of Ralph, which was delegated to Roger, bishop of Worcester, and Robert, prior of Kenilworth, was over the manor of Crich (Derbys.).[2] In 1205 the abbot and convent of St. Evroult charged R., a knight, and others about the church and manor of West Kirby and the chapel of Woodcott (Cheshire) before the dean and precentor of London.[3] The abbot and convent of Beaulieu brought Thomas de Pridias, knight, and Sibylla his wife before a delegated court in a suit about the manor of Rolonoydon (probably Cornwall) and certain lands. Beaulieu said that these lands belonged to the glebe of St. Kaveran.[4] A suit between the abbot and convent of Mont-Saint-Michel and Robert Marmion, a knight of York diocese, concerned the possession of the manor of Wath (Yorks. N.R.). In the presence of the king, presumably Henry III, there had been a duel between the two parties, which the abbot and convent had lost. They were, therefore, forced to renounce their suit, but the knight refused their renunciation until they should give a large sum of money to him as a token of their desire for peace. For this reason the abbot and convent of Mont-Saint-Michel appealed to Gregory IX, who on 26 February 1239 ordered the archbishop of York to examine the case and then to remit it to the pope, sending the parties to Rome.[5]

Monastic houses took suits about rents to Rome probably as often as they occurred. The abbot and convent of Thorney brought Walter de Trailly before the abbots of Vaudey and Bourne and Matthew, prior of St. Leonard's, Stamford, judges delegate of Honorius III, about an annual rent of thirty shillings. Walter confessed that he ought to pay the

---

[1] B.M. Add. Ch. 21888.   [2] *Darley Cart.* ii. 538–40.

[3] B.M. Wolley Ch. v. 27. The mandate included the subdean but there was no such office.   [4] Beaulieu Cart., ff. 134ʳ–5ʳ.

[5] *Reg. Greg. IX*, no. 4744, and see *Early Yorkshire Charters*, v, ed. C. T. Clay (Yorks. Archaeol. Soc. Rec. Ser., Extra Ser. ii, 1936), 224–5. Cf. *W.P.*, pt. ii. 267 n. 22 (KB 26/165 m. 36d).

rent, and because he had not paid it for a long time he gave Thorney the rent of sixty acres of some other land.[1] William son of Conan of Holbeach was questioned by the priors of St. Augustine's and St. Gregory's, Canterbury, and the prior of Faversham, in 1222, about an annual rent of four shillings from seven acres of land in Holbeach, which he was supposed to pay to the prior and convent of Christ Church, Canterbury. William confessed that he ought to pay the rent, and the prior and convent remitted arrears amounting to twenty-four shillings (they sought sixty-eight shillings).[2] Ralph, son of Lefwine, and Ivetta his wife, widow of Richard Villein, were brought by the priory of Thurgarton before Roger, dean of Lincoln, Philip, the subdean, and Master Walter Blund, canon of Lincoln, over a rent of half a mark in Eastgate (Lincoln). The settlement provided for the lease by the canons to Ralph and Ivetta of an oven in Sapergate for twelve years from Michaelmas 1206. The suit reopened before 13 November 1219, when a fresh commission of judges delegate was appointed by Honorius III to hear it.[3]

(ii) Advowson and Benefices

A large number of cases concerned all aspects of the parish church, its patron, its rector and vicar, its income, and its rights. It might be argued that any of these cases affected the right of patronage or advowson. From Henry II's reign advowson was classed as real property, that is as an immovable, and it was therefore subject to the jurisdiction of the temporal courts in England.[4] There is no

---

[1] Thorney Cart. ii, f. 299ʳ; and cf. East Riding Rec. Office DDEV/44/3, where Owston brought Hugh Paynel before judges delegate over the rent of a mill.

[2] Canterbury, Cartae Antiquae, H 120, pd. by K. Major in 'Some Early Documents relating to Holbeach', *Reps. and Papers of the Archit. and Archaeol. Socs. of Lincs. and Northants.*, xli (1935), 42–3. See also MS. Scrapbook A, p. 13, Ch. 25, a suit between the prior and convent of Christ Church and the brothers of Dunes in Sheppey about an annual rent of four shillings (1219–20).

[3] *Reg. Antiq. Linc.* viii, no. 2300, note on pp. 112–13.

[4] See *Glanvill*, ed. Hall, iv. 9 and 13. Henry had concerned himself with the question of advowson in England before 1158, see Haskins, *Norman Institutions*, p. 332, and for similar activities in Normandy, see pp. 171–2. See also B.M. Cotton MS. Otho B xiv, f. 66ᵛ: 'Item litera Ricardi regis Angl' [Richard I] de prohibitione directa priori de Ware quod non trahat causam juris patronatus qui (*sic*) pertinet ad curiam suam ex antiqua consuetudine in regno Angl' ad aliquam curiam Christianitatis extra regnum Anglie.'

doubt that in the latter part of Stephen's reign such suits had been heard in ecclesiastical courts, and decisions about the right of presentation as well as the actual possession of the benefice had also been made there.[1] Clause 1 of the Constitutions of Clarendon (1164) declared:

De advocatione et praesentatione ecclesiarum si controversia emerserit inter laicos, vel inter clericos, vel inter laicos et clericos, in curia domini regis tractetur vel terminetur.[2]

It has often been supposed that from 1164 onwards the claims of the ecclesiastical courts in England over this field of jurisdiction were decisively and completely rejected.[3] This is not so, although certain emphases of the dispute changed, for instance from possession to presentation.

The Church as a whole did not give up its claims.[4] The decrees of the 1179 Lateran Council were framed with the intention of increasing ecclesiastical control over the exercise of the right of patronage,[5] and the *Glossa Ordinaria* on the words *ecclesiasticum iudicem* of the decretal c. 11. X. II. 2 states that among the causes which lie within the competence of the ecclesiastical judge are causes concerning the *jus patronatus*.[6] Furthermore the papal Chancery did not have any scruples about issuing mandates to judges delegate to try English cases about advowson in courts Christian. Professor Cheney comments on the Harrold case that it shows 'how disputes which involved ecclesiastical patronage might, despite the Constitutions of Clarendon, come up repeatedly for settlement before ecclesiastical judges, provided that the words "patronage" and "advowson" were avoided'.[7] But little trouble was taken to disguise many of these pleas either in the mandates or the *acta*. For instance, on 27 February 1217 Honorius III delegated a suit about the advowson of

---

[1] Gray, '*Ius Praesentandi*', p. 484.   [2] *Select Charters*, ed. Stubbs, p. 164.

[3] For examples of suits about advowson coming before the delegated courts before and after 1164, see Morey, *Bartholomew of Exeter*, pp. 63–5, 72; *J.S.L.*, nos. 81 and 102; Abingdon Cart., f. 55ʳ⁻ᵛ; and Bodleian MS. DD Queen's College, Oxford, nos. 282, 285–6.   [4] See, e.g., *X*. III. 38—'De iure patronatus'.

[5] Gray, '*Ius Praesentandi*', p. 486.

[6] J. W. Goldsmith, *Competence of Church and State over Marriage—Disputed Points* (Catholic University of America, Canon Law Studies, no. 197, 1944), p. 9.

[7] Cheney, 'Harrold Priory', pp. 2–3, and Gray, '*Ius Praesentandi*', expresses the same view.

the church of Puttenham (Herts.), between the prioress and
the nuns of Stamford and the prior and convent of Canons
Ashby, to Simon, abbot of Thame, the prior of Abingdon,
and the dean of Stanton.[1] A suit between the prior and convent of Eye and John, clerk of Bedfield (Suff.),was delegated
by Gregory IX on 28 February 1237 to the dean, precentor,
and treasurer of Lincoln. The mandate was made out against
John, clerk, A., knight, and others, over patronage, debts,
and other things, in which Eye alleged that they were injured as patron of the church of Playford (Suff.).[2] A suit
delegated by Gregory IX on 18 January 1236 to the dean of
Lincoln (who subdelegated to Master Robert of Brinkhill,
canon) and the treasurer and subdean of Lincoln, was between the abbot and convent of Easby, and the archbishop
of York and Master Laurence of Topcliffe (Yorks.), and
concerned the advowson of the church of Stanwick (Yorks.).[3]
In another obvious question of patronage, Thomas of Ilderton swore before judges delegate not to move any question
in future against the prior and convent of Kirkham about the
church of St. Michael at Ilderton (Northumb.).[4]

By and large, however, the incidence of obvious cases of
advowson coming before papal delegated courts seems to
have been small. The evidence from the records of the delegated courts substantiates the assertion that the English
Church came in the course of the thirteenth century to tole-
rate the king's claim to exclusive jurisdiction over clear-cut
matters of advowson.[5] The king's court was showing itself
the more suitable to deal with these cases, and there was
anyway considerable risk in coming before a Church court,
as it was realized that a writ of prohibition could easily be
obtained by the defendant. Most advowson cases which
came before the papal courts called forth a writ of prohibition. The remaining handful of six or seven act as a reminder
against generalization. Their small number also supports

1 Canons Ashby Cart., f. 50ʳ⁻ᵛ (App. B (iv), no. 4).
2 Eye Cart., f. 41ʳ⁻ᵛ.
3 Easby Cart., ff. 291ᵛ, 292ʳ⁻ᵛ, and 293ʳ, and see another suit on f. 274ʳ⁻ᵛ:
'super . . . advocacione'.
4 Kirkham Cart., f. 82ᵛ, and *History of Northumberland*, xiv (1935), 256.
5 See G. B. Flahiff, 'Use of Prohibitions', p. 106 n. 27, and Gray, '*Ius Praesentandi*', pp. 487 and 502.

the argument that this kind of case had largely but not completely passed out of the competence of the Church court.[1]

During the late twelfth and early thirteenth centuries in England the evidence seems to support the contention that the crux of the quarrel about competence over advowsons changed. The royal courts had established successfully enough their claims to cases which directly affected the right of advowson. The really important innovation after 1180 was in the use of prohibitions to deal with actions between clerks which indirectly affected the right of advowson.[2] The type of advowson prohibition which became most frequent in the thirteenth century was not one directly about the right of advowson, but the *indicavit* where advowson was brought into question by a dispute over the possession of a church, or more frequently over a portion of the tithes due to the church.[3]

Quarrels about presentation to churches and the possessions of benefices were inextricably connected with the patron's rights. Evidence remains of many of these suits which came before judges delegate and in which no attempt seems to have been made by either party to obtain a writ of prohibition.[4] For instance, in a suit between the prior and convent of St. Andrew, Northampton, and Thomas de Eastleigh, clerk, which arose over his institution in the church of Wyville (Lincs.), St. Andrew's alleged that they were the patrons of the church and that Thomas had been presented against their wishes by the archdeacon of Salisbury and the dean of Wolverhampton. The judges declared on 15 December 1246 in the church of All Saints, Northampton, that this presentation should be regarded as null, that the presentee of the prior and convent should be admitted to the church, and that Thomas should be condemned to pay thirty pounds sterling expenses.[5]

---

[1] They are: Easby Cart., f. 301ʳ⁻ᵛ (1221–5); ibid., f. 274ʳ⁻ᵛ (1253); ibid., ff. 291ᵛ, 292ʳ⁻ᵛ, 293ʳ (1236–7); Eye Cart., f. 41 ʳ⁻ᵛ; Canons Ashby Cart., f. 50ʳ⁻ᵛ (1217); Torre Cart., f. 60ᵛ (c. 1243); Kirkham Cart., f. 82ᵛ; and *Bracton's Note Book*, ii, no. 62.

[2] Gray, '*Ius Praesentandi*', pp. 486–7.   [3] *W.P.*, pt. i. 275–6.

[4] e.g. Castle Acre Cart., f. 47ʳ; *Colchester Cart.* i. 100, 104; Dunstable Cart., f. 45ʳ, cal. *Dunstable Cart.*, no. 391; *Reg. Greg. IX*, no. 3229; Beaulieu Cart., f. 129ᵛ; Morey, *Bartholomew of Exeter*, pp. 59, 62, and 71; and *Glastonbury Cart.*, no.(xxii), mandate of delegation.   [5] Northampton, St. Andrew's Cart. (A), f. 208ʳ.

Over and above the local system of patronage was the papal right of provision, which constituted a more severe threat to secular claims to jurisdiction over advowson, as there was no possible legal interference with this right. It has been argued that the system of providing papal nominees to English benefices received much impetus from John's submission to the pope in 1213,[1] but it was also part of a general process. The earliest recorded instance, where a provision was asked, comes from 1137.[2] Mandatory provision was not used until the pontificate of Adrian IV (1154–9).[3] The final and most effective development was to reserve benefices before they became vacant. This method made its initial appearance in 1199, and it remained in use until the decretal 'Licet ecclesiarum' of 1265, which provided for general reservations of benefices.[4] A considerable number of cases, usually major ones, concern disputed benefices where one of the parties had been presented by the pope.[5] Albert, canon of Milan, was given a prebend at Salisbury by Martin de Summa, on the order of Pope Gregory IX, but the clergy of Salisbury and Lincoln objected that Albert had despoiled Ralph de Egham. An appeal was made to Innocent IV, who on 16 December 1243 ordered Master Henry, canon of St. Stephen's in Brolio, Milan, staying at Paris, to hear the cause or cite the parties to appear before the pope.[6] Similar trouble had arisen in another instance some time before 1237. Master Robert of Gloucester had been provided with the church of Eynsford (Kent) by the pope, but the official of Canterbury thrust in William de Plessi on the king's presentation, and the archbishop put in Master William de Cerneia. Robert obtained papal letters to the bishop of Worcester and

---

[1] Mackenzie, 'Anti-Foreign Movement', pp. 183–4.

[2] J. J. Haydt, *Reserved Benefices* (Catholic University of America, Canon Law Studies, no. 161, 1942), p. 14.

[3] Ibid., pp. 14–15.　　　　　[4] Ibid., pp. 16, 18, 22–3.

[5] e.g. *Reg. Greg. IX*, no. 630. The papal registers are full of examples.

[6] *Reg. Greg. IX*, no. 331. Cf. *Reg. Inn. IV*, no. 2537, a case between Godfrey de Toffetes, clerk of the bishop of Winchester, and Anthony, canon of St. Antoninus, Piacenza, about the church of Alresford (Hants). The sentence of the auditor, J., cardinal of St. Laurence in Lucina, was in favour of Godfrey. Pope Innocent IV, therefore, ordered the bishops of Winchester and Norwich to provide Anthony with another benefice in England.

his colleagues ordering them to hear the case, but the king then inhibited the process, as two of the judges informed the pope. On 5 January 1237 Gregory IX sent a mandate to the bishop of Chichester, the bishop elect of Valence staying in England (probably William of Savoy), and the abbot of St. Augustine's, Canterbury, ordering them to cite the archbishop of Canterbury and William de Plessi to appear at Rome. The case was heard by Thomas, cardinal of St. Sabina, and sentence was given in favour of Master Robert of Gloucester on 9 May 1239.[1] Another provision case began after John Sarracenus, dean of Wells, acting on a mandate of Innocent IV, had provided Matthew de Alperino, papal chaplain, with the church of Overton (Hants). Philip de Lucy, however, claimed that he was the rector there, and the case was brought before John, cardinal of St. Laurence in Lucina, who decided in favour of Philip.[2] The provision of John de Camezano, nephew and chaplain of Pope Innocent IV and *auditor litterarum contradictarum* during that pontificate, to the church of Lenham (Kent), initiated a suit between John and the abbot and convent of St. Augustine's, Canterbury, which was heard by John de Sancto Germano, papal subdeacon and chaplain. The decision declared in favour of John and was given by the auditor in May 1253 and confirmed by the pope at Assisi.[3]

(iii) *Tithes*

The greatest number of suits of which evidence remains concern tithes. It is likely that the preponderance of the evidence for tithe suits reflects the predominance of tithe cases over all other suits which went to Rome. The tithe system was based on the Jewish system of tithes, instituted by the Mosaic law. Tithes were the tenths of all produce, paid by the parishioners to the parish priest or to the monastery, for whom they formed an important part of the income.[4]

---

[1] *Reg. Greg. IX*, no. 3419; and see ibid., nos. 4882-3.

[2] *Reg. Inn. IV*, no. 2481.

[3] *Reg. Inn. IV*, no. 6990; and see above, p. 23.

[4] In general see John Selden, *Historie of Tithes* (1618), esp. chapters i and ii, and P. W. Millard, *Law relating to Tithes*, 3rd edn. (1938), p. 1. There were also disputes over other parts of the parson's income, such as burial fees and the right to

During the eleventh and twelfth centuries there was a widespread increase in the number of tithes owned by monks all over Europe,[1] and the thirteenth century was to reap the results of this expansion, in the number of tithe disputes. Greater tithes were those of corn of every variety, usually called garb tithes; the lesser tithes were those levied on every kind of natural commodity, hens, hay, hemp, flax, wood, honey, wax, salt, cabbage, and fish.[2] At least in the early years of the twelfth century, disputes over tithes were tried in both ecclesiastical and secular courts, although cases concerning oblations and obventions were regarded as purely spiritual.[3] Well before the thirteenth century, however, tithes too were established as spiritualities.

It was recognized by the royal courts that tithes might affect advowson, but in the mid-thirteenth century there was as yet no precise definition of the proportion of tithes which would bring into question the right of patronage.[4] In 1237, the clergy complained that clerks were unable to seek tithes which of common right belonged to their churches 'because patrons of churches or chapels owning the tithes said that the suit was derogatory to their right of patronage. Moreover, justices of the lord king did not wish to decide what part of the tithes could or should be sought before an ecclesiastical judge.'[5] Bracton, however, gives the form of a writ prohibiting a case touching a sixth part of the advowson of a church, and it seems that this amount was customarily accepted, although in 1253 and again in 1257 there were further complaints that lay judges were drawing actions of tithes into the lay court under colour of pleas of advowson.[6] The first official declaration as to the amount of tithes which would affect

---

loads of kindling wood at Christmas; see, for example, *Letters of Inn. III*, nos. 629, 665, and 674.

[1] G. Constable, *Monastic Tithes from their Origins to the Twelfth Century* (Cambridge, 1964), p. 107.

[2] See, e.g., Byland Cart., f. 107^r; Bradenstoke Cart., f. 147^v; Bayham Cart., f. 60^v; B.M. Harley Ch. 44 E 20; and Westminster Domesday, ff. 380^v and 381^r.

[3] On the vagueness but general intention of William the Conqueror's ordinance separating the Church courts from the secular courts, see now C. Morris, 'William I and the Church Courts', *E.H.R.* lxxxii (1967), 449–63.

[4] N. Adams, 'Judicial Conflict over Tithes', *E.H.R.* lii (1937), 6.

[5] *Ann. Mon.* i. 255, quoted by Adams, 'Judicial Conflict', p. 6.

[6] *W.P.*, pt. i. 295.

the right of advowson occurs in *Circumspecte Agatis* (1286), which fixed it at a quarter. Suits concerning a greater proportion were to belong to the lay court, while suits about the possession of tithes of less than a quarter of the value of the benefice were still to be tried in court Christian.[1]

The Hayling suit illustrates how a suit which was ostensibly about tithes might be claimed as affecting advowson.[2] Nicholas of Rye, rector of Hayling, brought an action against the bishop of Winchester and others about tithes before Master Simon the Norman and the dean of Cambridge, judges delegate,[3] but in 1242 Nicholas was served with a writ of prohibition.[4] When he came before the *Curia Regis*, Nicholas said that he had not continued the suit after prohibition. He declared that he was rector of the church, instituted by the bishop of Winchester, and that he sought the tithes belonging to it. Robert, prior of Hayling, proctor on behalf of the major defendants, the abbot and convent of Jumièges, asserted that Nicholas had only a vicar's portion and that Jumièges were the patrons of the church, which was a gift of King William. Nicholas was imprisoned until he acknowledged that he had no right to the tithes. He promised to be content with what his predecessor had had and to pay a pension of twenty shillings to the abbot and convent of Jumièges.[5] On his release, however, Nicholas took his suit again to Rome. On 23 February 1245, Innocent IV ordered Giles, cardinal of SS. Cosmas and Damian, to cite the abbot and convent of Jumièges and Robert, prior, to answer before the pope, probably for bringing the case before a secular court.[6] The suit was still not settled on 16 September 1253 when the abbot and convent of Jumièges obtained a faculty to appropriate the church and appoint a vicar after Nicholas's

---

[1] Adams, 'Writ of Prohibition', p. 292. The text of *Circumspecte Agatis* and the 'Addition' is printed in *W.P.*, pt. i. 312–13.

[2] Cf. *Bracton's Note Book*, ii, no. 536 (Easter 1231). When the plaintiff received a writ of prohibition he said that the suit was not about advowson but about tithes. The suit, however, was discontinued and the papal letters were renounced.

[3] Master Simon appears as a judge delegate, a litigant, and a proctor (see Powicke, *Henry III*, App. E, esp. pp. 775–8).

[4] P.R.O. KB 26/124 m. 27d (pd. *W.P.*, pt. ii. 284–5).

[5] P.R.O. KB 26/124 m. 27d.

[6] *Reg. Inn. IV*, no. 1122.

death or resignation,[1] and the case was committed to Aymer de Valence, bishop elect of Winchester, Geoffrey, dean of Chichester, and Hugh, warden of the Friars Minor at Chichester. On 28 December the judges made a settlement about the vicar's portion which was to apply after Nicholas's death.[2]

In many cases the judges were called upon to decide to whom the tithes belonged: rival claims to ownership were frequent. Thomas de Neville, chancellor of Lichfield and parson of Westmill (Herts.), charged the prior and canons of Holy Trinity, Aldgate, with taking tithes and offerings at Gatesbury (Herts.), which he said belonged to the church of Westmill. The prior and convent, however, showed that the tithes and offerings pertained to their church of Braughing (Herts.), and the judges delegated by Honorius III absolved them from the charge.[3] In another tithe dispute Richard, rector of Odell (Beds.), claimed in front of William, prior of Wymondham, in 1249–50, that a moiety of the tithes near Woodend and of the tithes of Allegho belonged to his church and not to the prior and convent of Canons Ashby. But the convent was able to show that it had been decided by the priors of Great Bricett, Holy Trinity, and St. Peter's Ipswich, judges delegate of Honorius III, on the confession of the parson, that neither he nor his church had any right to the tithes.[4] A tithe suit between the dean and chapter of St. Martin le Grand, London, and the master and brothers of the hospital of Santo Spirito in Sassia at Rome came before two sets of judges. The prior of Castle Acre decided in 1246 that the tithes of W., knight of Newelond, belonged to St. Martin's, and that the tithes from the church of Writtle (Essex) belonged to Santo Spirito.[5]

Suits about the tithes of newly cultivated land must be seen against the background of agrarian expansion and the

[1] Ibid., nos. 7002–3—these entries are misdated by Berger who gives 14 Sept. for 16 Kal. Oct. See also *Registrum Johannis de Pontissara episcopi Wintoniensis*, i, ed. C. Deedes (Canterbury and York Ser. xix, 1915), 166, cited by Hartridge, *History of Vicarages*, p. 47.

[2] B.M. Harley Ch. 83 C 32 (App. B (iv), no. 5). This charter was unknown to both Powicke and Flahiff who have commented on this case.

[3] P.R.O. E 212/28, and cf. a similar case in Northampton, St. Andrew's Cart. (A), f. 56ʳ.

[4] P.R.O. E 135/21/33.   [5] New College, Oxford, Writtle Ch. 401.

assarting of waste land in the thirteenth century.[1] In certain regions the opening of new lands was encouraged by allowing the cultivators to pay no tithes,[2] but according to a decretal of Alexander IV tithes of new lands could be demanded in proportion to the ordinary tithes received, and this seems to have been the standard practice from at least as early as 1198.[3] Imposition of tithes on goods from which no tithes had previously been exacted was a frequent source of trouble.[4] In England the Crown claimed the power to settle disputes over titheability, but it was not very successful in its claims during this period. If the litigant could show that the lands and chattels were not previously titheable, he was entitled to a writ of prohibition.[5] A dispute concerning the tithes of newly ploughed land arose between the prior and convent of Binham and Stephen, parson of Edgefield (Norf.), and was settled by Thomas, abbot of Coggeshall, Alard, dean, and Walter, precentor of St. Paul's, in 1202 × 1203. At the settlement Stephen renounced to the prior and convent the tithes of the new land in the wood of Edgefield and also some of the tithes of Coppingeshul.[6] A suit of 1199 between the abbot and monks of Crowland and Conan, knight of Holbeach, and R. and W., clerks of the diocese of Lincoln, concerned tithes due from a piece of land in Holbeach called Conan's newland, which Conan had first enclosed.[7] The abbot and canons of Bayham sought from the abbot and convent of Grestain in the diocese of Lisieux, France,[8] the tithes and proceeds of certain demesne lands, in conjunction with those from the new marsh, which they claimed by right of their church of Otham (Sussex). Before the abbot and prior of Boxley and the prior of Leeds, Bayham with-

---

[1] e.g. Spalding Cart., f. 418ᵛ; P.R.O. E 40/9649; Reg. Antiq. Linc. iii, no. 759; Glos. Cart. ii, no. dccxiii; and Peterborough, MS. 5, f. 82ʳ⁻ᵛ· (MS. 1, f. 112ʳ).

[2] G. Constable, 'Resistance to Tithes in the Middle Ages', Journal of Ecclesiastical History, xiii (1962), 179.

[3] c. 2. 6. III. 13, and Reg. Pont. Rom. i, ed. Potthast, no. 47.

[4] Constable, 'Resistance to Tithes', p. 176.

[5] See Adams, 'Judicial Conflict', pp. 17 and 18–20.

[6] Binham Cart., f. 90ʳ. See also Eye Cart., ff. 36ᵛ–7ᵛ.

[7] Crowland Cart., f. 94, and see K. Major, 'Conan son of Ellis, an Early Inhabitant of Holbeach', Reps. and Papers of the Archit. and Archaeol. Socs. of Lincs. and Northants.. xlii (1935), 1–28.

[8] See Cottineau, i, col. 1342.

drew all the claims which they had put to these places, and Grestain conceded to them the tithes of sixty acres in Otham.[1]

Tithes of assarted lands might be claimed in conjunction with the tithes of other pieces of land long held in cultivation, or of other commodities.[2] A long suit between Abbot Richard and the convent of Waltham and Prior Giles and the convent of Merton, which was placed before three papal commissions, about the tithes due to Stanstead Abbots church (Herts.) included the tithes of new lands, animals' food, the lesser tithes, and the tithes of hay and mills in the manor of Stanstead Abbots.[3] In another instance, W. de Roverio, parson of the church of Stoke Bruern (Northants.), sought in his libel the tithes of one virgate of land and of twenty-three acres of assart from the canons of St. James, Northampton.[4] Provisions were sometimes made about the disposal of the tithes if the land should be cultivated in future.[5]

A large number of laymen were brought before the delegated courts in tithe cases.[6] Roger d'Oilly was brought by the dean and chapter of Exeter before judges delegate in two separate instances: in 1235 about the tithes of a meadow in the parish of Bampton (Oxon.); and some time before 1247, again about the tithes of Bampton, before the prior of the hospital of St. John and the archdeacon of Wells, who subdelegated to Master Luke of Membury and Walter of Cossington, canons of Wells.[7] The prior and convent of Dunstable charged Alexander the younger, John his brother, Richard son of John, and William son of William about the

---

[1] Bayham Cart., f. 60ʳ. For other examples of suits about tithes of *novalia* see Westminster Ch. 2015 and *Letters of Inn. III*, no. 549.

[2] e.g. P.R.O. E 40/14044(2): 'super decimis Thome filii Rogeri militis . . . necnon super decimis assarti . . . nobis traxisset in causam'.

[3] Waltham Cart., f. 84ʳ.   [4] B.M. Add. Ch. 6109.

[5] Northampton, St. Andrew's Cart. (A), f. 120ʳ.

[6] Cooper, *Select Scottish Cases*, p. xxvi, says that in more than one half of the Scottish cases, which he has considered, one of the parties was a layman. He attributes this high percentage to the weakness of the lay courts in Scotland.

[7] Exeter Cart., p. 14, and Exeter Ch. 640. A suit between the prior and convent of St. Frideswide and Elias Ridel, canon of Salisbury and rector of Shipton, which was brought before the priors of Dunstable and St. Albans and the archdeacon of St. Albans, in 1226–7, concerned tithes of hay, fishing, and mills from the lordship of the same Roger d'Oilly in Ascot under Wychwood (*St. Frideswide's Cart.* ii, no. 1021).

tithes of a windmill, hay, and trade. It was settled by the abbot of Warden and his co-judges in February 1221/2 in the church of Dunstable.[1] When the prior and convent of Bradenstoke brought a tithe suit against Henry Heuse, before the prior of Ivychurch, the chancellor and the succentor of Salisbury, judges delegate of Honorius III, it was decided that Henry and his heirs should pay two shillings yearly for certain tithes of a quarry to Chilcompton church (Som.) and all other tithes.[2] In another Bradenstoke case, Roger Tyrel received a sentence against him when he defended a case about the tithes of a mill, which the prior and convent had brought before the same judges, probably off the same mandate of Honorius III.[3] Similarly Geoffrey d'Abitot was brought before a delegated tribunal by the abbot and convent of Westminster between 1216 and 1222 in a tithe quarrel about mills at Birlingham (Worcs.).[4] When Philip de Burnham was challenged by the abbot and convent of West Dereham between 1208 and 1210, his proctor admitted that the tithes of a marsh near Holme (Norf.) belonged to Dereham, although they had been taken by Philip, and as restitution Philip agreed to pay fifteen shillings to the canons.[5] Philip of Drayton (probably Drayton at Daventry, Northants.), a layman, appeared as the defendant before the abbot of Combe and G(eoffrey), prior, and the subprior of Coventry in 1222, and gave up his claim to the tithes of the courtyard and hay.[6] Henry of Earley (Berks.) and his chaplain were summoned on behalf of the prior and convent of Wallingford, by the prior of Barnwell and the chancellor of Cambridge, to answer their charges about the tithes of his demesne. The suit was settled on 10 July 1236 in the priory church at Wallingford.[7]

Frequently arrangements divided the tithes. Robert Passelew, archdeacon of Lewes,[8] charged the nuns of Chatteris

---

[1] Dunstable Cart., f. 50ʳ, cal. *Dunstable Cart.*, no. 451.

[2] Bradenstoke Cart., f. 120ʳ.   [3] Ibid., f. 119ᵛ.

[4] Westminster Domesday, f. 292ᵛ.   [5] West Dereham Cart., f. 260ᵛ.

[6] Daventry Cart., f. 17ᵛ. Geoffrey was prior of Daventry between 1216 and 1223, *Darley Cart.* ii. 630.   [7] Bodleian MS. Chs. Berks. a 1, Ch. 17.

[8] See Powicke, *Henry III*, pp. 104, 288 n., and 363 n. An important royal servant and baronial proctor at Rome, Henry III attempted to present him to a living in Northampton and later to secure his election to the see of Chichester, but he was at both times thwarted by Grosseteste.

about the tithes of one carucate of land in the parish of Barrington (Cambs.) in front of judges delegated by Innocent IV. In April 1249 at Balsham, Hugh, bishop of Ely, ordained that Robert, in the name of his church of Barrington, should receive all garb tithes and tithes of hay from the lands of the nuns in Barrington, while the nuns were to keep the tithes of one mill in the parish and other lesser tithes.[1] In a dispute between the prior and convent of Tonbridge and Ralph, rector of Wickhambrook (Suff.), about tithes belonging to the chapel of Denston (Suff.), it was decided in 1238 by the prior, precentor, and dean of Rochester that the prior and convent should have half the tithes from Aluredeffeld' and that the rector should have the other half.[2] Similarly, the priors of St. Albans and Dunstable and the archdeacon of St. Albans decided in September 1231 that the abbot and convent of Westminster and Martin, rector of Rotherhithe, should share the tithes of salmon caught in the Thames within the boundaries of the parish of Rotherhithe.[3] A composition was made before judges delegate in 1238, between the prior and convent of Bridlington and the abbot and convent of Bardney, about tithes at Bawburgh (Norf.), and a division was decided upon.[4]

(iv) Pensions and Portions

Fixed money payments known as pensions might be substituted for payment of tithes.[5] This was a fairly common arrangement. If suits broke out about the payment of tithes it was often found convenient for one party to farm out the tithes to the other for a fixed sum. For instance, the abbot and convent of Thorney let out the tithes which were in dispute between them and Master Paul, rector of Chesterton (Cambs.), for a payment of two and a half marks yearly.[6]

---

[1] Chatteris Cart., ff. 111ʳ⁻ᵛ, and 112ʳ.   [2] P.R.O. E 40/14036.

[3] Westminster Domesday, ff. 380ᵛ–1ʳ.

[4] Bardney Cart., f. 96ᵛ, and see *Reg. Antiq. Linc.* ii, no. 513.

[5] 'Originally pensions seem to have been a kind of feudal payment for a benefice. The large number of pensions owed to religious houses was, of course, due to the practice of appropriation of churches by monastic houses in the twelfth century and may be traced to the transference of part of the tithes.' (Adams, 'Judicial Conflict', p. 11 n. 5, contd. on p. 12.)

[6] Thorney Cart. ii, f. 383ʳ.

Similarly the priors of Thetford and Ixworth and the sacrist of Bury St. Edmunds decided that Master Alan of Beccles, rector of Bunwell (Norf.), should hold certain tithes that were said to belong to his church and should make an annual payment of five shillings to the prior and convent of Castle Acre.[1] John, rector of Brickhill (Bucks.), recognized that certain tithes and lands belonged to the prior and convent of Dunstable, and the tithes were farmed to him for twenty-six shillings yearly.[2] When the tithes from the demesne of a certain William of West Lavant (Suss.) were disputed between the prior and convent of Lewes and Master Simon, the rector of the church of East Lavant, and Matthew the vicar, they were confirmed by the judges delegate to Lewes and were farmed to Master Simon, who was to pay four shillings yearly for them, two shillings at Easter and two at Michaelmas.[3]

Many quarrels broke out over the non-payment of these pensions. In 1246 the abbot of Bayham settled a case between the prior and convent of Lewes and the rector of Canfield (Essex), over the detention of an annual pension of thirty shillings which, it was alleged and proved, had not been paid for three years. W., prior of Hatfield Regis and farmer of the rector, promised to pay sixty shillings of the money at the next feast of St. Thomas, and the other thirty shillings later, and he pledged thirty shillings yearly so long as he should be the farmer.[4] A suit between the abbot and convent of St. Valéry and James, rector of Compton (? Compton Beauchamp, Berks.), concerned the rector's payment of forty shillings sterling for the tithes in the parish of Compton. In a document dated 27 July 1245 at Isleworth, the rector, who had appeared before the prior of Hatfield Regis, promised to pay, under penalty of half a mark for

---

[1] Castle Acre Cart., f. 128ᵛ.

[2] Dunstable Cart., f. 62ᵛ, cal. *Dunstable Cart.*, no. 694. Cf. Christchurch (Twynham) Cart., f. 92ʳ, where the abbot and convent of Montébourg (dioc. Coutances, France) renounced the tithes in question in return for twenty shillings yearly to be paid to them by Twynham.

[3] P.R.O. E 40/14190. Cf. *Glos. Cart.* i, no. cclxiv, a similar arrangement.

[4] P.R.O. E 40/13875. See also, e.g., *St. Radegund Cambridge*, ed. Gray, Ch. 6; *Reg. S. Osmund*, i. 256–9; Bardney Cart., f. 92ʳ; and the Paxton case, *Reg. Antiq. Linc.* ii, nos. 385–6, and iii, nos. 830–1.

non-payment.[1] J. de Nerford, rector of Crundale (Kent), paid twenty-five shillings yearly to the prior and convent of Leeds in return for the benefice of the church of Crundale. A suit about this payment came before judges delegate, the priors of St. Andrew's, Rochester, and Lesnes and the archdeacon of Rochester, in 1224–5.[2]

Sometimes such arrangements were made to last only for the life of the incumbent. Professor Constable has pointed out that commutation of tithes to a fixed charge in either kind or money might cause trouble, especially if the yield increased or the crops were changed.[3] The tithes came to be worth more than the commuted payments when there was a rise in prices.[4] In a suit before the abbot of Langley and his colleagues between the prior and convent of Eye and William, vicar of Rickinghall (Suff.), about the tithes of the lordship of H. of Rickinghall, William confessed that the tithes belonged to the monks of Eye. They were leased to him for half a mark of silver a year. After William's death, however, the monks were to make what arrangement they liked about the tithes.[5] W., prior of Norwich, and Thomas, bishop of Norwich, reported a settlement made by the archbishop of Canterbury and his colleagues about the church of St. Martin Coslany in Norwich. The prior and convent of Norwich conceded the church to Richard de Bedeh, clerk, in perpetual farm for his life. Ten shillings yearly was to be paid to the infirmary of the monks in the name of the farm.[6] In 1213 a suit opened between the prior and convent of Lanthony and John, a priest of Salisbury diocese, about an annual pension from the church of Chirton (Wilts.). The mandate included the stipulation 'proviso attentius ne pensio

---

[1] New College, Oxford, Takeley Ch. 271. Cf. also *N.L.C.*, no. 9, and P.R.O. E 40/13873, cal. *Lewes Cart. S.P.* ii. 132–3.

[2] Leeds Cart., f. 10ʳ. Cf. Norwich Ch. 1686: Robert Buttamund, rector of Thornham, was charged by the prior and convent of Norwich about an annual payment for his benefice. He was ordered to pay in kind sixteen loads of corn, ten of barley, five of beans, and five of peas, and the arrears of eight years, and expenses of six marks.

[3] Constable, 'Resistance to Tithes', p. 178.

[4] Constable, *Monastic Tithes*, p. 107.

[5] Eye Cart., f. 36ᵛ. Cf. Lewes Cart., ff. 112, 116ᵛ, and 117, cal. *Lewes Cart. S.P.* ii. 27–8, 39, and 40.

[6] Norwich Ch. 1024. Probably Thomas Blundeville, bishop of Norwich, consecrated on 20 Dec. 1226, d. 16 Aug. 1236.

ipsa contra Lateranensis statuta concilii sit imposita vel adaucta'. Lanthony said in their intention that John had ceased to pay a pension of 100*s*. yearly. John held that the pension was against the Lateran Council enactment, but the canons disputed this. At the settlement, which was made on 2 October 1214 in Hereford cathedral, John resigned all right in the church. At the instance of the judges the canons conceded the church of Chirton to John for his lifetime in perpetual farm. In return John was to pay them ten marks of silver yearly, and a penalty of twenty shillings was imposed for non-payment at any term. He was to sustain all charges on the church, and both parties promised to keep this settlement.[1]

In the thirteenth century pension cases were frequent, and they form a large part of the business of the delegated courts. As with tithes, it was gradually realized that pensions could affect the right of patronage. For instance, when in 1237 the prior and convent of Eye endeavoured to remove John, clerk of Bedfield (Suff.), from the church of Playford, Eye held that John had occupied the church to the prejudice of their rights as patron, and that he had not paid a pension of five shillings yearly. John, contesting the suit, said that Thomas Blundeville, late bishop of Norwich, had conferred the church upon him, and he produced the instrument about this. He confessed before the judges, however, that he ought to pay the pension and that the convent of Eye was indeed the patron of the church.[2] By the fourteenth century, however, the lay courts were dealing with a large number of disputes between churchmen over pensions given in lieu of tithes, and by 1345 'pensions and other lay contracts were included on the list of pleas cognizable by the king's courts, pleas which must not be tried in the court of Rome'.[3]

---

[1] Lanthony Cart. A1, VIII, no. lxxx. No. lxxix is headed 'Testificatio' and appears to be a draft. In A2, on f. 221ᵛ, there is a mandate of Gregory IX, dated 16 Dec. 1235 at Viterbo and addressed to the prior of St. Oswald's and the archdeacon of Gloucester about the church of Chirton, tithes, rents, possessions, and other things in which the prior and convent of Lanthony charged the abbot and convent of Grestain and 'quidam alii'.

[2] Eye Cart., f. 41ʳ⁻ᵛ, and see above, p. 185.

[3] Adams, 'Judicial Conflict', pp. 11 and 14.

The rector received the main income of the parish church. The rector's deputy, the vicar, was either allotted a small sum out of the revenues of the benefice or granted a portion from the church's endowment in tithes, glebe, and offerings; how much he received depended on the individual arrangement.[1] Canon 32 of the Fourth Lateran Council (1215) declared that vicars should receive reasonable portions,[2] which the Council of Oxford of 1222 interpreted as a minimum salary of five marks, except in some parts of Wales.[3] Cases about vicarages and vicars' portions were common.[4]

On 30 November 1212 Innocent III ordered Richard, abbot of Woburn, Raymond, prior of St. Albans, and Richard, prior of Dunstable, to hear and decide a suit between Master Simon of London, rector of Launton (Oxon.), and Henry de Colewell, the vicar, about the vicar's portion in the church of Launton. Simon renounced his suit, saying that he had no right in the vicarage except to receive two marks of silver yearly from Henry. Henry promised to pay this, and sixteen shillings and eight pence to the abbey of Westminster, the patron, and also other charges on the church including *episcopalia*. The suit was settled in October 1214 in the church of St. Mary at Luton.[5] A suit between the prior and convent of Caldwell and the prior and convent of Little Dunmow, which came before the abbot and prior of Warden and the prior of Newnham, on a mandate of Innocent III dated 7 April 1215, concerned amongst other things the vicar's portion in the church of Tolleshunt (Essex). It was decided that the prior and convent of Dunmow should hold the church with all its appurtenances and should pay the priory of Caldwell a rent of thirty shillings a year.

[1] Hartridge, *History of Vicarages*, pp. 9, 22, 29, and Millard, *Law relating to Tithes*, p. 2.

[2] Hefele, *Conciles*, v, pt ii. 1359–60.

[3] *C.S.* ii, pt. i. 112–13, no. [21]. See C. R. Cheney, 'The Legislation of the Medieval Church', *E.H.R.* l (1935), 202, and *Reg. Inn. IV*, no. 1321, where a pension imposed by the archbishop was said to be against the Lateran Council enactment.

[4] e.g. Westminster Ch. 15684, chirograph, on dorse: 'Compositio facta inter Magistrum Simonem et Henricum de Colewell super vicaria ecclesie de Langetun'; Little Dunmow Cart., f. 73ʳ⁻ᵛ: the mandate reads 'Dilecti filii prior et conventus de Caudewelle nobis conquerendo monstrarunt quod canonici de Dunmawe Lond' diocesis vicariam ecclesie de Tholeshunt et alias res ad ipsos de jure spectantes contra justiciam detinent et reddere contradicunt'; and Lanthony Cart. A1, XVI, no. xvi.

[5] Westminster Ch. 15684.

A perpetual vicarage was to be established. If Dunmow could not or would not pay the thirty shillings, they were to restore the church.[1] When the suit between Master Baldwin, canon of Troyes, and Master W(illiam Scot), archdeacon of Worcester, about the possession of the church of Painswick (Glos.), was settled by judges delegate of Gregory IX in favour of Master Baldwin, the judges went on to provide that Master Baldwin was to possess the church in the name of the canons of Lanthony and was to pay an annual pension of fourteen shillings to them. A vicarage was to be ordained in the church, and Baldwin was to pay Master H. de Bruges, who was instituted vicar by the bishop, twenty marks yearly. The settlement took place on 22 August 1235 in the church of St. Paul, London.[2]

William, a clerk of Archbishop Richard le Grand of Canterbury, had been presented to the vicarage of the church of Chislet (Kent), by St. Augustine's. William, however, was not content with his vicar's portion and he retained the fruits as well. The abbot and convent of St. Augustine's therefore brought him before the priors of Waltham and Westminster in 1232. Their libel declared that the church of Chislet had been assigned to them by the pope for the uses of the infirmary, and that William by retaining the fruits had done them damage to the amount of fifty marks. William confessed *in jure* that what St. Augustine's said in their libel was correct, and sentence was given against him on 7 November 1233.[3]

Many livings were divided into several portions, and thus small sums were due to various people.[4] It was enacted at the Council of Oxford of 1222 that in future no more than one benefice was to be established in a church, and that

---

[1] Little Dunmow Cart., f. 73ʳ⁻ᵛ.

[2] Lanthony Cart. A1, XVI, no. xvi.

[3] St. Augustine's Cart., f. 75ʳ: St. Augustine's Red Book, f. 171ʳ: see *William Thorne's Chronicle of St. Augustine's Abbey Canterbury*, trans. and ed. A. H. Davis (Oxford, 1934), p. 196. Cf. *Buckland Cart.*, no. 13 (date: 1229). The sisters of the preceptory at Buckland complained that the vicar of their church of 'Pertuna' (?North Petherton, Som.) took so much from the issues of it that the residue was insufficient for their support. Gregory IX ordered the dean, chancellor, and treasurer of Salisbury to hear the cause.

[4] J. R. H. Moorman, *Church Life in England in the Thirteenth Century* (Cambridge, 1955), p. 7.

where a church had been divided between two or more clerks, the portions were to be consolidated on their death.[1] Thomas, rector of the church of St. Nicholas, Warwick, sought from the pope that the church, which had been divided into three by the canons of St. Mary's, should be restored to its original state according to the settlement of this provincial council.[2] The bishop of Worcester had refused, so Thomas appealed to Pope Gregory IX, who ordered the legate Otto to inquire into the case.

(v) Chapels

Chapels were the subject-matter of numerous suits. Many chapels were established during the thirteenth century, with the result that disputes about parish rights and claims to income were common. The prior and convent of Eye alleged that the brothers of the hospital at Jerusalem had built a chapel at Dunwich (Suff.) to the prejudice of their church of St. Leonard. At the settlement the brothers promised not to receive the parishioners of St. Leonard's, and not to take their dues or perform mass or baptism for them, while Eye promised to observe the privileges of the brothers.[3] The abbot and convent of Langdon erected a chapel at Newsole in the parish of Coldred (Kent). The prior and convent of Dover, who had parochial rights over the mother church of Coldred, therefore brought them before the abbot of Faversham and the priors of St. Gregory's and St. Augustine's, Canterbury. On 25 December 1219 a composition was made in the cathedral at Canterbury, in which Langdon promised not to injure Dover.[4] In 1236 the dean and chapter of St. Martin le Grand, London, challenged the abbot and convent of Walden about predial tithes and about a chapel in the parish of St. Botolph outside Aldersgate. It was decided that Walden might celebrate in the chapel, saving the rights of St. Botolph's church, but that they should not take oblations.[5] A case of the abbot and convent of Reading against the abbot and convent of Préaux and G. (a clerk) concerned the

---

[1] C.S. ii, pt. i. 111–12, no. [18].
[2] Reg. Greg. IX, no. 3614. See, e.g., Exeter Ch. 813 and Croxton Trans., f. 72ᵛ, for other suits about portions before judges delegate.
[3] Eye Cart., ff. 37ᵛ–8ᵛ.
[4] Langdon Cart., ff. 102ʳ–3ʳ.
[5] Walden Cart., f. 43ʳ.

chapel of Newbury, which Reading asserted was within their parish of Thatcham.[1]

The contention usually concerned also the question of the right to receive burial fees.[2] The abbot and convent of St. Augustine said that the rights of burial and the payments of the dead, in a fee held from the king in the parish of Milton (Kent), belonged to them. Master Jordan, vicar of the chapel of Iwade (Kent), confessed that this was so, and agreed that the men of this fee should receive burial at Milton. They were, however, to receive the sacraments and hear mass at Iwade, and the last mass for them was to be celebrated there.[3] The rights of the parish of Milton were asserted in another case about a chapel. Nicholas, abbot of Faversham, and the priors of Horton and Leeds, under a commission from Pope Innocent III, settled a case of burial fees between the abbot and convent of St. Augustine and Master Oliver, rector of Bapchild (Kent). The bodies of all men and women who were parishioners of Bapchild—for whose inheritance reliefs were given to the court of Milton—were to be buried in Bapchild graveyard, but for each a penny was to be paid to the rector of Milton. The parties compromised on the award, which was to remain valid until the end of Master Oliver's life, and both Master William, proctor of the abbot and convent, and Master Oliver swore to observe the arrangement.[4] H(ugh Nonant), bishop of Coventry, had consecrated a cemetery at the chapel of Corley (Warw.) which belonged to the monks of Coventry. The monks alleged later this was to their prejudice, and brought Philip the rector of Corley before A., abbot of St. James's, R., prior of St. Andrew's, and the dean of Northampton, by mandate of Pope Honorius III. In the presence of the monks, Philip swore to deliver to the mother church of Coventry half of each mortuary of all those who died within the parish of Corley. Burial rights were conceded to the chapel by the monks in return

---

[1] Reading Cart., ff. 112r, and 116v; and cf. f. 121v, another case about a chapel.
[2] See, e.g., Castle Acre Cart., f. 125v.
[3] St. Augustine's Red Book, f. 261v.
[4] *Chartulary of the High Church of Chichester*, ed. W. D. Peckham (Suss. Rec. Soc. xlvi, 1946), no. 278 (1214–16).

for one stone of wax.[1] In a suit between the prior and convent of Breedon and Philip of Staunton, their parishioner, about tithes and mortuaries, which was settled in Easter Week 1247 in the church of All Saints at Pontefract, it was decided that Philip and his successors were not to be compelled to be buried in the church of Breedon, unless they chose to be, and offices for the dead were to be celebrated at Staunton Harold chapel, saving the indemnity of the mother church of Breedon. Philip assigned to Breedon a rent of sixpence yearly.[2]

Chapels were usually allowed after an arrangement had been made about the income.[3] In a suit about the chapel of Mells in the parish of Wenhaston (Suff.), between Ralph of Mells and Hervey, rector of Wenhaston, it was decided that the chaplain should be presented to the rector of the mother church, and that he should swear faithfully to pay two shillings yearly to the church in token of his subjection. The men of the lord of Mells were to receive spiritual benefits from the mother church, and were to pay parish dues to it.[4] The celebration of offices had to be carefully arranged and stipulated. An arrangement between the nuns of Bullington and the parishioners of Burton-on-the-Wolds (Leics.), over the chapel of Burton, was made before the abbots of Louth Park (Cist. Lincs.) and Humberston (Ben. Lincs.) and the dean of Covenham, by order of Pope Innocent III. Hugh de Berges, on whose land the chapel was situated, gave to the church of St. Andrew, Prestwold, and to the house of Bullington (Gilb. Lincs.) one virgate of land and its appurtenances. The prior and nuns of Bullington, on the other hand, were to see that mass was celebrated on the sixth day of each week in the chapel of St. Peter at Burton, which belonged to the church of Prestwold, by the chaplain, his vicar, and clerk, unless the sixth day should fall on the feast of All Saints, St. Andrew, Christmas Day, the feast of the Purification of the Blessed Virgin Mary, Good Friday, or the Assumption of the Blessed Virgin Mary, in which case the Monday was to be substituted. Hugh, his heirs, and the men of Burton were to provide a chalice, missal, and

[1] St. John's College, Oxford, Ch. xix. 2.   [2] 'Breedon Cart.', no. 144.
[3] See Windsor, Arundel White Book, p. 174.
[4] Blythburgh Cart., ff. 44ᵛ–5ʳ.

other ornaments for the church.[1] When in 1240 William of Englefield took a case to Rome about the chapel of Shiplake (Oxon.), he asserted that the abbot and convent of Missenden failed to see that divine offices were celebrated in the chapel by one of the canons according to the terms of their agreement.[2]

Rights of patronage might be involved in cases about chapels. A suit about the chapel of Fleet (Kent) called forth a prohibition on account of the tithes in 1206.[3] A writ of prohibition was obtained also in a suit between Master William of Kilkenny, rector of Easton Maudit (Northants.), and Simon of Newark and Henry, chaplains, concerning the chapel of Yardley Hastings (Northants.), but the case was then delegated to Archbishop Edmund of Abingdon and the sentence, which was in favour of Master William, declared that the chapel belonged to the church of Easton.[4] Writs of prohibition which were aimed against cases relating to the dependent chapels of a church were included among the list of grievances drawn up by the clergy in 1237.[5] To judge from the *Curia Regis* rolls these were not numerous, and in spite of the implications of this protest, it does not seem as if there was any full-scale attack on such cases coming before Church courts.

4. *Spiritual Cases*

(i) *Marriage and Legitimacy*

Questions of matrimony indisputably belonged to the Church. Esmein is of the opinion that this was generally accepted by the end of the tenth century,[6] but the Church

---

[1] B.M. Harley Ch. 44 H 47 (pd. J. Nichols, *History and Antiquities of the County of Leicester*, iii, pt. 2 (1804), 831b). Cf. *Reg. of St. Augustine's Canterbury*, ii, ed. G. J. Turner and H. E. Salter (British Academy, Recs. of Social and Economic History, iii, 1924), 509–10: the parishioners of Faversham were obliged to attend the parish church on feast days and not the chapel of Ospringe. *Librum* is probably a missal (see Hartridge, *History of Vicarages*, p. 135).

[2] B.M. Add. Chs. 20370–3 (App. B (iv), nos. 6, 7, 8, and 9).

[3] *C.R.R.* iv. 198, and see also ix. 48, 52; *9 to 10 Henry III*, no. 168; and KB 26/107 m. 27 and 109 m. 6d.

[4] Bodleian MS. Chs. Bucks. a 3, Ch. 45. *Bracton's Note Book*, iii, no. 1387, may be connected in some way with this suit.   [5] *W.P.*, pt. i. 290.

[6] A. Esmein, *Le Mariage en droit canonique*, i, 2nd edn., revsd. R. Génestal (Paris, 1929), 27.

courts in England immediately after William the Conqueror's reorganization do not appear to have claimed marriage as belonging exclusively to their province, and the Laws of Henry I show that in cases of adultery the man's fine went to the king and the woman's to the bishop.[1] The transfer of this area of jurisdiction to the spiritual forum, however, was complete by the mid-twelfth century, as is clearly illustrated by this passage from the Anstey case:

Since a question of matrimony was involved, and matrimony is annulled or confirmed in accordance with ecclesiastical law, the court of our catholic sovereign Henry II, king of the English, decreed that the case should return for judgement to an ecclesiastical court, where the question of marriage might be duly determined in accordance with canon law, which the clergy know, whereas the common people do not.[2]

Cases about matrimony were almost certainly numerous, although the evidence does not survive in any abundance.[3] Until the marriage law of the Church was defined and made known, reference to Rome must have been frequent.[4] Gratian devoted only ten causes (nos. 27–36) to marriage. Compared with a whole book on the subject in the *Decretales* (Book IV) (where the law embraced questions of espousal, dowry,[5] legitimacy, and separation, as well as more obvious subjects) this was little, and until the triumph of Peter Lombard's theory that consent alone formed a marriage, the law was in a state of flux.[6] It was also recognized that marriage

[1] *Die Gesetze der Angelsachsen*, i, ed. Liebermann, 557 [11, 5].

[2] *J.S.L.*, no. 131 (c. Oct.–Nov. 1160), and see below, p. 209, and *Glanvill*, ed. Hall, vii. 15.

[3] Cooper, *Select Scottish Cases*, p. xxxii, says of his collection of cases that there is one feature common to them all, with one exception, namely that one of the parties was an ecclesiastic. The complete lack of marriage cases in this collection results from his reliance on cartulary evidence. See Haskins, *Norman Institutions*, p. 35, and Canterbury, Cartae Antiquae, M 364, where a considerable number of the appeals for the tuition of the see of Canterbury, while cases were being taken to Rome, concerned marriage.

[4] See, e.g., *Papal Decretals relating to Lincoln*, nos. viii, xviii, xxiii, and xxv (Cel. III to the bishop of Lincoln, 1191–8). See also S. Painter, *The Scourge of the Clergy, Peter of Dreux, Duke of Brittany* (Baltimore, 1937), pp. 37, 46–7; Morey, *Bartholomew of Exeter*, p. 67; and P.R.O. E 42/338 (an appeal of 1271).

[5] For a question concerning dowry, delegated to judges delegate in France, see *Letters of Inn. III*, no. 1052.

[6] *Papal Decretals relating to Lincoln*, pp. xxvi–xxvii; and J. Dauvillier, *Le Mariage dans le droit classique de l'Église depuis le Décret de Gratien (1140) jusqu'à la mort de Clement V (1314)* (Paris, 1933), pp. 5, 7, and 36.

suits as *causae majores* demanded special care. Marriage suits were often delegated because of the necessity of obtaining exact evidence.[1] Usually they demanded specific mandates. When, in a case of 1205, it was alleged by Juliana, wife of a certain W., that her husband had forced her to agree to his entering the abbey of Warden, and that he had later left the monastery and refused to take her back, the judges were given precise instructions how to act.[2] Appeal to Rome often took place in the course of the hearing. A case between Alan a knight, and Juliana, came before three sets of judges delegate: the abbot of Bruern and his fellow judges; the dean of Andover and others; and Stephen Langton, archbishop of Canterbury. Before the first judges, it was declared by witnesses that the marriage had been contracted, but Alan disputed it and appealed to the pope. He then renounced the appeal and continued to litigate before them, but at the same time he obtained a mandate to the dean of Andover and his colleagues. Before these judges, Juliana said that the letters to them had been obtained by misrepresentation, and that the case should be returned to the former judges. This exception was not allowed and so Juliana appealed to the pope. The first judges, from fear of the knight and also because of their inability to settle the case, returned it to Rome, ordering Juliana to appear there at the beginning of Lent 1224. This she did, and asked for judgement, but Honorius III, doubting the authenticity of the acts and attestations which she brought with her, ordered Stephen Langton to have the originals produced and to decide the matter, if Alan could not be induced to treat her as his wife. The outcome of this case is unknown.[3]

It is likely that many matrimonial cases were fought on the question of affinity. King John's marriage to Isabella of Gloucester was dissolved by judges delegate in Normandy, on the grounds that they were too closely related, but doubtless the lack of an heir was the king's prime reason for

[1] e.g. *Die Register Innocenz' III*, 1, Pontifikatsjahr 1198/9, ed. O. Hageneder and A. Haidacher (Graz–Köln, 1964), no. 380; and *Letters of Inn. III*, nos. 168, 409, and 600, the case between Llywelyn, prince of North Wales, and the daughter of the prince of the Isles.

[2] *Letters of Inn. III*, no. 614.

[3] *Reg. Hon. III*, no. 5349 (*C.P.L.* i. 101). Cf. *Oxford Formularies*, ii, no. 6.

bringing the suit.[1] Until 1215 marriage within the seventh
degree of relationship was forbidden. In that year Innocent
III in the Lateran Council reduced the affinity ban to the
fourth degree (third cousins).[2] A suit of Roger Bigod, fourth
earl of Norfolk and marshal of England, against his wife
Isabella, daughter of King William the Lion of Scotland, on
the grounds of consanguinity was brought finally before the
pope, but was not successful. The suit was probably pre-
cipitated by the absence of an heir, and Roger died childless
in 1270. Both sides had already obtained papal letters, and
the case had lasted for three years, with no possibility of its
termination in England, 'because of the tricks and deceits of
the parties'. On 3 April 1249 Innocent IV addressed a mandate to the bishop of Ely ordering him to cite the parties
to appear, or either in person by proctor, before the
Curia within two months.[3] Probably the most spectacular
marriage case of the first half of the thirteenth century was
that heard by the Savoyard bishop of Hereford, Peter of
Aigueblanche. He was commissioned as papal delegate at
Siena in 1251 to inquire into the contract of marriage which
had once been arranged between Henry III and Joan,
daughter of Simon, count of Ponthieu. The marriage had in
fact taken place by proxy in 1235, but the count had failed
to get the consent of his overlord the king of France, which
he had undertaken to seek on his restoration to Ponthieu.
Henry III had since married Eleanor of Provence in January 1236, and Joan had been betrothed to the king of
Castille. Peter of Aigueblanche ruled that the contract
should be regarded as null and void, on the grounds that
they were related in the fourth degree.[4]

Once the Church had settled whether a marriage was
valid or not, dependent questions might be referred to the
royal court.[5] A case about the seizure of a marriage portion
between husband and wife turned obviously on the question
of the validity of the marriage. The marriage between

[1] Cheney, *Hubert Walter*, p. 81.
[2] Can. 52. Hefele, *Conciles*, v, pt. ii. 1374–5, and c. 47. *X*. II. 20. See R. Naz,
'Mariage en droit occidental', *D.D.C.* vi, col. 742.
[3] *Complete Peerage*, ix (1936), 590–3; and *Reg. Inn. IV*, no. 4444.
[4] *Hereford Charters*, p. 90, and see p. xxi.
[5] See c. 7. *X*. IV. 17 (Alex. III).

William Basset and Beatrice de Taenden was declared to be null and void by judges delegate—R(ichard of Ely), archdeacon of Colchester, Master Richard of Stortford, master of the schools, and Master Benedict of Sawston, canon of St. Paul's—because a former wife of William was still living. After an appeal and some delays by William the case about possession of the property continued before royal justices.[1] The royal power was used also to enforce decisions. On 6 July 1244 Master E(?Eustace), archdeacon of Bath, wrote to Henry III asking him to see that Hugh de Olair restored to B., his former wife, her marriage portion, possessions, and lands. Papal judges, the bishop, succentor, and precentor of Salisbury, one of whom subdelegated to R. de Opere, vicar,[2] had declared that the marriage was within the forbidden degree, and had therefore nullified it.[3] In a marriage case in which a certain William was involved, the judge delegate Thomas Wallensis, bishop of St. Davids, asked the king to arrange for the seizure of William. As a result of an appeal by William from the judgement of Thomas, new judges—the bishops of Worcester and Bath and Wells—were delegated by Innocent IV on 17 December 1249. They asked Henry III to ignore the letters which sought the seizure of William, and they ordered Bishop Thomas to revoke his commands, and to appear before them in the church of St. Augustine, Bristol, on 14 January 1250.[4] In another suit, a letter dated at Hayfield (Derbys.) in 1252, which was sent by Roger of Weasenham, bishop of Coventry and Lichfield, who subdelegated to Master H. de Wysawe, his official, notified King Henry III of a sentence, presumably asking him to give effect to it in some way. This sentence, which concerned marriage, was in favour of Baldwin de Rumilly and Lucy de Estham, and against Robert de Curecun.[5]

The jurisdiction of the Church over cases concerning legitimacy followed logically from her competence over mar-

---

[1] C.R.R. ii. 267 and 298.

[2] It may be noted here that it was constantly repeated that matrimonial causes should only be handled by competent judges, see c. 1. X. IV. 14 (Alex. III); C.S. ii, pt. i. 113, no. [25] (Council of Oxford, 1222), and 255–6, no. [23] (Legatine Council of London, 1237).   [3] P.R.O. SC1, vol. 5, no. 84.

[4] P.R.O. SC1, vol. 5, no. 74.   [5] P.R.O. SC1, vol. 5, no. 81.

riage cases.[1] Alexander III had claimed cases of legitimacy
and bastardy to be of spiritual cognizance, and the much
celebrated case of the twelfth century, between Richard of
Anstey and Mabel de Francheville, is an example of a case
involving legitimacy which went to Rome.[2] There is no
evidence of these cases coming before the papally delegated
courts in England in the thirteenth century. This is almost
certainly due in some part to the lack of lay records, but the
kings undoubtedly attempted to prevent these cases being
taken outside the kingdom. In 1207 royal justices disregarded an appeal to the pope, because no appeal about
bastardy could be made outside the realm; and in 1223 a
bastardy appeal to the court of Rome, in an Irish case
concerning land, brought forth a severe rebuke from the
king.[3] The Church's views on legitimacy were not allowed
to affect the English laws of inheritance. The canon law
held that the subsequent marriage between two parties
legitimized their children, but when in 1236 the English
bishops urged the magnates to consent to this, they received
the reply 'We will not change the approved and customary
laws of England.'[4]

(ii) *Wills and Testaments*

Testamentary causes also came under the spiritual aegis of
the Church.[5] In the law of wills the Church greatly sim-
plified the civil law on the subject, so that the Church law
was attractive to the parties.[6] A suit about a will, which came

[1] See *X*. IV. 17, and *Glanvill*, ed. Hall, vii. 14.
[2] cc. 4–7. *X*. IV. 17. See *J.S.L.*, no. 131. For a thirteenth-century Scottish
case, see Cooper, *Select Scottish Cases*, no. 44, pp. 61–5. On the Anstey case see also
J. Boussard, *Le Gouvernement d'Henri II Plantagenet* (Paris, 1956), pp. 278–9;
English Historical Documents, ii (1042–1189), ed. D. C. Douglas and G. W. Green-
away (1953), 456; Voss, *Heinrich von Blois*, p. 141; and P. M. Barnes, 'The Anstey
Case', *Medieval Miscellany for Doris Mary Stenton*, ed. P. M. Barnes and C. F.
Slade (Pipe Roll Soc. N.S. xxxvi, 1960), pp. 1–24.
[3] *C.R.R.* v (1931), 48, and *Rotuli Litterarum Clausarum*, i, ed. T. D. Hardy
(1833), pp. xxxiv and 629.
[4] *C.S.* ii, pt. i. 201 n. 3, and the references cited there.
[5] See M. M. Sheehan, *The Will in Medieval England* (Pontifical Institute of
Mediaeval Studies, Studies and Texts, 6, Toronto 1963), pp. 163–76; *Glanvill*, ed.
Hall, vii. 8: 'quia placitum de testamentis coram iudice ecclesiastico tractari debet';
and *Henrici de Bracton de Legibus*, vi. 210 and 214.
[6] T. F. T. Plucknett, *Concise History of the Common Law*, 5th edn. (1956),
p. 304.

before judges delegate, the deans of Oxford and Abingdon and W., vicar of Cumnor (a subdelegate of the prior of Abingdon), is recorded in 1235–40. Unfortunately the charter mentioning it is badly damaged. The plaintiffs were the executors of the will of J. de St. John, knight, but it is not possible to decipher the names of the defendants or to glean any more details about the case.[1]

The royal court asserted its claims over cases about chattels and debt, but during John's reign they were gradually limited to exclude those connected with testaments and marriage.[2] In a suit of before 1210 about thirty marks, which Roger brother of Fulk Bainard left Hugh of Kerdiston in his will, Hugh impetrated letters from the pope. On the grounds that the subject-matter was chattels, a writ of prohibition was obtained from the king, and Hugh desisted from prosecuting his suit before the papal judges.[3] It seems, however, that as usual where both parties agreed to come before the Church, nothing could be done to prevent them. Henry d'Oilly and his wife Maud brought a case against Maud, countess of Hereford and Essex, wife of Roger of Dauntsey, about a debt of ninety pounds which William de Mandeville, earl of Essex, had owed them. The plea was probably testamentary although it is not directly mentioned as such. Maud, countess of Essex and Hereford, had married Henry de Bohun, earl of Hereford. Henry died on 1 June 1220, and Maud later married Roger. Maud was a daughter of Geoffrey fitz Piers, earl of Essex, and eventually heiress of her brother William de Mandeville, who was the last earl of Essex of that family.[4] The suit came before the prior of Luffield, the archdeacon and the dean of Buckingham on papal delegation, and it was decided that Maud d'Oilly was to have the manor of Gussage St. Michael (Dors.)[5] and its appurtenances until the debt was paid.[6]

---

[1] Bodleian MS. Chs. Oxon a 5, Ch. 294 (pd. *Oseney Cart.* ii, no. 1112).

[2] See *W.P.*, pt. i. 277 and its Appendix, and pt. ii. 261. See also Sheehan, *Will in Medieval England*, pp. 172–3.

[3] *C.R.R.* vi. 79, and see p. 121 for the continuation of the case.

[4] See *Complete Peerage*, v (1926), 134, and vi. 458–9.

[5] Gussage St. Michael was in the possession of the Bohuns in 1275. See A. Fägersten, *Place-Names of Dorset* (Uppsala, 1933), p. 81.

[6] P.R.O. DL 25/15 (App. B (iv), no. 10).

Most of the evidence remaining is of suits that indirectly concerned wills. At his death Richard de Ribof had granted his body and an annual payment of ten shillings to the abbot and convent of the Premonstratensian house of Welbeck.[1] In a suit brought by Welbeck before S., vicar of Blyth and subdelegate of the prior of Worksop, Walter de Ribof son of Richard confessed that he ought to pay this sum yearly to the convent, by reason of the will of Richard his father. He paid the arrears, which were estimated at fifteen shillings, and promised that he and his heirs would pay in future.[2]

In 1224, in front of the abbot and prior of Eynsham (Ben. Oxon.) and the dean of Oxford, suits were settled between the prior and convent of Christ Church, Canterbury, and the prior and convent of Clifford (Clun. al. Heref.), over the body of Walter of Clifford,[3] and between the prior and convent of Christ Church and the executors of the will of Walter of Clifford (M., prior of Clifford, R. of Clifford, and W. the goldsmith), over a certain sum of money. Walter of Clifford the younger[4] obtained that the the body of his father should remain buried in the monastery of Clifford amongst the bodies of his ancestors. He promised, however, to pay forty marks to the church of Canterbury for buying a rent, so that the anniversary of his father and of his mother, who was buried in the church of Canterbury, might be celebrated yearly.[5]

In 1214 a case concerning the lands and possessions of

[1] Welbeck Cart., f. 88ᵛ.

[2] Welbeck Cart., f. 89ʳ. Cf. Bradenstoke Cart., f. 105ʳ, a suit between the prior and convent of Bradenstoke and William, son of Everard de Ringesborn, about the payment of the arrears of an annual rent of 5s. from the will of Master William of Potterne, settled on 22 Apr. 1224.

[3] Walter of Clifford married Agnes daughter and heiress of Roger de Cundi, lord of the manors of Caenby and Glentham (Lincs.). His sister was Fair Rosamund, the mistress of Henry II and mother of William Longespée, earl of Salisbury. He died in 1222–3 (B. Burke, Genealogical History of the Dormant Abeyant Forfeited and Extinct Peerages of the British Empire (1883), p. 122).

[4] He took part in the rebellion of Richard Marshal, earl of Pembroke, and his lands were confiscated and he was outlawed. He was, however, soon restored to the royal favour, and to the castle of Clifford. He married Margaret daughter of Llywelyn, prince of Wales, and widow of John de Braose. (Burke, Dormant Peerages, loc. cit., and see also N. Denholm-Young, Richard of Cornwall (Oxford, 1947), p. 25).

[5] Canterbury, Cartae Antiquae, C 279 (App. B (iv), no. 11).

Alexander of All Saints was brought before judges delegate, the abbot of Leiston, the dean of Wangford, and the prior of Butley, by the abbot and convent of Sibton on the plea that those lands had been bequeathed to them in Alexander's will. The lands and possessions were adjudged to the monks against the defendants, Edmund of Norwich and Basilia his wife.[1] From this small amount of evidence it is difficult to estimate the proportion and importance of the number of marriage and testamentary suits that were taken to Rome, but it is possible to show the competence of the delegated courts over these spiritual cases in practice as well as in theory.[2]

5. The Litigants

As a survey of the business of the delegated courts has shown, religious houses, especially the Benedictines and Augustinians, were probably the most frequent litigants before papal tribunals.[3] But given the nature of the evidence, it is necessary to state this with caution, for the bulk of the information about monasteries and their suits comes from cartularies. Cartulary material suggests strongly, however, that the religious houses carried their suits straight to Rome and rarely favoured the diocesan courts. Their preferences for these courts can be explained by the desire of most monastic houses to exempt themselves as much as possible from the jurisdiction of the local diocesan. Most religious houses were litigious, and suits about property were common.[4] There is evidence that the regulars found these courts the

[1] Sibton Cart., ff. 81ᵛ–2ʳ. The date of the settlement, 1207 as given in the manuscript, must be a mistake for 1217, since the papal mandate is dated 13 Apr. 1214.

[2] Amongst spiritual cases breach of faith must be included. There is no evidence for these pleas except on the *Curia Regis* rolls, where it is often pleaded by one or other of the defendants that the case was not about lay fee or chattels, but about breach of faith. I have not, therefore, considered the question in any detail.

[3] Individual monks, as holders of a monastic office, sometimes brought cases: for instance the almoner of St. Albans initiated several suits in 1208 (St. Albans Almoner's Cart., ff. 131ᵛ–2ʳ, and 132ᵛ–3ᵛ). Otherwise they only appear as plaintiffs, and then very rarely, in suits about elections, monastic vows, and the like (e.g. *Reg. Inn. IV*, no. 5188, and *Letters of Inn. III*, nos. 525, 545, and 563).

[4] On their litigiousness over property see the remarks of R. Graham, *S. Gilbert of Sempringham and the Gilbertines* (1901), p. 132.

most suitable for their purposes.[1] Although the 1215 decree stated that all orders that were not already holding General Chapters should make arrangements to do so, the internal organization of the General Chapter for the settlement of suits never became very strong with the Benedictines and Augustinians, and for them the papally delegated courts remained the most frequented.[2]

With the Cistercians and some other orders, such as the Premonstratensians, on the other hand, the General Chapter had become by 1198 the main tribunal for hearing internal disputes.[3] Frequent decrees forbade appeal to Rome and the taking of cases before other courts.[4] Arrangements were also made for the private settlement of suits between Cistercians and Premonstratensians, Cistercians and Gilbertines, and Cistercians and Carthusians.[5] The extension of the Cistercian jurisdiction to cover cases with other orders and with laymen is one of the most interesting aspects of its influence,[6] and on occasion regulars and seculars and laymen brought Cistercians before Cistercian courts.[7] A suit between the Benedictine abbey of Lyre and the abbey of Quarr (Cist. Isle of Wight), in which the plaintiff appears to have been Lyre, was committed by the Cistercian General Chapter to the abbots of Waverley and Ford in 1201.[8] Similarly seculars—the dean and chapter of York and Jacob a clerk, for instance—challenged Cistercians before their own tribunals, and laymen occur as both plaintiffs and defendants.[9]

---

[1] Professor Cheney, working on the suits of Innocent III's pontificate, has come to a roughly similar conclusion on the proportion of plaintiffs, i.e. two thirds religious houses, less than a quarter parochial clergy, and about one fifteenth laymen, 'England and the Roman Curia under Innocent III', *Journal of Ecclesiastical History*, xviii (1967), 176.   [2] See my article 'Judicial Activities' i, esp. pp. 30–1.

[3] Ibid., and 'English Cistercian Cases'.

[4] 'Judicial Activities' ii, p. 178. Similar decrees were issued by the Premonstratensian and Carthusian General Chapters (ibid., p. 179).

[5] Ibid., pp. 180–2.

[6] See 'English Cistercian Cases', p. 94, and 'Judicial Activities' ii, pp. 171 and 182–3.

[7] In principle, according to the *Decretales*, a case should be brought before the defendant's tribunal, see cc. 8 and 20. *X*. II. 2, but there were countless exceptions to this ruling.

[8] *Statuta Ordinis Cisterciensis*, i and ii, ed. Canivez, 1201, 43; and cf. 1207, 48; and 1253, 20.

[9] Ibid., 1210, 42; and 1214, 41. See also 1203, 49; 1207, 62; 1213, 62; 1216, 55; and 1254, 15.

A considerable number of these laymen were wool merchants, such as Arnulph Canis whose case against the monks of Kirkstall 'qui lanam suam praevendiderunt' was delegated to the abbot of Fountains in 1209.[1] Burgesses from Bergen, Saint-Omer, and London were also involved in disputes with the Cistercians.[2] In choosing to bring a case before the Cistercian General Chapter, the lay impetrant must have been convinced of the reasonable fairness and competence of the Cistercian tribunals in dealing with cases about trading; and in consenting to come before a Cistercian tribunal other regulars and seculars and laymen must have been equally satisfied, and they may also have been attracted by its capacity to implement its sentence. At any rate there is evidence that the General Chapter was used in this way sometimes, being preferred to the courts of judges delegate.[3]

For the bishops the papal court had long been a court of first instance.[4] By 1198 archbishops and bishops, and archdeacons also, carried cases to Rome about election, jurisdiction, visitation, procurations and property, and about the exemption of religious houses, probably as often as it was necessary. The archbishop of Canterbury and the bishops of Coventry, Ely, Lincoln, Llandaff, London, Norwich, Rochester, and Worcester, in the southern province, all brought cases in the period between 1198 and 1254. The bishop of Lincoln was involved as plaintiff in six cases of this nature,[5] the archbishop of Canterbury in seven,[6] and bishops also appeared as defendants in cases brought by monasteries and secular clerks.[7]

---

[1] *Statuta*, 1209, 28.   [2] Ibid. 1206, 68; 1209, 34; and 1212, 55.

[3] There are also European examples of laymen coming as plaintiffs before Cistercian courts, e.g. ibid. 1211, 43; 1236, 49; and 1250, 53, and also as defendants without objection, 1237, 70 and 76.

[4] The first case taken to Rome by an English bishop appears to have been that of Wilfrid of York against Theodore, which came before Pope Agatho in 679, see A. J. Macdonald, *Lanfranc* (Oxford, 1926), pp. 72–3, and F. M. Stenton, *Anglo-Saxon England* (Oxford, 1943), pp. 135–6.

[5] *Acta Stephani Langton*, ed. Major, no. 43; *Reg. Antiq. Linc.* iii, nos. 645 and 653, ii, no. 374; and *Reg. Greg. IX*, nos. 3764 and 5023. Cf. Cheney, 'England and the Roman Curia', p. 179, who states that the bishops rarely appear as plaintiffs during Innocent III's pontificate.

[6] Canterbury, Cartae Antiquae, A 5; St. Augustine's Cart., f. 79ʳ; *Ann. Mon.* iii. 151; *Reg. Greg. IX*, nos. 4372, 5182, 5387; and *Reg. Inn. IV*, no. 5670.

[7] e.g. *Letters of Inn. III*, no. 434; and P.R.O. SC 7/19/12.

By the end of the pontificate of Alexander III, the passage
to Rome of secular clerks and parish priests with judicial
complaints had become quite common,[1] and throughout
the first half of the thirteenth century secular clergy were
frequent litigants. In seeking papal delegation they sought the
promise of a final judgement, free from diocesan restrictions.
If we break down into groups the number of secular clergy
who appear as plaintiffs, we find that the majority were
rectors. Of these about one third used the title of master.
Of only a handful do we know any subsequent history of
advancement, men such as Master William of Purleigh and
Master Robert de Gravele who became canons;[2] but it may
be true that many others were men of substance, as Professor
Cheney suggests.[3] About one sixth were dignitaries, deans,
archdeacons, chancellors, precentors, and canons, sometimes
appearing as litigant rectors; and another sixth was composed
of clerks, papal officers, and vicars. Their cases concerned
all aspects of the parish church. Any assessment of what
these figures mean is likely to be misleading: if we look at
the number of cases where secular clerks appeared as
defendants it is comparatively large but the only surviving
evidence is from cartularies. It is impossible to estimate how
many documents of cases in which rectors appeared as plaintiffs have perished and, similarly, how many records of
cases between one clerk and another. But all in all the chance
for the survival of their records is likely to be much smaller
than that for records of the religious houses.

For many parties the acquisition of mandates did not
present a difficult problem. Most of the larger religious
communities employed standing proctors at Rome. Higher
ecclesiastics and Church dignitaries visited Rome frequently,
and it was not unusual for lower clergy and laymen to make
the journey. A suit could be brought against many people
off one mandate,[4] and there was no limit to those who might
be challenged before a delegated court. The geographical
limits to diocesan justice, which often formed obstacles in

[1] e.g. *Papal Decretals relating to Lincoln*, nos. xv–xvi (1164 × 1181), and xix
(1174 × 1181).
[2] P.R.O. E 40/14044(2); and *Reg. Hon. III*, no. 2547 (*C.P.L.* i. 73).
[3] Cheney, 'England and the Roman Curia', p. 179.
[4] See above, pp. 66–8.

the litigant's way, could be superseded by a papal mandate, and the disadvantages of distance and expense might be outweighed if several suits could be settled in this way and further appeal obviated.[1]

One of the main attractions of the Church courts to litigants may have been the speed with which many suits were settled. In 1229 it was recorded on the plea rolls that a layman explained that he had brought a man to the court Christian in a case about a tenement 'because justice is to be had more speedily there'.[2] Before the papal delegated courts the minor suit was settled in one to two years on an average, and more suits became minor as the law was established.[3] This speed is all the more impressive when the time for the conveyance of the mandate to the judges is taken into account, and when it is recognized that the sittings of the delegated courts were inevitably controlled by other activities which might impede the judges, and by a procedure which insisted upon certain delays. The Alvingham suit illustrates how the meetings of a judge-delegate court were spread out in the course of a year between the issue of the mandate and the settlement. The papal mandate was dated 23 January 1245. The defendant was summoned to appear on 21 June (five months later) by a peremptory citation which would have allowed thirty days' grace. Therefore the mandate possibly did not arrive until the middle of May. On 21 June *induciae deliberatorie* were granted to the defendant. The next court day was about a month later, 17 July, and on that day several dilatory exceptions were proposed. October 7 was then appointed for putting forward all dilatory exceptions. A month later, on 5 November, the court sat again and interlocutory sentences on these exceptions were pronounced. On 12 November the court met, and appointed 4 December as the day on which the contesta-

---

[1] Maitland made these points in *Roman Canon Law* on p. 113.

[2] *Bracton's Note Book*, ii, no. 351. Cf. the remarks of Walter Map in '*De Nugis Curialium*', ed. M. R. James, *Anecdota Oxoniensia* (Mediaeval and Modern Ser. iv, pt. xiv, Oxford, 1914), p. 253.

[3] See App. A (iv), Examples of Time Taken for Settling Suits. Cooper, *Select Scottish Cases*, p. xxx, remarks that on the whole the papal system of justice exhibited promptitude and efficiency, and on p. xl he writes of 'a degree of expedition which could with difficulty be equalled in a modern court'.

tion of the suit was to take place before the principal judges. On that day the judges delivered sentence, thus completing the process within a year.[1]

Laymen are known to have brought parish priests and religious houses before judges delegate about the erection of private chapels, and about tithes, debts, and similar matters,[2] but on the whole the evidence of laymen using the papal courts is slight. Only one instance appears to survive of a group of parishioners taking a case to Rome. Here the parishioners of the church of All Saints, Thundridge (Herts.), brought a suit against the prior of Ware (Ben. al. Herts.) about a chantry in the church before judges delegate, the bishop of London, the prior of Holy Trinity, and the dean of St. Paul's, in 1229.[3] They were thus in fact appearing before their diocesan in company with two other judges, but it is possible that they believed that a settlement made by judges delegate would be the only kind acceptable to a religious corporation. William, son of Ralph of Hallow, took to Rome his case against the prior and convent of Worcester—that they without due process of law had deprived him of the office of prior's butler. Innocent III delegated the suit to three seculars, the archdeacon of Salop, Master R. Grosseteste, and the rural dean of Sapey.[4] Where laymen occur as plaintiffs in property suits before papal courts, it seems that they expected, and probably obtained, judgements as favourable as those available in other courts and also efficient enforcement. In about 1184 William knight of Hambleden brought the canons of Oseney before the abbot of Evesham and the prior of Reading in a case concerning the tithes of Whatcombe (Berks.). At the settlement the knight was freed from the vexations of the canons.[5] In 1237 Walter, son of Geoffrey, and others brought the prior and monks of Daventry before judges delegate, the prior of St. Frideswide's and

[1] Alvingham Cart., f. 5ʳ⁻ᵛ.
[2] e.g. Letters of Inn. III, nos. 94, 688, 889, 954, and 1187.
[3] Lambeth Palace Library, Arches F 3, f. 86ᵛ. Cf. Letters of Inn. III, no. 274, a case between a layman and a religious house about a chantry.
[4] Letters of Inn. III, no. 1156B.
[5] Oseney Cart. iv, no. 400A. Another early suit is mentioned in the Stixwould cartulary (f. 57ʳ), where William Fuc brought the convent of Stixwould before Richard, archbishop of Canterbury, acting as a judge delegate, about land and buildings which Master Syward had left the convent in his will.

the archdeacon and chancellor of Oxford. The suit, which concerned tithes, was resolved largely in favour of Walter, who, however, made another grant to Daventry.[1] W., called *pincerna*, and his sons brought the abbots of Margam and Neath (both Cistercians) before a papal court in 1222 in a case about land,[2] and William of Englefield, knight, brought the abbot and convent of Missenden (Aug. Bucks.), who had failed to provide a canon to serve his chapel at Shiplake (Oxon.) as agreed, before the priors of Reading, Sherborne, and Poughley.[3] Neither settlement was unfavourable to the lay party.

The case brought by William de Mowbray against the monks of Byland before Simon the dean and Hamo the treasurer of York, judges delegate of Innocent III, in 1204, is not so readily explicable. The suit concerned the forest of Middlesmoor in Nidderdale, and the king's court would have seemed the obvious forum for so influential a layman. The settlement provided that Byland was to give William 300 silver marks for the forest of Middlesmoor. Byland remitted a payment of 100 silver marks which William owed them, and in turn he allowed them to purchase a carucate of land in Airyholme for twenty marks. This arrangement was very favourable to William, for his grandfather had already gained 300 marks for the forest of Middlesmoor.[4] In the circumstances the choice of court can perhaps only be explained in the light of relationships between the Mowbray family, the Crown, and the chapter of York, and it is possible that a clerical adviser suggested this course of action to William. As one might expect, no evidence survives of property cases where both the parties were laymen being brought before papally delegated courts. It appears that papal mandates were not issued in property suits unless one of the parties was a clerk, except for the Tuscan patrimony where papal influence was much stronger.[5]

---

[1] B.M. Add. Ch. 21888.

[2] B.M. Harley Ch. 75 B 2 (App. B (iv), no. 3).

[3] B.M. Add. Chs. 20370-3 (App. B (iv), nos. 6-9).

[4] Byland Cart., f. 77^{r-v}. I am grateful to Dr. Diana Greenway for her help and comments on this case.

[5] See P. Herde, 'Papal Formularies for Letters of Justice (13th–16th Centuries)', *Monumenta Iuris Canonici*, Ser. C: Subsidia i (Vatican City, 1965), p. 340. But there is an interesting English case between two Christian knights and certain Jews about usury, which was delegated by Gregory IX in 1235 (H.M.C. *Var. Coll.* iv. 160).

Influential laymen undoubtedly favoured the papal courts in those suits that came under the Church's spiritual jurisdiction, such as suits about marriage and wills. The sources are so unbalanced that we have few lay records, but it is evident, from what material survives concerning marriage cases, that many of these went to Rome, if not in the first instance, then at least on appeal later.[1] William of Drogheda, whose assumptions owing to his position and experience command respect, apparently took it for granted that all important legal business would be taken to Rome.[2] It appears too that important litigants, lay as well as ecclesiastical, chose the papal courts where appropriate. Maud d'Oilly, daughter of Humphrey II de Bohun, for example, chose to bring Maud, countess of Essex and Hereford, and her husband before judges delegate in a case about a debt, when she could well have brought them before the archbishop's court.[3]

In bringing laymen as defendants before Church courts in certain cases, the religious were following an obvious course, and in choosing delegated courts they were simply taking advantage of a possibility open to them. Laymen appeared as defendants in suits about land, property, mills, rents, tithes, and chapels, in connection with their rights and duties as manorial lords, patrons of parish churches, parishioners, or tenants.[4] Knights frequently appear as defendants (for example, H., knight of Rickinghall, Fulk, knight, and William of Cheriton, knight),[5] often in the company of other laymen and of clerks, for a major attraction of a papal mandate was that it could be made to include an assortment of people. H., knight of Rickinghall, for instance, appeared in company with B., the parson, and W., the vicar.[6] Stephen de Marisco, knight, and other laymen and clerks were included in a mandate which the abbot and convent of Thorney acquired in 1248.[7] Simon of Lewknor, knight, and

---

[1] See, e.g., *Rotuli Hugonis de Welles*, ii. 204.   [2] Drogheda, pp. xix ff.
[3] See above, p. 210, and App. B (iv), no. 10.
[4] See above, pp. 181, 182–3, 193–4, and 203; and *Letters of Inn. III*, nos. 124, 387, and 513.
[5] Eye Cart., ff. 46ᵛ–7ʳ; *St. Frideswide's Cart.* i, no. 45, and *Acta Stephani Langton*, ed. Major, no. 62; and Canterbury, Cartae Antiquae, F 8.
[6] Eye Cart., ff. 46ᵛ–7ʳ.   [7] Thorney Cart. ii, f. 323ʳ.

other laymen and clerks of the cities and dioceses of Lincoln, Salisbury, and Winchester were the defendants named by the abbot and convent of Bec. This mandate was also made out against the abbot and convent of Dorchester.[1] These inclusive mandates do much to explain the presence of many such 'small fry' before the delegated courts, and probably provide the main reason why the monasteries chose to invade the delegated courts with their suits.

A suggestion that the religious sometimes compelled laymen to come before Church courts, both delegated and ordinary, in cases which belonged to the Crown, is contained in the inquiries of the itinerant justices at Stafford in 1255.[2] It is probable that the king was more worried at this turn of events than the lay defendants, who had means of removing any cases which they objected to answering to the royal courts. A passage in the *Chronica Majora* says that in 1247 the king, following the example of the French barons, prohibited ecclesiastical judges from hearing any pleas against laymen unless they concerned marriage or wills.[3] The French barons, headed by Hugh IV, duke of Burgundy, had protested in November 1246 against the extension of ecclesiastical jurisdiction, which they said should be limited to suits concerning heresy, usury, and marriage.[4] This suggests a general encroachment by the Church courts, but there is no evidence that lesser laymen objected to this. Like lesser clerks, they used the courts that suited them best in a particular instance.[5] It is probably true that knights and parish clergy, for example, cared very much less about which court they came before than did the magnates and the bishops, the king and the pope, who had a vested interest in maintaining their own jurisdictions.

---

[1] Windsor, Papal Bulls, no. 1; and see, e.g., two mandates on f. 223ʳ of Lanthony Cart. A 2.   [2] *Ann. Mon.* i. 337, cited by Flahiff, *W.P.*, pt. i. 296.
[3] *Chron. Maj.* iv. 614.
[4] See J. Richard, *Les Ducs de Bourgogne et la formation du duché du XIᵉ au XIVᵉ siècle* (Paris, 1954), pp. 234–5. See also Fournier, pp. 101–4, and *W.P.*, pt. i. 292–3.
[5] For clerks using the writ of prohibition as well as laymen see Flahiff, 'Use of Prohibitions', pp. 101–16, esp. pp. 101–9, and B.M. Cotton MS. Nero C iii, f. 199, and Bodleian MS. Chs. Bucks. a 3, Ch. 45. In France the device of 'l'appel comme d'abus' was used by both laymen and ecclesiastics, when it suited them, in much the same way as in England, see Dauvillier's introduction to Génestal's *Les Origines de l'appel comme d'abus*.

6. *The Proctors*

Proctors were representatives of the parties rather than professional counsel. In the 1150s one party complained 'that Gregory was always represented by a proctor when he went to law and that he never appeared in person, though he was in good health and lived close by'.[1] The proctor in fact was instituted to conduct the case instead of the party. This was in contrast to the advocates, *patroni*, who formed a professional body with duties of delivering advice and informing their clients about the law.[2] There are few references to the use of advocates in delegated courts in England.[3] They were, however, used in cases before the papal court.[4] Unlike proctors, advocates had no right of renunciation of a cause and they had to be learned in the law. Anyone charged in a criminal case employed an advocate, whereas proctors could act only in civil suits. A proctor could take an oath on behalf of his master; an advocate could not represent his client in this way.

At Rome there were two types of proctors: those constituted for impetrating or getting mandates, with powers to refuse or assent to a certain commission or place of hearing; and those appointed to present the case at the papal court if it was to be heard by an auditor or by the pope. The surviving evidence for both groups is extremely scanty, but it is probably correct to assume that on the whole they had more legal training than proctors used in England, who were treated as representatives of the party or as substitutes to act for him.[5]

Indeed the position of the proctors in the delegated Church courts is much more akin to that of the attorneys in

---

[1] *J.S.L.*, no. 81. Cf. no. 132: 'She sent her proctors and sought to excuse her absence; but the reasons put forward for her absence seemed insufficient.' Appearance was expected unless impossible, see also ibid., nos. 60 and 102 for other references.

[2] On advocates in general, see Fournier, pp. 32–6, and P. Gillet in *D.D.C.* i, cols. 1524–35.

[3] Magdalen College, Oxford, Findon Ch. t, mentions two advocates employed by the prior and convent of Sele as being paid £4 yearly.

[4] See, e.g., *Chron. Abb. Evesham*, pp. 152–3; and Binham Cart., f. 141ʳ⁻ᵛ.

[5] For proctors in the court of Rome see R. von Heckel, 'Das Aufkommen der ständigen Prokuratoren an der päpstlichen Kurie im 13. Jahrhundert', *Studi e Testi*, xxxviii (1924), 290–321, and my article 'Canterbury Proctors'.

the English royal courts.[1] Notices of parties appearing by attorney use the phrase 'ponit loco suo'.[2] The attorneys were generally appointed by the parties in the presence of the justices. At the same time the authority of the king's writ, or the justiciar's mandate in the king's absence, was recognized in appointment.[3] Attorneys were often engaged for a number of cases and it was not unusual to empower them to act either singly or together.[4] As soon as an attorney had been instituted, his principal could take no action of his own unless he cancelled the institution.[5]

The possibility, which was evident in England by the end of the twelfth century, that the proctors would gain a professional status was not fulfilled until the middle years of the thirteenth century.[6] The mobility of the courts, especially of the delegated courts, may have prevented the growth of groups of proctors round the courts. We may conclude from the legate Otto's enactment forbidding day appointments for proctors that until 1237 proctors were appointed frequently for day terms.[7] But certain factors suggest a growing professionalism. William of Drogheda, writing in 1239, insists that proctors should be paid.[8] The Council of Lyons, which was summoned by Gregory X in 1274, fixed at twelve pounds 'tournois' the maximum salary for a proctor for each affair.[9] There is evidence, too, that pleas were becoming more technical and procedural techniques more complicated, so that representation demanded a certain amount of experience of the practice of the delegated courts, and if it was to be done well, some legal knowledge.

[1] For attorneys see C. T. Flower, *Introduction to the Curia Regis Rolls (1199–1230)* (Selden Soc. lxii, 1944), chapter V. D. E. Queller, *The Office of Ambassador in the Middle Ages* (Princeton University Press, 1967), came to my notice after this section was written. On p. 34 he discusses the interchangeability of the proctor and the attorney.

[2] e.g. *Pleas before the King or his Justices (1198–1202)*, ed. D. M. Stenton (Selden Soc. lxvii–lxviii, 1952–3), no. 2637.

[3] Flower, *Introduction*, p. 396, citing *C.R.R.* ii. 133, and iii (1926), 284.

[4] Flower, *Introduction*, p. 401.   [5] Ibid., p. 403.

[6] Professional counsel existed in the common law courts by 1227 (see C. Johnson, 'Notes on Thirteenth Century Judicial Procedure', *E.H.R.* lxii (1947), 508–21), but they display ignorance of their position and the facts of the case, too, at times 'even in the reign of Henry III', see Flower, *Introduction*, pp. 402 and 405–6.

[7] See *C.S.* ii, pt. i. 256, no. [25].   [8] Drogheda, ciii, pp. 98–9.

[9] Fournier, p. 40, citing c. 19 of the Council of Lyons (*Sacrorum Conciliorum Collectio*, xxiv, ed. Mansi, col. 94).

(i) *Employers and their Representatives*

Contestants who employed proctors in the delegated courts can be separated into five main groups: foreign monastic houses and persons who lived or were staying abroad; religious corporations at home; nunneries; rectors and clerks; and laymen. The first group had property and interests in England but were absent from the country; for example, the abbots and convents of Fécamp, Fontevrault (dioc. Poitiers), St. Georges-de-Boscherville (dioc. Rouen), St. Pierre-de-la-Couture (dioc. Le Mans), Séez, Montébourg (dioc. Coutances), and Préaux, and the bishop and chapter of Le Mans.[1] The abbot and convent of Bec employed their general proctor in England, William de Ginevilla, to represent them from at least 1234 to 1254.[2] He was prior of Ogbourne, Bec's chief dependency in England, and a man of considerable administrative ability. He retired from office in 1254 and was granted the very considerable pension of nine manors. His death occurred in 1258.[3] Besides William de Ginevilla, Bec employed at least five others as proctors during this period: William of Wantage in 1222, A. of Exeter in

[1] *Chichester Cart.*, no. 273; *Reg. Antiq. Linc.* iii, no. 646; B.M. Campbell Ch. xxii. 11; Dunstable Cart., f. 75ᵛ, cal. *Dunstable Cart.*, no. 913; P.R.O. E 210/3736; Christchurch (Twynham) Cart., f. 92ʳ; Reading Cart., f. 112ʳ; and *Reg. S. Osmund*, i. 355.

[2] Windsor Ch. xi G 75 and *St. Frideswide's Cart.* ii, no. 1135, and probably Windsor, Arundel White Book, p. 174 (1233–4); P.R.O. DL 27/101 (1247); B.M. Campbell Ch. xxii. 11 (1252); Shaftesbury Cart., f. 116ᵛ (29 Apr. 1252); and *Godstow Reg.* i, no. [95] (1254).

[3] See M. M. Morgan, *English Lands of the Abbey of Bec* (Oxford, 1946), p. 43. The office of general proctor of the abbey of Bec and prior of Ogbourne seems to have been combined often, cf. Ranulph, *Godstow Reg.* i, no. [93], *c.* 1220, and *V.C.H. Wilts.* iii. 396. See also Christchurch Cart., f. 60ʳ⁻ᵛ, where the prior of Ogbourne and Andrew of Croydon, clerk, appear as general proctors in 1231–3. Andrew of Croydon had appeared as a clerk on behalf of Bec in 1222, witnessing a document of Stephen Langton, as arbiters, on an occasion when William of Wantage acted as proctor (Glynde Ch. 3370, cal. R. F. Dell, *Glynde Place Archives* (Lewes, 1964)). He occurs as a clerk of Archbishop Langton between 1222 and 1227, and possibly as late as 1228, and is described by Miss Major as being one of Langton's new clerks found after 1222 (*Acta Stephani Langton*, pp. xlviii n. 1, 121, 139, and 144). He was also parson of Croydon (see K. Major in *E.H.R.* xlviii, 532 and 534). A Master Andrew of Croydon attests an *inspeximus* made by Thomas, bishop of Norwich, on 15 Apr. 1230 and a confirmation of the same bishop made on 29 Mar. 1232 (Binham Cart., ff. 44ᵛ–5ᵛ, and 46ᵛ–7ᵛ, ibid; and Dugdale, *Mon. Angl.* iii, ed. Caley, Ellis, and Bandinel, 91, num. xxx).

c. 1225, Master Laurence in *c.* 1241, and Peter of Swyncombe and John of Bledlow in *c.* 1245, most of them on a temporary basis.[1] The abbot and convent of Fécamp appointed Roger, prior of Cogges (an alien cell dependent on Fécamp), as their proctor for a cause in *c.* 1220.[2] The abbot and convent of Grestain (Eure, France) were represented by Robert de Bulevilla, a monk of Grestain and presumably resident in one of their English cells, in a suit about the tithes of Conock (Wilts.) in 1224;[3] and the abbot and convent of Jumièges were represented by the prior of their dependency of Hayling (Hants) in 1242.[4] Ralph, the prior of the alien priory of St. Michael's Mount (Cornw.) which was dependent on the abbey of Mont-Saint-Michel, appeared as general proctor on behalf of the abbey in 1237;[5] and Hugh, monk (presumably of Takeley), acted as general proctor in England for the abbot and convent of St. Valéry in Picardy in *c.* 1220 and 1239–40.[6] Takeley in Essex was dependent on St. Valéry. There were also individuals abroad who needed proctors in England. Master William de Moy represented John of Colonna, cardinal priest of St. Prassede, and the abbot of Sawtry appeared for Leonard, chaplain of Stephen de Normandis, cardinal priest of St. Mary in Trastevere, who was also rector of Conington (Hunts.).[7] Master Laurence of St. Martin, rector of Abbots Ann (Hants), who was away at Bologna, had a proctor 'ad omnia eius tractanda negotia', and Berard de Secia constituted Master Reginald of London, rector of Orpington (Kent), as his general proctor in 1243.[8]

Secondly, monasteries used proctors to represent them as corporate institutions when a spokesman was needed; and their use of proctors, on account of the large number of their

---

[1] Glynde Ch. 3370; Windsor Chs. xi G 12; xi G 14, 16, and 37, and see xi G 22; and xi G 27.   [2] *Oseney Cart.* iv, no. 144.

[3] Lanthony Cart. A1, VIII, no. lxxxii. Neither of their two recorded cells at Creeting St. Olave in Suffolk and at Wilmington in Sussex (Knowles and Hadcock, *Religious Houses*, pp. 84 and 92) seem sufficiently near to the West Country.

[4] P.R.O. KB 26/124, m. 27d.

[5] Beaulieu Cart., ff. 132ᵛ–3ʳ (App. B (iv), no. 16).

[6] New College, Oxford, Takeley Chs. 139 and 229.

[7] *Glos. Cart.* ii, nos. ccccⅼxxxix–cccclxxxx; B.M. Add. Ch. 34033.

[8] Reg. Vat. 15, f. 86ʳ (*Reg. Greg. IX*, no. 630), and Ann. Tewkes. *Ann. Mon.* i. 129.

suits, was continual.[1] Two monks represented Burton in this period,[2] and W. de Millebroc, monk of Beaulieu, Roger de Soctindon and Adam of St. Albans, monks of St. Augustine's, Canterbury, R., monk of Margam, T. of Beccles, monk of Norwich, and Roger, monk of St. Andrew's, Northampton, all served as proctors for their respective houses.[3] Probably in large convents one monk was appointed to the office of proctor as to any other monastic position. The abbot and convent of Oseney had a general proctor, Master Walter de Bylendone, who served from at least 1240 to 1270.[4] He was preceded by William of Kilkenny, a canon of the house, who occurs in c. 1215–25 as general proctor.[5] Nicholas, monk of St. Martin's Dover, who was also cellarer of the convent, conducted suits on behalf of his house in 1224 and in 1228, and another monk, Thomas Lutren, represented St. Martin's in 1246.[6] R., who represented Reading abbey in 1234, was also sacrist of the house; and the precentor of St. John's, Colchester, acted for his abbey in a suit of 1240.[7] The abbot and convent of Malmesbury had as proctors John of Wales, monk, in c. 1218, Simon, monk, in c. 1219, and Master N. of Cirencester in c. 1229–30.[8] The last named was mentioned as 'datum ad totam causam', and it appears that several men in a convent might be seconded for temporary service of this kind if the general proctor was employed elsewhere. Ralph de Rokeburg, monk of Abingdon, was constituted only for a day and was

[1] c. 1. *X.* I. 39 (Greg. I): 'De syndico.' 'Religiosi debent habere syndicum, qui causas monasterii agat, et defendat, etiam, si oportuerit, constituto illi salario.' Abbots and priors often selected their monks as attorneys in the royal courts, see Flower, *Introduction*, p. 404.

[2] 'Burton Chs.', no. 58, and B.M. Stowe Ch. 58.

[3] Beaulieu Cart., f. 132ʳ; *Reg. Inn. IV*, no. 6990; B.M. Harley Ch. 75 B 2; Norwich Ch. 1686; and Northampton, St. Andrew's Cart. (B), ff. 39ᵛ–40ʳ.

[4] *Oseney Cart.* iv, no. 403, and v, no. 748. In vol. ii, no. 795, he occurs as an arbiter in 1265. See also ibid. iii, no. 1186, and v, no. 868B, for two other Oseney proctors.

[5] Bodleian MS. Chs. Oxon. a 4, Ch. 230, and cf. 300. A Master William of Kilkenny attests an Oseney charter of c. 1221, *Oseney Cart.* iv, no. 144; and someone of the same name was rector of Easton Maudit (Northants.) in 1237, see Bodleian MS. Chs. Bucks. a 3, Ch. 45. See also Emden, *Oxf. Reg.* ii. 1048–9, who has many entries under the same name but it is unlikely that they all refer to the same person.

[6] Dover Cart., ff. 5ʳ, 50ᵛ, 226ᵛ, and 229ᵛ.

[7] Reading Cart., f. 114ʳ, and P.R.O. E 42/384.

[8] *Malmesbury Reg.* i. 392, 402; and ii. 17, 31.

probably a stand-in.[1] A large religious house such as Christ Church, Canterbury, must have had several permanent proctors, but in a suit with the prior and convent of Clifford (Heref.) and the executors of the will of Walter of Clifford, which was heard probably at Oxford in 1224, before Oxfordshire judges, Christ Church used as their proctor Master Silvester, rector of St. Michael's, Oxford.[2] Presumably all their standing proctors were engaged elsewhere.[3]

The use of secular clerks as proctors was not infrequent. Master Alexander Walpole was a proctor of Lewes, probably for their Norfolk possessions.[4] Robert, clerk of Easton Neston (Northants.), appeared on behalf of the prior and convent of Luffield and Ralph, vicar of Thornborough, in 1251;[5] Master Alexander de Stanford on behalf of Thorney in c. 1224–5;[6] and Robert the Poitevin on behalf of Wymondham in 1249.[7] Master Adam of Barney, who represented Binham in 1251 in a case which came before a papal auditor, was probably the same Adam who as rector of Barney was the defendant in a suit brought by the prior and convent of Walsingham in 1252.[8] On the whole, these were probably not lengthy appointments.

Regular canons, too, represented their convents: W. de Bures, canon, on behalf of Bayham;[9] Henry de Rapendon, canon and abbot elect, on behalf of Darley;[10] Jordan, canon, for Merton;[11] Warin, canon, on behalf of Notley (in conjunction with Master S. de Melcheburne);[12] Roger de Stanford, canon, on behalf of Owston;[13] R. de Wassingburn,

---

[1] Abingdon Cart., f. 144ᵛ.

[2] Canterbury, Cartae Antiquae, C 279 (App. B (iv), no. 11). In *Oseney Cart.* v, no. 851C, a settlement is mentioned as having taken place in M. Silvester's house in 1225, and *St. Frideswide's Cart.* i, no. 276, records a Master Silurus (? Silvester), rector of St. Michael's, as an arbiter in 1228.

[3] The Canterbury proctors are hardly ever mentioned by name, see, e.g., Canterbury, Cartae Antiquae, C 280, F 8, F 31, H 120, L 351, and MS. Scrapbook A, p. 13: Ch. 25; and see Reg. C, f. 29ʳ for Ralph fitz Warin of Higham.

[4] Lewes Cart., ff. 252ʳ, 262ʳ⁻ᵛ, and see P.R.O. E 40/14067 and 14070. He had become archdeacon of Suffolk by 11 June 1240, *Lewes Cart. N.P.*, no. 112.

[5] B.M. Harley Ch. 84 F 36.   [6] Thorney Cart. ii, f. 257ᵛ.

[7] *Reg. Inn. IV*, no. 4645.   [8] Binham Cart., ff. 61ʳ and 141ʳ⁻ᵛ.

[9] Bayham Cart., f. 60ʳ.

[10] Belvoir, Wessington Ch. 331.

[11] Dunstable Cart., f. 53ʳ, cal. *Dunstable Cart.*, 501.

[12] N.L.C., no. 63.

[13] Bodleian MS. Dodsworth 76, f. 1.

canon of Shouldham, on behalf of Sempringham;[1] and Richard de la Lade, canon, for Holy Cross, Waltham.[2]

Priors might act on behalf of their convents if given special mandates from them for the purpose.[3] William, prior of Anglesey (Cambs.), acted on behalf of his convent in 1226–7;[4] R., the subprior, on behalf of the prior and canons of Canons Ashby in c. 1217;[5] the prior on behalf of the prior and convent of Leeds in 1225;[6] and the prior of Tutbury on behalf of the prior and convent in 1228–30.[7] Richard de Mores, prior of Dunstable, the procedural writer, appeared as proctor on behalf of his convent in 1214, 1222, and c. 1227.[8] If the papal mandate was made out against both the prior and the convent, separate representation might be necessary. The prior and J. (canon) represented Lanthony in c. 1224,[9] and the prior and subprior appeared on behalf of the master of Sempringham and the convent of Alvingham in 1245, presumably the prior for the master and the subprior for the convent.[10]

In a similar way deans and chapters appointed their own officers as representatives. Thomas, archdeacon of Totnes, appeared on behalf of the dean and chapter of Exeter.[11] Peter Picot, chancellor of Salisbury, was appointed to act on behalf of the chapter in 1215, and Master Abraham, the treasurer, acted in about 1218.[12] The dean and chapter of Wells were represented at Rome between 1243 and 1244 by the dean himself, the subdean, the archdeacon of Taunton, and numerous clerks;[13] while in the same suit the prior and convent of Bath employed monks, their precentor, Thomas, and other clerks.[14] The bishop of Worcester was represented at Rome in 1205 by his official, Robert de Clipstone.[15]

[1] Binham Cart., ff. 146v–7r.   [2] B.M. Egerton Ch. 409.
[3] See, e.g., Lanthony Cart. A1, VI, no. lxiii.   [4] N.L.C., no. 86.
[5] Canons Ashby Cart., f. 50r.   [6] Leeds Cart., f. 10r.
[7] Reg. Antiq. Linc. iii, no. 759.
[8] Dunstable Cart., ff. 45r, 46v, and 67v, cal. Dunstable Cart., nos.. 391, 405, and 767, and see above, p. 116.
[9] Lanthony Cart. A1, VIII, no. lxxxii.
[10] Alvingham Cart., f. 10r.   [11] Exeter Ch. 640.
[12] Reg. S. Osmund, i. 258; and Malmesbury Reg. i. 392 and 401.
[13] Wells, Lib. Albus i, ff. 72v, 75r, 77r, 79v and 95r–v.
[14] Two Chartularies of the Priory of St. Peter at Bath, ed. W. Hunt (Som. Rec., Soc. vii, 1893), pt. ii, nos. 182, 188, 197, 199, 200, 202, and 204.
[15] Chron. Abb. Evesham, p. 151.

Thirdly, nuns employed proctors on account of their inability to plead in court, although this canon could have been circumvented on the grounds that women might appear in order to defend their personal interests.[1] The abbess and convent of Godstow had five proctors between 1197 and 1254. Waleran, the abbess's chaplain, appeared on their behalf in 1197; Gilbert Vyam in 1234–5; William, chaplain, in 1236–7; Herbert, chaplain, in 1239; and W., clerk, in 1254.[2] The prioress and nuns of St. Michael, Stamford, were represented by their chaplain in *c.* 1217, and by a monk of Peterborough, Warin de Glinton, in a suit of 1235–6.[3] The abbess and nuns of St. Mary's, Winchester, also employed proctors, and the convent of Stixwould had as proctor Master H. de Mariseye.[4] Chaplains were appointed frequently;[5] and foreign nunneries used proctors in the same way as did foreign monasteries.[6]

The fourth group is formed by the rectors and clerks. The number of them appearing by proctor can be explained by the growing technicality of the law and by the fact that the court might be held at several days' distance. Some were represented by masters. Master Martin appeared on behalf of Adam, rector of Plumstead (Kent), in *c.* 1202×1226.[7] Master Roger de Boclande represented Geoffrey de Boclande, parson of Burnham Thorpe (Norf.), in 1224.[8] Master Henry de Trippeleawe acted for the rector of Great Wratting (Suff.) in *c.* 1245,[9] and Master Laurence of Lincoln for W., treasurer of York and vicar of Stradbroke (Suff.), in 1221.[10] Master William de Hanewrh', who acted on behalf of Richard Marescallus, rector of Tydd, in *c.* 1224–5, had

1 *C.* II. 12. 4. Women attorneys appear in the royal courts, and the word *attornata* was in use (Flower, *Introduction*, p. 404), but the prioress of Stainfield had a proctor to take her place in court (ibid., p. 405).

2 *Godstow Reg.* i, no. [309], and Westminster Domesday, ff. 378^v–9^r (App. B (v), no. 5); *Godstow Reg.* i, no. [92]; ii, no. [855]; ii, no. [775]; and Westminster Domesday, f. 379^r (App. B (iv), no. 12).

3 Canons Ashby Cart., f. 50^r, and Bodleian MS. Dodsworth 76, f. 1.

4 Godsfield Trans., f. 100^v; and Bardney Cart., f. 240^r.

5 e.g. Godstow and Stamford.

6 Canterbury, Cartae Antiquae, F31, and *Reg. Antiq. Linc.* iii, no. 646.

7 *Reg. Roff.*, p. 526 and St Augustine's Red Book, f. 237^v.

8 Lewes Cart., f. 241^v. This is almost certainly the Master Geoffrey de Boclande who was archdeacon of Norfolk and dean of St. Martin le Grand, London.

9 Windsor Ch. xi G 27.

10 Eye Cart., f. 37^r.

already been an arbiter (chosen by Richard) in the same case.[1]
Some rectors were represented by their chaplains. Peter,
chaplain of Tattingstone (Suff.), appeared for the rector,
Gilbert de Guines, in 1211 or 1213,[2] Richard de Sanford for
J. de Nerford, rector of Crundale (Kent), in 1225,[3] and A.,
chaplain, for Simon, rector of Brookland (Kent), in 1224.[4]
Others appointed clerks. Robert of Bury St. Edmunds, clerk,
represented Roger, the chaplain of St. Mary's, Dover, and
Andrew, the rector of St. John's, in 1246;[5] S. de Erderne,
clerk, appeared for the rector of Horwood (Bucks.) in
c. 1234;[6] and Ralph de Trikeb', clerk, for the rector of
Dalham (Suff.) in c. 1241.[7] When Laurence and William,
rectors of Wimborne All Hallows (Dors.), were a party in a
suit of c. 1225, Laurence appeared on behalf of them both;[8]
and W., the vicar, appeared on behalf of himself, B., the
rector, and H., knight, of Rickinghall in 1220.[9] No details
remain about the other representatives,[10] but although their
names are not always recorded, their occurrence is frequent.[11]

An even greater obscurity surrounds the few proctors
employed by the fifth group of contestants—the laymen.
Roger d'Oilly used proctors in c. 1229 and in 1246–7;[12]
John of Preston and Ralph Pudifet of Berkhamsted employed proctors in c. 1214 and 1221–8;[13] and Adam de Novo
Mercato sent his clerk, Roger, to answer the abbot and convent of Welbeck in 1242.[14] Thomas de Pridias and Ralph son
of Lefwine represented their wives.[15] Edmund of Norwich,
a layman, and Basilia his wife, who were contumacious for
a year, appear to have made no attempt to appoint and send
a proctor.[16] Philip de Burnham used a proctor 'datum tam ad

[1] Thorney Cart. ii, f. 257ᵛ. [2] Eye Cart., ff. 42ᵛ–3ʳ.
[3] Leeds Cart., f. 10ʳ. [4] Dover Cart., f. 226ᵛ.
[5] Dover Cart., f. 51ʳ. [6] N.L.C., no. 27.
[7] Windsor Chs. xi G 14 and 22. [8] Windsor Ch. xi G 12.
[9] Eye Cart., ff. 46ᵛ–7ʳ.
[10] B.M. Harley Ch. 84 F 45; Binham Cart., f. 186ʳ; and St. Neots Cart., f. 112ʳ.
[11] Eye Cart., f. 42ʳ; St. Frideswide's Cart. ii, no. 980; P.R.O. E 135/21/33;
St. Neots Cart., f. 130ᵛ; and Westminster Domesday, f. 576ʳ.
[12] St. Frideswide's Cart. ii, no. 1022, and Exeter Ch. 640.
[13] Northampton, St. Andrew's Cart. (A), f. 120ʳ, and Dunstable Cart., f. 46ᵛ,
cal. Dunstable Cart., no. 405. [14] Welbeck Cart., f. 79ᵛ.
[15] Beaulieu Cart., ff. 134ʳ⁻ᵛ; Thurgarton Cart., no. 1066 (cited Reg. Antiq. Linc.
viii. 113); and see Decretum, C. 3 qu. 7 c. 2; Drogheda, c, pp. 95–6; Tancred, p. 117.
[16] Sibton Cart., ff. 81ᵛ–2ʳ.

agendum quam etiam specialiter et expresse ad componendum et conficiendum . . .' for part of a suit; for the remain-
der he appeared himself.[1] William of Cheriton, Roger Tyrel,
and Walter de Ribof, to name only a few, put in a personal
appearance.[2] Laymen in fact appeared much more often to
argue their own cases than they sent proctors. This is true
both of important laymen such as Walter de Trailly, Geoffrey d'Abitot, and Philip de Kyme,[3] and lesser knights like
Nicholas, knight of Withybrook, Henry Heuse, Roger Curpeil of Hempnall, Ralph of Mells, and Philip of Staunton.[4]
The high proportion of laymen who came in person to plead
stresses the non-professional side of the proctor's duties.

(ii) *Appointment and Powers*

Terms of appointment varied considerably. Several proctors might be appointed simultaneously in any one of three
ways: *simpliciter, in solidum,* or *sub alternatione. Simpliciter*
meant that they all had to act together; *in solidum* implied
that one or more might act without the rest; and *sub alternatione* that two should act in turn. The first two methods
were rare in England, while *sub alternatione* was apparently
favoured.[5] Three of the documents appointing proctors
stipulate *sub alternatione,* including the proctorial constitution from the Alvingham suit of 1245.[6] Other instances
survive. The abbot and convent of Garendon appointed
Prior Richard and Robert Scot, monk, *sub alternatione*; and
in the same affair the master of the order of Sempringham
and the prior and convent of Bullington were represented
by the prior, it seems on behalf of the master, and the convent was represented by two canons, Richard and Luke, who

---

[1] West Dereham Cart., f. 260ᵛ.
[2] Canterbury, Cartae Antiquae, F 8; Bradenstoke Cart., f. 119ᵛ; and Welbeck Cart., f. 89ʳ.
[3] Thorney Cart. ii, f. 299ʳ; Westminster Domesday, f. 292ᵛ; and Bardney Cart., f. 95ᵛ.
[4] Combe Cart., f. 77ʳ; Bradenstoke Cart., f. 120ʳ; Thorney Cart. ii, f. 324ʳ; Blythburgh Cart., ff. 44ᵛ–5ʳ; and 'Breedon Cart.', no. 144.
[5] It was a common precaution to appoint more than one attorney in the royal courts, see Flower, *Introduction*, p. 401.
[6] Alvingham Cart., f. 5ʳ; B.M. Add. Ch. 28407 (App. B (iv), nos. 13 and 15); and *Sele Cart.*, no. 69.

were appointed to act in turn.[1] Theobald, vicar of Denham
(Suff.), and the prior and convent of Eye appointed two
proctors, Master Gilbert de Jakel and Master John de
Melles, to represent them in 1213–14. One proctor dealt
with the pleading and the other appeared at the settlement.[2]

A proctor could be constituted 'vel coram vel per nuntium,
vel per epistulam'.[3] The plaintiff or defendant might present
his proctor to the judge in court before the commencement
of any procedural act. Powers given to his proctor were
recited and noted. It is impossible to comment on the frequency of verbal mandates, but it is probable that written
testimonies were favoured, and examples survive of written
day constitutions.[4] Proctorial documents grew more precise
in terminology as proctors were more frequently used in
the thirteenth century.[5] Master Arnulphus says 'Quia
multotiens partes in iudicio per procuratores existunt, ideo
videamus, quomodo formantur procuratoria.'[6] A proctorial
document must include information on five points: who has
constituted the proctor, who is constituted, in what case,
against whom, and before whom.[7] The document must then
be sealed with an authentic seal.[8] Any proctor could be
asked to produce his credentials.[9] In one instance in 1245
an exception was made on behalf of the abbot and convent
of Bec, because the proctorial letters of the defendants, the
prior and convent of Dover, lacked a seal.[10] If the judges
were satisfied when they had scrutinized the document and
seal, they either appended their seals to the document, as

---

[1] P.R.O. E 135/6/13.

[2] Eye Cart., ff. 44ᵛ–5ʳ; and cf. *Reg. Greg. IX*, no. 4838: 'Deinde, procurator
[M. Laurence] archidiaconi, qui litem fuerat contestatus, reverso ad propria, Sadoch
procurator est constitutus ad sententiam audiendam.'

[3] *D*. III. 3. 1.

[4] B.M. Harley Ch. 84 F 43 gives an example of what appears to be a written
constitution lasting only one day for W. monk on behalf of Biddlesden, and see
Canterbury, MS. Scrapbook A, p. 86, no. 160 (1193×1205).

[5] Cf. A, f. 271ᵛ, col. ii (early thirteenth century), with *St. Frideswide's Cart.*
i, no. 740 (1346).   [6] Arnulphus, l, p. 52.

[7] Arnulphus, l, p. 53. Cf. Drogheda, cvii, cviii, and cx, pp. 102–5.

[8] Arnulphus, l, p. 54.

[9] See c. 1. X. I. 38 (Greg. I). Cf. Flower, *Introduction*, p. 396, citing *C.R.R.*
vii. 309: 'Robert de Burton, clerk, appeared and said that he was Robert de Percy's
attorney; since this appointment was not found in the rolls he was told to produce
his warrant; if he did not do so his default would be allowed to the other party.'

[10] Windsor Ch. xi G 27 (App. B (ii), no. 3).

when W., clerk of Calverley (Yorks. W.R.), was appointed
to represent Robert, rector of Ilkley (Yorks. W.R.), in
1215,[1] or they reported on the constitution in a document of
their own.[2] The method of approval seems to have been
determined by the intended duration of the document. If the
powers were granted only for one day, the judges simply
added their seals; otherwise, they made a new document.
Such careful examination was necessary because every proctor was bound strictly by the terms of his mandate, and in
the same way the mandatory was held to endorse the acts of
his proctor in so far as he had given him the powers to
perform them.[3]

In direct pursuance of the Roman law practice no mandate was given or accepted without pledges.[4] The plaintiff
gave his proctor authority to act as he had designated and
promised that he would abide by his proxy's actions so long
as they were mentioned in the mandate. From the proctor's
point of view this pledge, *de rato*, signified that he would
carry out the case faithfully and observe his mandate.[5] The
institution documents show clearly that it was a reciprocal
oath. A proctorial letter of the *actor*, according to Drogheda,
should contain the *ratum* clause and add in the final sentence
'iudicatum solvi si necesse fuerit', whereas for the defendant
'si necesse fuerit' is not added.[6] For the defendant and his
proctor the pledge 'de judicato solvendo' meant that the
defendant was bound to acquiesce in the enforcement of the
judgement, and that the proctor would stand firm in defend-
ing him until then.[7] Ricardus Anglicus said that *judicatum
solvi* included three clauses: *de re judicata* to have the judgement carried out, *de re defendenda* to appear at the hearing,

---

[1] Bodleian MS. Dodsworth 76, f. 44.

[2] B.M. Harley Ch. 44 F 24 (App. B (iv), no. 14).

[3] See c. 32. *X*. I. 29 (Inn. III).

[4] '*Institutiones*' (*Corpus Iuris Civilis*, i, ed. P. Krueger, 16th edn. (Berlin, 1954))
iv. 11. See also *C*. II. 56.

[5] Ricardus Anglicus, '*Summa de Ordine Iudiciario*', *Quellen zur Geschichte*, ii,
pt. iii, ed. L. Wahrmund (Innsbruck, 1915), xxi, pp. 26–7; Tancred, p. 119; and
Arnulphus, l, p. 53.

[6] Drogheda, cvii, cviii, and cx, pp. 102–5. For examples of each kind see Pipewell Cart. (C), f. 89ʳ, and Westminster Domesday, f. 379ʳ (App. B (iv), no. 12),
and cf. Windsor Ch. xi G 27 (App. B (ii), no. 3).

[7] Arnulphus, l, p. 53, and Tancred, p. 120.

and *de dolo malo* to act in good faith.[1] He holds: 'Nemo enim alienae litis idoneus defensor sine satisdatione intelligitur.'[2]

Appointments varied in the length of time that was conceded.[3] A proctor could be constituted merely for a day. Two surviving constitutions *ad diem* date from 1210 and 1230, and thus precede the legate Otto's directive in the Council of London of 1237, which was directed against this practice as wasting the time of the courts.[4] It was rarely possible to reach a state of passing sentence in such a short hearing, by which time the proctor's mandate would have expired. William of Drogheda echoes the legate's directions.[5] On the Continent, however, day constitutions appear to have been allowed: at any rate, Curialis provides a model form of a proxy for a day, and Arnulphus and Tancred mention the possibility.[6] There can have been no theoretical objection to constitution for a day, and the *ad diem* form may have been used principally when a party could not appear on a specific day but intended to represent itself for the rest of the suit, or when the business was likely to be short.[7] The latter was perhaps the case with the abbess and convent of Godstow who appointed W. their clerk as proctor for a day to appear before judges conservator, the priors of Blackmore and Tandridge, in 1254.[8]

The appointment might be made to last for a term, after which the powers could either be withdrawn or continued. R., brother of the abbot of Ramsey, and A. of Saltfleetby, chaplain, were appointed proctors by the prior and convent of Hatfield Regis until Michaelmas, in a suit with Benedict, chaplain of Sible Hedingham (Essex), in 1245.[9] The abbot and convent of Pipewell constituted a monk (N.) as their proctor until the next Christmas; his appointment being dated 12 October 1252.[10] Such delegation offered checks

---

[1] Ricardus Anglicus, '*Summa de Ordine Iudiciario*', xx, p. 25.
[2] Ibid. xix, p. 23, citing '*Inst.*' iv. 11. 4, and see *D.* III. 3. 46. 2.
[3] *D.* III. 3. 3 and 4.
[4] Abingdon Cart., f. 144ᵛ; and B.M. Harley Ch. 84 F 43; and see above, p. 222.
[5] Drogheda, cxxxviii, p. 168.
[6] Curialis, '*Ordo*', lxxiii and lxxiv, p. 24; Arnulphus, l, p. 52; and Tancred,
p. 115.   [7] See *D.* III. 3. 71.
[8] Westminster Domesday, f. 379ʳ (App. B (iv), no. 12).
[9] B.M. Add. Ch. 28407 (App. B (iv), no. 13).
[10] Pipewell Cart. (C) f. 89ʳ.

to both proctor and constituent.[1] Alien monastic houses, however, usually constituted proctors for an indefinite period of time, often until the proctor died or returned his mandate.[2] In 1251 the abbot and convent of St. Sever (dioc. Coutances) appointed Nicholas, monk, and Matthew, rector of Haugham (Lincs.), where they had a cell, as their proctors in England with general powers for an apparently unlimited time.[3] In a similar way the prior and convent of Lanthony had a general proctor in Ireland, who administered their properties, protected their interests, and defended their suits.[4] General appointment, however, may not have been common at the beginning of the period. In a case with J., clerk of Brant Broughton (Lincs.), and others, the parson of the neighbouring parish of Leadenham (Lincs.) represented the abbot and convent of Marmoutier, Tours, in 1204,[5] but by 1233 Marmoutier had general proctors in England, their priors Stephen of Holy Trinity, York, and Maurice 'de Malliaco'.[6] It is also demonstrable that proctors were sometimes appointed for specific purposes, to supplement the work of the general proctor. The abbot and convent of St. Germer-de-Flay (dioc. Beauvais) constituted a general proctor, Master John, with powers to appear before all courts in England and to appoint a substitute whenever he wished, in March 1246/7.[7] In the same year they also appointed one of their brethren, Matthew, with specific powers to sell, alienate, or exchange their rents in England.[8]

General powers for the proctor to do exactly what he thought fit in a given cause usually corresponded with a general mandate in time.[9] Such powers were to take oaths of speaking the truth and *de calumpnia*, to make exceptions, produce witnesses, substitute vice-proctors, make compositions, settle on arbiters and compromise before them, appeal, and prosecute such an appeal. The proctor might also grant and

[1] See *D*. III. 3. 8 and 14, and cf. Tancred, p. 120.
[2] Tancred, pp. 115 and 123.
[3] B.M. Harley Ch. 44 F 24 (App. B (iv), no. 14).
[4] Lanthony Cart. A2, ff. 264ʳ⁻ᵛ, and 266ʳ⁻ᵛ.
[5] B.M. Add. Ch. 11216. Brant Broughton is about 2½ miles west of Leadenham.
[6] *Rotuli Hugonis de Welles*, ii. 95–6. I have not been able to identify Malliaco.
[7] Lambeth Palace Library, Cartae Miscellaneae, II/53.
[8] Ibid. II/54.
[9] General powers could be granted for one case only, see Arnulphus, l, p. 53.

sue for expenses, seek restitution *in integrum*, confess, and promise observance of a settlement.[1] The extent of a proctor's authority varied from this general power to a more limited authority. If a proctor was constituted for one day to transact one or several small pieces of business, or if he was appointed for one specific cause, he was called a special proctor and had restricted powers granted by the party for waging that particular suit. For instance, the proctors of the abbot and convent of Ramsey and Master Robert de Ywardeby[2] were granted powers specially to compromise and submit to the jurisdiction of a certain judge or to an ordination.[3] It was quite common for proctors to be constituted 'ad componendum', 'ad agendum et componendum', and 'ad defendendum et componendum'.[4] When a certain Geoffrey, whose mandate did not include the power to make a composition, decided to accept this form of settlement, he agreed to seek ratification of his action from the dean and chapter of Lincoln.[5]

Empowering one's proctor to take oaths generally, 'ad praestandum quodlibet genus sacramenti in animam meam',[6] did not include the oaths of speaking the truth, *de veritate dicenda*, and avoiding vexatious actions, *de calumpnia*,[7] but it did enable him to take any other oath about the conduct of the cause and to promise that the settlement would be kept.[8] None of the canonists seems to have objected to proctors taking the oath to speak the truth, although general opinion seems to have considered it desirable for the parties to take it themselves. There is no indication that the parties actually did so. In fact documents of proctorial institution would

[1] See, e.g., B.M. Harley Ch. 44 F 24; and Beaulieu Cart., ff. 132ᵛ-3ʳ (App. B (iv), nos. 14 and 16).

[2] Professor Major suggests that this is Ewerby in Lincolnshire.

[3] Ramsey Cart., f. 41ᵛ, and see Canons Ashby Cart., f. 50ʳ⁻ᵛ (App. B (iv), no. 4). Cf. *D*. III. 3. 60: a general mandate does not include the right to compromise.

[4] B.M. Stowe Ch. 58; Windsor Ch. xi G 12; *Reg. Antiq. Linc.* iii, no. 759; and see also *N.L.C.*, nos. 62, 80, and 86.

[5] *Reg. Antiq. Linc.* ii, no. 386.

[6] e.g. B.M. Add. Ch. 34033.

[7] See, e.g., Chatteris Cart., ff. 142ʳ-3ᵛ; B.M. Harley Ch. 44 F 24, and Alvingham Cart., f. 5ʳ (App. B (iv), nos. 14 and 15).

[8] e.g. William, on behalf of St. Augustine's, Canterbury (1214–16), *Chichester Cart.*, no. 278, and William of Wantage, who promised to observe a composition on behalf of Bec, Glynde Ch. 3370, cal. Dell, *Glynde Place Archives.*

suggest the contrary. The oath concerning calumny was more vigorously disputed. Usually it was taken by the plaintiff and defendant in person, and not by their proctors;[1] but Innocent III in a decretal letter to the bishop of Piacenza declared that a proctor could take it.[2] Master Arnulphus mentions it as an example of a power which must be expressed in the mandate.[3] *Scientiam* insists that the principal persons ought to take it themselves, but he casts some doubt on the matter when speaking about those who plead in another's name. At any rate he holds that a special mandate is needed and that the proctor ought not to be compelled to swear it.[4] Innocent IV in the Council of Lyons decreed that parties could be compelled to appear personally to take both oaths.[5]

It is possible to catch a glimpse of the proctors at work. Some were contumacious, such as the proctor of the archbishop of Canterbury at Rome in 1241—the archbishop had died, which probably accounts for this—and Wimund of Deverill, proctor of the bishop and chapter of Le Mans, who against his oath did not come to judgement.[6] In an unusual curial case of 1250, the judge and one proctor waited in vain at the papal court for the other proctor to appear. Finally, after some warning, the case seems to have gone by default.[7] Contumacy in appearance, however, was rare among proctors.

Exceptions and appeals which were made by the proctors illustrate the growing complexity of pleading.[8] The most famous proctorial appeal of the period was that made on

---

[1] *Papal Decretals relating to Lincoln*, p. xxiii, and Ricardus Anglicus, '*Summa de Ordine Iudiciario*', xviii, p. 22.

[2] c. 6. X. II. 7: '. . . fecimus calumniae iuramentum ab ipsis procuratoribus utrinque praestari'.

[3] Arnulphus, li, p. 54.

[4] '*Scientiam*', *Quellen zur Geschichte*, ii, pt. i, ed. L. Wahrmund (Innsbruck, 1913), xxi, pp. 40–1: 'Utrum procurator iurare possit de calumpnia.' This treatise was finished between 1235 and 1240 (Stickler, col. 1137).

[5] c. 1. 6. II. 1.

[6] *Reg. Greg. IX*, no. 5387; and *Reg. S. Osmund*, i. 355 (c. 1199).

[7] Bodleian, Northants. Ch. 181, mentioned in *Cart. of the Mediaeval Archives of Christ Church*, cal. Denholm-Young, p. 50. On contumacy see Drogheda, cv, p. 100.

[8] See Reg. Vat. 19, f. 105ʳ⁻ᵛ (*Reg. Greg. IX*, no. 4838); Dunstable Cart., f. 67ᵛ, cal. *Dunstable Cart.*, no. 767; Eye Cart., ff. 36ᵛ–7ᵛ; and especially B.M. Harley Ch. 84 F 45.

behalf of Master Laurence of St. Martin, rector of Abbots
Ann (Hants), who was studying at Bologna. It formed the
subject of an important decretal letter, in which it was
established that a general proctor was to be allowed to
consult his master how to act, if he was absent, and that the
proctor might justifiably appeal if this was not allowed.[1]
Another instance of appeal is that made by the proctor of
the archbishop of Canterbury in a long case against Hugh
d'Aubigny, earl of Arundel, which was heard by three, and
possibly four, sets of judges delegate. The abbot of St.
Augustine's and the archdeacons of Wiltshire and Berkshire
were ordered by the pope to proceed in the cause if the
allegations of the proctor were true, otherwise the dispute
was to be returned to the former judges, presumably con-
demning the appellant to pay costs as was usual.[2]

Recognitions of the other party's right and the ground on
which he lodged his libel were not rare, and such recognitions might be made by the proctors. For instance, R. de
Dingel, proctor of T., rector of Brampton (Northants.), defendant in a case with the prior and convent of St. Neots in
1232, confessed that the rector ought to pay a pension of
100 shillings from his church;[3] and the proctor of Bruern in
1217 confessed that certain tithes in question belonged to
the convent of St. Frideswide at Oxford.[4] A similar confession was made by Robert of Bury St. Edmunds, clerk, proctor of two chaplains of Dover, who said that the charges of
the prior and convent of St. Martin about the payment of
yearly pensions from these chapels were true.[5] Similarly
Roger de Stanford, canon of Owston (Aug. Leics.), made a
confession on behalf of his convent in 1236/7.[6] Where the
continuance of a case seemed hopeless to the proctor, it was
his duty to inform his employer, so that if he mistrusted the

---

[1] *Reg. Greg. IX*, no. 630, and c. 11. *X*. I. 38. Cf. Flower, *Introduction*, p. 403:
'The attorney sometimes claimed the right to remain in touch with his client during
the process of an action and to consult him if necessary. The prior of Lenton's
attorney, being asked if he dared put himself on a jury, said that he knew not until
he could have counsel of his master'; citing *C.R.R.* v. 142.

[2] *Reg. Greg. IX*, no. 5182; and see c. 64. *X*. II. 28 (Hon. III).

[3] St. Neots Cart., f. 112r.

[4] *St. Frideswide's Cart.* ii, no. 1048, and for another example see no. 980.

[5] Dover Cart., f. 51r.

[6] Bodleian MS. Dodsworth 76, f. 1.

proctor's advice he might appear to defend himself. The practice of legal confession had its roots in Roman law procedure.[1]

Strangely contrary to the Roman law, which defined the position of the proctors in the Church courts, was the canon law. This law, which the proctors were helping to make, formed a growing antithesis, especially in legal theory, to the Roman *ratio scripta*. The greatest difference was that the canon law was expanding and developing, while the Roman law of the emperors lay long since dead. As the outline of a procedural machine the Roman law still had a part to play, but as a living law that could control human activities it had given way to a greater force. The institution of proctors illustrates how the Roman law, even if in a procedural aspect only, made itself felt far beyond the limits of its natural operation.

Such an investigation of the business of the courts, and of the litigants who came before them, incomplete as it must be, has suggested something of the volume of work with which the delegated courts dealt, and has shown the limitations that the royal court gradually endeavoured to impose on the growing jurisdiction of Rome. The special relationship between the monasteries and the papacy accounts for many of the suits that came before the papal delegated courts and that fill the main categories of business. Undoubtedly the late twelfth and early thirteenth centuries witnessed the high-water mark of Roman jurisdiction in England. The king claimed the right to decide when the jurisdiction was in question, but the exercise of this power of definition depended on one of the parties approaching his court for a decision as to competence, whereas the Church established the right to judge certain cases, and during this period the gains of canon law outnumbered its losses. By the middle of the thirteenth century, however, greater attempts were made to curtail its influence by increasing definition, as the secular authority reclaimed what it considered had been usurped by courts Christian.

[1] *C.* VII. 59: 'De confessis.'

V

THE EFFECTIVENESS OF
THE SYSTEM

1. *The Settlement or Sentence*

IN spite of the introduction of a sophisticated judicial
system and a refined procedure, some primitive facets
remained. Van Caenegem has said that 'The precedence
of compromise over judicial decision is a widespread charac-
teristic of primitive justice' and has compared the English
secular tribunal of the early twelfth century with the African
'palaver'.[1] This desire for compromise settlements is also
apparent in papally delegated courts, and was doubtless due
to the fact that execution was difficult.

It is noticeable that the majority of suits were ended by
compositions.[2] Here both the parties, on the whole, would
want to keep to their terms, and it was the policy of many
judges to prevail upon the parties to make compositions.
Richard, prior of Dunstable, and W., the subprior (a subdelegate of the archdeacon of Bedford), who had been
ordered by Gregory IX either to confirm or to declare null
the sentence of the subdelegates of the priors of St. Oswald's
and St. Bartholomew's, Gloucester, exhorted the parties at
the re-hearing to make a composition: 'cum perventum
esset ad sentenciam diffinitivam rogavimus diligenter partes
ut si fieri posset inter se componerent, et ipse ad nostram
instanciam in hunc modum composuerunt.'[3] This suggests
that compositions were regarded as more successful and
lasting arrangements than sentences.

---

[1] Van Caenegem, *Royal Writs in England*, p. 42.

[2] C. Morris, analysing cases which came before the consistory court of Lincoln
in 1430–1, says that out of ninety cases probably between one third and two thirds
were settled by compositions and only nine by sentences ('A Consistory Court
in the Middle Ages', *Journal of Ecclesiastical History*, xiv (1963), 158).

[3] Lanthony Cart. A 1, X, no. cviii: and cf. P.R.O. E 315/50, no. 48, where
the judges reported in Jan. 1246/7 'partes induximus ad concordiam'.

In compositions a leading role was assumed by the parties. Often it appears to be the parties who make the composition and the judges who confirm it. The judges reported in a case of 1249: 'Ne ergo ea que semel concordia mediante sopita sunt in iteratam redeant contentionem, nos hanc compositionem . . . confirmavimus.'[1] In 1230 the judges, reporting the composition made between the prior and convent of Christ Church, Canterbury, and William of Cheriton, knight, say that they confirm it.[2] When Simon, vicar of Hungerford (Berks.), made a composition with the prior of St. Frideswide's in c. 1190 in the presence of the abbot of Abingdon and others, he asked the judges delegate, the abbots of Reading and Thame and the archdeacon of Berkshire, to confirm it;[3] and a composition between the archdeacon of Lincoln and the convent of Bardney was confirmed by the judges delegate and also by the bishop and chapter of Lincoln.[4]

Such arrangements did not preclude renunciation of rights of impetration, appeal, and other benefits of law;[5] and the same paraphernalia of penalties and oaths is found as with sentences.[6] Subjection to the jurisdiction of ecclesiastics (local ones or the judges) for the observance of these compositions was not unusual.[7] When a composition was arranged between Dover priory and Langdon abbey, the judges induced the parties to observe what they had promised in a settlement already made about the church of Coldred (Kent), and they retained powers to coerce the parties to observe it.[8]

The prevalence of the compromise is illustrated by the number of proctorial constitutions which granted powers to compose as well as to litigate.[9] The power to make a composition was specifically included in the proxy given to Thomas de Pridias, knight, by his wife.[10] The popularity of

---

[1] Eye Cart., f. 42ʳ.   [2] Canterbury, Cartae Antiquae, F 8.
[3] *St. Frideswide's Cart.* ii, no. 1133.   [4] Bardney Cart., f. 30ᵛ.
[5] e.g. *Colchester Cart.* ii. 545; Windsor Ch. xi G 12; and Christchurch Cart., f. 92ʳ.
[6] e.g. Crowland Cart., f. 189; Lanthony Cart. A 1, IIII, no. cvii; and Windsor, Arundel White Book, p. 174.
[7] e.g. Lanthony Cart. A 1, IIII, no. cvii; and *Chertsey Cart.*, no. 92.
[8] Langdon Cart., ff. 102ʳ–3ʳ.
[9] e.g. Lanthony Cart. A 1, VIII, no. lxxxii; *N.L.C.*, nos. 62 and 86; and Windsor Ch. xi G 12.   [10] Beaulieu Cart., f. 134ʳ.

the compromise is also shown by the concessions which parties were prepared to make in order to arrive at a settlement.[1] Nor is it surprising that compositions were popular with the judges delegate and the administrators of the system. Suits could drag on and on and become wearisome for the judges, and final judgements could be deferred and deferred, as in the case of the abbess of Barking,[2] and of William who appealed to Rome for the third time 'without alleging any hardship and illegally, as it seemed to us', as Theobald wrote.[3] Even when the final sentence had been given there was always the possibility of another appeal and a reopening of the suit. This led Alexander III to declare in the Third Lateran Council 'lis sopita non debet resuscitari'.[4] In this context, and in a society where execution and enforcement were always precarious, it can be seen that the form of settlement by composition had much to offer.

Arbitrations and ordinations had similar attractions. After a suit before judges delegate in 1250, it was stated at the settlement that if there was a further disagreement between the parties, the matter should be decided by elected arbiters.[5] Possibly no differentiation can be made between arbiters and ordainers; the term is used loosely.[6] It does, however, appear that ordinations were usually before officers of the diocese, the bishops, archdeacons and officials of the localities where the parties lived.[7] It appears, too, that parties had to submit voluntarily to ordinations, which they promised to abide by, and to give up their rights of impetrating and appealing before such an arrangement would be undertaken.[8] The proctors in a suit between the abbot and convent of Ramsey and Master Robert de Ywardeby, who submitted to the ordination of Hugh of Northwold, bishop of Ely, are reported as doing such: 'ordinationi et jurisdictioni nostre se absolute et simpliciter summiserunt, renunciantes

---

[1] Bradenstoke Cart., f. 30ʳ; and Thorney Cart. ii, f. 384ʳ.

[2] J.S.L., no. 132.

[3] J.S.L., no. 84. See also no. 64, where Theobald wrote to the pope 'in order to escape from our hands he appealed to your court'.

[4] Sacrorum Conciliorum Collectio, xxii, ed. Mansi, pars. xxxvi, 3, cols. 264–393.

[5] Beaulieu Cart., f. 135ᵛ.   [6] See above, pp. 104–8.

[7] See, e.g., Magdalen College, Oxford, Selborne Ch. 326 (Macray, Calendar, i. 20).

[8] Bushmead Cart., no. 14; and Wells Ch. 31.

omnibus literis super premissis querelis hinc inde a sede
apostolica impetratis.'[1] Parties also subjected themselves to
accept ordinations under penalties, and they might submit
to the same ecclesiastics for compulsion to keep the arrangement, if necessary, allowing excommunication or seizure of
goods if the terms were not honoured.[2]

When the parties compromised on arbiters, they usually
pledged themselves to accept the settlement on pain of the
payment of a certain sum. Probably all arbitrations were
made under penalties. Surviving forms of compromise stipulate these sums,[3] which were usually high, ranging from
twenty shillings to one hundred marks.[4] No evidence survives of such a payment being made. Settlements were often
compositions, but provisions were made in case arbitrations
were broken, a fine of one mark being stipulated in one
instance.[5] Judges delegate confirmed arbitrations and reported them in documentary form.[6] The judges delegated
by Innocent III—Robert, abbot of Walden, William, prior
of Barnwell, and Master Robert, rector of Haddenham—
confirmed the compromise made between the prioress and
convent of Ickleton and the abbot and canons of West
Dereham, by the arbiters Eustace, bishop of Ely, and
Master Elias of Dereham.[7] In one instance, future jurisdiction was given to the bishop of Norwich if the composition which had been made by the arbiters, S(imon of
Elmham), prior of Norwich, Master Walter of Suffield,
and Thomas of Fakenham, was broken.[8] An arbitration in
another case, for which a form survives, appears to have been
disregarded. This arbitration was to have taken place on
1 November 1218, and if it did, then the suit must have
been reopened before judges delegate of Honorius III and
then again in 1249.[9]

[1] Ramsey Cart., f. 41ᵛ.
[2] *Bushmead Cart.*, no. 14 (10 marks); and Bradenstoke Cart., f. 155ᵛ (£20).
[3] Canons Ashby Cart., f. 111ʳ (10 marks); West Dereham Cart., f. 111ᵛ (100s.);
and B.M. Add. Ch. 28408 (£20).
[4] Dover Cart., f. 229ᵛ, and Glynde Ch. 3370.
[5] Pipewell Cart. (C), f. 147ʳ.
[6] St. Albans Cart. (B), f. 187ʳ; P.R.O. E 40/14198; and Thorney Cart. ii,
f. 257ᵛ.   [7] West Dereham Cart., f. 294ᵛ, and see ff. 293ᵛ–4ʳ.
[8] Eye Cart., ff. 45ᵛ–6ʳ, and cf. B.M. Add. Ch. 28408.
[9] Canons Ashby Cart., ff. 110ᵛ, 111ʳ⁻ᵛ, and P.R.O. E 135/21/33.

2. Safeguards for the Observance of the Settlement

(i) Documentary Evidence

Once an agreement had been arranged or a sentence declared in a judge-delegate case, the aim of the court was to see that it was enforced or observed and that the quarrel did not break out again. If it did break out again, it was important that documentary evidence could be found showing what the judges had decreed, that the recalcitrant party should be penalized, and that reappeal to Rome should be prevented if possible. All settlements before judges delegate were finally recorded in documentary form by the courts. These instruments were sealed by the judges and the parties. Usually three such documents were made, and they were frequently copied into cartularies. Sometimes the charters were sealed *alternatim*, that is to say each party put his seal on the other party's document,[1] and the judges too might append their seals and retain for themselves a copy sealed with the parties' seals.[2] But the making of records did not depend solely on the orders of the judges or the courts. The parties might make charters of their own, which they exchanged between themselves, and one party usually made a charter if it renounced its claims or defence. In July 1238 Master John, rector of Sibertswold (Kent), composed a document confirming the settlement between him and the prior and convent of St. Martin, Dover, which had taken place before the archdeacon, treasurer, and Master John, canon of Chichester.[3] Similarly Alexander, parson of Kerdiston (Norf.), caused a charter to be made in which he said, 'I declare publicly that I will never claim any right in the said tithes on behalf of my church.'[4] The charter of confession survives as a distinct form of document.[5] Probably it was an added safeguard. A report of the confession of Robert, rector of Maids Moreton (Bucks.), constituted a separate document, to which were appended the seals of the

---

[1] P.R.O. E 40/12969; and Stixwould Cart., ff. 46ʳ, 56ᵛ.

[2] Peterborough, MS. 5, f. 168ʳ⁻ᵛ; and Pipewell Cart. (A), f. 11ᵛ.

[3] Dover Cart., f. 176ʳ. 'Dupplicatur' is noted at the bottom of this document in the cartulary.

[4] Lewes Cart., f. 255ᵛ, cal. *Lewes Cart. N.P.*, no. 122. Cf. Walden Cart., f. 48ᵛ.

[5] Pipewell Cart. (A), f. 31ᵛ.

archdeacon and dean of Buckingham and of Robert himself.[1] A charter of Richard Marescallus, stating that he was bound to pay two marks yearly to Thorney for the church of Tydd, was made and sealed in the full chapter of Thorney.[2]

The Bendish (Herts.) case illustrates the number of documents which might be made at the settlement. Roger, bishop of London, confirmed the settlement on 31 December 1234.[3] Martin Camerarius, patron of Radwinter church (Essex), confirmed it and promised to abide by it;[4] and Baldwin of Bassingbourn, rector of Radwinter, made a charter, acknowledging the right of the prior and convent of Holy Trinity, Aldgate, to some of the tithes at Bendish, in which he quoted the settlement.[5] In an important suit between the abbot and convent of Malmesbury and the bishop and chapter of Salisbury in 1218–22, charters of both parties record that copies of the documents in the suit between them were deposited at Waverley abbey (Cist. Surr.).[6] A charter of Adam, abbot of Waverley, who had been one of the judges, records the receipt of these documents.[7] The deposit of copies of the legal *acta* of the court with one of the judges delegate must have been a usual arrangement, which was only by chance mentioned in the final *actum*. In the Great Paxton suit of 1252–3, which had come before a papal auditor, it was decided that the attestations and instruments of the case should remain with the judges delegate, the prior, archdeacon, and precentor of St. Albans.[8]

To stop the reopening of suits, deeds were often surrendered by one party, either to the other party or to the judges, at the time of the settlement. The papal rescript was resigned by the prior and canons of Rudham (Norf.), when they renounced all right that they had claimed to have in the

[1] *N.L.C.*, no. 40. It is not known who the judges delegate were in this suit, but that it was papally delegated is certain. The document is dated 14 Aug. 1251 in the chapter celebrated in the church of Maids Moreton.

[2] Thorney Cart. ii, f. 258ʳ.   [3] P.R.O. E 40/13828(d).
[4] P.R.O. E 40/13828(e).   [5] P.R.O. E 40/14301.
[6] *Malmesbury Reg.* i. 404.   [7] Ibid. 406.
[8] *Reg. Antiq. Linc.* ii, no. 386. Cf. P.R.O. E 40/14036, where the attestations of the witnesses, sealed by the examiners, were deposited in the priory of Stoke by Clare in case a further suit should be brought.

chapel and hermitage of Wiggenhall (Norf.).[1] When R., parson of Loughton (Bucks.), renounced his suit against the prior and monks of Newton Longville (Bucks.) and recognized the right of the monks to the tithes of the lordship, he resigned the papal letters into the hands of the judges —B(enedict), abbot of Stratford Langthorne, R(ichard of Ely), archdeacon of Colchester, and Master R., rector of St. Antoninus, London—who cancelled them.[2] On the settlement of their suit, the prioress of Farewell (Staffs.), the impetrant, gave the papal mandate which she had obtained to the prioress of Langley (Leics.).[3]

Instruments and deeds about lands or tithes that had been surrendered were also given to the judges. A. and S. de Skerlinges, sons of A., widow, renounced their claims to certain tithes and gave their deeds to the judges delegate, the abbots of Walden and Tilty. They promised to pay damages to the abbot and convent of Waltham, but these were remitted.[4] Thomas de Chelewrden resigned all right to some lands, pastures, and meadows, and surrendered the instruments which dealt with this to the proctor of the abbot and convent of Malmesbury, the plaintiffs.[5] Master Richard (de Marisco), archdeacon of York, and G., dean of Lynn, resigned certain tithes in Dereham (Norf.) to the abbot and convent and reported: 'Instrumenta etiam per que dictas possessiones et terras vendicavimus, cum literis pariter domini pape, in manu domini abbatis absolute renunciavimus.'[6] When William de Thornaco, dean of Lincoln, and the prior and convent of Tutbury reciprocally renounced suits in 1230, it was recorded in the judges' *actum*:

Prior insuper Tuttesbir' ad maius robur istius composicionis restituit decano scriptum apostolicum et acta quibus eundem coram iudicibus Stafford' convenerat similiter, et decanus restituit eidem priori

---

[1] Castle Acre Cart., f. 125ᵛ: date 1175×1200. Cf. Exeter Ch. 813.
[2] *N.L.C.*, no. 46.
[3] P.R.O. E 135/2/28. Cf. Peterborough, MS. 5, f. 135ʳ⁻ᵛ; *Malmesbury Reg.* ii 7; and *C.R.R.* xiv. 1336, where in 1231, when the subject of a case was admitted to be about advowson, the papal letters which had been obtained were surrendered to the justiciars.
[4] Waltham Cart., f. 149ʳ.
[5] *Malmesbury Reg.* ii. 7.
[6] West Dereham Cart., f. 17ʳ. For Master Richard de Marisco, see *York Minster Fasti*, i, ed. C. T. Clay (Yorks. Archaeol. Soc. Rec. Ser. cxxii, 1957), 46.

scriptum apostolicum et acta quibus eum et conventum suum coram
iudicibus Suwell' convenerat.[1]

Documents were frequently exchanged and deposited for
safe keeping. After a dispute between the abbot and convent
of St. Valéry and James, rector of Compton, which was
settled by the prior of Hatfield Regis, a chirograph was
made. The half which was sealed by the rector and the
judge was to be given to the prior of Takeley, the other half
with the seals of Takeley and the judge was to be kept by the
rector.[2] Similarly two documents were made, one to remain
at Christchurch and one at Breamore, by the prior of Poughley and the dean of Newbury, who had been ordered to hear
a suit between the prior and convent of Christchurch and
the prior and convent of Breamore on 27 February 1235.[3]
In a suit between William, abbot, and the monks of Bordesley and Walter, prior, and the canons of Kenilworth it was
reported that a chirograph was made. The monks sealed the
canons' half and the canons appended their seal to the monks'
part. The part of the chirograph which was to remain with
the canons was handed over to them in the chapter of
Bordesley, and a similar ceremony took place at Kenilworth.[4]
After settlement of a suit between the prior and convent of
Christchurch and the rector of Yarmouth (Isle of Wight),
which was heard by the prior of Milton and the dean of
Whitchurch (both Dors.), judges delegate of Honorius III,
one instrument was deposited at the abbey of Milton with the
judges and the other was placed with the canons of Christchurch.[5] It was recorded some time after 1228 in the final
actum of the abbot of Combe and the priors of Coventry
and Kenilworth that a tripartite chirograph had been made,
the chief part of which was to remain with the judges, who,
with the consent of the parties, were to compel them to keep
the composition.[6] A similar arrangement was made in a
1224 case. The parties, Stephen, rector of Brightwalton
(Berks.), and the abbot and convent of Battle (Suss.), were
each given an instrument, and the third was to be placed in
the treasury at Salisbury. The judges delegate had been the

---

[1] *Reg. Antiq. Linc.* iii, no. 759.   [2] New College, Oxford, Takeley Ch. 271.
[3] Christchurch Cart., f. 58[r].   [4] Kenilworth Cart., f. 78[r].
[5] Christchurch Cart., f. 91[v].   [6] Pipewell Cart. (A), f. 123[r].

dean, precentor, and chancellor of Salisbury.[1] When Eustace de Fauconberg, bishop of London, made an ordination in 1223/4, it was drawn up in the form of a tripartite chirograph. The parties, the prior and convent of St. Botolph, Colchester, and the prior and convent of Holy Trinity, Aldgate, had one each, and the third copy was to remain in the treasury at St. Paul's, London. It is written on the back of the St. Paul's document that it was to be kept there *in perpetuum*.[2] Three documents were made at the command of the judges, the priors of Monkton Farleigh and Bradenstoke (both Wilts.) and Master Richard de Sorestan, canon of Wimborne (Dors.): one was to be placed with each of the parties—at Iwerne Minster church (Dors.) and at Christchurch—and one was to be deposited in the treasury at Salisbury.[3] When a tripartite chirograph was made in a suit between the abbot and convent of Thame and Roger, rector of Oddington (Oxon.), one part was given to the abbot and convent, one part to the rector, and the other was placed amongst the archives of Holy Trinity priory, Aldgate. The judges had been the archdeacons of Colchester and Middlesex and the dean of Arches.[4]

The officers of the diocese were constantly being used by the judges delegate. They were also used to make confirmations, but probably at the instance of the parties. When a composition was made between the abbot and convent of Chertsey and Adam, rector of Cobham, in 1218, the bishop was to be asked to confirm it.[5] On 11 September 1241 while at Buckden (Hunts.), Robert Grosseteste confirmed a settlement which had been made between John, rector of Churchill (Oxon.), and the abbot and convent of Bruern (Cist. Oxon.) about tithes at Churchill,[6] and in 1242 × 1243, also at Buckden, he reported and confirmed the settlement of the treasurer and precentor of Chichester in a suit about the tithes

---

[1] P.R.O. E 327/51, and Salisbury D. and C. Muniments, 1st Press (H.M.C., *Var. Coll.* i. 340), pd. *Sarum Chs.* cxlv, but not from the original.

[2] St. Paul's, Press A, Box 23, Ch. 864 (App. B (iv), no. 2), and cf. *Early Charters of St. Paul's*, pp. 110–13, a similar arrangement.

[3] Christchurch Cart., f. 121ᵛ.

[4] *Thame Cart.*, no. 37.   [5] *Chertsey Cart.*, no. 91.

[6] *St. Frideswide's Cart.* ii, no. 1054 (and see no. 1053). Other letters of *inspeximus* and confirmations of Grosseteste of cases in which papal delegates were concerned are *Reg. Antiq. Linc.* ii, no. 356, and iii, no. 674; and Bodleian, Northants. Ch. 181.

of Offley (Herts.) between Master John, the rector, and the nuns of Elstow (Ben. Beds.).[1] An *inspeximus* of a settlement between the abbot and convent of Abingdon and Philip, rector of East Hendred (Berks.), which took place before the prior of Ivychurch, the succentor of Salisbury, and the dean of Wilton in 1231, was made by Robert, bishop of Salisbury, on 27 May 1231 at Ramsbury;[2] and Archbishop Edmund of Abingdon, acting as diocesan, issued letters of *inspeximus* for suits which had been heard before judges delegate in his diocese in 1227, 1238, and 1240.[3]

Confirmations were made sometimes by the bishop acting in concert with his dean and chapter. A case about the tithes of Barley (Herts.) between Herbert, the rector, and the nuns of Chatteris (Cambs.), which was heard by papal judges including the archdeacon of London, was confirmed by the bishop of London, G(eoffrey) de Lucy, dean, and the chapter of St. Paul's.[4] In July 1246 Robert (de Bingham), bishop of Salisbury, R(obert de Hertford) dean, and the chapter made an *inspeximus* and confirmation, as they said *auctoritate ordinaria*, of a settlement made by Master Henry Tessun, archdeacon of Bath, as judge delegate, and his subdelegates. The suit had been between John, rector of Sunningwell (Berks.), and the prioress and convent of Littlemore (Oxon.). It concerned the tithes of Bayworth, Sunningwell, and Chilswell.[5] A suit between the rector of Christian Malford (Wilts.) and the prior and convent of Bradenstoke (Aug. Wilts.) was inspected by Bishop William, the prior and convent of Bath, and the dean and chapter of Wells.[6] Deans and chapters might be approached directly for confirmations, and often they inspected the *inspeximus* of their bishops. On 8 February 1239/40 R(obert de Hertford) dean, and the chapter of Salisbury inspected an ordination made by their bishop on the previous day,[7] and the dean and chapter of Chichester made a confirmation of the *inspeximus* of Richard

[1] Bradenstoke Cart., f. 156ʳ.

[2] Abingdon Cart., ff. 53ʳ–4ʳ. For another example of an *inspeximus* by the same bishop of a judge-delegate arrangement, see Reading Cart., f. 115ᵛ, and f. 114ʳ.

[3] *St. Gregory's Cart.*, nos. 192, 219–20; and Dover Cart., f. 176ᵛ.

[4] Chatteris Cart., ff. 142ʳ–4ʳ.   [5] Bodleian MS. Chs. Oxon. a 8, Ch. 29b.

[6] Wells, Lib. Albus ii, f. 354ʳ, and Bradenstoke Cart., f. 65ʳ.

[7] B.M. Add. Ch. 19620 (App. B (v), no. 1); and see Reading Cart., f. 112ʳ⁻ᵛ.

II, bishop of Chichester, of a settlement before judges delegate.[1] Likewise Master Robert (de Arches), official of Eustace, bishop of London, made an *inspeximus* of an episcopal confirmation in 1226×1227.[2] On 23 October 1226 at the Strand, Bishop Eustace had confirmed the settlement made by Benedict of Sawston, bishop of Rochester, the archdeacon of Rochester, and the dean of Dartford, judges delegate of Honorius III in 1225–6, in a suit between the rector of Great Dunmow (Essex) and the prior and convent of Newton Longville about tithes in the parish of Great Dunmow.[3] Master Ranulf de Wareham, official of the bishop of Norwich, was approached directly to inspect a settlement which had been made by R(alph) and A(dam), abbots of St. Osyth's, and St. John's, Colchester, judges delegate of Innocent III, in a case between Geoffrey, archdeacon of Suffolk, and Roger, parson of Hardley (Norf.). The witnesses included Hubert, dean of Brooke, and R., dean of Yarmouth.[4]

Archdeacons might be asked to confirm judge-delegate settlements. In 1239 Hugh, archdeacon of Winchester, confirmed a settlement made by the prior of Hyde, the archdeacon of Surrey, and the dean of Winchester between the rector of Ringwood (Hants) and the prior and convent of Christchurch (Twynham, Hants). This suit concerned the tithes of Burley (Hants).[5] On 12 September 1241 at Exeter, Bartholomew, archdeacon of Exeter, acting on behalf of the bishop, made an *inspeximus* and confirmation of a settlement, reporting: 'Hanc autem transactionem acceptantes eadem imperpetuum valituram auctoritate dicti domini episcopi cujus vice fungimur confirmamus.'[6]

The pope was asked for confirmations by parties who feared the reopening of suits, but on the whole a confirmation by a near-by prelate was preferable, and was more quickly and less expensively obtained.[7] On 8 August 1224

---

[1] Magdalen College, Oxford, Buddington Chs., nos. 8 (cal. *Sele Cart.*, no. 30), 2, and 22.   [2] New College, Oxford, Lib. Niger, ff. 16ʳ, 67ʳ.

[3] *N.L.C.*, no. 81; see also no. 80. Cf. Reading Cart., f. 117ᵛ.

[4] H.M.C., *Var. Coll.* vii (1914), 80 (Duke of Norfolk's Muniments, Hardley Ch. 112), and see above, pp. 158–9.

[5] Christchurch Cart., f. 62ᵛ.   [6] Exeter Cart., p. 56.

[7] See, e.g., B.M. Add. Ch. 20373, and Cheney, 'Harrold Priory', no. 7.

Honorius III confirmed a composition between the prior and convent of Bradenstoke (Aug. Wilts.) and the rector of Steeple Aston (Oxon.);[1] and on 12 February 1200 Innocent III confirmed a sentence of the abbots of Barlings and Tupholme about certain tithes, after a dispute between Bardney (Ben. Lincs.) and Richard of Bassingham, parson of Burton by Lincoln.[2] Sentences might be confirmed by delegates who were specially appointed for the purpose. The prior and convent of Lewes requested Honorius III that he should confirm a sentence in their favour. Acting on a mandate from the pope, which was dated 2 March 1224, the priors of Pentney and Sporle and the dean of Lynn summoned the defendant William de Walda, rector of Lamport and Faxton (Northants.), to show why the sentence should not stand. As the proctor of William put forward no reason against the confirmation of the sentence, on 4 November 1224 the priors confirmed it and composed a document reporting this.[3] Papal commissioners, the abbots of Bordesley and Stanley and the prior of Stanley, confirmed the sentence of Pandulf, who was acting as a judge delegate, in the Oakley (Bucks.) case.[4] They wrote to Hugh, bishop of Lincoln, certifying the confirmation,[5] and sent a separate letter charging him to see that the sentence was observed.[6] Presumably following the advice of his commissioners, Pope Honorius III confirmed Pandulf's sentence on 5 October 1221.[7] The abbot of St. Albans had been asked to forward transcripts of all the proceedings in the matter to him.[8] The king also was commanded to see that the sentence was duly observed.[9]

Papal confirmations of sentences given by auditors were addressed to the successful party and were often followed by papal mandates ordering that the sentence should be observed.[10] On 22 June 1249 the pope sent a confirmation of a sentence to Master Walter, archdeacon of Norfolk, and on the same day he issued a mandate to the bishop and dean of St. Paul's, London, ordering them to see that the sentence

[1] Bradenstoke Cart., f. 31ᵛ, and see ff. 146ᵛ⁻7ʳ.   [2] Bardney Cart., f. 22ᵛ.
[3] P.R.O. E 40/14955.   [4] St. Frideswide's Cart. ii, no. 822.
[5] Ibid., no. 823.   [6] Ibid., no. 824.   [7] Ibid., no. 826.
[8] Ibid., no. 825.   [9] See ibid., no. 827.
[10] e.g. Reg. Greg. IX, nos. 4836-9, 4882-4; and Reg. Inn. IV, nos. 4601, 5194, and 6990.

was enforced.¹ Similarly on 22 April 1252 a copy of a papal sentence was addressed to the archbishop of Canterbury, one of the parties, and a papal mandate was dispatched to the abbot of Boxley ordering him to see that the archbishop was not molested in his rights of visitation and procuration in the churches of St. Bartholomew and Holy Trinity, Aldgate, London.² The value which was attached to a papal confirmation is well illustrated by a case which had been heard by a judge ordinary, Master John de Houton, archdeacon of Northampton, and had been settled by him in 1242/3 in the church of St. James, and in which the prior and convent of St. Andrew, Northampton, the plaintiffs, sought papal confirmation. The abbot of St. James's, Northampton, to whom this was committed, found the sentence just, confirmed it, and pronounced in a document of 1248/9 that it should be observed.³

Settlements could be confirmed by the parties. A charter of Margaret, prioress of Goring (Oxon.), confirmed the settlement made by the abbots of Warden and Woburn, between the nuns of Goring and the priest of Moulsoe (Bucks.) on the one hand, and the prior and convent of Newton Longville (Bucks.) on the other.⁴ W. de Girniges, parson of Careby (Lincs.), and his father, who was patron of the church, confirmed an arrangement about the garb tithes,⁵ and Thomas de Chimeli, rector of St. James's, Garlickhithe, London, in a charter of 1231, confirmed an agreement made between him and the abbot and convent of Westminster.⁶ This sort of document was by no means unusual.

(ii) Oaths, Penalties, and Renunciations

Oaths and penalties were further safeguards for the observance of settlements. Where compositions, agreements, and conventions were made, both parties took oaths to keep the

---

¹ Reg. Inn. IV, nos. 4645–6.
² Reg. Inn. IV, nos. 5670–1.
³ Northampton, St. Andrew's Cart. (A), ff. 204ʳ–5ʳ, and similarly Bushmead Cart., nos. 6 and 14.
⁴ N.L.C., no. 60, and see no. 59.
⁵ Peterborough, MS. 5, ff. 103ᵛ–4ʳ (MS. 1, f. cciiᵛ).
⁶ Westminster Domesday, f. 476ᵛ. For further examples see, e.g., N.L.C., no. 63; Blythburgh Cart., f. 44ᵛ; and Colchester Cart. ii. 547, 550, and 569.

settlement.[1] The dean, precentor, and Master Thomas Foliot, canon of Lichfield, the judges delegate in one case, recorded: 'Hanc autem compositionem firmiter observandam utriusque domus priorissei (*sic*) de assensu conventus sui tactis sacrosanctis juravit. . . .'[2] The abbot and monks of Crowland (Ben. Lincs.) and Conan, knight of Holbeach (Lincs.), and R. and W. clerks of Lincoln diocese, who had made a settlement before the abbot of St. James's and the prior of St. Andrew's, Northampton, and Master H. de Gylevylle, canon of Lincoln, promised to observe the composition: 'Hanc vero compositionem fideliter observandam utraque pars fide media confirmavit.'[3] In 1208 the plaintiffs, the abbot and convent of Combe (Cist. Warw.), and the defendants, the prior and convent of Monks Kirby (Ben. al. Warw.) and A., clerk of Withybrook (Warw.), promised to keep the composition which had been made between them.[4] Proctors, too, might take these oaths on behalf of their clients.[5] Where a sentence was decreed or a confession was made, the losing party was usually required to promise to abide by it.[6] In 1226 Simon, miller of North Aston (Oxon.), swore to observe the sentence against him, and he subjected himself to the perpetual jurisdiction of the judges, the priors of Monkton Farleigh and Malmesbury and the dean of Malmesbury.[7] Sometimes when compositions were made that entailed a definite concession by one of the parties in order to bring about an arrangement, the other party was required to swear to abide by it. For instance, when William de Pauelhi received at farm from the prior and convent of Lewes all the tithes of the lordship of Sculthorpe for an annual payment of twenty-eight shillings, he swore fealty on the gospels in the chapter-house and promised to make

---

[1] e.g. P.R.O. E 40/14036; P.R.O. E 42/426 (App. B (v), no. 2); P.R.O. E 210/9469; Tintern Cart., ff. 35ʳ–6ʳ; Exeter Cart., p. 14; and Thorney Cart. ii, f. 383ʳ.

[2] P.R.O. E 135/2/28 (App. B (iv), no. 1).

[3] Crowland Cart., f. 94.

[4] Combe Cart. (A), f. 76ᵛ.

[5] e.g. Christchurch Cart., f. 92ʳ; *N.L.C.*, no. 62; and Canterbury, Cartae Antiquae, F 31.

[6] Binham Cart., f. 138ᵛ; *Oseney Cart.* v, no. 802A; Lanthony Cart. A 2, f. 264ʳ; and Canterbury, Cartae Antiquae, H 120.

[7] Bradenstoke Cart., f. 29ᵛ.

the payments loyally.¹ When the archdeacon of Worcester promised to pay an annual rent of one mark from the church of Badingham (Suff.), it was stated in the judges' report that he should be compelled to do so, and that he should be punished if he went against his oath.² One or other party could also promise not to resuscitate the suit. J(ohn), abbot of Ford, one of the judges delegate, witnessed an oath of the archdeacon of Exeter never to seek four shillings again from Master M(ichael) de Buketon for the church of Colyton (Devon). The proctor of the archdeacon had remitted the four shillings sterling, which Master Michael was held to owe, for the sake of concord between them, and the judges had therefore absolved him from the payment.³

Where oaths were taken, penalties were sometimes included as well. Thomas de Pridias, knight, proctor for his wife Sibylla, promised that before the first feast of the Holy Cross she should take an oath to keep the composition with the abbot and convent of Beaulieu (Cist. Hants), under penalty of forty shillings.⁴ And on 1 August 1250 Richard Tregod, knight, the defendant, promised faith to the abbot and convent of Beaulieu, in the matter of payment of certain tithes from his lordship, under pain of one mark.⁵ When the abbot and convent of Bayham (Prem. Suss.) and the abbot and convent of Grestain (Eure, France) swore to keep a mutual arrangement, they did so under penalty of forty marks to be paid by the recalcitrant party to the other.⁶ Such penalties were often stipulated in the final *actum*, against the possibility of either party not keeping the settlement.⁷

Penalties were often included when the parties submitted themselves to the jurisdiction of the judges for coercion,

---

¹ P.R.O. E 40/14068, cal. *Lewes Cart. N.P.*, no. 136; and cf. Bardney Cart., f. 95ᵛ, where Philip de Kyme swore on the high altar at Bardney that he would observe the settlement.

² Eye Cart., ff. 35ᵛ-6ʳ.

³ Exeter Ch. 812; and cf. Castle Acre Cart., f. 47ʳ, where the prior and convent of Shelford (Notts.) gave up all claim to the church in question, promised to move no further suit, and declared that any charter of the bishop or patron about collation that they possessed should be held invalid.

⁴ Beaulieu Cart., ff. 134ʳ-5ʳ. Not dated.

⁵ Beaulieu Cart., f. 135ᵛ.

⁶ Bayham Cart., f. 60ʳ. Cf. *Oseney Cart.* iv, no. 144.

⁷ e.g. Binham Cart., ff. 146ᵛ-7ʳ; Stixwould Cart., f. 46ʳ; and Wells, Lib. Albus ii, f. 354ʳ.

because these persons were to enforce the payment.[1] At the settlement of a suit between the prior and convent of Box-grove (Ben. al. Suss.) on the one hand, and R., parson of the church of Bilton (Warw.), and R. de Crest, knight, on the other, the judges proclaimed a penalty of one hundred shillings for non-observance, and the parties subjected themselves to the judges and their successors, renouncing all appeal and contradiction.[2] In 1246, at the settlement of a suit before the prior of Castle Acre, it was decided that a penalty of one hundred shillings should be paid to the other party by the one who broke the composition, and the parties renounced the right of appeal.[3] When powers of coercion were granted by the parties, the abbot and convent of Bec and the rectors of Wimborne All Hallows (Dors.), some time after 1225, to the judges and their successors, it was also stipulated that if the rectors did not keep the convention, the monks of Bec were to seize the tithes.[4]

Penalties consisted usually of the payment of a fine, but they might also entail excommunication. The prior of Ivy-church, the succentor of Salisbury, and the dean of Wilton decreed a penalty of thirty marks and excommunication for the abbot and convent of Bec and Philip, rector of East Hendred (Berks.), if either should break the terms of the settlement.[5] The same judges delegate, in a suit between the same Philip and the abbot and convent of Abingdon, threatened a payment of ten marks sterling and excommunication for the party that did not keep the composition.[6] In 1238 the prior of Christchurch, judge delegate of Gregory IX, decreed sentence of excommunication for anyone upsetting an arrangement which he had made.[7]

In cases concerning money payments (such as pensions), where a composition had not been kept, an additional sum, over and above the fine, might be demanded if the payment

---

[1] See App. A (v), Examples of Submission to Ecclesiastics for Coercion, and, e.g., nos. 17, 21, 36–7.
[2] See App. A (v), no. 12.   [3] New College, Oxford, Writtle Ch. 401.
[4] App. A (v), no. 13; and cf. Reading Cart., f. 113ʳ, where it was agreed that Reading should take the tithes of East Ginge (Berks.), if no payment was made by Wallingford for three years, and should hold them until the pension and the fines were paid.   [5] Windsor Ch. xv. 41. 71.   [6] Abingdon Cart., ff. 53ʳ–4ʳ.
[7] Beaulieu Cart., f. 133ᵛ. Cf. Bradenstoke Cart., f. 119ᵛ, and see P.R.O. DL 25/563.

had not been made at the appointed time. It was ordered in a suit between the prior and convent of Holy Trinity, Aldgate, and the abbot and convent of Faversham, that Faversham were to pay double if they did not pay the specified sum at either of the two appointed terms, and that a penalty of sixty marks should be exacted from either party ignoring the arrangement. A further penalty of forty marks was to be imposed if they moved another suit.[1] Expenses and damages were to be paid by the abbess and convent of Shaftesbury to the abbot and convent of Alcester if there was non-payment of a pension or delay in making it.[2] Similarly the prior and convent of Newton Longville were to be made to pay expenses and the debt if they failed to give twelve shillings yearly to the rector of Horwood (Bucks.).[3]

Many documents recorded that the parties surrendered certain legal rights. Such renunciations might prevent a case from being carried to Rome again if it reopened. On making settlements the surrender of the right to impetrate was not infrequent. In 1238/9 Hugh de Lunde, rector of Brocklesby (Lincs.), renounced all claim to certain tithes and swore not to impetrate again against the nuns of Nun Cotham.[4] In a case between Richard, rector of Bucknall (Lincs.), and the abbot and convent of Crowland, both parties renounced present and future impetrations.[5] When James Saluage renounced his suit about the tithes of 'Codestede' against the abbot and convent of St. Augustine, Canterbury, he promised that he would never commence another about the same tithes;[6] and in another suit before judges delegate it was recorded: 'Promisit autem utraque pars se predictam composicionem fideliter observaturam et quod neutra contra formam composicionis predicte aliquid impetrabit. Et si fuerit impetratum iuribus carebit.'[7]

Renunciation of the right of appeal was usually coupled with surrendering impetation, and the right to seek a writ

[1] P.R.O. E 40/13828(f).   [2] Shaftesbury Cart., f. 29ʳ.
[3] N.L.C., no. 27.   [4] Nun Cotham Cart., f. 38ᵛ.
[5] Crowland Cart., f. 189.
[6] Reg. of St. Augustine's Canterbury, ii. 545–6. For further examples see also P.R.O. E 42/426, and Bradenstoke Cart., f. 156ʳ.
[7] Reg. Antiq. Linc. iii, no. 645.

of prohibition was often renounced as well.[1] At a composition made in 1237 in the church of St. Mary at the bridge, Stamford, the parties—the prioress and convent of St. Michael, Stamford, and William Erl of North Luffenham (Rutl.)—renounced rights of appeal, of impetration, and of seeking a writ of prohibition.[2] At another settlement, made on 10 July 1236 in Wallingford priory church, the parties subjected themselves to the judges' jurisdiction, renouncing legal benefits and the possibility of acquiring a royal prohibition.[3] Similarly Walter de Ribof, knight, who confessed that he ought to pay to the abbot and convent of Welbeck ten shillings yearly, as decreed in the will of Richard his father, and also arrears to the value of fifteen shillings, renounced legal remedies and royal prohibition.[4]

In a suit settled on 3 February 1243/4 at Hereford by the dean and chancellor of Hereford, the parties, Andrew of Wollaston, rector of Alvington (Glos.), and the prior and convent of Lanthony, surrendered all remedies of canon and civil law. These included the rights of impetration, appeal, the *privilegium fori*, and of applying for the writ of prohibition.[5] In another case it was recorded: 'Subjecit autem se dictus Rogerus jurisdictioni dictorum judicum, renuncians fori privilegio et appellationi et prohibitioni regie . . .'[6] This was a debt case which had been pleaded as testamentary before a delegated court. When in 1249 the abbot and convent of St. John, Colchester, renounced all varieties of legal rights, these included the right of tuitorial appeal.[7]

On renouncing all legal remedies, the parties often granted powers of coercion to the judges delegate and their successors.[8] The abbot and convent of Bec and the house of St. Frideswide at Oxford granted powers of coercion to the judges, the priors of Dunstable and Caldwell and the precentor of Dunstable, and their successors, notwithstanding appeal or legal remedies or impetration.[9] When the prior and convent of Wallingford (Berks.) and Henry of Earley (Berks.), knight, and his chaplain, renounced legal benefits

---

[1] *Glos. Cart.* i, no. ccxxxvi, and Combe Cart. (A), f. 77ʳ.
[2] P.R.O. E 326/2268 (App. B (v), no. 3).   [3] App. A (v), no. 43.
[4] Welbeck Cart., f. 89ʳ.   [5] Lanthony Cart. A i, IIII, no. cviii.
[6] P.R.O. DL 25/15.   [7] *Colchester Cart.* ii. 547.   [8] See App. A (v).
[9] App. A (v), no. 37, and see also P.R.O. E 326/2268 (App. B (v), no. 3).

and royal prohibition, and put themselves under the judges'
jurisdiction to keep the settlement, they exchanged documents to this effect.[1] William of Ingleby, a party in a suit
with the abbot and convent of Newsham (Lincs.), submitted
to the jurisdiction of the archdeacon of Stowe, the abbot of
Barlings, and the prior of St. Katherine's, Lincoln, presumably the judges delegate, allowing them to compel him
to observe the settlement which had been made, if compulsion should be necessary. He renounced appeal, the *privilegium fori*, and all exceptions, and he took an oath that he and
his successors would observe this. This document, a chirograph, was sealed by the judges and the parties, at their instance.[2] Such documents must have been common.

Submission could be made to local diocesan officers who
had courts in the territory where the parties resided. On 5
April 1234, in Canterbury cathedral, the parties Master
William de Weleburne, rector of Meopham (Kent), and the
prior and convent of Christ Church, Canterbury, renounced
appeal, exceptions, and other remedies of law and subjected
themselves to the jurisdiction of the archbishop of Canterbury. The papal judges had been the abbots of Langdon and
St. Radegund's and the prior of Monks Horton.[3] Simon,
rector of Compton (Berks.), and the abbot and convent of
Reading promised to submit to compulsion by the archdeacon of Berkshire and the dean of Newbury, if necessary.[4]
The abbot and convent of St. James, Northampton, and
John and Reginald, clerk, and other parishioners of Hartwell (Northants.), submitted to the coercion of the archdeacon of the place (Northampton) if the composition
should be broken.[5] On 4 August 1235 in the church of St.
Mary at Oxford, the parties in a case, the abbot and convent
of Notley (Bucks.) and the prior and convent of Newton
Longville (Bucks.), subjected themselves to the jurisdiction
of the archdeacons of Bedford and Buckingham for the observance of the composition.[6] In a suit of 1226, Thomas
Crispin, rector of Bytham (Lincs.), and William de Coleville
subjected themselves to the jurisdiction of the archdeacon

---

[1] App. A (v), no. 43.   [2] B.M. Harley Ch. 44 G 20 (App. B (v), no. 4).
[3] App. A (v), no. 34.   [4] Reading Cart., f. 114ʳ.
[5] App. A (v), no. 7.   [6] App. A (v), no. 38.

of Lincoln. William subjected himself and his successors *appellatione remota*.[1] In a similar way William Mansel and Ralph Taylebois, rectors of the church of Shenley (Bucks.), the defendants, in order to bind themselves to pay thirty-five shillings and sixpence a year to the prior and convent of Dunstable, placed their benefices under the jurisdiction of the archdeacon of Buckingham without appeal.[2] At the settlement of the suit between Master William of Purleigh, rector of Purleigh (Essex), and the prioress and convent of Wix (Essex), who had come before the priors of Merton, Bermondsey, and Southwark, judges delegated by Honorius III, the parties submitted themselves to the jurisdiction of the bishop of London, and renounced further suits about these tithes.[3] When the prior and convent of Christchurch (Twynham) and the abbot and convent of Montébourg made a settlement some time after 1235, they subjected themselves to the jurisdiction of the judges delegate, the prior of Poughley and the dean of Newbury, and also to the bishop of Winchester and his official, renouncing impetrations and appeal.[4] The bishop or the chapter of London or the successors in office of the judges delegate—the abbot of Lesnes and subprior of Lesnes (a subdelegate of the prior of Leeds)—were to enforce a yearly payment to be made by the abbot and convent of Colchester to Master William of Lichfield, clerk of London and rector of Barkway church.[5] Coercive powers were given to the chapter of Lincoln, over a pension from Sotby church (Lincs.), in a suit between the monastery of Bardney and Ralph (de Kyme), archdeacon of Cleveland (Yorks. N.R.). The settlement had taken place in the chapter of Lincoln in 1209, when the judges delegate had been the chancellor and two of the canons.[6]

The grant of coercive powers by the parties to the judges was a frequent occurrence. In 1234 judges delegate, the priors of Dunstable and Caldwell and the precentor of Dunstable, reported that with the consent of the parties, the abbots and convents of Bec and Tewkesbury, they had

---

[1] App. A (v), no. 18.
[2] Ibid., no. 20 (Fowler has this incorrectly as 25s. 6d. a year).
[3] Ibid., no. 5.   [4] Ibid., no. 40.
[5] *Colchester Cart.* i. 100, 104.   [6] App. A (v), no. 1.

reserved to themselves and their successors the authority to compel the observance of this peace, notwithstanding the exception that the power to compel the parties had not been granted in the papal mandate. All exceptions, delays, chicanery, the *privilegium fori*, and the right of appeal were to be renounced, and if either party did not keep the settlement it was to compensate the other for all the damages and expenses which had been caused:

Et reservavimus nobis et successoribus nostris de consensu partium potestatem, non obstante illa exceptione quod non habeamus copiam predicti rescripti apostolici compellendi partes, omni exceptione cavillatione dilatione fori privilegio et appellatione remotis, ad istius pacis observationem. Ita tamen quod, si alterutra pars quod absit predictam pacem non observaverit, alteri parti omnia dampna expensas et interesse sacramento observantis prefatam pacem declaranda persolvet, compositione nihilominus rata manente quocienscumque contra predicte pacis reformationem alterutra pars venerit. Et consenserunt sepedicte partes ut nos et successores nostri, qui pro tempore fuerint, possimus compellere partem contra predictam pacem venientem ad predicta dampna expensas et interesse persolvenda absque mora et dilatione, omni exceptione cavillatione et appellatione remotis, observanti prescriptam pacem.[1]

Usually such jurisdiction seems to have been assumed with the consent of the parties:

Ad hec sciatis quod ex utriusque partis consensu jurisdictionem partes ad istius compositionis observanciam cohercendi, si que illarum contra illam venire voluerit, nobis reservavimus,[2]

and it was for compulsion without coming again before a court:

Nos de consensu partium predictarum reservavimus nobis iurisdiccionem ad compellendum partes, sine strepitu iudiciali unica monicione tamen, premissa per censuram ecclesiasticam ad observacionem compositionis prenotate.[3]

In a suit about tithes in Waxham (Norf.) the judges reserved the power, with the consent of the parties, to compel the rector, Philip de Fleg, to observe what was contained in the

---

[1] App. A (v), no. 35.   [2] Ibid., nos. 2 and 39.
[3] *Reg. Antiq. Linc.* ii, no. 386.

instruments dealing with the case, without rights of appeal and the like.[1]

Sometimes just one of the parties subjected himself to the jurisdiction of the judges and their successors for retaining a settlement, as did William son of Everard de Ringesborn. In 1224 he put himself under the jurisdiction of Prior Walter of St. James's and Prior Martin of St. Augustine's, Bristol, for the payment of a rent to the prior and convent of Bradenstoke.[2] On 29 August 1220 in the cathedral at Canterbury, Lambert, proctor of the brothers of Dunes in Sheppey, submitted himself to the jurisdiction of the judges, the priors of St. Augustine's, Canterbury, Monks Horton, and Faversham, for compulsion if an annual rent of four shillings was not paid to the prior and convent of Christ Church.[3] Similarly in 1227 Osbert, vicar of Tew (Oxon.), subjected himself to the perpetual jurisdiction of the judges, the priors of Malmesbury and Monkton Farleigh and the dean of Malmesbury, giving them powers to force him to abide by the settlement.[4] These three submissions followed renunciations of suits.

Submission could be made not only to the judges delegate who had heard the case but also to their successors in office.[5] In theory, therefore, such jurisdiction could last for an unlimited time, provided that documentary evidence of the submission survived. Thus the priors of St. James's and St. John's, Northampton, reported in the suit between Richard, rector of Hanney (Berks.), and the abbot and convent of Abingdon, which was delegated to them by Gregory IX in 1237, that they reserved jurisdiction to compel the observance of the composition for themselves and their successors:

reservantes nobis et successoribus nostris jurisdictionem memorata auctoritate nobis attributam ut istius compositionis contradictores et rebelles ad ejus perpetuam observationem per censuram ecclesiasticam possimus compellere.[6]

In a case of the 1280s it was recorded that if a payment was not made by the nuns of Camestrum (al. Tarrant, Dors.),

---

[1] Bodleian MS. Chs. Norf. a 6, Ch. 623.   [2] App. A (v), no. 9.
[3] Ibid., no. 4.   [4] Ibid., no. 19.
[5] See, e.g., ibid., nos. 10, 35, 51, and 59.   [6] App. A (v), no. 47.

the canons of Christchurch were to have the permanent right of taking the suit back to the judges or their successors.[1]

3. The Observance of the Settlement

The existence of all these elaborate penalties and checks, and the profusion of these attempts to ensure observance suggest that settlements were not easily enforced. Most of the penalties and attempts to secure coercion depended on the willingness of the parties to renounce their legal rights, and on whether they wished to abide by the settlement. Some settlements made provisions for the future. In a case of 1242 between the abbot and convent of Welbeck and Adam de Novo Mercato, about the tithes of two mills, it was decided that Adam should pay Welbeck two shillings yearly for the tithes, that Welbeck should have possession of the mills, and that if the mills were burnt or destroyed at any future date, Adam should pay nothing.[2] Richard, prior of Dunstable, and A(lexander), archdeacon of Bedford, judges delegated by Innocent III, made a composition in which they provided that the canons of Walsingham were to pay one pound of incense yearly to Wymondham for the tithes of a marsh in Burnham. They also provided that if a quarter of the marsh was cultivated, the monks of Wymondham should receive a quarter of a mark, if a third, then one third of a mark, and one mark if all should be cultivated; and if there was any cultivation at all, the payment of the pound of incense was to be stopped.[3]

Information remains of settlements which were kept for considerable periods of time. Diocesan letters of *inspeximus* record settlements which had been made in some instances many years earlier. An instrument of Walter Reynolds, archbishop of Canterbury, which is dated 30 April 1320, records that Westminster said they received and alleged that they ought to receive a yearly pension of five marks from the church of Bloxham. Reynolds confirmed this.[4] He also confirmed to Westminster sixteen shillings and eightpence from

[1] Christchurch Cart., f. 136ᵛ.
[2] Welbeck Cart., f. 79ᵛ.   [3] Walsingham Cart., f. 2ᵛ.
[4] Westminster Domesday, f. 644ʳ, and see above, p. 92.

the church of Launton, which sum had been decreed to
Westminster by Richard, prior of Dunstable, Richard, abbot
of Woburn, and Raymond, prior of St. Albans, judges
delegate of Innocent III in 1214.[1] Settlements might receive successive confirmations. A confirmation of Prior
Henry of Eastry and the chapter of Christ Church, Canterbury, of 1314 confirmed an *inspeximus* of Archbishop John
Pecham (1279–92) which in turn had confirmed an arrangement made by the prior of Barnwell, judge delegate of
Innocent IV in 1250, about tithes claimed by the rector
of Harbledown.[2] Also copies remain of settlements made
several hundred years earlier. The Caversham settlement of
1235 was copied on a late paper title-deed;[3] and a fifteenth-
century copy of instruments, relating to Holbeach and belonging to Christ Church, Canterbury, records a settlement
made by judges delegate in 1222, which was presumably
still in force.[4]

On the other hand, some compositions and arrangements
were made only for the lifetime of the incumbent concerned.[5]
When a settlement was made between the convent of Newton Longville and Peter, chaplain of Chesham (Bucks.), that
Peter should have certain tithes for his lifetime in return for
half a mark of silver yearly, it was agreed that after the death
of Peter, Newton Longville should possess the tithes freely.[6]
A bargain of a similar kind was struck between the prior
and convent of Norwich and Walter, the rector of Swanton
(Norf.). The prior and convent conceded that the rector
should hold the two parts of all the tithes in the demesne of
Hubert de Ria in Swanton, and should pay them forty-four
shillings each year. Norwich were not committed to continue
this arrangement after Walter's death or transfer.[7] On 22
September 1229 Ralph de Sidesterne, defendant in a case
brought by the prior and convent of Lewes, promised to pay

---

[1] Westminster Domesday, f. 644ʳ, and Westminster Ch. 15684.

[2] C.U.L. Eastry Cart. MS. Ee v. 31, f. 148ʳ⁻ᵛ, and see Leeds Cart., f. 8ᵛ.

[3] *N.L.C.*, no. 63.

[4] Canterbury, Cartae Antiquae, H 121, and see H 120.

[5] See, e.g., Thorney Cart. ii, f. 322ʳ⁻ᵛ; Lewes Cart., ff. 116ᵛ, 112ʳ, and 117ʳ, cal.
S.P. ii. 27–8, 39, and 40; and Dunstable Cart., f. 33ʳ, cal. *Dunstable Cart.*, no. 266.

[6] *N.L.C.*, no. 47, and see Eye Cart., f. 36ᵛ.

[7] Norwich Ch. 680. Cf. P.R.O. E 40/14070, cal. *Lewes Cart. N.P.*, no. 140, and
Eton College, Cottisford Ch. C 37.

twenty shillings rent yearly from the church of Burnham Thorpe (Norf.) as long as he should hold the church.[1] A settlement had been made by judges delegate of Innocent III between Thomas Foliot, rector of Ashwell, and the monks of Westminster.[2] It is later recorded, on 11 October 1241, that on the death of Thomas Foliot the church of Ashwell was adjudicated and assigned to Westminster, towards the support of the brethren, guests, and poor. The vicar of Ashwell was to have forty-five marks from the fruits of the altar and other fruits, and was to pay a pension of two marks yearly to Westminster.[3]

Certain suits inevitably reopened as circumstances changed. For instance, new land might be brought under cultivation and this might upset an existing tithe arrangement, or a new rector might be appointed who was not prepared to abide by a settlement made by his predecessor.[4] When Richard (Foliot), archdeacon of Middlesex, a judge delegate of Innocent IV, confirmed a settlement made by his subdelegates, Master Robert de Pertona and Geoffrey of Thame, canons of Lincoln, he tried to guard against the reopening of the suit by reserving for himself the power of declaring and interpreting the sentence if necessary.[5] But although there were attempts to stop the reopening of suits, they were not always successful. A suit settled on 10 October 1228, in which the parties, the prior and convent of Bridlington and the abbot and convent of Bardney, subjected themselves to the jurisdiction of the archdeacon of the East Riding to observe the settlement, reopened before the bishop of Lincoln in 1294.[6] A quarrel about the tithes of Ottershaw between Richard Stapulford, rector of Walton-on-Thames (Surr.), and the abbot and convent of Chertsey, which was settled on 15 February 1227/8, was renewed by his successor Adam before the official of Winchester and then before the dean of Arches in 1279. Both sentences were in favour of Chertsey.[7] A suit between the prior and convent of Leeds and the rector of Crundale (Kent) provides a similar example.

[1] Lewes Cart., f. 240ʳ, cal. *N.P.*, no. 71.
[2] Westminster Domesday, f. 228ʳ⁻ᵛ (f. 452ʳ⁻ᵛ is the same).
[3] Ibid., f. 645ᵛ.   [4] See Chatteris Cart., ff. 142ʳ–4ʳ.
[5] Bardney Cart., ff. 213ʳ–14ʳ.   [6] Ibid., ff. 96ᵛ, 97ᵛ.
[7] *Chertsey Cart.*, nos. 93–5.

In October 1225 the priors of St. Andrew's, Rochester, and Lesnes, and the archdeacon of Rochester ordered J. de Nerford, rector of Crundale, to pay to Leeds twenty-five shillings yearly in the name of the benefice of Crundale. In this case, with the consent of the parties, the judges reserved the power to force the rector to pay.[1] On 31 May 1283 Master Martin de Hampton, the commissary of Canterbury, reported that Thomas, rector of Crundale, had confessed that he ought to pay twenty-five shillings yearly to Leeds for the church of Crundale. He ordered Thomas to pay in future and threatened excommunication if he dissented.[2] In 1314 Henry of Eastry, prior, and the chapter of Christ Church, Canterbury, confirmed the instruments of the Crundale case which had arisen in 1225 and again in 1283.[3] On 3 February 1234 in the church of St. Peter by the castle at Northampton, the priors of St. John's and St. James's and the dean of Northampton declared that the tithes in dispute in a case between St. Frideswide's and the rector of Beckley (Oxon.) belonged to the priory, and they reserved powers to compel the parties to observe this.[4] The same suit opened before the dean of Arches in 1270 on a charge of spoliation of the tithes by M., the vicar,[5] and once again, in 1303, sentence was declared in favour of St. Frideswide's and against James of Kirkham, the rector, by the official of Lincoln.[6] The Cliffe-at-Hoo case between the rector and the prior and convent of Christ Church, Canterbury, settled in May 1229, broke out again in 1277, but an *inspeximus* of 1291 and a notarial instrument of 1305 confirmed the first arrangement.[7] This was another case where powers to coerce had been granted to the judges, it seems ineffectually, because by this time most of the first commission would have been dead. Whether the grant of coercive rights to the judges' successors was more effective is hard to say.

A certain number of suits that reopened show the importance of the careful preservation of documents. In a case about Gatesbury, when the rector saw the document recording the

---

[1] Leeds Cart., f. 10ʳ.   [2] Ibid., f. 11ʳ.
[3] C.U.L. MS. Ee v. 31, f. 149ʳ⁻ᵛ.   [4] *St. Frideswide's Cart.* ii, no. 732.
[5] Ibid., no. 733 (734–6 deal with the same case).
[6] *St. Frideswide's Cart.* ii, no. 737.
[7] Canterbury, Cartae Antiquae, C 280, 286, 292, and 293e.

previous settlement, made some sixty to seventy years earlier by judges delegate of Honorius III,[1] he renounced his suit. This was in May 1288.[2] When a settlement was made in a case which came before papal judges delegate between 1198 and 1214, the judges recorded that they had inspected instruments which may well have included a previous arrangement made by Archbishop Richard (1174–84) as judge delegate.[3] A composition of 1236 between the rector of Christian Malford (Wilts.) and the prior and convent of Bradenstoke recorded that a previous settlement had been effected between the parties in 1229 (perhaps not through papal delegation), which shows that documentary evidence survived. This new arrangement, which reiterated the so-called 'old composition', that Bradenstoke were to pay the rector sixteen shillings yearly for the tithes, decreed that Bradenstoke were also to give fifty shillings and eightpence to the rector for arrears and expenses.[4] A charter of Nicholas de Longespée, rector of Iwerne Minster (Dors.), dated 9 September 1248, records that he had asked by what right the prior and convent of Christchurch held the garb tithes. They showed him documents of concession and confirmation of Hubert, bishop of Salisbury (1189–93), and the document of composition between them and his predecessor, R. de Maupaudr'. This composition had been made in response to a mandate of 14 May 1221, and documents recording it had been deposited at Iwerne Minster church (this copy was presumably lost by 1248, since the rector did not know of it), at Christchurch, and at Salisbury. The rector inspected the documents that Christchurch produced, and accepted the settlement made twenty-seven years previously, dropping his charges against the priory.[5]

The appointment by the pope of conservators for the protection of the rights of a particular person or monastic house might prevent unnecessary appeal or resort to the *Curia* where obvious reinforcement was needed and no question of law was involved. An instance that illustrates how they acted has survived at Westminster. On 14 June 1197

1 P.R.O. E 212/28.   2 P.R.O. E 42/232.   3 *Reg. Roff*, p. 384.
4 Bradenstoke Cart., f. 65ʳ, and Wells, Lib. Albus ii, f. 354ʳ.
5 Christchurch (Twynham) Cart., f. 121ᵛ.

Hugh (of Avalon), bishop of Lincoln, J(ohn de Cella), abbot of St. Albans, and B(enedict),[1] abbot of St. Mary's, Stratford Langthorne, delegates of Celestine III, reported that the abbot and convent of Westminster had conceded the church of Bloxham to the abbess and nuns of Godstow, saving an annual pension of five marks silver which was to be paid to them for providing the altar light.[2] In 1251, when Innocent IV confirmed certain pensions (presumably including that from Bloxham) to Westminster, he appointed the priors of Tandridge (Aug. Surr.) and Blackmore (Aug. Essex) as conservators.[3] They were to see that these pensions were paid and to censure anyone who should disobey. Three years later, in 1254, the prior of Tandridge and the dean of Southwark (who was acting on behalf of the prior of Blackmore) sat in the church of St. Magnus the Martyr, London, at the instance of Westminster. The matter before them was described as *negotio conservationis*, since the five marks from Bloxham had not been paid. The proctor of the abbess and convent of Godstow confessed that the pension ought to be paid, and a previous instrument was produced to prove this.[4] The conservators therefore reiterated the arrangement of 1197 as the Westminster scribe recorded in the *Domesday*.

It seems fair to assume that if settlements had not been generally observed before papally delegated courts, or had been less well observed than before the other courts, people would soon have stopped taking their cases to Rome. The number of cases between 1198 and 1254 that were taken to Rome, both on appeal and in the first instance, can in no way be estimated, but there is no visible decline in the number of cases during these years. In fact, cases before the delegated courts seem to have increased in number, especially after Innocent III's pontificate. Furthermore, an immense amount of expenditure could have been saved by keeping cases at

---

[1] Probably Benedict, although Ralph of Coggeshall (*Chronicon Anglicanum*, ed. J. Stevenson (R.S. lxvi, 1875), p. 187), describes him on his election as abbot of Coggeshall in 1218 as having been head of the abbey of Stratford for nineteen years, which the author of the entry in *V.C.H. Essex*, ii. 133, takes literally to mean that he was elected abbot of Stratford in 1199.

[2] Westminster Domesday, ff. 378ᵛ–9ʳ (App. B (v), no. 5), and see *Godstow Reg.* i, no. [308].

[3] *Reg. Inn. IV*, no. 5243.

[4] Westminster Domesday, f. 379ᵛ (App. B (v), no. 6).

home, and the parties sometimes state that they are tired of 'labours and expenses' in taking cases to Rome.[1] In the Bath–Wells election case the dean and chapter of Wells borrowed at least 2,600 marks ($£1,733. 0s. 8d.$) and probably nearer 3,600.[2] Similarly the resources of Bath were strained to the utmost, and the convent was involved in debt.[3] The convent of St. Nicholas at Angers alleged that their means were nearly exhausted in the course of a long legal struggle with the prior and convent of Spalding. Some seven years later, at the settlement, they asserted their expenses to be 1,000 marks. The judges decreed that sixty marks yearly should be paid by Spalding to Angers. This sum was increased from forty marks, the sum laid down in the *Compositio Prima*, because of the great expense that the abbey had suffered in the suit.[4] Likewise a Barnwell case which lasted for more than twenty years was said to have taken place 'non sine gravibus expensis et multis laboribus'.[5]

These were major cases, and the stakes, especially at Rome,[6] were consequently high, but an expense sheet for £56. 17s. 8d., in a case between the rector of Findon and the prior and convent of Sele, suggests that some of the lesser suits were also costly.[7] This is the only 'cost sheet' to have come to light. It was usual for the party who lost the suit to be condemned to pay the costs or expenses of the other. The Canterbury formulary includes a *forma litterarum pro expensis* with ten marks as the sum given in the example.[8]

[1] e.g. *Reg. Hon. III*, no. 1810 (*C.P.L.* i. 61), and *Reg. Greg. IX*, no. 2375.

[2] See C. M. Church, 'Roger of Salisbury, 1st Bishop of Bath and Wells, 1244–47', *Archaeologia*, lii (1890), 95, 100–1, and Wells, Lib. Albus i, ff. 69, 79, 95, and 97–8. The faculties to the proctors of bishops and monastic houses to contract loans at Rome are a common occurrence in the registers of Innocent IV (e.g. nos. 7051, 7306, and 7426). [3] *Bath Cart.* ii, nos. 139, 208–9, 228, and 399–409.

[4] *Reg. Greg. IX*, no. 2416; and Spalding Cart., f. 14ᵛ.

[5] *Lib. Memorandorum Ecclesie de Bernewelle*, ed. J. Willis Clark (Cambridge, 1907), no. 63, p. 143.

[6] See Matthew Paris, *Chron. Maj.* v (1880), 96, where he speaks of the *Curia* 'like an abyss' swallowing up gold; Grosseteste, *Epistolae*, p. lxxi: 'O money, money, how powerful thou art, especially at the court of Rome'; and *Die Chronik des Propstes Burchard von Ursberg*, ed. O. Holder-Egger and B. von Simson (Hanover and Leipzig, 1916), p. 82.

[7] Magdalen College, Oxford, Findon Ch. t, pd. W. D. Macray, *Notes from the Muniments of St. Mary Magdalen College, Oxford* (Oxford and London, 1882), pp. 13–14, who erroneously dates this 1264–6 for 1254–6.

[8] *C.F.*, no. (27).

In numerous *acta* of the courts the expenses are specified. They vary from one mark to one thousand marks.[1] The cost of making the journey to Rome, of obtaining mandates and confirmations, and of paying proctors cannot be estimated because of the lack of evidence, but it must have been more expensive than parallel procedure in the episcopal court.

4. *Interruptions in the Administration*

(i) *Local*

In England between 1210 and 1214 there were local interruptions to the judge-delegate system. On Sunday 23 March 1208 a Papal Interdict was pronounced over England which lasted until 2 July 1214.[2] It is not easy to discover what the practical implications and effects of the Interdict were, partly because of the discrepancies between the authorities as to its actual terms.[3] T. M. Parker has suggested that it is possible that no detailed instructions were issued from Rome for its observance. If this were so, he argues, the settlement of details would have fallen upon the ordinaries and might account for the confused documentary tradition, which was, perhaps, an echo of the diversity of practice of the time.[4] In assessing the effects by examining the practical results, Professor Cheney has concluded that, although the evidence is scanty, there was no deliberate obstruction to ecclesiastical business, with the notable exception of appeals to Rome in

---

[1] *St. Frideswide's Cart.* ii, no. 1048; *Reg. Antiq. Linc.* iii, no. 730; P.R.O. E 135/4/17; E 40/14953; and Bardney Cart., f. 30ᵛ.

[2] C. R. Cheney, 'King John and the Papal Interdict', *Bulletin of the John Rylands Library*, xxxi (1948), 295.

[3] Innocent's letter (in *Historical Works of Gervase of Canterbury*, ii, pp. lxxvi-lxxviii), speaks of it only in general terms. The commissioners, therefore, made inquiries about the details, which resulted in a letter of 14 June 1208. There are, however, two different versions of this letter (*P.L.* 215, no. cii (*bis*), cols. 1422-3; and Gervase, ii, p. xcii). Another document which professes to be the actual form of the Interdict of 1208 was discovered and printed by E. Martène and U. Durand, *Thesaurus novus Anecdotorum*, i (Paris, 1717), 812-13, and in *P.L.* 217, no. cxxxvi, cols. 190-2, from a manuscript of Mont-Saint-Michel. This gives greater detail and is more stringent in its prohibitions than the other documents. T. M. Parker, 'Terms of the Interdict of Innocent III', *Speculum*, xi (1936), 259-60, thinks that it is unlikely that it emanates from Rome, and says that its provenance and authority are uncertain.

[4] Parker, 'Terms of the Interdict', p. 60.

and after 1210. In this respect, if in no other, Church government was seriously impeded.[1]

Several chronicles record that in 1210 the king prohibited the hearing of papal causes in England.[2] Amongst the entries for that year, Richard de Mores, the writer of the *Annals of Dunstable*, reported: 'Ea tempestate jussit rex quod nullus placitet vel placitum teneat auctoritate Papae; et poenam corporalem transgressoribus indixit.'[3] Thomas Wykes, the Oseney chronicler, says, 'Rex Johannes prohibuit literas Apostolicas in Angliam differri et causas Apostolica auctoritate tractari.'[4] A further passage in *Walter of Coventry* records for 1210: 'Interdixit ergo publice ne auctoritate litterarum domini papae causae per Angliam tractarentur ecclesiasticae.'[5] Few cases were carried by English petitioners to Rome between 1210 and 1214 and few cases were delegated.[6] A further examination of the evidence substantiates Professor Cheney's thesis, but it also shows that records of few cases survive from the whole of Innocent III's pontificate compared with the quantity from the subsequent three pontificates.[7]

Already on 20 February 1203 Innocent III had accused King John of interfering with the activities of papal delegates hearing cases in England: 'Illud autem gravissimum reputamus quod, cum in regno tuo causas ecclesiasticas

---

[1] Cheney, 'Papal Interdict', pp. 308, 310.

[2] According to the Waverley annalist, the king placed a prohibition that pleas of the pope should not be held in England in 1207 (*Ann. Mon.* ii. 259). Professor Cheney has suggested that the chronicler has misdated the prohibition, 'Papal Interdict', p. 309 n. 2. *Chronica Johannis de Oxenedes* and the *Chronicon Anglicanum* of Ralph of Coggeshall do not give any specific references to this interference, but the latter records that in 1210 the religious, especially the Cistercians, were oppressed by John (p. 163).

[3] *Ann. Mon.* iii. 33.   [4] *Ann. Mon.* iv. 54.

[5] *Historical Collections of Walter of Coventry*, ii, ed. W. Stubbs (R.S. lviii, 1873), 202.

[6] Cheney, 'Papal Interdict', p. 309 and n.b. n. 2. Papal commissions survive from 1209, 1210, and 1212, but they are few in number. He gives as examples *Coucher Book of . . . Kirkstall*, ed. W. T. Lancaster and W. P. Baildon (Thoresby Soc. viii, 1904), p. 254, no. cccli (2 Nov. 1209); *P.L.* 216, no. ccviii, cols. 374–5 (13 Dec. 1210); Westminster Ch. 2596 (17 Dec. 1210); *St. Frideswide's Cart.* ii, no. 739 (25 Apr. 1212); H.M.C., *Var. Coll.* iv. 64 (7 May 1212); and 'Cartularium Prioratus S. Johannis Evang. de Brecon', ed. R. W. Banks, *Archaeologia Cambrensis*, 4th Ser. xiv (1883), 26–7 (9 Apr. 1214; settlement). See also *Letters of Inn. III* for these years.

[7] Cheney, 'England and the Roman Curia', p. 176, estimates some 267.

committimus cognoscendas, tu prohibes delegatis, ne in earum cognitione procedant jurisdictionem nostram impediens . . .'[1] Although Professor Cheney has suggested that this might be simply a complaint against writs of prohibition, the general tone of the letter, castigating John for refusing to allow legates into his lands and for interfering in certain episcopal elections, seems to hint at a more general obstruction to the business of the delegated courts. Whatever the truth of the matter, the interruptions in the exercise of papal jurisdiction, which it has been argued resulted from the Interdict, appear to have been considerably more widespread and severe after that censure was imposed.

The extreme difficulty of proceeding with papally delegated cases after 1208 can be seen in the following two instances. In 1209 Master John of Ramsbury[2] offered three palfreys to the king to have letters to judges delegate ordering them to proceed in a case;[3] and in a letter of 1210 Innocent III said that he stopped a case until the storm in the English Church should have ceased.[4] With the exile of most of the bishops from England from 1209 until the summer of 1213, and with the hostilities and war, the taking of lawsuits to Rome must have been almost impossible, and delegation virtually stopped.[5] Subsequently John's submission to the pope in 1213[6] and the lifting of the Interdict resulted in the complete re-establishment of papal control in England by the legates.

(ii) Central

Severe interruptions were caused in the central and local administration of the judge-delegate system from 1241 to

[1] *P.L.* 214, no. clx, col. 1176: 'Regi Angliae. Ne impediat ecclesiasticam libertatem', cited by S. Painter, *Reign of King John* (Baltimore, 1949), p. 158.

[2] This is probably the same Master John of Ramsbury as the one who was chosen as an arbiter or subdelegate in 1216–18, *St. Frideswide's Cart.* ii, no. 1020, and see Emden, *Oxf. Reg.* iii. 1544.

[3] 'The Staffordshire Pipe Rolls 1189–1216', ed. R. W. Eyton, *Collections for a Hist. of Staffs.*, ed. William Salt Archaeol. Soc. ii (1881), 148, 154, 161; and cf. *C.R.R.* vi. 189, cited by Cheney, 'Papal Interdict', p. 309 n. 2.

[4] *Memorials of the Abbey of St. Mary of Fountains*, i, ed. J. R. Walbran (Surtees Soc. xlii, 1863), 172, cited by Cheney, 'Papal Interdict', p. 309.

[5] Cheney, 'Papal Interdict', p. 311; the judges had ceased to act in a case of 1213 because of the outbreak of war (*Letters of Inn. III*, no. 1024).

[6] See *Foedera* i. 111–12.

1243 by the short reign of Celestine IV and by the following period *sede vacante*. Gregory IX died on 22 August 1241. After no little difficulty and many divisions of opinion among the cardinals, Godfrey Castiglioni, a nephew of Urban III, was elected to succeed him. The election took place on 25 October 1241 in the Septizonium, where the cardinals had been enclosed by Matthew Orsini, who it is said brought the corpse of Gregory IX amongst them to hasten their choice.[1] Godfrey took the name of Celestine IV, and occupied the chair of St. Peter for seventeen days including the day of his election and the day of his death. He was already an old man at the time of his election, and he died on 10 November 1241.[2]

Although the pope exercised full jurisdiction from the day of his election,[3] Celestine's pontificate was so brief that the reins of government can hardly have been taken up before they were allowed to fall again. No legates are known to have been sent out, and no legal pronouncements were made. According to several sources Celestine was never crowned or consecrated as pope: 'Qui [Celestinus] statim tercio die morbo correptus, nec pallio nec infula vel bulla functus, xvii. die, iv scilicet Idus Novembris, diem clausit extremum . . .',[4] and 'Cœlestinus qui morte praeventus, pallium non recepit more papali, munus consecrationis non habuit, neque bullam . . .'[5] As these passages assert, no *bulla* was cast for him. Even without a *bulla*, however, the pope elect could issue letters. It required some time to engrave

---

[1] K. Hampe, 'Ein ungedruckter Bericht über das Konklave von 1241 im römischen Septizonium', *Sitzungsberichte der Heidelberger Akademie der Wissenschaften*, Philosophisch-historische klasse, iv (1913), Abhandlung 1, 3–34; and O. Joelson, 'Die Papstwahlen des 13. Jahrhunderts bis zur Einführung der Conclaveordnung Gregors X', *Historische Studien*, clxxviii (1928), esp. 27 n. 47, citing Richard of San Germano: 'Cardinales qui in Urbe ad pape electionem convenerant, per senatorem et Romanos apud Septisolium includuntur, ut ad creandum papam inviti procedant'; 'Ryccardi de Sancto Germano Notarii Chronica 1189–1243', ed. G. H. Pertz, *M.G.H.*, *Scriptorum*, xix (1866), 381. See also R. B. Brooke, *Early Franciscan Government* (Cambridge, 1959), p. 207.

[2] Mercati, 'New List of the Popes', p. 78. On Celestine IV see also *Reg. Pont. Rom.* i, ed. Potthast, p. 940.   [3] Hinschius, *Kirchenrecht*, i. 291.

[4] '*Cronica S. Petri Erfordensis Moderna*', *Monumenta Erphesfurtensia*, ed. O. Holder-Egger (M.G.H., Scriptores Rerum Germanicarum in usum Scholarum, 1899), p. 237, cited by Hampe, 'Das Konklave von 1241', p. 16 n. 40.

[5] Nicholas de Curbio, '*Vita Innocentii IV*' in *Rerum Italicarum Scriptores*, iii, pt. i, ed. L. A. Muratori (Milan, 1723), 592a, cited by Hampe, loc. cit.

the face of the die with the pope's name, and the business of the Chancery could not be neglected for longer than was absolutely necessary. Before consecration, therefore, it was usual for the pope elect to use either the wax seal which he had used previously as cardinal or a *demi-bulla* (half seal), that is the counter seal of the *bulla*.¹ Innocent III, for instance, used a *demi-bulla* in the month and a half prior to his consecration (but no originals survive), and on 3 April 1198 he issued a general rescript confirming documents sealed by this method.² But it seems unlikely that any letters were ever issued from Celestine IV's Chancery. No letters which are indisputably Celestine IV's have yet come to light.³ The system of sending out mandates and appointing judges delegate, if not discontinued completely, must certainly have been jeopardized, and between the death of Gregory IX and that of Celestine IV there was a period of not quite three months in which contacts between Rome and the provinces were at a standstill.

The interregnum, or period *sede vacante*, that followed Celestine IV's death constituted an even greater threat to the judicial system of appeal and first instance. The vacancy lasted for more than eighteen months. There had been no such long interruption since the beginning of the appeal system. At the end of November 1241 some of the English bishops met at Oxford. The purpose of the meeting was to consult on the question of the Church being left so long without a pope. The prelates exhorted Christians to pray for the election of a successor to Celestine IV. A symbolic precedent was found in the passage recounted in Acts, which says that when St. Peter was in prison, the Church prayed without ceasing for him.⁴ The college of cardinals was weak. There were probably only about a dozen cardinals to take charge of the administration of affairs, and several of these,

¹ These 'half seals' bore the effigies of SS. Peter and Paul but not the name of the new pope. See P. M. Baumgarten, *Aus Kanzlei und Kammer* (Freiburg, 1907), pp. 163–74 and *Acta pontificum*, ed. I. Battelli (Exempla scripturarum, iii, Vatican, 1933), nos. 13, 17, and 28, cited in *Handbook of Dates*, ed. C. R. Cheney (1948), p. 33.
² Poole, *Papal Chancery*, pp. 201–2; and *P.L.* 214, no. lxxxiii, col. 72.
³ *Reg. Pont. Rom.* i, ed. Potthast, p. 940 n.
⁴ F. A. Gasquet, *Henry the Third and the Church, a Study of his Ecclesiastical Policy and of the Relations between England and Rome* (1905), pp. 199–200.

on hearing of Celestine's death, and fearing another long conclave, fled from Rome.[1] With such reduced numbers it is unlikely that the machinery of the administration continued to function. In any case, important questions and major cases could not be settled without a pope. After Innocent IV's election on 25 June 1243, he began at once to deal with several major lawsuits that had been pending, including the election cases at Wells, Winchester, Canterbury, and Coventry.[2] During the first few months of his reign he seems to have been occupied with much business.

This intermission in papal judicial government accounts for the protracted length of some major cases. On 1 April 1238 Gregory IX sent a mandate to the dean of St. Paul's, London, and Masters William de Sancte Marie Ecclesia and William of Lichfield, canons, ordering them to examine and make a full report on the case between the abbot and convent of St. Nicholas, Angers, and the prior and convent of Spalding.[3] The case had opened probably well before 22 January 1235, when the pope had ordered the abbots of Crowland and Peterborough to summon the prior and convent of Spalding to appear at Rome by proctors within the next Michaelmas term, furnished with all the documents, to receive the pope's decision.[4] The case seemed near decision on 1 April 1238, when Gregory also ordered the archbishop of Rouen to examine, make a full report, and summon proctors to appear before the pope by 1 April (1239) to hear sentence.[5] But it was not until 2 January 1242 that a settlement, which took the form of a private composition between the parties, was reached. It was confirmed by Innocent IV on 4 April 1245 at Lyons,[6] when an exemplification of the composition was addressed to the abbot and convent of St. Nicholas, Angers.

---

[1] The number is uncertain but the college of cardinals was certainly weak and diminished in numbers. Hampe, 'Das Konklave von 1241', p. 20, says that two of the cardinals were held prisoner by Frederick II, one was with the senators, three or four were in Rome, and the rest were at Anagni. *Chronica Iohannis Vitodurani*, ed. F. Baethgen (M.G.H., Scriptores Rerum Germanicarum, N.S. iii, 1924), p. 5, gives nine. See also 'Das Konklave von 1241', p. 17 n. 44, citing 'Cronica S. Petri', p. 237.
[2] Powicke, *Henry III*, pp. 271–3, 361; and *Reg. Inn. IV*, nos. 311, 935, 1120, 1369–70.   [3] *Reg. Greg. IX*, no. 4241.   [4] *Reg. Greg. IX*, no. 2416.
[5] *Reg. Greg. IX*, no. 4240.   [6] *Reg. Inn. IV*, no. 1203.

It might be thought that routine business could have been dealt with during the interregnum. The vice-chancellor of Gregory IX, brother James Buoncambio, a Dominican friar, is also found in office as vice-chancellor under Innocent IV.[1] Similarly the *auditor litterarum contradictarum*, Geoffrey de Trani, who is found occupying this position on 11 July 1240 under Gregory IX,[2] appears in the same office under Innocent IV, and presumably he continued as *auditor litterarum contradictarum* until his death in March 1245.[3] But possibly these officials were reappointed by the subsequent pope, their offices having lapsed with the death of the appointer. Potthast gives two bulls which were issued by the cardinals in 1242 and 1243 *sede vacante*,[4] but there are no examples of the delegation of suits between 22 August 1241 and 25 June 1243. Nor were cases taken to Rome during this period. Certain suits which were terminated in 1241 and 1242 do not record the delegator, although they are described as of papal delegation.[5] They were probably delegated by Gregory IX, since, according to canon law, on the death of the delegator the jurisdiction of the delegate did not expire if the suit had already been contested.[6]

The frequency with which suits were ended by com-

---

[1] Bresslau, p. 250. Likewise M. William de Cathadego was vice-chancellor under Innocent IV and Alexander IV (p. 251). Bresslau notes here, too, that there are no examples of the subscription of a vice-chancellor under Celestine IV.

[2] *Reg. Greg. IX*, no. 5250.

[3] J. Teige, 'Beiträge zum päpstlichen Kanzleiwesen des XIII. und XIV. Jahrhunderts', *Mitteilungen des Instituts für Oesterreichische Geschichtsforschung*, xvii (1896), 409 and 413. On p. 77 of *Reg. or Rolls of Walter Gray*, it is recorded that on 30 Aug. 1245 Innocent IV wrote to the abbot and convent of St. Mary's, York, stating that G., cardinal deacon of St. Adrian, being dead, he has given the church of Gainford (Durham) to his nephew and chaplain, Opitio de Sancto Vitali, canon of Parma; and see *Reg. Inn. IV*, no. 1460. Master Sinibald (Fieschi) *auditor litterarum contradictarum* under Honorius III continued under Gregory IX, Bresslau, p. 250.

[4] *Reg. Pont. Rom.* i, ed. Potthast, nos. 11074–5.

[5] Combe Cart., f. 77ʳ: 1241 (date of composition); Welbeck Cart., ff. 79ᵛ, 89ʳ: 23 June or 28 Aug. 1242 (2 cases, settlement); and A. F. Leach, *Schools of Medieval England* (1915), p. 176: July 1242 (settlement). Gregory IX had delegated this case on 20 Dec. 1235 (see *Glos. Cart.* i, no. ccxxxvi).

[6] c. 19. X. I. 29 (Lucius III to the archbishop of Canterbury). See *N.L.C.*, no. 45, where R., rector of Loughton, the impetrant, complained that he had got letters from Celestine III, who had died before the citation of the parties, and therefore he had not been able to obtain justice. New letters were obtained from Innocent III.

positions is a comment on the difficulties of enforcing and
maintaining legal arrangements. The elaborate precautions
to ensure observance, which were enshrined in the summarizing and confirmatory documents, point to the same
conclusion. Oaths, penalties, and renunciations were all
carefully detailed in the final documents. It is difficult to
determine how far the renunciation of judicial rights was
effective, but evidence survives of some arrangements which
were kept for considerable periods of time, and of some
which lasted in force until circumstances changed and they
became outdated. The survival of countless final *acta* demon-
strates a sufficient machinery for preservation, and in
general suggests a reasonably efficient enforcement, at least
an enforcement which did not compare unfavourably with
other systems. This enforcement depended mainly on the
diocesans and their subordinates, who witnessed documents,
carried out sentences, confirmed arrangements, and accepted
powers of compulsion. When the papal see was vacant and
the Interdict prevented intercourse with the *Curia*, mandates
could not be sought and dispatched, and judges delegate
could not be appointed. But when the papal judicial system
was functioning, the evidence suggests that it functioned as
effectively as, if not more effectively than, other judicial
systems, in spite of the distance between Rome and the
outlying provinces, such as that of Canterbury.

CONCLUSION

THE *Curia* in the twelfth and early thirteenth centuries had expounded and supervised a law and legal system that was required by the provinces, but by the middle of the thirteenth century it was tending to be administered for the gain of the administrators. The grievances connected with the maintenance of a superstructure at Rome, which was largely paid for by appropriating diocesan revenues and by appointing curial officers to the richer benefices and dignities, make it possible to understand the growing hostility of local churchmen. The judges delegate were not the men who would be promoted to the highest offices. These and their fruits were reserved for those at the centre of the administration, who had entered the service of the *Curia* as young men, and who were obviously not at the disposal of the bishop in the administration of his diocese. The monasteries, too, saw their wealth steadily diminished and absorbed by this central administration.

The movement of the monasteries for legal exemption from the diocesan originated in the twelfth century. The papacy championed the monastic cause during the thirteenth century and gave the monasteries judicial freedom. How far the bishops had ever exercised judicial powers over the great religious houses, hearing their disputes and giving judgements, is a question belonging to the twelfth century which cannot be answered here, but it does seem that the bishop's functions were often administrative rather than judicial. Certainly it was primarily as an administrative officer that he played a part in the judge-delegate system in the thirteenth century, confirming judge-delegate arrangements and enforcing them. Other ecclesiastics, and frequently regulars, might persuade the parties to compositions or pass sentences, but it was the bishop and the diocesan officers who, in the last resort, were responsible for enforcement and maintenance. In a sense this was the most important part of the system, so that episcopal objections, when they came, threatened to undermine the whole structure of papal judicial administration, and to create havoc of a more radical kind than dislocations caused by problems of papal succession or ecclesio-political upheavals.

The diocesans' criticism of the system was formulated mainly in the shape of objections against appeals which allowed the litigants to bypass the bishop. In 1250 Bishop Robert Grosseteste presented a speech to the pope and cardinals, attacking the system of papal provisions, monastic exemptions, and the wanton and irresponsible indulgence in appeals to Rome and to Canterbury. All these, he argued, led to the enfeeblement of pastoral power, a power which belonged especially to the bishops, and nowhere was this power more threatened than in England.[1] In 1284 Archbishop Pecham singled out appeals to Rome as one of the major abuses of the Church, speaking of the subterfuge of appeals which undermined the pastor's power of correcting clergy and people.[2] The decay of the papal judicial system resulted from the expansion and cost of the bureaucracy, and even more basically from the bishops' loss of confidence, but appellate government had been a powerful means of binding both the provinces to Rome and Rome to the provinces.

[1] Powicke, *Henry III*, pp. 283-4, pd. Edward Brown, *Appendix ad Fasciculum rerum Expetendarum et Fugiendarum*, ii (1690), 250-7.

[2] See *Registrum Epistolarum Fratris Johannis Peckham*, ii, ed. C. T. Martin (R.S. lxxvii, 1884), no. dxxx, pp. 694-7, a letter of 1284 comparing the abuses in the Church to the seven vials of the Apocalypse; the third abuse concerns appeals and is mentioned on pp. 695-6. The archbishop held, however, a contrary view to his diocesans on the place of his own Court of Canterbury, see Churchill, *Canterbury Administration*, i. 427.

APPENDICES

ABBREVIATIONS USED IN THE APPENDICES AND INDEX

abb.	abbot	nr.	near
abp.	archbishop	off.	official
archd.	archdeacon	pen.	penitentiary
bp.	bishop	pr.	prior
c.	chapter	preb.	prebendary
can.	canon	prec.	precentor
card.	cardinal	r.	rector
cath.	cathedral	relig. hos.	religious houses
ch.	church	sacr.	sacrist
chanc.	chancellor	subd.	subdean
chapl.	chaplain	subdeac.	subdeacon
d.	dean	subpr.	subprior
d. and c.	dean and chapter	succ.	succentor
deac.	deacon	t.	tempore
dioc.	diocese	treas.	treasurer
hosp.	hospital	unid.	unidentified
knt.	knight	v.	vicar
m.	master	*v.*	versus

APPENDIX A. LISTS

I. AUDITORS APPOINTED BY GREGORY IX AND INNOCENT IV TO HEAR ENGLISH LAWSUITS

Auditor	Parties	Suit	Date of appointment	Reference
1. M. Bernard, d. of Patrai (Greece), papal chapl.	Walter, archd. of Norfolk, and papal chapl. v. Wymondham (Norf.)	Visitation of Wymondham and Happisburgh chs. (Norf.)	before 10 June 1249	*Reg. Inn. IV,* no. 4645
2. Giles, card. deac. of SS. Cosmas and Damian (elected abp. of Toledo)	John de Vercellis, can. of Lincoln v. archd. of Buckingham	Buckingham ch.	before 30 Jan. 1236	*Reg. Greg. IX,* no. 2948
3. ,, ,, ,,	Master R., r. of Cliffe-at-Hoo (Kent) v. offs. of archd. of Canterbury	Archidiaconal rights in Cliffe-at-Hoo ch.	before 19 Dec. 1236	*Reg. Greg. IX,* no. 3406
4. ,, ,, ,,	Rochester v. abp. of Canterbury	Election of bp. of Rochester	before 20 Mar. 1238	*Reg. Greg. IX,* no. 4197
5. J., papal chapl. and subdeac.	Master R., r. of Somerton v. Master P., clerk of Brad' (Cant. dioc.)	Tetbury ch. (Glos.)	before 16 Jan. 1230	*Reg. Greg. IX,* no. 388
6. J. Spata, papal chapl. and subdeac.	Butley (Suff.) v. Campsey Ash (Suff.)	Tithes of ch. and mill at Dilham (Norf.)	before 28 June 1230	*Reg. Greg. IX,* no. 475

7. M. John Astensis, papal chapl. and subdeac.	Marmoutier (dioc. Tours, France) v. bp. of Lincoln	Bp.'s alleged excommunication of Newport Pagnell priory (Bucks.)	before 2 June 1249	*Reg. Inn. IV*, no. 4601
8. „ „ „	Cluny v. pr. of Daventry (Northants.)	Daventry's obedience to La Charité	before 27 May 1250	Bodleian, Northants. Ch. 181
9. John de Sancto Germano, papal subdeac. and chapl. of Gregory IX	John de Camezano, papal chapl. and *auditor contradictarum nostrarum* v. St. Augustine's, Canterbury	Lenham ch. (Kent)	before May 1253	*Reg. Inn. IV*, no. 6990
10. John of Toledo, card. priest of St. Laurence in Lucina	Godfrey de Toffetes, clerk of bp. of Winchester v. Anthony, can. of Piacenza	Alresford ch. (Hants)	before 30 Jan. 1247	*Reg. Inn. IV*, no. 2537
11. „ „ „	Philip de Lucy, r. of Overton v. Matthew de Alperino, papal chapl.	Overton ch. (Hants)	before 26 Mar. 1247	*Reg. Inn. IV*, no. 2481
12. „ „ „	Jacob 'Stephani Simeonis', chapl. of J., card. deac. of St. Nicholas in Carcere Tulliano v. M. John of Clanfield	'Bergwes' ch. (Bath dioc.)	before 13 June 1248	*Glastombury Cart.* (xxviii), p. (xii)
13. „ „ „	Cluny v. pr. of Daventry (Northants.)	Daventry's obedience to La Charité	before 27 May 1250	Bodleian, Northants. Ch. 181
14. „ „ „	M. Matthew de Alperino v. M. Alberic de Vitriaco	Freshwater ch. (I. of W.)	before 16 Sept. 1250	*Reg. Inn. IV*, no. 4833
15. „ „ „	M. Reginald, r. of Great Paxton v. Geoffrey, warden, and the ministers of the altar of St. Hugh in Lincoln cath.	Twenty marks yearly from Great Paxton ch. (Hunts.)	before 30 July 1252	*Reg. Antiq. Linc.* ii, no. 386

Auditor	Parties	Suit	Date of appointment	Reference
16. John Orsini, card. deac. of St. Nicholas in Carcere Tulliano (later Pope Nicholas III)	Godfrey de Toffetes, clerk of bp. of Winchester v. Anthony, can. of Piacenza	Alresford ch. (Hants)	before 30 Jan. 1247	*Reg. Inn. IV,* no. 2537
17. ” ”	Walter, archd. of Norfolk and papal chapl. v. Wymondham (Norf.)	Visitation of Wymondham and Happisburgh chs. (Norf.)	before 10 June 1249	*Reg. Inn. IV,* no. 4645
18. ” ”	Bp. of Worcester v. William de Beauchamp, sheriff of Worcester, and several of his household	Sentences of excommunication issued by the bp.	before 4 Jan. 1251	*Reg. Inn. IV,* no. 5194
19. Octavian, card. deac. of St. Mary in Via Lata (procurator of Bologna)	John de Vercellis v. Matthew, archd. of Buckingham and preb. of Sutton	Chs. of SS. Peter and Paul, Buckingham, and St. Margaret in Pottergate, Lincoln	before 19 Sept. 1245	*Reg. Inn. IV,* nos. 1517–18
20. Otto, card. bp. of Porto (formerly legate in England)	Evesham v. bp. of Worcester	Vale of Evesham chs. and others	before 11 Dec. 1248	*Reg. Inn. IV,* no. 4378
21. Peter de Barro, card. priest of St. Marcellus (later card. bp. of Sabina)	M. Angelo, can. of St. Laurence in Damaso, Rome v. bp. of Winchester	Collation to a church by the bp.	before 14 Oct. 1247	*Reg. Inn. IV,* no. 3335
22. Peter de Collemedio, card. bp. of Albano	Abp. of Canterbury v. d. and c. of St. Paul's, and St. Bartholomew's and Holy Trinity, Aldgate	Visitation, correction, and exemption	before 22 Apr. 1252	*Reg. Inn. IV,* no. 5670
23. Rainald, card. bp. of Ostia	M. Simon the Norman, papal subdeac. and chapl. v. R. de Blonville, archd. of Norfolk	Archdeaconry of Norfolk	before 4 Mar. 1239	*Reg. Greg. IX,* no. 4738

24. ,, ,,	Abp. of Canterbury v. chapter	Various questions	before 6 Mar. 1241	*Reg. Greg. IX,* no. 5387
25. Richard de Annibaldis, card. deac. of St. Angelo	Archd. of Buckingham v. John de Vercellis	Buckingham ch.	before 26 Mar. 1244	*Reg. Inn. IV,* no. 568
26. ,, ,, (accepted as arbiter)	Peter of Aigueblanche, bp. of Hereford v. d. and c. of Hereford	Jurisdiction	1252	*Hereford Charters,* pp. 93–4
27. Sinibald, card. priest of St. Laurence in Lucina	Master R., r. of Cliffe-at-Hoo (Kent) v. offs. of archd. of Canterbury	Archidiaconal rights in Cliffe-at-Hoo ch.	before 5 Dec. 1234	*Reg. Greg. IX,* no. 2375
28. Stephen de Normandis, card. priest of St. Mary in Trastevere (archpriest of St. Peter's)	Rochester v. abp. of Canterbury	Election of bp. of Rochester	before 29 July 1236	*Reg. Greg. IX,* no. 3261
29. ,, ,,	Walter (archd. of Norfolk) v. M. Simon the Norman, papal chapl.	Archdeaconry of Norfolk	before 18 June 1244	*Reg. Inn. IV,* no. 746
30. Thomas, card. priest of St. Sabina (abp. of Naples)	John de Vercellis, papal subdeac. and preb. of Walton in Lincoln cath. v. archd. of Buckingham	Buckingham ch.	before 20 Apr. 1239	*Reg. Greg. IX,* nos. 4836–9
31. ,, ,,	M. Robert of Gloucester v. William de Cerneia	Collation to Eynsford ch. (Kent)	before 9 May 1239	*Reg. Greg. IX,* nos. 4882–4
32. M. Vernacius, papal chapl.	Binham (Norf.) v. Herigettus, son of Perinus of Malachana	Westley ch. Waterless (Cambs.)	before 19 June 1251	*Binham Cart.,* f. 141r–v
33. William Fieschi, card. deac. of St. Eustace	Marmoutier (dioc. Tours, France) v. bp. of Lincoln	Bp.'s alleged excommunication of Newport Pagnell priory (Bucks.)	before 2 June 1249	*Reg. Inn. IV,* no. 4601

II. A LIST OF SOME OF THE MEETING-PLACES OF THE COURTS

Place	Judges	Parties	Date of settlement unless otherwise stated	Reference
1. Barnwell ch. (Cambs.)	Bp. and archd. of Ely	Pr. of Eye v. parson of Dennington (both Suff.)	1202–3	Eye Cart., f. 35ʳ⁻ᵛ
2. Barnwell (Cambs.)	Prs. of Barnwell, Anglesey (Cambs.), and d. of Cambridge	Walden v. r. of Pleshey (both Essex)	1223	Walden Cart., ff. 43ᵛ⁻4ʳ
3. Barnwell priory ch. (Cambs.)	Pr. of Barnwell	Leeds v. r. of Harbledown (both Kent)	1250	Leeds Cart., f. 8ᵛ
4. Boxley parish ch. (Kent)	Abb., pr. of Boxley, and m. Thomas of Maidstone	R. of Cliffe-at-Hoo (Kent) v. Christ Church, Canterbury	1229	Canterbury, Cartae Antiquae, C 280
5. Breedon ch. (Leics.)	Prs. of Leicester, Belvoir (Lincs.), and Breedon (Leics.)	Owston (Leics.) v. Stamford, St. Michael's (Northants.)	1236/7	Bodleian MS. Dodsworth 76, f. 1
6. Bury St. Edmunds (Suff.)	Prs. of Bury St. Edmunds, Ixworth, and Great Bricett (all Suff.)	Eye v. r. of Tattingstone and Bures (all Suff.)	1213	Eye Cart., ff. 42ᵛ⁻3ʳ
7. Bury St. Edmunds, chapel of St. Denis (Suff.)	Abb., pr. of Bury St. Edmunds, and pr. of Great Bricett (Suff.)	Eye (Suff.) v. archd. of Worcester	1218	Ibid., ff. 35ᵛ⁻6ʳ
8. Bury St. Edmunds (Suff.)	Abb. and pr. of Bury St. Edmunds	Binham v. r. of Bacton (both Norf.)	1222	Binham Cart., f. 185ʳ
9. Cambridge	Ds. of Cambridge, Wilbraham, and Chesterton (all Cambs.)	R. of Radwinter (Essex) v. Holy Trinity, Aldgate	1233	P.R.O. E 40/13828 (c); E 40/14302

10. Cambridge, All Saints ch. nr. the hosp.	D. of Cambridge	R. of Charwelton (Northants.) v. Biddlesden (Bucks.)	1253	B.M. Harley Ch. 84 F 45
11. Cambridge, St. Mary's ch.	Prec. of Barnwell (Cambs.), chanc. and d. of Cambridge	Anglesey (Cambs.) v. Newton Longville (Bucks.)	1227	N.L.C., no. 86
12. „	Prec. of Barnwell (Cambs.) and d. of Cambridge	St. Neots (Hunts.) v. r. of Brampton (Northants.)	1232	St. Neots Cart., f. 112r-v
13. „	Prec. of Barnwell (Cambs.) and d. of Cambridge	St. Neots (Hunts.) v. r. of Barton Bendish (Norf.)	1232	St. Neots Cart., f. 111v
14. „	„	St. Neots (Hunts.) v. parson of Barnwell (Northants.)	1232	St. Neots Cart., ff. 111r–12r
15. Canterbury, Christ Church	Pr. of St. Gregory's, Canterbury, archd. and pen. of Canterbury	Christ Church, Canterbury v. Guines (dioc. Thérouanne, W. Flanders)	1218	Canterbury, Cartae Antiquae, F 31
16. „	Abb. of Faversham (Kent), prs. of St. Gregory's, Canterbury, and St. Augustine's, Canterbury	Dover v. Langdon (both Kent)	1219	Langdon Cart., ff. 102r–3r
17. „	Prs. of St. Augustine's Canterbury, Monks Horton, and Faversham (all Kent)	Christ Church, Canterbury v. parson of Eythorne (Kent)	1220	Canterbury, Cartae Antiquae, L 351
18. „	„	Christ Church, Canterbury v. Dunes in Sheppey (dioc. Thérouanne, W. Flanders)	1220	Canterbury, MS. Scrapbook A, p. 13, Ch. 25
19. Canterbury	Prs. of St. Augustine's, Canterbury, St. Gregory's, Canterbury, and Faversham (Kent)	Christ Church, Canterbury v. William, son of Conan of Holbeach (Lincs.)	1222	Canterbury, Cartae Antiquae, H 120

Place	Judges	Parties	Date of settlement unless otherwise stated	Reference
20. Canterbury, Christ Church	Abb. of Langdon (Kent) and pr. of St. Gregory's, Canterbury	Dover v. r. of Brookland (both Kent)	1224/5	Dover Cart., f. 226ᵛ
21. " "	Pr. of St. Gregory's, Canterbury, off. and pen. of Canterbury	Christ Church, Canterbury v. William of Cheriton, knt.	1230	Canterbury, Cartae Antiquae, F 8
22. " "	Abbs. of Langdon, St. Radegund's, and pr. of Monks Horton (all Kent)	R. of Meopham (Kent) v. Christ Church, Canterbury	1234	Canterbury, Cartae Antiquae, M 123
23. " "	Abb. of St. Augustine's, Canterbury, pr. of St. Gregory's, Canterbury, and d. of Canterbury	Faversham (Kent) v. Holy Trinity, Aldgate	1234	P.R.O. E 40/13828(f)
24. Carlton cum Willingham (Cambs.)	Pr. of Merton (Surr.) and co-judges (unspecified)	Lewes (Suss.) v. r. of Weston Colville (Cambs.)	1236	P.R.O. E 40/9649, cal. *Lewes Cart. Camb. Portion*, ed. Bullock and Palmer, nos. 23, 73
25. Chertsey (Surr.)	Abb., pr. of Chertsey, and pr. of Reading (Berks.)	Westminster v. r. of St. James, London	1231	Westminster Domesday, f. 476ᵛ
26. Chichester, St. Faith's ch.	Bp., prec., and archd. of Chichester	St. Augustine's, Canterbury v. r. of Iwade (Kent)	1202	Canterbury, Cartae Antiquae, C 1270 and pd. *Reg. of St. Augustine's Canterbury*, p. 546
27. Chichester cath.	Prs. of Boxgrove, Arundel, and Tortington (all Suss.)	Bayham (Suss.) v. v. of West Greenwich (Kent)	1237	Bayham Cart., ff. 60ᵛ-61ʳ

28. Christchurch (alias Twynham) ch. (Hants)	Pr. of Christchurch	Beaulieu (Hants) v. St. Michael's Mount (Cornw.)	1238	Beaulieu Cart., ff. 132r-4r
29. Cirencester abbey ch. (Glos.)	Pr. of Cirencester (ordainer)	Malmesbury v. r. of Somerford (both Wilts.)	1251	*Malmesbury Reg.* ii. 218
30. Colchester, St. Botolph's ch. (Essex)	Prs. of Thoby and Tiptree (both Essex)	Colchester, St. John's v. r. of Easton (Suff.)	1240	P.R.O. E 42/384
31. Christian Malford (Wilts.)	Pr. of Bradenstoke (Wilts.), archd. of Bath, and d. of Cirencester (Glos.)	R. of Crudwell v. Malmesbury (both Wilts.)	1231	*Malmesbury Reg.* i. 386, and ii. 60
32. Dersingham (Norf.)	Pr. of Rudham and d. of Walsingham (both Norf.)	Binham v. Shouldham (both Norf.)	1232	Binham Cart., ff. 146v-7r
33. Dover, St. Peter's ch. (Kent)	Prs. of Dover and Folkestone (both Kent)	Bayham v. v. of Hellingly (both Sussex)	1240	Bayham Cart., f. 60v
34. Dunstable (Beds.)	Prs. of Dunstable, Caldwell, and prec. of Dunstable (both Beds.)	Bec (dioc. Rouen, France) v. William Estormy and Elias, chapl.	1234	Windsor, Arundel White Book, p. 174
35. Dunstable priory ch. (Beds.)	"	Bec (dioc. Rouen, France) v. St. Frideswide's, Oxford	1234	Windsor Ch. xi G 75 and pd. *St. Frideswide's Cart.* ii, no. 1135
36. "	"	Bec (dioc. Rouen, France) v. Tewkesbury (Glos.)	1234	Canterbury, Cartae Antiquae, L 381
37. "	Pr. and subpr. of Dunstable	St. Julian's hosp., St. Albans (Herts.) v. Lanthony (Glos.)	1239	Lanthony Cart. A 1, X, no. cviii
38. "	Pr. of Dunstable	Bec (dioc. Rouen, France) v. rs. of Withersfield and Dalham (both Suff.)	1241	Windsor Chs. xi G 14-16 and 37

Place	Judges	Parties	Date of settlement unless otherwise stated	Reference
39. Dunstable, St. Peter's ch. (Beds.)	Off. of archd. of Bedford	Dunstable v. r. of Cublington (Bucks.)	1239	Dunstable Cart., f. 55ᵛ, cal. *Dunstable Cart.*, no. 67
40. Exeter cath.	Not named	Prec. of Salisbury v. a can., the bp. and c. of Exeter	1236	Exeter Cart., p. 79
41. Faversham abbey ch. (Kent)	Sacr. of Faversham	Dover (Kent) v. chapl. of St. Mary's chapel and r. of St. John's chapel, Dover	1246	Dover Cart., f. 51ʳ
42. ,, ,,	,, ,,	Dover (Kent) v. chapl. of St. James's chapel, Dover	1246	Dover Cart., f. 50ᵛ
43. Flamstead (Herts.)	Abb. of Warden, pr. of Dunstable (both Beds.), and d. of Berkhamsted (Herts.)	R. of Covenham (Lincs.), and d. of Salisbury v. Chertsey (Surr.)	1218	*Chertsey Cart.*, no. 91
44. ,, ,,	Prs. of Dunstable (Beds.), St. Albans (Herts.), and archd. of St. Albans	St. Frideswide's, Oxford v. r. of Shipton-on-Cherwell (Oxon.)	1227	*St. Frideswide's Cart.* ii, no. 1021
45. Flitton (Beds.)	Prs. of Beadlow, Chicksands, and d. of Weston (all Beds.)	Dunstable (Beds.) v. Merton (Surr.), and r. of chapel of Whipsnade (Beds.)	1231 (mandate)	Dunstable Cart., f. 53ʳ, cal. *Dunstable Cart.*, no. 501
46. Flitwick ch. (Beds.)	Abb., pr. of Warden, and pr. of Beadlow (both Beds.)	Dunstable (Beds.) v. clerk of Bradbourne (Derbys.)	1223	Dunstable Cart., f. 77ʳ, cal. *Dunstable Cart.*, no. 937
47. Fornham All Saints ch. (Suff.)	Abb. and pr. of Bury St. Edmunds (Suff.)	Eye v. parson and v. of Stradbroke (both Suff.)	1221	Eye Cart., ff. 36ᵛ-7ᵛ
48. Frating (Essex)	Abbs. of Colchester and St. Osyth's (both Essex)	Binham v. r. of Bacton (both Norf.)	1218	Binham Cart., f. 185ʳ-ᵛ

49. Fressingfield, St. Peter's ch. (Suff.)	Prs. of Rumburgh, Mendham, and d. of Hoxne (all Suff.)	R. of Occold v. Eye (both Suff.)	1221	Eye Cart., f. 36^r
50. Gloucester, St. Mary's ch. in the south	Pr. of St. Oswald's, Gloucester, and ds. of Dymock (Glos.) and Gloucester	Lanthony (Glos.) v. r. of Alvescot (Oxon.)	1231	Lanthony Cart. A I, III, no. lv
51. Gloucester, St. Mary's ch. by the abbey gate	Subpr. of St. Oswald's, Gloucester, and d. of Gloucester	Lanthony (Glos.) v. St. Julian's hosp., St. Albans (Herts.)	1238	Lanthony Cart. A I, X, no. lxxiiii
52. Grimsby (Lincs.)	Abb. of Humberston, prs. of Thornton and Grimsby (all Lincs.)	Newsham v. Nun Cotham (both Lincs.)	1228	B.M. Harley Ch. 44 E 20
53. Hereford, St. Ethelbert's ch.	Bp., d., and prec. of Hereford	Bp. of Llandaff (Glam.) v. Gloucester	1204	*Glos. Cart.* ii, nos. dxix, dxx
54. Hereford cath.	Abbs. of Abbey Dore (Heref.), Flaxley (Glos.), and d. of Hereford	Lanthony (Glos.) v. chapl. of Chirton (Wilts.)	1214	Lanthony Cart. A I, VIII, no. lxxx
55. Hereford	D. and chanc. of Hereford	R. of Alvington v. Lanthony (both Glos.)	1243/4	Lanthony Cart. A I, IIII, no. cviii
56. Huntingdon, St. Mary's ch.	Pr., archd., and d. of Huntingdon	Lewes (Suss.) v. r. of Sculthorpe (Norf.)	1219 and 1225	P.R.O. E 40/14067 and Lewes Cart., ff. 260^v-r^r, cal. *N.P.*, nos. 112, 138
57. Hyde abbey ch. (Hants)	Pr. of Hyde, archd. of Surrey and d. of Winchester	R. of Ringwood (Hants) v. Christchurch (or Twynham, Hants)	1239	Christchurch (Twynham) Cart., f. 62^v
58. Ipswich, St. Matthew's ch. (Suff.)	Prs. of Holy Trinity, St. Peter's, Ipswich, and d. of Ipswich	Eye v. rs. of St. Martin's, Dunwich (both Suff.)	1226	Eye Cart., ff. 34^v-5^r

Place	Judges	Parties	Date of settlement unless otherwise stated	Reference
59. King's Lynn, St. Margaret's ch. (Norf.)	Abb. of Dereham and pr. of Castle Acre (both Norf.)	Waltham (Essex) v. Kirkstead (Lincs.)	1237/8	Waltham Cart., f. 142ᵛ, and Kirkstead Cart., f. 189ʳ
60. Lincoln chapter	Chanc. and two cans. of Lincoln	Bardney v. Stixwould (both Lincs.)	1208	Bardney Cart., ff. 240ʳ-1ʳ
61. ,, ,,	,,	Bardney (Lincs.) v. archd. of Cleveland (Yorks. N.R.)	1209	Bardney Cart., f. 92ʳ⁻ᵛ
62. Lincoln cath.	M. William de Novo Castro and Peter de Mixebyrii	Bolton v. r. of Ilkley (both Yorks. W.R.)	1215/16	Bodleian MS. Dodsworth 76, f. 44
63. Lincoln chapter	D., m. of the schools, and a can. of Lincoln	Treas. of York v. Eye (Suff.)	[1224]	Eye Cart., ff. 39ᵛ-40ʳ
64. Lincoln	Prec., subd., and m. of the schools of Lincoln	Bridlington (Yorks. E.R.) v. Westminster	1238	Westminster Domesday, f. 470ʳ
65. Lincoln cath.	D., m. William de Novo Castro, and a can. of Lincoln	Bullington (Lincs.) v. Garendon (Leics.)	1250/1 (intermediate acta)	P.R.O. E 135/6/13
66. ,, ,,	D., prec., and chanc. of Lincoln	Bullington (Lincs.) v. Garendon (Leics.)	1251	B.M. Harley Ch. 53 A 23
67. Lincoln	Can. of Lincoln	Bardney v. r. of Willoughby (both Lincs.)	c. 1251	Bardney Cart., ff. 105ʳ-6ʳ
68. Llandaff cath. (Glam.)	Pr. of Carmarthen (Carmarth.)	Clifford v. Abbey Dore (both Heref.)	c. 1252 (intermediate acta)	P.R.O. E 135/24/4
69. London	D. of Arches	R. of Stewkley v. Newton Longville (both Bucks.)	1238	N.L.C., no. 54

70. London, St. Magnus the martyr's ch.	Pr. of Tandridge and d. of Southwark (both Surr.)	Westminster *v.* Godstow (Oxon.)	1254	Westminster Domesday, f. 379^v
71. London, St. Paul's cath.	D. and prec. of London	St. Evroult (dioc. Lisieux, France) *v.* R., knt, of Coventry dioc.	[1206] (intermediate *acta*)	B.M. Wolley Ch. v 27
72. „	D. of London, archd. of Middlesex, and m. R. de Arcubus	Bp. of Norwich *v.* prs. of Binham and Wymondham (all Norf.)	1228	Binham Cart., ff. 47^v-8^r
73. „	Prs. of Waltham (Essex) and Westminster	St. Augustine's, Canterbury *v. v.* of Chislet (both Kent)	1233	St. Augustine's Cart., f. 75^r
74. „	Can. of St. Davids and a can. of St. Angelus, Ferentino (staying in England)	Master B., can. of Troyes (France) and r. of Painswick (Glos.) *v.* archd. of Worcester, and Lanthony (Glos.)	1235	Lanthony Cart. A 1, XVI, no. xvi
75. „	Archd. and chanc. of London	St. Valéry (dioc. Amiens, France) *v.* r. of Hinton Waldrist (Berks.)	1240	New College, Oxford, Takeley Ch. 229
76. Luton, St. Mary's ch. (Beds.)	Abb. of Woburn (Beds.), prs. of St. Albans (Herts.) and Dunstable (Beds.)	R. of Launton (Oxon.) *v. v.* of Launton	1214	Westminster Ch. 15684
77. Malmesbury, St. Paul's ch. (Wilts.)	Prs. of Monkton Farleigh (Wilts.), Malmesbury, and d. of Malmesbury	Bradenstoke (Wilts.) *v. v.* of Canford (Dors.)	1227	Bradenstoke Cart., ff. 112^v-13^r
78. Northampton, All Saints ch.	Prs. of St. John's, St. James's, and d. of Northampton	St. Frideswide's, Oxford *v.* r. of Souldern (Oxon.)	1236/7	*St. Frideswide's Cart.* ii, no. 980

Place	Judges	Parties	Date of settlement unless otherwise stated	Reference
79. Northampton, All Saints ch.	Pr. of Canons Ashby (Northants.) and m. of the hosp. of St. John, Northampton	St. Andrew's, Northampton *v.* Thomas de Esseby, clerk	1246	Northampton, St. Andrew's Cart. (A), ff. 208ʳ-9ʳ
80. Northampton, St. Peter's ch. by the castle	Prs. of St. John's, St. James's, and d. of Northampton	St. Frideswide's, Oxford *v.* r. of Souldern (Oxon.)	1233	*St. Frideswide's Cart.* ii, no. 978
81. „ „ „	„ „	St. Frideswide's, Oxford *v.* r. of Beckley (Oxon.)	1233/4	*St. Frideswide's Cart.* ii, no. 732
82. Northampton, St. Peter's ch.	Archd. of Northampton (ordainer)	St. Andrew's, Northampton *v.* r. of Yardley Gobion (Northants.)	1233	Northampton, St. Andrew's Cart. (A), f. 94ʳ⁻ᵛ
83. „ „	Pr. of St. James's, Northampton	Parson of Wytham (Berks.) *v.* Godstow (Oxon.)	1244/5	*Godstow Reg.* i, no. [31]
84. Norwich	Pr. of Norwich, m. Walter of Suffield and Thomas of Fakenham (arbiters)	Eye (Suff.) *v.* Horsham St. Faith (Norf.)	1240	Eye Cart., ff. 45ᵛ-6ʳ
85. Norwich cath.	Abb. and pr. of Langley (Norf.)	Eye *v.* parson, *v.*, and H., knt., of Rickinghall (both Suff.)	1220	Ibid., ff. 46ᵛ-7ᵛ
86. Nottingham, St. Mary's ch.	Subpr. of Lenton (Notts.)	Biddlesden (Bucks.) *v.* v. of Thornborough (Bucks.) and d. of Buckingham, and Luffield (Northants.)	1251/2 (intermediate *acta*)	Bodleian MS. Chs. Bucks. a 4, Ch. 91, and B.M. Harley Ch. 84 F 36
87. Oxford, All Saints ch.	D. of Oxford and m. Elias de Daneis	R. of Yatton (Som.) *v.* Malmesbury (Wilts.)	1230	*Malmesbury Reg.* ii. 30, 59

88. Oxford, St. Frideswide's priory ch.	Prs. of St. Albans (Herts.), Dunstable (Beds.), and chanc. of Oxford	Warden (Beds.) v. r. of Great Paxton (Hunts.)	c. 1233	*Reg. Antiq. Linc.* iii, no. 829
89. Oxford, St. Mary's ch.	Pr. of Oseney (Oxon.) and d. of Oxford	Abingdon (Berks.) v. r. of Chesterton (Warw.)	1210	Abingdon Cart., f. 144v
90. „	Pr. of Eynsham (Oxon.), chanc. and d. of Oxford	Lanthony v. r. of Painswick (both Glos.)	1229	Lanthony Cart. A 1, III, no. liv
91. „	Roger de Cantilupe and m. Philip de Hanneya	St. Frideswide's, Oxford v. certain burgesses of Oxford	1221 (mandate)	*St. Frideswide's Cart.* ii, no. 721
92. „	Chapls. of St. Peter's in the East, and of St. John the Baptist's, Oxford	Burton (Staffs.) v. Gresley (Derbys.)	early 13th cent.	*Burton Chs.* 58
93. „	Master J. de Poppleton, R. de Thetford, and S. de Dyham	R. of Charwelton (Northants.) v. Biddlesden (Bucks.)	c. 1230 (intermediate *acta*)	B.M. Harley Ch. 84 F 43
94. „	Pr. of St. Oswald's, Gloucester, archd. and d. of Gloucester	Notley v. Newton Longville (both Bucks.)	1235	*N.L.C.*, no. 62
95. „	Archd. and d. of Oxford	Abb. of Chertsey (Surr.) v. pr. of Newstead (Notts.)	1237	*Chertsey Cart.*, no. 92
96. „	D. and chanc. of Oxford	St. Martin's, London v. Walden (Essex)	1237	Walden Cart., f. 43r-v
97. Oxford, St. Peter's ch. in the east	M. Ralph of Sempringham	R. of Withcote v. r. of Pickwell (both Leics.)	1241	B.M. Cotton MS. Nero C iii, f. 199r
98. Peterborough, St. Thomas's chapel (Northants.)	Abb., pr. of Thorney (Cambs.), and pr. of Peterborough	Dereham (Norf.) v. Philip de Burnham, knt.	1210	West Dereham Cart., ff. 260v-1r

Place	Judges	Parties	Date of settlement unless otherwise stated	Reference
99. Peterborough (Northants.)	Pr. of Peterborough	Thorney (Cambs.) v. r. of Thurleigh (Beds.)	1251	Thorney Cart. ii, ff. 323ʳ, 325ʳ
100. Pinner ch. (Middx.)	D. of Middlesex and Baldric chapl.	Bec (dioc. Rouen, France) v. r. of Great Wratting (Suff.), and Dover (Kent)	1245 (intermediate acta)	Windsor Ch. xi G 27
101. Reading (Berks.)	D., prec., and chanc. of Salisbury	R. of Brightwalton (Berks.) v. Battle (Suss.)	1224	P.R.O. E 327/51
102. St. Albans abbey ch. (Herts.)	Pr., archd. of St. Albans, and pr. of Redbourn (both Herts.)	Dunstable (Beds.) v. r. of Bradbourne (Derbys.)	1214	Dunstable Cart., f. 45ʳ, cal. *Dunstable Cart.*, no. 391 (where it is wrongly dated 1215)
103. St. Albans, St. Andrew's chapel (Herts.)	Prs. of Dunstable (Beds.), St. Albans, and archd. of St. Albans	St. Frideswide's, Oxford v. r. of Noke (Oxon.)	1229	*St. Frideswide's Cart.* ii, no. 976
104. St. Albans abbey ch. (Herts.)	Pr. of St. Albans and d. of Hertford	Westminster v. v. of Pershore and the chapl. of Wick nr. Pershore (both Worcs.)	1234	Westminster Domesday, f. 576ʳ
105. ,, ,,	Archd. of St. Albans	Waltham (Essex) v. Chepstow (Mon.)	1251	B.M. Egerton Ch. 409
106. ,, ,,	Pr., archd., and prec. of St. Albans	R. of Great Paxton (Hunts.) v. warden and ministers of St. Hugh's altar in Lincoln cath.	1253	*Reg. Antiq. Linc.* ii, no. 386
107. St. Neots (Hunts.)	Pr. of Bushmead (Beds.)	St. Neots v. r. of Wimbish (Essex)	1247	St. Neots Cart., ff. 130ᵛ-rᵛ

108. Salisbury cath.	Pr. of Irychurch, d. of Wilton (both Wilts.), and succ. of Salisbury	R. of East Hendred (Berks.) v. Bec (dioc. Rouen, France)	1230	Windsor Ch. xv. 41. 71
109. " "	"	R. of East Hendred v. Abingdon (both Berks.)	1231	Abingdon Cart., f. 53r
110. Stamford, St. Mary's ch. at the bridge (Lincs.)	Ds. of Stamford (Lincs.), Rutland, and Carlby (Lincs.)	Stamford, St. Michael's v. William Erl of North Luffenham (Rutland)	1237	P.R.O. E 326/2268
111. Steppingley ch. (Beds.)	Abb., pr. of Warden, and pr. of Beadlow (both Beds.)	Pr. of Dunstable (Beds.) v. R. Pudifet of Berkhamsted (Herts.)	1222	Dunstable Cart., f. 46v, cal. *Dunstable Cart.*, no. 405
112. Wallingford priory ch. (Berks.)	Pr. of Barnwell (Cambs.) and chanc. of Cambridge	Wallingford v. Henry of Earley and his chapl. of Earley (Berks.)	1236	Bodleian MS. Chs. Berks. a 1, Ch. 17
X 113. Ware ch. (Herts.)	Pr. of Waltham (Essex) and colleagues (unspecified)	Lewes v. r. of Ovingdean (both Suss.)	1236	P.R.O. E 40/14227
114. Wells	Abb. of Muchelney, pr. and prec. of Taunton (both Som.)	R. of 'Cumton'' v. St. Valéry (dioc. Amiens, France), and r. of Hinton Waldrist (Berks.)	1220	New College, Oxford, Takeley Ch. 139
115. Wells cath.	Two cans. of Wells	D. and c. of Exeter v. Roger d'Oilly, knt.	1247	Exeter Ch. 640
116. Westleton (Suff.)	Abb. of Leiston, pr. of Blythburgh, and pr. of Wangford (all Suff.)	Eye (Suff.) v. clerk of 'Wltorp'' (? Woolsthorpe, Lincs.)	1218	Eye Cart., ff. 43r-4r
117. Westminster	Bp. of Lincoln, abbs. of St. Albans (Herts.) and Stratford (Essex)	Westminster v. Godstow (Oxon.)	1197	Westminster Domesday, f. 378v, and *Godstow Reg.* i, no. [308]

Place	Judges	Parties	Date of settlement unless otherwise stated	Reference
118. Westminster	Abp. and archd. of Canterbury	St. Frideswide's, Oxford v. Fulk, knt, and others	1224	Bodleian MS. Chs. Oxon. a 10, Ch. 79
119. Wilton, St. Nicholas's ch. (Wilts.)	D. and m. of the schools of St. Edward, Shaftesbury (Wilts.)	R. of 'Cumton' (? Compton, Berks.) v. Reading (Berks.)	1234	Reading Cart., ff. 114v–15r
120. Winchester cath.	Abb. and pr. of Waverley (Surr.), pr. of Sherborne (Dorset)	Reading (Berks.) v. Préaux (dioc. Lisieux, France) and G., clerk of Newbury (Berks.)	1216–27 (mandate)	Reading Cart., f. 112v
121. Worcester cath.	Bp. and prec. of Hereford	Malvern (Worcs.) and v. of Pershore v. Pershore (both Worcs.)	1204	Westminster Domesday, f. 574v

III. RICHARD, PRIOR OF DUNSTABLE, AS JUDGE DELEGATE

Colleagues	Parties	Suit	Date of mandate	Date of settlement	Reference
1. V., pr. of Latton (Aug, Essex), and W. Basset, d. of 'Wengh'	Abb. of St. Nicholas, Angers (Ben. France) v. parsons of Whaplode	Tithes in Whaplode (Lincs.)	..	before 17 June 1207	P.R.O. E 315/50 no. 216
2. A(dam), archd. of Dorset	Wymondham (Ben. Norf.) v. Walsingham (Aug, Norf.)	Tithes in Burnham (Norf.)	24 Apr. 1208	..	Walsingham Cart., f. 2v
3. ,, ,,	Wymondham (Ben. Norf.) v. Th., r. of Fring (Norf.)	Tithes of folds of Thomas of Ingoldisthorpe, knt., in Snettisham and Fring (Norf.)	t. Inn. III	..	Wymondham Cart., ff. 52v–3r

4. Richard, abb. of Woburn (Cist. Beds.) and William, d. of Berkhamsted	Almoner of St. Albans (Ben. Herts.) v. Hamelin de Andevilla, lord of Eversden, and the free tenants there, and v. Alexander Maugant and Maud Chine	Tithes in Eversden (Cambs.) and elsewhere	19 Dec. 1208	..	St. Albans Almoner's Cart., ff. 131ʳ-2ʳ, 132ᵛ-3ᵛ; and see f. 65ᵛ
5. Richard, abb. of Woburn, and Raymond, pr. of St. Albans (Ben. Herts.)	M. Simon of London, r. of Launton v. Henry de Colewell, v. of Launton	Launton ch. (Oxon.)	30 Nov. 1212	Oct. 1214	Westminster Ch. 15684
6. H., abb. of Warden (Cist. Beds.), and the d. of Salisbury	Hugh (of Northwold), abb. elect of Bury St. Edmunds (Ben. Suff.) v. bp. of Winchester and electors	Election of abbot	24 Mar. 1214 } 26 Jan. 1215 }	..	*Memorials of St. Edmund's Abbey*, ii, ed. T. Arnold (R.S. xcvi, 1892), pp. 118–21
7. Abb. and pr. of Warden	Thomas Foliot, r. of Ashwell v. Westminster (Ben.)	Tithes of Ashwell ch. (Herts.)	16 Mar. 1215	..	Westminster Domesday, ff. 228ʳ-ᵛ,452ʳ-ᵛ
8. W(illiam), abb. of St. Albans, and pr. of Missenden (Aug. Bucks.), all subdelegated	St. Frideswide's (Aug. Oxon.) v. Robert, r. of Shipton under Wychwood, and Elias Ridel, chapl. of Ascot d'Oilly	Tithes in Ascot d'Oilly (Oxon.)	22 Nov. 1216	1218	*St. Frideswide's Cart.* ii, no. 1020
9. Abb. and pr. of Warden	Sutton at Hone (Knights Hospitallers) v. Rochester	Tithes in Sutton at Hone (Kent)	1216-17	20 Nov. 1217	*Reg. Roff.*, p. 655
10. Abb. and pr. of St. Albans	St. Frideswide's v. W., son of Richard, clerk of Lincoln dioc.	Oakley ch. (Bucks.)	3 Mar. 1217	..	*St. Frideswide's Cart.* ii, no. 820, and *Reg. Hon. III*, no. 1680 (*C.P.L.* i. 60)
11. Abb. of Warden and d. of Berkhamsted	Adam, r. of Cobham, and d. of Salisbury v. Chertsey (Ben. Surr.)	Tithes in Cobham (Surr.)	21 Mar. 1217	17 or 21 Nov. 1218	*Chertsey Cart.*, no. 91
12. William, abb. of St. Albans, and Simon, abb. of Reading (Ben. Berks.) (Richard also acted as an arbiter in this case)	Westminster v. those who contravene their rights over certain churches	Staines ch. (Middx.)	5 May 1217	..	Westminster Ch. 16740

	Colleagues	Parties	Suit	Date of mandate	Date of settlement	Reference
13.	William, abb. of St. Albans (Ben. Herts.) and Simon, abb. of Reading (Ben. Berks.) (Richard also acted as an arbiter in this case)	Westminster (Ben.) v. those who contravene their rights over certain churches	Wheathampstead ch. (Herts.)	5 May 1217	21 Jan. 1221	Westminster Domesday, ff. 448ᵛ–9ʳ (Russell, pp. 112–13)
14.	Abb. of Warden (Cist. Beds.) and m. William Scot, doctor of canon law living at Oxford	A., abbess elect of Shaftesbury (Ben. Dors.) v. the electors	Election of abbess	31 Aug. 1217	..	*Reg. Hon. III*, no. 757 (*C.P.L.* i. 49) (Russell, pp. 112–13)
15.	Stephen, abp. of Canterbury, Peter and Richard, bps. of Winchester and Salisbury, and Thomas, pr. of Merton (Aug. Surr.) (ordainers)	Bp. and c. of London v. Westminster	Status of the abbey	..	25 Mar–20 Apr. 1222	*Acta Stephani Langton*, no. 54; and see *Chron. Maj.* iii, p. 75 (Russell, p. 113)
16.	Pr. of Abingdon (Ben. Berks.) and archds. of Bedford and Worcester	Oseney (Aug. Oxon.) v. Caldwell (Aug. Beds.) and m. R(ichard) de Tingehurst	Tithes in Clapham (Beds.)	..	10 Jan. 1224/5	*Oseney Cart.* v, no. 850
17.	William, abb., and E., archd. of St. Albans	Bec (Ben. France) v. Laurence and William, rs. of Wimborne All Hallows	Tithes in Wimborne All Hallows (Dors.)	15 Jan. 1225	..	Windsor Ch. xi G 12
18.	Pr. of St. Albans and d. of Luton ('Lovinton')	Roger de Moris, clerk v. abb. of Beeleigh (Prem. Essex) and others of London dioc.	Sum of money	18 Jan. 1225	..	P.R.O. SC 7 50(11)
19.	Pr. and archd. of St. Albans	St. Frideswide's (Aug. Oxon.) v. Elias Ridel, can. of Salisbury and r. of Shipton under Wychwood	Tithes in Ascot under Wychwood (Oxon.)	17 Dec. 1226	10 July 1227	*St. Frideswide's Cart.* ii, no. 1021
20.	Martin, abb. of Missenden (Aug. Bucks.), and Garin, d. of Berkhamsted (case went to arbiters)	St. Albans v. S., r. of Hemel Hempstead (Herts.)	Tithes in Redbourn (Herts.)	t. Hon. III	..	St. Albans Cart. (B), f. 187ʳ

21. Pr. of Redbourn (Ben. Herts.) and d. of Luton	Westminster (Ben.) v. Geoffrey d'Abitot, knt.	Tithes in Birlingham (Worcs.)	t. Hon. III	..	Westminster Domesday, f. 292v
22. H(arvey), pr. of Newnham (Aug. Beds.), and R(ichard), d. of Newport	Walter de Biden, clerk v. St. Andrew's, Northampton (Clun.)	Tithes in Wootton (Lincs.)	25 June 1228	..	Northampton, St. Andrew's Cart. A, ff. 56r, 270r, and B, ff. 39v–40r (Russell, p. 113)
23. Pr. and archd. of St. Albans (Ben. Herts.)	St. Frideswide's (Aug.Oxon.) v. Walter Foliot, r. of Noke (Oxon.)	Tithes	24 Dec. 1228	13 July 1229	St. Frideswide's Cart. ii, no. 976
24. „ „	St. Frideswide's v. Elias, r. of Ardley (Oxon.)	Tithes in Fritwell (Oxon.)	24 Dec. 1228	..	Ibid., no. 977
25. „ „	St. Frideswide's v. Richard, r. of Souldern	Tithes in Souldern (Oxon.)	24 Dec. 1228	13 July 1229	Ibid., no. 979
26. „ „	St. Frideswide's v. Roger d'Oilly, knt.	Tithes in Ascot d'Oilly (Oxon.)	25 Dec. (sic) ..	..	Ibid., no. 1022
27. Bp. of Rochester and m. Thomas, r. of Maidstone	Westminster v. bp. and c. of London.	Jurisdiction over Kilburn priory (Middx.)	15 May 1229	1231	Westminster Domesday, f. 637r–v; Dugdale, Mon. Angl. iii, pp. 427–8, nums. viii–ix, from B.M. MSS. Cotton Faust. A iii, f. 204f, and Vesp. A xix, f. 406r
28. R., pr. of St. Albans, and archd. of St. Albans	Westminster v. Martin, r. of Rotherhithe	Tithes at Rotherhithe (Surr.)	29 June 1230	Sept. 1231	Westminster Domesday, ff. 380v–1r
29. Prec. of Dunstable (Aug. Beds.) and archd. of St. Albans	W., r. of Ambrosden (Oxon.) v. Missenden (Aug. Bucks.)	Muswell chapel and tithes (Bucks.)	13 Mar. 1231	..	Reg. Greg. IX, no. 567
30. Abb. and pr. of Woburn (Cist. Beds.)	St. Mary de Pré hosp.(Herts.) v. r. of St. Michael's in St. Albans (Herts.)	Molesting nuns' privileges	2 Mar. 1232	..	P.R.O. SC7 15(30)
31. Subpr. of Dunstable	Oseney (Aug. Oxon.) v. Knights Hospitallers of Gosford	Gosford chapel (Oxon.)	14 July 1232	19 Mar. 1234/5	Oseney Cart. iv, no. 108
32. Pr. of St. Albans and chanc. of Oxford	Warden v. m. Reginald of Bath, r. of Great Paxton	Tithes in Great Paxton (Hunts.)	..	After Oct. 1233	Reg. Antiq. Linc. iii, no. 829

Colleagues	Parties	Suit	Date of mandate	Date of settlement	Reference
33. Pr. (William) of Caldwell (Aug. Beds.) and prec. of Dunstable	Bec (Ben. France) v. St. Frideswide's (Aug. Oxon.)	Tithes in Hungerford (Berks.)	27 Apr. 1233	4 Aug. 1234	Windsor Ch. xi G 75 and pd. St. Frideswide's Cart. ii, no. 1135
34. , ,	Bec v. Tewkesbury (Ben. Glos.)	Tithes in Lesser Ogbourne (Wilts.)	27 Apr. 1233	1 July 1234	Canterbury, Cartae Antiquae, L 381
35. , ,	Bec v. William Estormy and Elias, chapl.	Chapel and tithes in Shalbourne (Berks. now Wilts.)	27 Apr. 1233	1 July 1234	Windsor, Arundel White Book, p. 174
36. (William, pr. of Caldwell, subdelegated to sacr. of Dunstable)	Bec v. Godstow (Ben. Oxon.)	Tithes in Wycombe (Bucks.)	27 Apr. 1233	26 Sept. 1234	Eton College, Bledlow Ch. C 5 and pd. Godstow Reg. i, no. [94]
37. Abb. of St. Albans (Ben. Herts.) and archd. of Northampton	M. R(ichard), r. of Cliffe-at-Hoo (Kent) v. offs. of archd. of Canterbury	Archidiaconal rights	5 Dec. 1234	..	Reg. Greg. IX, no. 2375 (Russell, p. 113)
38. Archd. of Bedford, subdelegated to subpr. and prec. of Dunstable and m. Richard de Tingehurst	St. Julian's hosp. nr. St. Albans v. Lanthony (Aug. Glos.)	Tithes in Henlow (Beds.)	13 Oct. 1238	10 June 1239	Lanthony Cart. A 1, X, no. cviii
39. Not named	Hugh d'Aubigny, earl of Arundel v. abp. of Canterbury	Sentences of excommunication and interdict	..	before 15 Feb. 1240	Reg. Greg. IX, no. 5182
40. , ,	Abp. of Canterbury v. bp. of London	Visitation of monasteries	c. 1239	..	Ann. Mon. iii, p. 151 (Russell, p. 113)
41. Pr. of Wymondley (Aug. Herts.)	Wymondham (Ben. Norf.) v. d. of Waxham (m. Peter de Ware)	Jurisdiction in spirituals in the manor of Happisburgh (Norf.)	2 Mar. 1239	11 Feb. 1240/1	Wymondham Cart. ff. 69v-70r

| 42. | Pr. of Wymondley (Aug. Herts.) | Wymondham (Ben. Norf.) v. r. of Grimston | Tithes of earl of Arundel in Grimston (Norf.) | .. | 12 Sept. 1242[1] | Wymondham Cart, f. 56r–v |
| 43. | Archd. of St. Albans (Ben. Herts.) and d. of Flamstead (Herts.) (dean described as 'sublato de medio') | Westminster (Ben.) v. Pershore (Ben. Worcs.) | Tithes from the court of Henry de Hareleg' in Hendon (Middx.) | .. | .. | Pershore Cart., f. 112r |

OTHER OCCURRENCES CONNECTED WITH THE DELEGATED COURTS

44.	post 28 July 1210	attested the notification of a judge-delegate settlement made by the abbs. of Croxton (Cist. Staffs.) and Roucester (Aug. Staffs.) and B., pr. of Tutbury (Ben. al. Staffs.), in a suit between Darley (Aug. Derbys.) and W., r. of Morton (Derbys.), and possibly acted as legal adviser (Belvoir, Wessington Ch. 331)
45.	c. 1215	named as a possible arbiter; did not actually serve (Reg. S. Osmund i, p. 256)
46.	20 Aug. 1237	ordered to enforce the observance of an agreement acting with the abb. of St. Albans (Bushmead Cart., no. 6)
47.	1237	appointed with the master of the schools at Dunstable a delegate of the legate Otto (Oseney Cart., iv, no. 424)
48.	1241	acted as a subdelegate of Edmund, abp. of Canterbury (Windsor Chs. xi G 14–16, xi G 22, and xi G 37)

[1] According to the Dunstable Annals (p. 158) Richard died on 9 Apr. 1242, but there is a strong likelihood that the suit, which ended in a composition, was originally delegated to him.

IV. EXAMPLES OF TIME TAKEN FOR
SETTLING SUITS

Date of Mandate	Date of Settlement	Reference
8 May 1203	Aug. 1205	P.R.O. E 327/45
14 Apr. 1207	1208/9	Bardney Cart., f. 240ʳ
4 Dec. 1208	7 May 1210	West Dereham Cart., f. 260ᵛ
30 Nov. 1212	Oct. 1214	Westminster Ch. 15684
23 Jan. 1213	2 Oct. 1214	Lanthony Cart. A 1, VIII, no. lxxx
6 Sept. 1216	4 May 1218	Eye Cart., ff. 35ᵛ–6ʳ
12 Sept. 1216	7 Nov. 1218	Ibid., ff. 43ʳ–4ʳ
22 Nov. 1216	1218/19	*St. Frideswide's Cart.* ii, no. 1020
20 Dec. 1216	12 or 15 May 1220	Norwich Ch. 1686
15 Mar. 1217	21 July 1220	Eye Cart., ff. 46ᵛ–7ʳ
21 Mar. 1217	17 or 21 Nov. 1218	*Chertsey Cart.*, no. 91
5 May 1217	27 Apr. 1218	Binham Cart., f. 185ʳ–ᵛ
13 Dec. 1217	21 Sept. 1219	Tintern Cart., ff. 35ʳ–6ʳ
22 Feb. 1218	1221/2	*St. Gregory's Cart.*, no. 82
3 Apr. 1218	26 June 1219	*Reg. Antiq. Linc.* iii, no. 730
18 Sept. 1218	15 May 1225	Lewes Cart., f. 260ᵛ, cal. *Lewes Cart. N.P.*, no. 138
18 Sept. 1218	30 Oct. 1219	P.R.O. E 40/14067, cal. *Lewes Cart. N.P.*, no. 112
30 Mar. 1219	1 July or 5 Sept. 1221	Eye Cart., ff. 36ᵛ–7ᵛ
11 Nov. 1219	29 Aug. 1220	Canterbury, MS. Scrapbook A, p. 13, no. 25
11 Nov. 1219	24 Nov. 1220	Canterbury, Cartae Antiquae, L 351
30 Mar. 1220	Sept. 1227	*St. Gregory's Cart.*, no. 192
12 Jan. 1221	20 Oct. 1223	P.R.O. E 40/14953
3 Apr. 1221	6 Sept. 1221	Eye Cart., f. 36ʳ
10 Feb. 1222	July 1222	Canterbury, Cartae Antiquae, H 120
10 Mar. 1222	13 May 1223	Walden Cart., f. 43ᵛ
26 Mar. 1222	1225×1226	*N.L.C.*, no. 80
1 July 1222	1225/6	*St. Gregory's Cart.*, no. 169
9 Jan. 1223	13 Jan. 1231/2	*St. Frideswide's Cart.* ii, no. 731
20 Jan. 1223	July 1224	P.R.O. E 40/14253
7 Apr. 1223	26 Jan. 1224/5	Dover Cart., f. 226ᵛ
10 Apr. 1223	Oct. 1224	*Glos. Cart.* ii, no. dccxiii
31 July 1224	Oct. 1225	Leeds Cart., f. 10ʳ
3 Sept. 1225	8 Sept. 1226	Lanthony Cart. A 2, f. 4ʳ–ᵛ
23 Dec. 1225	2 Sept. 1226	Eye Cart., ff. 34ᵛ–5ʳ
23 Oct. 1226	10 June 1227	New College, Lib. Niger, f. 37ʳ
17 Dec. 1226	10 July 1227	*St. Frideswide's Cart.* ii, no. 1021
26 Mar. 1227	5 May 1229	Bradenstoke Cart., f. 30ʳ
31 Mar. 1227	20 June 1229	P.R.O. E 210/9469
23 Apr. 1227	11 Mar. 1229	Dover Cart., f. 229ᵛ
26 Jan. 1228	26 Apr. 1230	*Reg. Antiq. Linc.* iii, no. 759
16 Feb. 1228	23 July 1229	Lanthony Cart. A 1, III, no. liv

Date of Mandate	*Date of Settlement*	*Reference*
1 Dec. 1228	May 1229	Canterbury, Cartae Antiquae, C 280
24 Dec. 1228	13 July 1229	*St. Frideswide's Cart.* ii, nos. 976, 979
29 Mar. 1229	28 June 1230	*Malmesbury Reg.* ii, pp. 30, 59
9 May 1229	9 Apr. 1230	Leach, *Schools of Med. Eng.*, p. 176
18 June 1229	May 1230	Canterbury, Cartae Antiquae, F 8
9 Nov. 1229	1231/2	P.R.O. E 140/14190 (cf. 14189)
15 Mar. 1230	1231/2	*Malmesbury Reg.* i, pp. 386–90, and ii, pp. 60–4
29 June 1230	Sept. 1231	Westminster Domesday, f. 380ᵛ
27 Sept. 1230	2 Oct. 1231	Lanthony Cart. A 1, III, no. lv
27 Feb. 1231	1233/4	Christchurch Cart., f. 60ʳ
17 July 1231	30 June 1232	Binham Cart., ff. 146ᵛ–7ʳ
4 Apr. 1232	1239/40	*Glos. Cart.* ii, no. dxxvii
23 Dec. 1232	7 Nov. 1233	St. Augustine's Cart., f. 75ʳ
5 Feb. 1233	5 May 1237	P.R.O. E 326/2268
9 Feb. 1233	16 Sept. 1233	*St. Frideswide's Cart.* ii, no. 978
9 Feb. 1233	3 Feb. 1234	Ibid. ii, no. 732
9 Feb. 1233	17 or 24 Feb. 1236/7	Ibid. ii, no. 980
22 Feb. 1233	Dec. 1233	P.R.O. E 40/13828(c)
15 Apr. 1233	19 Oct. 1234	Westminster Domesday, f. 576ʳ
27 Apr. 1233	1 July 1234	Canterbury, Cartae Antiquae, L 381
27 Apr. 1233	1 July or 5 Sept. 1234	Windsor, Arundel White Book, p. 174
27 Apr. 1233	4 Aug. 1234	Windsor Ch. xi G 75: *St. Frideswide's Cart.* ii, no. 1135
15 July 1233	31 July 1234	P.R.O. E 40/13828(f)
3 Oct. 1233	22 Aug. 1235	Lanthony Cart. A 1, XVI, no. xvi
23 Mar. 1234	4 Aug. 1235	*N.L.C.*, no. 62
20 Dec. 1234	July 1242	*Glos. Cart.* i, no. ccxxxvi
10 Mar. 1236	10 Dec. 1237	Walden Cart., f. 43ʳ
10 June 1236	24 Nov. 1240	Dover Cart., ff. 228ᵛ–9ʳ
31 July 1236	1237/8	Bayham Cart., f. 60ᵛ
19 Dec. 1236	31 July 1237	*Chertsey Cart.*, no. 92
11 Apr. 1237	July 1238	Dover Cart., f. 175ᵛ
13 Apr. 1237	31 July 1238	Lanthony Cart. A 1, X, no. lxxiv
13 Oct. 1238 (2nd delegation)	10 June 1239	„ „ „ no. cviii
23 Mar. 1239	1241/2	*St. Frideswide's Cart.* ii, no. 1053
15 Nov. 1239	28 Sept. 1240	New College, Takeley Ch. 229
27 Jan. 1240	8 June 1240	P.R.O. E 42/384
24 July 1240	29 Nov. 1242	B.M. Add. Chs. 20371–2
11 May 1245	20 Dec. 1247	St. Neots Cart., f. 130ᵛ
16 Mar. 1246	25 Oct. 1246	*Thame Cart.*, no. 38
6 July 1247	Apr. 1249 (ordination)	Chatteris Cart., ff. 111ʳ⁻ᵛ, 112ʳ
8 July 1248	29 July 1251	Thorney Cart. ii, f. 323ʳ
15 Feb. 1250[1]	26 Apr. 1250	Leeds Cart., f. 8ᵛ
31 Oct. 1253	11 Feb. 1255/6	Bardney Cart., ff. 213ʳ–14ʳ

[1] Presumably misdated and should be 1249, or the settlement should be 1251.

V. EXAMPLES OF SUBMISSION TO ECCLESIASTICS FOR COERCION

Submission of	Judges	Submission to	Date of settlement unless otherwise stated	Reference
1. Bardney and archd. of Cleveland	Chanc. and two cans. of Lincoln	C. of Lincoln	1209	Bardney Cart., f. 92r
2. Cockersand and St. Martin, Séez	Subd., pr., and subpr. of St. Katherine's, Lincoln	Judges	1216	B.M. Add. Ch. 20512
3. Dover and Langdon	Abb. of Faversham, prs. of St. Gregory's, Canterbury, and St. Augustine's, Canterbury	Judges	1219	Langdon Cart., ff. 102r–3r
4. Proctor of Dunes	Prs. of St. Augustine's, Canterbury, Monks Horton and Faversham	Judges	1220	Canterbury, MS. Scrapbook A, p. 13, Ch. 25
5. R. of Purleigh, and Wix	Prs. of Merton, Bermondsey, and Southwark	Bp. of London	1221 (mandate)	P.R.O. E 40/14044(2)
6. Christ Church, Canterbury, and William, son of Conan of Holbeach	Prs. of St. Augustine's, Canterbury, St. Gregory's, Canterbury, and Faversham	Judges	1222	Canterbury, Cartae Antiquae, H 120
7. St. James's, Northampton, and parishioners of Hartwell	Chanc. and d. of Oxford	Archd. of the place, presumably Northampton	1222 (mandate)	Northampton, St. James's Cart., f. 109r
8. Thorney and H., clerk of Lincoln dioc.	Pr. of Holy Trinity, Aldgate, and d. of St. Paul's, London	Judges	1223 (mandate)	Thorney Cart. ii, f. 384r
9. William, son of Everard de Ringesborn	Prs. of St. James's and St. Augustine's, Bristol	Judges	1224	Bradenstoke Cart., f. 105r

10. Grestain (Eure, France) and Lanthony	Abb. of St. James's, pr. of St. Andrew's, and d. of Northampton	Judges and their successors	1224	Lanthony Cart. A 1, VIII, no. lxxxii
11. St. Laurence's, Canterbury, and St. Gregory's	Abb. of Faversham, pr. and archd. of Rochester	Judges	1225	*St. Gregory's Cart.*, no. 169
12. Boxgrove, and R., parson of Bilton, and R. de Crest, knt.	Unnamed	Judges and their successors	1225	Boxgrove Cart., f. 92r
13. Bec and rs. of Wimborne All Hallows	Abb., archd. of St. Albans, and pr. of Dunstable	Judges and their successors	1225 (mandate)	Windsor Ch. xi G. 12
14. Thorney and r. of Chesterton	Abb., pr. of Peterborough, and d. of Ness	Judges	1225 (mandate)	Thorney Cart. ii, f. 383r
15. Thorney and r. of Grafham	,, ,,	Judges	1225 (mandate)	,, ,,
16. Eye and rs. of St. Martin's, Dunwich	Prs. of Holy Trinity, St. Peter's, Ipswich, and d. of Ipswich	Judges and their successors	1226	Eye Cart., ff. 34v-5r
17. R. of Clapham and Bec	Abb. of St. John's, Colchester, off. and d. of Colchester	Judges and their successors	1226 (mandate)	Windsor, Arundel White Book, p. 215
18. William de Coleville and r. of Bytham	Chanc., d. of Oxford, and d. of Haseley	Archd. of Lincoln	c. 1226	*Reg. Antiq. Linc.* iii, nos. 1019-20
19. V. of Tew	Prs. of Monkton Farleigh, Malmesbury, and d. of Malmesbury	Judges	1227	Bradenstoke Cart., f. 147v
20. Rs. of Shenley	Prs. of St. Albans, Hertford, and d. of Luton	Archd. of Buckingham	1216-27	Dunstable Cart., f. 62v, cal. *Dunstable Cart.*, no. 695
21. Bradenstoke and Henry Heuse, knt.	Pr. of Ivychurch, chanc. and succ. of Salisbury	Judges	1216-27	Bradenstoke Cart., f. 120r

Submission of	Judges	Submission to	Date of settlement unless otherwise stated	Reference
22. R. of Lamport and Faxton	Pr. of Westminster and m. William of Purleigh	Off. of the abp. of Canterbury	1216–27	P.R.O. E 40/7896
23. Bridlington and Bardney	Archd. of E. Riding, prec. of York, and a can. of York	Archd. of E. Riding	1228	Bardney Cart., f. 96ᵛ
24. Pipewell and r. of Braybrooke	Abb. of Combe, prs. of Coventry and Kenilworth	Judges	1228 (mandate)	Pipewell Cart. (A), f. 123ʳ
25. St. Frideswide's and r. of Ardley	Prs. of Dunstable, St. Albans, and archd. of St. Albans	Judges	1228 (mandate)	*St. Frideswide's Cart.* ii, no. 977
26. St. Frideswide's and r. of Noke	„	Judges	1229	*St. Frideswide's Cart.* ii, no. 976
27. Lanthony and r. of Painswick	Pr. of Eynsham, chanc. and d. of Oxford	Judges	1229	Lanthony Cart. A I, III, no. liv
28. Christ Church, Canterbury, and William of Cheriton, knt.	Pr. of St. Gregory's, Canterbury, off. and pen. of Canterbury	Judges	1230	Canterbury, Cartae Antiquae, F 8
29. R. of E. Hendred and Bec	Pr. of Ivychurch, succ. of Salisbury, and d. of Wilton	Judges	1230	Windsor Ch. xv. 41. 71
30. R. of E. Hendred and Abingdon	„	Judges and their successors	1231	Abingdon Cart., ff. 53ʳ–4ʳ
31. Archd. of Oxford and St. Frideswide's	Abb. of Bardney, prs. of St. Katherine's and St. Mary Magdalene, Lincoln	Judges	1231/2	*St. Frideswide's Cart.* ii, no. 731
32. Roger of Dauntsey (on behalf of his wife)	Pr. of Luffield, archd. and d. of Buckingham	Judges	1232	P.R.O. DL 25/15

33. Christchurch (Twynham) and Bec	Abb., pr. of Milton, and d. of Whitchurch	Judges	1233	Christchurch Cart., f. 60ʳ
34. R. of Meopham and Christ Church, Canterbury	Abbs. of St. Radegund's, Langdon, and pr. of Monks Horton	Abp. of Canterbury	1234	Canterbury, Cartae Antiquae, M 123
35. Bec and Tewkesbury	Prs. of Dunstable, Caldwell, and prec. of Dunstable	Judges and their successors	1234	Canterbury, Cartae Antiquae, L 381
36. Bec and William Estormy and Elias, chapl.	,, ,,	Judges	1234	Windsor, Arundel White Book, p. 174
37. Bec and St. Frideswide's	,, ,,	Judges	1234	St. Frideswide's Cart. ii, no. 1135, and Windsor Ch. xi. G. 75
38. Notley and Newton Longville	Pr. of St. Oswald's, Gloucester, archd. and d. of Gloucester	Archds. of Bedford and Buckingham	1235	N.L.C., no. 62
39. M. Baldwin, can. of Troyes, and the archd. of Worcester and Lanthony	Can. of St. Davids and a can. of St. Angelus, Ferentino (staying in England)	Judges	1235	Lanthony Cart. A 1, XVI, no. xvi
40. Christchurch (Twynham) and Montébourg	Pr. of Poughley and d. of Newbury	Judges and bp. and off. of Winchester	1235 (mandate)	Christchurch Cart., f. 92ʳ
41. Owston and St. Michael's, Stamford	Prs. of Leicester, Belvoir, and Breedon	Judges	1236/7	Bodleian MS. Dodsworth 76, f. 1
42. St. Frideswide's and Robert de la Haye	Prs. of St. John's, St. James's, and d. of Northampton	Judges	1236/7	St. Frideswide's Cart. ii, no. 980
43. Wallingford and Henry of Earley, knt., and his chapl.	Pr. of Barnwell and chanc. of Cambridge	Judges	1236	Bodleian MS. Chs. Berks. a 1, Ch. 17
44. Abb. of Chertsey and pr. of Newstead	Archd. and d. of Oxford	Judges	1237	Chertsey Cart., no. 91

Submission of	Judges	Submission to	Date of settlement unless otherwise stated	Reference
45. St. Martin's, London, and Walden	D. and chanc. of Oxford	Judges	1237	Walden Cart., f. 43^r
46. Bayham and v. of W. Greenwich	Prs. of Boxgrove, Arundel, and Tortington	Judges	1237	Bayham Cart., f. 60^v
47. R. of Hanney and Abingdon	Prs. of St. James's and St. John's, Northampton	Judges and their successors	1237 (mandate)	Abingdon Cart., ff. 90^v–1^r
48. Eye and clerk of Bedfield	D., prec., and treas. of Lincoln	Judges	1237 (mandate)	Eye Cart., f. 41^r–v
49. Bridlington and Westminster	Prec., subd., and m. of the schools of Lincoln	Prec. and subd. of Lincoln	1238	Westminster Domesday, f. 470^r
50. Tonbridge and r. of Wickhambrook	Pr., prec., and d. of Rochester	Judges	1238	P.R.O. E 40/14036
51. Lanthony and hosp. of St. Julian near St. Albans	Pr. of Dunstable and archd. of Bedford	Judges and their successors	10 June 1239	Lanthony Cart. A 1, X, no. cviii
52. St. Peter's, Gloucester, and Montacute and pr. of Malpas	Abb. of Evesham, pr. of Pershore, and d. of Dumbleton	Judges	1239	Glos. Cart. ii, no. cxxvii
53. St. Valéry and r. of Hinton Waldrist	Archd. and chanc. of London	Judges and their successors	28 Sept. 1240	New College, Oxford, Takeley Ch. 229
54. Dover and r. of Snargate	Abb. and pr. of Battle, subdelegated to abbs. of Langdon and St. Radegund's	Principal judges	1240	Dover Cart., ff. 228^v, 229^r
55. V. of Hellingly	Prs. of St. Martin's, Dover, and Folkstone	Judges	1240	Bayham Cart., f. 60^v

56. R. of Churchill and Bruern	Pr. of Bradenstoke and his subdelegates: d. of Oxford and v. of Haseley—all hear the cause.	Judges and presumably subdelegates	1241	St. Frideswide's Cart. ii, no. 1053
57. Combe, and Nicholas, knt., of Withybrook and free tenants of the same place	Prs. of Newnham and Caldwell	Judges and the prs. of Coventry and Kenilworth	1241	Combe Cart., f. 77r
58. Pipewell and r. of Desborough	Abb. and pr. of Evesham	Judges and their successors	1246	Pipewell Cart. (A), f. 29v fol.
59. Thame and r. of Oddington	Pr. of Reading	Judge and his successors	1246	Thame Cart., no. 38
60. R. of Barley and Chatteris	Prs. of Royston and Leighs	Judges	1246 (mandate)	Chatteris Cart., ff. 142r–3v
61. Walsingham and r. of Barney	Pr. of Newnham	Judge	1252	Binham Cart., f. 61r

APPENDIX B. DOCUMENTS

I. DOCUMENTS CONCERNING LEGATINE DELEGATION

I

Report of a settlement by Master R(obert) de Clipstone, official of Worcester, and W., dean of Rissington (Glos.), delegates of the legate Guala, acting on his mandate dated on 23 January (?1217) at Gloucester, to hear a suit between the abbot and convent of Bruern (Cist. Oxon.) and the rector of Guiting (Glos.). n.d. but probably 1217.

(See above, Chapter I, p. 30, and Chapter III, p. 126)

Universis sancte matris ecclesie filiis presens scriptum inspecturis, Magister R. de Clipston' officialis Wigorn' et W. decanus de Risendon' Wigorn' diocesis salutem in domino. Mandatum domini Gual' legati domini pape in Anglia in hec verba suscepimus: Gual' miseratione divina tituli Sancti Martini presbyter cardinalis apostolice sedis legatus dilectis filiis Magistro R. de Clipston' officiali Wigorn' et .. decano de Risendon' Wigorn' diocesis salutem in domino. Dilecti filii abbas et conventus de Bruerne Cisterciensis ordinis suam ad nos transmiserunt querelam, quod rector ecclesie de Guting' Wigorn' diocesis quasdam decimas ab eis nititur extorquere contra suorum privilegiorum tenorem temere veniendo, ideoque discretioni vestre qua fungimur legationis auctoritate mandamus quatinus partibus convocatis audiatis hinc inde proposita, quod justum fuerit, salvis privilegiis pontificum romanorum cum moderamine concilii generalis, decernere procuretis, facientes quod decreveritis per censuram ecclesiasticam firmiter observari. Testes autem qui fuerint nominati si se gracia, odio vel timore subtraxerint per districtionem eandem cogatis veritati testimonium perhibere. Datum Glouc' x. kalendas Februarii. Hujus igitur auctoritate mandati partibus convocatis et coram nobis comparentibus lis tandem tali modo conquievit, videlicet quod prefati abbas et conventus decimas garbarum et feni ecclesie de Guting' tantum persolvent, et quia privilegiati sunt immunes a prestatione omnium aliarum decimarum existent, sicut in instrumento a Ricardo rectore ecclesie de

Guting' eisdem monachis confecto manifeste continetur. Et in hujus
rei testimonium presenti scripto sigilla nostra apposuimus.

Two tags for seals.

P.R.O. E 326/3943

2

Report of a settlement by Abbot John and the prior of
Sherborne, delegates of the legate Pandulf, in a suit between
the prior and convent of Bruton (Aug. Som.) and the abbess
and convent of St. Edward, Shaftesbury (Ben. Dors.). 1218×
1221.

(See above, Chapter I, p. 31.)

In red: De litera mandati legati super querimonia predicti prioris de
frumento predicto etc.

Omnibus ad quos presentes litere pervenerint Johannes dei gracia
abbas Sireborn' et ejusdem loci prior salutem in domino. Noveritis
nos suscepisse mandatum domini legati in hec verba: Pand' dei gracia
Norwic' electus domini pape camerarius apostolice sedis legatus dilectis
filiis abbati et priori de Sireborne Sar' diocesis salutem in domino.
Dilecti filii prior et conventus de Brwton' nobis conquerendo monstrarunt, quod abbatissa et conventus Sancti Edwardi Sar' diocesis tria
sextaria frumenti, in quibus annuatim tenentur eisdem, contra justiciam detinent et eis solvere contradicunt, ideoque discretioni vestre[1]
legationis qua fungimur auctoritate,[2] mandamus quatinus partibus
(f. 106ᵛ) convocatis audiatis causam et fine debito terminetis. Testes
autem etc. Dat' etc. Nos autem hujus auctoritate[2] mandati causam
secundum juris ordinem tractavimus, que in hunc modum tandem
quievit, videlicet quod domina abbatissa et conventus de Shaftebury
recognoverunt se solvere debere annuatim priori et conventui de
Brwton' tria sextaria frumenti variati, secundum quod carta eorum
quam de eadem abbatissa et conventu habent testatur. In hujus autem
rei testimonium hoc scriptum fecimus et sigillis nostris signavimus,
servata nobis potestate cogendi eandem abbatissam et conventum ad
predictam solutionem dictis priori et conventui faciendam, si forte
vellent contraire. Valete.[3]

Shaftesbury Cart., f. 106ʳ⁻ᵛ

---

[1] MS. 'nostre'.　　　[2] MS. 'auctoritote'.　　　[3] MS. 'valetis'.

3

Report of a settlement by John of Farthingstone, rural dean, and Master Thomas, rector of Badby (Northants.), delegates of the legate Pandulf, in a suit between the prior and convent of Daventry (Clun. Northants.) and Thomas, rector of Lubbenham (Leics.). 1 October 1218×1221.

(See above, Chapter I, p. 32.)

In red: Carta ecclesie de Lobenho.

Universis sancte matris ecclesie filiis ad quos presentes littere pervenerint, Johannes de Fardingestona decanus et Magister Thomas rector ecclesie de Babdeby salutem in domino. Noveritis nos mandatum domini legati suscepisse in hec verba: Pandulfus dei gracia Norwic' electus domini pape camerarius apostolice sedis legatus, dilectis[1] filiis decano de Fardinston' et Magistro Thome rectori ecclesie de Baddeby Linc' diocesis salutem in domino. Querelam dilectorum filiorum prioris et conventus de Daventre recepimus, continentem quod cum Thome rectori ecclesie de Lobenho Lincolnienc' diocesis quasdam decimas ad ipsos de jure spectantes, pro sex marcis et dimidia eisdem annuatim solvendis tradidissent ad firmam, idem Thomas licet quatuor marcas exinde persolverit, residuum tamen contra justiciam detinet et ipsis prout tenetur reddere contradicit; ideoque discretioni[2] vestre legationis qua fungimur auctoritate, mandamus quatinus partibus convocatis audiatis causam et fine debito terminetis. Testes autem qui fuerint[3] nominati si se gracia, odio vel timore subtraxerint per censuram ecclesiasticam cogatis veritati testimonium perhibere. Datum[4] apud Lond' kalendis Octobris. Hujus igitur auctoritate mandati partibus in presencia nostra constitutis, fundata intentione prefatorum prioris et conventus de Daventre, responsum fuit ex parte memorati Thome de Lobenho verum esse quod ipse fuit obligatus eisdem monachis de Daventre, juramento interposito, ad solutionem sex marcarum et dimidie annuatim nomine omnium decimarum garbarum de toto feodo Hugonis Poherii in Lobenho (f. 151ʳ),[5] quas ipsi tradiderunt[6] ei ad firmam et successoribus suis in ecclesia de Lobenho futuris personis sicut aliquando conpositum fuit inter ipsos coram quibusdam judicibus delegatis a domino papa Innocentio tercio. Set propositum fuit ab eodem Thoma quod non cessavit a plenaria solutione nisi propter guerram et propter alias inportunitates emergentes. Cumque diutius

---

[1] MS. 'delectis'.   [2] MS. 'discretionem'.   [3] MS. 'fuerunt'.
[4] MS. 'Data'.   [5] Folios 127ʳ–38ᵛ are sewn in between ff. 150ᵛ and 151ʳ.
[6] Written also at the bottom of f. 150ᵛ.

super detentione reragiorum coram nobis esset litigatum, tandem post multas altercationes hinc inde propositas inter eos amicabiliter lis ita conquievit. Scilicet quod idem Thomas juravit tactis sacrosanctis evangeliis coram nobis se decetero fore fidelem domui de Daventre in plenaria solutione prefate firme sex marcarum et dimidie, absque appellatione vel aliqua contradictione ad terminos statutos, scilicet ad pascha xx. solidos et xx. d., ad festum Sancti Johannis baptiste xx. solidos et xx. d., ad festum Sancti Michaelis[1] xx. solidos et xx. d., et ad natale domini xx. solidos et xx. d. Prior autem et dicti monachi remiserunt eidem Thome pro bono pacis quedam reragia que ab eo petebant. Ut autem ea que acta sunt coram nobis auctoritate litterarum domini legati perpetuam optineant firmitatem, tam sigilla nostra quam sigilla dictorum prioris et conventus de Daventre et ejusdem Thome rectoris ecclesie de Lobenho utrimque[2] duximus apponenda.

Daventry Cart., ff. 150ᵛ–1ʳ

4

Mandate of the legate Pandulf to the abbot and prior of Westminster, ordering them to hear a case between Maud de Herlaue, formerly nurse of King John, and her son Thomas, and the archdeacon of London. Cawood (Lancs.), 28 August 1219×1221.

(See above, Chapter I, p. 32.)

Pand' dei gracia Norwicen' electus domini pape camerarius apostolice sedis legatus, dilectis filiis abbati et priori Westmonaster' London' diocesis salutem in domino. Dilecta filia Matillda de Herlaue, quondam nutrix bone memorie J. regis Angl', et Thomas filius ejus nobis humiliter intimarunt quod .. archidiaconus London', post appellationem ad nos legitime interpositam, excommunicationis sentenciam contra justiciam promulgavit in ipsos. Quare nos ei nostris damus litteris in mandatis ut sentenciam ipsam infra octo dies post receptionem litterarum ipsarum, secundum formam ecclesie sine qualibet difficultate relaxet, ideoque discretioni vestre legationis qua fungimur auctoritate, mandamus quatinus dicto archidiacono in mandati nostri executione cessante vos extunc sentenciam ipsam judicantes penitus esse nullam audiatis causam et fine debito terminetis. Testes autem qui fuerint nominati si se gracia, odio vel timore subtraxerint per censuram ecclesiasticam cogatis veritati testimonium perhibere. Datum apud Kawod' v. kal' Septembr'.

P.R.O. SC1, vol. 62, no. 3

---

[1] MS. 'Micahelis'.   [2] MS. 'utrumque'.

5

Mandate of R (oger de la Lee), prior, and the chapter of Christ Church, Canterbury, to Master R., official of the archdeacon of Canterbury, delegate of the legate Otto, ordering him not to proceed in a case on account of an appeal which has been made to Rome and for the tuition of the see of Canterbury. Canterbury, 9 December 1241.

(See above, Chapter I, pp. 33–4.)

R. prior et capitulum ecclesie Christi Cant' discreto viro et amico in Christo Magistro R. officiali archidiaconi Cant', salutem in domino. Sua nobis S. de Sinethe civis Cant' petitione monstravit quod cum appellationis causa que vertebatur inter Gregorium palmer et ipsum, vobis fuisset a legato nuper Anglie delegata, idem S. a vobis indebite sensiens se gravari ex eo maxime quod ipsum invitum et contradicentem citavistis ad diem festum Sancte Margarite virginis et martiris, qui celebris est in civitate Cant', et fere ubique terrarum, ac etiam eodem die sicut voluistis et potuistis in causa processistis eadem, ad sedem apostolicam et pro tuitione appellationis ad sedem Cant' vocem appellationis emisit. Quo circa discretioni vestre auctoritate nostre Cant' ecclesie districte precipiendo, mandamus firmiter inhibentes quatinus cognitioni cause et ejusdem processui supersedeatis, omnino nec in illa ulterius procedatis, donec de appellatione predicti S. fuerit a judicibus auctoritate apostolica diffinitum, scituri quod[1] si quid post hujusmodi appellationem que omnino legittima est, et nostram inhibitionem que legittime apellantes tantum defendere intendit, nunciamus irritum et inane. Valete. Data apud Cant' die lune prime diei dominice de adventu anno domini m. cc. xli.

Canterbury, Cartae Antiquae, M 364, no. 9

II. INTERMEDIATE *ACTA*, A DRAFT, AND A FINAL *ACTUM*

A Note on the Documents

The judges' final *actum*, at the same time as recording the settlement or outcome of the suit, provides a résumé of the proceedings.[2] The amount of detail which is recorded presumably depended on the clerk's discretion. Some *acta* are generously informative; all include the *proem*,

---

[1] 'sicut' here, deleted.   [2] See, e.g., Norwich Ch. 1686 (below, no. 8).

a recitation of the papal mandate, the report of the composition or judgement, and the dating clause. The document was made authoritative by the seals of the judges, and sometimes of the parties; the chirograph form was often used.

While final *acta* survive in large quantities, intermediate *acta* are rare. Intermediate *acta* survive, however, from assorted cases to illustrate most stages of the suit at this period;[1] and two cases are particularly well documented. Fourteen original documents remain at Windsor from a long suit between the abbot and convent of Bec, and Marcellus, rector of Dalham (Suff.), and Gilbert, rector of Withersfield (Suff.), about tithes from the demesne of Hamo Pechie at Dalham and of John de Valle at Withersfield.[2] The mandate of Gregory IX was made out against those who had alienated the property of Bec, and neither of these two parties was specified by name. It was addressed to the archbishop of Canterbury (Edmund of Abingdon) and was dated 22 November 1234. The archbishop subdelegated to the prior of Dunstable (Richard de Mores). A settlement of the suit was made on 25 April 1241.[3] The documents include intermediate reports, appointments of proctors, and instructions to officers to cite, etc.

The Alvingham cartulary contains transcripts of a dozen documents from a suit between the convent of Alvingham (Gilb. Lincs.) and Peter, parson of Stainton-le-Vale (Lincs.), about two parts of the church.[4] From the papal mandate, dated 23 January 1245, it appears that St. Hugh, bishop of Lincoln from 1186 to 1200, had allowed the nuns of Alvingham to appropriate the church, and that this appropriation had been confirmed by Archbishop Hubert Walter. Bishop Hugh of Wells, however, had revoked the action of his predecessor and had instituted a certain Peter in the church. In 1245, therefore, the nuns appealed to Pope Innocent IV for restoration of the possession of two parts in the church, which had originally been given to them by Lambert de Scoteni.[5] The judges were the priors of Bridlington and Kirkham (both Aug. Yorks. E.R.) and the master of the schools at Malton (Yorks. N.R.). The prior of Bridlington subdelegated to the dean of Buckrose (Yorks. E.R.), and the prior of

---

[1] See, e.g., P.R.O. E 135/6/13; Windsor Ch. xi G 27; and B.M. Egerton Ch. 409 (below, nos. 2, 3 and 7). Cf. Morey, *Bartholomew of Exeter*, p. 50.

[2] Windsor Chs. xi G 14–16, 22, and 37 (1–10). Two of the documents are printed below (nos. 4 and 6).

[3] The documents in the case against the rector of Dalham peter out after his contumacy.

[4] Alvingham Cart., ff. 3ᵛ–6ʳ. Two of the documents are printed below (nos. 1 and 5).

[5] Alvingham Cart., f. 4ᵛ; *Transcripts of Charters relating to Gilbertine Houses*, ed. F. M. Stenton (Linc. Rec. Soc. xviii, 1922), p. 107 [10], and also *Reg. Antiq. Linc.* vi, App. II, pp. 171–81 for a history of the Scoteni family.

Kirkham to the subprior. Definitive sentence in favour of Alvingham was decreed on 4 December 1245 in Winthorpe church (Notts. or possibly, but less likely, Lincs.).

I

Intermediate *acta* in a suit between the prior and convent of Alvingham (Gilb. Lincs.) and Peter, parson of Stainton-le-Vale (Lincs.). St. Michael's chapel, Malton, 21 June 1245.

(See above, Chapter II, p. 79.)

Acta in capella sancti Michaelis Maltone, die mercurii proxima ante festum sancti Johannis baptiste, coram magistro scolarum ejusdem ville principali judice, et decano de Bokeros et subpriore de Kirkeham, de Brideligton' et de Kirham priorum dimissis[1] sub[de]legatis;[2] in causa que vertitur auctoritate apostolica inter magistrum ordinis de Sempingham (*sic*) et priorem et conventum de Alvingham ex una parte, et Petrum qui se gerit pro persona duarum partium ecclesie de Staynton' ex altera, prefatis religiosis per priorem de Alvingham procuratorem legitime constitutum comparentibus, prefato P. personaliter comparente, videlicet quod aprobatis litteris commissoriis et probato sigillo decani de Walecroft, ad cujus probationem magister scolarum sigillum suum litteris citatoriis ipsius decani apposuit, prefatus P. petiit copiam transcribendi autentici domini pape et habuit [de][3] verbo ad verbum et postea petiit quod sibi ederetur. Ad quod procurator magistri et conventus de Alvingham respondit quod voluit uti ad presens narratione facti contenta in litteris domini pape pro editione, quo audito, petiit prefatus P. inducias deliberatorias[4] et habuit. Judices vero diem partibus eodem loco de consensu partium prefixerunt, scilicet diem lune proximam ante festum sancte Margarete, ad faciendum quod jus dictaverit.

Alvingham Cart., f. 5ʳ

2

Intermediate *acta* in a suit between the prior and convent of Bullington (Gilb. Lincs.) and the abbot and convent of Garendon (Cist. Leics.). Lincoln cathedral, 15 February 1250/1.

(See above, Chapter II, p. 78.)

---

[1] MS. 'dimissim' or 'dimissivi'.   [2] MS. 'sublegatis'.
[3] Not included, but the sense demands it.   [4] MS. 'deliberatoriis'.

Acta in majori ecclesia Lincoln' die mercurii proxima ante festum quod dicitur cathedra sancti Petri anno domini m. cc. quinqua[ge]simo,[1] coram domino Ricardo de Wysebech', canonico Lincoln', decano Christianitatis[2] ejusdem ville, et magistro Willelmo de Novo Castro, gerentibus vices dominorum decani, precentoris et cancellarii secundum formam suarum commissionum; in causa que vertitur inter magistrum ordinis de Sempingam (*sic*) priorem et conventum de Bolington' ejusdem ordinis actores ex una parte, abbatem et conventum de Gerond' reos ex altera, priore de Bolington' personaliter comparente, dicto magistro per eundem priorem, et Ricardum et Lucam canonicos de Bolingt' procuratores suos, sub alternatione constitutos comparente, abbate et conventu de Gerond' per fratrem Ricardum priorem et Robertum Scotum conmonacos suos procuratores suos legitime constitutos, sub alternatione comparentibus. Et licet signum abbatis de Gerond' fuisset in judicio probatum, cum non constaret judicibus literas procuratorias de consciencia conventus de Gerond' fuisse signatas, ex habundanti cavit magister Johannes de Noting' pro conventu sub pena unius marce quod ratum habebit dictus conventus quicquid actum erat dicta die litis per dictos procuratores de Gerond'. Et cum petita esset copia judicialium instrumentorum ex parte rea, et etiam quod fieret sibi editio, judices post aliquas altercationes hinc inde habitas decreverunt parti ree editionem fore faciendam, et similiter copiam judicialium instrumentorum. Proposuit autem pars actrix se velle uti literis papalibus pro editione, petens canonicam justiciam sibi exhiberi, et expensas factas et faciendas in lite sibi adjudicari. Et datus est dies loco quo prius partibus in crastino dominice qua cantatur 'Letare Jerusalem' ad faciendum quod jus dictaverit.[3]

Acta in majori ecclesia Lincoln' die mercurii, proxima ante festum sancti Petri in cathedra, anno domini m. cc. quinquagesimo,[1] coram domino Ricardo de Wysebech' canonico Lincoln' domini decani ejusdem ecclesie commissario, et magistro Symone decano civitatis ejusdem domini precentoris Lincoln', et magistro Willelmo de Novo Castro domini cancellarii Lincoln', secundum formam suarum commissionum vices gerentibus; in causa que vertitur auctorita[te][4] apostolica inter magistrum ordinis de Sempingam (*sic*) priorem et conventum de Bolingtonam actores legitime comparentes ex parte una, abbatem de Gerond' per procuratores, scilicet Ricardum priorem suum et Robertum Scotum monachum suum comparentem, conventu suo licet ad diem illum legitime vocato non comparente. Petebat pars actrix dictum conventum ob sui contumaciam puniri, sed magister Johannes dictus Norman rector ecclesie de Fortonam, pro dicto conventu cavit, sub pena unius marce quod ratificabunt, proximo die litis quod actum fuit, eo die per eundem subiciens se et sua jurisdictioni judicum principalium vel commissariorum eorundem, ut possint compellere eundem ad dicte pene si commitatur solutionem, post varias altercationes.[1]

P.R.O. E 135/6/13

3

Intermediate *acta* in a suit between the abbot and convent of Bec (Ben. dioc. Rouen, France) and the rector of Great Wratting (Suff.). Pinner church (Middx.), 26 July 1245.

(See above, Chapter II, p. 81, III, pp. 153–4.)

Acta in crastino sancti Jacobi apostoli anno domini m. cc. quadragesimo quinto in ecclesia de Pinnore, coram dominis .. decano Middelsex' et Baldrico capellano, gerentibus vices sub alternatione de Benetleye[2] et de Hermodesworth'[3] priorum usque ad Pascha; in causis que vertuntur inter abbatem et conventum de Becco comparentes per Petrum de Suynecumbe et Johannem de Bleddel' procuratores eorum sub alternatione,[4] sine loci et temporis prefinitione legitime et apud acta constitutos ex una parte, et rectorem ecclesie de Magna Wroting', per magistrum Henricum de Trippeleawe comparentem, et priorem et conventum de Doure[5] non comparentes ex altera. Licet quidam pro eis literas quasdam procuratorias in judicio exhiberet, ut prima facie videbatur, contra quas allegatum fuit ex parte dictorum abbatis et conventus quod ipse non valebant, tum quia prior scribebat cujus signum dictis literis non erat appensum, tum quia certum nomen procuratoris non fuit expressum in litera procuratoria, tum quia cum esset ex parte rea deficiebat ibi clausula necessaria 'judicatum solvi'. Unde cum constaret dictis judicibus dictos reos legitime et peremptorie fuisse citatos petita instanter cautione idonea ab illo qui se gerebat pro procuratore dictorum prioris et conventus pro eis, quia eam vel noluit vel non potuit exhibere, decreverunt judices eos quantum ad diem illum esse indefensos, et propter hoc in expensis puniendos propter quod taxatione judicum prehabita sacramento procuratoris ad hoc specialiter constituti subsecuto, condempnaverunt ipsos in duabus marcis sterlingorum, demandantes decano de Doure ut citra festum

---

[1] The final *actum* in this case is B.M. Harley Ch. 53 A 23.
[2] Bentley (Aug. Middx.).   [3] Harmondsworth (Ben. al. Middx.).
[4] 'sub alternacione' is written in here with an omission mark.
[5] Dover (Ben. Kent).

assumptionis beate Marie[1] compellat eos per censuram ecclesiasticam satisfacere dictis abbati et conventui in dictis expensis, quem quidem decanum dictam pecuniam nomine dictorum abbatis et conventus recipere decreverunt; alioquin extunc dictos priorem et conventum denunciet esse suspensos et de die in diem non soluta ei pecunia, per singulas ecclesias de Doure puplice excommunicandos quousque super dictis expensis satisfacerint competentur. Nichilominus decreverunt eos iterato et peremptorie fore vocandos per eundem decanum, quod in crastino beati Mathei apostoli[2] coram eis loco quo prius compareant dictis abbati et conventui responsuri. In hoc autem processum est contra rectorem ecclesie de Magna Wrotting' quod ex decreto judicum porrectus est ei libellus in ju.....[3] ei copia omnium instrumentorum et data est ei dies in vigilia beati Mathei[4] ....[5] ad faciendum quod jus dictaverit non obstante illo interlineari sub alternatione.

Windsor Ch. xi G 27

4

Intermediate *acta* in a suit between the abbot and convent of Bec and the rectors of Dalham and Withersfield (Suff.). Dunstable priory church, 22 February 1235×14 February 1241.

(See above, Chapter II, p. 82.)

Acta in crastino cinerum in ecclesia conventuali de Donestapl', coram R. priore ejusdem loci, in causis que vertuntur inter abbatem et conventum de Becco comparentes per magistrum Laurencium procuratorem usque ad Pascha legitime constitutum ex una parte, et de Dalleham et de Wetherfeld ecclesiarum rectores non comparentes ex altera, videlicet cum datus esset dies predicto rectori de Dalleham ad proponendum omnes exceptiones dilatorias, libello ei porrecto, quia non comparuit, decrevit judex preclusam esse ei viam decetero ad easdem proponendas, et ipsum fore citandum per decanum de Clare, ut die veneris proxima post annunciationem beate Marie coram eodem judice loco quo prius ad litem contestandam precise compareat. Contra rectorem ecclesie de Wetherfeld in hoc est processum quod data ....[6] predicta ad proponendum omnes exceptiones dilatorias, et ad probandum eas que consistunt in facto, et ad signa inhibitionis probanda.

---

[1] 15 Aug. [2] 22 Sept.
[3] Document torn: about one word missing. [4] 20 Sept.
[5] Torn: about two or three words missing.
[6] Document torn: about two words missing.

Protestatus .... [1] abbatis et conventus quod propter predictorum rectorum contumaciam, debet ei fieri refusio expensarum.

On dorse: Daleham.

Windsor Ch. xi G 16

5

Intermediate *acta* in a suit between the prior and convent of Alvingham (Gilb. Lincs.) and Peter, parson of Stainton-le-Vale (Lincs.). St. Michael's chapel, Malton, 12 November 1245.

(See above, Chapter II, p. 82.)

Acta Maltone in capella sancti Michaelis, die sabbati proxima ante festum sancti Leonardi, coram magistro scolarum Malton' principali judice, et subpriore de Kirham et decano de Bukeros, de Brideligton' et de Kirham priorum dimissis[2] subdelegatis; in causa prescripta partibus religiosorum per priorem legitime constitutum procuratorem comparentibus ex una parte, et P. qui se gerit rectorem duarum partium ecclesie talis personaliter comparente ex altera, videlicet quod datus esset dies ad interloquendum super exceptionibus propositis et in retroactis contentis, judices auditis hinc inde rationibus communicato bonorum virorum et jurisperitorum consilio deliberatione prehabita predictas exceptiones interloquendo cassaverunt, et ad litem precise contestandam coram principalibus judicibus diem prefixerunt, scilicet diem lune proximam post festum sancti Andree in ecclesia de Winerthorp,[3] et hec facta sunt de consensu partium.

Alvingham Cart., f. 5ᵛ

6

Intermediate *acta* in a suit between the abbot and convent of Bec and the rector of Withersfield (Suff.). Dunstable priory church, 27 June 1235 × 27 June 1240.

(See above, Chapter II, p. 80.)

Acta in crastino beatorum Johannis et Pauli in conventuali ecclesia de Dunestapl', coram domino priore ejusdem loci gerente vices domini Cantuariens' archiepiscopi, in causa que vertitur inter abbatem et

---

[1] Torn: about three words missing.   [2] MS. 'dimissim' or 'dimissivi'.
[3] 4 December 1245, in the church of Winthorpe (Notts.).

conventum de Becco ex una parte, et G. rectorem ecclesie de Wether-esfeld' ex altera personaliter comparentem, dictis abbate et conventu per magistrum Robertum de Clare comparentibus; videlicet quod dictus rector literas procuratorias dicti magistri dicebat non valere eo quod procurator ante litis contestationem alium procuratorem con-stituere non potest, et ipse a fratre W. de Guinevilla procuratore Beccensi procurator esset constitutus. Ad quod dictus magister respon-dit dictum fratrem W. generalem esse procuratorem predictorum abbatis et conventus, et alium constituendi procuratorem specialem habere potestatem, quod bene constabat judici ut dicebat. Tandem dictus procurator intentioni sue priori hoc addidit, videlicet quod dictus rector spoliavit dictos abbatem et conventum in rebus contentis in libello, et injuriatus est eis super illis vi. annis elapsis, ob quod dictus rector sibi novas petiit dari inducias, dicto magistro R. hoc fieri non debere allegante eo quod lis nondum fuit contestata, et salvum esset ei beneficium juris, scilicet addendi, mutandi vel minuendi, usque ad litis contestationem. Et propter hanc temporis additionem, decrevit dictus judex novas inducias ei dari non debere, quod etiam dictus magister[1] fieri non debere prius allegaverat ut expresse probatur extra de dilationibus c[ap]. 'litere'.[2] Et ob has causas dictus rector ad priorem delegatum appellavit, cujus appellationem dictus judex, eo quod predicta causa ei appellatione remota non fuerat commissa, duxit deferendum diem lune proximum ante festum sancti Michaelis per ...,[3] predicto rectori prefigens infra quem, si sibi viderit expedire, suam prosequatur appellationem.

Windsor Ch. xi G 37(4)

7

Draft of a sentence in a suit between the abbot and convent of Waltham (Aug. Essex) and the prior and convent of Chepstow (Ben. al. Mon.). St. Albans abbey, 27 July 1251.

(See above, Chapter II, pp. 77, 93, and Chapter III, p. 157).

Acta die jovis proxima post festum sancti Jachobi anno gracie m. cc. quinquagesimo primo, in conventuali ecclesia sancti Albani, coram archidiacono ejusdem loci sui prioris judicis a domino papa delegati in totum commissario; in causa que vertitur inter abbatem et conven-tum sancte Crucis de Wauth' per Ricardum de la lade canonicum[4]

---

[1] 'magister' is written in here with an omission mark.   [2] c. 3. X. II. 8.
[3] Document torn: about three letters missing. Possibly a false start.
[4] 'suum' follows here but is crossed out.

procuratorem suum legitime constitutum conparentes ex una parte, et priorem et conventum de Strugull' nullo modo comparentes ex altera, videlicet cum constaret dicto judici eosdem ad audiendam sentenciam precise diffinitivam, dictis die et loco fuisse citatos, judex in penam contumacie eorundem sentenciando hoc modo pronunciavit.[1] In nomine patris et filii et spiritus sancti Amen. Ego Johannes archidiaconus sancti Albani, ejusdem loci prioris judicis a domino papa delegati commissarius in totum; in causa que vertitur inter abbatem et conventum sancte Crucis de Wauth' ex una parte, et priorem et conventum de Strugull' ex altera, super duabus partibus garbarum decimarum de dominico Odonis Bernard' provenientium in parochia de Alritheshereye,[2] auditis et[3] intellectis intentione abbatis et conventus sancte Crucis de Wautham et probationibus eorumdem et aliis ad juris ordinem spectantibus, de virorum prudentium et juris peritorum consilio michi assidentium (et ordine juris in omnibus diligenter observato),[4] supradictos priorem et conventum a dictarum decimarum percepcione sentencialiter condempno, easdem decimas ad prefatos[5] abbatem et conventum de jure[6] communi[7] pertinere declarans,[8] sentencia diffinitiva sepedictis[9] abbati et conventui sentencialiter adjudicando. Decrevit insuper dictus judex executionem istius sentencie inpedientes per decanum de Sefford excommunicationis et interdicti sentenciis fore coercendos. De qua coertione ab.. ....[10] certificari. Dat' anno et die predictis.

On dorse (in a late hand): de quibusdam decimis in alritheseya.

B.M. Egerton Ch. 409

8

Final *actum* in a suit between the prior and convent of Norwich (Ben. Norf.) and the rector of Thornham (Norf.). Norwich, 12 or 15 May 1220.

(See above, Chapter II, p. 93.)

[1] 'diffinitivam' follows here but is crossed out.
[2] Arlesey (Beds.).   [3] 'et' is written above the line here.
[4] 'et ordine juris in omnibus diligenter observato' is written above with an omission mark.
[5] Possibly an erasure here, and 'prefatos' written in.   [6] Text 'juri'.
[7] 'pronuncians' follows here but crossed out: 'declarans' is written above and also deleted.
[8] 'declarans' put in with an omission mark.
[9] 'prefatis' crossed out and 'sepedictis' written above.
[10] Several words missing: the document is torn.

Universis sancte matris ecclesie filiis ad quos presens scriptum pervenerit, R. de Teford'[1] et R. de Wimundham[2] et W. de Bukeham[3] priores salutem in domino. Noverit universitas vestra nos mandatum domini pape Honorii tercii suscepisse in hec verba: Honorius episcopus servus servorum dei dilectis filiis sancte Marie de Teford', de Wimundham et de Bukeham prioribus Norwic' diocesis salutem et apostolicam benedictionem. Querelam dilectorum filiorum prioris et conventus Norwic' recepimus, continentem quod archidiaconus Roffens' et de Tornham et de Possewic' ecclesiarum rectores et quidam alii Norwic' diocesis super quibusdam possessionibus, redditibus, decimis, debitis et rebus aliis injuriantur eisdem. Quo circa discretioni vestre per apostolica scripta mandamus quatinus, partibus convocatis et auditis hinc inde propositis, quod justum fuerit usuris cessantibus appellatione postposita statuatis, facientes quod statueritis per censuram ecclesiasticam firmiter observari. Testes autem qui fuerint nominati si se gracia, odio vel timore subtraxerint per censuram eandem cessante appellatione cogatis veritati testimonium perhibere. Quod si non omnes hiis exequendis potueritis interesse duo vestrum ea nichilominus exequantur. Datum Rome apud sanctum Petrum xiii. kalendas Januarii pontificatus nostri anno primo.[4] Hujus igitur auctoritate mandati constitutis in presencia nostra T. de Becles monacho et procuratore capituli Norwic' ex una parte, et Roberto Buttamund' rectore ecclesie de Tornham ex altera, tandem post multas dilationes predictus procurator petebat nomine annui beneficii de ecclesia de Tornham sexdecim summas frumenti et decem ordei, quinque fabarum et quinque pisorum insuper, et arreragia octo annorum, in quibus predictum R. nomine ecclesie de Tornham Norwic' ecclesie obligatum asserebat. Cumque ex parte predicti R. fuisset responsum priorem et conventum Norwic' injuste petere in petitione sua contenta eo quod de quibusdam terris domibus et homagiis quibus ecclesiam suam de Tornham per Gregorium clericum suum spoliatam asserebat, debuit predicta prestatio annua persolvi et hoc in modum reconventionis proposuisset. Lite in hunc modum contestata ad productionem testium diem partibus duximus prefigendum. Testibus igitur hinc inde productis et diligenter examinatis et post examinationem legitime factam attestationibus publicatis, dies ad dicendum in testes et testificata partibus per legitima intervalla prefiximus.[5] Dictis ergo testium rationibus etiam et allegationibus partium diligenter consideratis et legitime pensatis, cum tam per depositiones juratorum fide dignorum quam per tenorem instrumentorum didicissemus priorem et conventum Norwic'

---

[1] Thetford (Clun. Norf.). There were two priories in Thetford, one Cluniac and one Augustinian.   [2] Wymondham (Ben. Norf.).
[3] Buckenham (Aug. Norf.).   [4] 20 Dec. 1216.
[5] The 'p' has a stroke through it, but the sense demands 'pre'.

intentionem suam probasse, et predictum R. in probatione intentionis
sue defecisse, communicato virorum prudentum et juris peritorum
nobis assidentium consilio, ipsum R. Buttamund' ad solutionem predictarum summarum annuam, videlicet sexdecim frumenti et decem
ordei, quinque fabarum et quinque pisorum nomine annui beneficii de
ecclesia de Tornham priori et conventui Norwic' faciendam, necnon
ad arreragia octo annorum et expensas sex marcarum per diffinitivam
sentenciam condempnavimus; decernentes insuper ut a rectore ecclesie
de Tornham, qui pro tempore fuerit, in perpetuum predicte summe
sine contradictione prefatis priori et conventui Norwic' nomine annui
beneficii de predicta ecclesia integre, plenarie, et sine diminutione, ad
festum sancti Michaelis annuatim persolvantur. Et in hujus rei testimonium presens scriptum sigillis nostris duximus muniendum. Hiis
testibus domino Philippo de Leeston', domino Hugone de Langel',
abbatibus, Laurentio decano de Deppewad', Ricardo vicedecano
Norwic', magistro Waltero de Tirington', magistro Rogero de Cantel',
magistro Stephano de Ecclesfled, magistro Roberto de Bilneie, domino
Willelmo de Bec, Godefr' de Tiln'. Actum apud Norwic' anno ab
incarnatione domini m. cc. xx. feria sexta ante pentecosten.

3 tags for seals.

On dorse: Sententie judicum de Tornham.

Norwich Ch. 1686

III. DOCUMENTS CONCERNING THE JUDGES
AND THEIR ADMINISTRATIVE OFFICERS

I

Memorandum recording the prior of Dunstable's reply to
the revocatory letters sent to him by the prior of Langley
(Prem. Norf.) and his colleagues. 22 November 1234 ×
25 April 1241.

(See above, Ch. III, p. 104.)

Memorandum quod tales litere emanaverunt a domino[1] priore de
Dunestapl' priori de Langelee et suis collegis directe in hec verba.
Prior de Dunestapl' viris venerabilibus et discretis priori de Langelee et
suis collegis salutem. Miramur plurimum et movemur quod vos juris
ordine perturbato sub pena suspensionis nobis inibuistis ne in causa que
vertitur inter abbatem et conventum de Becco ex una parte et rectorem

———
[1] 'domino' is written above with an omission mark.

ecclesie de Wethresfeld' ex altera procederemus,[1] cum hoc facere non deberetis nisi primitus de vestra jurisdictione et signacione literarum inibicionis nobis constaret, cum habeamus majorem quam vos vel saltim parem vobis potestatem, propter quod vice versa vobis mandamus firmiter injungendo ne in causa inter predictas personas mota in nostre jurisdictionis prejudicium, cum de ea jurisdictione nobis constet procedatis quo usque de jurisdictione vestra et que litere secundum formam decretalium aliis prevaleant nobis constiterit evidenter, presertim cum litere abbatis et conventus secundum quod credimus sint priores usu tempore et primo iudici presentate quam litere predicti rectoris et etiam quoniam ejus litere sunt tacita veritate impetrate secundum quod hec omnia probare dicti abbas et conventus sunt parati. Valete in domino.

Windsor Ch. xi G 37 (9)

2

Notes about a suit between the prior and convent of Clifford (Clun. al. Heref.) and the abbot and convent of Abbey Dore (Cist. Heref.). On or after ? 15 November 1253.

(See above, Ch. III, pp. 139, 153.)

Innocentius episcopus servus servorum dei dilecto filio priori de Kem'[2] Menn' diocesis[3] salutem et apostolicam benedictionem. Dilectorum filiorum prioris et conventus de Cliff'[4] Cluniac' ordinis Heref diocesis precibus inclinati, presentium tibi auctoritate mandamus quatinus ea que de bonis ecclesiarum de Brendl'[5] et de Landevatl'[6] ad eos pleno jure spectantium alienata inveneritis illicite vel distracta ad jus et proprietatem ipsarum ecclesiarum legitime[7] revocare procuretis, contradictores per censuram ecclesiasticam appellatione postposita[8] compescendo. Testes autem etc. Dat' Perusii x. kalendas Augusti pontificatus nostri anno x.[9]

[1] On the whole case and the documents see above, p. 315.
[2] Probably Carmarthen, see *A History of Carmarthenshire*, ed. J. E. Lloyd (Cardiff, 1935), Map VI, and W. Rees, *South Wales and the Border in the Fourteenth Century* (Ordnance Survey Office, Southampton, n.d.), SW. sheet.
[3] St. Davids diocese.
[4] See Rees, *South Wales*, NE. sheet.
[5] Brwynllys (Brecon), one mile north-west of Talgarth, see *South Wales*, SE. sheet.
[6] Llandefalle (Brecon), 2 miles east of Brywnllys, *South Wales*, SE. sheet.
[7] A false start after this?   [8] False start.
[9] 23 July 1252.

F   Dies .... [1] et dies mercurii ante festum sancti Th[ome] apud Brecon'.[2]

F   Fuit propositum ex parte abbatis et conventus de Dora[3] quod vicarius de Talgard[4] judex esse non poterat, quia non fuit constitutus in aliqua dignitate, et ne ulterius congnosceret fuit ad principalem et papam appellatum.

F   Memorandum quod talis littera emanavit. Prior de Kem' judex a domino papa delegatus discreto viro decano Brecon' salutem in domino. Auctoritate domini pape qua fungimur, cujus autenticum vobis transmittimus inspiciendum, vobis mandamus firmiter injungentes quatinus peremptorie[5] citetis abbatem et conventum de Dora quod compareant coram nobis vel commissariis nostris, in cathedrali ecclesia Land' in crastino sancti Eaidmundi,[6] priori (et conventui)[7] de Cliff'[8] secundum formam mandati [apostolici][9] responsuri et juriparituri.

[Discreto viro priori de Kem' judici][10] a domino papa delegato vel quibuscumque commissariis .. decanus Brecon' salutem in domino. [Secundum][11] mandatum vestrum peremptorie citavi abbatem et conventum de Dora quod compareant coram vobis vel commissariis vestris, in cathedrali ecclesia Land' in crastino sancti Eadmundi regis, priori et conventui de Cliff' secundum formam mandati apostolici responsuri et juriparituri. In cujus rei testimonium etc. Dat' Brecon' die sabbati proxima post festum sancti Martini.[12]

P.R.O. E 135/24/4

F signifies where the scribe has begun a new paragraph.

3

Indult of Honorius III to the abbot and prior of St. Augustine's, Canterbury (Ben.), exempting them from hearing cases. Lateran, 27 April 1221.

(See above, Chapter III, p. 146.)

Honorius episcopus (servus servorum dei .. abbati et priori sancti Augustini Cantuarien' salutem et apostolicam benedictionem).[13] Cum sicut exhibita nobis vestra petitio continebat cognitioni causarum que

---

1 Illegible: ? 'martis'.   2 ? 18 Dec. 1252.   3 South Wales, SE. sheet.
4 Talgarth (Brecon), South Wales, SE. sheet.   5 Document 'peremtp".
6 21 Nov. (? 1253) at Llandaff cathedral.   7 'et conventui' is written above.
8 Possibly a false start.   9 Possible reading: the document is torn.
10 Document torn: about six words missing.
11 Document torn: probably one word missing.   12 Probably 15 Nov. 1253.
13 St. Augustine's Red Book: missing in St. Augustine's Cart. which has 'etc' instead.

vobis a sede apostolica delegantur, absque gravi vestri monasterii lesione ac turbatione regularis observancie intendere nequeatis, nos indempnitati monasterii vestri et vestre quieti providere volentes, auctoritate vobis presentium indulgemus ne de causis cognoscere compellamini vobis de cetero a sede apostolica delegandis, nisi forte in commissionis litteris de indulgencia hujusmodi mentio habeatur. Ne autem aliqui per ignoranciam ad vos commissionis (litteras)[1] impetrantes exinde dampnum incurrant, volumus ut per partes vicinas hanc indulgenciam publicetis. Data[2] Lateran' (v kalendas Maii pontificatus nostri anno quinto).[3]

St. Augustine's Red Book, f. 25ᵛ; and St. Augustine's Cart., f. 66ᵛ (also in Reg. Vat. 11, f. 114).

4

Indult of Honorius III to the abbot of Waltham (Aug. Essex) exempting him from hearing cases. Lateran, 19 April 1221.

(See above, Chapter III, p. 146.)

Honorius episcopus servus servorum dei dilecto filio .. abbati de Waltham ordinis sancti Augustini salutem et apostolicam benedictionem. Cum propter[4] rerum dispendia et labores quos in persona propria oporteret [m]ultotiens[5] te subire propter multiplicitatem causarum que tibi a sede apostolica delegantur, et quies tui ordinis perturbetur et grave immineat commisse tibi ecclesie detrimentum, nobis humiliter supplicasti ut tibi et ecclesie eidem super hoc providere de benignitate sedis apostolice dignaremur, nos igitur tuis postulationibus inclinati auctoritate presentium tibi duximus indulgendum ut auctoritate litterarum nostrarum de causis aliquibus congnoscere in posterum non cogaris que specialem non fecerint de hac indulgencia mentionem. Ita tamen quod per vicinas partes hoc facias publice nunciari. Dat' Lateran' xiii kalendas Maii pontificatus nostri anno quinto.

Waltham Cart., f. 73ʳ

5

Notification by H(enry) de Sandford, archdeacon of Canterbury, of the execution of a sentence at Crundale (Kent). October 1225×26 December 1226.

(See above, Chapter III, pp. 156–7.)

---

[1] Cart.: missing in Red Book.   [2] Cart. has 'Datum'.
[3] Red Book: Cart. has 'etc'.   [4] MS. 'preter'.   [5] MS. 'ultotiens'.

In margin: Executio ejusdem sentencie.

Omnibus Christi fidelibus presens scriptum inspecturis H. de Sandford archidiaconus Cantuariensis salutem in domino. Literas de Rofa[1] et de Lesnes[2] priorum et archidiaconi Roffensis judicum a domino papa delegatorum suscepimus in hec verba .. prior Roffensis et prior de Lesnes et archidiaconus Roffensis viro venerabili archidiacono Cant' salutem in domino. Cum inter priorem et conventum de Ledes[3] ex una parte, et Johannem rectorem ecclesie de Crumdale ex altera, super viginti quinque solidis annuis dictis priori et conventui ab ecclesia de Crumdale nomine beneficii debitis coram nobis auctoritate domini pape cognoscentibus questio mota fuisset, partibus in presencia nostra constitutis post plura hinc inde proposita, instrumentis dictorum prioris et conventus in medio exhibitis et aliis judiciis et eisdem fideliter indagatis virorum prudentium usi consilio, prenominatos viginti quinque solidos annuos dictis priori et conventui esse debitos, ab eo qui pro tempore dicte ecclesie rector extiterit, pronunciamus per sentenciam diffinitivam. Qua propter auctoritate domini pape qua fungimur vobis mandamus quatinus memoratos priorem et conventum in memorati possessionem beneficii annui induci faciatis et inductos illos tueri, contradictores si quos inveneritis aut rebelles per ecclesiasticam censuram compescentes.[4] Hujus igitur auctoritate mandati prenominatos priorem de Ledes et conventum in possessionem annui redditus memorati ab ecclesia de Crumdale singulis annis percipiendi per magistrum Rogerum officialem nostrum induci fecimus. In hujus rei testimonium presentibus literis sigillum nostrum apponi fecimus. Valete.

Leeds Cart., f. 10ᵛ

6

Letter of judges delegate to the dean of Gloucester ordering him to carry out a sentence at Painswick (Glos.), and to excommunicate the dean of Easton Neston (Northants.) for his contempt. 22 × 29 August 1235.

(See above, Chapter III, pp. 160–1.)

In red: De ecclesia de Wyka. Sentencia delegatoria super ordinatione facta inter priorem Lanth' et magistrum Baudinum.

Magister Rogerus de Cantilup' Meneven's[5] et Johannes de Fumon' sancti Angeli[6] de Ferentin'[7] canonici, judices a domino papa delegati,

---

[1] Rochester (Ben. Kent).	[2] Lesnes (Aug. Kent).
[3] Leeds (Aug. Kent).	[4] MS. 'composcentes'.
[5] St. Davids. [6] MS. 'angl'i'.	[7] St. Angelo, Ferentino.

dilecto sibi in Christo decano de Glouc' salutem in domino. Ecce mittimus vobis sentenciam latam in questione que quondam vertebatur inter Magistrum Baudinum canonicum Trecen'[1] et Magistrum W. archidiaconum Wygorn' super ecclesia de Payneswyk', necnon ordinationem factam super eadem ecclesia inter priorem et conventum de Lanth' et ipsum magistrum Baudinum et vicarium eiusdem ecclesie, cum litteris domini pape quarum auctoritate processimus, quare vobis sub pena excommunicationis districte mandamus quatinus dictam sentenciam et ordinationem cum dictis litteris de verbo ad verbum diligenter inspiciatis, et faciatis executioni mandari mandatum nostrum taliter impleturi, quod contra vos procedere non cogamur, quibus inspectis latori presentium restituatis. Insuper mandamus vobis sub pena predicta quatinus decanum de Hesteneston' propter ipsius inhobedienciam manifestam excommunicatum[2] faciatis publice nunciari, nichilominus citantes eundem iterato[3] peremtorio edicto ut coram nobis compareat per procuratorem legittimum die martis proxima post nativitatem beate virginis in ecclesia sancti Pauli London', Franconi procuratori Magistri Baudini canonici Trecen' super expensis quas occasione dicte inobediencie fecit satisfacturus, et nobis super contemp[t]um[4] prout justum fuerit responsurus. Qualiter autem mandatum nostrum in hac parte fueritis executi nobis per litteras vestras patentes faciatis constare. Valete.

Lanthony Cart. A 1, XVI, no. xiiii

IV. DOCUMENTS ILLUSTRATIVE OF THE BUSINESS OF THE COURTS, THE PARTIES, AND THE PROCTORS

I

Settlement of a suit between the convent of Farewell (Ben. nuns, Staffs.) and the prioress and nuns of Langley (Ben. Leics.), made by R(ichard de Dalham), dean, N., the precentor, and Master Thomas Foliot, canon of Lichfield, in a suit about conventual jurisdiction. 20 December 1209 × 2 February 1210.

(See above, Chapter IV, p. 175.)

Omnibus sancte matris ecclesie filiis ad quos presens scriptum pervenerit, R. decanus N. precentor et Magister T. Foliot canonicus Lichesfeldensis ecclesie salutem in domino. Mandatum domini pape in hec verba suscepimus: Innocentius episcopus servus servorum dei

---

[1] Troyes.
[3] MS. 'uterato'.

[2] MS. 'excommunicatam'.
[4] MS. 'contempm''.

dilectis filiis decano precentori Magistro Thome Foliot Lichesfelden' Coventren' diocesis salutem et apostolicam benedictionem. Lecta nobis monialium de Fairwell' conquestio patefecit quod prioressa et moniales ecclesie de Langeleia Lincolnien' diocesis cujus ordinatio ad ipsas de jure dinoscitur pertinere subjectionem ab eis sibi debitam subtrahere non formidant, ideoque discretioni vestre per apostolica scripta mandamus quatinus partibus convocatis audiatis causam et appellatione remota fine canonico decidatis, facientes quod decreveritis per censuram ecclesiasticam firmiter observari. Testes autem qui fuerint nominati si se gracia, odio vel timore subtraxerint per censuram eandem cessante appellatione cogatis veritati testimonium perhibere; nullis literis veritati et justicie prejudicantibus[1] a sede apostolica impetratis. Quod si non omnes hiis exsequendis potueritis interesse duo vestrum ea nichilominus exequantur. Datum Lat' ii nonas Aprilis pontificatus nostri anno xii. Hujus igitur auctoritate mandati partibus vocatis et presentibus, controversia mota inter moniales de Fairwell' et moniales de Langeleia in hunc modum amicabiliter conquievit; videlicet quod vacante domo de Langeleia vocabitur priorissa de Fairwell' a conventu de Langeleia ut electioni intersit et illa cum ceteris monialibus de Langeleia eliget priorissam majori et saniori parti consentiens, sine contradictione et impedimento ab ipsa priorissa facienda, regula tamen ordinis in omnibus observata, si autem vocata non venerit nec aliqua loco sui miserit nichilominus procedet electio. Priorissa vero de Langeleia retinebit in domo sua Aliciam de Ely et tractabit sicut alias moniales domus sue per quinquennium a purificatione beate Marie proxima post consecrationem Hugonis archidiaconi Wellensis in episcopum Lincolniensem, finito autem quinquennio predicta Alicia ad domum[2] propriam de Fairwell' redibit nisi de consensu utriusque domus ibi ulterius remaneat, et deinceps mittent et recipient domus de Fairwell' et domus de Langeleia moniales ad invicem prout ordo postulaverit. Priorissa vero de Fairwell' et conventus prelibatis solempnibus fideliter sibi reservatis omni juri quod tempore[3] hujus compositionis facte in domo de Langeleia se dicebant habere in presencia nostra imperpetuum renunciaverunt. Hanc autem compositionem firmiter observandam utriusque domus priorissei (sic) de assensu conventus sui tactis sacrosanctis juravit, et in hujus conpositionis testimonium signa sua una cum nostris huic scripto prefate priorisse apposuerunt, et autenticum domini pape priorissa de Fairwell' reddidit priorisse de Langeleia. Valete in domino.

Two tags for seals. Two slits for tags.

P.R.O. E 135/2/28

[1] Document 'predicantibus': corrected in another hand.
[2] Document 'domu'.   [3] Document 'temporo'.

2

Ordination by E(ustace de Fauconberg), bishop of London, in a suit between the prior and convent of St. Botolph, Colchester (Aug. Essex), and the prior and convent of Holy Trinity, Aldgate (Aug. London), over the relationship between the two houses. St. Paul's, London, 26 January 1223/4.

(See above, Chapter IV, p. 177 and Chapter V, p. 247.)

Omnibus Christi fidelibus presens scriptum inspecturis, E. dei gratia London' episcopus salutem in domino. Noverit universitas vestra quod cum prior et conventus Sancti Botulphi Colecestr' priorem et conventum Sancte Trinitatis London' coram abbate de Langeleya priore et decano Norwicens', judicibus a summo pontifice videlicet Honorio tercio delegatis, super subjectione, obediencia, professione, visitatione, procuratione et rerum ejusdem ecclesie dispositione traxissent in causam, tandem post multas altercationes utraque pars unanimi assensu et voluntate spontanea super premissis et omnibus dictos articulos contingentibus se nostre subjecerunt ordinationi. Nos igitur auditis hinc inde propositis inspectisque utriusque partis instrumentis et plenius intellectis, ex quibus omnibus liquido nobis constabat ecclesiam Sancte Trinitatis Lond' et canonicos ibidem deo servientes a cujuslibet ecclesie subjectione preterquam ecclesie Sancti Pauli London' a prima sui fundatione semper fuisse liberos, utriusque partis paci et tranquillitati providere volentes de consilio prudentium et jurisperitorum nobis assidentium ita duximus ordinandum; videlicet ut ecclesia Sancte Trinitatis et ejusdem loci canonici a subjectione obediencia et omnibus premissis liberi maneant in perpetuum mutuis orationum suffragiis inter memoratas ecclesias specialiter perseverantibus. Hanc autem nostram ordinationem utraque pars firmiter et bona fide se promisit observaturam, renuncians supplicationi, in integrum restitutioni, inpetratis et inpetrandis et omni beneficio juris contra hanc nostram ordinationem facientibus. In cujus rei testimonium sigillum nostrum et capituli nostri una cum sigillis partium huic scripto in modum cyrographi tripartite confecto duximus apponendum, cujus una pars penes dictos priorem et conventum Sancte Trinitatis et altera penes priorem et conventum Sancti Botulphi, et tercia in thesauro Sancti Pauli London' remanebit. Actum apud Sanctum Paulum London' anno ab incarnatione domini m. cc. xxiii. in crastino conversionis Sancti Pauli Apostoli. Hiis testibus E. priore de Meretun', Roberto decano London', Philippo archidiacono Huntedun', Willelmo archidiacono de Stowe, Philippo de Lucy, Magistro Roberto de Iwyardesby officiali domini Elyensis,

Magistro Reginaldo de Radenor' et Magistro Roberto de Arch' domini London' officialibus, Magistro Gregòrio de London', Magistro Adam de fontibus, Magistro Waltero de Tresgoz.

Tag with remains of seal.	Slit for seal tag.	Portion of seal on tag.	Seal on tag of Holy Trinity, Aldgate; counter seal.	Seal on tag of St. Botolph, Colchester; counter seal.

On dorse: Ordinatio Eustachii episcopi London' facta de ecclesia Sancte Trinitatis London' et ecclesia Sancti Botulfi Colecestr' habenda in perpetuum in thesauro Sancti Pauli London'.

St. Paul's, Press A Box 23, Ch. 864

3

Final *actum* of the judges delegate, P(eter de Cicester), dean, A(lard), chancellor, and L (?Lambert) subdean of Wells, reporting the course of a suit between W. called *pincerna*, a layman, and his sons, and the abbot and convent of Margam (Cist. Glam.), about land. n.d. but after 12 January 1222.

(See above, Chapter IV, pp. 181 and 218.)

Omnibus sancte matris ecclesie filiis P. decanus, A. cancellarius et L. subdecanus Wellenses salutem in domino. Mandatum domini pape suscepimus in hec verba: Honorius episcopus servus servorum dei dilectis filiis decano, cancellario et subdecano Wellens' Bathon' diocesis salutem et apostolicam benedictionem. W. dictus pincerna R. et J. filii ejus nobis conquerendo monstrarunt quod de Margan et de Neth abbates Cisterciensis ordinis Landavens' diocesis super terris et rebus aliis injuriantur eisdem, ideoque discretioni vestre per apostolica scripta mandamus quatinus partibus convocatis, audiatis causam et apellatione remota fine debito terminetis, facientes quod decreveritis per censuram ecclesiasticam firmiter observari. Testes autem qui fuerint nominati si se gracia, odio vel timore subtraxerint per districtionem eandem appellatione cessante cogatis veritati testimonium perhibere. Quod si non omnes hiis exequendis potueritis interesse duo vestrum ea nichilominus exequantur. Datum Lateran' ii idus Januarii pontificatus nostri anno sexto. Hujus igitur auctoritate mandati abbatem et conventum de Margan citavimus dictis W. pincerne R. et J. filiis suis coram nobis responsuros et juri parituros, quibus tandem per fratrem R. monachum ejusdem domus procuratorem suum in nostra presencia comparentibus et predictis W., R. et J. respondentibus, facta est eis sufficiens editio de terris et rebus aliis super quibus eis injuriari dicebantur, et postea prefixus est eis dies ad omnes exceptiones dilatorias que sibi conpeterent proponendas. Et ecce interim operante illo qui fecit utraque unum pax inter partes est reformata et concordia confirmata, ita scilicet quod prenominati W. et filii sui omnes questiones et exactiones super terris et rebus aliis quas habuerunt adversum domum de Margan omnino remiserunt, sicut litere eorumdem patentes ad nos misse protestantur. Nos autem hanc predictorum W. et filiorum suorum et domus de Margan concordiam et pacem gratam habentes et ratam in posterum fore volentes, sigilla nostra huic scripto apposuimus in testimonium.

Seal on tag (damaged):   Tag for seal.   Seal on tag (damaged):
(a seeded fleur-de-lis according   (an *agnus dei*).
to B.M. Cat.).

On dorse (in red): finalis compositio inter domum de Margan et domum de Neth et (? W) pincernam et R. et J. filios ejus.

B.M. Harley Ch. 75 B 2

4

Final *actum* of the judges delegate, the abbot of Thame (Cist. Oxon.), the prior of Abingdon (Ben. Berks.), and the rural dean of Stanton (probably Stanton Harcourt, Oxon.), in a suit between the nuns of Stamford (Ben. Northants.) and the canons of Canons Ashby (Aug. Northants.), about the advowson of the church of Puttenham (Herts.). n.d. but after 27 February 1217.

(See above, Chapter IV, pp. 184–5.)

Omnibus Christi fidelibus frater S. dictus abbas de Tham' et O. dictus prior de Abindon' et decanus de Staunton' salutem in domino. Noverit universitas vestra nos literas domini pape in hec verba sussepisse: Honorius episcopus servus servorum dei dilectis filiis abbati de Tam' priori de Abindon' et decano de Staunton' Linc' et Salesbir' diocesum salutem et apostolicam benedictionem. Priorissa et moniales ecclesie de Sanford nobis conquerendo monstraverunt quod cum jus patronatus ecclesie de Puteham sibi ab R. milite (f. 50ᵛ) vero patrono legitime fuisset collatum, prior et canonici de Esseby et quidam alii Linc' diocesis super eodem contra justiciam inquietant. Idcirco discretioni vestre per apostolica scripta mandamus quatinus vocatis qui fuerint evocandi et, auditis hinc inde propositis, quod canonicum fuerit appellatione postposita statuatis, facientes quod statueritis per censuram ecclesiasticam firmiter observari. Testes autem qui fuerint nominati si se gracia, odio vel timore subtraxerint, per censuram eandem appellatione cessante cogatis veritati testimonium perhibere. Quod si non omnes hiis exequendis potueritis interesse duo vestrum ea nichilominus exequantur. Datum Lateratum (sic) iii kalendas Martii pontificatus nostri anno primo. Hujus auctoritate mandati constitutis in presencia nostra literatorie procuratoribus datis ad componendum, videlicet ex parte monialium de Sanford domino A. capellano et ex parte canonicorum de Esseby domino R. suppriore, controversia inter eosdem mota super patronatu ecclesie de Putteham amicabiliter hoc fine quievit; videlicet quod moniales per dictum procuratorem suum liti et juri si quod habuerint in peticione sua renunciaverunt. Canonici vero de Esseby per predictum procuratorem suum specialiter ad hoc datum concesserunt dictis monialibus unam marcam argenti a domo sua de Esseby inperpetuum annuatim sine difficultate ad duos terminos anni percipiendam, videlicet ad festum sancti Michaelis dimidiam marcam et ad pascha dimidiam marcam per nuncium canonicorum de Esseby apud prioratum de Sanford. Et ad hec facienda dicti canonici per cartam suam dictis monialibus se obligaverunt et dicte moniales dictis canonicis super dicti juris renunciatione cartam suam confecerunt. Nos vero compositionem istam inter eos rationabiliter initam et ab[1] utraque parte juramento confirmatam acceptantes, auctoritate apostolica qua fungebamur illam presenti scripto duximus confirmare. Et ne aliqua partium futuris temporibus possit contra factum suum venire, de consensu parcium recuremus nos et successores nostri plenam potestatem auctoritate dictarum literarum domini pape coercendi partes ad dictam pacem observandam, si qua resilire voluerint, sub pena legibus et canonibus statuta. In hujus autem rei testimonium presenti scripto sigilla nostra apposuimus. Facta autem.[2]

Canons Ashby Cart., f. 50 r-v

5

Report of A(ymer de Valence), bishop elect of Winchester, Geoffrey, dean, and brother Hugh, warden of the Friars minor of Chichester, judges delegate of Innocent IV, of the

---

[1] 'omni' here: crossed out. [2] The text ends abruptly here.

suit between the abbot and convent of Jumièges (dioc. Rouen, France) and Nicholas of Rye, rector of Hayling (Hants), about the church there. Hayling, 28 December 1253.

(See above, Chapter IV, pp. 190–1.)

Universis presentes litteras inspecturis, A. dei gratia Wynton' electus, G. decanus et frater Hug' gardianus fratrum minorum Cycestr' salutem in domino. Noverit universitas vestra nos mandatum domini[1] suscepisse sub hac forma: Innocentius episcopus servus servorum dei dilectis filiis .. electo Wynton', decano et gardiano fratrum minorum Cycestr' salutem et apostolicam benedictionem. Cum dilectis filiis .. abbate et conventu Gemeticen' ordinis sancti Benedicti Rothomagen' diocesis in ecclesia de Heling' Wynt' diocesis, in qua ipsi jus optinent patronatus, duas partes omnium decimarum proponentibus se habere ac etiam a tempore cujus non extat memoria percepisse, et nos ecclesiam ipsam cum parte alia quam Nicholaus de Rya rector ipsius percipit eis ad supplicationem ipsorum post cessionem vel obitum rectoris ejusdem in usus proprios retinendam, de gracia concesserimus liberali; ita tamen quod in ecclesia ipsa perpetuus statuatur vicarius, cui pro sui sustentatione ac episcopalibus et archidiaconalibus aliis que omnibus ecclesie ejusdem supportandis congrua de ipsius proventibus portio assignetur. Quia de quantitate portionis hujusmodi posset contentio suboriri, discretioni vestre per apostolica scripta mandamus quatinus consideratis ecclesie predicte facultatibus portionem auctoritate nostra taxetis eandem prout secundum deum id circumspectio vestra viderit faciendum; contradictores per censuram ecclesiasticam appellatione postposita compescendo, non obstante si aliquibus a sede apostolica sit indultum quod interdici, suspendi vel excommunicari non possint per litteras apostolicas non facientes plenam et expressam de indulto hujusmodi mentionem. Quod si non omnes hiis exequendis potueritis interesse duo vestrum ea nichilominus exequantur. Datum Asisii xvi kalendas Octobris pontificatus nostri anno undecimo.[2] Hujus igitur auctoritate mandati nos apud Heling' personaliter accedentes, pensatisque ipsius ecclesie facultatibus de prudentium virorum consilio, taxamus et ordinamus perpetuam vicariam ecclesie de Helyng' videlicet in hunc modum; quod perpetuus vicarius qui pro tempore fuerit in eadem habeat totam curiam cum ipsius curie domibus et pertinentiis quam quondam Nicholaus de Rya tenuit et habere consuevit. Et quod habeat etiam totas terras arrabiles et incultas cum omnibus earum pertinentiis quas idem N. tenuit omnibus tenentibus cum eorum tenementis quos consuevit predictus N. habere exceptis.

---

[1] Erasure here, probably of 'pape'.   [2] 16 Sept. 1253.

Et quod habeat etiam omnes oblationes et oventiones cum ceteris proventibus altaris et minutas decimas totius insule de Heling' et quicquid pertinet ad jus parochiale sive consistat in decimis personalibus sive realibus, exceptis decimis garbarum et bladi et leguminum et decimis provenientibus de curia sive de dominico abbatis et conventus Gemeticen' ac prioris de Heling' quos a prestatione decimarum volumus esse inmunes, nisi aliquas possessiones de novo adepti fuerint, sive alique ad dominicum eorum pervenerint de quibus minute decime dari consueverunt.[1] Taxamus etiam auctoritate memorata concedimus et ordinamus quod abbas et conventus monasterii Gemet', sive procuratores ipsorum qui pro tempore fuerint, habeant et percipiant libere omnes majores decimas totius insule de Helyng' que consistunt in omni genere bladi et leguminum preter quam decimas de dictis terris vicarii quas volumus a prestatione decime esse immunes, et quod habeant omnes tenentes cum eorum tenementis quos habere consuevit quondam predictus N. de Rya. Statuimus etiam quod perpetuus vicarius, qui pro tempore fuerit in predicta ecclesia de Heling', onera episcopalia archidiaconalia et omnia alia debita ordinaria et consueta sustineat. Et ut hec taxatio et ordinatio nostra perpetue stabilitatis robur optineat sigilla nostra huic scripto duximus apponenda. Datum apud Helyng' die dominica proxima post natale domini anno gracie millesimo ducentesimo quinquagesimo tercio.

Slit for pendant seal.   Seal on silk cords   Seal on silk cords of Hugh,
                         of Geoffrey, dean   warden of the Friars minor
                         of Chichester.   of Chichester.

B.M. Harley Ch. 83 C 32

6

Mandate of Gregory IX to the priors of Reading (Ben. Berks.), Sherborne (Ben. Dors.), and Poughley (Aug. Berks.), ordering them to hear a suit between William of Englefield, knight, and the abbot and convent of Missenden (Aug. Bucks.). Lateran, 24 July 1240.

(See above, Ch. IV, pp. 204 and 218.)

Gregorius episcopus servus servorum dei dilectis filiis .. de Redinges .. de Shirburn' et .. de Pokheley prioribus Saresbirien' et Wintonien'

---

[1] Document 'consuevernt'.

diocesum, salutem et apostolicam benedictionem. Willelmus de Englefeld' miles nobis conquerendo monstravit quod cum .. abbas et
conventus monasterii de Messenden' ordinis sancti Augustini Lincolniensis diocesis teneantur in ejus capella de Sipplake,[1] que in proprio
ipsius fundo consistit, per aliquem ex canonicis ipsius monasterii sibi
et ejus familie facere celebrari divina, iidem id facere indebite contradicunt, propter quod eadem capella debitis officiis defraudatur et
ipsi patiuntur in spiritualibus detrimentum. Ideoque discretioni vestre
per apostolica scripta mandamus quatinus partibus convocatis audiatis
causam et appellatione remota fine debito terminetis, facientes quod
statueritis per censuram ecclesiasticam firmiter observari. Testes autem
qui fuerint nominati si se gracia, odio vel timore subtraxerint per
censuram eadem appellatione cessante cogatis veritati testimonium
perhibere. Quod si non omnes hiis exequendis potueritis interesse duo
vestrum ea nichilominus exequantur. Datum Lateran' viiii kalendas
Augusti pontificatus nostri anno quartodecimo.

Hemp cords for bulla.

B.M. Add. Ch. 20371

7

Final *actum* of the judges delegate, recording the settlement
made between William of Englefield, knight, and the abbot
and convent of Missenden, over the chapel of Shiplake
(Oxon.). The parties subjected themselves to the judges, the
bishop of Lincoln and the archdeacon of Oxford, and their
successors, who were to compel them to observe the arrangement if necessary. 29 November 1242.

Universis[2] Christi fidelibus presens scriptum visuris vel audituris, de
Radingia et Sireburne et de Poheley priores judices a domino papa
delegati salutem in domino. Mandatum domini pape suscepimus in hec
verba: Gregorius episcopus servus servorum dei dilectis filiis de Radinges de Sireburne et de Poheley prioribus Sar' et Winton' diocesum,
salutem et apostolicam benedictionem. Willelmus de Englefed miles
nobis conquerendo monstravit quod cum abbas et conventus monasterii de Messendene ordinis sancti Augustini Lincoln' diocesis teneantur in ejus capella de Sipplak', que in proprio ipsius fundo consistit,
per aliquem ex canonicis ipsius monasterii sibi et ejus familie facere

---

[1] Shiplake (Oxon.). [2] The 'U' is lacking.

celebrari divina, iidem id facere indebite contradicunt, propter quod eadem capella debitis officiis defraudatur et ipsi patiuntur in spiritualibus detrimentum. Ideoque discretioni vestre per apostolica scripta mandamus quatinus partibus convocatis, audiatis causam et eam appellatione remota fine debito terminetis, facientes quod statueritis per censuram ecclesiasticam firmiter observari. Testes autem qui fuerint nominati si se gracia, odio vel timore subtraxerint per censuram eandem appellatione cessante cogatis veritati testimonium perhibere. Quod si non omnes hiis exequendis potueritis interesse duo vestrum ea nichilominus exequantur. Datum Lateran' ix kalendas Augusti pontificatus nostri anno quartodecimo.[1] Cujus auctoritate mandati abbate et conventu de Messendene ad presenciam nostram vocatis, libelloque conventionali eisdem ex parte Willelmi de Engelfeld militis porrecto sub hac forma. Hec est intentio Willelmi de Engelfeld versus abbatem et conventum de Messendene. Dicit quod cum predecessores ipsius quandam dimidiam hidam terre que vocatur dimidia hida de laflexlond' sitam in teritorio suo de Sippelak dederunt et concesserunt dictis abbati et conventui ut in capella de Siplak', que in proprio ipsius fundo consistit, per aliquem ex canonicis suis sibi et familie sue facerent divina celebrari, cumque per quadraginta annos et amplius stetissent Galfridus filius Willelmi, Emma et Muriel de Langethot et Galfridus Dunstanwill' ipsius predecessores consequenter unus post alium in possessione ipsius cantarie secundum formam prescriptam, idem abbas et conventus cantariam premissam eidem injuste subtrahunt et divina celebrare in dicta capella injuste contradicunt, unde cum dicta cantaria per eos sit spoliatus petit restitui. Petit etiam dictos abbatem et canonicos ad inveniendum ibidem cantariam propriis eorum sumptibus judicialiter compelli possessorium recuperande possessionis et petitorium intentans, obligans se ad probandum utrumque vel eorum alterum quod elegerit quod sibi sufficere possit ad victoriam. Lite legitime coram nobis contestata in hunc modum, pars rea litem contestando dixit quod dicta dimidia hida terrre non fuit data domui sue ob predictam causam, set ob aliam causam translatum (*sic*) est in eos dominium, item si fuit aliquando in possessione non tamen quadraginta annis, item si fuit in possessione ipsa non fuit continua set interrupta, et propter hoc dicit se non spoliasse et dicit quod credit ipsius predecessores fuisse in possessione dicte cantarie qualiquali. Demum testibus hinc inde productis citra attestationum publicationem partibus in presencia nostra legitime constitutis, lis inter eosdem mota hoc amicabili fine quievit. Videlicet quod dictus miles liti mote et omni actioni sibi conpetenti inpetratis et inpetrandis sponte renuncians, omnes donationes tam in editione contentas quam alias a predecessor-

[1] 24 July 1240.

ibus suis dictis canonicis factas eisdem confirmavit, et ad uberiorem dicte cantarie sustentationem predictis canonicis octodecim[1] acras terre de dominico suo de Sipplak et annuas triginta sex solidatas redditus de camera sua apud Sipplak' percipiendas donec eisdem in loco conpetenti illas plene assignaverit et contulerit inperpetuum, pro ut in cartis suis super hiis confectis plenius continetur. Dicti vero abbas et conventus capellanum ydoneum cum ministro misse et omnia ad celebrandum necessaria tam in vestimentis quam libris et aliis excepto corpore edificii capelle site in curia de Sipplak' predicto Willelmo et heredibus suis perpetuo invenient. Et capellanus ibidem celebraturus ad optionem domini qui pro tempore fuerit cum presens fuerit vel uxor ejusdem diebus dominicis et ceteris diebus festivis missam de die seu aliam quam voluerint cum matutinis et horis diei cum cantu vel sine, nisi per inpotentiam fuerit prepeditus, celebrabit. Ceteris vero diebus sive presens seu absens fuerit, pro anima dicti W. et M. uxoris sue et animabus antecessorum et successorum suorum et omnium fidelium defunctorum celebrabit matutinas etiam et horas diei cum dominus vel uxor ejus presens fuerit dicet ibidem nisi ut predictum est per inpotentiam fuerit inpeditus. Et si dicta capella sita in curia de Sipplak' aliquo casu diruta fuerit, seu etiam deteriorata ita quod in ea non possint honeste celebrari divina, continuabitur dicta cantaria sine cantu in matrici ecclesia vel etiam in capella sita in cimiterio, si in ipsa possint honeste divina celebrari quousque dicta capella fuerit reedificata. Hoc sane adjecto quod per supradictam cantariam nullum matrici ecclesie de Sipplak' prejudicium seu dispendendium generetur. Reservata dictis judicibus ad omnium predictorum observationem secundum tenorem cartarum super hiis confectarum partem renitentem cohercendi potestate. Et ad uberiorem super premissis securitatem faciendam, subjecerunt se partes jurisdictioni domini Lincoln' episcopi et archidiaconi Oxonie, qui pro tempore fuerint ut uterque vel eorum alter, quem pars dicte parens conpositioni elegerit, eas ad predicta omnia observanda sine strepitu judiciali per censuram ecclesiasticam conpellat. Nos vero dictam conpositionem acceptantes et eandem auctoritate qua fungimur apostolica confirmantes, ipsam signorum nostrorum appositione una cum sigillis partium eidem alternatim appensis duximus roborandam. Hiis testibus magistris Johanne de sancto Egidio tunc archidiacono Oxonie, Roberto de Kadenay, Leonardo filio Alexandri, Giraudo de Wesenham, Rogero de Campedene, Roberto de Bukingeham, Willelmo de Radinges, Galfrido de Poterne, et dominis Waltero rectore ecclesie de Stokes, Willelmo vicario de Aldermanestone, H. rectore ecclesie de Tehdmerse, et Magistro Egidio rectore ecclesie beati Egidii de Rading', Rogero de Wimbrevile, Radulfo de

---

[1] Document 'octodocim'.

Englefeld et aliis. Actum in vigilia beati Andree apostoli anno gracie
m. cc. xl. ii.

Five seals on silk cords.

(1)	(2)	(3)	(4)	(5)
Prior of	Prior of	Prior of	The convent of	Roger, abbot of
Reading.	Sherborne.	Poughley.	Missenden.	Missenden.

B.M. Add. Ch. 20372 (pd. in *The Cartulary of Missenden Abbey*, pt. iii, ed.
J. G. Jenkins (Bucks. Rec. Soc. xii and H.M.C. JP i, 1962), no. 689, from
B.M. Harley MS. 3688, which is somewhat corrupt).

8

Charter of the abbot and convent of Missenden, acknowledging their obligation to William of Englefield to serve
his chantry in the chapel of Shiplake, and agreeing to certain penalties if they default. n.d. probably *circa* 29 November
1242.

Universis ad quos presens scriptum pervenerit, abbas de Messenden'
et ejusdem loci conventus salutem in domino. Noverit universitas
vestra nos obligatos esse Willelmo de Engelfeld' militi et heredibus suis
et eorum custodibus ad inveniendum (*sic*) eisdem et eorum familie
cantariam in capella sita in curia de Sipplak', per capellanum religiosum
seu secularem idoneum cum ministro misse et omnibus ad celebrandum
necessariis tam in vestimentis quam libris et aliis excepto corpore
edificii capelle site in curia de Sipplak' inperpetuum, secundum tenorem cujusdam cirograffi super hoc inter nos confecti. Ita sane quod
quotiens in inventione dicte cantarie aliquo tempore nisi justo inter-
veniente inpedimento cessaverimus, committatur pena unius marce una
cum dampnis expensis et interesse dicto W. et heredibus suis seu
eorum custodibus seu ipsorum assignatis solvende rata manente con-
ventione presenti. Liceatque statim episcopo Lincolniensi et archidiacono Oxonie qui pro tempore fuerint vel eorum alteri et etiam
priori de Radinges suisque collegis seu alicui omnium predictorum
quem dictus W. seu heredes ipsius seu etiam ipsorum custodes eleg-
erint, nos per sentenciam excommunicationis ad inventionem dicte
cantarie et ad solutionem pene dampnorum expensarum et interesse de
plano omni circumscripta cognitione conpellere. Ita quod citra ut
dictum est dicte cantarie inventionem et plenam ut dictum est solutionem in omnibus a dicta excommunicationis sentencia nullo modo
absolvamur super dampnis vero expensis et interesse credatur de plano
ipsius Willelmi et heredum suorum et etiam custodum procuratoris
sacramento sine alterius onere probationis. In cujus rei testimonium

presenti scripto sigilla nostra apposuimus. Hiis testibus Petro filio Ogeri, Reginaldo de Blancmust', Roberto de Anuers, Rogero de Wimbrewill', Simone tunc vicario de Sipplak', Thoma de Benfeld', Thoma Carbunel et aliis.

Seal on tag of Roger, abbot of Missenden.

Seal on tag of the convent of Missenden.

B.M. Add. Ch. 20370

9

Mandate of Innocent IV to the precentor of Reading (Ben. Berks.), ordering him to see that the agreement between William of Englefield and the abbot and convent of Missenden (Aug. Bucks.) over the chapel of Shiplake (Oxon.) is observed. Lyons, 1 April 1251.

Innocentius episcopus servus servorum dei dilecto filio .. precentori ecclesie de Radingia Saresbirien' diocesis, salutem et apostolicam benedictionem. Sua nobis Willelmus de Englefeld miles petitione monstravit quod cum ipse .. abbatem et conventum de Messendene Lincolniensis diocesis super eo quod ipsi in capella sua de Sipplake singulis diebus tenentur facere celebrari divina, coram .. priore de Radingia et conjudicibus suis auctoritate apostolica traxisset in causam, tandem mediante venerabili fratri nostro Lincolniensi episcopo diocesano loci amicabilis inter partes compositio intervenit, quam idem miles apostolico petiit munimine roborari. Ideoque discretioni tue per apostolica scripta mandamus quatinus compositionem ipsam, sicut sine pravitate provide facta est et ab utraque parte sponte recepta et hactenus pacifice observata, facias per censuram ecclesiasticam appellatione remota firmiter observari. Datum Lugdun' Kalendis Aprilis pontificatus nostri anno octavo.

Hemp cords for *bulla*.

On dorse: Cunforment de la chanterie de la chapele de Sipplake soient liuere a sire Willame de Englefeld.

B.M. Add. Ch. 20373

10

Letters patent including the composition made between Henry d'Oilly and Maud his wife, and Maud, countess of Essex and Hereford, wife of Roger of Dauntsey, over a

debt of ninety pounds, by papal judges delegate, the prior
of Luffield (Ben. Northants.) and the archdeacon and rural
dean of Buckingham. 30 November 1232.[1]

(See above, Chapter IV, pp. 210 and 219.)

Omnibus Christi fidelibus presens scriptum visuris vel audituris, prior
de Luffeld archidiaconus et decanus de Buchingham salutem. Noveritis quod cum ex delegatione apostolica mota fuisset causa coram nobis
inter dominum Henricum de Oili et Matildam uxorem ejus ex una
parte, et Matildam comitissam Essexie et Hereford' uxorem domini
Rogeri de Dant' ex altera, super demanda quater viginti librarum et
decem ex debito quondam Willelmi de Mandevill' comitis Essex';
tandem partibus coram nobis diu litigantibus in hanc formam pacis
dicte partes convenerunt. Hec est forma compositionis facte inter
dominum R. de Dantesi maritum M. comitisse Essexie et dominam M.
de Oili super demanda quater viginti librarum et decem ex debito W.
comitis de Mandevill' coram priore de Luffeld' et conjudicibus suis
a dicta M. petitis, scilicet quod dicta M. de Oili habebit manerium de
Gersich' cum omnibus pertinentiis sicut dicti R. et M. illud posse-
derunt singulis annis pro quindecim lib[ri]s sterlingorum donec totum
dictum debitum [fuer]it[2] persolutum dicte M. de Oili .... [3] assignare
voluerit. Si autem contingat quod oblitus asisus centum s[o]lid' quem
Wal...[4] de Ausevill' [? habe]t in predicto manerio revertatur vel sic
excaeta dicta M. de Oili habebit illum redditum solidorum centum
simul cum dicto manerio quousque dictum debitum fueri[t] persolutum ita quod ex tunc computentur viginti libre per annum. Si
autem dictum [m]anerium vel pars ejus fuerit distrangatum[5] ab aliquo
dicti R. et M. rationabiles excambias facient dicte M. de Oili in loco
competenti infra viginti dies postquam fuerint super hoc commoniti,
ita quod si culpa dicti R. dilata fueri[n]t excambia, rationabiles dicte M.
de Oili expensas reddent. Reddet autem dicta M. de Oli post debitum
dictum adquietatum dictum manerium cum terris seminatis et cultis
sicut ipsa M. de Oili idem recepit per visum legalium hominum.
Dictus autem R. fructus inventos in horreis et extra et totum instaur-
amentum que ibidem fuerunt tempore saisine inventa sibi retinet.[6]

---

[1] The date of the letters patent which announce the absolution of Roger from a
sentence of excommunication for not paying the debt is given as 30 Nov. 1232.
This cannot have preceded the composition, which is dated on the feast of St.
Nicholas in the seventeenth year of Henry III's reign (6 Dec. 1232), so it appears
that the scribe either mistakenly put 'm. cc. xxxii' for 'm. cc. xxxiii' or miscalculated
the regnal year.

[2] Document damaged.   [3] Document damaged: about 7 letters missing.
[4] Document damaged: about 3 letters missing.
[5] Document 'disrantgatum'.   [6] Document 'retinuit'.

Subjecit autem se dictus Rogerus jurisdicioni dictorum judicum renuncians fori privilegio et appellationi et prohibitioni regie ad hoc, ut possint eum compellere per censuram ecclesiasticam ad observationem istius compositionis si forte quod absit contravenire voluerit quam diu terras comitisse Essexie habuerit. Dicta autem M. de Oli conservabit dictum R. de Dantesi indempnem super dicto debito erga heredes quondam Henr' de Oili et erga ejusdem executores. Facta fuit autem hec compositio anno [domin]i regis Henrici tercii anno septimo decimo[1] die Sancti Nicholai. Et in hujus rei testimon[i]um huic scripto in modo cyrograffi confecto utraque dicta pars sigillum suum apposuit. Hiis testibus Magistris Henrico Teisun, Clemente Pighun, dominis Johanne filio Galfridi, Willelmo de Mandevill', Johanne Talebot militibus, domino H. filio justiciarii, Henrico de Lingivere, Daniel et aliis. Nos autem hanc formam pacis ratam habentes eam presenti scripto sigillis nostris signato munimus et confirmamus. Absolvimus etiam et absolutum denunciamus dictum Rogerum de Dant' a sentencia excommunicationis in ipsum a nobis lata pro contumacia sua, quia a nobis commonitus dictum debitum reddere contradixit. Et in hujus rei testimonium has litteras nostras patentes eidem Rogero habere fecimus. Datum anno gracie m. cc. xxxii ad festum Sancti Andree.

Slit for tag.   Two tags for seals.   Slit for tag.

P.R.O. DL 25/15

11

Final *actum* of the judges delegate, the abbot and prior of Eynsham (Ben. Oxon.) and the rural dean of Oxford, reporting the composition made between the prior and convent of Christ Church, Canterbury (Ben. Kent), and the prior and convent of Clifford (Clun. al. Heref.) and the executors of the will of W(alter) of Clifford. 1224.

(See above, Chapter IV, pp. 211 and 226.)

Omnibus ad quos presens scriptum pervenerit .. abbas .. prior de Eynesham et decanus Oxon' salutem in domino. Ad universitatis vestre noticiam volumus pervenire quod cum inter priorem et conventum ecclesie Christi Cant' ex una parte, et priorem et conventum de Cliff' ex alia, super corpore W. de Clifford, item inter dictos priorem et conventum Cant' et executores testamenti W. de Cliff' super

[1] Document 'decino'.

quadam summa pecunie, coram nobis auctoritate domini pape Honorii tercii questio verteretur, die tandem partibus prefixa sepedictorum prioris et conventus Cant' procurator, scilicet magister Silvester rector ecclesie sancti Michaelis Oxon', et M. prior de Cliff' et R. de Cliff' et W. aurifaber testamenti sepedicti W. executores, presente procuratore W. de Cliff' junioris, et idem asserente scilicet W. de Kinardell', confessi sunt quod dicte lites mote amicabili compositione quieverunt in hac forma: videlicet quod dictus dominus W. de Cliff', ad petitionem domini regis et domini Cant' archiepiscopi et aliorum magnorum virorum, a priore et conventu Cant' optinuit quod corpus W. patris sui in monasterio de Cliff' sepultum inter corpora predecessorum suorum ex dono predictorum prioris et conventus ibidem remaneret. Et predictus W. ad honorem Cant' ecclesie pro anima predicti W. patris sui obligavit se ecclesie Cant' ad solvendum xl. marcas intra annum istum ad emendum redditum, de quo aniversarium predicti patris sui [un]a[1] cum aniversario matris sue in ecclesia Cant' sepulte singulis annis in ecclesia Cant' honorifice possit celebrari. Nos igitur nolentes quod in presencia nostra actum est in dubium futuris temporibus posse revocari .....[1] auctoritate qua fungimur confirmamus, fac... [in pre]sencia[1] nostra predictorum confessiones presentibus litteris protestantes. Actum anno m. cc. xxiiii ab incarnatione domini.

Four slits for seal tags.

Canterbury, Cartae Antiquae, C 279

12

Notification by Abbess Emma and the convent of Godstow (Ben. Oxon.), the defendants, to the judges conservator, the priors of Blackmore (Aug. Essex) and Tandridge (Aug. Surr.), of the appointment of W., their clerk, as proctor for a day. Godstow, 25 June 1254.

(See above, Chapter IV, pp. 228 and 233.)

Littera Emme Abbatisse et conventus de Godestowe de procuratore faciendo.

Viris venerabilibus et discretis de Blakemore et de Tanrigg' prioribus, E. dei gratia abbatissa de Godest' et ejusdem loci conventus eternam in domino salutem. Quoniam multis et variis prepedite negotiis die sabbati proxima post festum sancti Johannis baptiste in ecclesia sancti

---

[1] Document torn.

Magni London', coram vobis seu quocumque alio vices vestras[1] gerente, in causa que vertitur inter dominos abbatem et conventum de Westm' ex una parte et nos ex altera, personaliter comparere non possimus (*sic*), dilectum clericum nostrum W. presentium latorem procuratorem nostrum constituimus, ratum et gratum habituri quicquid dictis die et loco coram vobis in dicta causa factum fuerit, judicatum autem pro eo solvi promittimus. Idem parti adverse significamus. Valeat reverencia vestra semper in domino. Datum apud Godest' in crastino nativitatis sancti Johannis baptiste anno domini m. cc. l. quarto.

Westminster Domesday, f. 379[r]

13

Notification by the prior of Hatfield Regis (or Hatfield Broad Oak, Ben. al. Essex) to the judges delegate of the appointment of proctors, R., brother of the abbot of Ramsey, and A. de Saltfletebi (? Saltfleetby, Lincs.), chaplain, for a term and 'sub alternatione', in a suit with the chaplain of Sible Hedingham (Essex). 29 March 1245.

(See above, Chapter IV, p. 233.)

Viris venerabilibus de Dunmawe[2] et de Tremhal'[3] prioribus judicibus a domino papa delegatis, prior et conventus de Haffeld' salutem in domino. In causa que coram vobis vertitur inter nos ex parte una, et Benedictum capellanum de Heyngham Sibille ex parte altera, dominum R. fratrem abbatis de Rameseya dominum A. de Saltfletebi capellanum procuratores nostros sub alternatione usque ad festum beati Michaelis constituimus, ratum habituri quicquid uterque vel eorum alter qui presens coram vobis fuerit in dicta causa nomine nostro usque ad prefinitum tempus duxerit ad agendum. Idem parti adverse significamus. Valete. Actum anno domini m. cc. xl. quinto quarto kalendas Aprilis.

> Seal on tongue presumably of Hatfield priory: pale brown wax, damaged, with traces of a seated virgin and child.

B.M. Add. Ch. 28407

---

[1] MS. 'nostras'.   [2] Little Dunmow (Aug. Essex).
[3] Thremhall (Aug. Essex).

14

Report by the judge delegate, H(enry de Lexington), dean of Lincoln, of a proctorial document of the abbot and convent of St. Sever (dioc. Coutances, France), constituting Nicholas, monk, and Matthew, rector of Haugham (Lincs.), to act on their behalf with general powers for an unlimited time. June 1251.

(See above, Chapter IV, p. 234.)

Noverint universi Christi fideles presens scriptum inspecturi vel audituri, quod hec est forma procurationis qua .. abbas et conventus de Sancto Severo usi sunt coram nobis H. judice delegato et decano Linc' ecclesie contra magistrum ordinis de Sempingh' priorem et conventum de Bolingt'. Universis presens scriptum visu[ris ve]l[1] audituris, P. dei miseratione abbas Sancti Severi et ejusdem loci conventus salutem in domino. Noveritis quod nos dilectum fratrem [nostrum][1] Nicholaum et dilectum clericum nostrum Matheum rectorem ecclesie de Hacham procuratores nostros constituimus, in omnibus negoti[is][1] et causis quas habemus vel habituri sumus in regno Anglie contra quoscumque coram quibuscumque judicibus ecclesiasticis [se]u[1] mundanis ordinariis seu delegatis seu etiam arbitris. Dantes eisdem specialem potestatem agendi, defendendi, transigen[di, auctoritate nostra][1] amicabiliter componendi, eligendi arbitros et compromittendi in ipsos, jurandi expensas et recipiendi eas s[i] ...[2] fuerint adjudicate, jurandi de calumpnia seu de veritate dicenda et faciendi cujuslibet generis sacramentum in animas nostras vel suas prout de jure fuerit faciendum, constituendi procuratorem vel procuratores unum vel plures in [universis][1] et singulis supradictis quociens ambo vel alter ei[s][1] viderint expedire, ita videlicet quod quilibet eorum potestatem ..... [ad omnia][3] supradicta facienda. Ratum habituri et gratum quicquid predicti aut alter eorum seu substitutus aut substituti ab eis ....[4] fecerint impremissis[5] vel fecerint, promittentes pro ipsis vel pro substituto ab eis seu substitutis sub ypoteca rerum nostrarum judicatum solvi. Et hec omnibus quorum interest significamus per presentes litteras sigilli nostri impressione munita. [Datum][1] anno domini m. cc. l. primo mense Junii.

Plica with slit for seal tag.

On dorse: Forma procuracionis abbatis sancti Severi.

B.M. Harley Ch. 44 F 24

[1] Document damaged.   [2] Document damaged: about 3 letters missing.
[3] Document damaged: about 5 letters missing.
[4] Document damaged: 2 words missing.   [5] ?read 'in premissis'.

15

Appointment of a proctor or proctors (unnamed by the
copyist but mentioned elsewhere on two occasions as the
prior), by the master of the order of Sempringham and
the prior and convent of Alvingham (Gilb. Lincs.), in their
suit with Peter, parson of Stainton-le-Vale (Lincs.). June
1245.

(See above, Chapter IV, p. 230.)

Universis Christi fidelibus presentes literas inspecturis, R. dei gratia
magister ordinis de loco et prior et conventus ejusdem loci salutem in
domino. Ad noticiam perveniat singulorum quod nos talem vel tales
constituimus[1] procuratores nostros sub alternatione, in causa que vertitur vel verti speratur inter nos ex una parte, et talem personam duarum
partium ecclesie de Staynton' ut dicitur ex altera, super duabus partibus reddituum ecclesie sancti Andree de Staynton', coram de Boe-
linton et de Kirham prioribus et magistro scolarum ecclesie de Malton',
concedentes eisdem plenam potestatem jurandi in animam nostram
de calumpnia et de expensis petendis et recipiendis quotienscumque
fuerint adjudicate. Damus etiam eis speciale mandatum transigendi,
compromittendi, componendi et prestandi in animam cujuslibet generis sacramentum et constituendi ad necessaria predicta alium procuratorem loco sui quotienscumque voluerint vel non potuerunt
interesse, sive contigerit ipsos abesse et faciendi necessaria alia que
possemus facere si presentes essemus, ratum et gratum habituri quicquid omnes predicti vel aliquis eorum quem judicio interesse contigerit egerit in predictis et idem parti adverse significamus. Datum
anno domini m. cc. xl. v. mense Junii.

Alvingham Cart., f. 5ʳ

16

Appointment of a proctor, Ralph, prior of St. Michael's
Mount (Ben. al. Cornw.), by the abbot and convent of Mont-
Saint-Michel (dioc. Avranches, France), granting him general
powers to appear before ordinary judges or judges delegate.
December 1237.

(See above, Chapter IV, p. 224.)

[1] MS. 'continuimus'

Universis Christi fidelibus presentes litteras inspecturis, R. humilis abbas Montis Sancti Michaelis de Periculo Maris et ejusdem loci conventus salutem in domino. Noverit universitas vestra quod nos dilectum monachum nostrum fratrem Radulfum custodem domus nostre Sancti Michaelis in Cornub' constituimus nostrum procuratorem, contra quoscumque coram quibuscumque judicibus ordinariis sive delegatis ad respondendum, defendendum et ad faciendum quicquid de jure fuerit faciendum. Damus etiam eidem plenariam potestatem paciscendi, transigendi, componendi, compromittendi, alium procuratorem[1] quocienscumque voluerit vel viderit expedire, promittentes si necesse fuerit pro ipso judicatum solvi, sub rerum nostrarum ypoteca, ratum et gratum (f. 133ʳ) habituri quicquid per ipsum factum fuerit justicia mediante. Et hoc partibus adversis significamus. Dat' anno domini m. cc. xxxvii mense[2] Decembri.

Beaulieu Cart. ff. 132ᵛ–3ʳ

V. DOCUMENTS CONCERNING THE OBSERVANCE OF THE SETTLEMENT

I

Confirmation by R(obert de Hertford), dean, and the chapter of Salisbury of an ordination made by their bishop, R(obert de Bingham), in a suit between the rector of Thatcham (Berks.) and the abbot and convent of Reading (Ben. Berks.). Salisbury, 8 February 1239/40.

(See above, Chapter V, p. 248.)

Universis sancte matris ecclesie filiis presens scriptum inspecturis vel audituris, R. decanus et capitulum Sar' salutem in salutis auctore. Literas venerabilis patris nostri R. dei gracia Sar' episcopus inspeximus in hec verba: Omnibus Christi fidelibus ad quos presens scriptum pervenerit Robertus miseratione divina Sar' ecclesie minister humilis salutem in domino. Universitati vestre presentibus innotescat quod

---

[1] Either the original document or the copy was carelessly written. The sense demands something like 'substituendi loco suo' or 'constituendi' here, and the rest of the document seems to be compressed into the shortest possible form.

[2] MS. 'Septemb'. The scribe has attemped first to change it to 'decemb' and has then deleted it.

cum magister Gilbertus de Byham rector ecclesie de Thacham dilectos filios abbatem et conventum de Rading' super tercia parte omnium terrarum, decimarum, fructuum et proventuum ejusdem ecclesie necnon et novem marcis annuis eisdem monachis ad hospitalitatis honera supportanda, capituli nostri Sar' accedente assensu in usus proprios et perpetuos de ecclesia supradicta concessis, et rebus aliis ad dictam ecclesiam spectantibus, coram archidiacono et decano Oxon' auctoritate domini pape traxisset in causam, partes in nostra presencia constitute litteris impetratis et impetrandis questionibus motis et movendis et predictarum rerum concessionibus sponte et absolute renunciantes, ordinationi nostre sese penitus submiserunt. Nos igitur ut paci et tranquillitati partium et earum successorum futuris et perpetuis temporibus provideatur, habita deliberatione ordinationem super premissis ad ipsarum partium instanciam in nos suscipientes, deum habentes pre oculis de consilio jurisperitorum, invocata spiritus sancti gracia, taliter duximus ordinandum; videlicet quod dictus Gilbertus rector predicte ecclesie de Thacham et successores sue habeant et possideant totam ecclesiam de Thacham cum omnibus juribus suis libertatibus et pertinentiis libere, quiete, integre et pacifice in perpetuum sustinendo honera ordinaria spectantia ad ecclesiam supradictam. Ordinavimus etiam de consensu dicti rectoris quod dicti abbas et conventus percipiant viginti marcas annuas nomine perpetui beneficii a dicto rectore et suis successoribus in perpetuum solvendas ad quatuor anni terminos, videlicet ad natale domini quinque marcas, ad pasca quinque marcas, ad festum nativitatis sancti Johannis Baptiste quinque marcas et ad festum sancti Michaelis quinque marcas; ita tamen quod dicti abbas et conventus cum aliquid extraordinarium prefate ecclesie de Thacham fuerit inpositum id pro portione sua subeant et agnoscant. Nulli ergo hominum hanc nostre ordinationis paginam audeant infringere vel ei ausu temerario contraire; si quis autem ausu temerario eam infringere temptaverit indignationem dei et beate virginis et omnium sanctorum se noverit incursurum. In hujus rei testimonium presens scriptum sigillo nostro duximus muniendum. Hiis testibus E. archidiacono Berk' tunc officiali nostro, Petro de Cumb', Waltero de la Wyle, Galfrido de Bedef', canonicis Sar', Th' de la Wyle senescallo nostro, Roberto Foliot, Roberto de Wichamt', Willelmo de Castellis, clericis nostris, et aliis. Actum apud Ramebir' vii idus Februarii anno gracie m. cc. xxxix.[1] Nos autem dictam venerabilis patris nostri ordinationem ratam et gratam habentes, eam quantum in nobis est approbamus et sigilli nostri appositione confirmando corroboramus. Hiis testibus dominis Roberto decano, Rogero precentore, Ada cancellario, Henrico thesaurario, E. archidiacono Berk', Th' subdecano, Magistris Elia de

---

[1] Ramsbury (Wilts.), 7 Feb. 1240.

Derham, Radulfo de Eboraco, et aliis. Datum Sar' per manus A. cancellarii nostri vi idus Februarii anno gracie m. cc. xxxix.[1]

Seal of the dean and chapter on silk threads;
counterseal of Adam the chancellor.

On dorse: Confirmatio Decani et capituli Sar' de xx. marcis de Ecclesia de Tacham.

B.M. Add. Ch. 19620

2

Final *actum* of the abbots of Sibton (Cist. Suff.) and Leiston (Prem. Suff.) and the prior of Blythburgh (Aug. Suff.), in a suit between the prior and convent of Holy Trinity, Ipswich (Aug. Suff.), and the nuns of Wix (Ben. Essex). 1198×1216.

(See above, Chapter V, pp. 251–2.)

Chirograph

Omnibus sancte matris ecclesie filiis ad quos presens scriptum pervenerit L. et Ph. de Sibetun' et de Leistun' dei gracia abbates et[2] W. prior de Blieburc' eternam in domino salutem. Ad universorum noticiam volumus pervenire quod cum causa que vertebatur inter canonicos ecclesie Sancte Trinitatis de Gypeswic' et moniales de Wikes super decimis bladi, de dominio quod fuit Gocelin' de Lodnes in villa de Prestun',[3] nobis a domino papa Innocentio tercio esset commissa, demum post multas et varias altercationes hinc inde habitas de assensu partium hoc fine quievit; videlicet quod dicte moniales decimas prenominatas in perpetuum pacifice possidebunt, solvendo exinde annuatim dictis canonicis nomine pensionis duos solidos ad festum sancti Michaelis apud Gypewic' in ecclesia Sancte Trinitatis, de blado tamen unius acre terre quam ecclesia de Prestun' de eodem dominio annuatim percipit et ex antiquo percipere consuevit dicte moniales nihil percipient. Prior autem et canonici sub hac forma dictam remittentes questionem in verbo veritatis firmiter promiserunt quod prenominata pensione contenti ipsis monialibus super predictis decimis nullam in posterum movebunt questionem. Similiter priorissa et moniales predicte

[1] There is a very short report of this *inspeximus* in the Reading Cartulary on f. 112ʳ. On this folio there is also the report of the ordination by Robert de Bingham.
[2] 'et' written twice.   [3] Probably Preston (Suff.).

se dictam pensionem in forma prescripta soluturas dictis canonicis in perpetuum firmiter et fideliter in verbo domini promiserunt. Ne autem ea que amicabiliter coram nobis sopita sunt tractu temporis aliquorum malignitate revocari possint in irritum, ea hoc scripto nostro tam sigillis nostris quam sigillis utriusque conventus communiter[1] testificari et corroborare dignum duximus. Valeat universitas vestra in domino.

> Tag for seal (detached): *agnus dei.*
> Seal on tag: abbot of Leeston (*sic*).
> Tag for seal (detached): (?) prioress of Wix.
> Tag: remnants of seal.

On dorse: Prestun.

P.R.O. E 42/426

3

Composition in the form of a chirograph between the prioress and convent of St. Michael, Stamford (Ben. Northants.), and William Erl of North Luffenham (Rutl.). St. Mary's church at the bridge, Stamford, 5 May 1237.

(See above, Chapter V, p. 256.)

Chirograph

Omnibus sancte matris ecclesie filiis presentes literas visuris vel audituris, de Stanford'[2] de Roteland'[3] et de Carleby[4] decani salutem in domino. Mandatum domini pape suscepimus in hec verba: Gregorius episcopus servus servorum dei dilectis filiis de Stanford' de Roteland' et de Carleby decanis Linc' diocesis salutem et apostolicam benedictionem. Dilecte in christo filie priorissa et conventus sancti Michaelis de Stanford' nobis conquerendo monstrarunt quod .. abbas et conventus de Osolveston'[5] et quidam alii Linc' diocesis super decimis, possessionibus, redditibus et rebus aliis injuriantur eisdem; ideoque discretioni vestre per apostolica scripta mandamus quatinus partibus convocatis, audiatis causam et appellatione remota fine debito terminetis, facientes quod decreveritis per censuram ecclesiasticam firmiter observari. Testes autem qui fuerint nominati si se gracia, odio vel timore subtraxerint per censuram eandem appellatione cessante cogatis veritati testimonium perhibere. Quod si non omnes hiis exequendis

---

[1] Document 'communito'. [2] Stamford (Lincs.). [3] Rutland.
[4] Carlby (Lincs.). [5] Owston (Aug. Leics.).

potueritis interesse duo vestrum ea nichilominus exequantur. Datum Anagnie nonis Februarii pontificatus nostri anno sexto.[1] Hujus igitur auctoritate mandati ad instanciam priorisse et conventus monialium sancti Michaelis de Stanford' Willelmum Erl' de Northluffenham sepe ac sepius et tandem peremptorie fecimus evocari, partibus vero in nostra presencia constitutis lis in hunc modum amicabiliter conquievit; videlicet quod dictus Willelmus concessit et carta sua confirmavit deo et ecclesie sancti Michaelis de Stanford' et monialibus ibidem deo servientibus in liberam et puram et perpetuam elemosinam unam bovatam terre cum pertinentiis in territorio de Northluffenham, quam Henricus nepos Everardi de Northluffenh' aliquando tenuit de feodo dicti Everardi cum tofto et crofto et cum omnibus pertinentiis infra villam et extra dicte bovate terre pertinentibus tenendam et habendam dictis monialibus et successoribus suis libere et quiete ab omni servicio et seculari demanda. Et dictus Willelmus et heredes sui warantizabunt, aquietabunt et defendent prenominatum tenementum cum omnibus pertinentiis predicte ecclesie et predictis monialibus contra omnes homines in perpetuum. Obligavit etiam dictus Willelmus se et heredes suos ad solvendum dictis monialibus et earum successoribus duodecim denarios ad quatuor anni terminos inperpetuum, videlicet ad festum sancti Michaelis 3 d'., ad Natale domini 3 d'., ad Pasch' 3 d'. et ad nativitatem sancti Johannis Baptiste 3 d'., pro quadam placea terre in villa de Northluffenh', continente in latitudine viginti pedes que jacet infra toftum et croftum dicti W., et pro prato quod pertinet ad tantam terram, et illa terra jacet in longitudine a via ville usque ad magnam aquam juxta toftum et croftum Henrici nepotis Everardi, et pro tribus dimidiis acris terre, quarum una dimidia acra jacet in campo ejusdem ville versus orientem juxta viam inter terram Ricardi de Attolfston' et terram Ade filii Ricardi et tres rode jacent in Upfeld' inter terram Rogeri filii Hugonis Edwardi et terram Roberti Wlrich, et una roda jacet inter terram dicti Ricardi de Attolfston' et terram Alani Basset, et pro quatuor rodis terre de bovata terre quam Henricus nepos Everardi tenuit, que scilicet rode ita jacent in campo apud orientem, una roda inter terram Alani Basset et terram Moysi filii Nich', et una roda juxta Boygrene, et una roda in Upfeld' inter terram Ricardi de Attolfston' et terram dicti W. Erl, et una roda inter terram Hugonis de Pilton' et terram Yvonis filii Galfridi. Preterea idem Willelmus resignavit dictis monialibus tres rodas terre in territorio de Northluffenham quas Everardus avunculus dicti W. eis legavit. Et sciendum est quod non licebit dicto Willelmo Erl vel heredibus suis dictas terras vendere vel invadiare vel aliquo modo alienare sine rationabili licencia dictarum priorisse et conventus, prestito ab eodem W. corporali

[1] 5 Feb. 1233.

sacramento pro se et heredibus suis ad hec omnia fideliter tenenda. Nos vero pacis amatores dictas compositiones coram nobis factas auctoritate domini confirmamus, retenta nobis et successoribus nostris de consensu partium cohertione ad faciendum premissas compositiones a partibus firmiter ac fideliter observari, renunciantibus eisdem in hac parte appellationi, exceptioni cuilibet et fori privilegio, literis etiam omnibus impetratis et impetrandis et maxime prohibitioni regie. Actum die martis proxima post inventionem sancte crucis in ecclesia beate Marie ad pontem Stanford' anno gracie m. cc. tricesimo septimo. In cujus rei testimonium presenti scripto in modum cirographi confecto sigilla nostra una cum sigillis partium apposuimus.

3 tags for seals.   Slit for seal tag.   2 tags for seals.

On dorse: Compositio inter priorissam et conventum sancti michaelis de Stanford' et Willelmum Herle de Lufinham coram judicibus facta.

P.R.O. E 326/2268

4

Charter in the form of a chirograph made on the completion of the suit between the abbot and convent of Newsham (Prem. Lincs.) and William of Ingleby (Lincs.). Early thirteenth century.

(See above, Chapter V, p. 257.)

Chirograph

Notum sit omnibus Christi fidelibus quod ita convenit inter abbatem et conventum de Neuhus ex una parte, et Willelmum de Engelby ex altera; videlicet quod dictus W. subjecit se jurisdictioni domini archidiaconi de Stowe, qui pro tempore fuerit, abbatis de Barlinge[1] prioris sancte Katerine Lincolnie,[2] per censuram ecclesiasticam cohercendum secundum qualitatem delicti, si forte non observaverit scriptum inter ipsos confectum super servicio capelle de Engelby, renunciando appellationi et privilegio fori et omnibus exceptionibus sibi competentibus. Et ad hoc fideliter observandum dictus W. pro se et heredibus suis corporale prestitit sacramentum. In hujus autem rei robur et testimonium ad instanciam partium prefati archidiaconus abbas et prior

[1] Barlings (Prem. Lincs.): a cell or daughter-house of Newsham.
[2] Gilb. Lincoln.

huic scripto in modum cyrographi confecto una cum sigillis partium
signa sua apposuerunt.

Seal (mutilated) on tag.	Slit for seal tag.	Two tags for seals.

B.M. Harley Ch. 44 G 20

5

Final *actum* of H(ugh of Avalon), bishop of Lincoln, J(ohn
de Cella), abbot of St. Albans (Ben. Herts.), and B(enedict),
abbot of Stratford Langthorne (Cist. Essex), judges delegate of Celestine III, recording an arrangement about
Bloxham church (Oxon.). 14 June 1197.

(See above, Chapter V, pp. 265–6.)

In red: Scriptum H. Linc' episcopi et J. abbatis sancti Albani et B.
abbatis sancte Marie de Stratford' super pensione predicte ecclesie.

Omnibus sancte matris ecclesie filiis tam presentibus quam futuris H.
dei gracia Lincoln' episcopus et J. abbas sancti Albani et B. abbas
sancte Marie de Stratford' eternam in domino salutem. Quod ad mul-
torum noticiam pervenire congruum duximus, literarum monimentis
tradere provida deliberatione decrevimus. Noverit ergo presens etas
omniumque secutura posteritas quod controversiam a domino papa
Celestino iii nobis delegatam que inter venerabilem virum dominum
W.[1] abbatem et monachos sancti Petri Westm' et inter sanctimoniales
de Godestowe super ecclesiam de Blockesham vertebatur, communi
partium assensu hujusmodi transactione coram nobis inperpetuum esse
sopitam. Prefatus W. abbas Westm' et totus conventus ejusdem loci
attendentes religionem et honestatem sanctimonialium predicte domus
de Godestowe et earundem paupertati compatientes, unanimi assensu
concesserunt et dederunt in perpetuam elemosinam prefatis sanctimonialibus ecclesiam de Blocchesham cum omnibus pertinentiis suis
plenarie et integre perpetuo habendam et possidendam et totum jus
quod in eadem ecclesia habuerunt ecclesie beati Johannis baptiste de
Godestowe et sanctimonialibus ibidem deo servientibus quietum clam-
averunt, salva pensione quinque marcarum argenti quas de eadem
ecclesia de Blokesham antiquitus percipere solebant. Quam pensionem
sanctimoniales annuatim reddere debent sacriste sancti Petri Westm'
ad duos terminos anni, scilicet intra octabas festivitatis omnium sanctorum duas marcas et dimidiam et intra octabas pentecostes duas

---

[1] William Postard, elected 9 Oct. 1191, d. 4 May 1201.

marcas et dimidiam ad luminare magni altaris. Porro Juliana abbatissa de Godestowe et sanctimoniales ejusdem loci promiserunt in verbo veritatis et in bona fide pura et simplici consciencia coram deo prestito etiam sacramento per os et manum Waleranni capellani earum in verbo veritatis in animas earum sacrosanctis evangeliis ab eodem inspectis, quod nunquam apud aliquem vel aliquos per eas vel interpositam personam artem aliquam fraudis vel ingenii querent unde predicta ecclesia Westm' prenominate pensionis ecclesie de Blockesham diminutionem incurrat vel alienationem vel quominus prefatus conventus Westm' per manum sacriste sui predictum annuum redditum ad statutos terminos integre et absque detentione et omni occasione percipiat. Et ut hec transactio fide et omnimoda securitate inperpetuum teneatur, eam presenti scripto et sigillorum nostrorum appositione communimus.[1] Facta est autem hec transactio inter eos anno ab incarnatione domini m. c. xc. vii. die tercia post festum sancti Barnabe apostoli, mediante ex parte domini Huberti Cant' archiepiscopi et apostolice sedis legati[2] viro (f. 379ʳ) venerabili Hugoni abbate Abbendonie[3] et huic compositioni opem et operam adhibente. Hiis testibus domino Hugone abbate Abbendonie, Nich' et Ricardo monachis et capellanis ejus, Waleranno capellano, Johanne de Kensinton' et Henrico de Kensinton' fratre ejus, Marino clerico domine regine, Godefrido de la Dene, Willelmo de Haggehurste, Roberto de Clere, Magistro Ernulfo Postard, Magistro Simone de Bareswrde', Theodbaldo senescallo Westm', Radulfo de Septem fontibus, et Henrico fratre ejus, et multis aliis.

Westminster Domesday, ff. 378ᵛ–9ʳ

6

Report by the prior of Tandridge (Aug. Surr.), and the dean of Southwark, acting on behalf of the prior of Blackmore (Aug. Essex), conservators of the privileges of the abbot and convent of Westminster, reaffirming an arrangement about Bloxham church (Oxon.). St. Magnus the martyr's church, London, 27 June 1254.

(See above, Chapter V, p. 266.)

In red: Confessio partis abbatisse et monialium predictarum ac condempnatio judicum super dicta pensione in forma actorum.

---

[1] MS. 'communinus'.
[2] Hubert Walter, acceded 29 May 1193, d. 13 July 1205.
[3] Abingdon (Ben. Berks.).

Acta in ecclesia beati Magni martiris in London' die sabati proxima post festum sancti Johannis baptiste anno gracie m. cc. liiii, coram priore de Thauregg' conservatore privilegii abbati et conventui Westm' indulti et decano de Suwerk', gerente vices prioris de la Blakemore similiter conservatoris predicti privilegii, in negotio conservationis quod vertebatur inter dictos abbatem et conventum ex una parte et abbatissam et conventum de Godestowe ex altera; videlicet dictis abbatissa et conventu per procuratorem legittime constitutum in judicio comparentibus, earundem procurator confessus fuit in judicio nomine dicte abbatisse et conventus eosdem in quinque marcis sterlingorum nomine annue pensionis prefatis viris religiosis teneri ad duos terminos anni solvendis, secundum quod in instrumento ex parte dictorum virorum religiosorum super prefata annua pensione inter eosdem confecto et exibito in judicio continetur. Ex cujus inspectione apparet quod in festo omnium sanctorum debent solvi due marce et dimidia sacriste Westm' et due marce et dimidia in festo pentecost' proximo sequenti de anno in annum. Cujus confessionem judices secuti ipsum in posterum ad dicte pensionis solutionem faciendam sentencialiter condempnarunt sub pena unius marce pro quolibet termino, si in solutione cessatum fuerit predictis abbati et conventui solvende rata manente principali obligatione. Et cum pars dictorum abbatis et conventus Westm' instanter peteret dictas reas in expensis condempnari, parata jurare ratione litere impetrationis facte necnon et expensarum in prosecutione confectarum decem et octo marcas sterlingorum, judices volentes eisdem intuitu dei et religionis parcere, judices de peritorum consilio hinc inde amicabiliter assidentium et de consensu partium prefatas abbatissam et conventum in xl. solidis pro expensis prefatis abbati et conventui intra festum beati Petri ad vincula[1] solvendis condempnarunt, descernentes executionem decreti sui decano Oxon' fore demandandam quatinus dictam abbatissam et moniales moneat quod intra dictum festum sub pena excommunicationis inferrende in dictam abbatissam satisfaciant, reservata eisdem potestate ad cohercionem faciendam super principali et pena si forte contingat eam committi. Hec omnia de consensu partium sunt confecta.[2]

Westminster Domesday, f. 379[v]

[1] 1 Aug.
[2] On f. 644[r] is copied an instrument of Walter Reynolds, archbishop of Canterbury, confirming a pension of five shillings yearly from the church of Bloxham to Westminster, and dated 30 Apr. 1320.

SELECT BIBLIOGRAPHY

(For the unprinted primary sources, which have been used frequently, see the list of abbreviations, pp. xv–xviii).

A. PRINTED PRIMARY SOURCES

AEGIDIUS DE FUSCARARIIS, 'Ordo Iudiciarius', ed. Ludwig Wahrmund, Quellen zur Geschichte des Römisch-Kanonischen Processes im Mittelalter, iii. 1 (Innsbruck, 1916).

Annales Monastici, ed. H. R. Luard, R.S. xxxvi, 5 vols. (London, 1864–9).

ARNULPHUS, MAGISTER, 'Summa Minorum', ed. Ludwig Wahrmund, Quellen zur Geschichte des Römisch-Kanonischen Processes im Mittelalter, i. 2 (Innsbruck, 1905).

AUGUSTINIANS, Chapters of the Augustinian Canons, ed. H. E. Salter, Canterbury and York Ser. xxix (London, 1922).

BARNWELL, Liber Memorandorum Ecclesie de Bernewelle, ed. J. Willis Clark (Cambridge, 1907).

BATH, Two chartularies of the priory of St. Peter at Bath, ed. William Hunt, Somerset Record Society, vii (1893).

BENCIVENNA OF SIENA, 'Invocato Christi Nomine', ed. Ludwig Wahrmund, Quellen zur Geschichte des Römisch-Kanonischen Processes im Mittelalter, v. 1 (Heidelberg, 1931). Also printed as: 'Summa de Ordine Iudiciorum', ed. F. Bergmann, Pillii, Tancredi, Gratiae Libri de Iudiciorum Ordine, 3–86 (Göttingen, 1842).

BERNARD, SAINT, 'De Consideratione', P.L. 182, cols. 727–808.

BRACTON, HENRY DE, Bracton's Note Book, ed. F. W. Maitland, 3 vols. (London, 1887).

—— Henrici de Bracton de Legibus et Consuetudinibus Angliae, ed. Sir Travers Twiss, R.S. lxx, vols. ii and vi (London, 1879–83).

BRECON, 'Cartularium Prioratus S. Johannis Evang. de Brecon', ed. R. W. Banks, Archaeologia Cambrensis, 4th Ser. xiii. 275–308, and xiv. 18–49, 137–68, 221–37, 274–311 (London, 1882–3).

BREEDON, 'The Cartulary of Breedon', ed. R. A. McKinley, Manchester M.A. thesis, 1950.

BRUTON, Two cartularies of the Augustinian priory of Bruton and the Cluniac priory of Montacute, ed. members of the Council, Somerset Record Society, viii (1894).

BUCKLAND, Cartulary of Buckland priory, ed. F. W. Weaver, Somerset Record Society, xxv (1909).

BULGARUS, 'Excerpta Legum edita a Bulgarino Causidico', ed. Ludwig Wahrmund, Quellen zur Geschichte des Römisch-Kanonischen Processes im Mittelalter, iv. 1 (Innsbruck, 1925).

BURTON, 'An Abstract of the Contents of the Burton Chartulary', cal. the Hon. G. Wrottesley, *Collections for a history of Staffordshire*, ed. William Salt Archaeological Society, v, pt. 1, 1–101 (1884).
—— 'Descriptive Catalogue of the Charters and Muniments belonging to the Marquis of Anglesey', compiled by I. H. Jeayes, *Collections for a history of Staffordshire*, ed. Staffordshire Record Society, 1–195 (1937).
BURY ST. EDMUNDS, *Memorials of St. Edmund's abbey*, ed. T. Arnold, R.S. xcvi, 3 vols. (London, 1890–6).
—— *The Pinchbeck register*, ed. Lord Francis Hervey, 2 vols. (Brighton, 1925).
BUSHMEAD, *The cartulary of Bushmead priory*, ed. G. H. Fowler and Joyce Godber, Bedfordshire Historical Record Society, xxii (1945).
CAMBRIDGE, *The priory of St. Radegund, Cambridge*, ed. Arthur Gray, Cambridge Antiquarian Society, xxxi (1898).
CANTERBURY, 'A Judge Delegate Formulary from Canterbury', ed. Jane E. Sayers, *Bulletin of the Institute of Historical Research*, xxxv. 198–211 (1962).
—— St. Augustine's, *The register of St. Augustine's abbey Canterbury*, ed. G. J. Turner and H. E. Salter, British Academy Records of Social and Economic History, ii and iii, 2 pts. (London, 1915–24).
—— St. Gregory's, *Cartulary of the priory of St. Gregory Canterbury*, ed. Audrey M. Woodcock, Camden Society, 3rd Ser. lxxxviii (London, 1956).
CHERTSEY, *Chertsey abbey cartularies*, pt. 1, Surrey Record Society, xii (1915).
CHESHIRE, *Early Cheshire charters*, ed. G. Barraclough, Lancashire and Cheshire Record Society (1957).
CHICHESTER, *The Acta of the bishops of Chichester 1075–1207*, ed. H. Mayr-Harting, Canterbury and York Ser. lvi (1964)
—— *The chartulary of the high church of Chichester*, ed. W. D. Peckham, Sussex Record Society, xlvi (1946).
CIRENCESTER, *The cartulary of Cirencester abbey*, ed. C. D. Ross, 2 vols. (Oxford, 1964).
CISTERCIANS, *Statuta Capitulorum Generalium Ordinis Cisterciensis*, ed. Dom J.-M. Canivez, Bibliothèque de la Revue d'histoire ecclésiastique, fasc. ix, x, 2 vols. (Louvain, 1933–4).
CLOSE ROLLS, *Close rolls of the reign of Henry III*, Record Publications, 14 vols. (London, 1902–38).
—— *Rotuli Litterarum Clausarum*, ed. T. D. Hardy, Record Commission, 2 vols. (London, 1833–4).
COLCHESTER, *Cartularium Monasterii Sancti Johannis Baptiste de Colecestria*, ed. Stuart A. Moore, Roxburghe Club, 2 vols. (London, 1897).
CORPUS IURIS CANONICI, *Corpus Iuris Canonici*, ed. E. Friedberg, 2 vols. (Leipzig, 1879–81).
—— *Decretales D. Gregorii Papae IX suae integritati una cum glossis restitutae* (Rome, 1582).
Corpus Iuris Civilis, ed. T. Mommsen and P. Krueger, 2 vols. (Berlin, 1954).
Councils and synods, ed. F. M. Powicke and C. R. Cheney, vol. ii, 2 pts. (Oxford, 1964).
Curia Regis rolls, Record Publications, 14 vols. (London, 1922–61).

CURIALIS, 'Ordo', ed. Ludwig Wahrmund, Quellen zur Geschichte des Römisch-Kanonischen Processes im Mittelalter, i. 3 (Innsbruck, 1905).

DAMASUS HUNGARUS, MAGISTER, 'Summa de Ordine Iudiciario', ed. Ludwig Wahrmund, Quellen zur Geschichte des Römisch-Kanonischen Processes im Mittelalter, iv. 4 (Innsbruck, 1926).

DARLEY, The cartulary of Darley abbey, ed. R. R. Darlington, 2 vols., Derbyshire Archaeological Society (1945).

DUGDALE, SIR WILLIAM, Monasticon Anglicanum, ed. J. Caley, H. Ellis, and the Revd. Bulkeley Bandinel, 6 vols. (London, 1846).

DUNSTABLE, A digest of the charters preserved in the cartulary of the priory of Dunstable, compiled by G. H. Fowler, Bedfordshire Historical Record Society, x (1926).

DURAND, WILLIAM, Speculum Juris (Frankfurt, 1668).

ERFURT, St. Peter's, 'Cronica S. Petri Erfordensis Moderna', ed. O. Holder-Egger, Monumenta Erphesfurtensia, M.G.H., Scriptores Rerum Germanicarum in usum Scholarum, 117–369 (Hanover and Leipzig, 1899).

EVESHAM, Chronicon Abbatiae de Evesham, ed. W. D. Macray, R.S. xxix (London, 1863).

EYNSHAM, The cartulary of the abbey of Eynsham, ed. H. E. Salter, Oxford Historical Society, xlix and li, 2 vols. (1907–8).

FOLIOT, GILBERT, The letters and charters of Gilbert Foliot, ed. A. Morey and C. N. L. Brooke (Cambridge, 1967).

GERVASE OF CANTERBURY, The historical works of Gervase of Canterbury, ed. William Stubbs, R.S. lxxiii, 2 vols. (London, 1879–80).

GIRALDUS CAMBRENSIS, Opera, iii, ed. J. S. Brewer, R.S. xxi (London, 1863).

GLANVILL, RANULF DE, The treatise on the laws and customs of the realm of England commonly called Glanvill, ed. G. D. G. Hall. (London, 1965).

GLASTONBURY, The great chartulary of Glastonbury, ed. Dom A. Watkin, Somerset Record Society, lix, lxiii, and lxiv, 3 vols. (1947–52).

GLOUCESTER, Historia et Cartularium monasterii Sancti Petri Gloucestriae, ed. W. H. Hart, R.S. xxxiii, 3 vols. (London, 1863–7).

GLYNDE, The Glynde Place archives, cal. R. F. Dell (Lewes, 1964).

GODSTOW, The English register of Godstow nunnery near Oxford, ed. Andrew Clark, Early English Text Society, cxxix, cxxx, and cxlii, 3 pts. (London, 1905–11).

GRATIA OF AREZZO, 'Summa de Iudiciario Ordine', ed. F. Bergmann, Pillii, Tancredi, Gratiae Libri de Iudiciorum Ordine, 319–84 (Göttingen, 1842).

GRAVESEND, RICHARD, Rotuli Ricardi Gravesend Episcopi Lincolniensis, ed. F. N. Davis, Lincoln Record Society, xx (1925).

GRAY, WALTER, The register or rolls of Walter Gray, Lord Archbishop of York, ed. J. Raine, Surtees Society, lvi (1872).

GREGORY IX, Les Registres de Grégoire IX, ed. Lucien Auvray, Bibliothèque des Écoles françaises d'Athènes et de Rome, 4 vols. (Paris, 1896–1910).

GROSSETESTE, ROBERT, Epistolae Roberti Grosseteste, ed. H. R. Luard, R.S. xxv (London, 1861).

—— Rotuli Roberti Grosseteste, ed. F. N. Davis, Lincoln Record Society, xi (1914).

GUALA (BICHIERI), CARDINAL, 'Der Libellus petitionum des Kardinals Guala Bichieri', ed. R. von Heckel, *Archiv für Urkundenforschung*, i. 500–10 (Leipzig, 1908).

HEFELE, C.-J., and LECLERQ, DOM H., *Histoire des conciles d'après les documents originaux*, 11 vols. (Paris, 1907–52).

HEREFORD, *Charters and records of Hereford cathedral*, ed. W. W. Capes, Cantilupe Society (Hereford, 1908).

HISTORICAL MANUSCRIPTS COMMISSION, *Reports of the Royal Commission on Historical Manuscripts*.

HONORIUS III, *Regesta Honorii Papae III*, ed. Petrus Pressutti, 2 vols. (Rome, 1888–95).

INNOCENT III, *The letters of Pope Innocent III (1198–1216) concerning England and Wales*, cal. C. R. and Mary G. Cheney (Oxford, 1967).

—— *Die Register Innocenz' III*, i, ed. O. Hageneder and A. Haidacher, Publikationen der Abteilung für Historische Studien des Österreichischen Kulturinstituts in Rom (Graz–Köln, 1964).

INNOCENT IV, *Les Registres d'Innocent IV*, ed. Élie Berger, Bibliothèque des Écoles françaises d'Athènes et de Rome, 4 vols. (Paris, 1884–1911).

JOCELIN OF BRAKELOND, *The chronicle of Jocelin of Brakelond*, ed. and trans. H. E. Butler (London, 1949).

JOHN DE OXENEDES, *Chronica Johannis de Oxenedes*, ed. Sir Henry Ellis, R.S. xiii (London, 1859).

JOHN OF SALISBURY, *The letters of John of Salisbury*, i, ed. W. J. Millor and H. E. Butler, revsd. C. N. L. Brooke (London, 1955).

LANGTON, STEPHEN, *Acta Stephani Langton*, ed. Kathleen Major, Canterbury and York Ser. l (London, 1950).

LEWES, *The Cambridgeshire portion of the chartulary of the priory of St. Pancras of Lewes*, ed. J. H. Bullock and W. M. Palmer; issued to members of the Cambridge Antiquarian Society and the Sussex Record Society (Cambridge, 1938).

—— *The chartulary of the priory of St. Pancras of Lewes*, ed. L. F. Salzman, Sussex Record Society, xxxviii and xl, 2 vols. (1933–4).

—— *The Norfolk portion of the chartulary of the priory of St. Pancras of Lewes*, ed. J. H. Bullock, Norfolk Record Society, xii (1939).

LICHFIELD, '*Magnum Registrum Album*', ed. H. E. Savage, *Collections for a history of Staffordshire*, ed. William Salt Archaeological Society (1926 for 1924).

LIEBERMANN, F., ed., *Die Gesetze der Angelsachsen*, i (Halle, 1903).

LINCOLN, *Papal decretals relating to the diocese of Lincoln in the twelfth century*, ed. Walther Holtzmann and E. W. Kemp, Lincoln Record Society, xlvii (1954).

—— *The Registrum Antiquissimum of the cathedral church of Lincoln*, ed. C. W. Foster and Kathleen Major, Lincoln Record Society, xxvii, xxviii, xxix, xxxii, xxxiv, xli, xlii, xlvi, and li, 8 vols. + plates (1931–58).

LONDON, *Early charters of the cathedral church of St. Paul London*, ed. Marion Gibbs, Camden Society, 3rd Ser. lviii (London, 1939).

MALMESBURY, *The register of Malmesbury abbey*, ed. J. S. Brewer and C. T. Martin, R.S. lxxii, 2 vols. (London, 1879–80).

MANSI, GIOVANNI DOMENICO, *Sacrorum Conciliorum Nova et Amplissima Collectio, in qua . . . ea omnia . . . exhibentur quae J. D. Mansi . . . evulgavit, etc.*, vols. xxi–xxiv (Florence and Venice, 1776–80).

MARINUS OF EBOLI, *Die Formularsammlung des Marinus von Eboli*, ed. F. Schillmann, Bibliothek des Pruessischen Historischen Instituts in Rom, xvi (1929).

MIDDLEWICH, *A Middlewich cartulary*, ed. Joan Varley and James Tait, Chetham Society, n.s. cv and cviii, 2 pts. (Manchester, 1941–4).

MISSENDEN, *The cartulary of Missenden abbey*, ed. J. G. Jenkins, Bucks. Archaeological Society, ii, x, and xii, 2 pts. (1939–62).

MONTACUTE, see BRUTON.

NEWNHAM, *The cartulary of Newnham priory*, ed. J. Godber, Bedfordshire Historical Record Society, xliii (1963).

NEWTON LONGVILLE, *Newington Longeville charters*, ed. H. E. Salter, Oxfordshire Record Society, iii (1921).

OSENEY, *The cartulary of Oseney abbey*, ed. H. E. Salter, Oxford Historical Society, lxxxix–xci, xcvii–xcviii, and ci, 6 vols. (1929–36).

OXFORD, *Cartulary of the mediaeval archives of Christ Church*, cal. N. Denholm-Young, Oxford Historical Society, xcii (1931).

—— *The cartulary of the monastery of St Frideswide at Oxford*, ed. the Revd. S. R. Wigram, Oxford Historical Society, xxviii and xxxi, 2 vols. (1895–6).

—— 'Collection of Brackley Deeds at Magdalen College, Oxford', cal. W. D. Macray, *Bucks. Advertiser* (1910).

—— *Formularies which bear on the history of Oxford*, ed. H. E. Salter, W. A. Pantin, and H. G. Richardson, Oxford Historical Society, n.s. v, vol. ii (1942).

—— *Oriel College Records*, ed. C. L. Shadwell and H. E. Salter, Oxford Historical Society, lxxxv (1926).

PAPAL REGISTERS, *Calendar of entries in the papal registers illustrating the history of Great Britain and Ireland*, vol. i (1198–1304), ed. W. H. Bliss, Record Publications (London, 1893).

Papsturkunden in England, ed. Walther Holtzmann, Abhandlungen der Gesellschaft der Wissenschaften zu Göttingen, Philologisch-historische Klasse, Neue Folge, Bd. xxv, 1, 3. Folge, nr. 14 and nr. 33 (Berlin, 1930–5, Göttingen, 1952).

Papsturkunden in Frankreich, ed. J. Ramackers, Abhandlungen der Gesellschaft der Wissenschaften zu Göttingen, Philologisch-historische Klasse, 3. Folge, nr. 21, nr. 23, nr. 27, and nr. 35 (Göttingen, 1937–56).

PARIS, MATTHEW, *Chronica Majora*, ed. H. R. Luard, R.S. lvii, 7 vols. (London, 1872–83).

PARIS, UNIVERSITY OF. *Chartularium Universitatis Parisiensis*, ed. H. Denifle et E. Chatelain, t. i (1200–1286) (Paris, 1889).

Patent Rolls of the Reign of Henry III 1216–1232, Record Publications, 2 vols. (London, 1901–3).

Patrologiae Cursus Completus—Series Latina, ed. J.-P. Migne, 221 vols. (Paris, 1844–64).

PEAK DISTRICT, 'Ancient Documents relating to Tithes in the Peak', ed.
J. C. Cox, *Journal of the Derbyshire Archaeological and Natural History
Society*, v. 129–64 (London and Derby, 1883).

PRYNNE, WILLIAM, *An exact chronological vindication and historical demon-
stration of our British, Roman, Saxon, Danish, Norman, English Kings
supream ecclesiastical jurisdiction*, vol. ii (London, 1665).

Quinque Compilationes Antiquae, ed. E. Friedberg (Leipzig, 1882).

RALPH OF COGGESHALL, *Chronicon Anglicanum*, ed. J. Stevenson, R.S. lxvi
(London, 1875).

RICARDUS ANGLICUS, '*Summa de Ordine Iudiciario*', ed. Ludwig Wahrmund,
Quellen zur Geschichte des Römisch-Kanonischen Processes im Mittelalter,
ii. 3 (Innsbruck, 1915).

RIEVAULX, *Cartularium Abbathiae de Rievalle*, ed. the Revd. J. C. Atkinson,
Surtees Society, lxxxiii (1889 for 1887).

ROCHESTER, *Registrum Roffense*, ed. John Thorpe (London, 1769).

ROME, CHURCH OF. *Die Papstlichen Kanzleiordnungen von 1200–1500*, ed.
M. Tangl (Innsbruck, 1894).

—— *Regesta Pontificum Romanorum 1198 ad annum 1304*, ed. A. Potthast,
2 vols. (Berlin, 1874–5).

—— *Regesta Pontificum Romanorum—Italia Pontificia*, ed. P. F. Kehr,
8 vols. (Berlin, 1906–35).

Royal and other historical letters illustrative of the reign of Henry III, ed. the
Revd. W. W. Shirley, R.S. xxvii, 2 vols. (London, 1862–6).

RYMER, THOMAS, *Foedera, Conventiones, Litterae etc.*, Record Commission,
vol. i (London, 1816).

SALISBURY, *Charters and documents illustrating the history of the cathedral . . . of
Salisbury*, ed. W. H. Rich Jones and W. D. Macray, R.S. xcvii (London,
1891).

—— *The register of S. Osmund*, ed. W. H. Rich Jones, R.S. lxxviii, 2 vols.
(London, 1883–4).

'*Scientiam*', ed. Ludwig Wahrmund, *Quellen zur Geschichte des Römisch-
Kanonischen Processes im Mittelalter*, ii. 1 (Innsbruck, 1913).

SELBORNE, *Calendar of charters and documents relating to Selborne and its
priory*, ed. W. D. Macray, Hampshire Record Society, 2 vols. (1891–4).

SELE, *The chartulary of the priory of St. Peter at Sele*, cal. L. F. Salzman
(Cambridge, 1923).

STUBBS, WILLIAM, ed., *Select Charters*, 9th edn., revsd. H. W. C. Davis
(Oxford, 1913).

TANCRED, '*Tancredi Bononiensis Ordo Iudiciarius*', ed. F. Bergmann, *Pillii,
Tancredi, Gratiae Libri de Iudiciorum Ordine*, 89–316 (Göttingen, 1842).

THAME, *The Thame cartulary*, ed. H. E. Salter, Oxford Record Society, xxv–
xxvi, 2 vols. (1947–8).

THORNE, WILLIAM, *William Thorne's chronicle of St. Augustine's abbey
Canterbury*, ed. and trans. A. H. Davis (Oxford, 1934).

VACARIUS, *The Liber Pauperum of Vacarius*, ed. F. de Zulueta, Selden
Society, xliv (London, 1927).

VOLTERRA, *Regestum Volaterranum*, ed. Fedor Schneider, Regesta Chartarum
Italiae, i (Rome, 1907).

WELLES, HUGH DE, *Rotuli Hugonis de Welles Episcopi Lincolniensis*, A.D. *1209–1235*, ed. W. P. W. Phillimore and F. N. Davis, Canterbury and York Ser. i, iii, and iv (1907–9).

WILLIAM OF DROGHEDA, *'Summa Aurea'*, ed. Ludwig Wahrmund, *Quellen zur Geschichte des Römisch-Kanonischen Processes im Mittelalter*, ii. 2 (Innsbruck, 1914).

WINCHESTER. *The chartulary of Winchester cathedral*, ed. A. W. Goodman (Winchester, 1927).

B. SECONDARY AUTHORITIES

ADAMS, NORMA, 'The Judicial Conflict over Tithes', *E.H.R.* lii (1937), 1–22.

—— 'The Writ of Prohibition to Court Christian', *Minnesota Law Review*, xx, no. 3 (Feb. 1936), 272–93.

ANDRIEU-GUITRANCOURT, PIERRE, *Essai sur l'évolution du décanat rural en Angleterre d'après les conciles des XIIe, XIIIe et XIVe siècles* (Paris, 1935).

BARNES, P. M., 'The Anstey Case', *A Medieval Miscellany for Doris Mary Stenton*, ed. P. M. Barnes and C. F. Slade, Pipe Roll Society, N.S. xxxvi (1960), 1–24.

BARRACLOUGH, GEOFFREY, *'Audientia Litterarum Contradictarum'*, *Dictionnaire de droit canonique*, i (1935), cols. 1387–99.

—— 'Formulare für Suppliken aus der ersten Hälfte des 13. Jahrhunderts', *Archiv für Katholisches Kirchenrecht*, cxv (Innsbruck, 1935), 435–56.

—— 'The Making of a Bishop in the Middle Ages', *The Catholic Historical Review*, xix (Washington, 1933), 275–319.

—— Review of *Repertorium der Kanonistik* by S. Kuttner, *E.H.R.* liii (1938), 492–5.

BAUMGARTEN, P. M., *Aus Kanzlei und Kammer* (Freiburg, 1907).

BERLIÈRE, DOM URSMER, 'Les Élections abbatiales au Moyen Âge', *Académie royale de Belgique*—Classe des lettres et des sciences morales et politiques, t. xx, fasc. 3 (Brussels, 1927).

BOCK, P. COLOMBAN, 'Les Cisterciens et l'étude du droit', *Analecta Sacri Ordinis Cisterciensis*, vii (Rome, 1951), 3–31.

BOUIX, D., *Tractatus de Curia Romana* (Paris, 1859).

BRENTANO, ROBERT, 'An Endorsed Subdelegation: 1284', *Traditio*, xiii (New York, 1957), 452–6.

—— *York metropolitan jurisdiction and papal judges delegate (1279–1296)*, University of California Publications in History, lviii (University of California Press, Berkeley and Los Angeles, 1959).

BRESSLAU, HARRY, *Handbuch der Urkundenlehre für Deutschland und Italien*, 2nd edn. i (Leipzig, 1912).

BROOKE, Z. N., 'The Effect of Becket's Murder on Papal Authority in England', *Cambridge Historical Journal*, ii (1928), 213–28.

—— *The English Church and the papacy* (Cambridge, 1931).

BUCKLAND, W. W., *A Textbook of Roman Law from Augustus to Justinian*, 3rd edn., revsd. P. Stein (Cambridge, 1963).

BURKE, SIR BERNARD, *A genealogical history of the dormant abeyant forfeited and extinct peerages of the British Empire* (London, 1883).

BURN, RICHARD, *The ecclesiastical law*, 9th edn., revsd. R. Phillimore, 4 vols. (London, 1842).

CAENEGEM, R. C. VAN, 'Notes on Canon Law Books in Medieval Belgian Book-Lists', *Studia Gratiana*, xii (Bologna, 1967), 265–92.

—— *Royal writs in England from the Conquest to Glanville*, Selden Society, lxxvii (London, 1959).

CANIVEZ, J.-M., 'Étonnantes Concessions pontificales faites à Cîteaux', *Miscellanea historica in honorem Alberti de Meyer*, i (Louvain, 1946), 505–9.

The Canon Law of the Church of England, being the Report of the Archbishops' Commission on Canon Law, by the Hon. Mr. Justice Vaisey (S.P.C.K., London, 1947).

CERCHIARI, E., *Capellani Papae et Apostolicae Sedis Auditores Causarum Sacri Palatii Apostolici seu Sacra Romana Rota ab origine usque 20 Sept. 1870*, 3 vols. in 2 (Rome, 1919–21).

CHENEY, C. R., *From Becket to Langton* (Manchester, 1956).

—— 'Cardinal John of Ferentino, papal legate in England in 1206', *E.H.R.* lxxvi (1961), 654–60.

—— 'Decretals of Innocent III in Paris, B.N. MS. Lat. 3922A', *Traditio*, xi (New York, 1955), 149–62.

—— 'England and the Roman Curia under Innocent III', *The Journal of Ecclesiastical History*, xviii (1967), 173–86.

—— *English bishops' chanceries, 1100–1250* (Manchester, 1950).

—— 'Harrold Priory: a Twelfth Century Dispute', *Bedfordshire Historical Record Society*, xxxii (1952), 1–26.

—— *Hubert Walter* (London, 1967).

—— 'King John and the Papal Interdict', *Bulletin of the John Rylands Library*, xxxi (Manchester, 1948), 295–317.

—— 'The Papal Legate and the English Monasteries in 1206', *E.H.R.* xlvi (1931), 443–52.

CHENEY, MARY, 'The Compromise of Avranches of 1172 and the Spread of Canon Law in England', *E.H.R.* lvi (1941), 177–97.

CHRISTOFORI, F., *Storia dei Cardinali di Santa Romana Chiesa* (Rome, 1888).

CHURCHILL, I. J., *Canterbury administration*, 2 vols. (London, 1933).

CIACONIUS, A., *Vitae et Res Gestae Pontificum Romanorum et S.R.E. Cardinalium*, ii (Rome, 1677).

COLLINET, PAUL, *La Procédure par libelle* (Paris, 1932).

COLVIN, H. M., *The White Canons in England* (Oxford, 1951).

The Complete Peerage, ed. Vicary Gibbs, H. A. Doubleday, G. H. White, and others, 12 vols. in 13 pts. (London, 1910–59).

CONSTABLE, G., *Monastic tithes from their origins to the twelfth century* (Cambridge, 1964).

—— 'Resistance to Tithes in the Middle Ages', *The Journal of Ecclesiastical History*, xiii (1962), 172–85.

COOPER, LORD (Thomas Mackay), *Select Scottish cases of the thirteenth century* (Edinburgh and London, 1944).

COTTINEAU, DOM L. H., O.S.B., *Répertoire topo-bibliographique des abbayes et prieurés*, 2 vols. (Mâcon, 1935–7).

CRISCI, G., '*Evolutio historica delegationis a jure*', *Apollinaris*, ix (Rome, 1936), 270–99.

DAUVILLIER, J., *Le Mariage dans le droit classique de l'Église depuis le Décret de Gratien (1140) jusqu'à la mort de Clément V (1314)* (Paris, 1933).

DICKINSON, J. C., *The origins of the Austin Canons and their introduction into England* (London, 1950).

Dictionnaire de droit canonique, 7 vols., published under the direction of R. Naz (Paris, 1924–65).

DUGGAN, CHARLES, *Twelfth-century decretal collections and their importance in English history*, University of London Historical Studies, xii (London, 1963).

The ecclesiastical courts. Principles of Reconstruction, being the Report of the Commission set up by the Archbishops of Canterbury and York in 1951, at the request of the Convocations (S.P.C.K., London, 1954).

EDWARDS, K., *The English secular cathedrals in the Middle Ages*, 2nd edn. (Manchester, 1967).

EMDEN, A. B., *A biographical register of the university of Cambridge to A.D. 1500* (Cambridge, 1963).

—— *A biographical register of the university of Oxford to A.D. 1500*, 3 vols. (Oxford, 1957–9). Additions in the *Bodleian Library Record*, vi (Oxford, 1957–61).

ESMEIN, A., *Le Mariage en droit canonique*, 2nd edn., revsd. R. Génestal, 2 vols. (Paris, 1929).

EUBEL, C., *Hierarchia Catholica Medii Aevi*, i (Munich, 1898).

FLAHIFF, G. B., 'The Use of Prohibitions by Clerics against Ecclesiastical Courts in England', *Mediaeval Studies*, iii (Toronto, 1941), 101–16.

—— 'The Writ of Prohibition to Court Christian in the Thirteenth Century', *Mediaeval Studies*, vi (1944), 261–313, and vii (1945), 229–90.

FLOWER, C. T., *Introduction to the Curia Regis rolls (1199–1230)*, Selden Society, lxii (London, 1944, for 1943).

FOSTER, J., 'The Activities of Rural Deans in England in the Twelfth and Thirteenth Centuries', Manchester M.A. thesis, 1955.

FOURNIER, E., 'L'Accueil fait par la France du XIIIᵉ siècle aux Décrétales pontificales: leur traduction en langue vulgaire', *Acta Congressus Iuridici Internationalis*, iii (Rome, 1936), 247–67.

FOURNIER, MARCEL, *Essai sur l'histoire du droit d'appel* (Paris, 1881).

FOURNIER, PAUL, *Les Officialités au Moyen Âge* (Paris, 1880).

GABEL, L. C., *Benefit of clergy in England in the later Middle Ages*, Smith College Studies in History, xiv, nos. 1–4 (Northampton, U.S.A., 1929).

GAMS, P. B., *Series Episcoporum Ecclesiae Catholicae* (Regensburg, 1873).

GAUDEMET, J., 'Das römische Recht in Gratians Dekret', *Österreichisches Archiv für Kirchenrecht*, xii (1961), 177–91.

GÉNESTAL, R., *Les Origines de l'appel comme d'abus*, Bibliothèque de l'École des hautes études—sciences religieuses, lxiii (Paris, 1951).

—— *Le Privilegium Fori en France*, Bibliothèque de l'École des hautes études—Sciences religieuses, xxxv, vol. i (Paris, 1921).

GIBBS, M., and LANG, J., *Bishops and reform, 1215–1272* (Oxford, 1934).

GOLDSMITH, J. WILLIAM, *The competence of Church and State over marriage—disputed points*, The Catholic University of America, Canon Law Studies, no. 197 (Washington, 1944).

GRAHAM, ROSE, *English ecclesiastical studies* (London, 1929).

GRAY, J. W., 'The *Ius Praesentandi* in England from the Constitutions of Clarendon to Bracton', *E.H.R.* lxvii (1952), 481–509.

HAMILTON THOMPSON, A., 'Diocesan Organization in the Middle Ages: Archdeacons and Rural Deans', *Proceedings of the British Academy*, xxix (London, 1943), 153–94.

—— *The English clergy and their organization in the later Middle Ages* (Oxford, 1947).

HAMPE, K., 'Ein ungedruckter Bericht über das Konklave von 1241 im römischen Septizonium', *Sitzungsberichte der Heidelberger Akademie der Wissenschaften*, Philosophisch-historische Klasse, iv (Heidelberg, 1913), 3–34.

HARTRIDGE, R. A. R., *A history of vicarages in the Middle Ages* (Cambridge, 1930).

HASKINS, C. H., *Norman institutions* (Cambridge, Mass., 1918).

HAYDT, REVD. JOHN J., *Reserved benefices*, The Catholic University of America, Canon Law Studies, no. 161 (Washington, 1942).

HECKEL, R. VON, 'Das Aufkommen der ständigen Prokuratoren an der päpstlichen Kurie im 13. Jahrhundert', *Studi e Testi*, xxxviii (Rome, 1924), 290–321.

HERDE, P., *Beiträge zum Päpstlichen Kanzlei und Urkundenwesen im 13. Jahrhundert*, Münchener Historische Studien, i (Kallmunz, 1961).

—— 'Papal Formularies for Letters of Justice (13th–16th Centuries)', *Proceedings of the Second International Congress of Medieval Canon Law 1963, Monumenta Iuris Canonici*, Series C: Subsidia i (Vatican City, 1965), 321–45.

—— 'Der Zeugenzwang in den päpstlichen Delegationsreskripten des Mittelalters', *Traditio*, xviii (New York, 1962).

HINSCHIUS, P., *Das Kirchenrecht der Katholiken und Protestanten in Deutschland*, 6 vols. (Berlin, 1869–97).

HOLDSWORTH, W. S., *A history of English Law*, 3 vols., 3rd edn. (London, 1922–3).

HOLTZMANN, W., 'Über eine Ausgabe der päpstlichen Dekretalen des 12. Jahrhunderts', *Nachrichten der Akademie der Wissenschaften in Göttingen*, Philologisch-historische Klasse, for the year 1945 (Göttingen, 1948), pp. 15–36.

HOVE, A. VAN, *Prolegomena*, Commentarium Lovaniense in Codicem Iuris Canonici (Malines-Rome, 1945).

HUNT, R. W., 'English Learning in the Late Twelfth Century', *Transactions of the Royal Historical Society*, 4th Ser. xix (London, 1936), 19–42.

JOELSON, OLGA, 'Die Papstwahlen des 13. Jahrhunderts bis zur Einführung der Conclaveordnung Gregors X', *Historische Studien*, clxxviii (Berlin, 1928.)

JOHNSON, CHARLES, 'Notes on Thirteenth Century Judicial Procedure', *E.H.R.* lxii (1947), 508–21.

KANTOROWICZ, H., and BUCKLAND, W. W., *Studies in the glossators of the Roman Law* (Cambridge, 1938).

KER, N. R., *Medieval libraries of Great Britain. A list of surviving books*, Royal Historical Society Guides and Handbooks, iii, 2nd edn. (London, 1964).

KNOWLES, DOM DAVID, and HADCOCK, R. NEVILLE, *Medieval religious houses* (London, 1953).

KUTTNER, STEPHAN, '*Analecta Iuridica Vaticana* (Vat. lat. 2343)', *Studi e Testi*, ccxix (Vatican City, 1962), 415–52.

—— 'Bernardus Compostellanus Antiquus. A study in the Glossators of the Canon Law', *Traditio*, i (New York, 1943), 277–340.

—— 'Notes on a Projected Corpus of Twelfth-Century Decretal Letters', *Traditio*, vi (New York, 1948), 345–51.

—— 'Repertorium der Kanonistik (1140–1234)', *Studi e Testi*, lxxi (Vatican City, 1937).

—— and RATHBONE, ELEANOR, 'Anglo-Norman Canonists of the Twelfth Century: An Introductory Study', *Traditio*, vii (New York, 1949–51), 279–358.

LA DUE, WILLIAM J., *Papal rescripts of justice and English royal procedural writs 1150–1250. A comparative study.* An excerpt; Pontificia Universitas Lateranensis Institutum Utriusque Juris, Theses ad Lauream, no. 155 (Rome, 1960).

LAWRENCE, C. H., *St. Edmund of Abingdon*, (Oxford, 1960).

LEACH, A. F., *The schools of medieval England* (London, 1915).

LE BRAS, G., 'Le Droit romain au service de la domination pontificale', *Revue historique de droit français et étranger*, 4ᵉ série xxvii (Paris, 1949), 377–98.

—— ed., *Histoire du droit et des institutions de l'Église en occident*, vii (Paris, 1965).

LEE, R. W., *Elements of Roman Law*, 3rd edn. (London, 1952).

LEFEBVRE, C., 'Les Origines romaines de la procédure sommaire aux XIIᵉ et XIIIᵉ s.', *Ephemerides Iuris Canonici*, xii (Rome, 1956), 149–97.

—— *Les Pouvoirs du juge en droit canonique.* Contribution historique et doctrinale à l'étude du canon 20 sur la méthode et les sources en droit positif (Paris, 1938).

LEWIS, C. E., 'Ricardus Anglicus: A "Familiaris" of Archbishop Hubert Walter', *Traditio*, xxii (New York, 1966), 469–71.

LUCHAIRE, A., *Innocent III*, vol. i (Paris, 1904).

MACKENZIE, HUGH, 'The Anti-Foreign Movement in England, 1231–2', *Anniversary essays in medieval history by students of C. H. Haskins* (New York, 1950), 183–203.

MAHN, J.-B., *L'Ordre cistercien et son gouvernement des origines au milieu du XIIIᵉ siècle (1098–1265)*, Bibliothèque des Écoles françaises d'Athènes et de Rome, clxi (Paris, 1945).

MAITLAND, F. W., *Roman canon law in the Church of England* (London, 1898).

MAJOR, KATHLEEN, 'Conan Son of Ellis an Early Inhabitant of Holbeach', *Reports and Papers of the Architectural and Archaeological Societies of the County of Lincoln and the County of Northampton*, xlii (Lincoln, 1936), 1–29.

—— 'The "Familia" of Archbishop Stephen Langton', *E.H.R.* xlviii (1933), 529–53.

—— 'The "Familia" of Robert Grosseteste', *Robert Grosseteste Scholar and Bishop*, ed. D. A. Callus, App. 1 (Oxford, 1955).

—— 'Some Early Documents relating to Holbeach', *Reports and Papers of the Architectural and Archaeological Societies of the County of Lincoln and the County of Northampton*, xli (Lincoln, 1935), 39–45.

MARTI, OSCAR A., 'Popular Protest and Revolt against Papal Finance in England from 1226 to 1258', *The Princeton Theological Review*, xxv, no. 4 (Princeton, 1927), 610–29.

MAYR-HARTING, H., 'Hilary, Bishop of Chichester (1147–69), and Henry II', *E.H.R.* lxxviii (1963), 209–24.

MERCATI, A., 'The New List of Popes', *Mediaeval Studies*, ix (Toronto, 1947), 71–80.

—— 'La prima relazione del Cardinale Niccolò de Romanis sulla sua legazione in Inghilterra', *Essays in history presented to R. L. Poole*, ed. H. W. C. Davis (Oxford, 1927), 274–89.

MILLARD, P. W., *The law relating to tithes*, 3rd edn. (London, 1938).

MOLLAT, G., 'Contribution à l'histoire de l'administration judiciaire de l'Église romaine au XIVᵉ siècle', *Revue d'histoire ecclésiastique*, xxxii (Louvain, 1936), 877–928.

MOORE, N., *The history of St. Bartholomew's hospital*, 2 vols. (London, 1918).

MOORMAN, J. R. H., *Church life in England in the thirteenth century* (Cambridge, 1955).

MOREY, DOM A., *Bartholomew of Exeter* (Cambridge, 1937).

—— and BROOKE, C. N. L., *Gilbert Foliot and his letters*, Cambridge Studies in Medieval Life and Thought, n.s. xi (Cambridge, 1965).

MORGAN, M. M., 'Early Canterbury Jurisdiction', *E.H.R.* lx (1945), 392–9.

—— *English lands of the abbey of Bec* (Oxford, 1946).

MORRIS, C., 'A Consistory Court in the Middle Ages', *The Journal of Ecclesiastical History*, xiv (1963), 150–9.

—— 'William I and the Church Courts', *E.H.R.* lxxxii (1967), 449–63.

PACAUT, MARCEL, 'Les Légats d'Alexandre III (1159–1181), *Revue d'histoire ecclésiastique*, l (Louvain, 1955), 821–38.

PAINTER, S., *The scourge of the clergy, Peter of Dreux, duke of Brittany* (Baltimore, 1937).

—— *The reign of King John* (Baltimore, 1949).

PARKER, T. M., 'The Terms of the Interdict of Innocent III', *Speculum*, xi (Cambridge, Mass, 1936), 258–60.

PAVLOFF, GEORGE G., *Papal judge delegates at the time of the Corpus Iuris Canonici*, The Catholic University of America, Canon Law Studies, no. 426 (Washington, 1963).

PHILLIMORE, SIR ROBERT, *The ecclesiastical law of the Church of England*, 2nd edn., 2 vols. (London, 1895).

Phillips, Georg, *Kirchenrecht*, 7 vols. (Regensburg, 1845–72).

Plucknett, T. F. T., *A concise history of the common law*, 5th edn. (London, 1956).

Poole, R. L., *Lectures on the history of the papal Chancery down to the time of Innocent III* (Cambridge, 1915).

Powicke, F. M., *King Henry III and the Lord Edward* (Oxford, reprinted, 1966).

Rambaud-Buhot, J., 'Le Décret de Gratien et le droit romain: influence d'Yves de Chartres', *Revue historique de droit français et étranger*, 4ᵉ série xxxv (Paris, 1937), 290–300.

Rathbone, Eleanor, 'The Influence of Bishops and of Members of Cathedral Bodies in the Intellectual Life of England 1066–1216', 2 vols., London Ph.D. thesis (1936).

Rees, W., *South Wales and the border in the fourteenth century*, Ordnance Survey Office, Southampton, n.d.

Riaza, R., and Torres Lopez, M., 'Versiones Castellanas de las Decretales de Gregorio IX', *Acta Congressus Iuridici Internationalis*, iii (Rome, 1936), 291–6.

Richard, J., *Les Ducs de Bourgogne et la formation du duché du IXᵉ au XIVᵉ siècle* (Paris, 1954).

Richardson, H. G., 'Azo, Drogheda and Bracton', *E.H.R.* lix (1944), 22–47.

—— 'Letters of the Legate Guala', *E.H.R.* xlviii (1933), 250–9.

—— 'The Oxford Law School under John', *The Law Quarterly Review*, lvii (London, 1941), 319–38.

—— 'An Oxford Teacher of the Fifteenth Century', *Bulletin of the John Rylands Library*, xxiii (Manchester, 1939), 436–57.

—— 'The schools of Northampton in the twelfth century', *E.H.R.* lvi (1941), 595–605.

Ruess, K., *Die Rechtliche Stellung der Päpstlichen Legaten* (Paderborn, 1912).

Russell, J. C., 'A Dictionary of Thirteenth Century Writers', *Bulletin of the Institute of Historical Research*, suppl., no. 3 (London, 1936).

Saltman, A., *Theobald, Archbishop of Canterbury*, University of London Historical Studies, ii (London, 1956).

Sayers, Jane E., 'Canterbury Proctors at the Court of *Audientia Litterarum Contradictarum*', *Traditio*, xxii (New York, 1966), 311–45.

—— 'English Cistercian Cases and their Delegation in the First Half of the Thirteenth Century', *Analecta Sacri Ordinis Cisterciensis*, xx (Rome, 1964), 85–102.

—— 'The Judicial Activities of the General Chapters', *The Journal of Ecclesiastical History*, xv (1964), 18–32 and 168–85.

Schaller, H. M., 'Eine Kuriale Briefsammlung des 13. Jahrhunderts . . .', *Deutsches Archiv für Erforschung des Mittelalters*, xviii (Köln–Graz, 1962), 171–213.

Schierse, P. J., 'Legislation on Sequestration in Roman Law and in the Decretals of Gregory IX', *The Jurist*, xxiii (Washington, 1963), 291–313.

Schmid, T., 'Canon Law in Manuscripts from Medieval Sweden', *Traditio*, vii (New York, 1949–51), 444–9.

Schneider, F. Egon, *Die Römische Rota* (Paderborn, 1914).

SELDEN, JOHN, *The historie of tithes* (London, 1618).

SENIOR, W., 'Roman Law Manuscripts in England', *The Law Quarterly Review*, xlvii (London, 1931), 337–44.

SERÉDI, I. G., Cardinal, '*De Relatione inter Decretales Gregorii Papae IX et Codicem Iuris Canonici*', *Acta Congressus Iuridici Internationalis*, iv (Rome, 1937), 11–26.

SHEEHAN, M. M., *The will in Medieval England*, Pontifical Institute of Mediaeval Studies, Studies and Texts, vi (Toronto, 1965).

SPAETHEN, M., 'Giraldus Cambrensis und Thomas von Evesham über die von ihnen an der Kurie geführten Prozesse', *Neues Archiv der Gesellschaft für ältere deutsche Geschichtskunde*, xxxi (Hanover, Berlin, 1906), 629–49.

STENTON, D. M., *English justice between the Norman Conquest and the Great Charter, 1066–1215*, Jayne Lectures for 1963 (London, 1965).

STENTON, F. M., '*Acta Episcoporum*', *Cambridge Historical Journal*, iii, no. 1 (1929), 1–14.

STICKLER, A.-M., '*Ordines Judiciarii*', *Dictionnaire de droit canonique*, vi (1957), cols. 1132–43.

SWEET, A. H., 'The Control of English Episcopal Elections in the Thirteenth Century', *The Catholic Historical Review*, n.s. vi (Washington, 1927), 573–82.

TEIGE, JOSEF, 'Beiträge zum päpstlichen Kanzleiwesen des XIII. und XIV. Jahrhunderts', *Mitteilungen des Instituts für Oesterreichische Geschichtsforschung*, xvii (Innsbruck, 1896), 408–40.

TESSIER, G., 'Note sur un manuel à l'usage d'un officier de la Cour pontificale (XIIIe siècle)', *Études d'histoire du droit canonique dédiées à G. Le Bras* (Paris, 1965), 357–71.

THORNE, S. E., 'Le Droit canonique en Angleterre', *Revue historique de droit français et étranger*, 4e série xiii (Paris, 1934), 499–513.

TIERNEY, B., *Foundations of the conciliar theory*, Cambridge Studies in Medieval Life and Thought, n.s. iv (Cambridge, 1955).

TILLMANN, H., *Die Päpstlichen Legaten in England bis zur Beendigung der Legation Gualas* (1218) (Bonn, 1926).

ULLMANN, WALTER, 'A Forgotten Dispute at Bridlington Priory and its Canonistic Setting', *Yorkshire Archaeological Journal*, xxxvii (1948–51), 456–73.

—— *The growth of papal government in the Middle Ages* (London, 1955).

VETULANI, A., 'La Pénétration du droit des Décrétales dans l'Église polonaise au XIIIe siècle', *Acta Congressus Iuridici Internationalis*, iii (Rome, 1936), 385–405.

VOSS, LENA, 'Heinrich von Blois, Bischof von Winchester (1129–1171)', *Historische Studien*, ccx (Berlin, 1932).

WALEY, D., *The papal State in the thirteenth century* (London, 1961).

WILLIAMSON, D. M., 'Some Aspects of the Legation of Cardinal Otto in England, 1237–1241', *E.H.R.* lxiv (1949), 145–73.

WINKELMANN, E., 'Die Legation des Kardinaldiakons Otto von S. Nicolaus in Deutschland, 1229–1231', *Mitteilungen des Instituts für Oesterreichische Geschichtsforschung*, xi (Innsbruck, 1890), 28–40.

WOODCOCK, BRIAN L., *Medieval ecclesiastical courts in the diocese of Canterbury* (Oxford, 1952).

ZIMMERMANN, H., *Die Päpstliche Legation in der ersten Hälfte des 13. Jahrhunderts* (Paderborn, 1913).

ZULUETA, F. DE, 'William of Drogheda', *Mélanges de droit romain dédiés à Georges Cornil*, ii (Ghent, Paris, 1926), 641–57.

INDEX

For abbreviations see above p. 279